GREEK AND ROMAN ACTORS

This collection of twenty essays examines the art, the profession and the idea of the actor in Greek and Roman antiquity, and has been commissioned and arranged to cast as much interdisciplinary and transhistorical light as possible on these elusive but fascinating ancient professionals. It covers a chronological span from the sixth century BC to Byzantium (and even beyond to the way that ancient actors have influenced the arts from the Renaissance to the twentieth century) and stresses the enormous geographical range of ancient actors. Some essays focus on particular themes, such as the evidence for women actors or the impact of acting on the presentation of suicide in literature; others offer completely new evidence, such as graffiti relating to actors in Asia Minor; others ask new questions, such as what subjective experience can be reconstructed for the ancient actor. There are numerous illustrations and all Greek and Latin passages are translated.

PAT EASTERLING is an Honorary Fellow of Newnham College and a Fellow of the British Academy. She was Regius Professor of Greek at Cambridge from 1994 to 2001, and Professor of Greek at University College London from 1987 to 1994. She has been a General Editor of Cambridge Greek and Latin Classics since its foundation over thirty years ago, and has published an edition within this series of Sophocles' *Trachiniae* (1982), co-edited, with B. M. W. Knox, Volume 1 of the *Cambridge History of Classical Literature* (1985) and edited *The Cambridge Companion to Greek Tragedy* (1997). She is currently writing a commentary on Sophocles' *Oedipus at Colonus*.

EDITH HALL is Leverhulme Professor of Greek Cultural History at the University of Durham and has previously taught at the Universities of Cambridge, Reading and Oxford, where she was Fellow of Somerville College from 1995 to 2001. She is Co-Director of the Archive of Performances of Greek and Roman Drama at the University of Oxford and author of *Inventing the Barbarian* (1989), editor of Aeschylus' *Persians* (1996) and co-editor of *Medea in Performance* (2000). She is currently working, with Fiona Macintosh, on a history of Greek tragedy on the British Stage for Oxford University Press.

GREEK AND ROMAN ACTORS

Aspects of an Ancient Profession

EDITED BY

PAT EASTERLING

Regius Professor of Greek Emeritus, University of Cambridge

AND

EDITH HALL

Leverhulme Professor of Greek Cultural History, University of Durham

PUBLISHED BY THE PRESS SYNDICATE OF THE UNIVERSITY OF CAMBRIDGE
The Pitt Building, Trumpington Street, Cambridge, United Kingdom

CAMBRIDGE UNIVERSITY PRESS
The Edinburgh Building, Cambridge CB2 2RU, UK
40 West 20th Street, New York, NY 10011-4211, USA
477 Williamstown Road, Port Melbourne, VIC 3207, Australia
Ruiz de Alarcón 13, 28014 Madrid, Spain
Dock House, The Waterfront, Cape Town 8001, South Africa

http://www.cambridge.org

First published 2002

Printed in the United Kingdom at the University Press, Cambridge

Typeface Baskerville Monotype 11/12.5 pt. *System* LaTeX 2ε [TB]

A catalogue record for this book is available from the British Library

ISBN 0 521 65140 9 hardback

Contents

PART TWO THE PROFESSIONAL WORLD

PART THREE THE IDEA OF THE ACTOR

Illustrations

Contributors

PETER G. McC. BROWN is a Lecturer in Classics at Oxford University and a Fellow of Trinity College. He is a Director of the Archive of Performances of Greek and Roman Drama, with particular responsibility for Roman Comedy. He has published extensively on both Greek and Roman Comedy.

ERIC CSAPO is Associate Professor of Classics at the University of Toronto, co-author of *The Context of Ancient Drama* (Ann Arbor 1995) and author of numerous articles on the history of the ancient theatre, ancient Greek literature, and ancient culture.

PAT EASTERLING was Regius Professor of Greek at Cambridge from 1994 to 2001; she spent the previous seven years as Professor of Greek at University College London. She edited the *Cambridge Companion to Greek Tragedy* (1997), and is currently writing a commentary on Sophocles' *Oedipus at Colonus.*

CATHARINE EDWARDS teaches Classics and Ancient History at Birkbeck College, University of London. Her publications include *The Politics of Immorality in Ancient Rome* (Cambridge 1993) and *Writing Rome: Textual Approaches to the City* (Cambridge 1996). She is currently working on a commentary on selected letters of Seneca for the Cambridge Greek and Latin Classics series.

THOMAS M. FALKNER is Professor of Classical Studies and Dean of the Faculty at The College of Wooster. In addition to articles on Greek and Latin literature, he is the author of *The Poetics of Old Age in Greek Epic, Lyric, and Tragedy* (Oklahoma 1995) and a commentary on Euripides' *Orestes* (Bryn Mawr 1984) and co-editor of *Old Age in Greek and Latin Literature* (Albany 1989) and of *Contextualizing Classics: Ideology, Performance, Dialogue* (Lanham 1999).

ELAINE FANTHAM was born in Liverpool and educated mostly at Oxford before emigrating with her husband to the USA (Indiana University), then the University of Toronto, Canada (1968–86) and finally Princeton University, where she was Giger Professor of Latin until June 1999. She began with a love of Roman comedy, and has never lost it while adding interests in Roman rhetoric, epic and tragedy. Her most recent books are *Roman Literary Culture* (Johns Hopkins 1996, pbk 1998) and a Cambridge Greek and Latin Classics commentary on Ovid's *Fasti* Book IV. She is writing a book on Cicero's *De Oratore*, while dividing her retirement between Toronto and Cambridge.

RICHARD GREEN is Professor of Classical Archaeology at the University of Sydney and a Senior Research Fellow attached to the Dramatic Archive at the Institute of Classical Studies, School of Advanced Study, University of London. With Eric Handley, he is preparing a major study on Greek theatre performance.

EDITH HALL is Leverhulme Professor of Greek Cultural History at the University of Durham and a Director of the Archive of Performances of Greek and Roman Drama at Oxford. Her publications include *Inventing the Barbarian* (Oxford 1989), an edition of Aeschylus' *Persians* (Warminster 1996), and (co-edited with Fiona Macintosh and Oliver Taplin) *Medea in Performance 1500–2000* (Oxford 2000).

ERIC HANDLEY is a Fellow of Trinity College, Cambridge and Professor of Ancient Literature at the Royal Academy of Arts. He was Regius Professor of Greek at Cambridge, 1984–94; before that, Professor of Greek at University College London and Director of the Institute of Classical Studies. His publications include a commentary on Menander's *Dyskolos* (1965; repr. Bristol Classical Press 1992), editions of fragments of drama in *The Oxyrhynchus Papyri*, and (with Richard Green) *Images of the Greek Theatre* (British Museum Press 1995; repr. 2001).

RICHARD HUNTER is Regius Professor of Greek at the University of Cambridge and a Fellow of Trinity College. He has published extensively in the fields of ancient comedy, Hellenistic poetry and the novel. His most recent books are *Theocritus: A Selection* (Cambridge 1999) and (with Marco Fantuzzi) *Muse e Modelli: La poesia ellenistica da Alessandro Magno ad Augusto* (Rome/Bari 2002).

JOHN JORY was born in Cornwall and educated at Penzance and University College London. Since 1959 he has worked in the Department of

Classics and Ancient History at the University of Western Australia, since 1979 as Professor, and he was Executive Dean of the Faculty of Arts 1999–2000. He is currently writing a book on pantomime.

ISMENE LADA-RICHARDS is Lecturer in Classics at King's College London. She is the author of *Initiating Dionysus: Ritual and Theatre in Aristophanes' Frogs* (Oxford 1999) and articles on tragedy, aspects of Greek acting and Brecht. She is presently engaged in a project which aims to explore the cultural construction of acting and viewing in Greek and Roman literature.

JANE L. LIGHTFOOT holds a Post-Doctoral Fellowship at All Souls College, Oxford, where she has been since 1994. Her first book was *Parthenius of Nicaea* (Oxford 1999), and she has recently completed an edition and commentary on Lucian's *De Dea Syria* which she also hopes to publish with Oxford. Her research interests include Hellenistic and imperial poetry and prose, especially in the Near East, and she intends to turn her attention next to the Sibylline Oracles.

WALTER PUCHNER is Professor and head of the Department of Theatre Studies in the University of Athens. He also teaches Theatre History at the Institut für Theaterwissenschaft in Vienna. He has published several critical editions of Christian drama in Greek in addition to numerous books and articles on theatre history, dramatic theory, and Byzantine Studies, including *Popular Theatre in Greece and the Balkans* (1989).

CHARLOTTE ROUECHÉ is Reader in Classical and Byzantine Greek at King's College London. Her principal interests lie in the inscriptions of the Greek-speaking world, particularly those of the Late Antique period, and the literature of the Byzantine Empire. She has published the late antique inscriptions of Aphrodisias in Turkey and has been working more recently on similar material excavated at Ephesus.

G. M. SIFAKIS is A. S. Onassis Professor of Classical Greek Literature at New York University, and the author of 'The one-actor rule in Greek tragedy', in A. Griffiths (ed.), *Stage Directions: Studies Presented to E. W. Handley* (London 1995), 'Formulas and their relatives: A semiotic approach to verse making in Homer and modern Greek folksongs' (*JHS* [117] 1997) and *Aristotle on the Function of Tragedy* (Herakleion 2001).

KOSTAS VALAKAS is Associate Professor of the theory and interpretation of ancient Greek drama at the Department of Theatre Studies in the University of Patras, Greece. He has published papers on the three extant tragedians, and is currently working on language and performance in ancient Greek theatre as well as on Menander.

RUTH WEBB was formerly Assistant Professor of Postclassical Greek in the Department of Classics at Princeton, and is currently Honorary Research Fellow at Birkbeck College, University of London. Her research interests include rhetorical theory in the Second Sophistic and Late Antiquity, and theatrical performance in the Eastern Mediterranean during the Roman period. She has published numerous articles and is currently working on books on ekphrasis in ancient rhetorical theory and the Late Antique theatre.

PETER WILSON is Lecturer in Classics at the University of Oxford and Fellow of New College. He is the author of *The Athenian Institution of the 'Khoregia': the Chorus, the City and the Stage* (Cambridge 2000) and of various articles on Greek society and drama. Current projects include a volume on *Mousikē* edited with Penelope Murray (Oxford University Press, forthcoming).

Preface

One of the most exciting developments within Classics over the last twenty-five years has been the rediscovery of the important truth that many of the masterpieces of ancient literature were originally designed to be appreciated not by isolated individual readers but by spectators grouped at performances. Scholars have been casting off the prejudices against the performative dimension of ancient literature which they inherited from Plato, the Christian fathers and (for different reasons) Aristotle. Interest in the ways in which arenas and modes of performance conditioned the forms taken by literary texts has penetrated even to the study of oratory, epic and choral lyric: recent publications have demonstrated the extent to which ancient authors were creating words whose meaning had to be realised and transmitted through the voices and physical movements of performers – orators, rhapsodes, chorus-members.[1] Dramatic texts, most of all, demand to be interpreted as scripts for players, which can show in often surprising detail how meaning was articulated and mediated through theatrical performance.

Alongside this growing interest in performance, several discrete trends are currently rendering the study of ancient theatre one of the most important avenues by which to explore ancient Mediterranean society, an approach pioneered in Eric Csapo and W. J. Slater's innovative sourcebook *The Context of Ancient Drama* (1995). Besides supplementing the evidence analysed in the fundamental works of A. W. Pickard-Cambridge, especially in *The Dramatic Festivals of Athens* (1st edition 1953, revised and updated by John Gould and David Lewis in 1968, re-issued with addenda in 1988), Csapo and Slater have cast new and thought-provoking light on the social and institutional history of ancient drama and have made it available to a wider public by translating previously inaccessible texts.

[1] See (e.g.) Scodel (1993), Goldhill and Osborne (1999).

Another of these mutually complementary trends is towards a sharper awareness that new material finds not only supplement but significantly alter our picture of the place of theatre in ancient society, in a manner unprecedented except by the papyrus finds of the tragedians and Menander over the past hundred years. The evidence for the ever-increasing volume of empirical data is provided by the expanded 3rd edition (1995) of T. B. L. Webster's *Monuments Illustrating New Comedy* (1st edition 1961),[2] by the publication by L. Bernarbò Brea and his colleagues of the hundreds of terracotta masks and masked figurines found since 1965 in a necropolis on the island of Lipari[3] and by Charlotte Roueché's work on new inscriptions of Asia Minor in *Performers and Partisans at Aphrodisias* (1993).

Closely associated with this acknowledgement of the importance of new finds is the emphasis on the impact of theatre on society. Richard Green, in *Theatre in Ancient Greek Society* (1994), has cogently argued that the depictions of actors and theatrical images on artefacts throughout antiquity reveal a much broader social enjoyment of theatre than is suggested by the written sources, whose consumers tended to come from more élite groups. For the Roman world the work of Richard Beacham and Shadi Bartsch has directed attention to audiences and the way they responded to very varied kinds of performance and spectacle.[4]

At the same time, interest has been growing in the reception, influence and social role of individual 'classic' theatrical works and authors, showing their durability over hundreds of years of performance, adaptation and interpretation. Many articles in the *Lexicon Iconographicum Mythologiae Classicae* illustrate the artistic evidence for the popularity of particular plays, and scholars are now seeing the value of combining the visual data with evidence drawn from ancient commentaries, and from quotations, parodies and allusions in other authors.[5] The story is being extended far beyond antiquity to cover the after-life in performance of ancient plays from the Renaissance onwards.[6]

Yet although the theatre as institution and practice has found a place at the centre of classical scholarship, the ancient actor and acting techniques

[2] = *MNC*³. See Hall (1997b) for a review article noting Webster's 'dogged and precociously modern insistence on drawing interdisciplinary connections between what used to be called "art" and "life" '. The long-term influence of Webster's work can be traced in much contemporary research on ancient theatre practice, notably the Ancient Theatre Project at the Institute of Classical Studies in London.

[3] See Bernabò Brea (1981) and Bernabò Brea and Lavalier (1991).

[4] See Beacham (1991); Bartsch (1994).

[5] See (e.g.) for the *Oresteia* Prag (1986) and Knoepfler (1993).

[6] See (e.g.) Flashar (1991), Hartigan (1995), Hall, Macintosh and Taplin (2000).

remain elusive and relatively under-appreciated phenomena. This is particularly surprising because the actor is a privileged figure in scholarly terms, standing at the intersection between the different sub-disciplines within Classics, and implicitly undermining the distinctions between them. There has been no full-scale exploration of actors in the Greek world since Paulette Ghiron-Bistagne's *Recherches sur les acteurs dans la Grèce antique* (1976). Although this was a fine attempt at synthesising diverse types of evidence into a broad historical overview, it is now outdated; for the Roman world Charles Garton's *Personal Aspects of the Roman Theatre* (1972) made a significant contribution, but it never set out to be comprehensive. More recently, I. E. Stephanis has brought together a vast amount of relevant material in his catalogue of ancient theatrical performers in Διονυσιακοὶ Τεχνῖται (*Artists of Dionysos*, 1988). This is a collection of testimonia rather than a work of interpretation, but besides admirably serving its intended purpose it has had the good effect of widening horizons, since it includes many types of theatrical performers in addition to tragic and comic actors. There have been other recent publications, usefully annotated in Richard Green's *Lustrum* bibliography for 1987–95 (published in 1998),[7] but we believe that there is a real need now for a more sustained study. As we went to press there was published a substantial new two-volume treatment of the evidence for the Hellenistic Artists of Dionysus (B. le Guen, *Les associations de technites dionysiaques à l'époqve hellénistique*, Nancy 2001), revealing how much interest there currently is in our subject. Unfortunately the book did not appear in time for us to take full account of it.

Our aim in editing this volume has been to produce neither a comprehensive reference work nor an historical narrative but a series of complementary essays by experts in different areas – literature, archaeology, art, history – arranged so as to cast as much interdisciplinary light as possible on the diverse aspects of a fascinating social and artistic phenomenon. Now that scholars are no longer inhibited by the assumption that 'late' must mean 'decadent', or that only a few select types of artistic entertainment count as 'theatre', it is easier to gain a sense of the extraordinary staying power and adaptability of the acting profession over the whole period of Greco-Roman antiquity. We have been particularly interested in the light that evidence from the late antique and early Byzantine centuries can throw on these processes of continuity and change.

7 Although this report covers only nine years it is over twice the length of its predecessor for 1971–86 = Green (1989).

Definitions are difficult to make, of course, when one is dealing with such a long period – nearly a thousand years – as well as with a great geographical spread and a wide range of different types of entertainment. By and large we have included under the heading 'actors' artists who played roles in public for (mainly) theatre audiences. This rather broad category is capacious enough to include performers of mime and pantomime, genres which have been too easily neglected in the past, largely because there is much less primary evidence to throw light on their content, but also because they have often seemed to be marginal in various ways: 'post-classical', 'low', or 'sub-literary'. We have tried to avoid using very strict category distinctions so as to allow for significant changes in performance practice which are not necessarily reflected in vocabulary. Thus a solo singer in the Hellenistic period and a pantomime artist under the Empire might both be categorised as 'tragic' performers, though neither would function in the same way as actors who took part in tragic competitions in the fifth or fourth century BC.

Above all we have been concerned, through this 'holistic' approach, to look for the different kinds of illumination that evidence about actors and acting can offer to students of ancient society. Some of the 'marginal' genres, after all, can bring access to a wide range of social classes via the entertainments they enjoyed, and anecdotes about actors can suggest ways in which the experiences of spectators coloured collective awareness and imagination at different periods. A book of this size must also have its limits. Much work remains to be done on the figure of the performer and the acting metaphors that haunt genres of writing not investigated here: the novel, for example, or medical writers.[8] There are other large fields that we have also had to leave unexplored: comparative theatre studies, the theory of performance at its most general, and the anti-theatrical tradition in antiquity and beyond.[9]

The tripartite division of the volume is essentially thematic, although the chapters within each of the three Parts are arranged in broadly chronological order. In Part One the emphasis is on types and styles of ancient performance so far as they can be reconstructed or imagined from a variety of sources. The musical element in ancient dramatic performances is easily neglected in modern discussions, largely because the music has disappeared; we have deliberately chosen to begin with singing actors and with accompanying musicians in order to bring this

[8] See (for the novel) Paulsen (1992), (for medical writers) Lloyd (1979) 89–90, King (1998) 42.
[9] See (e.g.) Barish (1981), Barba and Savarese (1991), Goldhill and Osborne (1999).

important aspect into focus. Other chapters in this section study body movement, costume and acting style from different angles, using the play texts themselves (the nearest thing we have to scripts), vase paintings, and secondary evidence, such as Aristotle's writings on drama, to help recapture something of past experiences and traditions.

Part Two addresses questions of professional organisation, from the Hellenistic to the early Byzantine world. Cumulatively the papers in this section bring out the long-term resilience of some traditions and institutions as well as emphasising differences in social practice and perceptions. In predominantly Greek communities, for example, there was no history of translating ambivalence or anxiety about actors into legal categories like the Roman concept of *infamia*. And yet the growing mobility and cosmopolitanism of actors, and the spread of Roman imperial power, must have created new circumstances which performers had to learn to manage to their advantage, just as later the adoption of Christianity brought ideological challenges which could be met (to some extent, at least) by drawing on the public's deeply felt needs for what performers had to offer. The opening of the profession – some branches of it, at any rate – to women is another significant development which deserves attention. Two chapters in this Part contribute new evidence to the story of change and adaptation: Jory on representations of pantomime masks and Roueché on graffiti showing mime performers.

Part Three explores some of the many ways in which actors, acting and theatre acquired symbolic power in Greco-Roman culture. The sources here are mainly literary, but the focus switches from dramatic texts themselves to biography, scholarly commentary, oratory and history, and the final chapter begins to take the story forward, towards reception in the modern world, and the important role that ancient actors have played in the creation of more recent genres of theatre and literature.

Editing this book has taught us how much there is already to be learned and how much more still to be explored: a full and systematic account of the subject as we have defined it would have entailed many more years of preparation. We hope the twenty chapters offered here, juxtaposing material from different places and periods, will be a stimulus to further efforts to understand ancient acting traditions in all their diversity. The suggestions for further reading, attached, where appropriate, to individual chapters, and the consolidated bibliography, attempt to give both an overview of current scholarship and some flavour of its interdisciplinary nature.

Note on text

The perennial editorial problem of dealing consistently with Greek names has been particularly acute in a volume covering Greek, Roman and early Byzantine culture. We have identified performers by the Greek or Roman form of their names according to their origins, thus Polos not Polus, even though this actor became famous in Latin literary tradition. For well known authors and places we have chosen the forms most familiar in English, but otherwise we have generally followed the practice of the *Oxford Classical Dictionary* (3rd edition 1996) and the *Oxford Dictionary of Byzantium* (1991). For epigraphical publications we have followed the conventions of LSJ, except where indicated in the list of abbreviations. All translations are the contributors' own unless otherwise indicated.

Acknowledgements

For help, advice and support of all kinds in the preparation of this volume we are grateful to the contributors, who have been cheerfully patient and co-operative, and to Nikos Charalabopoulos, Aidan Foster, Stuart Hall, Johannes Haubold, Pat Kelly, Fiona Macintosh, June McCall, Thalia Papadopoulou, Richard Poynder and the Principal and Fellows of Somerville College, Oxford. Our colleagues at Cambridge University Press have given us imaginative guidance and much practical help; we thank two Classics editors, Pauline Hire and her successor Michael Sharp, our scrupulous copy-editor Linda Woodward, our indexer Barbara Hird and our proof reader Henry Maas.

Abbreviations

AP	*Anthologia Graeca Epigrammatum Palatina cum Planudea*, ed. H. Stadtmüller. 3 vols. Leipzig 1894–1906
Arnott	Arnott, W. G., ed. and trans. (1979–2000) *Menander*. 3 vols. Cambridge, MA and London
*ARV*²	Beazley, J. D. (1963) *Attic Red-Figure Vase Painters*. 2nd edn. Oxford
Beazley Addenda	Carpenter, T. H. (1989) *Beazley Addenda: Additional References to ABV, ARV², and Paralipomena*. 2nd edn. Oxford
CEG	Hansen, P. A. (1983/89) *Carmina Epigraphica Graeca*. 2 vols. Berlin
CHCL	*Cambridge History of Classical Literature*. Vol. I: *Greek Literature*, eds. P. E. Easterling and B. M. W. Knox, Cambridge 1985. Vol. II: *Latin Literature*, eds. E. J. Kenney and W. V. Clausen, Cambridge 1982
CIL	*Corpus Inscriptionum Latinarum* (1863–). Berlin
DFA	Pickard-Cambridge, A. W. (1953) *The Dramatic Festivals of Athens*. Oxford (2nd edn, revised by J. Gould and D. M. Lewis, Oxford 1968; 3rd edn with supplement and corrections, Oxford 1988)
DK	Diels, H. and W. Kranz, eds. (1951–52) *Die Fragmente der Vorsokratiker*, 2 vols. 6th edn. Berlin and Zurich
Edelstein–Kidd	Edelstein, L. and I. G. Kidd, eds. (1989) *Posidonius, The Fragments*. Vol I. 2nd edn. Cambridge
FD	*Fouilles de Delphes* (1902–). Paris
FGrH	Jacoby, F. (1923–58) *Fragmente der griechischen Historiker*. Berlin
FR	Furtwängler, A. and F. Reichhold (1904–32) *Griechische Vasenmalerei*. Munich

GLP — Page, D. L. (1942) *Greek Literary Papyri*. Cambridge, MA

IG^2 — *Inscriptiones Graecae*^{2}, eds. F. H. de Gaertringen et al. Berlin 1924–

IGD — Trendall, A. D. and T. B. L. Webster (1971) *Illustrations of Greek Drama*. London

IGUR — Moretti, L., ed. (1968–90) *Inscriptiones Graecae Urbis Romae*. Rome

IK — *Inschriften griechischer Städte aus Kleinasien*. Bonn 1972

IMagn. — Kern, O., ed. (1900) *Die Inschriften von Magnesia am Maeander*. Berlin (repr. Berlin 1967)

KA — Kassel, R. and C. Austin (1983–) *Poetae Comici Graeci*. Berlin and New York

Kaibel — Kaibel, G. (1899) *Comicorum Graecorum Fragmenta*. Berlin

K–T — *Menandri quae supersunt*, ed. A. Koerte (Leipzig 1938); ed. with revisions and addenda by A. Thierfelder. 2 vols. Leipzig 1957–59

LCS — Trendall, A. D. (1967) *The Red-Figured Vases of Lucania, Campania and Sicily*. Oxford

Marm. Par. — *Marmor Parium* (*IG* 12(5).444), ed. F. Jacoby, *Das Marmor Parium*. Berlin 1904

Michel — Michel, C. (1900–27) *Recueil d'inscriptions grecques*. Brussels

MMC^3 — Webster, T. B. L. (1978) *Monuments Illustrating Old and Middle Comedy*. London. 3rd edn, revised and enlarged by J. R. Green and A. Seeberg (*BICS* Suppl. 39). London

MNC^3 — Webster, T. B. L. (1995) *Monuments Illustrating New Comedy*. 3rd edn, revised and enlarged by J. R. Green and A. Seeberg (*BICS* Suppl. 50) 2 vols. London

MTS^2 — Webster, T. B. L. (1967) *Monuments Illustrating Tragedy and Satyr-Play*. 2nd edn (*BICS* Suppl. 20). London

Nauck — Nauck, A. (1889) *Tragicorum Graecorum Fragmenta*. 2nd edn. Leipzig (repr. with Supplementum by B. Snell, Hildesheim 1964)

OGIS — Dittenberger, W., ed. (1898–1905) *Orientis Graecae Inscriptiones Selectae*. Leipzig

Paralipomena — Beazley, J. D. (1971) *Paralipomena. Additions to Attic Black-Figure Vase-Painters and to Attic Red-Figure Vase-Painters*. 2nd edn. Oxford

Paroemiogr.	*Corpus Paroemiographorum Graecorum*, eds. E. L. Leutsch and P. G. Schneidewin. Göttingen 1839
Passion for Antiquities	*A Passion for Antiquities. Ancient Art from the Collection of Barbara and Lawrence Fleischman*. Malibu 1994
PG	Migne, J. P. (1857–1912) *Patrologia Graeca*. Paris
PCG	Kassel, R. and C. Austin, eds. (1983–) *Poetae Comici Graeci*. Berlin
PhV²	Trendall, A. D. (1967) *Phlyax Vases*. 2nd edn (*BICS* Suppl. 19). London
PL	Migne, J. P. (1844–65) *Patrologia Latina*. Paris
PMG	Page, D. L. (1962) *Poetae Melici Graeci*. Oxford 1962
Powell, *Coll. Alex.*	Powell, J. U. (1925) *Collectanea Alexandrina*. Oxford
P Oxy.	*Oxyrhynchus Papyri* (1898–). London
RE	*Real-Encyclopädie der classischen Altertumswissenschaft*, eds. A. Pauly, G. Wissova and W. Kroll. Stuttgart and Munich 1893–1980
Robert, *OMS*	Robert, L. (1969–90) *Opera Minora Selecta*. 7 vols.
RVAp	Trendall, A. D. and A. Cambitoglou (1978/82) *The Red-Figured Vases of Apulia*, 2 vols. Oxford
RVAp Suppl. ii	Trendall, A. D. and A. Cambitoglou (1992) *The Red-Figured Vases of Apulia, Supplement* II (*BICS* Suppl. 60). London
RVP	Trendall, A. D. (1987) *The Red-Figured Vases of Paestum*. London
RVSIS	Trendall, A. D. (1989) *Red Figure Vases of South Italy and Sicily*. London
SEG	*Supplementum Epigraphicum Graecum* (1923–). Leiden
SIG	Dittenberger, W. (1915–24) *Sylloge Inscriptionum Graecarum*. 3rd edn. Leipzig
Studies . . . Trendall	Cambitoglou, A., ed. (1979) *Studies in Honour of Arthur Dale Trendall*. Sydney
Suppl. Hell.	Lloyd-Jones, H. and P. Parsons, eds. (1983) *Supplementum Hellenisticum*. Berlin and New York
SVF	von Arnim, H. (1903–) *Stoicorum Veterum Fragmenta*. 4 vols. Leipzig
TrGF	Snell, B., S. Radt and R. Kannicht, eds. (1971–) *Tragicorum Graecorum Fragmenta*. Göttingen
Vahlen	Vahlen, J. (1854) *Ennianae Poesis Reliquiae*. Leipzig (3rd edn Amsterdam 1963)

1. *The Aegean World*

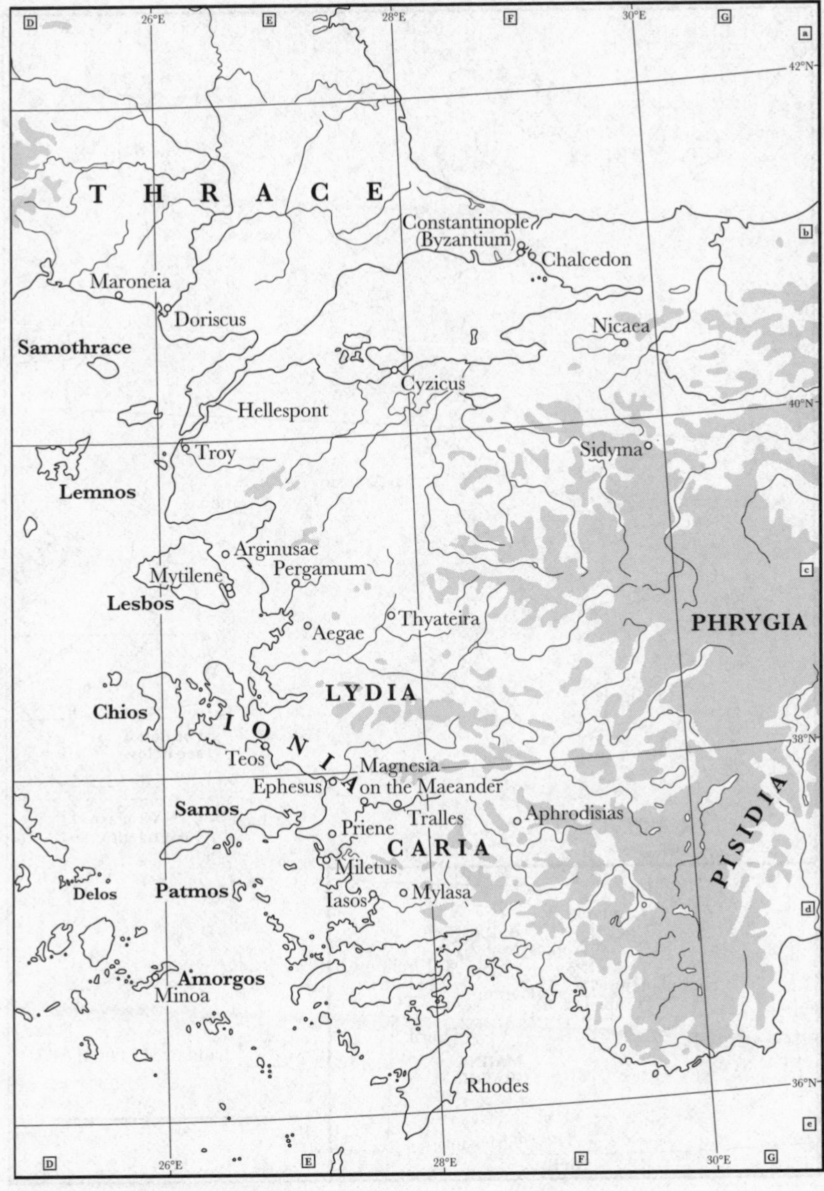
THRACE
Constantinople
(Byzantium)
Chalcedon
Maroneia
Doriscus
Samothrace
Nicaea
Cyzicus
Hellespont
Troy
Sidyma
Lemnos
Arginusae
Pergamum
Mytilene
Lesbos
Aegae
Thyateira
PHRYGIA
LYDIA
Chios
IONIA
Teos
Magnesia
on the Maeander
Ephesus
Samos
Tralles
Aphrodisias
Priene
CARIA
PISIDIA
Miletus
Delos
Patmos
Iasos
Mylasa
Amorgos
Minoa
Rhodes
26°E
28°E
30°E
42°N
40°N
38°N
36°N

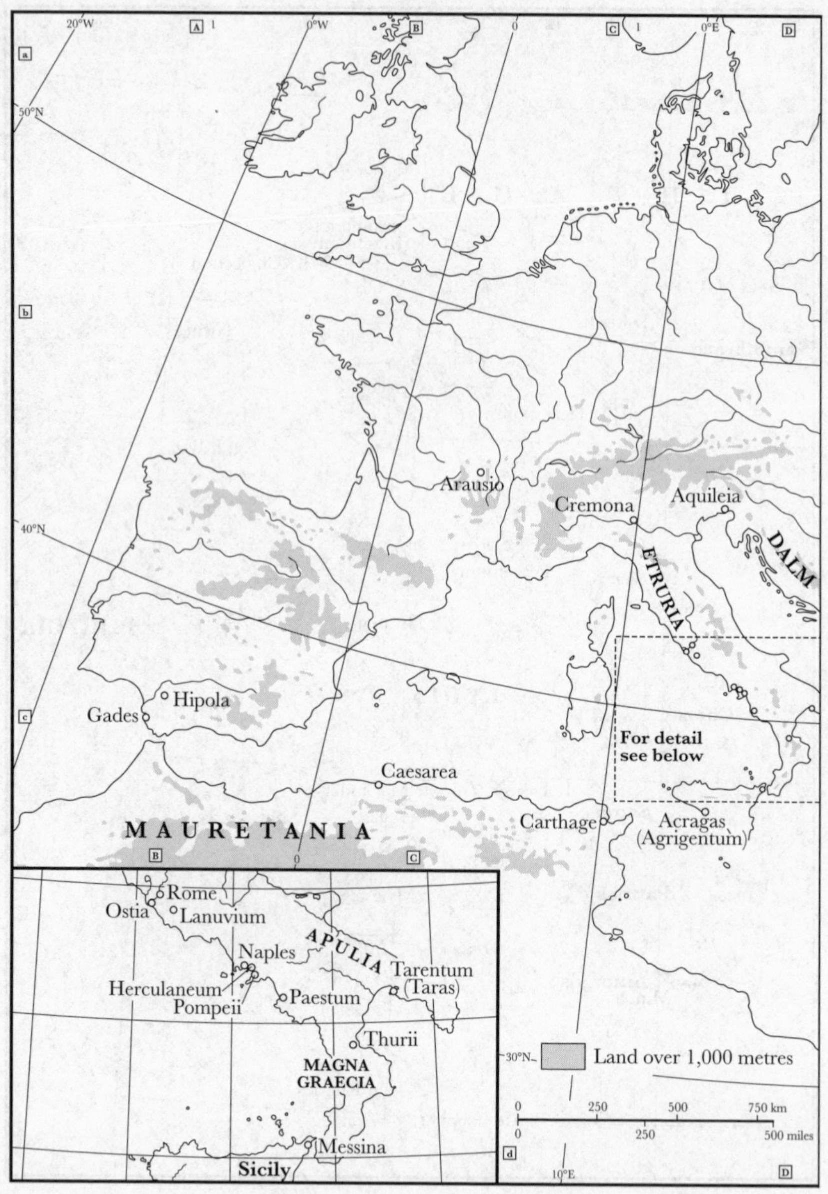

2. *The Mediterranean World*

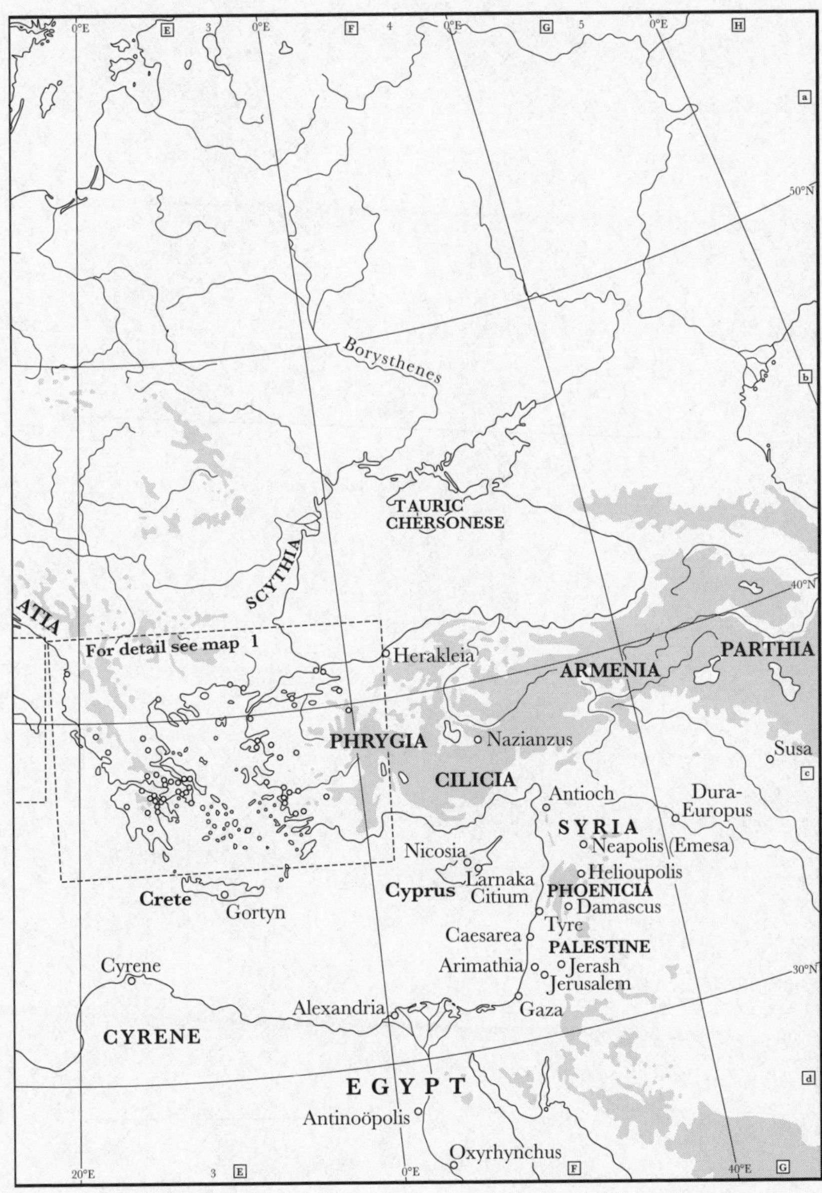
Borysthenes
TAURIC CHERSONESE
SCYTHIA
ATIA
For detail see map 1
Herakleia
ARMENIA
PARTHIA
PHRYGIA
Nazianzus
Susa
CILICIA
Antioch
Dura-Europus
SYRIA
Neapolis (Emesa)
Nicosia
Helioupolis
Larnaka Citium
Cyprus
PHOENICIA
Damascus
Crete
Gortyn
Tyre
Caesarea
PALESTINE
Arimathia
Jerash
Jerusalem
Cyrene
Alexandria
Gaza
CYRENE
EGYPT
Antinoöpolis
Oxyrhynchus
50°N
40°N
30°N
20°E
40°E

PART ONE

The art of the actor

CHAPTER ONE

The singing actors of antiquity

Edith Hall

INTRODUCTION

At the turn of the fifth century AD Augustine confesses to having sometimes neglected the spiritual content of the psalms of David because he has been distracted – even moved to tears – by the beauty of the voices he has heard singing them. Augustine therefore approves of the Alexandrian bishop Athanasius, who attempted to protect his congregation's spiritual purity by instructing 'the reader of the psalm to sound it forth with such slight vocal modulation (*flexu vocis*) that it was nearer to speaking than to singing' (*Conf.* 10.33).

Augustine's supposedly shameful passion for vocal music had been fed by his successful participation, as a young pagan, in theatrical singing competitions (*Conf.* 4.2). He recalls a solo he used to sing entitled *The Flying Medea* (*Medea volans*, 3.6). The tragic theme implies that Augustine performed in costume and with gestures as a *tragoedus* or *tragicus cantor* (a 'tragic singer').[1] We do not know whether this aria was composed in the first person, requiring the singer to impersonate Medea as she flew, but it was certainly much performed (4.3). Augustine's testimony opens a fascinating window on the late Roman theatre, where famous songs on mythical themes were still being sung by expert singers, more than eight centuries since the first actor to impersonate Euripides' Medea had flown off to Athens in the chariot borrowed from the Sun. In antiquity, when our modern genres of musical theatre, opera and the musical, had not yet been invented, but which relished expert singing to a degree unsurpassed by music lovers today, the relationship of the art of acting to the art of singing was often inextricable. This chapter leads into the book's reappraisal of the profession of the ancient player via an unorthodox but illuminating route, which traces the history

[1] If he could play the cithara *Medea volans* just might have been a 'citharoedic' performance (Kelly (1979) 27–8).

of the singing actor from democratic Athens to beyond Augustine's day.

This story is co-extensive with ancient theatrical activity, which can still be documented at Epidauros and Athens in the late fourth century AD, and at Aphrodisias as late as the seventh.[2] Theatrical singers are attested from tragedies of Thespis in the sixth century BC to the Byzantine theatres in which Theodora performed in the sixth century AD, when the word 'tragedy' gave rise to what is still the word for 'song' in the Greek language (*tragoudi*, see Puchner, this volume). Vocal performances thrilled audiences not only across many centuries but also across a huge geographical area, for the Roman empire saw theatres built from Britain and western Portugal to North Africa and the far east of modern Turkey. Even some small cities had an Odeion in addition to one or more theatres (on the fascinating graffiti depicting performers drawn on the Odeion at Aphrodisias see further Roueché, this volume). It is revealing that in the second century AD Pausanias says that one reason Panopeus scarcely deserves to be called a city is because it had no theatre at all (10.4.1); two centuries later, when Eunapius wants to illustrate the primitivism of some Spanish barbarians, he portrays their astonishment at the singing of a travelling tragic actor (see below, 'Conclusion').

Although it is fashionable to stress that the ancient Greek and Latin words for a theatrical audience (*theatai*, *spectatores*) prioritised the act of watching, many ancient authors acknowledge the importance of the aural impact of drama on the 'spectator'. The discussion of tragedy in Aristophanes' *Frogs* focuses extensively on music and rhythm, Plato disapprovingly refers to spectators' sympathy with heroes 'delivering long speeches or singing (*aidontas*) and beating themselves' (*Rep.* 10.605c10–e2), Aristotle regards songwriting (*melopoiia*) as a more significant source of tragic pleasure than the visual dimension (*Poet.* 1450b15–18, see Sifakis, this volume), and Plutarch describes the experience of watching tragedy as 'a wonderful *aural* and visual experience'.[3]

The solo singing voice was particularly associated with Greek tragedy. Early tragic actors' roles may have consisted almost entirely of singing;[4] by Hellenistic times the Athenian guild of actors worshipped Dionysus under the title 'Melpomenos' (see Lightfoot, this volume), and

[2] See Green (1994a) 161–2.

[3] θαυμαστὸν ἀκρόαμα καὶ θέαμα (*On the Renown of the Athenians* 5 = *Mor.* 348C). By the end of the fourth century AD, when tragic songs had become dissociated from staged production, it is natural to Jerome to refer in his commentary on Ezechiel to the pleasure of people 'who *listen to* either tragic or comic actors' (*vel tragoedos audiunt vel comoedos*, 10. 33, 23–33, Migne, *PL* vol. 25 (1845) col. 326).

[4] In the earliest extant tragedy, Aeschylus' *Persians*, King Xerxes' entire role is in song or recitative (Hall (1996a) 169), and it is just possible that some truth lies behind the statement in Philostratus

Melpomene, the muse who represented tragedy, derived her name from the same basic verb meaning 'sing'.[5] But the singing voice was heard in all the other types of ancient drama and their adaptations – satyr play, Old Comedy, Greek and Roman New Comedy, Atellan farce,[6] Roman tragedy, virtuoso recitals of excerpts from old dramas, pantomime, mime,[7] and such curiosities as Philoxenus' *Cyclops*, a light-hearted work on a mythical theme for two solo singers and an aulete, which has been compared with a chamber opera.[8] There were also innumerable sub-theatrical entertainers whose acts involved singing, including jugglers (Theophr. *Char.* 27.7), the hilarodes and Simodes who sang risqué parodies of highbrow musical compositions, and the magodes who banged cymbals and drums while impersonating such figures as a drunk singing a serenade.[9] Nor did theatrical singers confine their art to theatres: *tragōidoi*, for example, are found performing on board Alcibiades' trireme when he returned from exile in 408 BC (Duris, *FGrH* 76 F 70), at the five-day wedding celebrations of Alexander the Great at Susa (Chares, *FGrH* 125 F 4), and at symposia throughout antiquity from Macedonia to Mauretania.[10]

TRAGEDY IN CLASSICAL ATHENS

Tragedy developed in what Herington stressed was 'a song culture'.[11] Many fifth-century spectators of drama will themselves have sung at one of the several Athenian festivals where fifty-strong choruses of men and

that it was Aeschylus who invented spoken dialogue (*antilexeis*) for the actors, 'discarding the long monodies of the earlier time' (*Life of Apollonius* 6.11).

5 It probably has implications for the way tragedy was being performed by late antiquity that on artefacts Melpomene represents tragedy in contrast to Pol(h)ymnia, the new muse of pantomime (see further below). On a third-century Roman mosaic at Elis there are images symbolising all nine muses, including Melpomene, Thalia and Polymnia, who are represented by theatrical masks: see Yalouris (1992). On a fourth-century silver casket found on the Esquiline these theatrical muses are depicted holding their masks (Jory (1996) 12–13 and figs. 7 and 9).

6 In Petronius, *Sat.* 53 Trimalchio says he had bought a troupe of professional (Greek) comic actors but compelled them to perform Atellan farces and his *choraules* (see below n. 69) to sing in Latin: *malui illos Atellaniam facere, et choraulen meum iussi Latine cantare.*

7 See e.g. the canticum from the mime *The Silphium Gatherer* (*Laserpiciarius Mimus*), sung in a foul voice (*taeterrima voce*) by Trimalchio at his dinner party (Petronius *Sat.* 35, Bonaria (1965) 81). Although it has been argued that Greek mime did not involve much use of music (Cunningham (1971) 5), it is difficult to see what other genre the so-called 'Charition mime' might belong to, and it is preserved on a papyrus (*P Oxy.* 413, edited in Grenfell and Hunt (1903)) which may well have been a musician's copy: it contains signs at several points which are almost certainly instructions to play percussion instruments and probably *auloi* (see *GLP* 338–9).

8 *PMG* frr. 815–24. See Arist. *Poet.* 1448a14–16, West (1992a) 366.

9 See Maas (1927) and Hunter, this volume.

10 See Easterling (1997d) and Easterling, this volume.

11 Herington (1985) 3–10.

boys competed.[12] The Athenians knew many songs by heart – hymns, songs to congratulate athletes and military victors, processional songs, drinking songs, work songs, lullabies, medical and magical incantations, and songs to mark courtship, marriage, birth, and death. They sang them more often than modern individuals whose personal repertoire scarcely extends beyond *Happy Birthday* and *Auld Lang Syne* can possibly imagine. Many songs in tragedy (and comedy, see below) are derived from one of these pre-existing genres of 'ritual' or 'activity' song and are in the lyric metres appropriate to them. But tragedy's material was mostly drawn from the world of myth, inherited, rather, from epics and from choral lyrics, especially those of Stesichorus.

Tragic poetry is 'adorned with various rhythms and includes a wealth of metres', observed the Byzantine scholar Psellus.[13] Tragedy's innovation was to *integrate* genres into a complicated artistic pattern: spoken verse alternated with various types of sung poetry, performed to the accompaniment of *auloi* by both a chorus and individual actors. The tragic actor made use of a metre long associated with marching armies, the 'recitative' anapaest, whose basic unit is repeated pairs of ⏑⏑ –. Anapaests predominate at times of physical movement, especially entrances and exits such as the airborne departure of Euripides' Medea. The anapaestic metre there indicates that Medea and Jason performed their interchange to *aulos* accompaniment in a rhythmical, semi-musical type of vocal delivery, in antiquity designated by the verb *katalegein*, and perhaps comparable with the intermediate form of enunciation later recommended to Christian psalmodists by Bishop Athanasius. Like rhapsodes and citharodes, the tragic actor also needed mastery over the dactylic hexameter, at least when impersonating mythical bards such as Thamyras or Amphion (see further Wilson, this volume). But in addition he had to perform new sung metres, especially the excited dochmiac (based on ⏑ – – ⏑ –). Dochmiacs make no appearance prior to tragedy and virtually disappear after it, but often characterise the genre's most emotionally lacerating moments.[14]

The actor of fifth-century tragedy had to sing in a variety of metres in rapid succession,[15] and to negotiate the delicate transitions between

[12] A thousand citizens will have performed every year at the City Dionysia in dithyrambic choruses alone, even before the tragic and comic choruses are taken into account (West (1992a) 17).

[13] ἡ τραγικὴ ποίησις διαφόροις τε ῥυθμοῖς κοσμουμένη καὶ μέτρα ποικίλα λαμβάνουσα (Dyck (1986) 21–4).

[14] West (1992a) 142.

[15] See e.g. Soph. *Philoctetes* 1169–1217 and the comments of West (1992a) 153. This skill would have been considered remarkable by Aristoxenus' day, when the emphasis on rhythmical intricacy had been superseded by a love of melody ([Plut.] *On Music* 1138B–C).

them: the shift between recitative and lyrics was regarded as particularly emotive ([Arist.] *Probl.* 19.6). Anapaestic and lyric verses repeatedly alternated with iambic trimeters, and these were spoken. Besides some important external evidence,[16] tragic poetry offers internal clues to the way in which the voice was being used; in iambics people constantly use such verbs as *legein* and *phrazein* in reference to their own speech and that of their interlocutors, whereas the semantic range referring to lyric utterance, which includes *melpein* and *aidein*, is quite different.[17]

Tragedy thus offered the dramatist a palette of vocal techniques with which to paint his sound pictures, and certain patterns can be discerned in the way that he handled them. Gods and slaves, for example, rarely sing lyrics in tragedy, but they do recite anapaests. Sophoclean leads all sing at moments of great emotion, female characters frequently sing, but middle-aged men in Aeschylus and Euripides (with the exception of distressed barbarians) prefer spoken rhetoric to extended lyrics.[18] This complex metrical and vocal prosopography was unprecedented. Athens invented tragedy at a time when it was staking claim to be the cultural leader of the Greek world, and it is possible, from a sociological angle, to view tragedy's appropriation of metres associated with other places as Athenian cultural imperialism manifested on the level of form.[19] But it is equally important to stress the *aesthetic* achievement represented by tragedy's elaborate design.

Expert singers, rhapsodes and citharodes, had been singing Greek myths long before the emergence of the specialist *tragōidos*: the *Iliad*, after all, opens 'Muse, sing (*aeide*) of the wrath of Achilles'. But the term *aeidein* demonstrates how close an affinity was perceived between the performances of the epic and the tragic singer, for together with its cognates *aeidein* provided many of the basic words for 'singing' both epic and drama in Greek literature, and formed the second half of the compounds denoting almost all specialist singers, including *kitharōidos*, *tragōidos* and *kōmōidos*. Etymologically related to *aeidein* are both *audē* (the human voice, endowed with speech), and *aēdōn*, 'nightingale', a bird whose plaintive song brought it into association with lachrymose women from Penelope of the *Odyssey* onwards (19.518–23). But it was with female

[16] Two important passages in Aristotle associate the iambic metre with speech (*Poet.* 1449a19–28, *Rhet.* 3.1408b24–6); in Lucian's caricatures of *tragōidoi*, he complains that the performers contemporary with him 'even' sing their iambics, implying that this practice is a decadent modern development (see below).

[17] Although Barner (1971) 292 collects some of the Greek tragic terms designating song, much work remains to be done on the numerous different words used in tragedy to describe vocal performance, and on how they might illuminate actors' techniques of singing and speaking.

[18] See Hall (1999a) 108–20 and Csapo, this volume.

[19] Hall (1997a) 100, 111; Hall (1999a) 120–2.

singing in tragedy that the nightingale, formerly Procne, the infanticidal mother, became most closely connected.

The story of Procne's murder of her son Itys was staged in Sophocles' famous *Tereus* (the music of which seems to have been memorable, see below) and by the Roman tragedians Livius Andronicus and Accius. Elsewhere tragedy alludes to this myth when describing women's singing. In Aeschylus' *Agamemnon*, for example, Cassandra's dochmiac singing is likened by the chorus (also using dochmiacs) to the song of the nightingale (1140–9):

CHORUS You are crazed, possessed by a god, and singing a tuneless tune about your own fate, like some shrill nightingale, insatiable in lament – alas! – who in the misery of her heart mourns 'Itys, Itys', whose death was full of evil for both his parents.

CASSANDRA Ah, ah, for the life of the clear-voiced nightingale! The gods clothed her in winged form, and gave her a sweet life with nothing to cry about, whereas for me there awaits the blow of a two-edged weapon.

The comparison was presumably reinforced by the lost melody, and certainly by the 'twittering' effect produced by the high proportion of short syllables in the resolved dochmiacs of this particular interchange; the chorus' description of Cassandra's melody as a 'tuneless tune' (*nomon anomon*) itself scans as five short syllables consecutively. Cassandra, however, shifts the focus from the bird's voice to her winged body, reminding us that the singing actor playing her is engaged in an emphatically physical activity.[20]

The actor playing Cassandra needed skill in antiphonal singing, which requires a solo voice with a timbre distinct from that of the choral group but minutely adjusted to its tonality and pace of delivery. Cassandra's sung dialogue with the chorus consists of serial pairs of metrical units of similar length, which respond strophically. The structured rhythmical character of Aeschylus' music is suggested by Dionysus' description in *Frogs* of his melodies as appropriate for 'someone drawing water from a well' (1297). But tragic music evolved alongside that of citharody and dithyrambic choruses, which had already been composed without strophic responsion by the middle of the fifth century (Arist. *Rhet.* 3.1409b).

In Euripides' dateable plays actors' songs increasingly replace strophic responsion with asymmetric, 'freeform' metrical structures,

[20] Segal (1995) 68. See Valakas, this volume. See also Aeschylus' Danaids, who compare their own singing with the voice of the nightingale, the wife of Tereus (*Supp.* 58–67), and the comments below on Sophocles' *Electra*.

characterised by repetition of individual words.[21] Euripides' astrophic monodists are mostly self-absorbed women, who use song to express intimate and passionate emotions.[22] Astrophic song is much harder to learn than song in a repeated metre, which is one reason why it was associated with the solo voice rather than with choruses ([Arist.] *Probl.* 19.15). But it also increased the ornamentation and mimetic element (see Csapo, this volume) and affected the vocal timbre. Timotheus, the citharode most closely associated with the 'New Music' influencing Euripides, differentiated his own relaxed, beguiling sound from that of older, out-of-date singers, 'the maulers' of songs 'who strain and yell with the far-ringing voices of heralds' (κηρύκων λιγυμακροφώνων τείνοντας ἰυγάς, *Persians PMG* 791, 218–20).

A plausible tradition held that the earliest tragedians were star actors and took the principal roles in their own plays. Sophocles is said to have played the lead in his own *Thamyras*, in which this mythical bard performed hexameters and played the cithara (*Life* 5; fr. 242 *TrGF*, see also Wilson, this volume). Sophocles' *Thamyras* is probably illustrated on a hydria from the middle of the century (fig. 1). It has the words 'Euaion is beautiful' inscribed over the figure of an agitated woman, probably Thamyras' mother Argiope, dancing under the influence of his music. Since we know that Aeschylus' son Euaion was a tragic actor, we may be looking at a picture of characters played in the original production by a singing, strumming Sophocles and by Aeschylus' dancing son.[23]

Sophocles is supposed to have given up performing in his own plays because of his weak voice (*Life* 4), a tradition which functioned as an aetiological narrative for the emergence of the specialist tragic singer. Sophocles is also said to have taken the talents of his actors into account when composing their roles (*Life* 6), and the vocal skills of the available lead actors (for example, the Tlepolemos who often acted for Sophocles (schol. on Ar. *Clouds* 1266)) must have influenced all the tragedians;[24] any competent singer, for example, knew the exact range of his own voice and

[21] E.g. *IA* 1289–90, Ἰδαῖος / Ἰδαῖος ἐλέγετ' ἐλέγετ', on which England (1891) 130 comments: 'probably it was the music which was mainly responsible for this double repetition'. On this kind of diction and repetition in Euripidean monodies see Barlow (1986b). But Euripides was not the only tragedian to experiment with the new, freer form of actor's song. Io in the Aeschylean *PV* (566–73) is an interesting early example of an astrophic monodist.

[22] Damen (1990) 134–5. In Electra's monody at *Orestes* 960–1012, for example, Euripides moves his actor from strophic to astrophic form at the point where Electra's grief moves beyond control to hysteria (982, see Collard (1975) vol. II, 359).

[23] Rome, Vatican 16549 (*IGD* 69, no. III. 2.9). On the vase and on Euaion see further Green, this volume and Kaimio (1993) 22.

[24] Owen (1936) 150, 153.

Fig. 1 Thamyras and his mother Argiope: played by Sophocles(?) and Aeschylus' son Euaion (Photo: J. R. Green)

needed to have his singing pitched accordingly.[25] Actors who performed alongside star protagonists also had to be able to sing. In Euripides' *Orestes* the deuteragonist who originally played Electra and Helen's Phrygian servant, in support of the protagonist Hegelochos' Orestes, must have possessed a remarkable singing voice with a high tessitura.[26] Aeschines had to sing an antiphonal lament as Sophocles' Creon in *Antigone* (probably a tritagonist's role, see Easterling, this volume), but also a striking monody as the blinded Polymestor in Euripides' *Hecuba* (Dem. 18.267, see fig. 2).[27]

[25] Callicratidas in Thesleff (1961) 106.21.

[26] See further Falkner, this volume. Information from several sources tells us more than usual about the music to Euripides' *Orestes*, an exceptionally popular play on the ancient stage. An important papyrus of the third or second century BC (Vienna G 2315, see Pöhlmann (1970) 78–82) preserves the sung melody and accompaniment to seven lines delivered by the chorus (338–44), and there is no reason to suppose that this music was not composed by Euripides himself. Dionysius of Halicarnassus, writing in the Augustan era about the relationship of words to music, seems to have been able to make a detailed consultation of a 'score' of Euripides' *Orestes* (*On Composition of Words* 5.11.63, see Pöhlmann (1960) 19–24). And a scholiast happens to have recorded the information that the actor playing Electra sang at a very high pitch (*oxeiai phōnēi*), appropriate to a dirge, when asking the entering chorus to be quiet (schol. on *Or.* 176). See also Damen (1990) 141–2.

[27] Stephanis (1988) no. 90.3a.

Fig. 2 The blinded Polymestor in Euripides' *Hecuba* (©The British Museum)

VIRTUOSO *TRAGŌIDOI*

Actors were becoming famous for their virtuoso specialisms by the fourth century – Nikostratos for his recital of tetrameters to the *auloi* and his messenger speeches,[28] and Theodoros for his 'natural' delivery and female roles, which included several with important lyrics, such as Sophocles' Electra and Antigone.[29] But it is in the third century that inscriptions recording the constitution of theatrical companies at festivals such as the Delphic Soteria, combined with the Hellenistic *Problems* attributed to Aristotle, begin to present a clear picture of a new kind of travelling professional actor whose special expertise was in singing.[30] He was to remain a feature of cultural life in the Mediterranean region for eight hundred years.[31]

Travelling professional *tragōidoi*, if successful in competitions, could enjoy huge earnings and fame, and be honoured by statues and civic rights in the cities where they performed.[32] Their only rivals were rhapsodes, and, later, star dancers of pantomime (see below). It is not surprising that a skilled singer might participate in several different types of event at festivals, for example the Athenian Xenophantos of the first century BC, a rhapsode, tragic actor, and singer of paeans and choruses.[33] The

[28] Xen. *Symp.* 6.3; it was proverbial to 'tell everything like Nikostratos' (*Paroemiogr.* 1.395). See also Csapo, this volume.

[29] Plut. *Sympotic Questions-Moralia* 737B, Dem. 19.246 (Stephanis (1988) no. 1157). Theodoros was also famous for his performances of female roles in Euripidean tragedy (see Lada-Richards, this volume). On the enormous importance of the public opinion of an actor's vocal skills, see Easterling (1999). On actors' specialisms see also Green, this volume, Dihle (1981) 29–30, Ghiron-Bistagne (1976) 157. Other actors may have specialised in male roles: see, for example, the enterprising third-century boxer/actor whose documented (all male) winning roles included heroes renowned for the physical prowess, such as Heracles and Antaeus (Stephanis (1988) no. 3003). This impressive person may have been an Arcadian named Apollogenes (see Stephanis (1988) no. 239).

[30] Gentili (1979) 22; Sifakis (1967) 156–65.

[31] By the late Roman period the theatres came to be dominated by pantomimes and mimes, but a certain diversity of entertainment was maintained, and there are still references to 'tragic actors' in the fourth century (John Chrysostom, *Homily on the Acts of the Apostles* 30, *PG* 60.226) and even as late as the sixth (Choricius *Syn. Mim.* 118, where they are listed with conjurors): see Theocharidis (1940) 50–2. At Byzantium, at any rate, excerpts from old tragedies continued to be sung by actors who wore high shoes and elaborate costumes, and took both female and male roles (Theocharidis (1940) 49–62).

[32] See e.g. Stephanis (1988) nos. 1272, 2001.

[33] Stephanis (1988) no. 1913, see also nos. 2137, 822. Outside the context of competitive festivals, the distinctions between performers of tragedy and performers of epic must in practice often have been blurred. See, for example, the travelling professional actor in Achilles Tatius' *Leucippe and Cleitophon* (3.20), of the second century AD. He gave vocal displays of passages from Homer (τις . . . τῶν τὰ Ὁμήρου τῷ στόματι δεικνύντων ἐν τοῖς θεάτροις). But the performances were theatrical enough to require props (σκευή), which the context implies consisted of armour and

singing profession was often practised by more than one member of the same family, for example the third-century brothers Ouliades and Aristippos of Miletus, or the Theban rhapsode Kraton and his son Kleon, a *tragōidos*.[34] Such singers may have begun as infant prodigies, perhaps specialising in sung children's roles such as that of Alcestis' son in her Euripidean name-play: a boy actor from Cyzicus in the third century AD (*pais tragōidos*) was honoured by the citizens of Ephesus.[35]

The performances of *tragōidoi*, although masked and costumed, must often have resembled what we call concerts or recitals rather than theatrical productions. The nineteenth Aristotelian *Problem* implies that the growing popularity of the *tragōidos* as entertainer, and the increasing ascendancy of his solos over choral lyric, resulted from the greater expressive and mimetic possibilities of the solo aria. Hellenistic *tragōidoi* concentrated the pleasure their performances offered by excerpting the most delicious solo lyric highlights from tragedies. Solo recitals were first to rival and, together with pantomime, eventually to supersede the performance of whole tragic texts.[36]

A papyrus of the third century BC shows a programme, for example, which not only consists of excerpted lyrical highlights from *Iphigenia in Aulis*, but rearranges their order.[37] Another possibility was to extract several scenes from different tragedies on the same mythical figure, such as the excerpts apparently linked by Achilles' son Neoptolemus in the 'Oslo papyrus', a beautiful document from which some ancient *tragōidos* learned the words and melodies for a recital (fig. 3).[38] A star Samian aulete named Satyros, after his victory at a Pythian festival (probably in 194 BC), demonstrated his versatility by offering his audience one song with a chorus called *Dionysus*, and another on a presumably similar theme, from Euripides' *Bacchae*, which he accompanied on the cithara.[39] A *tragōidos*, Kanopos, appears on a papyrus from Oxyrhynchus alongside the aulete Epagathos, who is named as the accompanist to forty 'odes' from six

weapons. They certainly included, for stage murders (πρὸς τὰς κιβδήλους σφαγάς), a trick dagger with a retractable blade, which saves the heroine's life.

34 Stephanis (1988) nos. 322, 1968 (see also nos. 2810–12), 1502, 1464.

35 Stephanis (1988) no. 1779.

36 A practice for which there is no firm evidence after the early third century AD (Barnes (1996) 170–3, Easterling and Miles (1999) 96).

37 Leiden papyrus inv. 510. Thanks to Martin West for helpful advice on the musical papyri.

38 Gentili (1979) 28–30, first edited by Eitrem, Amundsen and Winnington-Ingram (1955). The text, which contains more than one version of some phrases, may have been written by the music's composer (West 1992a) 312. For further discussion of the possible links between the excerpts in this papyrus see Pöhlmann (1970) 118–19.

39 Stephanis (1988) no. 2240.

Fig. 3 The 'Oslo' papyrus showing words and melodies for a recital of songs about Neoptolemus (Photo: Adam Bülow-Jacobsen/AIP Archive)

'dramas'. These seem to have been excerpts from (mostly Euripidean) plays, including *Hypsipyle*, *Medea* and *Antiope*.[40]

Tragic singers appear at significant moments in the literature of the Second Sophistic. Anecdotes concerning *tragōidoi* (usually singing the songs of Euripidean heroines) demonstrate the charisma, status and authority these actors could acquire (see further Easterling, this volume). Plutarch's account of the display of the dead Crassus' head at a feast in Armenia is enlivened by a sung performance of part of Euripides' *Bacchae*, thus inviting the reader to draw a comparison between the

[40] See Cockle (1975) with plate xv. Cockle notes that one Claudius Epagathus was a member of the embassy of Dionysiac artists to the emperor Claudius in AD 42 (p. 64, with references).

slaughter of Crassus and the murder of Pentheus (the actor was Jason of Tralles, Plut. *Life of Crassus* 33.2–4); another *tragōidos* anecdote functions to underline the cultural aspirations of Juba II, a Mauretanian client king of the Roman empire in the early first century AD (Leonteus of Argos sang from Euripides' *Hypsipyle*, Athenaeus 8.343e–f).

Despite the ancients' voracious appetite for tragic singing, the most detailed description of a *tragōidos*' performance is an unflattering caricature. It is placed by Lucian in the mouth of Lykinos, an advocate of the danced versions of tragedy offered by pantomime (*On Dancing* 27):

> What a repulsive and at the same time frightful spectacle is a man tricked out to disproportionate stature, mounted upon high clogs, wearing a mask that reaches above his head, with a mouth that is set in a vast yawn as if he meant to swallow up the spectators! . . . The man himself bawls out (κεκραγώς), bending backward and forward, sometimes singing even his iambic lines (ἐνίοτε καὶ περιᾴδων τὰ ἰαμβεῖα) and (what is surely the height of unseemliness) melodising (μελῳδῶν) his calamities, holding himself answerable for nothing but his voice, as everything else has been attended to by the poets, who lived at some time in the distant past.[41]

However exaggerated, some of these colourful details are illuminating. The singing actor provided a striking spectacle, wearing a mask with a distortedly gaping mouth, a view the dialogue elaborates by saying that the pantomime dancer's masks, with their closed mouths, are much more beautiful (29). This important difference between tragedy and pantomime is indeed supported by the depictions of masks on artefacts (see figs. 4 and 5 and Jory, this volume). The information that both words and music have been provided by the poets of long ago also accords with other evidence from Lucian's period, which implies that melodies were still in circulation which were by (or at least believed to be by) Euripides and Sophocles.

In the first half of the second century AD the Milesians dedicated an inscription to their fellow countryman G. Ailios Themison. They commemorated his victories at the Isthmian and other games, adding that he was the 'first and only' individual to set Euripides, Sophocles and Timotheus to music of his own.[42] Ailios might simply have used *themes* from these famous poets in original new vocal works, but Latte was probably correct in arguing that he provided his own music to old,

[41] Translation adapted from Harmon (1936).

[42] μόνον καὶ πρῶτον Εὐριπίδην Σοφοκλέα καὶ Τιμόθεον ἑαυτῷ μελοποιήσαντα. The inscription was published by Broneer (1953) = Stephanis (1988) no. 1132. See also Wilson, this volume.

Fig. 4 Ivory with mask of singing actor of tragedy (By permission of the National Museum of Wales)

famous words in the classic repertoire.[43] Did Ailios compose new music for the old lyric sections, for iambic trimeters, or for both? Here a problem arises. What was (or was at least believed to be) the original music to old tragedy was still familiar, but as far we know the fifth-century tragedians

[43] Broneer (1953); Latte (1954). Some *tragōidoi* were creative artists of another kind, victorious both as performers of 'old' tragedies from the classic repertoire and as poets of 'new' tragedy (e.g. Stephanis (1988) no. 274).

Fig. 5 Glass jug with mask of singing actor of tragedy (Soprintendenza Archeologica per la Toscana – Firenze)

had not composed the music which by this time was often accompanying 'even' iambic trimeters.

In an oration on his liking for music Dio Chrysostom says that he prefers listening to citharodes and actors than to orators. One reason is that orators often extemporise, whereas citharodes and actors offer poetry composed by ancient poets (*Or.* 19.5):

And the most of what they give us comes from ancient times (ἀρχαῖά ἐστι), and from much wiser men than those of the present. In the case of comedy everything is kept; in the case of tragedy only the strong parts (τὰ μὲν ἰσχυρά), it would seem, remain – I mean the iambics and portions of these that they still give (διεξίασιν) in our theatres – but the more delicate parts (τὰ δὲ μαλακώτερα) have fallen away, that is, the lyric parts.

Dio's context in this dialogue is Cyzicus, a Milesian colony in which G. Ailios Themison himself may have performed a few decades later. Dio states that only selected iambic portions of tragedy were being 'given'. The context of the dialogue, which is comparing music to oratory and is inspired by the visit of a citharode to Cyzicus, suggests that these iambic parts are being *sung*, and sung, moreover, to music believed to be the work of the original poets.

So where did singers (other than the innovative Ailios) get the music for their iambics from? Ancient tunes were repetitive and conformed to traditional melodic patterns.[44] In the current state of our evidence we must imagine that singers performing passages from 'old' tragedy used original (or at least plausibly old-sounding) and *recognisable* scales and cadences from the lyrics and recitative, somehow transferring them to the different rhythm of the iambics; Roman connoisseurs, at any rate, could tell from the notes produced by the first breath of the accompanying pipe whether a tragedy was *Antiope* or *Andromache*.[45]

THE ART OF THE *TRAGŌIDOS*

Papyrus discoveries allow us to sketch in outline the technical demands made on tragic singers. A fragment of a scene from a post-classical tragedy on the fall of Troy implies that *tragōidoi* could be competent at musical 'improvisation'. Cassandra deliriously describes Hector's last battle against Achilles, but the papyrus includes the word 'song' (ᾠδή) on seven occasions before verses probably delivered by her. These seem almost certain to be musical directions to the actor playing Cassandra to improvise sung preludes to the words he had to memorise.[46]

[44] Comotti (1989b) 8. The papyri of Euripidean music show repeated playing up and down within the cluster of notes close together in pitch.

[45] Cicero, *Acad.* 2.20 = fr. 31 in Jocelyn (1967), who believes, however, that Cicero is referring to theatrical displays at, for example, funerals, rather than fully staged performances of entire tragedies (pp. 253–4).

[46] *TrGF* fr. adesp. 649 = *P Oxy.* 2746, first edited by Coles (1968). Perhaps the improvised singing consisted of the type of exclamations Cassandra delivers in Aeschylus' seminal *Agamemnon*

However outlandish the lyric snatches improvised by Hellenistic actors playing Cassandra, most of the original music of fifth-century tragedy had used the 'manly' enharmonic scale.[47] This means that the tragic singer will have sung melodies based around the tonic and the fifth, which repeatedly contrasted tiny steps in pitch with a larger one of approximately a major third. Euripides and Agathon began using the chromatic scale, which somewhat evened out the gaps between the notes and was regarded as more effeminate than the enharmonic. Both these scales gradually gave way to the diatonic, which dominated in the Roman period, and which, since its notes were at more equal distances apart, more closely resembled the modern western scale. But the tragedians' old enharmonic remained in use to accompany their works, even though only the most outstanding musicians could attempt it, since the tiny intervals it entailed demanded strict precision.[48]

The melodies sung by tragic actors generally rose and then fell again in pitch, rather than beginning with a descent. While singing the same note repeatedly was rare, most tunes predominantly moved stepwise in the scale to an adjacent note, and thus would now seem to be continuously in motion (which perhaps illuminates the comparison with the nightingale), sinuous and writhing.[49] In the tragic melodies preserved on papyri the occasional leaps or dives of up to a ninth, on the other hand, seem designed to create an emphatic special effect. An important musical papyrus at Yale contains a dramatic Greek lyric song performed by a highly skilled baritone of the imperial era, quite possibly a *tragōidos*;

(e.g. 1214, 1256; see Gentili (1979) 71–3). Coles (1968) 116, suggests the possibility that the musical direction 'is not contemporary with the composition of the play but a later interpolation which reflects later methods of production'. However, at *Cyclops* 487, the Laurentian manuscript's stage direction to the actor playing Polyphemus to sing from within (ᾠδὴ ἔνδοθεν) may go back as far as Euripides (Seaford (1984) 195).

47 It was seen as a paradox that martial peoples like the Aetolians, who used the diatonic scale, were more manly and courageous 'than singers in tragedy, who have [always] been accustomed to singing in the enharmonic' (so the classical polemic on music preserved in the third-century BC 'Hibeh' papyrus 2.1–4, edited by Grenfell and Hunt (1906), pt. I no. 13, pp. 45–58, col. ii, translated by Barker (1984) vol. I, 184). The enharmonic divided the octave into two tetrachords (in modern terms, say, *e* to *a* and *b* to *e*), but within the tetrachords bunched the other available notes just above the bottom at tiny intervals of only about a quarter-tone, leaving a big gap above them: getting from *e* to *f* took two steps, but from *f* to *a* only one.

48 Aristid. Quint., *On Music* 16.10–18, translated in Barker (1989) vol. II, 418. The difficult melodies of tragic songs were made easier to perform by the supporting *auloi*: it was believed that too many instruments obscured a voice, but *auloi* or a lyre could define a sung melody ([Arist.] *Probl.* 19.43, 19.9, see also Euripides' *Electra* 878). In the fragment of the musical score from Euripides' *Orestes* (see above n. 26), the instrumental notes suggest that the two pipes for the most part played the same note, but occasionally diverged to play at an interval of a fourth (West (1992a) 103–4).

49 West (1992a) 191–2, 194.

the melody involved a sudden leap down no less than an octave and a third. The editor of the papyrus argues that the sudden descent in pitch was designed to represent the voice change caused by spirit possession, and that it marked the beginning of the first-person representation of a prophet or prophetess' utterances.[50] This florid song is most unusual in requiring its performer to cover two octaves; most melodies seem to have been composed within the compass of little more than one. Some recently published papyrus fragments, which may record the vocal music to a tragedy on Achilles by Sophocles or his homonymous grandson, reveal a striking tendency for the melody to 'oscillate' between two notes separated by an interval ranging between a semitone and a fifth.[51] It is possible that such oscillation suggested the use of the verb *elelizesthai* ('trill' or 'quiver') used in sung descriptions of the nightingale's song in both Aristophanes' *Birds* (213–14, see further below) and Euripides' *Helen* (1111).

The songs sung in these scales were in one of the musical 'modes', which entailed recognisable ways of selecting notes (probably with distinctive melodic formulae and cadences), and a particular tessitura. The exciting Phrygian mode, which Sophocles is supposed to have introduced to tragedy, required high-pitched singing. The dignified Dorian was often used in tragic laments, the emotive Mixolydian was used for many choruses, and the 'soft' Ionian, compared in Aeschylus' *Supplices* with the nightingale's song (69), is associated by Aristophanes with the seductive songs of prostitutes (*Eccl.* 883). The active Hypophrygian and the magnificent Hypodorian, introduced by the innovative tragedian Agathon, were not used by choruses, but only by actors playing heroic roles;[52] virtuoso *tragōidoi* thus needed to be able to sing in special (and perhaps specially difficult) modes which distinguished their solo singing from the collective choral voice.

Songs seem to have been sung at a speed similar to that at which they would have been intuitively spoken: when a Greek poet wanted his poetry to be delivered at a slower or faster pace, he used more long or short syllables respectively. These two types of syllable provided the two basic note values of Greek vocal music as they did Greek speech, one twice as long as another – in modern terms, a crotchet and a quaver.[53] Most

[50] Johnson (2000) 75.
[51] West (1999) 49. These musical fragments are inscribed on the other side of cartonnage scraps containing tragic lyrics.
[52] [Arist.] *Probl.* 19.48. See also the Byzantine treatise on tragedy edited by Browning (1963) par. 5.
[53] West (1992a) 154, 131.

Greek music did not stretch out individual words by spreading their syllables over more than one note. Euripides, however, experimented with this kind of ornamentation, a development parodied in *Frogs* where the verb *heilissō* ('twirl') becomes *heieieieieilissō* (1314, 1348). This ornament became popular for proper names, where a syllable is sometimes spread over several notes. In a papyrus scrap of a dramatic lament for Ajax, his name is sung '*Ai-ai-i-an*' rather than '*Ai-an*'.[54]

Although Aeschylean tragedy provides occasional internal musical directions,[55] the early *tragōidos* learned his tunes by hearing other men – in theatrical families (see above) a father, brother, or uncle – sing them.[56] But as traditional melodic forms were replaced by more modern music after the fifth century BC, it became important to record the music to tragedy. From at least as early as the fourth century Greek singers had a system of musical notation based on a modification of the Attic alphabet. Significantly, the papyri containing literary texts with musical notations are almost all copies of texts of *drama*, presumably designed for use by *tragōidoi* and associated performers – instrumentalists, a chorus, or a theatrical company.[57]

Tragedy sometimes makes bodily demands on its singing actors; the actor playing Hecuba, for example, had to sing some of her laments from a prone position on the ground (see Valakas, this volume). Yet in ancient visual art singers stand erect, with their heads thrown back, as if to open up the throat and windpipe. Theophrastus says that when people sing high notes they 'draw in the ribs and stretch out the windpipe, narrowing them by force'.[58] The mouth was also opened wide: in an ekphrasis the citharode Amphion 'shows his teeth a little, just enough for a singer'.[59] The tragic actor's mask had a gaping mouth to allow the sound to emerge, and the actor's own mouth to be visible (see Green, this volume). The convention of the mask may have survived partly because it concealed the facial distortion necessary to the production of a voice big

54 West (1992a) 203, 320.

55 *Supplices* 69, for example, suggests the use of the Ionian mode. On the musical modes see also Wilson, this volume.

56 Aural lessons in both song and instrumental playing appear on fifth-century vases, such as the famous kylix by Douris in Berlin (Berlin 2285, see Comotti (1989b) 8–9). Henderson (1957) n. 1, observes that a singer reads from a scroll on a vase of about 425 BC, but points out that there is no evidence that the scroll contains any notation other than words.

57 Comotti (1989b) 11 (see e.g. this chapter, fig. 3).

58 He adds that when singing low notes they widen the windpipe to shorten the throat (Porphyry, *Commentary on Ptolemy's Harmonics* 63, translated in Barker (1989) vol. II, 114).

59 Philostratus, *Imagines* 1.10–25. I owe this reference to Peter Wilson.

enough to fill outdoor theatres,[60] although a good actor could exploit the mask to intensify the awesome impression he made: Prudentius compares the mendacious but potent orator with 'a tragic singer (*tragicus cantor*) who conceals his face beneath a hollow wooden mask, but breathes some great crime through its gaping hole (*hiatus*)', (*Contra Symmachum* 2.664–8).

The sound produced by singers was admired for its loudness, resonance, clarity, precision, and security of hold on notes (Plato, *Rep.* 8.568c3; Arist. *De aud.* 804a9–32). Voices are admired for being 'sweet' or 'honey-like'; the nightingale in Aristophanes' *Birds* is said to sing a 'liquid' melody in a 'clean' voice (213–15); the most common epithet of praise is *ligus* or *liguros*, which refers to a clear sound, free from roughness, and is also used to describe the sound made by cicadas, birds, orators, *auloi*, lyres and panpipes.[61] According to Isidore of Seville in the seventh century, who drew on earlier authors, the 'perfect' voice is male and 'high, to be adequate to the sublime; loud, to fill the ear; sweet, to soothe the minds of the hearers'.[62]

Isidore says that women, like children and the sick, have 'thin' voices, which lack sufficient breath and sound like stringed rather than wind instruments. Such a perception of female vocal weakness may partly explain the dearth of women dramatic singers, despite the extensive evidence for ancient female instrumentalists and dancers.[63] The best candidate for a female *tragōidos* is the *diva* Athenion, celebrated in an epigram by Dioscorides for her stunning performance of a work entitled the *Horse* (*AP* V.137). This just might have been the Greek prototype of Livius Andronicus' tragedy *Equus Trojanus*, in which case Athenion might have sung the role of Cassandra.[64] But other evidence implies that Athenion's *Horse* was more likely a concert aria. The heroine of the second-century novel *Leucippe and Cleitophon* is able to perform, in private at least, both epic and lyric songs.[65] A unique musical papyrus fragment

60 Hunningher (1956) 326–8.
61 West (1992a) 42.
62 *Etymologiarum sive originum libri xx* 6.20. Isidore proposes that there are ten categories of singing voice: the sweet (fine, full, loud and high), penetrating (those which can sustain a note evenly an unusually long time and continuously fill a place, like trumpets), thin, fat, sharp, hard, harsh, blind, prettily flexible (*vinnola* from *vinnus*, a softly curling lock of hair), and perfect.
63 See Webb, this volume, and e.g. the elder Seneca's report of women dancing on private pantomime stages all over Rome (*Q.Nat* 7.32.3). The Kleopatra listed with tragic and comic actors at Delos in 268 BC was not an actress but a specialist trick dancer (Webster (1963) 539).
64 Rostagni (1956) vols. 2.1, 384–7 and 2.2, 3–22.
65 2.1; she sings part of the sixteenth book of the *Iliad* and a lyric in praise of the rose. See also Tarsia's autobiographical monody in *The Story of Apollonius King of Tyre* (41).

of a tragic lament for Ajax, set in the register of a female voice, may well be a new setting of a solo from an old tragedy made for a female concert singer in the Roman imperial period.[66] In Theocritus' fifteenth Idyll an expert and apparently professional woman singer (*aoidos*), the daughter of a well-known Argive woman, sings a hymn in praise of Adonis at his Alexandrian festival (100–44).

The singer trained his voice for years with daily exercises, including singing scales while lying down (Cic. *De or.* 1.59.251); Hermon, a comic actor contemporary with Aristophanes, did a prolonged vocal workout before performing (Pollux *Onom.* 4.88). Tragic actors could mature slowly, as their voice developed: Aesopus was performing until well over the age of sixty, although his voice finally failed him at Pompey's festival games of 55 BC.[67] Alcohol was avoided (as by the orator, Ar. *Knights* 347–9); the singer often fasted, dieted, or practised before breakfast, since food was held to roughen the windpipe (Plato, *Laws* 2.665e8, [Arist.] *Probl.* 11.22, 11.46). Artichokes were shunned, but conger eels, gargling and special linctuses were thought helpful.[68] Nero went to great lengths to improve his 'slight and husky' voice (*exiguae vocis et fuscae*): he would develop his breathing by lying with lead sheets on his chest, purge himself with enemas and emetics, and avoid foods liable to cause obstruction (Suet. *Nero* 20; Pliny *NH* 282.237).

Some singers seem to have gone even further. A little evidence links expert singing with infibulation (a procedure usually associated with athletes), entailing a metal device inserted into or round the foreskin to inhibit erection. The use of the *fibula* to spare the voice is associated by Juvenal with *comoedi* (6.73, see also 6.379), and by Martial with *comoedi*, *citharoedi*, and a *choraules* (7.82, 11.75.3, 14.215). The explanation must be connected with the information in Celsus that adolescents are infibulated 'sometimes for the sake of their voice, sometimes for the sake of their health' (7.25.2).[69] Sexual activity was thought by Aristotle to *deepen* the pitch of the male voice, but if youths 'are forcibly restrained from their desires, which some people concerned with chorus

[66] Berlin Papyrus 6870, lines 16–19 = *TrGF* adesp. 683a. See West (1992a) 320–1.

[67] Cic. *Fam.* 7.1.2. See Lebek (1996) 41–2. Polos is said to have been still able to perform eight tragedies in four days at the age of seventy, shortly before his death (Plut. *Whether an Old Man Should Engage in Public Affairs* 3 = *Moralia* 785B–C).

[68] Persius, *Sat.* 1.17–18 (thanks to Chris Kraus for this reference). See also Antiphon's speech *On the Choreutes*, *passim* and the emphasis on the singer's need to clear the throat in Theocritus' *Idyll* 15 (διαχρέμπτεται, 99).

[69] The term *choraules* here probably has the wider application of *cantator* (see *Corp. Gloss. Lat.* 5.12.32, Kay (1985) 231).

production do, their voice stays unbroken longer and on the whole changes less'.[70]

It is unfortunately not clear whether *tragic* singers were ever infibulated. Some ancient tragic actors, including the Andronikos who taught Demosthenes, were reputed to be highly sexed (Athen. 13.584d), but Aelian praises a tragic actor named Diogenes for avoiding sex before performing (*On Animals* 6.1 and *VH* 3.30). We do not even know whether tragic actors were normally (rather than in exceptional cases such as that of the deuteragonist of *Orestes*, see above) expected to sing at an 'unnaturally' high pitch.[71] It is generally thought unlikely that male actors playing female parts used a true falsetto voice, which would have been difficult to project to the back of the theatre.[72] But they could have used a high tenor range.[73] Perhaps the register of tragic song varied considerably according to the character being impersonated. The baritone register is suggested by, for example, some papyrus scraps of tragic lyrics recently published by Martin West.[74] Old men such as Oedipus in *Oedipus at Colonus* or Peleus in Euripides' *Andromache* may well have sung at a relatively low pitch, since Aristotle remarks that 'it is not easy for those whose powers have failed through years to sing the high scales, and their time of life naturally suggests the use of the low' (*Pol.* 8.1342b20–3).

SINGING IN ROMAN TRAGEDY

When Greek tragedy arrived in Italy it was transformed by free translation into the Latin language and by a sizeable increase in the use of non-iambic metres. A significant proportion of early Roman tragedy was musically accompanied by the *tibicen*, whose pipes may have originated in Etruria.[75] The subject of singing in early Roman drama has long been

[70] *Hist. An.* 7.581a21–7. See Kay (1985) 230–1; Courtney (1980) 272. I am extremely grateful to Peta Fowler and the late Don Fowler for help on this issue.

[71] Although we know little about the singing voices of ancient comic actors (see below), tragic tunes were lower pitched than the citharodic style of melody (Aristid. Quint. *On Music* 30.2, 23.3, although Sifakis (1967) 77 thinks that this refers to tragic music for the chorus rather than to actors' solos).

[72] Slater (1997) 101.

[73] The Hibeh papyrus says that tragic actors are not very 'manly' (see above n. 48), and Sophocles' Ajax is described prior to his great sung scene on the *ekkuklēma* as being forced by grief to use a higher pitch of vocal delivery than the 'manly' deep groaning he advocated (*Ajax* 317–20). See further Hall (1999a) 112.

[74] West (1999) 49.

[75] See further Wilson, this volume. The scarcity of information about theatrical activities in Etruria and in the Greek-speaking cities of Southern Italy of course makes it impossible to be sure exactly how much the musical nature of Roman tragedy owed to indigenous performance styles and

confused by Livy's apparent claim that the Roman *histrio* merely mimed his *cantica* while another performer, an expert singer, accompanied the *tibicen*, a phenomenon Livy traces to the day when the early tragedian Livius Andronicus allegedly lost his voice and needed a substitute vocalist (7.2.8–10). Since it is, however, virtually impossible to believe that tragedy and comedy were performed in this way, Livy's anecdote is best understood as an aetiological narrative explaining the invention of pantomime, which was popular by the Augustan era (see Jory, this volume), and did indeed separate the tasks of movement and song, allocating them to different performers.

It is regrettable that we understand so little about Republican Roman tragic music, for ancient authors bear witness to its impressive *severitas* and simplicity (see e.g. Horace, *AP* 202–7). Its arias could be exquisitely moving; Cicero says that the appeal made by the ghost of Deiphilus to his mother in Pacuvius' *Iliona*, if sung in 'measured and plaintive' tones, could inspire sadness in entire audiences (*Tusc.* 1.106). These imposing scores were not composed by the tragic poets, but by musical specialists.[76] Famous arias were to some extent 'detachable' from their original plays; the actor Aesopus, at least, once inserted into Accius' praetexta *Brutus* an entire aria from Ennius' tragedy *Andromacha* (Cic. *Sest.* 120–3, see further Fantham, this volume).

The titles and exiguous fragments of early Latin tragedy suggest a strong interest in lyrical virtuosity. Livius Andronicus, whose tragedy *The Trojan Horse* has been mentioned above, also adapted Sophocles' *Tereus*, although a more famous Roman *Tereus*, first performed in 104 BC and much revived during the following century, was by Accius.[77] Livius Andronicus also wrote an *Andromeda* (as did Ennius and Naevius), presumably modelled on Euripides' lyrical tragedy of that name. The titles of Ennius' *Andromacha*, *Hecuba*, *Iphigenia*, and the prolific Accius' *Alcestis*, *Hecuba*, and *Bacchae* also imply a Roman attraction to Euripidean plays with important solo singing. The fragments include a few actual vestiges of striking *cantica*, sung, for example, by Ennius' Alcumene, Pacuvius' Ajax in *The Judgement of Arms*, and Accius' Antigone and Althaea.[78] Poets adapting Greek tragedy for the Roman stage could make characters sing

how much to the way in which Greek tragedy was being performed by this date. See Jocelyn (1967) 32; Wille (1967) 169–75.

76 Cf. Donatus, *De com.* 8.9, *cantica vero temperabantur modis non a poeta sed a perito artis musicae factis*, Wilson in this volume.

77 See Cic. *Att.* 16.2.3, 16.5.1, *Phil.* 1.36. For the fragments and testimonia relating to Accius' *Tereus* see frr. 639–55 in Warmington (1936) 542–9.

78 For a list see Wille (1967) 166–7; on the complex metres of these *cantica* Fraenkel (1922) 321–73.

passages that they had spoken in the original: Ennius' Medea sings some of the crucial scene with her children (fr. 282 Vahlen) which she speaks as iambic trimeters in Euripides.

Singing in imperial Latin tragedy is also a problematic area, but for different reasons. Despite the preservation of Senecan drama, controversy surrounds nearly every dimension of the theatre of the Empire except the degree to which histrionic metaphors penetrated élite culture and literature (see Edwards, this volume). Although Senecan tragedy is dominated by highly wrought, epigrammatic rhetoric, it certainly contains material in lyric and anapaestic rhythms. Cassandra unsurprisingly sings in the Senecan *Agamemnon*, the Senecan *Trojan Women* includes an important lyric solo for Andromache,[79] and *Phaedra* opens with Hippolytus' excited anapaestic leading of attendants to the hunt (1–84). Most modern scholars believe that Senecan tragedy was performed, even if they prefer to think in terms of private theatricals. And the close Roman association of dramatic performances with the *tibicen* makes it difficult to believe that the lyrics and anapaests were not sung, or at least recited to musical accompaniment.[80]

Yet Senecan tragedy is not wholly compatible with the external evidence for 'tragic' performances in the same era, which mostly centres around the Emperor Nero and emphatically points to the prominence of music in the theatre.[81] A mythical narrative could be danced to choral music as a pantomime (*tragoedia saltata*), sung by a tragic singer (*tragoedia cantata*), or sung to the cithara (*citharoedia*), and Nero seems to have experimented with all these forms. Tacitus speaks of him only as a *citharoedus*,[82] but others say that Nero composed tragic works such as an *Oresteia* and an *Antigone*, and acted and sang tragic roles in private and public theatres in both Rome and Greece.[83] The roles, evidently selected for their emotional flamboyance, included *Canace in Childbirth*, *Orestes the Matricide*, *Oedipus Blinded*, and *Hercules Distraught* (Suet. *Nero* 21). There are, moreover, reasons for believing that these roles did not just consist of

[79] 705–35. For an appreciation of the musical impact of this play see Boyle (1997) 74–5.

[80] So Boyle (1987) 7–11 and 135.

[81] Much of the written testimony is assembled in Wille (1967) 338–50.

[82] See especially 16.65 (which appears to contrast Nero's citharody with Piso's singing in tragic costume), and Kelly (1979) 28–9. Dio asserts that it was in citharodic garb Nero notoriously sang his composition *The Sack of Troy* while Rome burnt (61.20.1–2, 62.18.1). I am very grateful to Miriam Griffin for help on Nero.

[83] Philostratus *Life of Apollonius* 4.39, 5.7, Dio Cassius 62.29.1, 3.8.2, 9.6, 22.5, Suetonius, *Nero* 10.2, see also Juvenal *Sat.* 8.220–1.

excerpted arias, but included mimetic gesture and spoken dialogue with an attendant *hypocrita*.[84]

PANTOMIME

Nero also aspired to *dance* the role of 'Virgil's' *Turnus*, which implies a pantomime version of part of the *Aeneid* (Suet. *Nero* 54); other evidence suggests that book 4 of that epic was adapted into both ballet and *tragoedia cantata* (Macrobius *Sat.* 5.17.5). The same mythical material could be performed in quite different ways: Suetonius reports that on the day before Caligula was assassinated the *pantomīmus* Mnester danced the 'same' tragedy as the *tragōidos* Neoptolemos had once sung for Philip of Macedon.[85] Although it is not clear whether the text of an 'old' tragedy 'belonged' to anybody in terms of bringing in fees when it was performed, by the first century AD authors seem to have resembled modern novelists who hope to sell the rights for their book to be adapted into a script for TV, a screenplay for the cinema, and/or a libretto for a musical. Poets wrote 'tragic' texts which could be danced, sung by a choir, or acted and sung by a *tragoedus*, in the hope that someone would buy them to perform, just as Paris the pantomime dancer bought from the poet Juvenal a libretto entitled *Agave*.[86] Presumably the music was commissioned or composed by the individual who made the purchase.

The nature of any performance (whether a rhetorical five-act tragedy, a sung recital or a pantomime) will have varied depending upon the venue, audience and available histrionic talent. Different actors at different times and in different places performed even the standard tragic repertoire in very different ways, just as the musical element in Shakespearean drama has been variously curtailed, expanded, or transformed into various types of opera and dance.[87] There is evidence for almost every conceivable combination of performers of 'tragedy' under the Roman empire. In Dio Cassius, for example, we read that the entertainment ordered by Caligula just before his assassination consisted of 'a ballet and the enactment of a tragedy'. Although this could mean

[84] Lesky (1966) followed by Kelly (1979).

[85] See above and Suetonius, *Caligula* 57.3: *Pantomimus Mnester tragoediam saltavit quam olim Neoptolemus tragoedus ludis quibus rex Macedonum Philippus occisus est egerat.* There are problems with this passage (Easterling (1997d) 220–1).

[86] Juv. *Sat.* 7.82–7. Lucan and Statius also wrote for the pantomime stage (Kelly (1979) 43, 28).

[87] Neighbarger (1992) xx–xxi.

two separate shows, it could also refer to an elaborate entertainment involving a combination of dance, song and spoken dialogue.[88]

The most important cultural development was nevertheless the rise of pantomime. Much earlier authors describe glamorous dancing entertainers, such as Homer's Phaeacians and the acrobatic dancing girl who thrills the diners at Xenophon's *Symposium* by somersaulting over upright sword-blades (2.11). Fifth-century tragic actors had sometimes been required to dance,[89] and those who performed the roles of, for example, Cassandra in *Trojan Women* or Jocasta in *Phoenissae* (let alone the more boisterous roles in satyr drama) must have been able to both dance and sing. Actors of Old Comedy had cut jolly and obscene capers (*Clouds* 540) and parodied virtuoso tragic dancing (*Wasps* 1474–1515). But pantomime offered the public something similar to modern balletic realisations of serious drama. In Lucian's *On Dancing* we hear that 'the themes of tragedy and the dance are common to both, and there is no difference between those of the one and those of the other' (31). It has even been argued from an epigraphic term for a pantomime dancer, 'actor of tragic rhythmical movement',[90] that fierce rivalry between the pantomime dancer and the *tragōidos* was a fact of life as well as the rhetorical premise of Lucian's *On Dancing*.[91]

Pantomime's origins in mimetic danced interpretation of myth go back at least as early as the middle of the third century BC (see further Jory, this volume), and the genre becomes identifiable as a separate art form by the 80s BC, when the *pantomīmos* Ploutogenes danced at the Hellenistic city of Priene, near Miletus.[92] It was to be found in Latin-speaking western theatres by the end of the first century AD, was later accepted into the programmes of the Greek festivals, and is attested until the sixth century AD. Tradition held that pantomime dancers had originally sung as well as danced, but had given up singing when it was discovered that dancing left the performer too out of breath to sing well, and handed this part of their role over to a choir (Lucian, *On Dancing* 29–30; see above on Livy 7.2.8–10). The art was certainly arduous and required severe training.[93]

88 Dio Cassius, *Roman History* 59.29.6: καὶ ὀρχήσασθαι καὶ τραγῳδίαν ὑποκρίνασθαι ἠθέλησεν; Kelly (1979) 21–2.

89 See above on Argiope in Sophocles' *Thamyras*.

90 τραγικῆς ἐνρύθμου κινήσεως ὑποκριτής (Robert (1930). See Stephanis (1988) nos. 236, 475, 1504, 2007.

91 This view is strongly stated in Brooks (1981) 288–92.

92 Stephanis (1988) no. 2075; see Robert (1930).

93 Weismann (1972) 44.

Not a single pantomime libretto survives, which makes reconstructing the way it used singing difficult.[94] But it is clear that there was no single 'correct' way to stage a pantomime: although usually featuring a star (male) *saltator* (Lucian, *On Dancing* 66),[95] the genre could add a second dancer (Quintilian 6.3.65), a herald to broadcast the actions beforehand (Augustine, *De doct. Christ.* 2.38.97), or an actor. His vocal contribution was aesthetically important: Lucian says that he added 'euphony' (ὑποκριτοῦ εὐφωνία) to the aural delight offered by the choir's plural voice (ὁμοφωνία, *On Dancing* 68, see also *The Mistaken Critic* 19). In Apuleius' novel *Metamorphoses* the marriage of Cupid and Psyche is celebrated on Olympus with a show (*scaena*) in which Venus dances, the Muses sing choral melodies, Apollo sings to the cithara, while Satyrus and Paniscus speak to the pipe (*ad fistulam dicerent*, 6.24). If, as seems likely, pantomime is reflected in this Olympian entertainment, it could clearly accommodate both solo singing and accompanied recitation.

Choral music, however, seems to have been crucial to pantomime's popularity.[96] The *cantica* sung by the pantomime choirs were presumably less difficult than the virtuosic libretti of the tragic singer, and the overall effect must have been rather different on account of the number of decibels produced, for the choir was often reinforced by large-scale instrumental accompaniment (*symphoniaci*), even by the organ. But the choirs must have included competent singers, and pantomimes that involved mythical figures famous for their vocal performance, like Orpheus, Cassandra, or Philomela,[97] are likely to have offered opportunities for solo singing. This view is supported by the high-pitched (*acidum*) aria sung by an individual Alexandrian slave-boy to Trimalchio's dinner guests at precisely the point where the proceedings are likened to a pantomime (Petronius *Sat.* 31). Crinagoras, moreover, addresses an

94 The problem is compounded by the tendency for late antique authors to call authors of pantomime 'tragedy writers'. When they refer to performances of tragedies familiar to us, for example Arnobius' apparent reference to Heracles' (sung) death lament in Sophocles' *Trachiniae*, the reference could have been inspired by a pantomime (Arnobius 4.35), a citharodic performance (Weismann (1972) 35), or even a text of Cicero (*Tusc.* 2.20).

95 In *The Judgement of Paris*, danced in a Corinthian theatre, there is a different dancer for each role and women perform female parts (Apuleius, *Metamorphoses* 10.29–34); on evidence for female performers in pantomime see further Webb, this volume.

96 Joshua the Stylite (sixth century) says that a festival involving this form of entertainment was one at which 'the heathen tales were *sung*' (30, pp. 20–1, 46, p. 35), and spectators sometimes picked up the songs to repeat at home (Libanius *On Dancing* 93).

97 Lucian *On Dancing* 51, Claudian *In Eutrop.* II 405, Apuleius *Apol.* 78. For a fairly comprehensive list of ancient titles and subjects of pantomimes, with their sources, see Wüst (1949) 847–50, supplemented in Kokolakis (1959).

epigram to one Philonides, who sang, presumably a solo aria, to accompany a pantomime dancer named Bathyllos (*AP* 9.542); another late epigram refers to an individual (*tis*) singing a 'new song' about Hector to accompany a woman dancer named Helladia (*Anth. Plan.* 287).[98]

SINGING IN ANCIENT COMEDY

Old Comedy was fascinated by vocal performance, and contains some of the oldest assessments of actors' voices, such as the 'extremely bitter voice' of Melanthios (πικροτάτην ὄπα γηρύσαντος), and 'woman-voiced' (γυναικόφωνος) Agathon in *Thesmophoriazusae*.[99] Agathon's role demanded an enterprising singing actor (he had to imitate alternately the singing of a tragic actor and of his chorus), even if his skill primarily lay in female vocal impersonation rather than lyrical technique (101–29). Indeed, much of the solo singing in Old Comedy is parody of virtuoso singing by female tragic characters.[100] In *Birds* Aristophanes used Sophocles' famous lost tragedy *Tereus*, which dramatised the story of Procne, the woman–nightingale associated with the art of the *tragōidos*. The tragedy had probably related rather than enacted the triple transformation of Tereus into a hoopoe, Procne into a nightingale, and her sister Philomela into a swallow,[101] but in the comedy Tereus and Procne are birds, living as a married couple. Aristophanes chooses to represent the nightingale's voice by the playing of the aulete after 222, giving to the hoopoe the most extraordinary sung performance in his dramas. It consists of both an anapaestic run (209–22) and an elaborate astrophic lyric invocation of the bird-chorus (227–62), whose several metres include dochmiacs.

The difficulty of this aria raises the question of the level of singing skill required of the actors of Old Comedy; it has even been suggested that a professional singer temporarily replaced the actor playing the hoopoe.[102] It is unfortunate that we know little about how this aria related to the metre and music of the Sophoclean *Tereus*. There is, however, a similarity between the hoopoe's anapaests and those of the heroine of Sophocles' *Electra* (who, suggestively, compares her voice in both the anapaests and her subsequent lyrics with the laments of the nightingale (107–9, 147–9));

[98] See Rotolo (1957) 16, 115, 119.
[99] *Peace* 804–9; *Thesm.* 192. See Vetta (1993) 706–7.
[100] See Rau (1967), Parker (1997).
[101] *Birds* 100–1; see Dunbar (1995) 164–5.
[102] Russo (1994) 156; Sommerstein (1987) 212. For a discussion of the controversial staging of this scene see Craik (1990a) 83–4.

the hoopoe, moreover, avoids the incongruities and exaggerations typical of Aristophanes' other monodists.[103]

The leading actors of Aristophanes' plays also faced the lesser challenge of simpler types of song familiar from the rituals and social practices of Athens. In *Acharnians* the peasant Dicaeopolis sings an unsophisticated iambic hymn to Phales at his rustic festival of Dionysus (263–79). In *Wasps* Philocleon practises *skolia*, drinking songs for the symposium (1224–48). At the end of *Peace* the bridegroom Trygaeus performs a processional wedding song antiphonally with the chorus, complete with a refrain and sequences of question-and-answer in the manner of folk-song (1329–59, 1337–40).[104] *Lysistrata* features a Spartan singing and dancing a Laconian song, apparently to bagpipe accompaniment (1242–6). In the second half of *Ecclesiazusae* (from 893 onwards) solo singing replaces choral lyric altogether, as actors playing an old woman, a teenage girl and a youth perform popular songs. Most are sympotic, but one is a remarkable love-duet in which the youth responds to sexual advances made by the girl.[105]

Aristophanes represents himself as an opponent of the 'New Music', while himself reducing choruses and increasing actors' lyrics over the course of his career. Yet by the time of Menander both scenes accompanied by music and lyric song became rare in Greek comedy.[106] Roman comedy, on the other hand, contains far more verse in either lyric metres or 'recitative' metres (iambo-trochaics and cretico-bacchiacs). It is as true of Roman comedy as of Roman tragedy (see above) that passages from a Greek prototype could be transformed from iambic trimeters into lyrics.[107] This type of 'translation' is assumed to indicate that for reasons

[103] Dunbar (1995) 202–3, 212. Musical notation to some words of the hoopoe's song may be inscribed on an ostrakon found at the Maximianon in Upper Egypt, and soon to be published by Annie Bélis, Director of Research at the CNRS.

[104] See Parker (1997) 293. The third hypothesis to *Peace* (41) reports that the comic actor Apollodoros was the protagonist of the play's first production in 421 BC (= Stephanis (1988) no. 247). See Olson (1998) 3 and 66. Apollodoros must have been a versatile vocalist, because Trygaeus also performs paratragic lyrics and hexameters.

[105] This may reflect an authentic form of traditional serenade, sung by an *exclusus amator* (see further Hunter, this volume), but with the sex roles reversed in line with the new sexual politics of Praxagora's communistic utopia. See Olson (1988), Parker (1997) 546. Bowra (1958) rather charmingly argued that it is a reflection of a type of bawdy duet sung in the less respectable quarters of Athens.

[106] On the exceptions see Handley, this volume. One fragment is so unusual that Handley has suggested that it was sung by a professional singer within the play (Handley (1992)). The noisy revel which concludes *Dyskolos* (on which see Hunter, this volume) also seems to have been exceptional.

[107] An important example is Caecilius Statius' polymetric song, quoted by Aulus Gellius (2.23), which was a free adaptation of an iambic passage from Menander's *Plokion* (fr. 333 K–T).

to do with indigenous Italian forms of entertainment and popular taste Latin dramatists liked to make Greek comedy more musical. Most of the characteristically ebullient Plautine monodies belong to slaves, for example, while no evidence has yet emerged for Menandrean slaves expressing their feelings in monodies.[108]

Towards the end of the nineteenth century the current consensus emerged that much more of Plautine comedy than just the passages in lyric metres was musically accompanied. Following Donatus' *Preface to Adelphi* 1.7, the markings *DV* and *C* in a few of the manuscripts of Plautus, which are associated with scenes in iambic senarii and with scenes in other metres respectively, have been assumed to indicate that iambics were spoken (*diverbium*) and other metres sung (*canticum*, see also Wilson, this volume). It has been argued that these markings go back to at least as early as grammarians of the second century AD, which might make them reliable guides to the way the plays were performed.[109] Those who are convinced that the important distinction was between the 'spoken' iambic senarii and all the other (musically accompanied) metres have studied how this type of shift in performative gear can aid interpretation of the plays.[110] Yet this sort of work does not solve the tantalising problem of the vocal skills required of the Roman comic actor. It is interesting that Roscius is recorded as saying that as he grew older he needed the pipe music to be slower and more gentle (*De oratore* 1.254, see further Fantham, this volume), suggesting that the fast pace of accompanied passages of Roman comedy was physically demanding. But the evidence for the performance of Roman comedy is both slight and difficult to interpret

108 Fraenkel (1922) 321–73, especially 335–8. But this argument from silence is vulnerable, since masks and figures of Greek comic slaves were popular ornaments, and by the first century BC an Athenian actor named Alexander has a slave mask on his gravestone (Webster (1963) 543).

109 Questa (1984). Cicero says that comic iambic senarii are hardly distinguishable from ordinary spoken prose (*Orat.* 55.183–4). Internal evidence for this view is the scene in *Stichus* where the slaves are having a party; when they decide the *tibicen* should have a drink, too, the metre changes to iambic senarii for exactly seven lines while he is drinking (762–8). Another argument is that although some plays make polymetric *cantica* important (they constitute nearly a third of *Casina*), several of the comedies contain none at all (e.g. *Miles Gloriosus*), and it is impossible to believe that these plays were completely unaccompanied. The same goes for the plays of Terence and early dramatic fragments, which reveal nothing like Plautus' variety of metres. I am extremely grateful to Malcolm Willcock for his help on this question.

110 Accompaniment was used in emotional scenes such as Pamphilus' description of his wife giving birth (*Hecyra* 336–409), for certain types of character (slaves and young lovers such as Argyrippus in Plautus' *Asinaria*), and for some stock scene-types (episodes of knockabout violence, e.g. *Amphitruo* 984–1005). The shift between accompanied and unaccompanied verse can also be shown to emphasise exits and entrances such as the arrival of the *servus currens* or the slave-dealer Ballio's stunning musical entrance in *Pseudolus* (133–229); particular attention is called to this by the eavesdropping presence of Pseudolus and Calidorus (Slater (1987) 7). In general see Moore (1998b) 248–59.

(see Brown, this volume), and there are certainly no equivalents of the musical papyri used by Greek *tragōidoi* to help in this regard.

There has therefore been a long-standing debate about what kind of accompaniment and delivery we are to understand for the 'recitative' metres. Just because they were accompanied does not mean that Gentili was correct in arguing that the actor was required to 'sing' them, at least as we understand the word.[111] In one crucial respect the Latin of the 'recitative' metres resembles the iambic senarii: their prosody is more sensitive than that of the lyrics to quantitative gradations. This strongly suggests that 'recitative' was delivered in a manner nearer speech than the lyrics, even though it was almost certainly accompanied. That is, the recitative metres were probably not delivered melodically; the accompanist in the recitative probably helped to define rhythm, cola, pacing, pauses, phrasing, emphases, and shifts in speaker rather than a sung tune. Roman actors had to master complex timing and phrasing in their recitative, and the *tibicen* gave this special form of delivery extra shape and definition.

Unfortunately the meaning of the words *canere*, *cantare*, *carmen* and their cognates is particularly ambiguous in Latin,[112] and a few scholars have gone so far as to deny that there was any song at all in Plautus.[113] While such an extreme view is counter-intuitive, it is important to acknowledge the close affinity the ancients perceived between the arts of singing and of speaking.[114] Orators and actors faced similar challenges and found similar solutions (see also Sifakis and Fantham, this volume). The ancients had no artificial means of amplifying the volume of voices: Timotheus compared old-fashioned singers with heralds (see above), who entered competitions in which the criterion of assessment was volume (Poll. *Onom.* 4.91), and sheer volume was arguably even more important in singing: Dio Chrysostom says that the actor's voice, in comparison with the orator's, was 'larger and undoubtedly better modulated' ἥ τε γὰρ φωνὴ μείζων καὶ δῆλον ὅτι ἐμμελεστέρα.[115] Breath control was equally important to actor and to orator, and the writers of both dramatic poetry and

[111] Gentili (1960).

[112] For a discussion and bibliography see Allen (1972).

[113] Beare (1950) 224.

[114] This is indicated, for example, by the Aesopic fable about the untalented citharode who thought he had a beautiful voice after hearing it echo inside a house with thickly plastered walls, but was driven from the theatre because he sang so badly: the 'moral' the ancients appended to this fable was that *orators*' incompetence is often only revealed when they enter the public arena (fable no. 123, Hausrath and Hunger (1970)).

[115] *Oration* 19.4. The *tragōidos* Neoptolemos is described by Diodorus as 'supreme in *megalophōnia* and in reputation' (16.92). It is interesting that several ancient tragic actors are known to have competed as heralds (e.g. Stephanis (1988) nos. 822, 1870, 2137).

oratory needed to script 'rests' during arduous vocal performances.[116] The affinities even included pitch: choruses were given the pitch of the starting note of the song by their trainers, just as the slave of the orator C. Gracchus quietly provided his master with appropriate notes on a pitchpipe called the *tonarion*.[117]

Yet the differences between acting and public speaking need to be accepted. There are ancient descriptions of the technical distinction.[118] But, more importantly, actors performed *memorised* speech, which was viewed as a different type of performance from those types of oratory (legal and political) into which changes or extemporaneous remarks were customarily introduced: indeed Dio Chrysostom argues that this is one of the major reasons why actors, whose words are not thought up on the spot (ἥ τε λέξις οὐκ αὐτοσχέδιος), give more pleasure than orators (*Oration* 19.4). Moreover *all* poetry necessitates a pattern of intonation divergent from the sound of ordinary conversation. Although gifted actors like Theodoros could give the illusion of talking naturally, all the poetry ever delivered in the ancient theatre was heightened and artificial: the stage whisper often required of Roman comic actors reinforces this point. The language of the senarii and septenarii in Plautus, Terence (and indeed the fragments of Republican tragedy) is a long way from constituting an accurate metrical charting of the cadences of everyday Roman speech. Metrical conventions of 'stage Latin' were established which, in order to be intelligible, demanded expertise in actors and basic familiarity in audiences.[119]

Just to compound the confusion it must, however, be added that a papyrus fragment containing a phrase from an iambic trimeter in

[116] Hall (1995) 46–9. See Lysias 12.61, and the scholion to *PV* 472, which says that choral lines are inserted into Prometheus' long *rhesis* on his philanthropy (between 436–71 and 476–506) 'to give Aeschylus' actor a rest' (see Falkner, this volume).

[117] Quint. *Inst.* 1.10.27. See West (1992a) 113.

[118] Aristoxenus, for example, argues that the fundamental difference between speech (τὸ διαλέγεσθαι) and singing (τὸ μελῳδεῖν) is that in singing the voice moves at clear, discrete intervals and becomes stationary on each note (*El. Harm.* 1.3, 9–10); see further Hall (1999a) 104–5.

[119] This is shown by various technical features including elision *across* punctuation, and enjambement of sense at colon-boundary or line transition. I am extremely grateful to Adrian Gratwick for his indispensable assistance on this topic. Performing poetry in a marked and 'artificial' style at a great volume, regardless of whether there is melodic accompaniment, necessarily takes the voice far away from everyday spoken prose even when it is in a direction we would not recognise as melodic song: this is probably what Tertullian has in mind when he is describing a tragic actor who utters his verse with particular vocal extravagance (*tragoedus vociferans exclamationes*, *Spect.* 23.4, cf. Apul. *Flor.* 18, *tragoedus vociferatur*).

Menander's *Perikeiromene* (796), provided with three different musical settings, may confirm the truth of Gentili's hypothesis that even *Menander*'s iambic dialogue was eventually set to music.[120] This raises the interesting possibility that the musical character of Roman comedy was at least in part derived from the musical way that Greek New Comedy, including its iambic dialogue, was (sometimes at least) being performed by the second century BC. This would have a major implication for the performance of Roman comedy. It would undermine the consensual view that Latin iambic senarii were always unaccompanied, since if Greek comic iambic trimeters could be set to music then so could their Latin equivalents. That would entail the startling possibility that in Roman comedy the *tibicen* could have been playing continuously, or at any point. Such a picture would not be wholly incompatible with that of a noisily musical form of entertainment suggested by occasional remarks in literary sources, such as the statement that the games were not considered to have been properly performed if something went wrong, the dancer stopped, and the *tibicen* 'suddenly went silent' (Cic. *De haruspicum responso* 23).

CONCLUSION

At least one ancient *tragōidos*, Herakleides of Thyateira, seems to have suffered from stage fright. When preparing to perform in a competition at Rome he was afflicted by a nightmare. This correctly predicted that the audience and the judges would give him a hostile reception (Artemidorus *Oneir.* 4.33). But there is little other evidence for the psychological experience undergone by singing actors.[121] The situation is not much better when it comes to the emotional impact they could have on an audience, which is surprising given the phenomenal power attributed to the singing voice in the ancient world. This power was early personified in the sirens of the *Odyssey*, whose beguiling voices lured strong men to their deaths, and whose aid was summoned to assist the vocal performance of the outstanding monodist who in 412 BC must originally have acted the lyrical leading roles in Euripides' *Andromeda* and *Helen* (*Hel.* 167–73). In Lucian's *On Dancing* tragic singers (along with pantomime dancers) are called 'sirens of the theatre' (3), but the evidence for the *emotions* evoked by these thespian sirens is extremely meagre.

[120] Gentili (1979) 22–45; Huys (1993). Certainly, by the second century BC, it is not unusual to find Greek comic actors attested as competing at festivals in the singing of paeans (Stephanis (1988) nos. 253, 583, 794).

[121] The material Lada-Richards assembles later in this volume to reconstruct the ancient actor's subjective experience is, however, of general relevance here.

Aristotle thought that tragic music could improve the moral character of the people in the audience (see further Sifakis, this volume). Plutarch records that pity, aroused by a solo performance of lyrics from Euripides' *Electra*, prevented the Spartans from destroying Athens in 404 BC (*Life of Lysander* 15.2–3, see further Hall, ch. 20). Excitement was Dioscorides' reaction when Athenion's singing set him on fire 'as badly as Troy' (*AP* 5.137). Physiological disturbances including an epidemic of monody-singing, fever and nosebleeds followed the performance of *Andromeda* by the actor Archelaos in Abdera (Lucian, *How to Write History* 1), even if the epidemic was not directly caused by it. Terror was the reaction of the barbarian natives of Hipola (Seville) to the gaping mask, buskins, costume and reverberating voice of a travelling *tragōidos* in Nero's time (Philost. *Life of Apoll.* 5.9). In a different version recounted by Eunapius, the actor won the audience round by first keeping his voice and the melody (from *Andromeda*) 'moderate', then gradually letting go the restraint on his volume, singing with much greater intensity (ἐπήγαγεν ἁρμονίαν σύντονον), before reverting to the 'sweetness' (γλυκεῖαν) of his former singing. This audience was not equipped to appreciate the poetry or plot, but he 'so conquered them with the beauty of his voice and his singing' that they honoured him as if he were a god, and weighed him down with money, before succumbing to a gastrointestinal contagion during which they yelled out the tragic melody with its words indistinct.[122]

The existence of these narratives shows, of course, that the pagan Greco-Roman world saw the tragic singer as an important symbolic bearer of the values and tastes of civilised culture. The stories also show that ancient pagans were well aware that he was capable of making a huge psychological impact on his audience, even if they preferred to think about that impact taking effect on inexperienced provincial barbarians. Much more revealing evidence for the emotive power of the theatrical singing voice appears, perhaps paradoxically, in Christian sources, such as the confession of the reformed *tragoedus* Augustine with which this chapter began. The early Christian writers created 'a Christian civic identity in direct opposition to the classical model, with church representing the former and theatre, the latter'.[123] The visual arts and the visual dimension of theatre, as forms of pictorial representation associated with idolatry, were of course fundamental to the early church's

[122] Eunapius fr. 54, in Dindorf (1870) vol. 1, pp. 246–8. For a careful contextualisation of this scene within Eunapius' own time, see Easterling and Miles (1999) 101–2.

[123] Easterling and Miles (1999) 100.

disapproval of polytheistic culture (see Puchner, this volume). But differences between styles of *singing* also came to symbolise the confrontation between Christian and pagan.

St John Chrysostom expounded St Paul's injunction to be filled not with wine but with the Spirit, which is caused by 'singing and making melody in your heart to the Lord' (*Ephesians* 5.18, 19). The bishop explicitly associates Christian households with psalm-filled churches, and pagan households with theatres attended by harlots and entertainers.[124] St Jerome, expounding the same Pauline passage, goes further even than the edict of Bishop Athanasius mentioned in the first paragraph of this chapter, by recommending that Christians appointed to perform the psalms in church scarcely sing out loud at all:[125]

> Sing to God, not with the voice, but with the heart; not, after the fashion of the *tragoedi*, in smearing the gullet and throat with a sweet drug, so that theatrical melodies and songs are heard in the church, but in fear, in work, and in knowledge of the Scriptures.

Here, towards the end of pagan antiquity, a Christian scholar from Dalmatia, a quite different corner of the Roman world from Augustine, emphatically reasserts the continuing attractions of the art of the singing actor, whose beautiful, artificially medicated voice sang spiritually bankrupt theatrical melodies. The very vehemence of the discussion of singing in these early Christians testifies more strongly than any pagan source to the intense appeal of the solo songs of the ancient theatre, which, as we have seen, enthralled thousands upon thousands of audiences for well over a millennium.

SUGGESTIONS FOR FURTHER READING

On music in ancient Greek culture generally see Comotti (1989b), the collection of sources translated in Barker (1984–9), and especially Martin West's outstanding survey (1992a). West's book also transcribes and translates the Greek musical papyri, for the texts of which see now Pöhlmann and West (2001). For Roman music see Wille (1967) and Comotti (1989b). On the importance of ancient actors' vocal skills see Vetta (1993) and Easterling (1999). On the songs of Greek tragedy see Barner (1971), Pintacuda (1978) and Hall (1999a); for Greek comedy see Parker

[124] *PG* 55, 155–9. It has been argued that the invention of the Christian hymn was a pragmatic response to popular demand for music in worship (MacMullen (1984) 74–5).

[125] *Commentary on the Epistle of Paul to the Ephesians*, in Migne, *PL* vol. 26 (1845) section 652, cols. 527–8.

(1997). Hellenistic *tragōidoi* are discussed in Gentili (1979), Dihle (1981), Xanthakis-Karamanos (1993), and especially in the fundamental work of Sifakis (1967). For Roman comic actors' singing, see Beare (1950) and Moore (1998b); for Roman tragedy see Jocelyn (1967) and Kelly (1979). On Nero's singing see Lesky (1966); on pantomime see Roueché (1993), Jory (1996) and Easterling (1997b). For references to tragic singers in late antiquity see Weismann (1972) and Easterling and Miles (1999); for Byzantium see Theocharidis (1940).

CHAPTER TWO

The musicians among the actors

Peter Wilson

Ancient Greek theatre was a fundamentally musical experience. Whether it took its origins from the cultic dance-songs performed for Dionysus, from ritual masquerading as the satyric companions of the god, from informal celebrations at the vintage or at some important sacrifice, an essential component of the early matrix of drama was music. Origins do not explain historical forms; but music never leaves ancient drama, which at least until Plato's day remains within the broad Greek category of *mousikē* (that integral unity of poetry, music and dance whose many manifestations constituted one of the basic forms of socialisation in Greek society). Tragedy was much closer to what we might term 'choral opera' than 'theatre': all of its poetry – even the purely spoken dialogue – had the rhythmical and musical quality given by metre,[1] while its choral core – the songs and dances of the chorus that interwove the spoken parts – were full-scale, complex productions of rigorous, highly trained dance steps, group singing from the twelve or fifteen choreuts (twenty-four in the case of Old Comedy), all to the penetrating sound of the *aulos*. The role of instrumental music also extended beyond these purely choral songs to the exchanges between the chorus (or its leader) and actor(s) in certain passages of heightened emotionalism; and to passages of 'recitative' – again, normally associated with the crescendo on stage of emotional pressure; and even to songs sung entirely by actors, 'lyric monodies' that became increasingly characteristic of tragedy towards the end of the fifth century BC, at a time when the choral parts of drama were shrinking.[2] By far the most important and intimate musical relationship, however, was that between the musician and the chorus – a fact most readily exemplified by the depiction of the virtuoso Pronomos of Thebes on the famous late fifth-century vase named after him, seated in the centre of

[1] Cf. Dion. Hal. *On the Arrangement of Words* 11.

[2] Discussion of the elements of drama accompanied by music: *DFA* (1988) 156–67, ch. 5; Csapo and Slater (1995) 331–48; Comotti (1989b); Hall (1999a) and this volume, ch. 1.

Fig. 6 The famous piper Pronomos of Thebes, seated with his satyr chorusmen (Drawing reproduced from FR III. 143–4)

his company of satyr-choreuts, and at a marked distance from the actors in the upper register (fig. 6).

The importance of music is submerged from sight, however, by the historical development of the genres towards the increased preponderance of dialogue and speech – that is, by the rise of the roles accorded the actor; and, much more significantly, by the inevitable evanescence of sound. All the more or less credible reconstructions of ancient musical instruments and their music have given us very little sense of the ancient quality – and, more importantly, the ancient *reception* and *perception* – of the sounds they made. A tune on the most authentically reconstructed *aulos* is, in isolation, almost as meaningless to the modern ear as a recitation of a speech of Euripides to someone ignorant of the structure of ancient Greek, let alone of the whole historical and social environment in and for which it was created. The 'language' of music changes over time just as does ordinary language.[3] Another factor in the sidelining of music in drama is a result of the enormous influence of Aristotle's *Poetics*, with its general displacement of the pragmatics of performance. Music is placed firmly at the bottom of Aristotle's hierarchy of the six essential components of tragedy (1450a8). Music and spectacle are seen as features which make tragedy more effective than epic (1462a14), but the effect is not regarded by the philosopher as a 'good' one, and music is for him clearly tainted by what is seen as its principal function of producing pleasure in the audience (*idem*; cf. 1449b24ff.; 1450b16; Xen. *Symp*. 6.3).

Despite this marginalisation, more can be said of the musical resources of the ancient theatre than is usually imagined. In this chapter I focus on the figure of the musician himself, the *aulētēs*, largely to the exclusion of the music he played. To some extent it represents a false distinction to isolate *aulētai* as 'the' musicians of drama: the poet was the musical composer; choreuts needed to be highly expert in song and dance. However, the distinction is made meaningful, as we shall see, by the very particular role attributed to – and, more importantly, the attitudes expressed towards – the pure instrumentalist of dramatic music. Although largely anonymous for most of the classical period, his importance to dramatic performance was always recognised. And with the radical innovations in music of the later fifth century – innovations that generated such hostility in conservative social critics but seem to have won widespread popular

3 'There is no subject on which it is more difficult – if it is not virtually impossible – to reach a clear understanding, not to speak of appreciation, than that of the music to which the words were set and the character of the instrumental accompaniment': *DFA* (1988) 257. Cf. Hall (1999a) 102.

favour – the musician occupied a more conspicuous, and increasingly contentious, position.

One constant in the history of the music of the Greek theatre is the *aulos*. (Indeed, the *tibia* of the later Roman stage seems to represent essentially the same instrumental resource.) More properly termed *auloi*, since almost always played in pairs, this pipe with finger-holes and double-reed mouthpiece provided the entire musical support of all the major Dionysian performance-genres, of tragedy (and satyr-play), comedy, and dithyramb. Its penetrating sound was also heard in dozens of other important social functions, and its use and familiarity in at least some of these, with echoes of the tunes traditionally played in them, must have impinged on its perception within drama: it was a constant at the ritual heart of sacrifice; in contexts of lament and mourning, including the funeral, as well as on more joyous occasions of celebration and release, such as the wedding and symposium.[4] From the earliest days of formal drama (and, to judge from iconography, from possible 'prototheatrical' precursors) to the period when theatre had been exported to all corners of the Greek world and beyond, the principal and, quite probably, the sole musical resource deployed in performance was provided by a single instrumentalist, playing this distinctive set of double pipes (fig. 7).

The familiar expression 'tragic lyric' is thus in fact little more than a time-honoured scholarly misnomer. If the lyre and other instruments were ever used, it was only for local and specific effect – and an effect which in some cases depended on the assumed presence of the *aulos* and even on a deeply-entrenched polarity, amounting at times to an imagined hostility, between lyre and *aulos*. The chorus of Dionysus at the heart of drama seems never to have had any other instrument accompany its actions but the one which, in Aristotle's words, belonged to 'all bacchic activity (*baccheia*) and all movement of that sort' (*Politics* 8.1342b 4–5). When stringed instruments do appear on stage, it is significant that they were in the hands of (or especially associated with) heroic figures – individual actors rather than the chorus – especially given the much more socially elevated status of both lyre and cithara in contemporary Athenian life, clearly indicated by the foundational role that 'learning one's strings' from an early age played in the formation of the élite citizen, a skill that would be further honed in the competitive world of the symposium.

4 Sacrifice: cf. Herodotus 1.132; Nordquist (1994). West (1992a) 81–107 for full treatment of the instrument; cf. Wilson (1999); Landels (1999) ch. 2 (a).

Fig. 7 Piper with double pipes (Photo M. and P. Chuzeville)

The best-known example of such mythic musicians on the tragic stage is Thamyras the Thracian lyre-player, the story of whose musical *hybris* was most famously dramatised in Sophocles' play named after him, perhaps following an Aeschylean precedent.[5] Expertise on the lyre was doubtless essential for dramatic as for properly lyric poets, and part of the fame of the *Thamyras* may have derived from the fact that Sophocles himself took up the cithara on stage in the lead role; he was said to have been depicted holding a cithara in Athens' illustrious civic 'picture gallery', the Painted Stoa in the Agora.[6] Most of the small number of surviving fragments of this play focus on matters musical, including the tantalising *TrGF* 4, 245:

5 Hall (1989) 135–6 on the evidence for an Aeschylean *Thamyras* (possibly satyric), or at a minimum a treatment of his story within a play (the *Edonoi* and *Bassarai* have been proposed).

6 Sophocles as Thamyras, and depicted with cithara in the Stoa Poikile: *Life* 5. The association of this image, possibly as a dedicatory *pinax*, with the production of the *Thamyras* is entirely hypothetical, and iconographic convention (following compositional practice) tends to identify tragic (and perhaps even comic: cf. *Knights* 531–6) poets with the lyre or cithara (and not the *aulos*). The youthful Sophocles also famously danced naked and played the lyre around a victory monument following Salamis: Athenaeus 1.37.16; *Life* 3. Reference to the image of a lyre-playing Sophocles may have been made in a representation of the heroised poet in Neoptolemos' monument for Asclepius: Beschi (1967–8) 422–8; Connolly (1998) *contra*. (See also Fig. 1.)

And I was seized by an urge to be mad for music, and went to the place of assembly, an urge inspired by the lyre and by the measures with which Thamyras makes music supremely.

The evidence from a good number of lost plays suggests that the fates of such heroic *lyrikoi* (lyre-players) were a significant concern of Greek tragedy. Others include the Orpheus of Aeschylus' *Bassarids*; Euneus, a student of Orpheus, and the son of Jason and Hypsipyle who, at the close of Euripides' *Hypsipyle*, is possibly told by Dionysus to found a clan of Athenian religious musicians;[7] and Amphion, the musical twin brother of the military man Zethos: the two conduct a fully fledged *agōn* on the virtues of music (or its lack of them) in Euripides' *Antiope*, with Amphion ultimately instructed by Hermes to construct the walls of Thebes by the power of his lyre-music (fr. 48 Kambitsis (1972) col. iv. 90–7). In these and other cases it is fair to suppose that the relevant actors held and probably played their string instruments, but more significant than this largely banal fact of staging is the way that these figures were doubtless used to explore important social and religious aspects of the highly contested domain of contemporary *mousikē*.[8]

The theatrical *aulētēs* will have used a type of instrument specially suited to the musical range required: we hear of 'tragic *auloi*' as a distinct type,[9] but that may not be much more than a later classification based on the settled usage over a long period of a type of *aulos* not originally designed specifically for drama. The instrument used in tragedy was very probably described in other ways. There was a classification of types of *auloi* as old as the third century that distinguished at least four kinds according to their different pitches. These in turn depended on the kinds of choral voice they were to accompany, since the vocal and instrumental line of early Greek music tended to be the same. Alongside the 'maiden-*auloi*' and 'child- (or 'boy'-) *auloi*' we have the 'man-*auloi*' (also known as 'complete' or 'extra-complete').[10] It was doubtless one of these latter 'masculine' instruments that was the standard for tragedy and comedy, given that the voices they were to accompany were those

7 The Euneidai: see Bond (1963) 20; Burkert (1994).

8 The claim often made (on the basis of *Frogs* 1281–1300) that Aeschylus employed the cithara in performance under certain conditions is answered by West (1992a) 352: the point of comparison 'seems to lie in Aeschylus' occasional use of rolling dactylic rhythms of an epical cast'. Cf. Herington (1985) 255 n. 14; Snyder (1979) 86.

9 Athenaeus 4.182c–d, citing Ephorus (*FGrH* 70 F 3), Euphranor and Alexis.

10 Athenaeus 4.176e–f, cf. 14.634e–f (from Aristoxenus); cf. Arist. *Hist. An.* 581b; Poll. 4.74–7, 81 with West (1992a) 89–94. Elsewhere a more basic distinction seems to be between a 'choral' *aulos* and a type designed for solo performance: West (1992a) 93–4.

of men.[11] At the level of *mīmēsis*, however, the tragic choral voice was very frequently that of 'maidens', and it is possible that the *aulos* – always regarded as a highly 'mimetic' and 'polyphonic' instrument (cf. Pind. *Ol.* 7.12, *Isth.* 5.27; Plato *Rep.* 3.399d) – played an important part in evoking registers and tones not easily available to the singing adult male voice. An instrument with an extended technical range is also indicated by the wide variety of types of song mimicked in drama, from across the entire emotional, social and performative spectrum.[12]

Another piece of equipment used by the theatrical musician was the *phorbeia*: this was a set of leather straps or 'halter' that generally went both around the cheeks and over the top of the head of the player, and at the mouth was pierced so as to accommodate the mouthpieces of the pipes.[13] The *phorbeia* assisted in securing a firm oral control over the instrument, especially important in outdoor performance where the maximum volume of sound – and hence of air to the reeds – was demanded; and when, as was possibly the case with drama, a certain degree of vigorous movement was involved on the part of the player.

But who were these *aulētai*? We can speak with some confidence about the identities, the familial and social backgrounds of not only poets of theatre but also of many actors. Of musicians we can say much less, at least in the early period. And a very important part of the reason for this early anonymity is to be found in dominant Athenian attitudes towards music and musicians. The metropolis of ancient drama seems to have had, as it were, a collective problem with the *aulos*. Although its much-lauded and socially elevated poets did indeed also compose the music for their magnificent productions, and although participation at the 'musical' level, by dancing and singing in the chorus, was a highly valued form of socio-political participation (as well as probably maintaining a certain cachet as a largely élite activity), there was a high and strong ideological barrier between the Athenian and the *aulos*. In Athenian mythology – especially the story of Athena's own rejection of the instrument and ban on its subsequent use in the realm of good civic comportment – as well as in a wide range of other texts reflecting on Athenian attitudes, it emerges

[11] Cf. Arist. Quint. *On Music* 1.12 with Comotti (1989a) 43.

[12] The claim of the Byzantine treatise *On Tragedy* 12 (Browning 1963) that there could be three *aulētai* present at dramatic performances, one for each of the *genera*, is probably no more than a poor deduction, especially given that it was technologically possible by the final third of the fifth century to play all the *harmoniai* on a single instrument: Athenaeus 14.613e (attributed to Pronomos). However the possibility that the *aulētēs* employed more than one kind of *aulos* before that time cannot be dismissed.

[13] Bélis (1986); on the possible use of a 'clapper' see below.

that around the *aulos* crystallised a set of broadly 'educational' ideas and issues concerning the way a citizen should control his body. In particular, the *aulos* came to be associated, in part through its strong Dionysian ambience, with the loss of control, and more particularly, with the loss of the power of articulate speech. The instrument that blocked the mouth and so prevented the use of *logoi* was bound to be problematic in the city that so prided itself on the pre-eminent role and quality of its speech.[14]

The important musical services that the good Athenian 'gentleman' could never provide had thus necessarily to be delivered by others. The instrument and its craft were touched with the banausic slur of 'technology'. Such attitudes are helpful in probing the darkness surrounding the identity of early musicians of the theatre. Aristotle's surprise, verging on horror, that a member of the fifth-century Athenian élite actually played the *aulos* to accompany a comic chorus for which he was paying (*Pol.* 8.1341a33–7) is very suggestive: it implies (an implication supported by other evidence) that the musicians who kept close company with the élite Athenian poets, *chorēgoi* and performers were usually, and normatively, of a very different status. Many, probably most, were not Athenians. Some were perhaps from the lower orders of Athenian society: Athens also needed scores, if not hundreds, of players of the *aulos* to supply the time for the (lower-class) rowers of its triremes, and for the numerous sacrifices that took place across the city and countryside every day. Some of these were certainly slaves. There were many slaves in the city and its élite homes among whose duties was to provide musical services in a range of contexts, though whether any appeared in the theatre we cannot say.[15] The fact that there were so many slave players of the *aulos* in the city, male and female, seems to have attached an indelible slur on the whole range of players, and made the business of differentiating status and occupation between players themselves a pressing matter. There is even a faint possibility that female players may have entered the *orchēstra* from time to time. If they did, it is telling that the little and ambiguous evidence for their presence points to comedy rather than tragedy.[16]

[14] Wilson (1999).

[15] Cf. e.g. Andocides 1.12; *SEG* 25 no. 178: 'Hope' (Elpis) the *aulētris* manumitted *c.* 320 by a rich Athenian; cf. the regulation on the price of renting (slave) *aulētrides* in [Arist.] *Ath. Pol.* 50.

[16] For possible 'official' female comic *aulos*-players: Taplin (1993) 76–8. No female is ever recorded among the players on dedicatory inscriptions; none certainly appears in Attic theatre-related iconography (but see now the fragmentary *chous* which may show a female player with a comic chorus, although the identification of gender depends on one delicate hand (no good guide) and white paint for skin-colour: Pingiatoglou (1992)). Given the better-known tasks of *aulētrides*, a hierarchy among players is likely to have seen females excluded from the more prestigious events in Athens. Female players were however not universally excluded from 'public' roles in Greece. Full prosopography of Greek theatre-musicians: Stephanis (1988).

Like their divine patron Dionysus himself before them, many *aulētai* who played at Athenian dramatic festivals came there from across the Boeotian border.[17] Certainly by the later fifth century, Thebes (and Boeotia more broadly) was the recognised centre of excellence on the *aulos*, Pronomos its recognised master. The reeds around lake Copais proved ideal for the instrument.[18] In an earlier period, many *aulētai* in Greece may have come from Phrygia and Lydia, the original home of the instrument, places that gave their names to two of the principal musical 'modes' or *harmoniai*.[19] Only in the late Hellenistic period do we find Athenians starting to turn their hands (and mouths) to the instrument. The absence of Athenians from this major sphere of musical *technē* throughout the classical period, when thousands of performances of tragedy, comedy and dithyramb needed huge resources of *aulētai*, is highly marked – especially given the city's prominence in most other musical areas.

As if in conformity to this dominant attitude towards the *aulos* and its players, it appears that the city of Athens itself – so careful to record the details of not only the victors but also of all who competed at its major dramatic festivals – appears never to have perpetuated the names of these important musicians.[20] We do however know the names and the places of origin of a good number of *aulētai* who contributed to victorious performances in Athens, largely because (from around the beginning of the fourth century) individual *chorēgoi* chose to include them on the monuments they erected after victory. The single largest group are Thebans, and the relevant performances are almost all of dithyramb.[21]

17 Cf. Lucian *Harmonides* 1.

18 Pindar *Pyth.* 12.22–3; Theophrastus *Hist. Plant.* 4.11.8ff.

19 [Plutarch] *On Music* 1132; Athenaeus 14.624b.

20 On these records: *DFA* (1988) 101–25. Ghiron-Bistagne (1976) 84 entirely misrepresents the situation when she writes: 'le nom de l'aulète est presque toujours cité sur les dédicaces. Cette reconnaissance officielle montre qu'ils ont bénéficié d'une situation privilégiée que les acteurs mirent longtemps à conquérir.' The dedications she refers to are choregic, erected by individuals successful in their support of a Dionysian chorus, and are not at all of the same status as 'official', polis-sponsored documents. If *IGUR* 219, one of the Athenian didascalic fragments from Rome, contains a reference to an *aulos*-player for (?) comedy in the (?) fourth century, it will be unique in surviving polis records:] τατον γυμν[ ]/[ῳ̣]ι ηὔλησε Με [ ]/[μ̣]ια καὶ 'Αλε [ ]/[ ] καὶ πρ[ ]).

21 Scheithauer (1997) 111 for detailed prosopography; add Epigonos the Aeginetan from *SEG* 44 no. 129. I suspect that the decision to record the *aulētēs* in this way is connected to an increasingly significant role, perhaps especially as a musical composer and certainly as a virtuoso performer. From around the 330s the *aulos*-player and poet (*didaskalos*) vie for priority of placement in these memorials: Wilson (2000) 214–15, 367. A further important development sees the terms that describe dithyrambic contests (esp. the familiar abbreviation of simply *andres* 'the men' / *andrikos choros* 'male chorus' or *paides* 'the boys' / *paidikos choros* 'boy chorus') shift to *aulētai andrōn* / *paidōn* 'the *aulētai* for the men / boys': on this change see now Slater (1997). Whatever was happening in practice, this shift strongly suggests a further increased emphasis on the importance of the musician, perhaps to the extent of their being the focus of competition instead of the singing and dancing chorus.

The somewhat neglected Dionysian genre of dithyramb required twenty musicians for the City Dionysia alone every year, and by around 420 BC it had spread to the celebration of various other gods in Athens, including Apollo, Athena, Hephaestus and Prometheus, further increasing the demand. Part of the explanation for this expansion was the fact that dithyramb of this age hosted radical developments of musical form and style which, while abhorred by conservatives, were evidently extremely popular in the theatres.[22]

Other places represented among the homes of *aulētai* appearing in Athens include Sicyon (six known victors – including an Alkathous, a Kleanthes and the Pantaleon who performed the *Elpenor* of Timotheus, some eighty years after its composition, in a successful performance for the Kekropis tribe and its extremely lavish *chorēgos*, Nikias Nikodemou[23]); Argos (two); Aegina (two – including one Epigonos who only very recently surfaced on a choregic monument, having played for the victorious tribe, Leontis, at the Dionysia around 350[24]); Tegea (two); Epidamnos, Ambracia, Oreos, Heraclea (second century); possibly one from Delphi; a Rhodian called Sokrates (who was awarded Athenian citizenship); and a Boeotian.[25] These musicians were a highly mobile group, and although Athens, with its massive requirements for Dionysian *aulētai* from the end of the sixth century, was a major and highly attractive destination for them, it was far from the only one. Players of a certain standing will also have done the rounds of the various important *mousikoi agōnes* – the specifically 'musical' (and non-choral) contests – which offered to outside contestants the possibilities of individual prestige and, often, lucrative prizes. An early example of a successful travelling player is Midas from Acragas in Sicily, a master *aulētēs* for whom Pindar composed his only surviving epinician ode not for an athlete, *Pythian Twelve*, after Midas' victory on the *aulos* at Delphi in (probably) 490. Midas had success there again four years later, and on another occasion at the Panathenaia in Athens.[26] Significantly, unlike the rest of Pindar's clients, Midas seems not to have come from an illustrious family. His name may recall servile origins. It at least points to origins, real or imaginary, in the east.[27] In a later period, there is Euios of Chalcis, an *aulētēs* with an appropriately Dionysiac name who caught Alexander's eye and was singled out for mention among the hundreds of musicians summoned to

[22] On dithyramb in Athens see now Ieranò (1997); Wilson (2000) especially 65–70, 244–6; on the 'New Music' and dithyramb Csapo and Slater (1995) 332–4.

[23] Stephanis (1988) no. 1997; Wilson (2000) 226–9. [24] See note 21 above.

[25] On the use of Βοιώτιος in such inscriptions see Roesch (1982) 444–7, (1989).

[26] Schol. Pind. *Pyth.* 12 inscr. [27] Strauss (1992).

Susa in 324 to play for his mass royal wedding, and who turns up four years later in Athens (after Alexander's death) to play with success at the Dionysia of 320/19.[28] The presence in Athens of such well-travelled experts in the art of the *aulos* in the late archaic and early classical periods may well have been one of the (neglected) avenues by which the special capabilities of the instrument, and certain of the tunes specific to it, took root in the fertile soil of the burgeoning theatrical culture of Athens.

When identifiable festival *aulētai* appear in any numbers in surviving records, many of their names reveal at least two very striking characteristics (both perhaps exemplified already by Midas): social origins not among the élite; and an identifiable professional self-consciousness. The two are clearly related: pride in professional status acts as an alternative to pride in one's prestigious paternity. Names like Tekhnon, Deinon, Ariston and Nikon are especially evocative, as are the more specifically 'Dionysian' professional names like Bromias, Satyros and Euios.[29] Like many *technai* (including that of actors), auletic musical skill was often transmitted through family tradition. The great Antigeneidas of Thebes had his two daughters Melo and Satyra follow in their father's footsteps, the latter at least presumably in anticipation from birth.[30] A fine illustration of the professional pride and familial traditions of *aulētai* is the early fourth-century funerary stele, with epigram and relief sculpture, of the Theban *aulētēs* Potamon (fig. 8).[31] The epigram explicitly claims that the son's fame will add to that of his father, Olympichos – 'such a son did he produce, a touchstone for the discerning'. This was, interestingly, found in Athens, where the player had presumably become a resident, and its relief image shows the dignified, standing, younger man wearing a long *hīmation* and holding in his left hand a set of *auloi*, while with his right shaking the hand of his seated, bearded father (on a *klismos* (chair) almost identical to that on which Pronomos sits), who also holds *auloi* in his left hand. The family pride was evidently shared by Potamon's wife, who survived him: this relatively unspectacular but moving monument appears to have been dedicated, or in some way altered, by 'Patrokleia, the wife of Potamon', whose name and relation to Potamon appear under the epigram.

28 Stephanis (1988) no. 952.

29 Scheithauer (1997) 110.

30 Scheithauer (1997) 109, 115; Chaniotis (1990) 94–5 on 'Kunsterfamilien' in the Hellenistic and imperial periods. An even more illustrious father and son are Pronomos and Oiniades of Thebes.

31 The relief, found near Phaleron: Nat. Mus. 1962; the inscription: *IG* II² 8883 = *CEG* II, 509. . . . πατρὸς δὲ μνήμαισιν 'Ολυνπίχου αὔξετ' ἔπαινος / οἷον ἐτέκνωσεμ παῖδα σοφοῖς βάσανον.

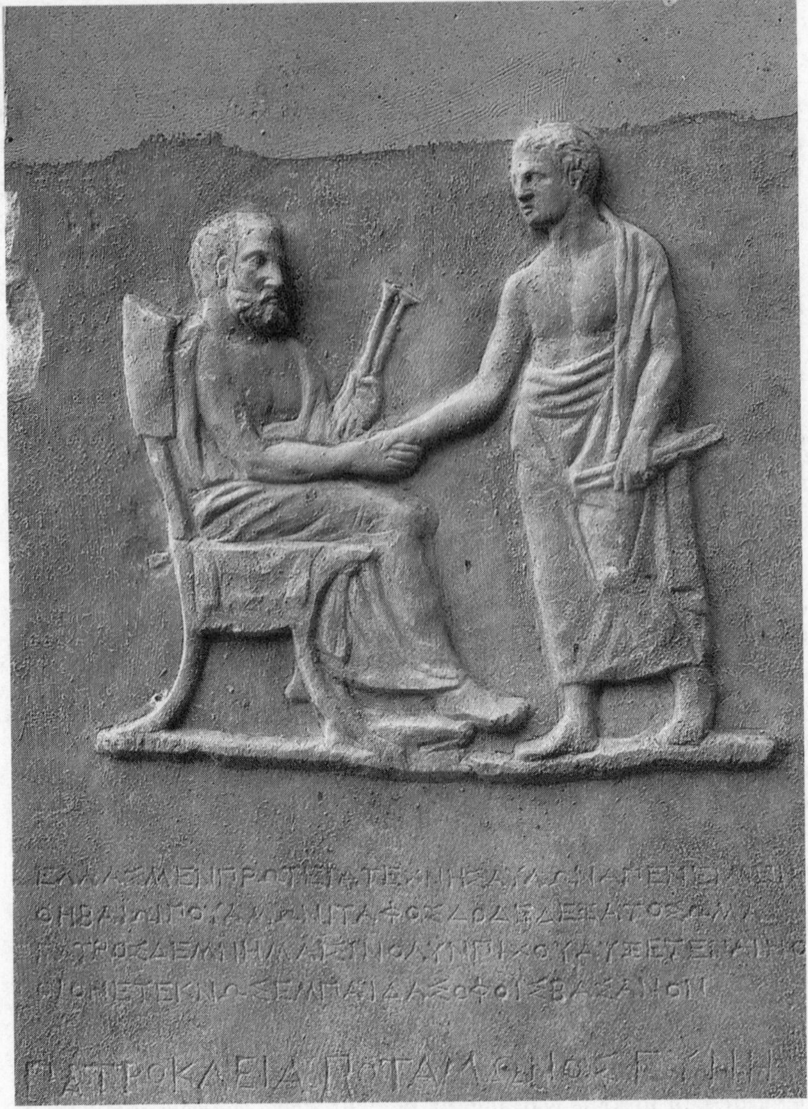

Fig. 8 Potamon of Thebes with his father Olympichos (© DAI Athens)

As 'craftsmen' and not members of the leisured élite, *aulētai* depended, more certainly than poets and many actors, on the return they received for their services. Playing the *aulos* may have constituted little more than a subsistence living for most of its practitioners. The topos of the *aulētēs* as parasite was so widespread as to generate the proverb 'You live the life of an *aulētēs*', referring to 'those who live off others; inasmuch as *aulētai* keep watch over those who perform sacrifices and live *gratis*'.[32] Non-slave *aulētai* were evidently often paid. The craft of the *aulētēs* was in demand in many more, and more socially diverse, contexts than that of the actor, who (like the poet) long remained a specialist within one or another of the Dionysian genres. In the *Peace* of Aristophanes (955), it is feared that the Theban *aulētēs* Chairis, reviled elsewhere as a poor player, will turn up unasked to play at a sacrifice in the hope of some return.[33] While this joke may depend precisely on the fact that Chairis was a serious, 'concert' instrumentalist who would never stoop to such work, the anxiety evident elsewhere on the part of musicians to differentiate the 'high' from the 'low' *aulētēs* must depend on a genuinely blurred region in practice. Illuminating in this context is the anecdote told of a fourth-century player, Dionysodoros,[34] who is said to have boasted that none of his melodies (*kroumata*) had ever been heard on a trireme or at a spring, unlike those of Ismenias (his great rival). And two other items in the anecdotes concerning Ismenias himself show how constantly open to contestation the status of the player was; how on the one hand there was a need for players at the upper levels to fortify their positions by a sharp demarcation from those at the lower levels, and how in turn even the greatest of virtuosi – like Ismenias – were never entirely free from slurs. Ismenias is said to have complained that the noble title of *aulētēs* was given to the hacks who blew hornpipes at funerals;[35] while the philosopher Antisthenes, when told that Ismenias was an expert *aulētēs*, replied 'But a base person; otherwise he wouldn't be an expert *aulētēs*.'[36]

One way in which the star musician sought to distinguish himself from his lesser colleagues was at the visual level, in the dress he wore during performance.[37] A number of vases with 'theatrical' imagery from Athens

32 *Suda* Prov. 4438. Evidence exists from the mid-third century for the regular payment of the *aulētris* on Delos who accompanied the famous chorus of women, the Deliades: one Bromias was paid 180 dr. a year (195 for a leap year) – hardly princely sums, though the work here is regular, and 'star' (male) musicians at major competitive events attracted much higher sums.

33 Stephanis (1988) no. 2594.

34 Diogenes Laertius 4.22; Stephanis (1988) no. 753.

35 Dio Chrysostom 49.12. The same story is told of Antigeneidas: Apuleius *Flor.* 1.4.

36 Plutarch *Life of Pericles* 1.5.

37 *Skeuē*, the term also used for the costume of choreuts and actors, could be used of the elaborate dress of musicians. A good example is from the provisions for new *mousikoi agōnes* at the festival of Artemis in Eretria *c.* 340, where all the contestants are required to participate in the processional song 'with the *skeuē* which they wear in the contest' (*IG* XII 9 189.12–14).

Fig. 9 *Aulētēs* in performance (Reproduced from Stephanis (1988), fig. 11)

show that *aulētai* in performance in large-scale festival contexts, including drama, wore a special and at times highly elaborate outfit (fig. 9).[38] In addition to his innovations in musical technique, the great Theban *aulētēs* Antigeneidas, perhaps second only to Pronomos (his senior by a few decades), was credited with introducing the wearing of Milesian shoes, and is said to have worn a *krokōtos* during his performance of *The Komast*. This is a yellow-gold robe more familiar from the wardrobe of women and of Dionysus.[39] Such 'effeminacy' and 'foreignness' of dress is all of a part with the somewhat 'alien' quality of the musical performer, and his music, at the heart of Athenian theatrical performance.[40]

But this was an area where skill could, at least for a small group of real virtuosi, secure considerable sums, both as prizes in the major musical contests and as payment for supporting choruses. In Athens, Dionysian *aulētai* were never, as far as we know, offered any prize by the city as competitors. They were thus probably perceived as banausic recipients of a 'wage' rather than active contenders for the prestige of a prize. Payment,

38 Beazley (1955); Taplin (1993) 69–70. Nordquist (1992) on the appearance of sacrificial *aulētai*.

39 *Suda* α2657. The wearing of effeminate footwear on stage and the allegation of 'softening the whole *technē*' are both reported of the *aulētēs* Battalos of Ephesos: Stephanis (1988) no. 519.

40 For an allegation of a lack of 'manliness' among tragic singers in classical Athens cf. the speech preserved in the Hibeh papyrus [?] *Against the Harmonikoi* (Barker (1984) 184, see also Hall, this volume), and Plato's description of tragedians as 'children of soft Muses' at *Laws* 7.817d 4.

however, and the relationships it implied, were open to different evaluations. We are told that in the early period (until about 440), *aulētai* were paid by poets.[41] The relationship of pay is clearly understood to suggest control and subordination: *aulētai* were hired technicians, the music they played subordinate to the word. At some point, however, both the financial and the performative relationship changed. We are ill informed as to the details, and our sources may in any case be making deductions from polemic embedded in early poetry, but it is revealing that this change is presented in that poetry in the language of a musico-political revolution, or of violent sexual assault on the figure of *Mousikē* herself (in terms that might also further recall, in the political register, the topos of tyrannical violence against women.[42]) A likely scenario is that, as the importance of the musical component increased and became more elaborate in the intensely competitive performance-context of the Athenian Dionysia in the fifth century, the performing musician experienced a corresponding increase in status. This process continues for the musician, as it certainly does for the actor, with the rise of the unions of *technītai* at the end of the fourth century (see further Lightfoot, this volume). The unions were able to negotiate favourable financial terms for musicians at festivals, and the other considerable privileges they arranged for their members (including exemption from military service and various taxes) were extended to them.[43] The social standing of *aulētai* was probably markedly improved through their association with the *technītai*. An important contractual agreement between *technītai* and the four major cities of Euboea (made in about 290) shows an *aulētēs* engaged for the Dionysia and Demetria apparently receiving the very handsome sum of 2,400 drachmas per performance.[44] The privileges won by the *technītai* evidently had antecedents in the earlier period: it is a fairly safe assumption that the many visiting musicians who supported drama and other performances in Athens were granted some form of safe passage to reach their

[41] The date depends on the date of Melanippides ([Plut.] *On Music* 1141 c), for which see West (1992a) 357. There are difficulties in correlating this date with the implication of Athenaeus 14.617b–c that during the time of Pratinas of Phlius (*c.* 500) *aulētai* abandoned their traditional, subordinate role and 'instead, choruses sang accompaniments to the *aulētai*'. One solution is to understand the Melanippides in question to be the maternal grandfather who won a dithyrambic victory in Athens in 493 (*Marm. Par.* Ep. 47) – preferable to the attempt to redate Pratinas. Alternatively we might suppose that such motifs of musical 'insurgence' – especially of the *aulos* – were prone to repetition.

[42] See references in previous note. The fragment of Pherecrates in which *Mousikē* recounts the violence worked on her is 155 KA. For discussion see also West (1992a) 360 and Barker (1984) 236–7nn. 200–1. Cf. Hall (2000).

[43] *DFA* (1988) 279–80; Lightfoot, this volume.

[44] *IG* XII 9 201.20–1: 600 dr. from each city; cf. Nordquist (1994) 83–4.

destination, and immunity from taxes once there (especially the tax on resident aliens that became payable after a month's sojourn – unless this was shouldered by *chorēgoi*). We do not hear until much later, however, of citizenship being granted to *aulētai*, long after this honour had been won by some actors.[45]

In the classical period, by the time we find clearer evidence for the position of the *aulētēs* – around the middle of the fourth century – the characteristic democratic institution of the lot is being used to allocate a choice of player to the competing *chorēgoi*. Presumably a pool of sufficient *aulētai* had already been preselected by the archon from among the aspirants who came for the great festival. This may represent a development from a stage during which the securing of a musician for a theatrical team was left entirely in the hands of *chorēgoi* and their agents. And the change may reflect a desire on the part of the city to curtail the excessive influence of a rich *chorēgos*' purchasing power. The lot may have been the polis' way of ensuring that the distribution of musical skills was fair, because random. It will have been modelled on the procedure already in place for the allocation of poets. Whether the polis also became the paymaster of the *aulētēs* at this juncture is not known. He is perhaps more likely to have remained the responsibility of the *chorēgos*, for his music was much more of a part with the chorus than with the actors. The importance of good relations between musician, *chorēgos* and the rest of the performing team was paramount.[46]

It was at a meeting of the democratic assembly that 'the lawgiver requires the archon to allot the *aulētai* to *chorēgoi*' (Dem. 21.13): only the genre of dithyramb is mentioned in this passage, but that is because Demosthenes' legal grievance arose out of his dithyrambic *chorēgia*, and it was presumably here too, in a meeting of the major organ of democratic government, the assembly, that dramatic *chorēgoi* were united with their musicians. It is possible that securing the 'best' available player under this system was something for which there was competition *between* genres.[47] A much sought-after musician could in theory have participated in all three Dionysian performances, since they were all held at different times, but

45 Scheithauer (1997) 116; the evidence for a possible fourth-century case in Phaon (Stephanis (1988) no. 2465) is far too doubtful to be considered seriously; Alexippos the Argive (Stephanis (1988) no. 123) who played with (at least) three victorious Athenian Thargelian choruses in the fourth century (363, 361, and an unknown year) is a faint possibility: he may have been granted citizenship by the time he played for the third, since in it he is mentioned without his ethnic.

46 Cf. Dem. 21.17 quoted below; Amphis fr. 14 KA.

47 The author of the eleventh-century Byzantine treatise *On Tragedy* edited by Browning (1963), some of whose material at least has roots in the Hellenistic period, writes that the 'best *aulētai*' (οἱ κράτιστοι) used to accompany tragic choruses.

one wonders whether this would have been feasible given the demands on the player and the need for extended rehearsals with the different teams. And *chorēgoi* and poets may have been unwilling to 'share' their musician even across the boundaries of performance (and so of formal competition). It is possible too that some *aulētai* may have tended to specialise in particular genres.

The question of specialisation raises once again issues of status. Perhaps only a minority of players are likely to have enjoyed the luxury of being able, through inherited wealth or lucrative remuneration, to have confined their activities to the poetic realm, and in particular to one of its 'high' forms such as tragedy.[48] Some of these, certainly in the later fifth and fourth centuries, were also composers in their own right: both of musical *nomoi*, innovatory new musical forms and, in a few notable instances, of fully fledged poetic compositions.[49]

Although the picture is complex, and open to major change over the classical period, (and although most of the important parts of the picture are missing), it is clear that this distinctive status of the musicians among the theatrical troupes chimes in interesting ways with the role of the music they played within drama. As I mentioned above, their instrument, with its many uses outside drama, brought with it to drama a rich baggage of social and emotional meaning. Tragic music was not, or at least not entirely, *sui generis*: to a significant degree it was constructed from a vast array of pre-existent musical forms, which came with their own powerful and varied associations.[50] This musical variety and elaboration (*poikilia* is the term of aesthetic criticism most often used for these qualities) made of the medium an immensely flexible tool for generating mood and emotion, as well as associative connotations of all kinds.

[48] Specialist 'tragic' or 'comic' *aulētai* are very rare, and evidence for them appears only with the arrival of the unions of *technītai*: e.g. in Egypt in the earlier period, *c.* 240, a 'tragic *aulētēs*' appears on the books of the local association: *OGIS* 50.63; at the Delphic Soteria in the third century: e.g. Stephanis (1988) nos. 121, 785, 1224, 1471, 1541, 1574, 1637, 1897, 1961, 1994; and cf. the '*aulētai* who [?produced] the tragedy . . . and the comic ones' at the Sarapieia in first-century AD Tanagra: *SEG* 19 no. 335.47. However, even in these late cases this evidence is only of their formal 'job description' within the unions at a particular time or occasion. Scheithauer (1997) 114, 119–26 assembles evidence for specialisation; Chaniotis (1990) 89–108 for its increase in the later period.

[49] *Aulētēs* and musical composer: e.g. Euios of Chalcis (Stephanis (1988) no. 952), known for his '*kyklioi nomoi*' – tunes for dithyramb (Polyd. 4.78). *Aulētai* also poetic composers: e.g. Sakadas of Argos (sixth century): [Plut.] *On Music* 1134A – a composer of *melē* and elegies; Pronomos of Thebes: Paus. 9.12.5–6 – a *prosodion*; cf. Stephanis (1988) no. 2149 for his musical innovations; his son Oiniades: Douris *FGrH* 76 F 36 – a dithyramb, the *Kyklops*; Telesias of Thebes: [Plut.] *On Music* 1142B–C – composer of *melē* as well as a player.

[50] Herington (1985); Comotti (1989a) 60.

It requires an enormous effort on the part of a modern reader to evoke any sense of these subtle and powerful nuances, not only because we have as good as no idea of the actual tunes and tempos used, but also because we have little in the way of a comparable musical idiom that patterns the activities of our own lives. Nor does modern music have any of the profoundly ethical and formative qualities ascribed (not without controversy) to ancient music: here certain modes or styles of tuning (*harmoniai* – 'melodic types' –) were felt to have a strong and specific moral, psychological and almost physical effect on their hearers and performers. Among the various 'modes' used in drama, the Dorian was the only one named for an unambiguously 'Hellenic' cultural tradition, and so it is no surprise to find that it is also the only one whose effect is described by critics in unambiguously positive terms: it was regarded as an austere and solemn tonal ambience which was felt to make men braver, more 'manly'.[51]

The musician was to an important degree the manager of this highly emotionally charged medium, the producer, or inducer, of its varied psychological and ethical effects.[52] He provided the crucial ambience within which the choral group of Athenian citizens took on the identities so often alien to their own: of women, often young women; of foreigners (whether non-Athenian Greeks, as in Sophocles' *Oedipus Tyrannus*, or non-Greeks); of slaves – or any combination of these; of old men beyond their political prime; even, at times, of semi-divine figures like the Oceanids of the *Prometheus Bound*. This role of the theatrical musician as a kind of intermediary is clear from theatre-related iconography. Here, in his elaborate dress that seems to fall short of being a strictly 'theatrical' costume on a par with that of the chorus (but see note 3 above), he is represented at the 'edge' of the properly mimetic, theatrical zone, on the margin between the Dionysiac world and the 'ordinary' world beyond. Consider for instance the image on an Attic hydria in Boston (fig. 10): in front and under the influence of the playing musician, the performing chorus has truly become a group of satyrs inside their mythical world. Immediately behind him, on the other hand – and as it were 'out of range' of the effects of his playing – stands a figure who is generally described as a 'civilian' (because of his non-theatrical garb and demeanour), and who is clearly not an integral member of the Dionysiac scene.[53]

[51] Arist. *Pol.* 8.1342b12–17; cf. Pl. *Rep.* 3.399c, [Plut.] *On Music* 1136; below.

[52] Cf. West (1992a) 106.

[53] This figure is often assumed to represent a *chorēgos*, whose position on the 'border' of the theatrical world would be altogether appropriate, given his highly active role in its organisation: Wilson

Fig. 10 Chorus performing as satyrs with piper and a standing figure (© Museum of Fine Arts, Boston)

The satyr-chorus, it should be added, while to some extent an 'extension' or component of the tragic team, and sharing its forms of *mousikē* in the same somewhat parasitic manner that it shares in tragic language and style, also had its own special performance idiom in terms of dance and music. The name *sikinnis* is often used of satyr-dance, and it seems to have involved rapid leaping movements.[54] The music that went with it was doubtless correspondingly rapid in tempo. We hear for instance of a kind of *aulos*-tune called the *sikinnotyrbē* (Athen. 14.618c) – the 'satyrs' whirl'.

With its connections to sacrifice, to lament and the funeral, the music of the *aulos* had strong associations of extreme grief. The combination of

(2000) 257–8; cf. also the image (fig. 11) on the neck of the Attic volute-krater of *c.* 450 in Spina, *ARV*² 612.1; and Nordquist (1992) 167.

54 See esp. Athen. 14.630b–c, citing Aristocles' treatise *On Choruses*. Seaford (1984) 103–4.

Fig. 11 Chorus performing as satyrs with piper and standing figure (far right) who may be a *chorēgos* (Photo: Hirmer Verlag)

aulos music and solo voice (*aulōidia*) proved too 'elegiac' a performance-category, we are told, for the Pythian festival of Apollo.[55] From the other side, with its links to the world of Dionysiac release and joy, and to celebrations of different kinds – in marriage, victory in war, the symposium and so on – it came into the orbit of extremes of happiness. The technical development of such an emotionally expressive register would have served well the ends of the new tragic genre, to which the expression and exploration of heightened extremes of emotion was always central. Similarly with the connotations of 'foreignness' and the alien that came with the instrument and its practitioners: the 'foreign' and alien were after all very much central to the thematics of tragedy, ever modulated in a complex and historically shifting dialectic with an implicit notion of the norms of Attic (civic) identity. The *aulētai* of drama provided a rich array of 'foreign' tunes;[56] while the 'modes' in which they did so were, with the significant exception of the Dorian, all characterised as more or less exotic, named for more or less foreign cultures (Mixolydian, Phrygian, Lydian, Hypodorian, Hypophrygian, Ionian).[57]

I sketched at the start of this chapter the principal areas of a dramatic performance in which its musician was probably active. It is possible to say a little more about the practicalities of his role. In the months leading up to the actual event, the *aulētēs* was evidently a crucial figure in the *chorēgeion*, the training-space of the choral or theatrical team. As much is clear from the (admittedly unusual) events of Demosthenes' dithyrambic *chorēgia* around the middle of the fourth century, during which for some reason Demosthenes lost the support of his own poet–trainer (*didaskalos*). Demosthenes claims his poet had been 'corrupted' by his enemy Meidias,

55 Introduced in 586 BC and dropped at the next festival: Paus. 10.7.3–5.

56 In addition to the modes with their foreign 'coloration', tragedy is full of references to specific foreign forms of musical expression, many of which will have involved a form of auto-description of the music being played at the time: a small selection – the great dirge which closes the *Persians*, for which some (e.g. Comotti (1989a) 54) believe the *aulētēs* picked up a set of special Mariandynian *auloi* around 935ff. whose tuning and timbre would have at once evoked the Asiatic ambience; cf. Hall (1989) 83–4; Soph. fr. 412 (from the *Mysoi*); Eur. *Trojan Women* 544; *IA* 576–8. See also the long list of suggestive references to mostly foreign musical instruments made by Comotti (1989a) 52–4.

57 Mixolydian: especially suited to lamentation (Pl. *Rep.* 3.398–9); said to have been an inheritance of the tragedians from Sappho (Aristoxenus: [Plut.] *On Music* 1138D); Phrygian: described as both peaceful and calm (Pl. *Rep.* 3.399), and in Aristotle (*Pol.* 8.1342a) as orgiastic and 'pathetic': see Comotti (1989a) 46, Barker (1984) 168; Lydian: said by Plato to be conducive to drunkenness, softness and sloth, though associations with lament are also known (*Rep.* 3.398–9); Hypodorian and Hypophrygian: (apparently not in choral parts; [Arist.] *Probl.* 19.30, 48, see Hall, this volume); the Ionian: perhaps with an austere and noble gravity (Heracl. Pont. in Athen. 14.625b), although see West (1990a) 130–1 and Pl. *Rep.* 3.398e. On the difficult question of the modes and their use in tragedy see Comotti (1989) 44–9.

'and if Telephanes, the *aulētēs*, had not been a very good friend to me then and, when he saw what was happening, turned the man out and taken upon himself the co-ordination and direction of the chorus, we should have been out of the running . . . ' (21.17). This was an age – and dithyramb was a genre – in which music and the musician played a major role. But that does not diminish the likelihood that the musician for drama played a similarly important role in maintaining discipline during training.

As for the performance itself, the musician almost certainly led the chorus into the *orchēstra* at its first (and any subsequent) appearance, piping the appropriate accompaniment for their *parodos* or 'song for the entrance' in the many cases where there was such a choral entry.[58] We know that he led them off at the end, and this frame of close contact between *aulētēs* and chorus very probably reflects the nature of their relationship throughout.[59] He is likely to have played an important role, in close concert with the leading choreut, in steering the group through their complex dance formations during choral odes, giving them their 'keynote' (*endosimon*) and acting somewhat in the capacity of a conductor. We hear of a kind of wooden slipper (or rattle, *kroupeza*) worn by an *aulētēs* to give time to his chorus. Already by about 430, Cratinus apparently associates it – pejoratively – with Boeotians: 'these are the Pig-Boeotians, the race of clapper-wearers' (οὗτοι δ' εἰσὶν συοβοιωτοί, κρουπεζοφόρων γένος ἀνδρῶν).[60]

Just where the musician was positioned during choral singing and dancing is entirely unknown, one aspect of our profound ignorance about the nature of dramatic dance. When, as seems to have happened on at

[58] The mode of delivery of the tetrameters (iambic, trochaic and anapaestic) of the *parodos* was probably in most cases the recitative 'chant' in-between speech and full song: Csapo and Slater (1995) 332. The description of the *parodos* as an ᾠδή at Arist. *Poet.* 1452b22 (cf. Schol. Eur. *Phoen.* 202) may imply however that a fully sung *parodos* was a possibility.

[59] *DFA* (1988) 244; Schol. Ar. *Wasps* 582; Cratinus fr. 308 KA (cf. *Suda* ε1784, Hesych. E3934, Poll. 4.108): τοὺς ἐξοδίους ἵν' αὐλῶ τοὺς νόμους, 'so that I may pipe you the tunes for the exit-song'. Was this spoken by the stage *aulētēs*? Taplin (1993) 108 reckons not even Cratinus would have 'dared . . . to let the official *aulētēs* speak within the play', and so takes this as a likely case of 'another player playing at playing'. However, in a comedy whose chorus may have in some sense 'been' '*Nomoi*' (if this came from the *Nomoi*, though most editors leave it as *adespoton*), there will have been all sorts of potential for metatheatrical overlap between musical and legal–conventional meanings, and we might entertain the possibility of a speaking *aulētēs*, perhaps serving as *koryphaios*? In that case, his 'piping' of the 'exodic *nomoi*' could refer both to familiar tunes and the members of the chorus physically leaving the *orchēstra*.

[60] Cratinus fr. 77 KA (from the *Thracian Women* of *c.* 430). The title suggests women worshipping Bendis. Cf. Poll. 7.87, 10.153; Phot. s.v. κρουπέζαι; Schol. Aeschin. 1.126. Further on this instrument: Bélis (1988). For the possibility of the *koryphaios* giving the 'keynote' cf. [Arist.] *De mundo* 6.399a14; Aelian *NA* 15.5.

least some occasions, the tragic and comic chorus abandoned their regular rectangular formation to dance in a circle, the *aulētēs* is likely to have followed the practice of his dithyrambic colleagues, and positioned himself in their centre.[61] It seems in any case scarcely imaginable that he remained motionless throughout, and we probably should imagine some degree of direct involvement in the movements of the chorus. At least from the later fifth century some *aulētai* practised extravagant physical movement of a mimetic nature. Aristotle complains of their habit of 'rolling round to represent a discus, and mauling the coryphaeus if their music concerns Scylla' *Poet.* 1461 b 30–2.[62] Although not to the philosopher's taste, it is clear that this new corporeal dimension to musical *mīmēsis* was successful in the theatres. The great Pronomos was remembered with pleasure for his facial expressiveness as he played (Paus. 9.12.4). Possibly the *technē* of *aulos*-playing was beginning to learn from – even to infringe upon – that of the actor, which saw a major expansion of its technical resources in this period.

It is, however, probably more fitting to think in terms of a loosening or general reconfiguration of forms of musical structure and performance in the late- and post-classical period. The usual account of the dramatic form posits a decline in the fully choral *mousikē* of both tragedy and comedy in the last decades of the fifth century, and although any interpretation which sees a wholesale withering of the chorus is open to serious qualifications, it is certainly true that by the last third of the fifth century tragic poets were expecting their actors to sing more often and to perform more musically elaborate passages than before.[63] Even the purely choral form of the dithyramb saw the introduction of extended passages of solo song some time in the fourth century.[64]

Despite the probable reduction in fully orchestrated choral song and dance, music remained extremely important to comedy in Menander's day. Far from indicating its absence, the appearance of the term XOPOY in the text of his *Dyskolos* (produced in 316 BC) shows that a chorus did still

61 Possible circular dance-formation in drama: Ar. *Thesm.* 953ff. is an especially striking example; cf. Davidson (1986). The dithyrambic *aulētēs* at the centre of the circle: Schol. Aeschines, *Against Timarchus* 10.

62 The innovation may have come from Sicily: Athen. 1.22c.

63 Hall (1999) and this volume, ch. 1; Rothwell (1992) against the standard image of 'choral decline'. If the *Rhesus* is a fourth-century work, the management of its chorus – which has ample odes and is moreover a notably 'engaged' participant in the action – almost has the air of a considered intervention in a current 'debate' about the proper degree and nature of choral performance in drama.

64 This is associated with Philoxenus of Cythera (*c.* 435–380): [Plut.] *On Music* 1142A; West (1992a) 364–6. The potential, and perhaps a version of the practice, had long been there: cf. Bacch. 18.

perform 'between acts' in this age, whatever it may be taken to imply concerning the originality of the odes it sang and danced. Music also figures prominently in the latter stages of the same play, as the old man is forced to participate in dancing after his accident (see further Handley and Hunter, this volume). The shift to an eight-foot iambic line (and a possibly authentic direction at 879 indicating that 'the *aulētēs* plays') shows that the end of the drama was given an extensively musical treatment (as with many an Old Comedy), though whether delivery at this point was in song or recitative is unclear.[65] In more general terms, comedy of Menander's day, as well as among his immediate predecessors and successors, shows a thematic fascination with music and its practitioners. We know of comedies called *The Aulētris* by Alexis, Diodorus, Antiphanes and Menander, and of an *Aulētrides* by Phoenicides; a *Kitharistria* by Anaxandrides; a *Kitharōidos* by Alexis, and eight others by later poets (Antiphanes, Sophilus, Theophilus, Clearchus, Diphilus, Apollodorus, Anaxippus and Nicon); and a *Kitharistēs* by Menander. There are in addition many scenes in other plays where musicians figure prominently. It is almost as though, with the decline of *choreia*, music needed to find other areas for its dramatic expression. The prominence of sympotic and erotic themes explains this phenomenon only in part. One might also point to a degree of continuity with Old Comedy's practice of including prominent *mousikoi* in its critical sights, largely for their cultural and intellectual significance: thus Konnos the *kitharistēs* who tried to teach Socrates how to play the lyre in advanced age appeared in the chorus of *phrontistai* ('thinkers') in the play by Ameipsias named after him.[66] Whereas tragedy's form meant that it could only comment indirectly, via its mythic medium, on the controversies surrounding the social role of music of its time, comedy was as ever much more up-front.[67]

The post-classical picture is much more complicated, in music as in all aspects. Already by the later fourth century there was an extensive demand for dramatic performances in many places well beyond Attica,[68] and this loosening of the Athenian grip on dramatic production encouraged the further loosening of form. The travelling unions of players which were to become the preponderant providers of drama certainly

[65] See the full discussion of Handley (1965) 283–6.

[66] Of 424. A comedy of the same name is attributed to Phrynichos; cf. Plato's *Sophistai*, which included the *aulētēs* Bacchylides of Opountis, and Xenokles Karkinou; also relevant is Cratinus' *Archilochoi*: see fr. 2 KA.

[67] The satyr-play's representations of musical inventions and practices deserves further study in this connection. See e.g. Iophon fr. 1 (from his satyric *Singers to the Aulos*).

[68] Le Guen (1995); Taplin (1999).

included musicians among their ranks, and in some cases, specialised choreuts, but there seem also to have been occasions on which choreuts were recruited locally, perhaps to supplement those 'professionals' in the travelling group.[69] On the other hand, the virtuosic actor–singer – who now took on the title of *tragōidos* once the preserve of chorus-members – rises to a prominence that will remain his for centuries.[70] An example of the kind of versatility and mobility expected of performers in this age is to be found in the career of the third-century singer and choral star Pythokles from Hermione.[71] His brother [Pan]takles, also a choreut,[72] set up a statue in his honour which boasts *inter alia* of his success at a wide range of festivals (at Thespiae, the Isthmus, the Theban Agrionia and the Delphian Pythia among others) as a (?) singer to the *aulos*, a choreut and perhaps as a rhapsode or *kōmōidos*, as well as 'in the cyclic choruses' (*IG* IV 682).[73] From the remains of another commemorative statue, erected in Athens, we hear of the agonistic musical career of one Nikokles, almost certainly the third-century citharode from Taras 'who achieved the greatest fame of all citharodes' as Pausanias comments when, in his narrative, he passed Nikokles' memorial near the Sacred Way (1.37.2). Among victories at the Pythia, Great Panathenaia, Isthmia, Hekatomboia, the Basileia in Macedonia, the Basileia in Alexandria, the Helleia and the Asklepieia, is a victory 'with a dithyramb at the Lenaia' (*IG* II^2 3779.7–8). This is clearly not the familiar massed choral performance of the classical age, but rather a citharodic interpretation of a dithyramb. A pure instrumentalist rather than a singer, early in the second century we find Satyros of Samos ceded the honour of a special uncontested performance on the *aulos* at Delphi – 'this man was the first person to play the *aulos* in the contest alone, without competitors'. Satyros' appearance at Delphi included an 'extra' performance of a song – the '*Dionysus*' – with choral accompaniment (a configuration increasingly common in this period), as well as a *kitharisma* from the *Bacchae* of Euripides.[74]

The great increase in performance opportunities occasioned by the 'agonistic explosion'[75] in the later Hellenistic period and under the Empire offered the theatrical musician broader horizons of prestige: witness as a final instance the manner in which the union of Ionian *technītai* honoured one Moirios from Miletus, apparently a musician, in the middle

69 Wilson (2000) 289–90. 70 Gentili (1979) 26; Hall, this volume, ch. 1.

71 Stephanis (1988) no. 2174. 72 Stephanis (1988) no. 1993.

73 Nachtergael (1977) 317–23, 429–30 has full discussion of the activities of this pair and judicious commentary on the inscription.

74 Stephanis (1988) no. 2240; cf. Sifakis (1967) 96–7. 75 Robert (1984) 38.

of the second century 'for his excellence and good-will towards it'. The statue erected for him included this epigram, with its emphatic statement of the 'internationalism' of his career:[76]

> The Ionian cities set up this image of Moirios,
> a highly skilled practitioner of his melodious craft.
> He boasts that he's laid his hands on the crowns of lasting memory
> through all the cities for his well-staged choral song.
> Most divine Miletus, you nurtured the prestigious tribes of *Technītai*
> and have been adjudged the leader in theatrical performance.

The music of the Roman stage should not be regarded as nothing more than a crude appropriation by the 'unmusical' Romans of this essential performative element of the Greek theatre.[77] The picture of the theatrical inheritance and forging of a Roman idiom is much more complex than the old idea of a simple 'translation' of Greek models allows, and the realm of music is one where Roman innovation may well have been as important as the influence of Greek traditions, not to neglect the input from other 'local' sources, notably the Etruscans.

The spread of Greek drama, tragic and comic, to the Italian peninsula and to the Greek cities of Sicily was well under way by the early fourth century, and by the time (240 BC) that *ludi scaenici* were added to official Roman games, classical Athenian drama performed in its original language, as well as Latin (and possibly Etruscan)[78] adaptations, was probably quite widely known and enjoyed. Despite a clear attachment to 'classics' of the Athenian theatre, especially Euripides among tragedians and Menander in comedy, it is not at all clear to what extent the original musical form of their works was preserved (especially as regards the chorus).[79] It is widely held that the Hellenic theatre of Magna Graecia did not have a chorus, but the matter is open to some debate.[80]

[76] Stephanis (1988) no. 1736. On the *technītai* see further Lightfoot, this volume.

[77] For a recent stereotyping of the 'unmusicality' of the Romans cf. Landels (1999) 172–3: 'The Romans themselves do not seem to have been troubled or embarrassed by their lack of interest and proficiency in music . . . they were prepared to admit that when they came across the Greeks' very sophisticated tastes and techniques in music they had chosen to be listeners and admirers rather than competitors.' For a detailed survey of the – very extensive – role of music in Roman life in general see Wille (1967).

[78] Jocelyn (1967) 14.

[79] This is also an issue relevant within the Greek context. It seems likely that musical scoring of dramas was not preserved in written form until the fourth century, and transmission of fifth-century music probably depended on oral means, via the poet and his associates, including the *aulētai* who worked with him.

[80] Taplin (1993) ch. 6 makes the case for a comic chorus; Pöhlmann (1997) and Dumont (1997) *contra*.

However, whatever the status of the theatrical chorus, as we have already seen, Hellenistic drama in Greece was exploring and expanding its musical potential in other ways, and it is perhaps wisest to think, with Csapo and Slater, in terms of a general trend in performance both in Rome and in the eastern Mediterranean in the late third and second centuries.[81]

The *tibia* and its player, the *tibicen*, were as much a fixture of the Roman theatre as the *aulos* and *aulētēs* of the Greek. But despite their omnipresence in Roman theatrical mosaics and painting, even less is known about their background and roles than for their Greek counterparts.[82] The texts of Roman comedy do give a fair indication of where and how music figured in performance, and it was extensive (see also Hall, this volume). Like its Greek models, the drama of Plautus and Terence shows a basic metrical distinction between spoken verse (a six-foot iambic line generally known as the *senarius*) and a range of longer 'lyric' metres, the latter accompanied by the music of the *tibia*.[83] There were, further, passages of 'mixed metres' where various of these longer lines mixed with iambic dialogue – a feature generally regarded as a Roman contribution to the theatrical tradition.[84] The accompanied metres of Roman comedy were, of course, delivered by actors, not a chorus.[85] But rather more than two-thirds of a Plautine comedy will probably have been accompanied by music – a significantly higher proportion than that for all surviving Greek tragedies and comedies.

The dramatic significance of the employment of music in Roman drama remains to be explored further. Some have argued convincingly for its role as a major structuring device for the comedies of Plautus

[81] Csapo and Slater (1995) 331.

[82] See Landels (1999) ch. 8; Howard (1893) and Beare (1955) ch. 26 remain useful.

[83] That the metrical distinction reflects a performance distinction between accompanied and unaccompanied verse is shown by the presence of possibly authentic annotations in some Plautine manuscripts of '*DV*' and '*C*' for '*diverbium*' ('speech') and '*cantica*' ('song'): Moore (1998b), see further Hall, this volume.

[84] Beare (1955) esp. 226. Dumont (1997) downplays its originality. The mode of vocal delivery of the 'mixed metres' is unknown, but a combination of full song and recitative or 'chant' of some kind is usually supposed. They were however almost certainly accompanied by the *tibicen*: Moore (1998b) 246–8; Landels (1999) 186.

[85] Although Senecan tragedy did have a chorus, the fact that its metrical patterns are highly homogeneous, combined with the strong suspicion that the plays were designed for reading or 'declamation' rather than full dramatic staging, leaves little room for a fully 'musical' chorus. The practice of earlier Roman tragedy in this regard is very unclear, but there are 'unmistakable signs' that Ennius, for instance, retained the original chorus of Corinthian women in some form in his version of Euripides' *Medea*: Jocelyn (1967) 19. As to whether there was any '*entr'acte*' music in Roman comedy (Plautus *Pseud.* 573ff. is the most likely case) see Landels (1999) 182; Moore (1998b) 246 against 'act breaks' of any kind.

(which, like many Aristophanic works, always end to musical accompaniment); and have noted, for instance, the way that less sympathetic characters tend not to have music, like Diabolus (and his parasite) in the *Asinaria*, the rival to the play's young lover. The only scenes without music in the entire play are those in which these two appear (746–827). On the other hand, scenes of heightened emotion are routinely accompanied, a continuity of a sort with their Greek predecessors, but probably not one which demands explanation in terms of direct imitation or borrowing.

About the sociology of Roman theatrical musicians – the main interest of this chapter – frustratingly little can be said. It seems that from its earliest days the Roman theatre was organised in self-sufficient troupes, with none of the centralised 'state' support and management clear in the early Greek context.[86] Each troupe will have had its own instrumentalist(s), who was also probably the composer as well as the performer of music. Many early Roman musicians and other theatre people were probably slaves and immigrants, 'and it is unlikely that their names carried much weight while they lived'.[87] One precious testimony from the production records of Terence's comedies indicates that his musician – one Flaccus Claudi – was (or had been) a slave, and that he was the composer as well as the player of Terence's music (*modos fecit*). It seems likely that it was never a tradition for Roman dramatists to compose their own music, unlike their Greek counterparts – a fact of some consequence for Roman attitudes to the practice. However, if the author of the *De comoedia* is to be believed, the very considerable importance of the musician within the theatrical world is signalled by the fact that 'the name of the person who composed the music was placed at the beginning of the play after those of the author and actor'.[88] The production records also provide important details of the varieties of *tibia* used in six of Terence's comedies: these are described as either 'equal' (a category apparently further distinguished as between 'right-' or 'left-hand') or 'unequal'; and in one case – the *Self-Tormenter* – a shift between 'unequal for Act 1 then two right-hand for the rest' is prescribed (*primum imparibus deinde duabus dextris*). The difference between 'left' and 'right' is almost certainly one of size and so of pitch, while the use of different pipes together may imply a melody and

[86] See Brown, this volume.

[87] Jocelyn (1967) 6, with reference to the early 'adapters' of Greek drama in Rome.

[88] *De comoedia* 8.10: *eius qui modos faciebat nomen in principio fabulae post scriptoris et actoris superponebatur.* The *Excerpta de comoedia* are published with Euanthius' *De fabula* in Wessner's 1902 Teubner edition of Donatus, vol. 1. pp. 22–31. At 8.9 the author appears to make the generalisation that the music of *cantica* was composed by a musician, not the poet: *diverbia histriones pronuntiabant, cantica vero temperabantur modis non a poeta sed a perito artis musicae factis.* See also Hall, this volume.

accompaniment of some kind.[89] The right-hand *tibiae* were evidently the deeper in pitch, and they were said to accompany the 'serious speech of comedy', while the left-hand were better suited to the more light-hearted parts.[90]

The evident importance of the musician and his craft to the Roman theatre – clearly, in its way, no less substantial than its place in the Greek – should banish any notion of the 'unmusicality' of the Romans, who for instance appear to have enjoyed and employed purely instrumental music on many more occasions than the Greeks. Their attitude to music and its practitioners may have been fissured by a deep ambivalence, but as we have seen, neither were the attitudes of the highly 'musical' classical Athenians towards the *aulētai* of their prized drama altogether straightforward. The variety and subtlety of the deployment of music in Roman drama are evidence of a refinement of appreciation among at least a significant part of its audience. The same is suggested by a somewhat neglected passage of Cicero's *Academica* (2.20), which is also a valuable indication of the role of music in Roman tragedy.

As part of his defence against scepticism, Lucullus stresses the importance and degree of knowledge that can be derived from the senses: those practised in certain of the arts which depend on the senses develop a more acute understanding. The illustration he turns to shows that there were clearly some Romans whose musical sensibilities were highly refined:

> How many things in music that escape us are caught by the hearing of persons trained in that department, who when the *tibicen* blows his first note say 'That is the *Antiope*' or '*Andromache*', when we have not even a suspicion of it![91]

SUGGESTIONS FOR FURTHER READING

The testimonia relevant to the classical Greek theatre are collected in *DFA* (1988) 257–62, and, in translation, in Csapo and Slater (1995) 331–48. Pages 331–4 of the latter are an excellent general introduction to the material in its historical context. For the broader canvas against

89 Landels (1999) 188. Of another type mentioned – the *Serranae*, used in the *Adelphoe* – very little is known. Further on the didascalic records and the slightly different information provided by Donatus see Howard (1893) 41–3.

90 *De comoedia* 8.11: *dextrae autem tibiae sua gravitate seriam comoediae dictionem pronuntiabant, sinistrae [Serranae] acuminis levitate iocum in comoedia ostendebant.*

91 Although some scholars believe that the situation envisaged here is that of a 'concert' performance of individual arias excerpted from different works (see e.g. Jocelyn (1967) 253), it is equally possible that Cicero bases his remarks on observed theatrical practice.

which Greek theatrical music and musicians operate see Barker (1984) and West (1992a).

Sociological study of Greek music is an underdeveloped field. Stephanis (1988) is a scholarly prosopography of theatrical and musical performers which will provide an invaluable resource for future research. Csapo (forthcoming b) is an important study of the momentous fracture in Greek musical and social practice that is summed up by the expression the 'New Music'. Wilson (2000) has much discussion of the sociology of the Greek theatre. On *auloi* and *aulētai* see Wilson (1999), Taplin (1993) and Scheithauer (1997). Wille (1967) is the most comprehensive treatment of music in Roman culture.

CHAPTER THREE

The use of the body by actors in tragedy and satyr-play

Kostas Valakas

THE BODY AT THE CENTRE OF PERFORMANCE

In an essay of 1907 the Russian director and actor Vsevolod Meyerhold commented on the modern 'stylised theatre' which he intended to produce: 'since the stylised theatre wants . . . to subordinate acting to the rhythm of dialogue and plastic movement; since it anticipates the revival of the dance and seeks to induce the active participation of the spectator in the performance, then clearly the stylised theatre is leading to a revival of the Greek classical theatre . . . : it has three-dimensional space, no scenery, and it demands statuesque plasticity'.[1] Meyerhold was influenced by Georg Fuchs' book *The Stage of the Future* (1904–05), in which the German director used the ancient Greek and Japanese theatrical traditions in support of his argument that acting originated from dance, and that modern theatre, too, should mainly focus on 'the rhythmical movement of the human body in space'.[2]

Yet until the 1960s researchers and directors took one of two views of Athenian performances in the fifth century BC: either that they were as realistic as possible, or that they were more or less static, based on the poetic use of speech and on limited, conventional movements by actors and dancers.[3] The latter view seems to have been best formulated in 1943 by the Czech formalist Jindřich Honzl in a useful critique of modern realistic performances of ancient tragedy. Acting 'was an aesthetic system of vocal and gesticulatory signs, and the techniques used by the players were, no doubt, differentiated as to use in tragedy or comedy',[4] but in fact only poetry could 'become "actor" or "scenery"',[5] for 'verbal deixis serves as a semantic filter that enables the dramatist to create an image of the world and of people from . . . the few artistic resources that the ancient

[1] In Braun (1991) 63–4. [2] Braun's phrase in Braun (1982) 115.
[3] Taplin (1977a) 31–9 and his references. [4] Honzl (1976) 125.
[5] Honzl (1976) 123.

actor and ancient stage technology were able to provide'.[6] Honzl neglects any possible difference between drama and poetry in performance, and claims that in the hierarchical order of theatrical devices poetic speech was paramount.[7]

In *The Dramatic Festivals of Athens*, first published in 1953, A. W. Pickard-Cambridge noted the surprising range of movements and gestures attested in the preserved dramatic texts, but seriously doubted whether mobility was expressed in stylised ways other than by speech. He drew attention to the example of weeping as a common linguistic motif to which the mask did not correspond.[8] Peter Arnott's book of 1962, *Greek Scenic Conventions in the Fifth Century BC*, takes this approach further. In his investigation of the abstract theatrical devices typically used in performances, Arnott treats the logocentricity of the performance as an essential criterion of quality, and praises Sophocles because 'he exploits the imaginative possibilities of his medium to the full, and relies little on stage effect'.[9] By contrast, he detects the influence of comedy, if not of the bad taste of the audience, on Euripides, for example in his frequent use of torches in tragedy as an indication of time.[10] Such a device, Arnott writes, 'shows the growing trend from convention to illusion, and the desire to establish that the action involved real people in a real place. This change, common to all Greek art of the time, marked the beginning of the decline'.[11]

It was Roland Barthes who shifted the emphasis to the somatic aspect of acting, in a brief account of fifth-century Athenian theatre published in 1965. Barthes described acting in terms of what he called *choreia,* a complex synthesis of stylised elements from the semantic codes of poetry, music and dance, which ancient Greek education used as a means 'of transforming [the] body into an organ of the spirit'.[12] In tragedy the actor's and dancer's use of the body and of the voice through the mask followed a sign-system of acting, which, along with theatrical devices, aimed at creating mythical pictures both 'real and unreal'.[13] This 'dialectical realism' of Athenian tragedy, as Barthes defined it, served the representation of a 'surreal' theatrical world, which questioned mythology and

[6] Honzl (1976) 121.
[7] Honzl (1976) 122–3: 'The poem (which is what ancient tragedy has always been) was transformed from a dithyramb into drama by a device that Aristotle characterized as "action, not pure narration". But the means for realizing that "action" remained within the domain of the dithyramb.'
[8] *DFA* (1988) 171 and 176. Cf. Arnott (1962) 69–70.
[9] Arnott (1962) 114. Arnott seems to contradict himself, since just before, he stresses the suicide scene in *Ajax* as a most remarkable example of stagecraft.
[10] Arnott (1962) 120–1.
[11] Arnott (1962) 121.
[12] Reprinted in Barthes (1982a) 78.
[13] Barthes (1982a) 78–81.

reality at the same time.[14] Barthes' adoption of contemporary terminology can be explained by his intention to offer practical suggestions for staging.[15] From my point of view, his use of the term 'dialectical realism' might better render the local colour of Athenian comedy, but it allows me to propose the concept of 'dialectical anti-realism', in order to describe both the mythical context of tragedy and satyr drama and the *monde renversé* of comedy. Most importantly, Barthes' interpretation seems to have been the first attempt to consider ancient Greek acting on a dialectical, non-logocentric, basis of semantic codes, which involved the bodies of the performers and the text on equal terms. To some extent, it is possible to draw a parallel between Barthes' view and Jerzy Grotowski's acting system in the 1960s, in which the actor's body was used as the essential defining element of theatrical reality.[16]

More recently, however, *theatricality* has been given less stress in research focusing on Athenian drama's *textuality*.[17] Sheila Murnaghan, for example, notes the tendency of body imagery in both the Homeric epics and tragedy to draw attention to heroism rather than to corporeality, and she interprets this tendency as an aspect of the logocentricity in the performance and ideology of both genres. Tragedy, for Murnaghan, 'inherits from epic a peculiar status as speech that represents – both in the sense that it is and in the sense that it depicts – the displacement of the body by speech'.[18] Her interesting view of Sophocles' *Oedipus at Colonus*, as the only play which centres attention on the visible body of the hero,[19] seems to contradict her main idea of the 'generic ambivalence' of tragedy under the influence of epic narrative.[20] For example, Murnaghan interprets the trial scene of Orestes in Aeschylus' *Eumenides* as an artificially stylised action based on civilised speech,[21] suggesting that this 'situation in which the characters are by definition speakers rather than actors deflects attention from the body' of the mother whom Orestes killed. I think it is important, however, to lay greater stress on the differences between the two genres in terms of performance and ideology. *Eumenides* could well have contained a messenger's speech narrating either the trial, or decision-making by a Homeric-style assembly of gods. In fact, it shows chorus men dressed as Erinyes, and male actors in the roles of a goddess, a god, a hero, and Athenian citizens performing a legal procedure on stage.

14 Barthes (1982a) 83, cf. 67–8.
15 Barthes (1982a) 83–5.
16 Braun (1982) 193–5.
17 Both terms in Taplin (1995) 93.
18 Murnaghan (1987–88) 29.
19 Murnaghan (1987–88) 36–41.
20 Murnaghan (1987–88) 31.
21 Murnaghan (1987–88) 34.

The transformation of poetry into theatre necessarily involved the use of the body by performers as the kinetic and sounding instrument, no longer of narratives, as used to be the case in epic and lyric poetry, but of action. Reciting a text, which offers the audience the means that they need in order to create a literary or dramatic world in their imagination, is different from the bodily presence of theatrical performers, which makes possible the representation of a world of the imaginary in a visibly changing form.[22] The Athenian male performer was a citizen, and not necessarily experienced in acting; there is no evidence of how playing a role in the theatre could affect his consciousness and the way he used his body. Nor is it known precisely how spectators understood these aspects of the experience of the performer through their eyes, or how they reacted to them. But Gorgias' remarks on the power of poetic and rhetorical speech,[23] as well as on the deceptive power of tragedy,[24] are traces, at least, of late fifth-century theoretical discussions about the means and purposes of constructing different forms of reality. The transformation of poetry into theatre was likely to be felt as a new frame of experience by spectators as well as by performers,[25] who had to exploit existing vocal and dancing techniques for the development of acting, that is of the bodily means of theatricality.

One enduring link between the performance of the tragic tetralogy and the choral poetry from which it originated was the continuing presence and involvement of a choral group. The few occasions when an actor could be alone on stage were in the prologue, or during a purposeful short exit of the chorus.[26] The possible, though infrequent, participation of a second chorus and, more often, the presence of one or more mute actors, both emphasise the idea of a large-group performance, in which main roles, like the ones played by the *prōtagōnistēs*, can either be at the centre of attention or merged with the group. In this kind of theatre the speaking actor always uses his body primarily in relation to the other figures within the scenic area, and the play entails continuous interaction between numerous performers.

[22] Vernant in Vernant and Vidal-Naquet (1986) 23 and 85–6.
[23] 82 B 11 DK. Cf. Kennedy's translation in Sprague (1972) 50–4.
[24] 82 B 23 DK. Cf. Kennedy's translation in Sprague (1972) 65.
[25] Elam (1980) 87–92.
[26] A monologue comes after the so-called *metastasis* (exit) of the chorus, implied by the text in Aeschylus' *Eumenides* 231, Sophocles' *Ajax* 814, Euripides' *Alcestis* 746 and *Helen* 385. On the instances of *metastasis* and *epiparodos* (the re-entry of the chorus), see Taplin (1977a) 375–6, and *DFA* (1988) 240.

Even in a case like the prologue of Sophocles' *Ajax*, when only the three actors are visible, extremely intense interaction between the performers is implied. The theatrical space represents the area in front of Ajax's tent on the seashore, as the goddess Athena defines it at the very beginning of the play (3–4). Odysseus, who is first presented as circling around, looking for Ajax's traces (18–20, cf. 5–6), listens to her voice. The goddess commands him to watch in silence while she mocks Ajax's madness in the dialogue during which she pretends to be his 'ally' (90 and 117). The text of the prologue makes it explicit that Athena sees both heroes (1–3 and 94), while Odysseus can see only Ajax (14–16, 81 and 118–26), and Ajax can see only the goddess who has damaged his vision (69–70, 83–5, 92 and 117). Thus, the text implies that the actor in the role of Odysseus directs his body and mask mainly towards the actor playing the insane Ajax; the body and mask of the actor who plays Ajax are mainly directed towards the actor in the role of Athena, to whom Ajax expresses gratitude and devotion. The symbolic and ironical situation during the dialogue between the goddess and the mad hero can be interpreted metatheatrically: the goddess controls every action of the two heroes like a theatrical director,[27] while Ajax appears transformed by her, like an actor, into a madman, and Odysseus watches and listens as terrified, pitying and silent as the spectators. The scene emphasises the intense interdependence of these figures, even though the actors move at some distance from each other.[28]

IN SEARCH OF THE TEXTUAL EVIDENCE

Scholars have always stressed the lack of clear evidence relating to the use of the body by performers in fifth-century theatre. Mythological scenes on vases suggest a variety of 'theatrical' bodily signs, at least in terms of

[27] Easterling (1993b) 80–4. The concept of the director is obviously a modern one, but, as Braun (1982) 7, remarks, it has antecedents in different theatrical traditions, including the case of Aeschylus (see Athenaeus, *Deipn.* 1.21 d–e, with the cautious remarks in *DFA* (1988) 201, 250–1). In fifth-century Athenian theatre the so-called *didaskalos* ('teacher') taught the group of performers how to recite, sing, move and dance. The *didaskalos* was usually the poet himself, who could also be an actor in the performance.

[28] Hourmouziades (1984) 167, interprets the dialogue of Athena and Ajax as a rare instance of the hierarchical placing of the actors at the three levels of the scenic area: Odysseus in the *orchēstra*, Ajax on stage, and Athena on the roof of the stage building. If so, the positions of the actors would have defined key points of the sizeable theatrical space. But most critics stress that the goddess is meant physically to approach her favourite heroes on their own level (as in the Homeric epics and on archaic vase paintings). See Easterling (1993b) 81 and her references in note 7.

the shapes of the body, positions of the limbs and gestures, which could be visible from a distance.[29] Yet vase-painters never aimed principally at reflecting specific theatrical scenes, and we know nothing but the title of the treatise *Peri chorou* (*On the Chorus*) attributed to Sophocles, which may – or may not – have referred to acting. Whatever their limitations, the dramatic texts themselves are the only actual parts of performances which have survived, however altered they may have been.[30] Recent research on silences, entrances and exits of personages in the plays as well as on what Oliver Taplin called 'stage blockings',[31] namely performance pictures suggested by the text, has proved extremely useful. Of course, there are significant limitations to the use of the text as evidence for the performance: one problem, as Taplin has pointed out, is that 'inferred stage directions . . . cannot be verified for the production'.[32] The other, more fundamental, problem is the validity of Taplin's principle that 'for Greek tragedy and for Shakespeare, there are good reasons for taking a general, if not total "identity" of text and stage action as a *working hypothesis*'.[33] With this we should contrast Honzl's claim that 'the Greek theater operated on the basis not of parallelism but of polarity of impressions. That is why the ancient actor's wholly unchanged expression and immobile mask are a fitting accompaniment for [the] text'.[34] The validity of research based on inferred stage directions evidently needs further testing.

An example can demonstrate the usefulness of the text as evidence of performance elements. Search, which Hans Diller identified as the introductory motif of all surviving Sophoclean tragedies,[35] is also the central motif of the action in the preserved half of Sophocles' satyr-play *Ichneutae* (*Trackers*): the text repeatedly stresses how Silenus supervises the chorus' search for traces of the stolen cattle of Apollo, and how the satyrs soon fail to follow the instructions of their father. There can be little doubt about explicit and implicit stage directions in this case: the text describes the *action* of the chorus as *performing or failing to perform* the choreographical design suggested by Silenus (fr. 314.93–130 and 174–220 *TrGF*). Commentators have stressed linguistic analogies between the descriptions of the search performed by the chorus of *Ichneutae* and the search-scenes in *Ajax*, in which Odysseus at the beginning (1–33),[36] and

29 Green and Handley (2001) 22–9, 36–48.
30 Taplin (1995) 110. See Green, this volume.
31 Taplin (1995) 105–8.
32 Taplin (1995) 108.
33 Taplin (1995) 105, cf. Taplin (1977) 28–31.
34 Honzl (1976) 123.
35 Diller (1979) 88.
36 Kamerbeek (1963) 20, on line 6.

the Salaminian sailors in the epiparodos (866–90), desperately look for traces of the hero.[37] As the tragic actors and dancers must also have performed the satyr-play at the end of a tetralogy,[38] the comparison between tragic and satyric scenes in terms of performance is clearly legitimate. In this particular case it suggests that the searching for traces both by Odysseus[39] and the chorus in *Ajax* was performed, as in *Ichneutae*, by visible changes in the use of the actor's or dancer's body. Moreover, this comparison allows one to think of possible analogies between the ways actors and dancers used their bodies, the only clear difference being that the chorus danced more often than actors did.[40] As in other kinds of traditional theatre, performers had to be actors, singers and mimes as well as dancers.[41]

BODIES WITH PROPS, MASKS, COSTUMES

Contemporary theorists, when analysing the ways in which an actor or dancer uses his body in performance, take into account more concretely the body's physical form and costume; its positions and displacements within the theatrical space; its orientation and relation to the public, to other actors and to theatrical objects; the direction of the axis of the body; the positions of the limbs and the distribution of weight; the visible and audible expressions of the body, mainly movements and gestures, speech and song.[42] Consequently, acting techniques and styles need to be conceptualised in terms of the functions or purposes which the performer's body and verbal delivery fulfil.

In the first place, the definition of space and the sense of perspective, created by the performers' bodies and their shadows, are characteristic functions of group performance. In daylight the all-embracing architectural design of the fifth-century wooden theatre aimed to lead the gaze of the spectator through the *orchēstra* to the acting area in front of the stage building (*skēnē*), to the door at the centre of its façade, and to the invisible depth behind that door. The use of painting as scenery on the façade of the stage building during the fifth century is a matter of hypothesis; it is usually taken for granted that the audience identified the place thanks to the more or less descriptive words of characters, which served as

37 Sutton (1971) 60–7, and Sutton (1980) 47–8. Sutton also notes similarities between the prologues of the two plays.

38 Easterling (1997a) 38 and n. 11.

39 Taplin thinks of it as a 'dumb show' in Taplin (1978) 40–1.

40 Fuchs in Braun (1982) 115.

41 Barba and Savarese (1991) 192.

42 Pavis (1996) 53 and 62.

'word-scenery'.[43] Aristotle notes that Sophocles invented *skēnographia*:[44] scene painting, following the tendency of mural painting in Athens before the mid-century, could emphasise the sense of perspective and spatial depth by presenting an architectural design of 'a three-dimensional façade on a two-dimensional wall', as Ruth Padel has remarked.[45] But the sense of three dimensions would in any case be there thanks to the forms and shadows of the bodies of the group of performers, which defined the space of the *orchēstra* and the stage as a whole for most of the performance. Thus an actor on stage could use his body almost as a sign of spatial closure, as when the heroine in Sophocles' *Electra* declares before the female chorus her desperate decision to spend the rest of her life at the Mycenaean palace entrance (817–19), represented by the central stage door.

Theatrical objects emphasised in the text can also play a significant role in defining space and meaning. What is less commonly stressed is that theatrical objects essentially operate in relation to the bodies of actors. In Aeschylus' *Agamemnon* Clytemnestra's female slaves spread purple fabrics from the king's chariot in the *orchēstra* to the entrance of the palace, represented by the stage door; Agamemnon accepts the invitation to walk on them, but first he demands that 'someone' should take off his boots (944–5). The text does not indicate who takes off Agamemnon's boots; it clearly implies the danger that he runs through his domineering attitude, evident both from his demand for this servile action and from his decision to tread bare-footed on the valuable blood-coloured fabrics.[46] The removal of the boots seems to centre attention less on the hands of the helper who takes them off than on the feet of the actor who plays Agamemnon. For several moments, as he walks, his feet and the purple fabrics will be the focus of attention. As the bare feet come into contact with them, these blood-coloured theatrical objects, marking the route to be followed by the actor within the theatrical space, acquire their full significance as ambiguous symbols of power and death. On the one hand, they define the space, and the dangerous dimension, of Agamemnon's actions, and, on the other, like his costume and the removal of his boots, they stress nuances of his theatrical character. Clearly, though, the role of the purple fabrics is fulfilled only in relation to the body and, in particular, to the bare feet and steps of the actor who plays the king: it is as though

[43] Pfister (1988) 267. See, for example, Athena's description in *Ajax* 3–4, which I have already mentioned.

[44] *Poetics* 1449a19–20.

[45] Padel (1990) 354, cf. 346–54, and 353 figs. 1–2.

[46] Reinhardt (1949) 96.

the fabrics were the blood spilled on the ground from Agamemnon's body, a picture on stage of what will soon happen out of sight within the palace.

This scene suggests that the apparently simple form of mythical action and plot in ancient Greek plays is best defined as symbolic, concentrated and suggestive of meaning at multiple levels during the performance. As Agamemnon walks in silence from his chariot in the direction of the palace entrance, moving among his attendants, the chorus of old citizens, and Clytemnestra and her slaves, he is joined in silence by all of them except for Clytemnestra: her ambiguous, if not ominous, speech, ending with a prayer to Zeus, is pronounced as a seemingly joyful response to Agamemnon's action (958–74). From the parallel and interdependent actions of the two actors in focus, it becomes obvious that the dynamics of the performance are defined both by the voice (and, presumably, the body language) of the actor who renders the words and rhythm of Clytemnestra's speech and by the body of the actor playing Agamemnon as he walks in silence towards the palace door. The whole scene shows that for the definition of space in three dimensions, of time and of action as well as for the operation of theatrical objects, the role of the bodies of performers is just as fundamental at any moment during the performance as the formal and semantic role of speech. Throughout the performance actors and dancers are the living agents who express by means of their bodies and voices all the symbolic elements necessary for the creation of the metaphorical world of theatre in front of the eyes of the spectators.

A most important function of the performer's body and voice is to realise each of the different roles prescribed for him by the text. In ancient Greek theatrical tradition performing a role involves in the first place a metamorphosis of the body by the mask and costume. Evidence from vases indicates that these symbolic constituents of theatricality, however stylised, tend to be individuated and differentiated, and seem not to have become standardised in the course of the fifth century.[47] In comedy a grotesque costume and unnatural mask[48] deliberately distort and transform the performer's body and head. This is not the case in satyr-plays: the appearance of Silenus, and the masks, shorts, phalloi and tails of the satyrs make them look like both men and animals at the same time. In both tragedy and satyr-play the modification of the performer's body by a simple mask and a more or less elaborate dress produces a theatrical image which is meant to evoke the anthropomorphic world of myth in

47 *DFA* (1988) 180–209; more particularly, on masks, 189–93. See Green, this volume.

48 Aristotle, *Poetics* 1449a34–7.

an unrealistic, but not wholly unnatural, way. Mask, costume, theatrical objects (such as a staff, a bow, or a chariot) used in relation to a specific role, the variable voice of the male actor or dancer,[49] and the words of his role or of other personages referring to his role, are the differentiating elements of theatricality; they can represent the gender, mythical status,[50] and perhaps the geographical provenance and some individual characteristics of a tragic or satyric character or chorus.[51] But it is less commonly accepted that the gait and body language of performers were as significant for the expression of individual characteristics and feelings.

Hecuba's first lines of lament in Euripides' *Troades* (98–101) provide a telling example of such characteristics: 'Up, you poor one; lift your head and neck from the ground. This is no longer Troy nor we the Queen of Troy. Bear with your fortune as it changes.'[52] Hecuba's self-admonition implies that the chest and mask of the actor are now raised and visible, while at the same time her desperate words about no longer being Queen of this non-existent Troy confirm who she is. The text does not indicate how soon she is to stand up; the anapaestic metre suggests some movement, and she later refers to aching parts of her body, as if she had perhaps had to sleep on the ground (112–19) in Agamemnon's tent (138–9). The heroine's first lines make it explicit that when the actor raises his chest, neck and mask[53] from the ground it is a somatic expression of being in command of one's senses and finding the courage to endure. Hecuba's character and feeling at a moment of desolation are depicted equally by the text through the actor's voice and by his parallel use of body language.

CLASSICAL DYNAMISM

In ancient Greek theatre posture could be as expressive as movement. Aeschylus was renowned for exploiting a major character's silence over a long section of a play, as in the famous cases of the heroine of the lost *Niobe*, mourning by her children's tomb, and of the angry Achilles

49 On speech, recitative, song, and the variable use of the voice, see *DFA* (1988) 156–71, Csapo and Slater (1995) 265–6 under IV 66–8, Hall (1999a) and Hall, this volume.

50 Hall (1997a) 103–18.

51 *DFA* (1988) 187 (on the late fifth-century Pronomos vase), 202–3, 208–9.

52 Translation by Barlow (1986a) 61. In lines 36–8 Poseidon points to Hecuba lying down and weeping in front of the central door. But the text does not make clear exactly when she entered, and whether later she is asleep or in a faint. Barlow (1986a) 162, notes that Hecuba 'has been asleep throughout the dialogue between the two gods and now raises her head'.

53 See Barba and Savarese (1991) 118, for examples from other theatrical traditions, in which training and experience helped the actor learn how to use his mask for different purposes.

in the lost *Myrmidons*.[54] These figures sat veiled, speechless, almost motionless, looking like statues for half of the performance; their presence amongst speaking performers was disturbing and dynamic.[55] The undated *Prometheus Bound* attributed to Aeschylus provides an extant example of pathos and dynamism expressed by a standing figure's virtually static position as well as by his language. Two other possible examples occurred in lost tragedies by Euripides: in *Andromeda*, performed in 412, the heroine was fixed to a rock at the beginning of the play so as to be offered as a sacrifice to a sea-monster; in *Ixion*, performed in the 410s, it seems that the torture of the hero, who was fastened to a wheel, was shown on stage.[56] The actor would have to stand in a fixed position, probably on the *ekkuklēma*, throughout the final scene of *Ixion*, while in *Prometheus Bound* the actor would have to do so throughout the play.[57] Jan Kott remarked that the body of the Titan fixed by chains on a Scythian rock is a symbolic picture of the vertical axis of the universe: Prometheus' body both divides and unites the upper world of Olympus, where the gods live, and the abyss of Tartarus, where the hero is to disappear after the earthquake at the end of the play.[58] As these examples show, the meanings of body language can be expressed through postures as much as through gestures and movements, and the dynamic aspect of a character could depend on the particular symbolic shape taken by the axis of the performer's body.

In their comments on postures of actors and dancers in different cultures, Eugenio Barba and Nicola Savarese remark that there is something important to be learned from studying Polyclitus' bronze statues and theoretical views on statuary as well as 'the body's architecture' in classical Greek sculpture: 'the dynamic representation of the body by means of motion which winds around a central axis remains a fundamental principle of an artistic work's "life"... A combination of movement and rest, balance and asymmetry, a dance of oppositions'.[59] A similarly dynamic style, based on antithetical and mutually balanced bodily signs, may well

54 'Euripides' ridicules this Aeschylean technique in Aristophanes' *Frogs* 912–24. Aeschylus fr. 154a6–7 *TrGF* may refer to Niobe also *crying* by the grave.

55 Hourmouziades (1984) 191–4. Most often the body language of silent roles, even impressive ones, is impossible to consider in detail. In the important case of Pylades, one can only guess that Orestes' omnipresent companion from Phocis in Aeschylus' *Libation-bearers* and the *Electras* by Sophocles and Euripides is meant to impersonate in silence the imperative of the Delphic oracle. This is suggested by the only three lines he is given in *Libation-bearers* (900–2).

56 See Plutarch, *How the Young Man Should Study Poetry* 3 = *Moralia* 19E; Green and Handley (2001) 39–40.

57 Green and Handley (2001) 39.

58 Kott (1974) 3–42.

59 Barba and Savarese (1991) 180.

have been used to animate stage figures in classical Greek theatre. This is suggested in the text of Cassandra's part in Aeschylus' *Agamemnon*, a fine instance of the demands made on a tragic actor's physical and vocal versatility.[60] Throughout the scene dramatising Agamemnon's arrival, Cassandra remains veiled and silent, like an object, on his chariot in the *orchēstra*. She evidently does not move even during the following stasimon. She then behaves as though she were in a state of mania, and both the queen Clytemnestra and the chorus of old Argive citizens regard her as a barbarian who cannot understand Greek. Clytemnestra leaves (1060–4) and Cassandra gets down from the chariot, dressed in her prophetic garments, with sacred bands around her neck and a staff in her hands as another sign of her art;[61] as she moves towards the statue of Apollo, next to the palace entrance, which is represented by the door of the stage building, she unexpectedly breaks her silence, shouting out in a state of prophetic mania, and singing a pathetic lament in the agitated dochmiac metre.

This is the earliest attested lyric *amoibaion* (1072–1177) which gives the leading role to the actor:[62] every stanza begins with Cassandra's lyric lines, perhaps accompanied by her dancing movements, followed by the chorus' response in iambic trimeters. This apparently novel form in the order of sung and recited dialogue between the actor and the chorus emphasises the interaction between the Trojan slave and the old men from Argos as well as the gradual reversal of their roles. In the second half of the song (1114–77) the reactions of the chorus are also expressed in dochmiacs, suggesting Cassandra's influence on their words and movements (see also Hall, this volume, ch. 1). In the absolute solitude of her prophetic madness she sings a fragmented soliloquy about the blood from the palace of Argos and the blood from the palace of Troy, without ever addressing the old men. They keep asking her anxiously about the meaning of the nightmarish imagery in her song, and their last word in both halves of the lyric dialogue is *amēchanō*, 'I am at a loss' (1113 and 1177). The audience, by contrast, are unable to resist Cassandra's disarming truth and agitation.

The scene continues with four iambic speeches of Cassandra, within which three exchanges of stichomythia between her and the chorus are interposed. The iambic dialogue develops and clarifies the themes of the lyric *amoibaion* in a different tone, as the prophetess tries to communicate

60 On the text and movements of the Cassandra scene see the remarks of Taplin (1978) 59–60 and 103–4.

61 See lines 1265–70, and Fraenkel (1950) on 1264–5.

62 Fraenkel (1950) vol. III, 488.

with the old men by explaining her meaning and referring overtly to the killing of Agamemnon (1246). The chorus now try to silence her again, refusing to accept the truth: as she says, it is now they who have become insane and unable to understand Greek (1247–55). Cassandra is again lonely in her prophetic vision, and in a spectacular expression of protest at her treatment by Apollo, she throws on the ground the prophetic symbols which the god had given her (1264–72). Now ready to enter the palace where, as she knows, death awaits her, Cassandra shows that she is not being driven to the sacrifice like an unsuspecting animal as Agamemnon was, arrogant and ignorant, trapped by both gods and men.[63]

Cassandra's body language and alternating song and speech suggest an exceptionally demanding role, full of antithetical elements: it includes silence and immobility, delirious shouts and gestures, ecstatic singing and choreographed steps, logically structured narratives, arguments and meditations, the conscious rejection of prophetic symbols as an indication of freedom, and physical wavering to and fro on stage as she is repelled by the smell of death at the palace gate (1305ff.). Cassandra's role seems to have involved acting both in the 'archaic' style of oracular pronouncement and in the 'classical' style of dynamic performance.[64] Moreover, it implies that acting had already reached a high level as an expression of character through the variable use of the body and voice by the time of the *Oresteia* in 458 BC, nearly a decade before the institution of the prize for the best tragic actor in 449.

THE ACTING OF PHYSICAL AND MENTAL STATES

Physical and mental states could be conveyed solely by language or by abstract theatrical means. In Sophocles' *Oedipus Tyrannus* the damage to

63 Reinhardt (1949) 101–5; Taplin (1978) 141–3.

64 Aristophanes' *Frogs* is among the texts used by Csapo and Slater (1995) 259–65, as evidence for the 'grand' style of acting in the plays of Aeschylus and for the 'realistic' style of acting in the plays of Euripides. Both styles could perhaps be best investigated though distinguishable levels of linguistic style in the texts. But I propose to adopt the terms 'archaic' and 'classical' respectively, which are often used with an analogous, though broader, reference in relation to ancient Greek history, art and literature. The Cassandra scene suggests that the two acting styles co-existed at the time of the *Oresteia*; a third style of 'mannerist' acting can be traced in plays after 420 BC (see below). What I call the 'archaic' style of acting is to be related to the influence of ritual, rhapsodic, lyric, choral and folk performances on theatrical acting throughout the fifth century. It can be traced in extant tragedy and satyr-play in those levels of poetic style which depend on the religious, epic and lyric traditions of poetry. Most typical forms of this style are the ritualistic techniques, which, for instance, seem to have been important for the parts given to the choruses throughout the history of ancient Greek theatre. By contrast, what I call the 'classical' style of acting is suggested by the tragic and satyric language which evokes aspects of everyday political, cultural and private life in fifth-century Greece.

Oedipus' unseen feet is only evoked in the text (1031–6, cf. 718) and present in his name; his self-blinding is fully described in a messenger's speech (1275–9) before it is shown on the mask. However, it is a remarkable indication of the *physicality* of ancient Greek acting that the texts also suggest that the actor's body could be used to represent both bodily and mental conditions. Besides the case of Cassandra in *Agamemnon*, the actor playing Clytemnestra in *Libation-bearers* 896–8 directed attention to his chest under the royal dress as an expression of the queen's appeal to Orestes to feel pity for the breast that fed him.[65] Elsewhere, too, a combination of verbal and corporeal indications, rendered by covered or uncovered parts of the actor's body, is chosen to mark the vulnerable point of a hero's body as a marker of his vulnerable human self: the actor's torso becomes a sign of mortality in the Sophoclean dramatisation of the hero's suicide in *Ajax* (834) and of Heracles' sickness in *Trachiniae* (1036, 1053–5, 1081–4, cf. 767–70); the diseased foot is a sign of the bodily and inner suffering of Philoctetes throughout Sophocles' play, as it may well have been in Aeschylus' and Euripides' homonymous tragedies.

The symbolic meaning of the hands of the actor who plays the heroine in Euripides' *Medea* is different. The linguistic theme of hands and physical contact by the actor playing Medea is first emphasised in the two supplication scenes, in which she apparently touches Creon's and Aegeus' knees (respectively 324 ff. and 709–13).[66] The effect of her touch will prove fatal for Creon,[67] while Aegeus, who has guaranteed a safe refuge for her, is to go safely back to Athens. Medea's hands are also in focus in the speech in which she tries to take her final decision: 'I shall not let my hand be weak' (1055). Towards the end of the speech, when she embraces her two silent sons (1069–77),[68] Medea caresses the boys, referring to each one's right hand, head, skin and breath: her words sound like a farewell lament,[69] implying that the caresses of these hands provide an ominous picture on stage of what is soon to happen inside the house.

A satyric use of physical acting and contact can be traced in the 'sympotic' scene from Euripides' *Cyclops*, in which Polyphemus is invited

65 For this motif in the *Iliad* and the three tragedians see Segal (1986) 351–7.

66 Kaimio (1988) 51 and 56 respectively.

67 Medea's touch is seemingly innocent. In 947–61 she gives her boys the gifts which she asks them to take to Jason's wife, and Jason's first reaction is that Medea should not be left with empty hands by sending the gifts. When Jason's wife later uses the gifts she will die, and so will Creon after embracing his dying daughter.

68 Kaimio (1988) 28, and on the physical contact suddenly interrupted at the end, 46.

69 These lines and images are recalled at the end of the tragedy, when Medea, on her chariot with the corpses, repeatedly rejects Jason's plea to touch the bodies of his sons (1397–1412).

by Silenus to lie down next to him and enjoy more wine and the sunshine as they talk with Odysseus and the chorus of satyrs (540–81). The text strongly implies the gradual effect of wine on the Cyclops' body and mind (483–589)[70] as well as his vehement physical action when he finally regards Silenus as Zeus's favourite Ganymedes, seizes and pulls him into the cave (582–9).

The representation of bodily and mental states by more literally physical means is strongly suggested in the course of the action of *nosos* scenes in extant tragedies by Sophocles and Euripides. The text of these scenes focuses on the body of a heroic figure in pain, and on the physical support offered by other personages. In the exodos of *Trachiniae* Heracles is brought on stage senseless, like a corpse (971–1278); when he wakes up, his son Hyllus tries to help him, following the advice of the *paidagōgos*, but Heracles' pain seems unbearable throughout. In *Philoctetes* the crisis caused to the hero by the agony of his wounded foot ends when he falls into a deep sleep (730–899); after the stasimon Neoptolemus helps Philoctetes to stand up and walk, and proves to be deeply affected by the physical contact, too. In the initial scene of the first episode of *Hippolytus* the nurse and female attendants help Phaedra to cope with her sickness, caused, as will be revealed, by her desperate passion (170–372); in the exodos the dying Hippolytus is brought on by attendants so as to be seen by his father Theseus (1342–1466). During the prologue and parodos of *Orestes* Electra describes her brother's illness as he sleeps on stage (1–207). In the first episode Orestes wakes up and manages to stand with Electra's help. But then, being in a state of mania, he fantasises that the Erinyes are threatening him, until he recovers his sanity (208–315). Pylades is later to support Orestes so that he can stand up and walk as they exit to the Argive tribunal (790–806; cf. 879–83).

In all these scenes the text, marked by changes of metre and pathetic interjections, goes into detail about the suffering of both body and mind, and suggests the movements of the actor playing the sick or dying character and of those who are to help physically.[71] The fact that the helpers prove deeply moved emphasises the dynamic sense of physical suffering and contact: in scenes of this kind character and action are conveyed most intimately through the words, postures, gestures and movements of actors.

70 See Seaford (1984) 199, on line 503; 205, on line 543; and 208–11, on lines 572–86.

71 Besides iambic trimeters, the scenes from *Trachiniae* and *Hippolytus* contain lengthy sections in other metres. The scene from *Philoctetes* contains a stasimon, and the first scene from *Orestes* is preceded by the parodos, while the other scene is in trochaic tetrameters. For the motif of physical contact in these scenes see Kaimio (1988) 17–20 and 83–5.

The purpose of *nosos* scenes seems to be to represent mythical figures discovering their bodily identity and inner state;[72] this can explain why these scenes are designed to be as strongly based on physical acting and contact as on language and on abstract elements of theatricality. Another example of a hero discovering his bodily identity is the less typical *nosos* scene in the exodos of *Oedipus Tyrannus*, where the self-blinded king comes out of the palace with a visible lack of orientation and balance (1307–15), and gives the chorus of Theban citizens a full account of his painful actions. His plea for exile is more welcome to the chorus than his request to be touched by them (1409–18). It is only thanks to Antigone and Ismene, who come in support of Oedipus, embrace him and listen to him without speaking, that his unexpected and repeated wish for physical contact is fulfilled (1462–1523). Oedipus, deprived of his vision, is thus to discover, if only for a few moments, a new bodily identity and stability on stage.

MANNERISM

In the plays surviving from the last two decades of the fifth century there is a clear tendency for the protagonist's roles to become lengthier and increasingly virtuosic. Presumably, pressure from the by now highly versatile leading performers, who were solo singers and dancers as well as actors, could cause playwrights to adopt more complex techniques, tending towards the gradual stylisation of acting in the direction of 'mannerism'.[73] Long, sophisticated lyric songs sung and danced by actors now become indispensable parts of the most impressive roles. The virtuosic monodies, duets or *amoibaia* with the chorus in Euripides' *Ion*, *Phoenissae*, and *Orestes*, and in Sophocles' *Philoctetes* and *Oedipus at Colonus*, are instances of what I would call the mannerist style of acting. The comic portrait of Agathon in the prologue of Aristophanes' *Thesmophoriazusae* (87–265) is evidence of the conscious choice on the part of dramatists

[72] Loraux (1985) 83, points out that women in Athenian tragedy become conscious of their bodies before dying; so do Heracles in *Trachiniae* and the hero in *Hippolytus*, whose agony is described in terms of female pain: see Loraux (1981) 58–64. Cf. Zeitlin (1990) 72–3.

[73] Given the anti-classical connotations of 'mannerism', critics tend to avoid using this term in relation to fifth-century Greece. Yet in analysing Athenian art during the Peloponnesian War, Strocka (1988) 166 and 177, refers to mannerism in the case of the sculptor Callimachus, the supposed inventor of the Corinthian capital. Pollitt (1972) 115, compares late fifth-century Greece with 'Italy after the sack of Rome in 1527', namely in the late Renaissance period of mannerist art, but does not use the term 'mannerism' in his chapter on the 'decorative manner' of late fifth-century Greek art (Pollitt (1972) 111–35), already evident on the marble reliefs of Nikai on the Acropolis temple of Athena Nike, dating from around 420 BC.

and actors to make the performance of tragedy look and sound *theatrical*. A development along these lines is not surprising in a period when every original play and performance would – almost inevitably – echo and allude to, or even parody, previous dramatic texts and acting techniques used in all dramatic genres,[74] which by this time were identifiable as the long-standing traditions of a solid institution. Mannerist techniques in textual form seem prominent, too, in fourth-century tragic fragments and in *Rhesus*, most probably a work of the fourth century. At the centre of this tragedy Athena makes her appearance as helper of the Greek heroes (595–626). The scene may recall the beginning of Sophocles' *Ajax*, but it soon takes on an astonishing turn when Athena explains that she will reappear transfigured as Aphrodite in order to deceive the Trojan Alexander (627–41).

The possibility of interplay between a tragic performance and, at least, the tragic and satyric traditions, presupposing familiarity with their respective acting styles, is evident in Euripides' *Bacchae*. E. R. Dodds emphasised the 'archaism' of this tragedy in terms of its mythical theme, language and basic structural techniques, such as the clear distinction between episodic and lyric parts, and the arrangement of the action in episodes on the basis of messenger speeches and other long narratives.[75] These traces of 'rhapsodic' technique, as well as the ritualistic choruses, are aspects of archaic performance; a dynamic style of acting is traceable, however, in the miraculous earthquake scene (585–603), probably rendered by choreographic movements,[76] and in the agitated dochmiac *amoibaion* between Agave and the chorus (1168–99). In the fourth episode Pentheus appears disguised as a maenad (912–17); this is according to the plan earlier proposed by the Stranger, who gave a full description of the appropriate costume, and promised that the king would thus remain unrecognised while watching the bacchants on Cithaeron (821–39). In fact, the king's change of costume signifies his alienated state of mind

74 *Cyclops*, which seems to date from this period, is marked by the influence of both tragedy and comedy, and satyric fragments after the fifth century show the dominating influence of comedy. See Seaford (1984) 38–51 and 18–20.

75 Dodds (1960) xxxvi–xxxviii.

76 Collard, Cropp and Lee (1995) 189, commenting on Euripides' *Erectheus* fr. 370K.45–54, where Poseidon causes an earthquake in order to destroy Athens, compare *Bacchae* 585–603, *Heracles* 904–9, and *Prometheus Bound* 1080–90. They note that the fifth-century theatre 'could have supported such scenes with sound-effects but hardly with physical ones'. Cf. Honzl (1976), 124. But the phrases of the chorus in *Erectheus* fr. 370K.48, ὀρχεῖται δὲ πόλεως πέδον σάλῳ, 'the city's ground is set dancing by the quake' (Collard, Cropp and Lee (1995), 171) and in *Bacchae* 600–1, δίκετε πεδόσε δίκετε τρομερὰ / σώματα, 'throw to the ground your trembling bodies', allow one to suppose that choreographic movements emphasising the loss of balance could also express the dynamic effect of the earthquake described by the language.

under the Stranger's influence (918–24); and it is likely that Pentheus' disguise as a maenad would make him look very much like the Stranger, whose womanish bacchic appearance he earlier criticised (453–9),[77] even threatening to cut a lock of the Stranger's hair and to remove the thyrsus from his hand (493–6).[78] Quite often in *Bacchae* the Stranger acts as the director of the action,[79] and this is obvious in the ironic dialogue of the fourth episode, where he arranges Pentheus' hair, head, dress, posture and thyrsus, to make him look exactly like a maenad. Textual details imply different bodily postures and movements of the actor in the role of Pentheus:[80] the king intends to imitate postures of his bacchant mother and aunt (925–7), and is taught how to use his body and costume more convincingly (928–44). This is a fine example of mannerism in acting: the emphasis on sophisticated details in the actor's use of the body and costume aims first and foremost to make him look theatrical.

In this scene the theme of physical contact is based on the hands of the actor who plays the Stranger, and his touch proves as ominous as Medea's: the effect of the Stranger's hands will be realised when we next see Pentheus' head on his mother's thyrsus. This device of horror may have actually been modelled on an earlier play. In a fragment from Aeschylus' *Theori* or *Isthmiastae* (78a1–22 *TrGF*) the singer, probably the satyric chorus, is surprised by the gifts offered to the satyrs, which are copies of their heads; the satyrs are prepared to fasten these masks, perhaps on stakes,[81] as votive offerings to be fixed on Poseidon's Isthmian temple. The singer's mask is so much like himself, he says (13–17), that, if his mother saw it, she would be terrified by the spectacle of her son's severed head: this, in turn, could be the satyric version of a scene from a tragedy of Aeschylus' time. But *Bacchae* is the only surviving tragedy in which the emphasis on the body, mask and costume of an actor in a dressing-up scene is later recalled by the sight of theatrical objects, in

77 As Dodds (1960) xxxi–xxxiii, notes, Dionysus was also 'taunted with his effeminate appearance and costume' in *Edonians*, a tragedy from Aeschylus' lost tetralogy *Lycurgeia*, on which several motifs in *Bacchae* were modelled. The whole ritual appearance of Dionysiac worshippers, which seems to have been the same for both sexes, looked womanish and oriental to the Greeks; it seems to have been recalled by costumes in performances of plays on Dionysiac themes (Dodds (1960) 134, 176–8, 181). Dodds also remarks on *Bacchae* 854–5 that 'the specific ritual reason for the disguising of Pentheus is perhaps that . . . the victim, like the priest, is often invested with the dress of the god'. From a theatrical point of view, there is a strong and ominous sense of reversal in that the disguised Pentheus is like a mirror of the Stranger and of each maenad in the chorus whom he has persecuted.

78 Dodds (1960) 192, stresses the reversal of this earlier situation in the latter scene.

79 Easterling (1993b) 81, with her references in n. 6.

80 Taplin (1978) 76.

81 Fr. 78a19; cf. Agave's wish in *Bacchae* 1214.

this case representing parts of Pentheus' dismembered body, which is put back in order and ritually lamented by his mother. A further daring device of mannerism occurs in this tragic exodos, where the physicality of the actors gives way to miraculous theatrical effects on the bodies of the two main heroes: the Stranger is transfigured as Dionysus *ex machina*, and Pentheus is now a dismembered puppet.

THE ACTOR'S BODY IN FLUX

The use of the body and the text by performers, for the purposes and in the styles that I have sketched, seems on the whole to express, in a symbolic sense, inner and bodily transformations undergone by tragic and satyric characters. There is already an obvious sense of metamorphosis in that the actor is transformed into different theatrical bodies and voices by his different costumes and masks, in order to play several male or female tragic and satyric roles in the course of the performance of a tetralogy, and this is also the case with the dancers who played the four different roles of the chorus. But this principle of metamorphosis is further intensified by the ways in which an actor or dancer can express the motif of character metamorphosis itself in the process of the action of each play. Agave's poignant return to sanity through her father Cadmus' questioning in *Bacchae* 1263–97 is a prime example. In Euripides the inner and external transformation of a personage can be sometimes made visible by a change of mask: this is implied by the text, as Pickard-Cambridge noted,[82] in the cases of Admetus in *Alcestis* (512, cf. 425ff.), of the heroine in *Helen* (1186), and of two personages who reappear blind, Polymestor in *Hecuba* (1049), and Polyphemus in *Cyclops* (663). The use of the mask for a blinded figure is also traceable at the beginning of the exodos in *Oedipus Tyrannus* (1297). The device there seems ironically foreshadowed by a paradoxical phrase which the blind Teiresias earlier addresses angrily to Oedipus: οὐ τὸ σὸν / δείσας πρόσωπον ('without fearing your face', 447–8).[83] The context indicates that Teiresias means to stress how changed Oedipus is soon to appear, and in the end Oedipus could have used the same mask as Teiresias wore before. These examples show how abstract linguistic and theatrical means are chosen to indicate the process of self-metamorphosis, which was fundamental for the construction of

[82] *DFA* (1988) 173.

[83] 'Mask' as a meaning of *prosōpon* is not attested before the fourth century; the comic mask is referred to as a *geloion prosōpon* at Aristotle, *Poetics* 1449a36, cf. b4. One could still consider a *double entendre* in *Oedipus Tyrannus* 448 possible, as Burian does in *Bacchae* 1277 (Burian (1997) 198 n. 34).

characters and the dramatic structure in most ancient Greek plays. This inner and outward change is the definition of the fifth-century actor's role: it is precisely this process that the actor has to express by physical as well as linguistic means, namely by the variable use of his body and voice.

Illuminating thoughts about acting are attested in Plato's early fourth-century dialogue *Ion*. The fact that the rhapsode Ion is described as an actor, ὁ ῥαψῳδὸς καὶ ὑποκριτής (536a1, cf. 532d7), suggests the major influence of theatrical acting on rhapsodic techniques in the performances of the period. Socrates first takes into account epic and lyric poets as well as musicians (533e5–534c5), then rhapsodes identified with actors, and finally dancers and spectators (535e7–536a7): he thus formulates a theory of performance as an unconscious human action wholly dependent on divine inspiration. Plato's rejection of poetry and theatre in later dialogues is foreshadowed by the ambiguous critique in *Ion*, where the performer is depicted by Socrates as the unconscious carrier of a gift of the gods. But Ion describes his performance of sad Homeric narratives and speeches in terms which strongly evoke theatrical acting, and tries to explain how his whole body expresses strong emotions under the influence of poetic pathos, while, at the same time, he makes a calculated effort to move the responsive audience deeply and so win the prize (535b1–e6). Socrates treats Ion as a charlatan unable to explain his divine art, and, at the end, compares him with the mythical Proteus, who changes himself 'into every possible form, shifting all ways' (541e7–8).[84] This final philosophical picture of the rhapsode–actor as morally changeable and unreliable implies how his character is determined by such professional techniques as changing the sound of his voice and the image of his body. And it is worth noting that the comparison evokes the mythical figure whose body can be repeatedly transformed into a different image of being, to the extent that he seems to lack identity.

From my point of view, it is significant that the critical theory of performance in *Ion* ends by emphasising the protean metamorphosis of the body and voice of the performer. The variable identity of roles, and, indeed, of the world in the theatre seems to have been a fundamental theoretical principle of ancient Greek performances, broadly related to Heraclitean dialectics and Protagorean relativism. The sense of unity in the performance of each play or of a complete tragic tetralogy depended

[84] The comparison is also used in a critical tone in Plato's *Euthydemus* 288b7–8, where Proteus is called a bewitching sophist.

on the repetition of thematic and scenic imagery, but the stylistic variation of the performance aimed at creating a sense of heterogeneous unity in transformation. Theatre represented an imaginary counterpart of the world in a changing form, and gave it a changing meaning: Plato's critique was precisely against this unstable and dynamic depiction of man, of the world and of truth in poetic performances at the turn of the fifth century.

ANCIENTS AND MODERNS

This analysis of uses of the body in acting, on the evidence of stage directions inferred from tragic and satyric texts, has cast doubts on the view that poetic speech had always the main role in fifth-century Athenian performances. Several writers nowadays think that the logocentric interpretation of ancient Greek theatre was based on the *Poetics* of Aristotle, and they try to explain his lack of interest in the visual dimension (*opsis*) of tragedy as a result of the theatrical, historical and social context in which the *Poetics* was written.[85] It is true that the preserved half of Aristotle's essay is the first instance of theatrical performance texts approached as though they were essentially literary texts.[86] But this may have been a matter of choosing where to put the emphasis in codifying the poetics of a dramatic genre. It was rather the neoclassical theorists, actors and dramatists in Europe who, following Aristotle (as they believed), insisted on rhetorical uses of the body and voice to match stylised speech in theatrical performances. Ever since the end of the seventeenth century neoclassicist ideas have repeatedly determined the perspectives from which directors, actors and scholars have revived and interpreted Athenian plays.

In 1899 D. B. Laflotte published pictures of ancient Greek vases and of contemporary actors of the Comédie Française in order to prove the close dependence of the staging of Athenian and French tragedy on the ancient vase-painting models (fig. 12). Savarese republishes the pictures and notes how clearly they show that 'there was no real connection made with the body behaviour of the Greek models, whose physicality seemed rather to be denied, almost contradicted, by the more clearly rhetorical physical attitudes of the two French actors'.[87]

85 Taplin (1995) 94–6; Hall (1996b).
86 Barba in Barba and Savarese (1991) 68.
87 Barba and Savarese (1991) 166, pictures 1–6 and caption.

Fig. 12 Contrasts in physical attitudes: the actors of the Comédie Française Jean Mounet-Sully and Sarah Bernhardt as Creon, Medea and Phaedra respectively in the 1890s and the ancient Greek vase paintings they used as models (Reproduced from Barba and Savarese (1991), 166)

The French surrealist theorist of theatre, actor and director Antonin Artaud, has been perhaps the most influential among modernists who have emphasised the physical aspects of acting and the abstract devices of theatricality rather than the role of the text. Artaud proposed as a model the oriental show traditions which gave priority to clearly visual performance elements and to the use of the actor–dancer's body, while he categorically rejected the predominance of the text and of speech as a psychologising and manipulative device of the western theatrical legacy.[88] The purpose of Artaud's 'theatre of cruelty' was to reach what he

[88] Artaud (1958) 68–83. [89] Artaud (1958) 80 and 92–3, cf. 90.

considered to be the metaphysical background of ancient tragic myths,[89] but he believed that the tragedies of classical Athenian dramatists and of Shakespeare could make no sense nowadays, unless they were to be performed with emphasis on physical acting: 'we have lost the sense of their theater's physics. It is because the directly human and active aspect of their way of speaking and moving, their whole scenic rhythm, escapes us. An aspect that ought to have as much, if not more, importance than the admirable spoken dissection of their heroes' psychology'.[90] This point is quite close to my own conclusion that fifth-century performances of tragedy and satyr-play were as much based on the somatic and vocal role of the actor or dancer as on the text and theatrical devices.

Contemporary theatre research emphasises the significant similarities of pre-industrial theatrical traditions both in the East and the West.[91] In fact, some western theatrical traditions, such as the Commedia dell' Arte by the eighteenth century, as well as twentieth-century acting systems under the influence of oriental show traditions, have been based on the use of the body and voice by performers and on abstract theatrical elements. But modernists frequently adopt an opposition between the iconocentricity of oriental show traditions and the logocentricity of theatre in western industrial societies, which they inaccurately attribute to the influence of the ancient Greek and Roman theatrical traditions. The reason seems to be that neoclassicist European theatre, following the principle of rationalism, invented the logocentric, static and rhetorical performance of those Athenian and Roman plays which it chose to reproduce and imitate, ignoring completely, though understandably, the physical traces they had left behind.

SUGGESTIONS FOR FURTHER READING

All the evidence for the formal elements of ancient Greek theatrical performances and acting is discussed in *DFA* (1988); the ancient testimonies are translated into English, further evaluated, and discussed in Csapo and Slater (1995). Taplin (1978) uses a characteristic sample of preserved tragedies to investigate and categorise aspects of fifth-century performances on the basis of the texts. Sutton (1980) refers to performance elements in his presentation of the fragments and texts preserved from the tradition of satyr drama. The form and meaning of the ancient texts and performances of tragedy, and, to some extent, of satyr drama are

90 Artaud (1958) 108. 91 Barba and Savarese (1991) 165, 192.

analysed in Easterling (1997a). This *Companion to Greek Tragedy* also contains discussions of the reception and performances of tragedy in later antiquity and from the Renaissance to modernity. From the perspective of theatre anthropology, Barba and Savarese (1991) offer a selective analysis of views on acting, actors and theatrical performances in different cultures from antiquity to the present.

CHAPTER FOUR

Towards a reconstruction of performance style

Richard Green

Recent scholarship has quite properly put an increasing emphasis on interpreting and evaluating ancient drama in terms of its impact in performance, and yet, despite the identification of more and more material evidence for the physical appearance of actors and their masks, a great deal of work remains to be done on such issues as the semiotics of costume, the perception of mask-types, the use of gesture and, for that matter, of body language more generally. All these need to be explored in terms of the attitudes and prejudices of a given community at a given period. It is a difficult area for many reasons, not least because it involves attempting to understand the conventions of physical appearance, dress and behaviour as they evolved through time, doubtless with regional variations, while deconstructing the artistic conventions through which the material evidence was presented.[1]

ACTORS AND THEIR COSTUME: TRAGEDY

All too few pictures survive of classical Greek actors acting tragedy. There are good reasons for this, the principal of which is the convention that vase-painters (and doubtless, therefore, the purchasers of their vases) were governed by the sense of the story conveyed by the performance. Thus, what is usually depicted on vases is not the process of performance but what the audience was persuaded to see, as it were the 'real' Agamemnon of Greek myth–history rather than the actor playing that role. It is something modern viewers experience from a good performance, whether on stage or in film, and there is some evidence to suppose that members of the fifth-century audience felt it even more strongly – if only because the experience was less frequent, because they were less exposed and

[1] On the visual codes of fifth-century Athenian vase-painters, see Green (1991). I am grateful to Eric Csapo, Pat Easterling, Edith Hall and Eric Handley for their helpful advice and criticism in the preparation of this chapter.

Fig. 13 Detail from the Pronomos Vase depicting Heracles and other members of the cast of a satyr-play (Photo: J. R. Green after FR)

therefore in some ways less critical. We may think, by analogy, of early cinema, which we now find stilted and not very convincing, but which was found absorbing by its contemporaries.

The earliest explicit depictions appear on the series of vases, like the Pronomos vase (fig. 13), which seem to show performers in the sanctuary of Dionysus celebrating success in the dramatic festival (see 'List of objects cited', nos. **1–7**[2]). They date to the last decade of the fifth century and perhaps the beginning of the fourth. The Pronomos vase and at least one of the others show the cast of a satyr-play, and we may guess that

[2] In this chapter, bold numerals refer to items listed in 'List of objects cited', pp. 121–6 below.

the performers were shown in this context since the satyr-play was the last of the set of four plays put on by the successful team. At the same time, the group of vases as a whole can be taken to give a fair idea of the appearance of actors at this period.

The costume is elaborate. If we take the bearded figure standing by the head of the couch with Dionysus, we can see from the mask that he has played a male role. He wears soft boots which were doubtless like those worn by the actor of Heracles by the foot of the couch. They have slightly long, turned-up toes, and there are white dots, probably reflecting the means of tying them up (they are calf-length). The skirt of the *chitōn* seems light in weight and is fussily decorated with wave-pattern, palmettes and psi-motifs. The upper part has white dots, more wave-patterns, and a figured upper border with horse-*protomai* (foreparts). It has sleeves to the wrist decorated with what one might describe as double-wave. The *hīmation* has broad borders again with the foreparts of horses combined with Eros-like figures, edged here too with wave motifs.[3] While some of the details are common to the painter's repertoire when dealing with non-theatrical figures, the general effect must surely be similar to that seen on stage.

Three important observations already suggest themselves. The first raises the question of professionalism. It is arguable that, by comparison with those of the succeeding generation, the figures shown here are still gentleman amateurs. They have their beards, unlike the actor on the fragments in Würzburg (fig. 16) of the middle years of the fourth century. He is by contrast a regular performer, as other aspects of the depiction imply (see below). This is not to say that the actors seen in representations of the late fifth century were not skilled or famous, and it may be relevant that the prize for actors at the Dionysia was instituted half a century earlier. On the other hand their activity was still confined to a limited number of festivals, mostly still in Athens. They are shown as mature figures. This may have been normal, for acting was an arduous activity and must ordinarily have demanded some years of training.[4] Twentieth-century experience might lead us to suppose that the audience preferred the fullness of a mature, deep voice – although this was not so, for example, for the heroes of eighteenth-century opera. There is some evidence for lighter-voiced actors and, depending on one's view of the naturalism of performance, there was considerable scope with female roles in Greek tragedy (see Hall, ch. 1, this volume). It is difficult to know if Aeschylus'

3 For a recent study of this kind of clothing, see Manakidou (1997).

4 There are some excellent observations, though in the context of a later period, in Sifakis (1979).

Fig. 14 The Choregos Vase, showing a tragic actor with three comic actors (Photo: Museum)

son Euaion, as an actor in the 440s, was exceptionally young. He had presumably had experience in the theatre from an early age; but young he was if he could still be described as *kalos* ('beautiful') by the Phiale Painter when he played the part of Perseus in Sophocles' *Andromeda* (**8**).[5] His youth may be explained by his exceptional circumstances and the good fortune of his father, and/or by the age in which he lived. What was possible then may not have been possible later.

The second point to be made from these representations is that the style of costume matches the general trends observable in contemporary art, the so-called Rich Style. That this is not simply a result of an individual vase-painter's style seems clear not only from the general consistency across this series of depictions, but also from the next representation

5 Other vases have him playing the hero's mother Argiope in Sophocles' *Thamyras* (see Hall ch. 1, fig. 1 (*IGD* III 2, 9)), a part for which his voice may have suited him), and the youthful role of Actaeon in his father's *Toxotides* (*IGD* III 1, 28). For other vases with *Euaion kalos*, see *ARV*[2] 1579 and Shapiro (1987). On the *Thamyras* vase, see Oakley (1990) 20–2 and no. 92. He notes that there is a hint that the figure of Argiope wears a mask.

of a tragic actor, the Aegisthus-figure on the Choregos Vase of about 390–380 BC (**9**, fig. 14), where he is contrasted with the comic performers who follow the comic convention of being depicted in the actuality of their appearance on stage. The style of contemporary painting and sculpture is elaborate in this same way and it is interesting to see that tragic costume is given a similar sort of treatment. It is also worth remembering Webster's observations on the comparability of Euripidean lyric.[6] This elaboration also seems to have infected contemporary music.[7] This is the style of the age and it transcends particular modes.[8]

The third point is that this style of costume is in apparent contrast with what the sources suggest about the 'realism' of contemporary drama. It in fact emphasises the relativity of 'realism' and forces us to question the extent to which Kallippides was actually ape-like, and the degree to which any actor could be said to mimic low-level behaviour.[9]

Earlier than this there are of course depictions of chorusmen. Some of the earliest, like those on the hydria in St Petersburg and the column-krater in Basle (of about 490 and soon after 480 BC respectively), can have relatively elaborate costume, in both cases for youthful warriors (**10, 11**). On the other hand the maenad on the pelike in Berlin (about 460 BC, **12**) is dressed simply, as is the pair depicted by the Phiale Painter on the well-known pelike in Boston (about 440 BC, **13**, fig. 15) or the other pair on the bell-krater in Ferrara (about 460–450 BC, **14**). One has the impression that just as vase-painting and sculpture of the early classical period show dress that is simple compared with that of late archaic, so too was that employed in the theatre. Equally, the series of five vases by different vase-painters which seem to reflect Sophocles' *Andromeda* in the 440s and which, through their similarity one to another, may be argued to give a reasonable idea of the way the figures were dressed, again appear to reflect a style in keeping with the general style of the classical period proper.[10] It is the vases of the later fifth century which appear to demonstrate the development of a distinctive theatre costume of a kind that is both different in cut and composition from, as well as more elaborate than, that of the well-dressed person of everyday life.

[6] Webster (1939) 189ff. More recently Zimmermann (1991) 19–20, and articles in Murray and Wilson (forthcoming).
[7] Webster (1967) 17ff.; West (1992a) 351–4.
[8] See Hall and Valakas in this volume, pp. 8–9 and 84–7.
[9] See Csapo in this volume, pp. 127–31. [10] Green (1991).

Fig. 15 Two tragic chorusmen preparing for performance (Photo: Museum)

Something of the same would appear to be true of tragic masks. Again there are all too few depictions of them, but those used by the chorusmen on the vases just mentioned as well as the frontal one held by an assistant on the widely published oinochoe fragments from the Athenian Agora are of very simple, almost plain appearance (**15**). Like all Greek masks, they enclose the head, extending beyond the crown on top, hiding the person of the performer. The features and hair are not in any way exaggerated. They have the same general style as we find in contemporary sculpture and vase-painting, as Halliwell (1993) has already observed. In this case we can be sure that the similarity to contemporary art is deliberate, indeed that it has meaning. A classic example which demonstrates the point is the west pediment of the Temple of Zeus at Olympia (completed by 456 BC) where the Apollo in the centre and the surrounding Lapiths have calm, untroubled expressions despite the fierceness of the battle. The centaurs, on the other hand, have distorted faces, reflecting the struggle in which they are engaged. Another similar case is found on the southern metopes of the Parthenon (perhaps of the mid- to later 440s) where the Lapiths again look calm in their tussles with the centaurs. One could point to many other examples. 'Proper' Greeks and the gods they created show calm and control even in the most adverse situations, whereas aliens, the outsiders of society, exhibit their emotions. It is an aspect of the 'classical Ideal'. Similarly, and as we shall observe again below, 'proper' Greeks have trim, well-proportioned bodies – as we see throughout most fifth- and fourth-century art. By contrast slaves and other outsiders are often shown with fat bellies. We should expect that on stage the figures of serious drama also looked 'proper'. This is surely an aspect of the decorum expected of tragedy as explained recently, for example, by Easterling (1997b: 167).

The Gnathia fragment in Würzburg (**16**, fig. 16) is one of the finer examples of Greek vase-painting, both in the skill of the drawing and in its depiction of the engaging contrast between the mean, rather shabby person of the actor and the heroic quality of the figure he has just portrayed. The piece probably dates to about 350–340 BC. What is curious about him is that he shaves or at least trims his beard close. Adult men did not usually shave before the time of Alexander. The stubble on his face has usually been taken as a sign of his shabbiness, a growth he had not bothered to remove for the last several days.[11] In fact this is not so, but a heavily trimmed beard, and it was trimmed like this because a beard was a nuisance when one regularly wore a mask during one's professional activity.[12] Compared with him, earlier actors were amateurs.

[11] For example Dumont (1982) 126–7: 'la barbe qui s'est remise à pousser sur son menton rasé'.

[12] On those Myrina figurines where the actor's head is visible below the mask at the back, the hair is shown as trimmed short.

Fig. 16 Tragic actor holding his mask (Photo: Museum)

It is worth putting alongside this a roughly contemporary depiction of a tragic messenger (**17**, fig. 17) witnessing the death of Hippolytus as his chariot crashes on the seashore. Although he is shown as the actual messenger rather than as an actor playing the role, he is one of about fifty such figures preserved in vase-painting, and they are depicted with such consistency that we may reasonably assume an accurate depiction

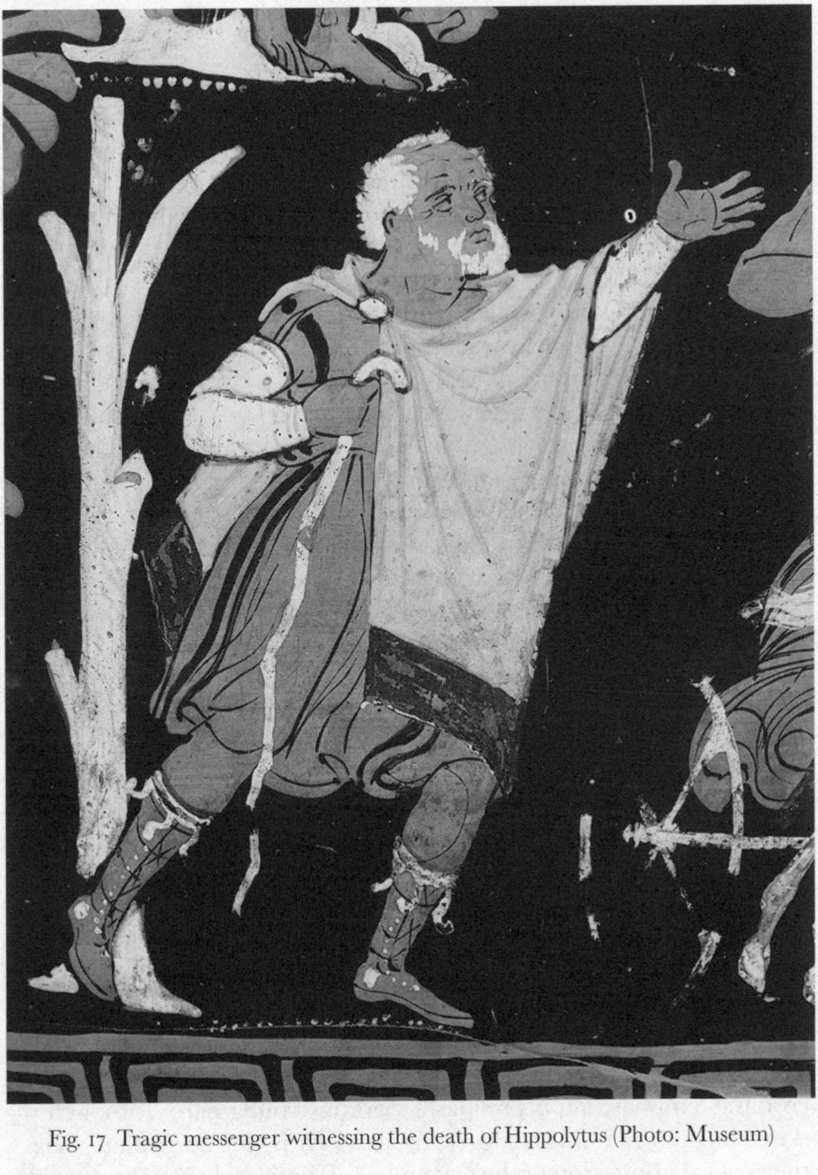

Fig. 17 Tragic messenger witnessing the death of Hippolytus (Photo: Museum)

of the character as he appeared on stage.[13] Within the conventions of the time, he is far from heroic. He has scruffy hair and beard (contrast the luxuriant hair of the mask in fig. 16), he carries the stick of an old man

[13] See Green (1996), (1999).

and he wears a cloak of heavy cloth and simple cut. He is a servant. At the same time he wears the elaborate boots of tragedy, just like those of fig. 16, his cloak has a purple border with white trim (note the purple of the clothing of the king in fig. 16), and it is fastened with a gold brooch. He is a servant in a royal house, but more importantly from our perspective, he is seen within the context of the performance of tragedy with its rich costume. He also has the long sleeves of the stage performer. This last is something seen already on the actors of the Pronomos vase (fig. 13) or, earlier still, on the actors of comedy.

While we from our perspective may regret that we have no depictions of actors of serious drama earlier than the ones we have been considering, their appearance at this point is probably not pure chance. It is the beginning of a process by which Athenians and others begin to distinguish the performers from the play, the early manifestation of the emergence of a star-system, also seen in the evolving consciousness of the figures like Mynniskos, Kallippides and Nikostratos as individuals.[14] It is a process that reached a peak in the middle and third quarter of the fourth century with actors such as Polos and Theodoros.[15]

Later than this depictions of tragic actors become more common, a phenomenon which coincides with the public perception of their being if anything more important than the work performed.[16] We may take as a random example a terracotta figurine in Nicosia (**18**, fig. 18). It does not preserve the colour of the costume, but the other details are reasonably clear. The mask has the early version of the high-arching *onkos*, in this case with wavy hair; it has a furrow on the forehead, sloping brows, a wrinkled nose and a gaping mouth (through which the actor's mouth must have been visible[17]); it is beardless. The type is that of a young male, and it is interesting that his *chitōn* reaches rather lower than it would have earlier, down to the top of his boots.[18] It is high-girt, with a broad belt on the lower chest. The figure has a *chlamys* (also implying he is an active, young man) fixed by the right shoulder, and he holds its edge with his left hand. The right hand is also visible. He has sleeves from some kind of undergarment. The stance, frontal, with feet apart, goes with the mask type and the costume, emphasising his role as a vigorous young hero. Although the skirt hangs in fine folds, suggesting its cloth is not particularly heavy, the general impression of the costume is of increased formality, and this

[14] See Stefanis (1988) nos. 1757, 1348 and 1861 respectively. It is worth observing that Eubulus (fr. 134 KA) says that Nikostratos was notable for his playing of messenger parts.

[15] Stephanis (1988) nos. 2187 and 1157.

[16] Easterling (1997d) puts it neatly at 215–16.

[17] See Hall, ch. 1, in this volume, p. 15.

[18] Note that the boots do not yet have platform soles.

Fig. 18 Tragic actor in the role of a young man (Photo: Museum)

is something which will continue in the ensuing centuries. The piece should be dated within the early Hellenistic period.

ACTORS AND THEIR COSTUME: COMEDY

Actors of comedy are easier to deal with, not least since they are much more commonly depicted, and they are shown in more explicit fashion. The earliest, which belong to about 430 BC, show a figure dressed in a loose body-stocking with, underneath it, padding on the belly and backside. At the front is attached a large leather phallus. This costume represents stage-nakedness and over it the actor would usually wear clothes appropriate to the part played. In the later fifth century it is often a short jerkin (leaving the phallus exposed), and perhaps a cloak. The contrast with the propriety of tragic costume is surely deliberate. Comic performers are placed outside the normally acceptable appearance of the citizen as we see it in art (whether of official art such as we see in temple-reliefs or in free-standing sculpture or, for that matter, in vase-painting) or as we read it in texts. They are gross, uncouth, as is made clear by their fat appearance or even more especially by the large and obvious phallus which contrasts with the preternaturally small ones of males in fifth- and fourth-century art. The comic performer stands outside the accepted norm, and this is doubtless part of the convention which allows the characters of comedy to behave in ways and to say things which also fall outside the accepted norms of public behaviour.

The development of comic costume over the next hundred years or so, to the end of the fourth century, is one of increasing couthness. Clothing becomes slowly more naturalistic and more in keeping with the parts played, and, from the rare and casual surviving evidence, one has the impression that colour of dress becomes more significant in helping define the characters. Costume becomes longer. By the end of the fourth century, mature men often have their cloak down to at least mid-calf, young men to just below the knee, women to the ankle; only slaves and their equivalents still have it short. The padding seen in Old Comedy is slowly decreased during Middle: young men and women lose it first, for older citizen males it becomes less pronounced, though they still remain portly. (Slaves keep the padding throughout the history of comedy, as a signifier of their status.) The phallus comes to be covered by longer dress. When exposed, as it still is for slaves, cooks and so on until late in the century, it becomes markedly small during the course of the third quarter, and disappears very soon after. This must have been part of what made New Comedy seem more naturalistic.

The range of masks grows greater until, by the time of Menander, the full complement numbers something in the region of forty. While more naturalistic than they were in Old Comedy, they were nonetheless designed according to a series of conventions. For example most males were divided according to a primary division by hairstyle, whether in a tight roll or loose and wavy, and this convention in turn indicated something of their dramatic function, whether they belonged to one or another stage household; this division by hair was applied across the categories of males, mature, young and slave. At the same time, those with wavy hair seem to have been regarded, in accordance with contemporary physiognomics, as having more outgoing personalities.[19] Within these primary sets, various other factors were applied, such as darker or lighter complexion, raised brows and frown (implying extrovert inquisitiveness or strength of personality) or level and/or drooping brows (implying a more modest or even introvert personality), and so on. Younger people's masks show the greatest range, and this doubtless reflects the interests of comedy in the later years of the fourth century, and, at the same time, a shift in the interests of society as a whole. Women's masks are defined by different principles, a combination of facial features, age and hairstyle, from the maiden with more severe hair, straight nose and a small, proper mouth, to varying degrees of hetaira (shape of nose – the snub being cheeky, width of mouth – larger being more sexually promising, and elaboration of hairstyle – the simple, more modest mistress to the party girl). Then the more wrinkled, older women like nurses or concubines. The whole represents a naturalism of a kind that is based on a systematised set of conventions.

STYLES OF PERFORMANCE: TRAGEDY

Styles of performance, or the rules of deportment on the Greek stage, must have been developed relative to the conventions held proper in everyday life. We know something of the rules of deportment for upper-class Athenian males of the later fifth and earlier fourth centuries. When, at the beginning of the *Republic*, Polemarchus sends his slave to catch Socrates and Glaucon whom he sees walking ahead of him back to Athens, we may

[19] Fundamental is Krien (1955). Among other relevant work on physiognomics in the Greek world, see Pfuhl (1927), Evans (1969), Yalouris (1986), Kiilerich (1988), Krierer (1988), and not least Decleva Caizzi (1993) on self-presentation by philosophers through physical appearance.

suppose he does so not merely as a matter of convenience, but because a gentleman could not be seen to run, or even hurry (Plato, *Rep*. 1.327b2–5). *Eurythmōs badizein*, as Alexis put it, implies walking with a steady step, neither dawdling nor hurrying, and certainly not turning about and gawking, as Aristophanes accuses Socrates of doing.[20] *Sōphrosynē* ('self-control') implied behavioural restraint as much as any other kind.

The same restraint applied to gesture, as is still the case for the upper classes in most western societies.[21] And it was reinforced by dress codes. The *hīmation*, which was the regular outdoor wear for mature 'free' males in the fifth century, was heavy and enveloping, and certainly did not encourage free or violent movement.[22] Gloves had not yet been invented, but, except in special cases, some care was taken to conceal at least one of the hands (usually the left). Of representations in contemporary vase-painting, the ubiquitous draped youths found on the reverse of calyx- and bell-kraters are a case in point.[23] Another example is to be found on the Choregos Vase (fig. 14). The two *chorēgoi* are on the one hand costumed as normal comic actors of the period with short dress which exposes the phallus, but on the other they wear the equivalent of long *hīmatia*, with the left hand bound up invisibly within. They are wealthy, upper-crust gentlemen, as one would expect of *chorēgoi* who have to perform a liturgy. It is a good case of the conventional nature of stage costume: the audience is trained to read the relevant aspects. The messenger of tragedy also has his left hand hidden as a rule: fig. 17 is an exception and it thereby helps to express his strong emotion at the terrible event, the death of Hippolytus, which he sees occurring. The slaves of comedy rarely have their hands hidden in this way, and when it happens it is always worth asking why, what is particular to their behaviour at that point.

Women's public behaviour was of course even more circumscribed. We shall come back to it later, but for the moment we may note the way that generally in vase-painting, proper ladies (and some others) have their gaze slightly lowered, presumably as a sign of modesty, and commonly,

[20] Alexis fr. 265 KA with essential further references to Plautus, *Poenulus* 522 and to Arnott and others in their note. It is possible that *arhythmōs* is a semi-technical term here, given the importance of *eurhythmia* for the deportment of young men: see Dickie (1993) 111–13 and 118–28 (especially, for the fifth century, 125). See also Aristophanes, *Clouds* 362, Plato, *Symp.* 221b and the comments of Handley (1985a) 376. See also Bremmer (1991).

[21] Compare the observation that the upper-class French gesticulate less than the lower classes: Wylie (1977) viii–ix.

[22] Cf. Geddes (1987).

[23] A useful area for those investigating the proprieties of deportment is grave reliefs, especially because they are so bound by convention. For steps in this direction, see Breuer (1994), Bergemann (1994), (1997).

when they do not, a point is being made. If they look a man in the eye, there is a strong reason.

That is, to attempt to understand what is represented in the images of theatre, one has to understand the background of expectations, the norm, against which stage behaviour might be judged. One of the most striking extant examples of reaction against the accepted norm is the key scene of Sophocles' *Andromeda*. In this case it is possible to gain some reliable idea of what the performance looked like on stage, despite the way that the scenes are shown, as usual, as mythological reality (Green (1991); **8, 19–22**). Five different vases decorated by five different painters seem to reflect independent observations of a single performance. They share many elements of characters, costume and action. There is an element of spectacle in the depiction of the Ethiopian attendants as Africans, their bringing of wedding/funerary gifts, and the dress of Andromeda in eastern hat, short tunic and trousers. Nonetheless it is more than just spectacle. The contrast between whites and blacks is designed to add to the horror of the occasion, as are the wedding gifts which are the same as can serve as funerary offerings. And Andromeda is being tied to stakes on stage, frontal, with her arms apart, unprotected and exposed for the monster's pleasure. As treatment of a woman, it was shocking.

We may look at two other examples from tragedy, even if they are not unproblematic. They may be treated as a pair since they are both by a single painter and share a number of elements in presentation. They date to soon after the middle of the fourth century, that is about a century after the first production of *Andromeda*. Fig. 19 (**23**) is unusually explicit in that it shows the figures on a stage,[24] and that in turn helps interpret fig. 20 where there is something resembling a stage floor at the bottom of the scene, and there are columns in the background which perhaps are to be thought of as deriving from the façade of the stage building like that of the so-called Lycurgan Theatre of Dionysus in Athens.[25] Both have a messenger bringing news, another clear link with tragedy. None of the figures, however, is shown as wearing a mask, and we have to be wary of interpretation by the vase-painter into the parts played, beyond the actuality of the performance.

Fig. 19 is generally, and probably rightly, taken as representing a key scene from *Oedipus Tyrannus* (924ff.). This is therefore a performance of classic theatre, and we cannot know if the staging attempted to recreate the conventions of performance in Sophocles' time or was done in

[24] Alan Hughes points out to me that the 'blocks' below the stage at each end are in fact stairs.
[25] See Townsend (1986).

Fig. 19 A messenger bringing news. Scene of a tragedy in performance: *Oedipus Tyrannus*? (Photo: E. W. Handley)

contemporary style. (The latter seems more likely.) The messenger wears much the same costume as his colleagues in figs. 16 and 17, including the boots. He makes the conventional gesture of address with his left hand, two fingers and the thumb raised. (It is one which will later pass into Christian liturgy.) The gesture makes it clear that the person he is addressing is the king, Oedipus, but he is turned to face the spectator: he is performing for the audience. The king's role is signified by his sceptre. As a respectable figure, his left hand is concealed within his cloak. He is taller than the servant, which is as it should be – given the distribution of parts, one may wonder how this could be achieved on stage beyond the rounding of the messenger's shoulders. He has full, luxuriant hair (compare the white-haired version in fig. 16 and contrast that of the messenger). While his cloak is relatively simple, but for its coloured border, his principal garment is elaborately decorated. He stands evenly balanced, with his legs straight and fairly close together. He is a respectable and respected figure. More specific to the moment are the lowered head and the hand to chin, gestures of puzzlement. One may guess that the left hand to hip may in this case mean something similar. The figure of Jocasta, as is proper for a woman, draws her arms in about herself so as to take up the least possible space. Her feet are close together, her ankles invisible, her head slightly lowered. Her hands are out of sight. Though as tall as Oedipus (she is as important), she is less obtrusive and she stands in a secondary position. Her clothing has the same degree of elaboration as that of Oedipus. The gesture of covering the face is one of shock or anxiety, one common to much of western culture.

The other vase (fig. 20, **24**) is another calyx-krater by the same painter. The surface is poorly preserved and therefore many of the details difficult to make out, but the main outlines are clear. In terms of costume, it is worth noting first the decoration of the skirts of the two standing women and the sleeves of the one on the right; they are also dressed somewhat unusually, with loose cloaks held by a brooch at the neck.[26] Their hair is exposed and this may indicate that they are found in a domestic situation. They are approached by a messenger dressed in the normal boots of the tragic stage, but in the traveller's hat of a poor man, the *pīlos*, and with a skin about his body, under the cloak. He is again small. (It is odd that he should appear from the right: the country is conventionally thought of as on the left of stage.) His left hand is barely visible as it gathers the cloak, but his right hand is open, palm up, in a gesture which conveys speech and surprise. He brings bad news which shocks the women, and the painter put some effort into depicting their reactions. The one on the left turns away, head bowed, her right hand raised towards her companion as if she cannot accept the news, an idea reinforced by the gesture of left hand on hip (the hand itself is wrapped within the cloak). The woman in the centre of the group has thrown herself to her knees in a way all too familiar to us from images of recent events in the Balkans, and here too it must imply extreme distress, perhaps at the news of the death of a loved one. She spreads her arms in a gesture which, for a respectable woman, indicates the enormity of the situation. The hairstyle should imply that she is either a wife or a betrothed, and it is not surprising that she should be at the centre of the picture. The woman immediately in front of the messenger

26 We may therefore ask if they are normal heroines or conceived as non-Greek. It is also hard to say if the sleeves they wear are intended as the costume of foreign women (as worn by Andromeda for example), or a reflection of what the actors actually wore on stage. For sleeved costume in the East, see Knauer (1985).

Fig. 20 Three women responding to a messenger's news. Scene of tragedy in performance (Reproduced from *IGD*, III. 6, 1)

raises her hands at the shock of the news. Her palms are turned towards her; the gesture is strong without being extravagant, and the upper body leans back, presumably indicating her difficulty in accepting the news.[27] In terms of stage action it is perhaps noteworthy that she stands between the messenger and the more important figure in the centre.

There is no means of knowing in any absolute sense how much of the scene is interpretation by the painter of a performance he witnessed, but the fact that he puts it on a stage should imply that he thought the actions of the figures he drew compatible with what he saw in the theatre at Syracuse about 340 BC.

STYLES OF PERFORMANCE: COMEDY

While tragedy of the fifth and fourth centuries seems to have become, for a while, more naturalistic in its presentation, comedy seems to have developed from more knock-about, with rapid and even violent movement, to more subtle and considered. This is surely a gross oversimplification, but overall it appears to hold true. Menander is arguably closer to Euripides than he is to Aristophanes. Among depictions to be associated with the later phases of Old and the earlier phases of Middle Comedy, there are certainly more that show vigorous action.[28] One may think of the Vlasto oinochoe in Athens with (it seems) Perseus dancing on stage (**25**), or of the well-known Tarentine bell-krater in the British Museum with the old man Chiron being heaved up the steps onto the stage (**26**), or again of the Tarentine bell-krater in Sydney with a frenzied pursuit including a pretend Heracles (fig. 21, **27**). There are figures beating or threatening to beat one another (**28–30**), men rowing fish (**31–2**), and a range of figures in other sorts of vigorous activity (e.g. **33–7**), as well as others who are simply dancing or running wildly (e.g. **38–40**). As we saw above, after the middle of the fourth century, it is only slaves who continue to run. For others it becomes improper behaviour.

There are of course many calmer scenes, even if they may carry implicit dispute. The Choregos vase (fig. 14) is a case in point. Both the *chorēgoi* are respectably dressed, and although there is a contrast between the younger and the older, they are both mature figures, leaning on their staffs with slightly rounded shoulders. The older one addresses the tragic

27 On the other hand, Ghiron-Bistagne (1974b) 366–7 took this woman as welcoming the news.
28 See MacDowell (1988).

Fig. 21 Comic performance: naked male pursued by pretend Heracles (Photo: Museum)

paradigm, Aegisthus (as he seems to be in this case), with a confidence which is signified by his relaxed pose, weight on one leg, whereas his counterpart on the right of the scene is given a turn of the head and a balance on his feet that might enable him to move quickly. The slave Pyrrhias standing on the up-turned basket is less confined in the way he carries himself, making a quasi-authoritative gesture with his right hand and indicating a certain force of character with his left. The improbability of his role as stand-in archon is emphasised by the elaborate detail of his slave-garment, the *exōmis*.

A bell-krater in Copenhagen dates from two or three decades later, towards the middle of the century (fig. 22, **41**). Quite typically, the scene

Fig. 22 Comic performance: hetaira, old man, slave carrying chest (Photo: Museum)

is less specifically Athenian in content and more concerned with life in general. The stage has four supports in the form of Doric columns, a stairway from the *orchēstra* in the middle, and a curtain hiding the underneath of the stage. The column shown above may indicate a columnar façade for the stage-building in an abbreviated fashion, but it is more likely symbolic of the house-entrance. From the right comes a slave wearing the normal short *chitōniskos* and carrying a chest. The weight of the chest is conveyed by the leaning forward of his body and the bend in the knees. It must represent the worldly wealth of the man in the centre of the scene, and his reactions have to be judged in the context of the action and of the glamorous hetaira at the left (for her costume and pose,

Fig. 23 Comic performance: woman, youth, slave in disguise as young woman, old man with stick (Photo courtesy Professor Umberto Spigo)

compare some of the figures discussed below). He sags at the knees and his stick hangs loose; his head is tilted back. The woman's gesture suggests that she is the one who is in control of the situation.

A calyx-krater excavated in Messina in 1989 takes us to the later phase of Middle Comedy (fig. 23, **42**). It is decorated by the Manfria Painter or someone close to him and should be dated to the third quarter of the fourth century. The scene is shown taking place on a stage with, as usual with this painter, a pair of stairs leading up to it. Four columns are shown behind the figures, as in the tragic scene of fig. 20, and between the two central figures is an incense-burner indicating that the setting is a sanctuary, or at the very least that the occasion is a special one. At the far right is an old gentleman with white hair and beard, closely wrapped in his cloak, neither of his hands visible though he partially supports himself on a stick in front of him. The cloak is still short and he wears a small phallus. His legs should imply that he is approaching the central event, although, to judge by the poses of the other figures, at this moment he is not a direct participant in it. His counterpart at the far left is a young woman, and it is worth observing that her dress reaches the ground. She too is closely wrapped in her *hīmation*, her feet together. One hand holds the folds of her *hīmation*, and the other is stretched forward towards a young man, possibly grasping his arm. Her hair is shoulder-length and wavy. It is not covered, though it is held by a band on top of the head. The young man in front of her (note that his garment comes to just below his knees) turns round towards her, his legs apparently swinging, his arms forward from the elbows and the fingers of his left hand in a distinctive gesture: the thumb, first and fourth finger are extended, the other two held in. Finger-gestures are the most culturally specific of all human gestures and it is unsafe to interpret them through contemporary analogy.[29] One might nonetheless guess that he is startled and that the gesture is a speaking one, perhaps interrogatory. He is looking back to her from the figure in front of him, and the reason is explicable. This figure is dressed in women's clothes, reaching to the ground, but the pose is hardly decorous: the legs are apart and the hands are raised in front. Although the head is covered with tresses of hair visible at the sides, the mask is that of a slave. It is a slave in disguise as a young woman, and at this point we may also note that the figure is fat-bellied, as all stage-slaves are. By the conventions of stage disguise, the audience has to be able to see the original character of the figure even if the other participants in the drama cannot. We might speculate that he has impersonated the young woman on the left, and, given the incense-burner, that an event such as a marriage was about to take place. The young man is shocked and doubtless anticipates the reaction of the old man approaching from the right, most probably the person at the receiving end of the trick. It is the crux of the play.

The vase is an important one for what it tells us of developments in costume, of the nature of disguise on stage, and of the use of body language.

Let us now look at five other young women (figs. 24–8). All are terracotta figurines, ranging in height between about 8 and 12cm. Most date within the first half of the fourth century, although one or two may be slightly later. They are characterised by their masks as *pseudokorai* ('pretend maidens') and young hetairai. All wear the same basic clothing, and part of the interest lies in seeing how it is used. It is unfortunate that the colour of the garments is rarely preserved, but where traces survive, the mantle is a bright blue.

29 See the useful overview of this gesture in Csapo (1993) 50–1, with further references.

Fig. 24 Comic actor playing young woman (Photo: Museum)

Fig. 25 Comic actor playing young woman (Photo: Museum)

Fig. 26 Comic actor playing young woman (Photo: J. R. Green after Bieber)

Fig. 27 Comic actor playing young woman (Photo: J. R. Green)

Fig. 28 Comic actor playing young woman (Photo: J. R. Green)

A potential problem in their interpretation rests in the fact that they are figurines, not vase paintings, and they therefore do not belong to particular situations in particular plays, but may be supposed to encapsulate a character found fairly often on stage. They are not quasi-photographic likenesses, either, and it is always possible that the makers of the figurines applied some degree of interpretation or standardisation, but they must have done so within certain conventions, and these conventions must have reflected stage practice. All are Athenian or derive directly from Athenian prototypes.

In brief, the critical elements include basic deportment (the positioning of legs and feet, the placing of hands and arms, the carriage of the head), the use of clothing, and the degree to which hands and arms are exposed. For these purposes the protrusion of the belly is meaningless: it is part of the padding standard to the comic actor at this period.

In the first, fig. 24 (**43**) known in sixteen surviving examples, with many other variants) the actor plays a modest character. The legs are straight and placed reasonably close together (a maiden or 'proper' woman would have had them still closer); the distribution of weight is even. The figure is completely enveloped in the *hīmation* and the hands are hidden, except possibly a little of the left where the garment is held across. The mouth is hidden and only the eyes are seen. The head is tilted sideways.[30] The figure stands in marked contrast with fig. 25 (**44**, known in seven examples) despite some superficial similarity. In this case both hands are used to hold up the *hīmation*, as if to raise or lower it before the mask (the right and perhaps the left are visible). The body has an S-curve, the weight on the left leg, the right relaxed with the knee pushed forward. The shoulders are pushed sideways but the head tilts back in a way that could be read as communicating directly with the interlocutor. The drapery hangs more loosely at the side. Much of the hair is exposed, and it is fairly loosely worn. (It is well worth comparing the Jocasta of fig. 19 with both these.)

Fig. 26 (**45**, known in twelve examples) is from early in the Middle Comedy sequence despite the lack of prominent padding. Here the pose can be read as more sexually aggressive, straightforward rather than coy. The left leg is forward and out, a feature which is emphasised by the coroplast (maker of the figurine) in the contrast with the closely-hanging folds of the *chitōn* over the right leg. To have the left hand on the hip seems to have been read as provocative in Greek as in later western culture, and it is something which respectable young women are never seen to do in Greek art in general. Similarly, the right arm is exposed (the actor of course wears the normal close-fitting sleeves to his wrist, but they count as stage-skin); and to hold the mantle at the side of the head may also be taken as an immodest gesture. The head is held up and the gaze is direct (and again, therefore, immodest). The *hīmation* is loose and allowed to hang down at the front revealing the form of the left breast. Much of the hair is uncovered, and a tress hangs outside the *hīmation* at the left shoulder. There is no doubt that hair was read as symbolically in classical Athens as it was in Victorian England.

Similar in approach to the last is fig. 27 (**46**) which may be taken as an example of a long-running series. The principal difference is that here it is the right leg which is out and forward (and possibly thereby carrying a stronger message), and the *hīmation* is held forward at the side of the face in a manner which echoes the shyer version seen when brides meet their husbands. In this case the total pose makes the gesture rather stronger in its intent. At the same time the whole of the upper chest is uncovered to the thin *chitōn*. Tresses of hair hang down over the shoulders.

The fifth piece, fig. 28 (**47**, known in six examples), is more difficult to read. Our immediate, subjective impression is that the figure conveys

30 For later derivatives, see *MMC* 3 ST 15, 16, 17.

sorrow or despair, probably due to the angling of the head and the way the right arm is held across the chest. This may be right, but we should note, nonetheless, the thrusting forward of the left leg, the exposure of much of the right arm and the fact that the head is essentially uncovered. It is just as possible that the pose suggested aggressive complaint, whether at a lack of success or as a means of achieving success. Again, we may misinterpret the angle of the head which could be intended as deliberate coyness, or, for that matter, a use of the head which goes with aggressive complaint, indicating a lack of straightforwardness. But compare fig. 29 (**48**), which gives a very different impression though very similar in pose.

These are examples from limited series in which actors play the role of a particular kind of young woman. They demonstrate the degree to which deportment and the manipulation of costume were used to indicate character and/or mode of behaviour, without any use of words. We should remember at the same time that they are genre- and time-specific: they belong to comedy and we should not automatically assume that actors performed in the same style in tragedy, even at this period; they belong to comedy at a time when it was developing an ever greater

Fig. 29 Comic actor playing young woman (Photo: J. R. Green)

subtlety in the portrayal of character, in a way that would be picked up and treated with even more careful definition by Menander and his performers. A task which remains is to expand our examination of the material evidence, to develop subtle readings of what it represents, and to write a history of performance style. It is a task which would also reveal a great deal about the attitudes and preferences of the audience, both in the theatre and at the market-stalls where they bought these objects.

SUGGESTIONS FOR FURTHER READING

Most of the relevant references are cited in this chapter. For fuller, annotated coverages, see J. R. Green, 'Greek theatre production, 1971–1986', *Lustrum* 31 (1989) 7–95, and 'Theatre production: 1987–1995', *Lustrum* 37 (1995b [1998]) 7–202.

LIST OF OBJECTS CITED

(The bibliographies given are selective.)

1 The Pronomos vase (fig. 13). Attic red-figure volute-krater. Naples inv. 81673 (H 3240), from Ruvo. Cast of a satyr-play in the sanctuary of Dionysus. FR iii, 147 (with Buschor's discussion at 132ff.); Arias, Hirmer and Shefton (1962) 377–80 (with good analytical bibliography); *IGD* II.1; Green (1994a) figs. 2.19 and 3.25; Green (1994b) 158–60, fig. 169; Green and Handley (2001) no. 5; Taplin (1997) 73–4, fig. 7; *MTS*² 49, AV 25; *ARV*² 1336, 1. Pronomos Painter; late fifth century BC.

2 Attic red-figure volute-krater fragments. Samothrace 65.1041, from Samothrace. Cast of a satyr-play in the sanctuary of Dionysus. *Hesperia* 37 (1968) 204, pl. 59c (McCredie); Froning (1971) 12–13, pl. 1.2; *RevArch* (1982) 237–41, figs. 2–4 (Green); *Hesperia* 61 (1992) 506ff. and pll. 119–20 (Dinsmoor); Green (1994a) fig. 3.17. Not in *ARV*². Late fifth century BC.

3 Attic red-figure volute-krater fragment. Switzerland, private collection. [Actor] in the sanctuary of Dionysus. Green (1982). Late fifth century BC.

4 Attic red-figure volute krater fragments. Würzburg H 4781, from Taranto. Performers in the sanctuary of Dionysus. *Corolla Curtius* (Stuttgart 1937) 150, pll. 54–6 (Bulle); Froning (1971) pl.1.1; *DFA* (1953) fig. 40, (1968) 187, fig. 50a–c; *CVA* (2) pl. 41.1–5; *MTS*² 49, AV 27; *ARV*² 1338. Near the Pronomos Painter; late fifth century BC.

5 Attic red-figure bell-krater. Actors with Dionysus. Ferrara inv. 20483 (T 161 C VP), from Spina (Valle Pega). Berti and Gasparri (1989) 132–3, no. 63 (ill.); Green (1994a) fig. 3.18; Himmelmann (1994) 147, fig. 79; Green (1994b) 160, fig. 170; Green (1995a) 99, pl. 7c. Not in *ARV*². Late fifth or early fourth century BC.

6 Attic red-figure oinochoe (shape 3, chous). Athens NM 1165, from Athens. Dionysus, Nike and two youths in tragic costume but with bare feet. van Hoorn (1951) no. 14, fig. 144; *MTS*² 50, AV 31. Not in *ARV*². About 400–390 BC.

7 Attic red-figure oinochoe (shape 3, chous). Paris, Louvre, from Italy. Dionysus, Nike and two youths in tragic costume but with bare feet. van Hoorn (1951) no. 836, fig. 142; *MTS*² 50, AV 31. Not in *ARV*². About 400–390 BC.

8 Attic white-ground calyx-krater. Agrigento AG 7, from Agrigento. Andromeda tied to stakes, addressed by Perseus, Kepheus standing near. *IGD* III 2, 1; Oakley (1990) 19–20 and no. 53, pl. 37; *ARV*² 1017, 53. Phiale Painter; about 450–440 BC. Inscr. ΕΥΑΙΩΝ ΚΑΛΟΣ ΑΙΣΧΥΛΟ

9 Tarentine red-figure bell-krater (fig. 14). Malibu, J. Paul Getty Museum 96.AE.29 (ex coll. Fleischman, F 93). Three comic actors and a tragic. Rasmussen and Spivey (1991) 164–5, fig. 67 (Trendall); Taplin (1993) pl. 9, no. 1; Schmidt (1993) 36–9, fig. 3; *Passion for Antiquities* 125–8 no. 56 (colour ill.); Green (1994a) 46, fig. 2.21; *AntK* 41 (1998) pl. 7, 1–2 (Schmidt); *RVAp* Suppl.ii, 7 no. 1/124, pl. 1, 3. Choregos Painter; early fourth century BC.

10 Attic red-figure hydria. St Petersburg 627 (B 201: St. 1538), from Vulci. Two tragic chorusmen taken by Hermes to meet Dionysus. *AntK* 10 (1967) 78, pll. 19.3 and 21.2 (Schmidt); Follmann (1968) no. 95, pl. 5.1; Green (1994a) 84, fig. 3.22; Green (1995b) pll. 1–2; *ARV*² 555, 95; *Beazley Addenda* 258. Pan Painter; about 500 BC.

11 Attic red-figure column-krater. Basle BS 415. Tragic chorus raising a dead hero from his tomb. *AntK* 10 (1967) 70, pll. 19.1–2 and 21.1 (Schmidt); *CVA* (3) pll. 6.1–2 and 7.3–5; Green (1991) pl. 6; Green (1994a) fig. 2.1; Green (1994b) 154–5 fig. 162; Taplin (1997) 70, fig. 4. Soon after 480 BC.

12 Attic red-figure pelike. Berlin inv. 3223. A and B: chorusman in the role of a maenad, dancing before a piper. *Hesperia* 24 (1955) 312–13, pl. 87 (Beazley); Green (1991) pl. 5; *MTS*² 46, AV 15; *ARV*² 586, 47. Early Mannerist; about 460 BC.

13 Attic red-figure pelike (fig. 15). Boston 98.883, from Cerveteri. Two tragic chorusmen preparing for performance. *DFA* (1953) fig. 34; Oakley (1990) 39, 73–4 no. 46, pl. 6a; *MTS*² 47, AV 20; *ARV*² 1017, 46. Phiale Painter; about 440 BC.

14 Attic red-figure bell-krater. Ferrara, from Spina (Valle Pega, Tomb 173c). Two tragic chorusmen preparing for performance. *Arte Antica e Moderna* 2 (1959) 37, pll. 17–18 (Riccioni); *DFA* (1968) 181, fig. 33; Simon (1982) pl. 6.2; *CHCL* I, pl. 5b; *MTS*² 46, AV 10, pl. 1a. About 460–450 BC.

15 Attic red-figure oinochoe frr. Athens, Agora P 11810, from Athens, Agora. Youth holding a tragic mask. *Hesperia* 8 (1939) 267ff., fig. 1 (Talcott); *DFA* (1953) fig. 25, (1968) 180, fig. 32; Bieber (1961) fig. 74; *CHCL* vol. I, pl. 7a; Moore (1997) no. 623, pl. 67; *MTS*² 46, AV 9; *ARV*² 495. Hermonax; about 470 BC.

16 Tarentine Gnathia bell-krater fr. Würzburg H 4600 (L832), from Taranto (fig. 16). Tragic actor holding his mask. Bulle (1930); *DFA* (1968) fig. 54; Simon (1968); Simon (1982) pl. 4, 3; *MTS*² 80, GV 3. Konnakis Painter; about 340 BC.

17 Tarentine red-figure volute-krater (fig. 17). London 1856.12–26.1 (F 279). Death of Hippolytus observed by a *paidagōgos*. *IGD* III.3.24; Oakley (1991); *MTS*² 158; *RVAp* II, 487 no. 18/17, pl. 173, 1; Green and Handley (2001) no. 21. Darius Painter; third quarter of the fourth century BC.

18 (Athenian?) terracotta figurine (fig. 18). Nicosia, Cyprus Museum CS 1661/16, from Soloi (tomb 11). Tragic actor. Ht 21 cm. *BCH* 92 (1968) 284 fig. 52 (Karageorghis); *ArchReports* (1968–69) 49, fig. 17; *RDAC* (1970) 142 (Christodoulou); Nicolaou (1989) 280 fig. 29. The mask seems to be type 11 of Pollux's list. Perhaps about 300 BC.

19 Attic red-figure hydria. London 1843.11–3.24 (E 169), from Vulci. Andromeda brought forward by Ethiopian servants, Cepheus, Perseus. *CVA* (5), pll. 75.1 and 76; *IGD* III.2.3; Green and Handley (2001) no. 17; *LIMC* I Andromeda-I 3*; *MTS*² 117 and 147, AV 56; *ARV*² 1062. Workshop of the Coghill Painter; about 450–440 BC.

20 Attic red-figure pelike. Boston 63.2663. Andromeda being tied to the stakes. *AuA* 13 (1967) 1–7, pll. 1–2 (Schauenburg); *IGD* III.2.2; *LIMC* I Andromeda-I 2*; *MTS*² 117 and 147, AV 54; *Para* 448. Kensington Painter and Kensington Class; about 450–440 BC.

21 Attic red-figure calyx-krater. Basle BS 403. Andromeda tied to the stakes, Cepheus. *CVA* (3) pl. 10, 1–6 (with refs.); *GRBS* 32 (1991)

43, no. 4, pl. 8 (Green); *LIMC* I Andromeda 6*; *ARV*² 1684.15 *bis*. Kleophon Painter; about 440 BC.

22 Attic red-figure bell-krater. Caltanissetta V 1818, from Caltanissetta T. 52. Andromeda tied to a stake. *AuA* 13 (1967) 1–7, figs. 8 and 10 (Schauenburg); *MTS*² 117 and 147, AV 55. Circle of Polygnotos; about 450–440 BC.

23 Sicilian (Syracusan?) red-figure calyx-krater (fig. 19). Syracuse 66557, from Syracuse. Scene of a tragedy in performance (*Oedipus Tyrannus*?). *IGD* III.2.8; *RVSIS* fig. 429; Taplin (1993) fig. 6.112; Green (1994a) 60, fig. 3.6; Green and Handley (2001) 43, no 20 (ill.); Taplin (1997) 87, fig. 17; *LCS* Suppl. 3, 276, no. 98a. Gibil Gabib Group; third quarter of the fourth century BC.

24 Sicilian (Syracusan?) red-figure calyx-krater (fig. 20). Caltanissetta, from Capodarso. Scene of a tragedy in performance. *IGD* III.6.1; Pugliese Carratelli (1990) 112, figs. 143–4; Taplin (1993) fig. 6.111; *MTS*² 126, SV 2; *LCS* 601, no. 98, pl. 235.2–3; *LCS* Suppl. 1, 105. Gibil Gabib Group in the Lentini-Manfria Group; third quarter of the fourth century BC.

25 Attic red-figure oinochoe. Athens, coll. Vlasto, from Anavyssos. Comic Perseus on stage before two onlookers. *PhV*² 20, no. 1; *JHS* 65 (1945) pl. 5 (Karouzou); Brommer (1959) figs. 21–3; *IGD* IV. 1; Hamilton (1978); Schmidt (1995); *MMC*³ 31, AV 4; *ARV*² 1215, 1. Group of the Perseus Dance; *c.* 420 BC. Schmidt is rightly sceptical of the possibility of 'correct' interpretation.

26 Tarentine red-figure bell-krater. London F 151 (1849.6–20.13). Comic performance: old Chiron being helped up the stairs. *PhV*² 35 no. 37; *IGD* IV, 35; Taplin (1993) pl. 12, no. 6; Green and Handley (2001) 54 fig. 28 (colour); *RVAp* i, 100, no. 4/252. McDaniel Painter; about 380–370 BC.

27 Tarentine red-figure bell-krater (fig. 21). Sydney 88.02. Comic performance: naked male pursued by pretend Heracles. Trendall (1995) pll. 39, 40, 1 and colour pl. 5, 1; *RVAp* Suppl. ii, no. 5/200b. Lecce Painter; towards the middle of the fourth century BC.

28 Metapontine red-figure calyx-krater, Berlin F 3043, from Apulia. Comic performance: slave held by a rope about his neck and beaten by another. *PhV*² 49 no. 75; *IGD* IV, 15; *LCS* 43, no. 212, pl. 16, 5–6. Amykos Painter; end of the fifth century BC.

29 Metapontine or Tarentine red-figure calyx-krater, New York 24.97.104. Comic performance: capture of a thief before Scythian policeman. *PhV*² 53–4 no. 84; *IGD* IV, 13; *AntK* 41 (1998) pl. 5, 2 and

pl. 6, 1 (Schmidt); *RVAp* i, 46, no. 3/7. Tarporley Painter; early in the fourth century BC.

30 Tarentine red-figure bell-krater, Malibu, J. Paul Getty Museum 96.AE.114 (ex coll. Fleischman, F 98). Comic performance: old man with raised stick pursuing running slave. *Passion for Antiquities* 134–5 no. 59 (colour ill.); *RVAp* Suppl. ii, 74 no. 11/133b, pl. 12, 5–6. Meer Group; *c.* 360–350 BC.

31 Attic plainware oinochoe, London 1898.2–27.1, probably from Athens. Comic performance: man rowing a fish. *PhV*² 24 no. 9; *Hesperia* 24 (1955) pl. 37a; Green and Handley (2001) 51 fig. 26; *MMC*³ 33, AV 10. Late fifth century BC.

32 Shape and whereabouts unknown. Comic performance: man on a fish. *PhV*² 70–1 no. 144; *Hesperia* 24 (1955) 83 fig. 2 (Crosby). Probably Tarentine.

33 Tarentine red-figure bell-krater. Bari 3899, from Bari. Comic performance: man splitting giant egg with an axe. *PhV*² 27–8 no. 18; *IGD* IV, 26; Taplin (1993) pl. 19, no. 20; *RVAp* i, 148 no. 6/96. Dijon Painter; about 380–370 BC.

34 Tarentine red-figure bell-krater. Ruvo, coll. Jatta 901, from Ruvo. Comic performance: man and slave waving swords over a woman. *PhV*² 43 no. 57; *RVAp* i, 70 no. 4/46, pl. 24, 3–4. Reckoning Painter; second quarter of the fourth century BC.

35 Paestan red-figure calyx-krater. Berlin F 3044, probably from S. Agata. Comic performance: youths pulling old man off chest. *PhV*² 50 no. 76; *IGD* IV, 14; *RVSIS* ill. 352; *RVP* no. 2/125, pl. 44. Asteas (early work); *c.* 350 BC.

36 Paestan red-figure calyx-krater frr. Rome, Villa Giulia 50279, from Buccino. Comic performance: rape of Ajax. *PhV*² 54–5 no. 86; *IGD* IV, 30; *RVSIS* ill. 354; Taplin (1993) pl. 17, no. 17; *RVP* no. 2/130, pl. 54b. Asteas; *c.* 350–340 BC.

37 Paestan red-figure bell-krater. Salerno Pc 1812, from Pontecagnano. Comic performance: Pyronides dragging the citharode Phrynis. *PhV*² 43 no. 58, pl. 3b; *IGD* IV, 34; Taplin (1993) pl. 16, no. 16; *RVP* 65 no. 19, pl. 20c–d. Asteas (early); mid-fourth century BC.

38 Attic red-figure bell-krater, Linares, from Baños de la Muela, t. XVI. Comic performance: four males dancing and running. Blázquez (1975) 192–3, fig. 108, pll. 36–7. Perhaps about 380–370 BC.

39 Tarentine red-figure bell-krater, St Petersburg 2074. Comic performance: slave (B) and cook (P) running with spit and situla. *PhV*² 34

no. 34; Taplin (1993) pl. 14, no. 12; *RVAp* i, 148 no. 6/97. Dijon Painter; second quarter of the fourth century BC.

40 Tarentine red-figure calyx-krater, Rome, coll. Malaguzzi-Valeri 52. Comic performance: two slaves dancing and piping about an altar, old man looking on. *Studies* . . . *Trendall* 107–10, pl. 29 (Lo Porto); Taplin (1993) pl. 14a–b, no. 11; *RVAp* i, 400 no. 15/28, pl. 140, 5. Suckling-Salting Group; 360–350 BC.

41 Tarentine red-figure bell-krater (fig. 22). Copenhagen NM 15032. Comic performance: hetaira, old man, slave carrying chest. *Nationalmuseets Arbejdsmark* (1970) 131–40 (H. Salskov-Roberts); *RVAp* i, 133 no. 5/295. Jason Painter; towards the middle of the fourth century BC.

42 Sicilian (Syracusan?) red-figure calyx-krater (fig. 23). Messina, Soprintendenza, from Messina. Comic performance: woman, youth, slave dressed as a female, old man with stick. Ht 42.5cm. Spigo (1992) pl. IV (colour); *MeditArch* 5–6 (1992–93) 34–9, pll. 32, 2–3 and 33, 1 (Spigo). Manfria Painter; third quarter of the fourth century BC.

43 Athenian terracotta figurine (fig. 24). St Petersburg BB 166, from Great Bliznitza, Tomb 4. Ht 10.7cm. Peredolskaya (1964) pl. 4.1; *MMC*[3] 48, AT 10h. Early fourth century BC.

44 Athenian terracotta figurine (fig. 25). Oxford 1922.207, bought in Athens. Ht 10cm. Hetaira. *MMC*[3] 88, AT 74b, pl. 13a. Perhaps second quarter of the fourth century BC.

45 Athenian terracotta figurine (fig. 26). New York 13.225.21, from Athens. Ht 12.4cm. Bieber (1961) fig. 192; *DFA* (1968) fig. 96; *MMC*[3] 52, AT 16a. Beginning of the fourth century BC.

46 Terracotta figurine (fig. 27). London 1951.7–31.1. Ht 8cm. Higgins (1954) no. 1520, pl. 206; *MMC*[3] 125, AT 113d. Corinthian copy of an Athenian original; near the middle of the fourth century BC.

47 Athenian terracotta figurine (fig. 28). Athens 6068, from Tanagra. Ht 7.7cm. Hetaira. Winter (1903) 421/3; *MMC*[3] 126, AT 115b. Yellow-brown hair, red on lips and shoes, blue chiton. Near the middle of the fourth century BC.

48 Athenian terracotta figurine (fig. 29). London 1865.7 – 20.43 (C 5), probably from Athens. Ht 14cm. Pseudokore? Higgins (1954) no. 746, pl. 98; Green and Handley (2001) no. 39; *MMC*[3] 126, AT 114. Third quarter of the fourth century BC.

CHAPTER FIVE

Kallippides on the floor-sweepings: the limits of realism in classical acting and performance styles

Eric Csapo

THREE WINDOWS ON A DEBATE ON ACTING AND PRODUCTION STYLES

Evidence for acting in the fifth and fourth centuries comes from two sources: iconography, which is examined by J. R. Green in ch. 4 of this volume, and literature, including the texts of the plays, and various, passing references in other genres. The written sources offer little direct comment on acting and production in the classical Greek theatre. If we omit the schematic and dubious claims, mainly in the scholia and poets' biographies, which are derived from Hellenistic and later authors, and confine ourselves to classical authors, we are left with a few comments by Aristotle, many anecdotal, and some extended but distorted descriptions in comedy. Among these, three independent *testimonia* give evidence for broad developments in acting and production and all three indicate that in the late fifth century BC there occurred a significant movement towards something we may provisionally call 'realism'.

Mynniskos versus Kallippides

Mynniskos called his fellow actor, Kallippides, an ape (Arist. *Poetics* 1461b34–5). Mynniskos was the senior colleague. He had begun his career in the time of Aeschylus – is even said to have been Aeschylus' actor (*Life of Aeschylus* 15). Kallippides was the *enfant terrible* of the new generation. Mynniskos probably delivered his insult, if at all, in the 420s BC. The anecdote gives direct testimony to controversy already within the second or third generation of 'professional' actors.

The value of the anecdote does not depend on its historicity. Whether Mynniskos really called Kallippides an ape is beyond proof. Though anecdotes (and comedy) are not reliable as concerns specific truths, they usually owe their survival to success in expressing general perceptions.

The anecdote neatly captured a perceived shift in aesthetic sensibilities between generations. This is why Aristotle tells the tale – it illustrates 'how the older actors perceived the younger generation of actors'. Even if the anecdote is not much older than Aristotle, we will see that it perpetuates a debate which goes back to the late fifth century BC.

The meaning of Mynniskos' insult is frequently misunderstood. In Aristotle's words Mynniskos called Kallippides an ape 'because he went too far' (. . . ὡς λίαν ὑπερβάλλοντα). The Greek expression can mean either overdoing something or transgressing some boundary. Translators almost invariably take Aristotle's words here to refer to overacting, i.e. the use of grotesquely loud gestures. But the broader context of the passage shows that Aristotle understood the slur to refer not to *excessive* or *exaggerated gestures*, but rather to an *excess of gesture*,[1] i.e. excessive *mīmēsis*; not overacting, but imitating actions that are best not imitated at all (*Poetics* 1461 b26–1462a14, with my italics):

> One may well be at a loss to decide whether epic imitation is better than tragic. For if the less vulgar is the better – the less vulgar being always that which is directed to the better part of the audience – it is only too clear that the vulgar art is that which *imitates everything*. Supposing that their audience will understand nothing unless they *incorporate it in their representation*, some artists *will produce any gesture* . . . Now tragedy is just this sort of art. So too the older actors perceived the younger generation of actors: Mynniskos used to call Kallippides an ape because he went too far; the same opinion might be held of Pindaros. The relation of these actors to their older contemporaries is arguably the same as tragedy generally to epic. Epic, so the argument goes, is directed to a superior audience that has *no need for such gestures and postures*, but tragedy is directed toward an inferior. If then tragedy is vulgar, clearly it would be worse. We may answer, first of all, that this charge has nothing to do with poetry but with acting, since one can be intrusive with one's use of gestures even in an epic recitation . . . Secondly, *not all movement is objectionable – one would not condemn dance, for example – but only that which is in imitation of inferior people: Kallippides was censured, as are others today, for representing lower-class women.* Tragedy does its work even without movement, just like epic: by reading it you can tell what kind of tragedy it is. If then tragedy is superior in other respects, it is not necessarily subject to this fault.

Kallippides is not an ape because he immoderately reproduced gestures which might have been acceptable in moderation, but because, like an ape that *imitates everything* and *will produce any gesture*, Kallippides produced gestures that non-vulgar sensibilities would rather not see in tragedy, specifically the gestures of the non-élite.[2]

[1] As it is translated by *DFA* (1988) 174.

[2] 'Ape' in the late fifth century BC was a colloquial synonym for *panourgos*, namely someone who knows no limits to their behaviour: see Taillardat (1962) 19, 227–8; Eire (1997) 202.

Taken in context, it is clear that the complaint about Kallippides has less to do with some transhistorical criterion of good taste (who would argue for excessive gesture?), than with the specific disgust of an upper-class Greek at seeing heroes behave with the mannerisms of social inferiors. Even for Aristotle *mīmēsis* has its limits, in this case ideological ones, which are difficult to reconcile with the strict logic of his theory of art, and especially tragic art, as *mīmēsis*.[3] In the past scholars and translators have attempted to reconcile Aristotle's words to their own middle-class ethical standard by interpreting the words I translate as 'lower-class women' as referring to sluts or harlots (who never appear in tragedy).[4] But the expression 'οὐκ ἐλευθέρας γυναῖκας' refers, in Aristotle's sociolect, to all women below leisure class, and hence lower than the élite status appropriate to tragic heroines and Aristotle's readers.[5] What Aristotle complains about is not what we would term the unseemly or pornographic, but imitation of the simple gestures of ordinary women.

It is worth insisting upon a contextual reading of this anecdote because the usual reading in terms of 'excessive gestures' is often inserted into a traditional picture of tragedy's decline in the fourth century,[6] when 'the actors are more important now than poets' (Arist. *Rhet.* 3.1403b31), and the vulgar masses 'once silent, became vocal, pretending to know what is good art and what not, and instead of aristocracy in the arts a degenerate theatrocracy came into being' (Plato, *Laws* 3.700e6–701a3). According to this theory an increasingly self-assertive mass audience came to exercise a form of democratic control over music and drama (which meant that the mob dragged it down to the level of their vulgar tastes). The theory is of little value for cultural history beyond attesting the cultural alienation of the élite in the fourth-century Athenian democracy and is

3 Cf. the puzzlement of Lucas (1968) 251: 'ἡ ἅπαντα μιμουμένη [= "imitates everything" in the quotation above]: a strange phrase, since it is the business of a mimetic art to imitate. Possibly *mīmēsis* here is impersonation . . . In the light of what follows the meaning seems restricted to the over-playing of parts by actors'.

4 E.g. Dacier (1692) 505: 'les gestes des femmes deshonêtes et corrompuës'; Butcher (1929) 109: 'representing degraded women'; Potts (1962) 60: 'imitate women who are not respectable'; Hutton (1982) 78: 'their women were anything but ladies'. This interpretation of Aristotle is doubtless influenced by Aristophanes' portrayal of Euripidean heroines as 'whores' (*Frogs* 1043), to say nothing of his Muse (*Frogs* 1305–63), and of Euripides himself as an aged procuress (*Thesm.* 1172–1231), a comic distortion of characters like Phaedra's nurse.

5 Cf. ἀνελεύθερος. For *eleutheros* meaning 'leisure-class', as more frequently *eleutherios*, see the comments by Wood (1996) 129–31. This usage (see Arist. *Rhet.* 1.1367a30; *Pol.* 8.1341b13, 8.1342a19, *Probl.* 19.918b21) is most common in discussions of aesthetics, where it is less likely than in political or ethical discussions to generate confusion with the technical sense of 'free', antonym to 'slave'. If Aristotle simply meant 'slave women', he would have written *doulas*.

6 E.g. Haigh (1907) 277; Lesky (1983) 401–2. Vetta (1995) 66–7 alone correctly reads the anecdote as evidence of the development of gestural realism.

based on the problematic assumption that actors (who by this time were not élites) were more inclined to cater to the masses than poets (who still were).[7] For the modern reader (for whom realism is perhaps still a default style) it is not easy to sympathise with the notion that the first step to tragedy's moral and aesthetic decline was due to 'excessive *mīmēsis*'. In effect this must mean 'too much realism', if not simply 'too much acting'. Modern proponents of the theatrocracy theory must contend with the fact that Kallippides and his generation did what they did to drama at the time of the first production of the majority of Euripides', if not Sophocles', extant plays, and that these are usually not thought degenerate.

Possibly Mynniskos' slur on Kallippides was meant to signify something other than the meaning Aristotle sets upon it. If so, that is beyond our control. Certainly nothing encourages us to doubt that Mynniskos intended what Aristotle implies. Indeed, a comic fragment of the fifth (or very early fourth) century, and so contemporary with Kallippides, makes a similar complaint about the actor's style. The fragment is cited from Aristophanes' *Skēnas Katalambanousai* ('Women who take Control of the Stage-Building' [or possibly 'the Tents']):

> Like Kallippides I sit upon the ground on the floor-sweepings.[8]

Kassel and Austin point out that the language is similar to the description in the *Odyssey* of Odysseus as a helpless suppliant at the Phaeacian court, 'sitting on the ground at the hearth in the dust' (7.160), and Kock was doubtless right to suggest that Aristophanes alludes to Kallippides' role in a tragedy, Euripides' *Telephus*, for example, in which Kallippides

[7] The view that drama declined in the fourth century BC because of greedy actors and '*theatrokratia*, that tyranny of the spectators' is repeated most notably by Ghiron- Bistagne (1974a) 1335. Wallace (1997) has a partly (and in my view excessively) sympathetic discussion of the *theatrokratia* theory and its reception in modern scholarship (on his own evidence, the audience of the fifth century BC differed little from that of the fourth). The theatre did not, in fact, degenerate in the fourth century BC (cf. Easterling (1993a)).

[8] There are difficulties with the text. Kassel and Austin (*PCG* F 490) print the reading of the manuscripts of Pollux ὥσπερ ἐν Καλλιπίδῃ ἐπὶ τοῦ κορήματος καθέζομαι χαμαί, which must mean 'I sit on the ground upon the floor-sweepings as in *Kallippides*', a reference to the play *Kallippides* by Aristophanes' contemporary Strattis. I prefer Brunck's emendation which is printed by Kock (fr. 474): . . . ὡσπερεὶ Καλλιπίδης etc. 'like [the actor] Kallippides . . . ' For the metatheatrical (and paratragic) reference to tragic actors, cf. Eubulus *PCG* F 134 'I will do everything in the style of Nikostratos', presumably said by a comic messenger in reference to the tragic actor Nikostratos' famed skill in delivering messenger speeches. Either text supports the present argument. With Kassel and Austin's text we would have to imagine a character in Aristophanes' play (which, judging by the title, may have been about the theatre) who also appeared in an undignified posture in Strattis' play, and this character would surely be none other than the *kōmōidoumenos* Kallippides himself.

portrayed the hero as a suppliant or beggar.[9] If this is right, Aristophanes ridicules Kallippides for realistically portraying the degradation of a mythological hero which an older actor like Mynniskos would have shown, if at all, with genteel restraint. This willingness to 'imitate anything' doubtless also contributed to the proverbial tale of Kallippides' dismissal as a 'buffoon' (*deikēliktas*) by the Spartan (hence conservative) king Agesilaus.[10]

Aeschylus versus Euripides

The contest of Aristophanes' *Frogs* sets Euripides against Aeschylus for the 'chair' of tragedy in the underworld. It is our first extended extant piece of ancient dramatic criticism. What most strikes the modern reader is that the criticism is entirely axiological (who is the better poet?) and that the criteria of value are predominantly moral and political, not aesthetic. It has sometimes been asked why Aristophanes did not make Sophocles part of this debate. Some even infer that *Frogs* was substantially written before Sophocles' death and that Aristophanes' lines excusing Sophocles' non-participation in the contest were last-minute additions (786–94). But the assumption that Aristophanes would have pitted Euripides against Sophocles, if only death had made him available in time, fails to see that the power and resonance of this debate, at least for the Athenian audience, went far beyond merely dramatic values. Aeschylus and Euripides represent positions, not poets, and these positions have all the social and ideological depth we find in other Aristophanic debates, that of the *Clouds*, for example, where classes, generations, moral codes and conceptual universes clash head on.[11] The choice of Aeschylus and Euripides to represent the poles of the debate in *Frogs* had a political logic which overshadows the poetic. Aeschylus represented tradition and the values of a heroic past. Euripides represented modernity and the values of a 'radically' democratic present.

The binarism which governs the caricatures of Aeschylus and Euripides is expressed mainly in social and political terms; the binarism which governs the caricature of their dramatic styles extends to subject-matter, dramaturgy, costume, gesture and diction. Euripides is low class

9 A text and translation, with commentary, of Euripides' *Telephus* is available in Collard, Cropp and Lee (1995) 17–52.

10 Plut. *Life of Agesilaus* 21, *Apophth. Lacon.* 212F; Apostol. 13.66 in *CPG* vol. II, 593.

11 Cf. Dover (1993) 32: 'Comparison with *Clouds* indicates that Aristophanes has assimilated the contrast between Aeschylus and Euripides to the generalized contrast between old and new . . .'

(947), self-professedly democratic (951), and supported by the demos of the underworld (779). He is a technician: his words are not the products of inspiration, but banausic craftsmanship (826–9, 956–7; cf. *Thesm.* 52–7). He is likened to a sophist, giving exhibitions of his skill to the bedazzlement of the degenerate 'mob' (771–6). Aeschylus by contrast is presented as a friend of the élite of the underworld (783), hostile to the leaders of the democracy, whom he refers to as 'demo-chimps' (1085), and no friend of the Athenian majority (807–8). His advice for saving Athens is to turf out the current democratic leaders and bring back the exiled aristocrats and oligarchs (1446–8), essentially the same advice as Aristophanes himself gives in the parabasis.[12] The political colour of Aeschylus' portrait is best marked in his complaint that Euripides taught the sailors of the ship *Paralos* to talk back to their superiors (1071–2). *Paralos* is a revealing example. At the time of the oligarchic coup at Athens in 411, the ship played a leading role in the democratic mutiny of the Athenian fleet at Samos, and this mutiny eventually led to the restoration of democracy at Athens. The sailors of the *Paralos* were 'all of them free men and Athenians', says Thucydides, 'and eternally opposed to oligarchy, even when it did not exist' (8.73). This caricature of Aeschylus as an alienated aristocrat is complemented by his overwhelming passion (816), which appears as the source of his inspiration, and especially by his indignation and rage (814, 838, 855–6, 859, 994, 998, 1006), which Dionysus must repeatedly restrain (843, 851, 927, 1132–4, cf. 922). This of course suits the caricature of his dramas as pervaded by the military ideals of earlier generations, whom he fostered with his 'drama filled with Ares', while Euripides created a generation of draft-dodgers and swindlers (1013–42).

Frogs gives the impression that Aeschylus wrote only on military themes in an imposing style, with verbal and visual magnificence designed to stun the audience (833–4, 862, 911–20). He maintains that heroes should wear uncommonly elegant costumes (1061) and use 'bigger words' than ordinary mortals (1060). Euripides and Dionysus find his language pompous, grandiose and unintelligible (923–6, 929–31, 940, 1056–7), while at the same time primitive and inarticulate (836–9).

Euripides, by contrast, boasts that he introduced to the stage the things of everyday life, which the audience knew and could judge by experience to be true to life or not (959–61). Aeschylus claims that, unlike Euripides, he never introduced anything as unseemly as women in love (1043–4). Here the poet of Ares is opposed to the poet of Aphrodite (1021, 1045).

[12] *Frogs* 718–37. See Dover (1993) 75, who notes that the advice is set in cautiously ambivalent terms.

Euripides defends himself by insisting that Phaedra's love for Hippolytus was a 'true story'; Aeschylus replies 'yes, true, by Zeus, but a poet must hide what is unseemly and not bring it on stage nor produce it' (1053–4). This also applies to the realistic portrayal of lame heroes and the 'rags' with which Euripides costumed his down and out (or disguised) heroes (842, 846): Aeschylus charges that Euripides 'first dressed kings in rags, so they would seem more piteous' (1064). Showing their halting gait is characterised as an act of *thraseia*, 'impudence' (846), a transgression of proper restraint. Euripides boasts that he also reduced the grandiose language of tragedy to make his heroes speak 'like ordinary human beings'.[13] Euripides is particularly abused for having modelled his verse on different literary genres (943), speech genres (841, cf. *Ach.* 398) and musical genres, some very low (843, 1297). He claims that his use of language was 'democratic' (952) insofar as he gave equal voice to women, slaves, young and old (949–50). For this audacity, says Aeschylus, he should have been killed (951).

Sophocles versus Euripides

We might compare a third document. Chapter twenty-five of Aristotle's *Poetics* is devoted to celebrated problems in ancient literary criticism and chiefly the defence of poetic authorities against the charge of representing immoral, improbable, or impossible objects. Such charges, says Aristotle, can often be dismissed by recognising that an artist may imitate three different categories of objects: 'either the way things were or are, or the way things are said or seem to be, or the way things ought to be' (1460b10–11). To illustrate the point Aristotle reports that 'Sophocles said he portrayed men as they should be, but Euripides portrayed them as they are' (1460b34). The meaning of the passage is much disputed. Suffice it here to say that more controversy attaches to the first term of the opposition than to the second: Euripides portrayed people 'realistically', but what is the sense of 'should' in Sophocles' alleged portrayal of people as they 'should be'? The statement is often over-interpreted as an unqualified opposition between 'idealism' and 'realism'.[14]

Aristotle introduces the statement as a possible defence against the charge of 'false reproduction', and an appeal to idealism is no defence in Aristotle's books against amimetic practice (though it might have satisfied Plato (*Rep.* 5.472d)). Verisimilitude (τὸ πιθανόν) is a central concern

[13] Dover's translation for ἀνθρωπείως (1993) 325. [14] See Halliwell (1986) 135–6, n. 39.

of Aristotle's theory of art, and verisimilitude is produced by what is possible, and, since we do not consider things possible which have never happened, real models are indispensable if art is to have its proper effect (*Poetics* 1451 b16–19).

Nevertheless, Aristotle surely understood some aspect of what we mean by 'idealisation' to lie behind the statement ascribed to Sophocles. This is probably the same kind of cosmetic surgery upon the real which Aristotle himself recommends to the tragedian. Tragic heroes, he says, should be both like ordinary men and better than ordinary men (*Poetics* ch. 15). In creating them, the poet should act as do good portrait painters, who 'while making men similar, paint them more beautiful'. 'In the same way', continues Aristotle, 'a poet imitating men who are irascible or too easy-going or of some other such quality, makes them good, while yet such as they are' (1454b 10–13). Heroes must be believable, but also better, in order to arouse pity and fear. There is also some concern for what Aristotle imagines to be the cognitive function of drama. The cognitive function of poetry in general requires the excision of unnecessary details of material reality: where history is concerned to represent particular truths, poetry is more serious and philosophical insofar as the poet attempts, by stripping his models of all that is contingent and idiosyncratic, to represent a universal truth (*Poetics* ch. 9). Thus some have interpreted Sophocles' self-assessment to mean that he portrayed characters 'as they should be [portrayed]'. In this case 'should be' has less to do with an ideal world, than a different criterion for accessing the real.

If Sophocles ever made such a statement he is likely to have meant considerably less by it than did Aristotle. Since Aristotle gives no context for Sophocles' putative statement, we may guess that Sophocles intended his opposition to be taken morally. This is certainly suggested by the context supplied by the *Gnomologium Vaticanum* (*TrGF* T 53b), where the *bon mot* is Sophocles' response to the question: 'Why, Sophocles, do you make human characters good, while Euripides makes them worthless?' A moralising context is also implied by a version in which Philoxenus responds to the question why his women are worthless, while Sophocles' are good (*TrGF* T 172).

However Sophocles may have conceived his own practice, the anecdote once more associates Euripides with a style of production which was perceived by contemporaries or near-contemporaries as 'realistic' and placed in opposition to a more restrained style of production, which only admitted what was consistent with good taste or moral decency.

The anecdotes and the comic contest in *Frogs* attest to a perceived opposition in dramatic values, diachronically between generations, and synchronically between individual actors and poets. They indicate, further, that the period of greatest polarisation was approximately 425 to 405 BC, and that the second term of this opposition can be characterised as the rise of 'realism' in the use of language, costume, gesture and characterisation.

In contrasting Euripides to the other tragedians, comedy to tragedy, or New Comedy to Old, classical scholars have never hesitated to use the term 'realism', or the often synonymous 'naturalism' (beyond occasionally placing the terms in 'scarequotes' as I have done), particularly in discussions of characterisation, stagecraft, and the dramatic use of time and space.[15] The terms are indeed helpful for understanding the development of classical drama, notwithstanding the occasional error (necessary to realists, but fatal to their critics) of confusing the art-historical term with its ontological cognate. One must keep in mind, however, that the term is a metaphor comparing ancient drama to a dominant style of Western art and literature in the eighteenth and nineteenth centuries. Like all metaphors, it has its utility, but also its limitations. Like its more modern counterpart, ancient drama developed a much richer typology of human character, and a more variegated means of portraying its diversity. Unlike its modern counterpart ancient drama was far more selective in the types of social diversity it described. This selectivity is all the more striking because, as we will see, the criteria of selection and avoidance change *toto caelo* from the late fifth to the late fourth century BC.

Since costume and gesture have been studied by J. R. Green in chapter 4, the greater part of the discussion which follows focuses upon verbal mimicry. The concluding section of this chapter will briefly compare trends in the actor's use of language with those of costume and gesture.

PERFORMING LANGUAGE

Some recent scholarship denies that ancient acting included verbal mimicry.[16] It argues that, because the protagonist competed for a prize, his chief interest lay in remaining conspicuous behind the roles he played.

[15] For example, the particularly useful discussion by Fantuzzi (1990) of tragic time and space.

[16] Pavlovskis (1977), Jouan (1983), Damen (1989) and others have argued that the main actor did not alter the quality of his voice in order to be recognised by the public and increase his chances of winning the acting competition; Ringer (1998) speaks confidently of 'non-naturalistic delivery' in ancient theatre. Their views are criticised by Vetta (1995) 68–78 and Sifakis (1995).

Given the convention of masked acting, actors were most readily identified by their voices. It would seem to follow therefore that the actor's interest in winning the competition prevented him from altering his natural speaking voice to suit any particular role.

The argument wildly exaggerates the difficulty experienced by ancient audiences in following the main actor's part in a drama where two or three (speaking) actors played a very limited cast of characters, and, especially so, given the tendency of most fifth-century drama to focus the action upon a single dominant character, which in practice seems generally to have been played by the protagonist.[17] But quite apart from this, the basic premise is wrong. Not the protagonist, but the acting troupe competed for the prize. True, only the name of the protagonist was officially recognised, but he won the prize not for his individual performance in competition with his subordinates, but for the performance of his troupe in competition with other troupes. It was therefore never imperative that the identity of any individual actor be transparent behind his mask.[18] Yet even supposing these scholars are correct regarding the practices of tragic protagonists, there is nothing to justify their generalised claim that ancient actors never altered the character of their voice. Their argument permits no conclusions about the practices of subordinate actors, who generally played far more roles than the protagonists, and no conclusions about the practices of comic actors. The actor's competition is indeed irrelevant for many comedies: the comic actor's prize was not introduced to the Dionysia until after 329 BC.[19]

Comedy provides ample evidence for vocal mimicry. Here characters frequently impersonate others. At times instruction in the art of mimicry even forms part of the comic action. At *Thesmophoriazusae* 267 the Kinsman (the protagonist) is instructed to 'feminize the tone of his voice', and then immediately enters the Thesmophorion chattering like a housewife to an imaginary maid;[20] in *Ecclesiazusae* the disguised women, exhorted to speak 'like men' (149), march out singing an 'old man's song, imitating the manner of countrymen' (277–9). In some cases the alteration of the actor's voice is necessary to avoid confusion. The sharing of a single role between two actors, though generally avoided in tragedy, is frequently necessary in comedy and especially in Menander.[21] The audience would presumably have difficulty recognising the identity of

[17] *DFA* (1988) 135–53. [18] Sifakis (1995).

[19] This is not to diminish the importance of the Lenaea, where a comic actor's prize was awarded from about 432 BC.

[20] Handley (1985a) 395–6. [21] *DFA* (1988) 154; Gomme and Sandbach (1973) 18.

the character unless both actors sharing the role acted with one voice. At *Lysistrata* 879 the actor playing Cinesias must supply the voice of the baby he holds by 'ventriloquism' – unlikely to succeed if the actor refuses to change the quality of his voice.[22] In Menander's monologues characters frequently quote one or more other characters in direct speech, sometimes with no introductory words such as 'he said', an act impossible to follow unless all the voices employed by the actor were audibly different.[23] Quintilian indeed complains of precisely this excess of mimicry in Menander's speeches: 'even if [comic actors] play the part of a youth they nonetheless speak with a quavering or effeminate voice when reporting in a narration the speech of an old man, as for example in the prologue of *Hydria*, or a woman, as in *Georgos'* (*Inst.* 11.3.91). This direct testimony for voice modulation by actors belongs to a much later date,[24] but Menander is unlikely to have written this way unless mimicry were already an established part of the actor's art. Similar juxtaposition of different voices appears in Agathon's song in *Thesmophoriazusae* (101–29), where only the modulation of the voice could show that Agathon is singing both parts of a duet between a priestess and female chorus (both voices are described as effeminate (131, 192)). The texts of Old Comedy also represent dialect and non-standard speech in direct quotation by Athenian characters of non-Athenians or the speech patterns of known individuals.[25] Are we to imagine that comic poets freely indulged an appetite for linguistic realism shunned by their actors? In antiquity dramatic poets wrote for dramatic performers, and it is an old, bad habit of traditional philology to suppose otherwise. We should rather infer that the poets' motive for introducing into their dramas such a medley of often clearly differentiated speech patterns was precisely to allow actors to display virtuosity in parading a patter of distinct voices. Clearly vocal mimicry was an important part of the comic actor's art by the late fifth century BC.

Slight and unevenly scattered as it is, the evidence shows an overall growth of interest in vocal mimicry among comic actors from the later fifth to the fourth and third centuries BC. This emerges not only from evidence for the form of delivery (as above), but from changes in the form and structure of the comic narrative. Increasingly common from

22 Marshall (1997).

23 E.g. Men. *Samia* 256–7; *Sikyonios* 257–8, 264–6; *Misoumenos* 698–700, 799 (Arnott). Handley (forthcoming) has an excellent discussion; see also Handley, this volume. The sparse use of 'quotatives' in direct speech is a distinctive feature of Menander's drama (Bers (1997) 117–18).

24 In addition to Quintilian, cited above, see Plut. *Sympotic Questions* = *Mor.* 711 C, Lucian *Nigrinus* 11.

25 Colvin (1999) 265–95.

411 BC are comedies involving themes of disguise and (especially cross-gender) role-playing, which make large demands upon the actor's mimic talents. Soon afterwards there is also a striking change in the pattern of role distribution in Aristophanic comedy. Earlier comic protagonists were content with a single dominant role, but after 405 BC Aristophanic comedy assigns the protagonist a much greater diversity of roles; Vetta at least explains this change as a response to the chief actor's desire to display his powers of mimicry.[26] In the fourth century BC skill at vocal mimicry might be the basis of an actor's claim to fame, as was the case with the comic actor Parmenon (said to have been 'emulated by many'), whose imitation of a squealing pig became proverbial. By this time even tragic actors cultivated such skills: Theodoros, the most famous tragic actor of the century, was particularly remembered for his success in imitating the sound of a windlass.[27] Plato cites these actors in a complaint about the tendency of narrative in direct speech, of which drama was the most extreme form, to involve 'imitation in voice and gesture' requiring 'every kind of pitch and rhythm if it is to be delivered properly, since it involves all manner of shifts'.[28] Such effects were evidently popular among contemporary theatre audiences – like Aristotle, Plato associated this mimetic excess with the tastes of men of low birth and breeding.

The refinement of the actor's powers of vocal mimicry was only part of series of developments in the language of dramatic performance. The texts of the plays show a marked turn towards realism in vocabulary and speech rhythm, especially from the last quarter of the fifth century onwards. Aristophanes' Euripides justly boasted that he tamed the high-flown language of tragedy and brought it closer to ordinary speech. Aristotle recommends natural speech to orators as most convincing and least likely to arouse suspicion – the illusion of natural speech 'succeeds when one composes from a vocabulary chosen from normal conversation' – and he adds that 'Euripides was the first to do this and showed the way' (*Rhetoric* 3.1404b24–5). As Aristotle implies, later dramatists followed his lead: Menander's vocabulary is far closer to ordinary speech than that of either Aristophanes or Euripides.[29] Euripides also led

[26] Vetta (1995) 77.
[27] Plut. *How the Young Man Should Study Poetry* 3. = *Mor.* 18B–C. Cf. Pl. *Rep.* 3.397a–b, *Laws* 2.669c–d.
[28] Plato *Rep.* 3.397a–c. Further evidence for tragedy is hard to find, but it is noteworthy that tragic messengers usually use direct quotation for characters played by the same actor (Dicken (1999)), presumably to get the voice right. The scholiast to *Orestes* 176 (a play whose musical notation survived till the Roman period) informs us that Electra's monody is 'sung on the top and very high' (see Hall, ch. 1, n. 26 and Falkner, this volume).
[29] *Rhet.* 3.1404a 30–5; Del Corno (1979) 280–1.

the way in modifying the iambic trimeters (and trochaic tetrameters) of tragedy to sound less stiff, deliberate and artificial.[30] Cropp and Fick are surely right to associate this development 'with Euripidean "realism" ' and with 'Euripides' determination to reflect his own world in the inherited and stylised world of the tragic legends'.[31] This loosening of metrical forms increases radically and consistently from the 420s until the time of Euripides' death. Speech rhythms are also measurably freer in the late plays of Sophocles. The concern to bring dramatic verse closer to natural language finds its proper culmination in early Hellenistic comedy, which avoids metres other than iambic trimeter and trochaic tetrameter, and nearly dispenses with song altogether.

The dramatic texts also show an increasing interest in language as a vehicle for characterisation, especially from the 420s onwards. Scholarship tends to treat this phenomenon in isolation as a more or less fortuitous poetic or literary achievement. Historical explanation is only really possible if we view the 'literary' evidence in the larger context of the trend towards realism in dramatic *performance*. In large part the growing realism of the language of our texts presupposes the developing skill of contemporary actors in capturing different personalities through voice and gesture. The actor's interest in developing the precision and diversity of his mimetic talents is in turn largely driven by the large economic incentives of the developing star system. The initial most powerful stimulus to the development of the star system for actors was the spread of theatre from Attica to the rest of Greece, which can be dated to the final decades of the fifth century BC.[32] For this reason the characters of Euripides and New Comedy are generally better individualised by their vocabulary, style, register, dialect, mode of delivery, metre, and syntax than the characters of Aeschylus and Sophocles, tragedy, and Old Comedy, respectively. By the time of Menander the mimicry of individual speech patterns is systematic and extensive.[33]

Despite this, ancient 'realism' falls short of its modern counterpart in the extent of its development. This is partly because it also differs in kind. Modern realism strives to reveal character inwardly as a private and unique essence. But, as Bakhtin acutely observed, the ancients generally constructed character outwardly as a public persona defined by a broad typology oriented less to psychological than to the sociological

30 Devine and Stephens (1981) and (1983); Cropp and Fick (1985).
31 Cropp and Fick (1985) 3.
32 The evidence and implications of this development are studied by Csapo (forthcoming).
33 For Menander's individualisation of speech: Sandbach (1970), Del Corno (1975), Arnott (1995).

distinctions that define one's *état civil.*[34] In the fifth century BC the differentiation of language is generally limited to broad categories of sex, age, ethnicity and social class. Even in New Comedy, the most realistic of the traditional dramatic genres, linguistic portraiture seems only to have diversified within the received typological framework, especially in the category of social class, adding more precise markings to distinguish the citizen from the slave, and the leisure-class gentleman from various representatives of the working class (the latter is curiously divided into a limited set of 'professions'). Yet in contrast with the universal and steadily incremental development towards more familiar vocabulary or freer verse, the development of realism in the linguistic representation of character shows interesting anomalies over the course of the fifth and fourth centuries BC.

THE LIMITS OF ANCIENT REALISM

Interest in representing women's speech seems to have grown steadily in the fifth and fourth centuries BC: several recent studies demonstrate that women's speech is more distinctive in Euripides than in Sophocles or Aeschylus, more distinctive in Aristophanes than in Euripides, and most distinctive in Menander.[35] The anomalies appear when we consider linguistic differentiation by ethnicity or class.

The direct representation of foreign speech is not attested in any genre of Greek literature before tragedy.[36] Paradoxically, it is our earliest extant tragedian, Aeschylus, who offers the most extensive representations of the tone, syntax and vocabulary of barbarian speech. *Persians* attempts to imitate the Greek spoken by Persians through formalities, frequent Ionicism, and the use of Persian words, names and exclamations.[37] In the highly emotional choral song preceding and accompanying the attack made by the Egyptians on the Danaids in *Suppliants* (776–871), we find Egyptian and North African Greek (Cyrenean) words, as well as a number of 'unusual, archaic, and cacophonous' words, all peppered with a great density of 'cries, repetition, and alliteration to substantiate

[34] Bakhtin (1981) 130–46.

[35] McClure (1995), cf. McClure (1999); Sommerstein (1995); Bain (1984).

[36] The fragments of Hipponax contain Lydian and Phrygian words. Since he is an Ephesian, this could equally be characterised as colloquialism. See Colvin (1999) 39–54, esp. 50–2.

[37] Hall (1989) 76–84, (1996) 22–3; cf. Colvin (1999) 77. The high incidence of words with long alphas may also represent an Aeschylean attempt to imitate the aural impact of Iranian: see Morenilla-Talens (1989).

his Egyptians' claim to be heterophone'.[38] Such characterisation is uncommon in the later tragedians. 'Only one reference to the fact that a character speaks a foreign language exists in the extant plays of Sophocles (*Ajax* 1263) . . . Tecmessa's foreignness might . . . have been developed by drawing attention to her speech, but Sophocles does not raise the point.'[39] Three fragmentary plays of Sophocles, not certainly tragedies, included items of foreign vocabulary.[40] Euripides revives some of the Aeschylean effects in his late monodies and choral odes, especially those influenced by the New Music (which had an Eastern flavour), but not in dialogue.[41] Realism in the characterisation of foreign speech in tragedy can therefore be said to decline over the course of the fifth century. Moreover, despite incipient realism in the characterisation of foreign non-Greek speech, foreign Greek dialect is never used to characterise non-Athenians in tragedy. Even after he announces in the *Libation-bearers* that he will 'imitate the Phocian dialect', Orestes speaks a perfectly normal poetic Attic.[42] Late fifth-century comedy is, by contrast, very free in its representation of both non-Greek and non-Attic speech: Colvin finds 'no example in extant Old Comedy of a non-Athenian Greek or barbarian whose speech is not marked as foreign in some way' (and he argues that dialect imitation, at least, has more to do with the genre's realism than with humour).[43]

The representation of sociolect presents a still more anomalous picture. Stevens found that Aeschylus was most concerned to differentiate the speech of lower-caste characters, which he did 'partly by colloquial expressions, partly by touches of naïveté, garrulity or sententiousness'.[44] The same is true of Sophocles, where 'colloquialisms are sometimes admitted, particularly in the speech of servants or messengers' as in

38 Hall (1989) 120, 118; cf. Colvin (1999) 78. 39 Bacon (1961) 64.

40 Phrygian and Persian words appear in *Shepherds* (*TrGF* Sophocles F 515, 519, 520), *Wedding of Helen* (F 183), both of which may be satyr-plays – see Heynen and Krumeich (1999) 391–3 – and *Troilus* (F 631, 634), which is more probably, but not certainly, a tragedy. Eastern colouring is also attested in *Prisoners of War* and *Triptolemus*, where the word 'Ionian' was used for 'Greek' (F 56, 617). See Colvin (1999) 81–3.

41 Hall (1989) 119–21, 126–7.

42 *Cho.* 563–4. See Dover (1987) 240 *contra* Stevens (1945) 96. It would be a disturbing anomaly if Orestes' lines were delivered in Phocian dialect despite our text: see Revermann (1997) 36–41; Colvin (1999) 75–6.

43 Colvin (1999) 295, 302–6.

44 Stevens (1945) 95; cf. Arnott (1995) 160–1. According to West (1990b) 5, the use of colloquialism as a means of characterisation appears to be a diachronic development even within Aeschylus' oeuvre, and does not appear before the *Oresteia:* 'minor characters in the earlier plays do not seem to be treated to these touches of the demotic', but 'on the contrary . . . seem to speak with a rather stiff formality'.

Aeschylus, but more rarely.[45] Low-caste characters account for 60 per cent of Aeschylus' colloquialisms but only 24 per cent of Sophocles'.[46] Yet even when Sophocles gives colloquialism to upper-caste heroes, it is frequently for the purpose of revealing them to be vulgar and undignified, like Menelaus in *Ajax*, or to be losing their composure through such emotions as anger or excitement.[47] Colloquialism thus remains associated with plebeian qualities more often than the bare statistics suggest. Satyr drama may also use colloquialism to distinguish the bestial (satyrs, Silenus, ogres) from heroic characters who speak a more uniformly tragic language.[48] By contrast, Euripides and Aristophanes are very free with colloquialism and apply it indiscriminately to both high- and low-caste characters, contributing 'to a general scaling down of heroic splendour to something nearer to the ordinary life of men'.[49]

Here is a paradox for any who might have expected to see a steady progression in the realism of linguistic portraiture. Euripides may be said to champion the trend insofar as it involves a general devolution of style to the level of common speech. Yet in the use of language to differentiate social status the opposite is true. As Stevens says, 'there is a greater degree of realism [in Aeschylus and Sophocles] than in much of the work of Euripides, whose tendency is to reduce the legendary heroes and heroines to a more everyday level both in thought and in speech, so that there is less room for distinction between them and the characters of humbler status'.[50] Similarly, students of Old Comedy have not failed to contrast the exuberant characterisation of non-Greeks and speakers of other Greek dialects with the surprising fact 'that comedy did not exploit the humorous potentialities of solecism and malapropism in the language of slaves or illiterate citizens . . . even the Sausage-seller of *Knights*, whose hold on reading and writing is shaky (188–9), speaks as well as anyone else'.[51] That Old Comedy was capable of such realism is shown by its use of non-standard Attic to characterise prominent real-life Athenian politicians like Cleophon and Hyperbolus when the comic poets wished to intimate their foreign birth or poor education. Non-standard Attic

[45] Stevens (1937) 183. [46] Stevens (1945) 95.

[47] Fraenkel (1977) 34–7, 44–5, 49, 52, 61, 64–5, 69–72; Rossi (1989). Resolution is sometimes also used by Sophocles to mark vulgar and undignified characters: see, for example, Webster (1970) 161; Fraenkel (1977) 75–6.

[48] Seaford (1984) 47–8; Seidensticker (1999) 15–16.

[49] Stevens (1945) 97, cf. Stevens (1937) 182–3. The incidence of colloquialism does vary between plays, being proportionately much higher in *Orestes* than elsewhere: Stevens (1979) 64–5.

[50] Stevens (1945) 95.

[51] Dover (1987) 19, cf. 241–4. See also Halliwell (1990); Del Corno (1997); Colvin (1999) 295.

was also used to mock the high social pretensions of real-life celebrities like Alcibiades. The odd thing is that sociolect, which was freely used to (mis)represent specific (élite) individuals, was avoided in the linguistic representation of social groups within the polis.[52]

New Comedy, by contrast, offers the fullest and freest dramatic representation of sociolect in the traditional dramatic genres. Plutarch, indeed, found Aristophanes' use of language completely inept in contrast with Menander's genius for discriminating the language appropriate to each age, gender, class and profession.[53] Unlike Aristophanes, Menander was careful to mark the language of slaves and working-class characters with obscenity, frequent oaths, vivid, colourful, colloquial, or technical language, and, especially in the case of poor rustics, laconic, syntactically disjointed or rhetorically inept speech.[54] Conversely, however – and, once again, in total contrast with Old Comedy – New Comedy shows little interest in portraying foreign speech, even despite the fact that many plays are set outside Athens or revolve around non-Athenian characters. The one notable exception seems to prove the rule: in Menander's *Aspis* a character puts on a Doric accent (430–64), but only because he is pretending to be a doctor: the dialect sooner characterises the working-class professional than the foreigner.[55]

As Green shows in this volume, the history of dramatic costume and gesture shows a similar pattern of developing realism combined with a highly selective and shifting focus. The best evidence is provided by comic costume. Barring props and clothing, Old Comic costume allowed no closer social distinctions than male and female, old and young, citizen and foreigner (though specific individuals received portrait masks). A uniform body served all Old Comic actors, with padded stomach, breast and buttocks, and an enlarged and (for male characters) normally exposed phallus (see Green, this volume). The iconographic evidence shows that these features gradually gave way to a more naturalistic costume over the course of the fourth century BC, but, significantly, at different rates and to different degrees. The phallus, padding and the more grotesque

52 Colvin (1999) 281–94. One exception may be the precious speech of the upper-class youth, Pheidippides (Ar. *Clouds* 872–3), but the passage is not easy to interpret. A passage of the comic poet Plato's *Metics* may be another, but there is no reason to think the chorus was composed of metics, rather than, say, citizen *kōmōidoumenoi*, nor any reason to suppose that the solecism of *PCG* Plato F 83, was spoken by one of them.

53 Plut. *Comparison of Aristophanes and Menander* 853D–E.

54 See esp. Arnott (1995), though his catalogue is by individual rather than type.

55 The chief medical schools were in Doric Sicily and Cos. It is not known whether Plautus or Alexis is responsible for the pseudo-Punic in *Poenulus* 930–49, though Plautus is the more likely candidate.

facial features of the traditional comic mask became markers of social inferiority. They disappear first (*c.* 350 BC) in the costume of the young man of good family who is the focal point of audience sympathy. Some time later old men (of the sort who in New Comedy are normally of the leisured class or wealthy merchants) acquire decent shin-length tunics, shed all their body padding, beyond a residue around the belly, and lose the more grotesque of their facial features. At the other end of the social hierarchy, slaves always retained pot bellies, though, by the late fourth century BC, there was a general reduction in the volume of body padding and especially the (for males) improbably prominent breast and buttocks. Similarly, though the slave's tunic grew just long enough that the phallus was not normally visible, it was still short enough to expose the (now smaller) genitals when a slave adopted a seated position, and short enough that the phallus could easily be withdrawn for the purpose of an occasional joke.[56] The physiognomy of the free working-class males in New Comedy was carefully positioned somewhere between the poles of upper-class decency and servile deformity. Parasites (a 'profession' in later comedy) often, soldiers and pimps sometimes, and cooks generally retained bellies. The tunic of parasites, cooks, farmers and soldiers is shorter than that of élite characters. Moreover, the distorted features of fifth-century comic masks, which differed only in terms of sex, age, or ethnicity, became highly differentiated in the later fourth century in conformity with currently fashionable physiognomic ideas. The toadies and parasites (i.e. free unemployed dependents of the élite families) have a hook nose which is said to show shamelessness, a short neck which indicates treachery, raised eyebrows to show malevolence, and to these the actor added hunched shoulders to indicate an 'unfree' disposition.[57] His semi-servile status is further emphasised by his broken ears (frequently boxed by his patron), and the strigil and oil bottle which serve as his regular attributes (he uses them to rub down his patron). In this world an undistorted body was the privilege of the free, and freedom meant economic independence.

Though New Comedy also admits foreign physiognomies, they are only visible in the masks of slaves and working-class characters. Of the latter category the best attested is the foreign cook called the 'Cicada',

[56] E.g. *MNC*³, vol. II, 4 (1 AT 3), Plautus *Rudens* 429. It is not clear that the phallus ever disappeared entirely from comic costume. There is good later evidence which cannot easily be dismissed as iconographic archaism or survival: see, for a good example, Herrmann (1994) no. 108.

[57] For the description of the mask and attributes, see Pollux, *Onomasticon* 4.148, 120, with *MMC*³, vol. I, 22–3. The physiognomic 'readings' appear in [Aristotle] *Physiognomonica* 811 a 4 (hunched shoulders), 17 (short neck), 34–5 (hooknose). Cf. Green, ch. 4 above, n.16.

who has an African physiognomy, but 'the monuments make it clear that the foreign cook was a far less common – or conceivably less interesting – character in the plays than his native fellow tradesman'; the 'Sicilian' parasite and the foreign 'Portrait-Like' masks, both attested by Pollux, are similarly rare, if they appear at all, in the monuments.[58] It would seem, in any case, that New Comic costume, like New Comic language, showed little interest in ethnicity for its own sake and used foreign physiognomy primarily as a marker of social status.

The history of tragic costume, though much more elusive, seems consistent with this pattern. For fifth-century tragic costume and gesture we must rely on Aristophanes and Aristotle to capture some of the sense of scandal that accompanied the levelling of the tragic hero's dignity when Euripides dressed him in rags and Kallippides portrayed him with the gestures of commoners. By the mid-fourth century, however, the archaeological evidence studied by Green shows that the costumes of the non-heroic caste, of tragic messengers, for example, are clearly differentiated from the growing magnificence of the masks and costumes of heroes. From about this time there is also a concern to use gesture to mark 'respectability' and to distinguish the restrained, graceful, and inexpressive gestures of heroes from the loud and busy movements of social inferiors.

In seeking an explanation for the anomalous development of ancient realism we should recall the self-consciously political and ideological terms with which ancient contemporaries expressed their attitudes towards the growth in acting realism (and which we explored in the first section of this paper). When Kallippides mimicked the language and behaviour of lower-class women, or imitated the manners of real beggars in performing the part of a king reduced to mendicancy, he did much more than offend against good taste. He uncovered deep divisions in the Athenian body politic about both the constitution of reality and the etiquette of its representation. We find evidence of the same divisions not only in conservative hostility to performance realism, but in the partiality and gaps in 'realist' representations. Aeschylus experimented with the means of distinguishing characters both by class and ethnicity. For Sophocles, the most important distinction was the horizontal division between the heroes and the lower classes, and relatively little attention was paid to the vertical divisions between different ethnicities and linguistic groups. Euripides and Aristophanes, by contrast, are much more

[58] *MMC*³ vol. I, 32, 25.

interested in representing the vertical divisions between Athenians and non-Athenians and even go so far as to erase the horizontal divisions between strata within Athenian society.

Within the context of the political and ideological polarisation of Athens during the time of the 'radical democracy' in Athens, the debate surrounding Kallippides can now be seen to have less to do with an opposition between 'realist' and 'idealist' aesthetics, than with two opposed concepts of the real, one belonging to a conservative, residually aristocratic–hierarchic mentality, the other to an emergent democratic–egalitarian mentality. The anecdotes with which we began this investigation criticise Euripides and the younger generation of actors for erasing the horizontal division separating tragic heroes from characters of low social status. The language of Euripidean and Aristophanic performance in the last decades of the fifth century tended towards social realism in the representation of common speech, but this produced no slice of life, since the diversity of language within the *polis* was misrepresented as a homogeneous common speech without social distinctions. The emergent aesthetic was a realism limited by the perspective of the democratic citizen, whose 'other' was an outsider, a foreigner, or possibly a woman. But he shunned the linguistic representation of social difference within the citizen body, and even within the resident population. This was a distinction which appealed, rather, to anti-democratic élites who readily equated the cultural difference between élite and mass with that between citizen and slave.[59] The effacement of social difference stands in stark contrast to the growing realism in the linguistic portraiture of women and foreigners (abetted doubtless by the sexist and xenophobic tendencies of Athenian democratic ideology).

Both trends left their mark on later dramatic performance. Though Kallippides' techniques were imitated by later actors, his contribution seems generally to have been contained within the framework of the more conservative aesthetic. Our evidence suggests that Kallippides' later imitators tended to raise rather than lower the profile of the heroic caste by using his gestural realism to mark the mannerisms of low characters within the world of tragedy.

Certainly, this élite aesthetic came to dominate comedy even as the status of the comic genre began to rise within the dramatic hierarchy. The homogenising tendencies of Old Comic linguistic portraiture of the citizen classes was reversed by Menander's style of New Comedy, which

[59] See esp. Raaflaub (1983) and (1984) 305–13.

paid much closer attention to sociolect and idiolect, and particularly in its characterisation of slaves and working-class professionals. This change is often ascribed to widespread changes in political structure, theatrical organisation, and spectatorship at the time of Demetrius of Phaleron (317–307 BC). The renewed focus upon the realistic depiction of difference within the social composition of the polis certainly brought dramatic representation in closer harmony with the viewpoint of a new governing élite, defined by wealth more than breeding (though it appropriated many of the values and attitudes of the early fifth-century aristocracy). The artefacts, however, show that the representation of social difference in costume began two or three decades earlier than Demetrius, and suggest a more complex causal relationship between the ideological and political changes that occurred in Athens in the later fourth century BC.

SUGGESTIONS FOR FURTHER READING

DFA (1988) 126–76 is still the standard general introduction to Greek actors and acting, although the discussion confines itself to technical details and is, in many respects, out of date. Taplin (1977a) is an invaluable mine of information on all aspects of tragic production in the time of Aeschylus and after, though, as the title suggests, it is focused on stagecraft rather than acting, as are the contributions of Dearden (1976), Taplin (1978), Seale (1982), Halleran (1985), Frost (1988), and, with a wider ambit, Rehm (1992). Bremmer (1991) provides useful background to the study of gesture in his survey of the literary evidence for gesture in Greek culture generally. The most promising approach to gesture in ancient acting is through iconography, as urged by Hughes (1991) and Csapo (1993). Steps in this direction have been taken by Neiiendam (1992), and, more cogently, by Green (1997).

CHAPTER SIX

Looking for the actor's art in Aristotle[1]

G. M. Sifakis

When Aristotle wrote his treatises on the art of rhetoric and the art of poetic composition (focusing on the making of tragedy), he recognised that the arts of poetic performance, *rhapsōidia* and *hypokritikē*, had come into existence after the poets had set in motion their own arts and performances (*Rhet.* 3.1404a20–3), but he did not attempt to write systematically about acting, the principles of which had never been worked up into an 'art' (a technical manual). However, because orators skilled in delivery were always successful 'in the contests of public speaking on account of the weakness of the audience', 'just as in dramatic contests the actors nowadays are more powerful than the poets' (*Rhet.* 3.1403b 32–5), Aristotle was forced (for he would have preferred a rhetoric based on plain facts and logical argument alone) to introduce certain remarks about delivery in his discussion of prose style, such as the definition of *hypokrisis* in terms of voice management (at *Rhet.* 3.1403b26–31) and the references to its influence on the style of public speaking.

On the other hand, he refuses to discuss what he calls *opsis* (the visual elements of theatrical production) in the *Poetics* on account of its being 'the least technical of the parts [i.e. undefined and as yet unregulated by an art], and having least to do with the art of poetry', since 'the accomplishment of the visual aspects (of production) depends more on the art of the mask maker than the art of the poets' (*Poet.* 1450b17–20). And yet he does include *opsis* among the six formative constituents of which the fabric of a play consists (1450a10), obviously because drama is intended to be performed on the stage by actors whose appearance was indeed fashioned by the mask maker. The philosopher recognises this,[2]

[1] I would like to thank the editors of this volume for their extremely useful suggestions and editorial improvements on the form and content of this paper.

[2] ἐπεὶ δὲ πράττοντες ποιοῦνται τὴν μίμησιν, πρῶτον μὲν ἐξ ἀνάγκης ἂν εἴη τι μόριον τραγῳδίας ὁ τῆς ὄψεως κόσμος, 'as they carry out the imitation by acting, it necessarily follows that in the first place the organisation of spectacle must be a part of tragedy' (1449b31–3; translations of Greek passages not attributed to specific translators are my own).

even if he also states that tragic poetry may be equally effective 'without performance and actors' (1450b18).[3] Now if *hypokrisis* influences the *lexis*, diction, of rhetoric (especially when the orator is to address a large audience), we must assume (*a*) that it would influence even more the construction of drama which is to be *enacted* before a large audience, and (*b*) that we should be able to detect that influence in what Aristotle says about how a play ought to be constructed. The philosopher himself implies that much when he says that the playwright should work out plot, diction and body movements by visualising the action as if he were an eye-witness to the events he wants to represent (1455a22–30).

ĒTHOS AND CHARACTER DRAWING

Of the six constituents of drama, *mythos* corresponds to plot, *melos* and *opsis* roughly correspond to musical composition and stage production respectively, but none of the three remaining formative parts – *ēthos* (usually translated as character), *dianoia*, *lexis* – corresponds to our (modern) concept of dramatic character; nor does their combination for that matter. *Ēthos* comes closest to character; but, then, how are we to understand why actual dramatic characters in tragedy employ a language and manner of speaking unrelated to their regional origin, social class or upbringing (with very few exceptions), while their reasoning is as sharp as if they have been thoroughly coached by a logographer?[4] Some scholars tend to see these qualitative parts – particularly the first two, *ēthos* and *dianoia* – as subdivisions of (dramatic) character, and then either criticise Aristotle for having separated them in the first place[5] or think that *dianoia* (thought or reasoning) is subsumed under *ēthos*,[6] despite Aristotle's clear distinction of them, which is actually consistent with the teachings of his ethical works.[7] Thought and diction (or poetic style, *lexis*), however, relate more to tragedy as a genre of poetry (as much as they do to epic) than to individual *dramatis personae*. Once this is acknowledged, our expectations as to how the latter should speak or justify their choices and actions should be less influenced by our modern assumptions of how the characters of literature ought to be drawn.

3 This should not be taken to mean that Aristotle underestimates the importance of performance but, as Halliwell (1986) 341 rightly observes, that 'the poet's art cannot strictly be tied to the conditions of production or be judged by theatrical standards'.

4 Cf. Dale (1954) xxii–xxix. 5 Dale (1969) 143–4.

6 Held (1985); see however Schütrumpf (1987). 7 See Schütrumpf (1970).

To take first things first, '*ēthos* is the kind of thing that manifests choice (...) hence speeches have no *ēthos* when there is nothing in them that the speaker chooses or avoids'; conversely, a dramatic character 'will have *ēthos* if, as has been observed, the speech or the action makes clear a choice (whichever it may) be, and [it will be] a good [*ēthos*] if [the choice is shown to be] good'.[8] As drama imitates people in action, dramatic characters must be such or such in accordance with their *ēthos*, and to some extent their thought (1449b37–8), but as Aristotle writes in his *Rhetoric*, even an orator should speak so as to suggest that his choices issue from his good *ēthos* rather than from his thought, unless what he has to say may sound incredible, in which case the speaker should also state his reasoning. The philosopher adduces an example of this from tragedy (not an unusual practice for him): 'as Sophocles does in the *Antigone*, [when Antigone says] that she cared more for her brother than for a husband or children, for if the latter were lost they might be replaced, "But since my mother and father have passed away / no brother can ever be born to me"' (*Rhet.* 3.1417a24–33, see Soph. *Ant.* 911–12).

However, Aristotle clearly thinks of categories of people rather than individuals. His basic division is between *spoudaioi* and *phauloi* (good or admirable and bad or unimportant men, respectively), 'the diversities of human character being nearly always derivative from this primary distinction, since it is by badness and excellence men differ in character' (1448a2–4, trans. Bywater). The *spoudaioi*, being generally better than 'men of the present day', are suitable as characters of tragedy; the *phauloi*, being worse than ourselves, are suitable as characters of comedy (1448a17). Therefore, Aristotle's advice to tragic playwrights was that regarding the *ēthē* to be involved in their plays 'there are four points to aim at. First and foremost, that they shall be good. [...] Such goodness is possible in every type of personage, even in a woman or a slave, though the one is perhaps an inferior, and the other a wholly worthless being. The second point is to make them appropriate. The character before us may be, say, manly; but it is not appropriate in a female character to be manly, or eloquent. The third is to make them like the reality, which is not the same as their being good and appropriate, in our sense of the

[8] Because these literal translations differ from Bywater's and other more recent ones, I quote here the original text: ἔστιν δὲ ἦθος μὲν τὸ τοιοῦτον ὃ δηλοῖ τὴν προαίρεσιν (...) διόπερ οὐκ ἔχουσι ἦθος τῶν λόγων ἐν οἷς μηδ' ὅλως ἔστιν ὅ τι προαιρεῖται ἢ φεύγει ὁ λέγων (1450b8–10); ἕξει δὲ ἦθος μὲν ἐὰν ὥσπερ ἐλέχθη ποιῇ φανερὸν ὁ λόγος ἢ ἡ πρᾶξις προαίρεσίν τινα <ἥ τις ἂν> ᾖ, χρηστὸν δὲ ἐὰν χρηστήν (1454a17–19).

term. The fourth is to make them consistent and the same throughout' (1454a16–26, trans. Bywater, slightly adapted).[9]

Despite his great interest and pioneering work in psychology, Aristotle leaves no doubt that he thinks of *ēthē* not in terms of individual dramatic characters, but in terms of *moral qualities characteristic of broad categories of people*,[10] which is confirmed by his detailed discussion of emotions and *ēthē* in the *Rhetoric*, where he begins his account of *ēthē* as follows: 'Let us now consider the various kinds of people with regard to their *ēthē* in relation to the emotions, states [or habits], ages of life and fortunes' (2.1388b31). He then proceeds to analyse the *ēthē* of youth and old age, 'the *ēthē* following upon wealth' (2.1390b32), power, good fortune, etc.

Regarding his specifications for character drawing in the *Poetics*, Aristotle adds the very important requirement that characters are to be subordinate to the plot, 'for tragedy is an imitation not of people but of actions and life . . . therefore [the tragedians] do not act in order to portray characters, but include the characters [in the plays] for the sake of the actions' (1450a16–22). It is primarily the plot that should imply the *katholou*, which is to say, the 'kind of thing that might happen, i.e. what is possible as being probable or necessary' (1451a37–8); but the acting agents should also 'probably or necessarily say or do' what would be expected on the part of 'such or such a kind of person' (1451b8–9, also 1454a35–6) under the constraints of specific circumstances, and what they say and do should thus reveal their *ēthos* (1454a17–19). It is this interplay between plot and characters that results in the statement of the *katholou*, the universal; this, together with the requirement that the *ēthos* of the *dramatis personae* should be made clear by what they say and do in relation to the action in which they are involved, makes the characters of tragedy into the morally specified archetypes they are (in contrast to the stereotypes of, mostly, popular literature: usually minor character types or tokens of types found across many specimens of a genre of fiction).[11]

9 For the concept of *ēthos* in the *Poetics*, see (in addition to the editions of the text with commentaries) Schütrumpf (1970); Halliwell (1986) 138–67. In the quotation from Bywater's translation I have changed 'clever' to 'eloquent' (for δεινή) following Schütrumpf (1987) 178, with a reference to Grube (1965) 81.

10 Cf. Jones (1962) 40–2.

11 For Aristotle's subordination of characters to plot and his concept of 'human beings' that are typical in their *ēthos* and yet extraordinary as to the tasks they have to perform, Jones' insightful comments are still indispensable (Jones (1962) 29–46). On action and character in the *Poetics* see also Halliwell (1986) 138–67. For some modern discussions of the construction of tragic characters see Gould (1978), Easterling (1990), Goldhill (1990), Gill (1986).

DICTION AND CHARACTERISATION

I move now to diction (*lexis*), and an actor's delivery (*hypokritikē* or *agōnistikē lexis*) which is discussed in the *Rhetoric*. *Lexis* is defined in *Poetics* (*a*) very generally as 'the composition of verses' (1449b35), and (*b*) as 'the expression of meaning through the use of (the proper) language which has the same potential in the case of either verse composition or prose' (1450b13–15).

The style of tragic poetry must be lofty and clear at the same time, which is a matter of subtle balance as 'the clearest diction consists of literal wording, but is mean,' while 'the diction becomes distinguished and non-prosaic by the use of unfamiliar terms, i.e. strange words, metaphors, lengthened forms, and everything that deviates from the ordinary modes of speech. But a whole statement in such terms will be either a riddle or a barbarism' (1458a18–24, trans. Bywater, slightly adapted). However, as the natural evolution of tragedy hit upon the appropriate metre when the dramatic dialogue emerged at the expense of parts that were sung, namely, the iambic trimeter (which 'is the most speakable of metres' (1449a24) for, as Aristotle explains in the *Rhetoric* 'the iambic is the very language of ordinary people' and 'in common talk iambic lines occur more often than any others'[12]) so tragic poets can limit the unfamiliar forms to a minimum (and use them as style markers, to put it in modern terms[13]) and, because iambic verse 'imitates as much as possible the spoken language', poets should use 'the vocabulary one would employ in prose speeches, i.e. words in their literal sense, metaphors, and [some] ornament' (1459a12–14). This is as far as Aristotle will go regarding the relationship of tragic diction to ordinary language. He does point out that the former models itself on the latter, but he does not anticipate or recommend linguistic realism, and stops short of considering the possibility that dramatic dialogue or set speeches might be written in prose (the partly rhythmical prose style, for instance, appropriate to rhetorical speeches which he discusses in his *Rhetoric* 3.1408b21 ff.) rather than in metrical verse; nor does he make any allusion to the effect that tragic *lexis* might be varied on the basis of different speakers – that it might be used, in other words, as a means of characterisation.

This is all the more remarkable given the finer distinctions he makes in the *Rhetoric* with regard to prose style: '[Rhetorical] *lexis* will be appropriate if it expresses emotion and *ēthos* and is equal to the underlying

[12] *Rhet.* 3.1408b33–5, trans. Roberts, cf. *Poet.* 1449a26. [13] See p. 154 and n. 17 below.

subject-matter' (i.e. neither casual about serious matters nor solemn about trivial ones). The aim of the orator is to persuade, and so he helps his case by displaying emotion, which his audience is invited to share, and by offering indications of good character. This kind of rhetorical demonstration 'from signs' (as opposed to logical reasoning) is ethical (i.e. it reveals the character of the speaker) insofar as there is a way of presenting one's case in a manner appropriate to each class of men and each state of habituation. 'By class' (*genos*), Aristotle writes, 'I mean a division according to age, such as boy, man or old man; and then man or woman, and Spartan or Thessalian. By states of habituation (*hexeis*) I mean those which determine the kind of persons we are in life; [. . .] therefore, if a speaker uses the language that is proper to his state he will create the character [he wants to project]; for a rustic and an educated man would not say the same things *nor speak in the same way*' (*Rhet.* 3.1408a10–13, 25–32). This is precisely the difference between prose style and the diction of tragedy, namely, that the latter is supposed to present '*what* such or such a kind of man will probably or necessarily *say* or do' (*Poet.* 1451b8–9, cf. p. 151 above), but allows for smaller differentiations regarding the manner in which tragic characters express themselves. In fact, Aristotle does not mention such variations of tragic *lexis* in the *Poetics*, but when he compares the styles of prose and poetry in the *Rhetoric* he writes that 'even here [sc. in poetry] it would be less appropriate for a slave or a very young man to express himself in fine language, or [to use fine language] about very small matters. But in these cases, also, what is fitting may be lessened or enlarged; therefore [poets] must not attract attention to what they do, and must appear to speak not artificially but naturally [. . .] which, for instance, happens to the voice of Theodoros as opposed to that of the other actors: his voice seems to be that of the speaker [sc. the impersonated character], theirs sound alien. Now this deceit is successful if one picks [one's phrases] from the ordinary language while composing, which is what Euripides does and was the first to indicate' (3.1404b15–25, cf. 3.1408a19–21). This imperceptible passage from actor to poet will be taken up again later.

To conclude and summarise, in tragedy 'well made ethical speeches as far as diction and thought are concerned' (*Poet.* 1450a29–30) should not be taken to characterise the speakers linguistically, except insofar as persons of different classes and habits in Aristotle's sense – e.g. queen and nurse in *Hippolytus*, or *Medea* for that matter – have different things to say; what they do is to reveal the choice of speakers and thus indicate their *ēthos* (1450b10). This is why the speeches of messengers more often than not have no *ēthos* or, to be precise, do not reveal any choice[14] and thus do not characterise the speakers, who use exalted language because of their emotional excitement,[15] but often remain nameless.[16] On the other hand, the choices of the main characters should be clearly motivated in terms of *ēthos* and, occasionally, reasoning (see above, p. 150). In the development of tragedy, though, Aristotle notices a movement from the highly poetic and embellished to a simpler language that culminates in Euripides' use of 'common dialect'. In the mouth of a good actor such as Theodoros, this simple style of speaking might even give the impression (or create the illusion) that the voice belonged to the character who spoke rather than to his or her impersonator. But the diction of tragedy could never become truly colloquial and idiomatic because it was poetic by definition, and Aristotle also praises Euripides for being able to attain the proper nobility of style by substituting a single poetic gloss for an ordinary word in a line from the lost *Philoctetes* of Aeschylus and thus turning what was an inferior line into a fine one.[17] However, style elaboration, Aristotle repeats, should be confined to 'inactive parts' (possibly messenger speeches, prologues, and other parts without ethical content) and be avoided in parts that are supposed to convey moral qualities or intellectual reasoning, 'for the very brilliant diction obscures both *ēthē* and thoughts (*dianoias*)' (*Poet.* 1460b4–5).

Yet the reason why tragic diction could not or would not make similar differentiations of vocabulary and language as prose diction, so as to represent character realistically, can be surmised from what Aristotle says about the unsuitability of metrical verse for rhetoric: 'The form of [rhetorical] diction must be neither metrical nor devoid of rhythm.

14 The obvious exception is, of course, the Corinthian messenger in Sophocles' *O.T.*

15 Cf. what Aristotle says about emotional language in the *Rhetoric*: 'We forgive an angry man for talking about a wrong "heaven-high" or "colossal" [οὐρανόμηκες, πελώριον, both words being Homeric]', etc. (3.1408b12–13, trans. Roberts).

16 How such characters were visualised and presented on the stage is a question which is partly answered, with regard to fourth-century performances in South Italy, by a large group (over fifty examples) of red-figure vases (mostly Apulian from Taranto plus a couple of Sicilian) recently studied by Green (1999). Cf. Green, this volume, ch. 4. The vases are decorated with mythological scenes, usually identifiable as subjects of tragedies, in which a white-bearded old man (sometimes balding, but maskless like everybody else) with laced boots, short chiton, cloak, and staff, is shown as 'an observer of great events that he reports onstage, rather than a direct participant' (Green (1999) 44). Inscriptions on several pictures identify him as *paidagōgos* (tutor, which Green adopts as a generic description), *tropheus* (nurse), *botēr* (herdsman), *aipolos* (goatherd), or simply *angelos* (messenger).

17 Euripides substituted θοινᾶται for ἐσθίει to produce φαγέδαιναν ἥ μου τὰς σάρκας θοινᾶται (fr. 792 Nauck).

The former does not carry conviction (for it seems artificial) and at the same time diverts attention because it makes the hearer attend to the recurrence of the similar [rhythmic elements] . . . the unrhythmical, on the other hand, is without limits' etc. (*Rhet.* 3.1408b21–6). So, despite the fact that the iambic trimeter is recognised by Aristotle as the verse closest to ordinary speech, and placed among the changes that led tragedy to full development, its metrical regularity was an impediment to further development towards linguistic realism, to say nothing about the other metres and music which made up the 'seasoned language' (cf. p. 161 below) of tragedy found in its parts other than the iambic scenes.

Now if *lexis* is the diction and style of poetry (and by implication tragic *lexis* is the style of tragic poetry as a genre), it follows that its corresponding delivery in performance must be in a comparable style of acting, free of the individual idiosyncrasies or shades of characterisation found in realistic dramatic dialogue. In addition, the tragic actor ought to be able to switch styles of delivery and move freely between three levels of language, all elevated in different degrees above ordinary speech: the normal level of tragic delivery in scenes in the iambic trimeter, the recitative of anapaests or long trochaic lines, and the singing of lyric parts.

Unfortunately, Aristotle says nothing about the style of lyric parts and their delivery, since tragic *lexis* in *Poetics* refers only to the iambic parts. We must, therefore, look elsewhere in his works for what he calls *hypokrisis* (acting, oral delivery, *Rhet.* 3.1403b22) and, also, for the mimetic power of music,[18] which he does recognise as one of the six formative elements of tragedy (*melopoiia*, literally, the composition of *melē*, songs, i.e., the lyric parts of tragedy) and one of the two such elements (together with *lexis*) by means of which tragic imitation is effected,[19] although *melopoiia* is later ignored – at least, ignored in the surviving book of *Poetics*.

HYPOKRISIS IN THE *RHETORIC*

In the third book of the *Rhetoric*, Aristotle discusses *hypokrisis* with respect to public speaking, but makes so many references to tragedy as to leave

[18] At the very beginning of the *Poetics*, 'most of the art of *aulos* playing and of *kithara* playing' is classified together with epic, dithyramb and dramatic poetry, as *mimēseis*, modes of imitation (1447a15).

[19] ἐν τούτοις γὰρ ποιοῦνται τὴν μίμησιν (1449b33), οἷς μὲν γὰρ μιμοῦνται, δύο μέρη ἐστίν (1450a10).

no doubt that much of what he says about oratory is also relevant to theatrical performance. *Hypokrisis*, he writes,

> is related to the voice: how it should be used so as to express each emotion, e.g., when the voice should be loud, when it should be soft and when between the two; or how it should be used with regard to pitch, e.g., when it should be high pitched, or low pitched, or between the two, and regarding the rhythm appropriate in each case. For there are three aspects [of voice management] to which they pay attention: loudness, pitch modulation, rhythm. One might almost say that the prizes in the [dramatic] contests are carried by those [who attend to the above], and as the actors nowadays are more powerful there [i.e., in the dramatic contests] than the poets, the same is done in the contests of public life on account of the baseness of the citizens.[20]

Much as he would have preferred public speaking to be based on facts and logical argument rather than on refinements of style and delivery – after all, 'nobody teaches geometry this way' (3.1404a12) – Aristotle recognises the great power of *hypokrisis*. He considers it to be a natural gift rather than a skill or art, and says that it had not as yet been subjected to technical study (3.1404a15), although the human voice is 'the most imitative of our organs', 'words are imitations of things', and it was the poets, naturally enough, who set things in motion, and thus 'epic delivery and dramatic performance, and other [arts of poetic performance], came into existence' (3.1404a20–3). Acting developed eventually into a proper art (*hypokritikē*), which rubs shoulders with poetics insofar as it deals with such 'forms of *lexis*' (in this case, modes of oral expression) as 'what is command, what is prayer, and narrative and threat, and question and answer, or anything similar, which are for the *hypokritikē* to know and for the master of this kind of art' (*Poet.* 1456b9–13). On the other hand, this art had never been systematically studied until Aristotle's time, hence he considers *opsis* as the least technical of the formative parts of tragedy, while as far as rhetorical delivery is concerned 'only very slight attempts to deal with [it] have been made and by a few people, as by Thrasymachus in his "Appeals to Pity"' (*Rhet.* 3.1404a13–14, trans. Rhys Roberts).

In any case, Aristotle correlates different kinds of rhetoric with different styles of diction and, by implication, delivery. Thus, he observes, 'the style of written prose and that of speeches intended for public

[20] *Rhet.* 3.1403b26–35. I accept (with Ross) Spengel's emendation of the last word in this passage, πολιτειῶν, to πολιτῶν, on the basis of 1408a8, a few lines below, where the same idea is repeated: the great power of delivery is due to the baseness, or weakness, of the hearer, διὰ τὴν τοῦ ἀκροατοῦ μοχθηρίαν.

performance is not the same', and among the latter 'the style of political speeches is not the same as that of the forensic ones' (3.1413b4–5). The style of written prose (*lexis graphikē*) is the most precise, that of public performance is the closest (or most suitable) to acting[21] and comes in two varieties, ethical and emotional, that is to say, it aims either at representing character or at representing emotion. Obviously, both varieties can be found in both species of public speaking, the political and forensic. The 'agonistic' / 'hypocritic' style in question is clearly the style of dramatic diction (unmetrical though it is in rhetoric and less elevated in tone and vocabulary than the tragic *lexis* proper) because Aristotle suddenly moves at this point from rhetoric to drama and asserts that 'for this reason [sc. because the agonistic style is most suitable to acting] the actors look out for such plays and the poets for such actors' (*Rhet.* 3.1413b11–12). 'Such plays' in this context evidently means plays containing ethical speeches, and 'such actors' means masters of the art of *hypokrisis* [sc. *hypokritikē*] who could perform speeches expressive of *ēthos* or emotion.

The significant point implied here is the interrelation between the style of tragic writing, which was the business of the poet, and the style (and art) of dramatic delivery, which was the business of the actor. And the key word (and potential source of confusion) is *lexis*, which Aristotle employs to indicate both poetic style and style of delivery.[22] A text intended to be performed before an audience (in a dramatic contest or in a political assembly) has to be composed in a different manner from a text intended for reading (such as the speeches of epideictic rhetoric).[23] The mode of delivery thus interacts with the style of writing, as 'in a performance the devices of acting are pertinent [but] if acting is removed they will not be performing their function and will appear silly' – if the text is only read, that is.[24] Then, Aristotle, in his customary manner, gives some

21 ἀγωνιστικὴ δὲ [λέξις] ἡ ὑποκριτικωτάτη (3.1413b9–11).

22 Its English equivalent, diction, can also refer both to writing and speaking, but *lexis* is more transparently related to *legein* (to speak) in Greek, not to mention that poetry was mostly communicated orally / aurally.

23 *Rhet.* 3.1414a18–19. Aristotle mentions the tragic poet Chaeremon as *anagnōstikos* (suitable to reading) earlier (3.1413b13), which is usually taken to mean that he (possibly among others) wrote tragedies with a reading public in mind, not to be performed in a dramatic contest. I very much doubt if Aristotle's assertion that Chaeremon wrote in a precise style ('like a speech writer') is to be taken as evidence for the composition of tragedies that were not to be performed in the theatre, in the fourth century, since there is no other evidence whatever for such a strange notion, while there is some evidence that Chaeremon's plays were performed (his *Achilleus* was performed in Dodona in the third century BC, *SIG*³ 1080, Stephanis (1988) no. 3003).

24 *Rhet.* 3.1413b17–19. I translate ἀγών as performance (cf. Sifakis (1997) 27) and τὰ ὑποκριτικά as devices of acting.

(deceptively simple) examples of what he means by devices related to acting: (*a*) a string of words unconnected by conjunctions (an 'asyndeton' such as 'I came, I met [him], I pleaded'), which makes one thing appear to be many, although it takes the same length of time to be stated as the single thing that results from the use of conjunctions which make the many into one; besides, the same device 'creates a climax: I came, I talked, I entreated – they seem many' (*Rhet.* 3.1413b30–4); (*b*) repetition of the same thing with small variations 'which paves the way as it were to acting' (e.g. 'this is the one who stole from you, this is the one who cheated you, this is the one who attempted the utmost by betraying you', 3.1413b24). In either case, to render such passages well 'acting is necessary, and the speaker must not deliver them as if he were saying one thing, in the same character and tone of voice' (3.1413b30–1, cf. 22).

Aristotle concludes his discussion of prose diction in the *Rhetoric* by comparing the style of political oratory to shadow or outline painting (*skiagraphia*, sometimes translated, though wrongly, as 'scene painting') which was intended to be seen from a distance: 'The greater the crowd the more distant is the point of view, therefore the exact details seem superfluous and detrimental in both cases. Juridical diction is more precise, and even more so when it is addressed to a single judge [. . .]. But wherever acting is most required there is least room for precision; and this is where a voice is needed, and big one at that.'[25]

There must surely have been many more acting devices interacting with diction and style than asyndeton, repetition and climax; and *hypokrisis* must have been a more elaborate art than the management of a big voice, but we will have to return to the subject when we summarise Aristotle's assumptions in the last section of this paper.

MELOPOIIA AS A MEANS OF IMITATION

I shall now turn briefly to the non-iambic parts of tragedy, either sung or delivered in recitative by the chorus or actors or both in alternation. Aristotle has very little to say about the lyric parts,[26] although in the

[25] *Rhet.* 3.1414a15–17. The ability to speak loudly (*megalophōnia*) was a great asset for an orator as well as an actor since both had to address big crowds (despite the good acoustics of Greek theatres) and often had to cope with the noise the audience was likely to generate. Socrates repeatedly asked the jury to be quiet (Plato, *Apology* 17d, 20e, 21a, 27b, 30c); Sophocles gave up acting because of his weak voice (*mikrophōnia, Life of Soph.* 4). On 'dicastic *thorubos*' see Bers (1985).

[26] He enumerates them, and offers some formal definitions, in the parenthetical chapter 12 (on the quantitative parts of tragedy), which interrupts abruptly the flow of argument from chapter 11 to chapter 13 and has often been athetised by editors; see Else (1967) 360.

Poetics he includes *melopoiïa* in the six formative elements of tragedy – and groups it with *lexis* as one of the two such parts by means of which imitation is effected[27] – and also says that the chorus should be 'considered as one of the actors, and to be part of the whole and participate in the action, not as in Euripides, but as in Sophocles' (1456a25–7).[28] *Melopoiïa* (composition of songs) he does not define because, as he says, its function is perfectly obvious (i.e. implied by the name itself, 1449b35). Later on, he calls it the greatest of *hēdysmata* (sweeteners, condiments, 1450b16) and, more specifically, he defines *hēdysmenos logos*, sweetened language, as 'that which has [i.e. includes, incorporates] rhythm and melody' (1449b29). I disagree with scholars who interpret Aristotle's food metaphor as 'pleasurable accessories' (Bywater) or embellishment of language (Butcher, Halliwell, Janko) and the like,[29] because speech, rhythm and melody are specified as *means of imitation* (already in the first chapter of the *Poetics*, 1447a22), which tragedy and comedy use in different combinations (either rhythm and speech or all three together) in their various quantitative parts, (1447b25–7; 1449b26) and they are, therefore, integral to drama as imitation.

However, we have to turn to other works of Aristotle in order to inquire what he means by calling music an imitative art, and it is in the last book of the *Politics* that he discusses music with reference to education and argues that it is capable of contributing to virtue and excellence because, just as *gymnastikē* disposes the body in a certain way, so can music affect our *ēthos* in a comparable manner. Aristotle follows Plato and, most likely, Damon (cf. Plato, *Rep.* 3.400b ff.), in considering that musical modes, melodies and rhythms directly set forth likenesses or imitations of *ēthē* and emotions (*Pol.* 8.1340a33–9), but to present his views in this chapter, in any meaningful way, would require a great detour away from our main concern, which is the style of acting the philosopher had in mind when he wrote his *Poetics*. Still, because the *Poetics* is a descriptive as much as prescriptive treatise (as is the *Rhetoric*), Aristotle's assumptions, definitions and guidelines are based on a close examination of classical plays and observation of contemporary theatre practice. We may, therefore, be sure that just as he acknowledges the function and role of the chorus as used by Sophocles in the fifth century, he must have also recognised the necessity (and reality) of musical delivery by actors of the lyric parts of

[27] See p. 155, n. 19 above. [28] For the chorus as a character in Sophocles, see Gardiner (1987).

[29] They constitute, of course, the great majority of interpreters; cf. Halliwell (1986) ch. viii on 'The chorus of tragedy'.

tragedy enumerated in *Poetics* 12. Now why he has so little to say about these parts is anybody's guess, although we should not forget that we have lost the second book of the treatise and do not really know much about its possible contents.

TRACES OF THE ART OF ACTING IN ARISTOTLE

In the final section of this paper I shall try to review the evidence so far discussed, and draw certain conclusions by way of summing up the vestigial traces of the actor's art found in Aristotle. To begin with, his separation of *ēthos* from thought and diction in his discussion of the constituent elements of tragedy is highly suggestive with regard to the style of tragic acting. Dramatic enactment (*hōs mimountai*, the manner of imitation in Aristotle's scheme of qualitative elements) in Greek theatre was carried out by actors who had their heads completely covered by masks representing the characters of a play, at least as far as the facial characteristics of the characters were concerned, and their bodies hidden by rich and elaborate costumes. The costume and mask concealed an actor's indifferent, insignificant (or, at times, even misleading) features, but revealed the *ēthos* of the character he impersonated, albeit in universal terms.[30] Characters, of course, were created (or mostly recreated) by the dramatist, visualised by the mask maker and costumier, working under the directions of the *didaskalos* (as dramatists were invariably referred to with regard to their function as theatre producers), and impersonated by the actors – also directed by the *didaskalos* who initially was one of the performers (actually, the main performer).

An actor should, then, be able to use his voice (and to some extent movement and gesture[31]) to enliven that same *ēthos* and deliver his lines in a variety of modes – rhythmic speech, recitative and, occasionally, song – which corresponded to different style registers and levels of emotional states, but might at times suit less the representation of any single character and more the moral and emotional tenor of a highly idealised dramatic situation, such as the *kommos* in Aeschylus' *Libation-bearers* or the

[30] Cf. Jones (1962) 43–6, 59–60; Gould (1978) 49; Halliwell (1993).

[31] But Aristotle shows no awareness of any stylisation of gestures into a system of signification as found in later rhetoric, for which see Katsouris (1989) and Graf (1991). On the other hand, we should keep in mind that deportment, body movement and gestures are on the whole culturally specific, and movements that may be perfectly natural in one culture may appear very stylised to a viewer from a different culture. For a good account of 'Walking, standing, and sitting in ancient Greek culture' see Bremmer (1991); see also Hall (1995) 53 on deportment.

exodos of Sophocles' *Antigone*; or the rhetoric of a situation, such as the *agōn* between Admetus and Pheres in Euripides' *Alcestis*.[32] The key to the style of Greek acting is to understand that the actor was at the same time an impersonator as much as he was a performer of poetry, conscious of the audience to which he addressed his utterance directly or indirectly.[33] This is why his art, *hypokrisis* proper, was used as a reference in discussions of the art of public speaking, which came to be called *hypokrisis*, also.[34] This kind of acting style corresponds to and is required by a language adjusted – in regard to both thought and diction – to the poetic genre rather than to the representation of individual character, even though Aristotle recognises (in the *Rhetoric*) that people who belong to different categories should be somewhat differentiated by the way they speak (p. 153 above). It follows that skilful use of voice ('the most imitative of human organs', see p. 156) was a Greek actor's principal qualification, hence it should hardly surprise us that Aristotle equates *hypokrisis* with voice management. We can also suppose that voice manipulation with regard to loudness, pitch modulation and rhythm would not be concerned with realistic representation of character aspects and peculiarities that were not already present in the text, such as, for instance, the pitch gamut or timbre of a female voice, because that would undermine the main aim of dramatic delivery, which was to represent emotion (p. 156).[35]

On the other hand, we should not presume that tragic delivery of the spoken parts was excessively stylised. Aristotle clearly prescribes that

32 Cf. Dale (n. 4 above).

33 The extent and importance of narrative in tragedy has rightly been pointed out by Bremer (1976). Narrative, however, is not confined to messenger speeches, but can also be found in prologues and set speeches, not to mention choral songs. Furthermore, Greek drama was not simply played before an audience (whose existence is tacitly ignored in modern realistic drama), but *to* an audience which was directly addressed so often that its presence was taken for granted by the actors throughout the performance.

34 We do not know whether it was Aristotle who first applied the term to public speaking or one of the sophists whom he recognises as early students of oratorical delivery, Glaucon of Teos and Thrasymachus of Chalcedon (*Rhet.* 3.1403b26, 3.1404a15). Aristotle's successor, Theophrastus, wrote a treatise on *hypokrisis* (Diog. Laert. *Vit. philos.* 4. 48.12), which was a study of oratorical delivery rather than dramatic acting (Fortenbaugh (1985)). The theatricality of lawcourt procedures is examined by Hall (1995), who extends the comparison of 'lawcourt dramas' to theatrical performance beyond the main 'protagonists' in both cases, to cover all other factors and functions of juridical proceedings.

35 This view does not preclude some occasional pitch modulation to hint at the voice of a female character or a hero (low-pitched) in generic terms as the anonymous scholiast on the *Rhetoric* suggests, although he draws his examples, not from Byzantine rhetoric as such (an important discipline in its own right), but from church readings (*Comm. in Arist. Graeca* xxi.2, pp. 158. 23, 159. 3, 224. 25–7).

the poet should not attract attention to his own craft by making his characters speak in a contrived, artificial style; he should have them speak naturally (*pephykotōs*), which is what happened in the case of the voice of Theodoros as compared to other actors; Theodoros seemed to have spoken with the voice of the character he impersonated, while the others sounded incongruous (p. 153). Now this is a double-edged piece of testimony: uncontrived verisimilitude in dramatic delivery was rare, it seems, but is quoted with approval by Aristotle evidently because it represents a tendency, or a step in the process of evolution. But what is more remarkable is Aristotle's subtle movement to and fro between poetry and delivery. For he ends his discussion of 'speaking naturally' with another reference to the use of ordinary language that was first introduced by Euripides, who is credited with starting this tendency towards a more realistic *lexis* (p. 154). Dramatic writing and delivery are thus seen to be intimately connected, at least down to the time of Aristotle. Things may not have remained the same after the end of the classical period, because visual evidence for actors and masks from Hellenistic (particularly late Hellenistic) times suggests a much greater stylisation of acting, but we have lost the texts of 'new' tragedy, so we cannot be sure.

As regards movement and gesture on stage, we have two indications in the *Poetics*. The first is found in chapter 17, where we read that the poet should work out the diction of a play while visualising the action (1455a23). He should also work out, at the same time, the *schēmata* (figures of movement and gesture). There follows a difficult passage in which Aristotle seems to suggest that a poet who feels the emotions to be described, such as distress and anger, will be most convincing in that he will be able to portray them most truthfully with regard to *schēmata* (1455a30–2). This passage has generated some controversy as to whether it is the poet who should feel the emotions and imagine the corresponding body movements of his characters while composing his play, or whether it is the actor who should experience the emotions in order to present them convincingly to the audience. The majority of interpreters side with the former view (and Else, the chief modern exponent of the latter,[36] actually harmed his argument by taking *schēmata* to refer to figures of diction rather than to gesture and movement) but, although the whole of chapter 17 is indeed about the construction of the plot and clearly refers to the art of the poet, perhaps a latent reference to production

[36] Else (1967) 490–5.

and acting should also be recognised in lines 1455a30–2.[37] Two passages from the *Rhetoric* support this view. As noted in the previous paragraph, Aristotle passes from poetic diction to delivery by (the actor) Theodoros and then back to Euripides, and in another passage the same key words for working out the appropriate gestures (*synapergazesthai, schēmata*) are used with reference to the orator who tries to look pitiful: 'Those who work out at the same time (as writing a speech) the figures and voices and dress and matters of delivery in general are necessarily more pitiful' (2.1386a31–2). We recall that Athenian logographers did not appear in lawcourts, but are spoken of here as if they were the same persons as their clients.[38] The same conflation ought to be recognised in the *Poetics* between dramatist and actor, its implication being that – according to Aristotle, anyway – an actor was bound by the text as far as the style of performance was concerned, from *lexis* (meaning both diction and manner of delivery) to movement and gesture, which were originally conceived by the poet/*didaskalos* and executed by the actor. The close dependence of the art of acting upon the art of playwriting goes against the grain, as it were, of modern theatre practice, in which each producer and actor (to say nothing of set or costume designers) is expected to offer an original interpretation of old and new plays alike, but even in modern realistic drama many authors are known to make enormous and detailed demands on performers. Witness the detailed directions accompanying the plays of, say, Eugene O'Neill or Henrik Ibsen.

The other reference to movement and gesture in the *Poetics* comes in the last chapter of the work (26. 1461b26 ff.), in which Aristotle makes his comparison of epic to tragic poetry and finds the latter superior to the former. The charge of vulgarity, he writes, sometimes levelled against tragedy, should actually be addressed, not to tragic poetry, but to bad acting. Vulgar movement and gesticulating can also be found in rhapsodes and even pipe players, but in theatre not every kind of movement should be disapproved – because then dancing should also be condemned – but only the excessive mimicry of some actors (such as Kallippides who was called a monkey by Mynniskos[39] because of that) or the impersonation of worthless characters, another accusation levelled

37 πιθανώτατοι γὰρ ἀπὸ τῆς αὐτῆς φύσεως οἱ ἐν τοῖς πάθεσίν εἰσιν, καὶ χειμαίνει ὁ χειμαζόμενος καὶ χαλεπαίνει ὁ ὀργιζόμενος ἀληθινώτατα.

38 Cf. Russell (1990).

39 An early actor who perhaps had learned his art in the proximity of Aeschylus; see Stephanis (1988) no. 1757. See also Csapo, this volume, ch. 5.

against Kallippides and other actors, contemporary with Aristotle, on account of their imitation of un-free women. I take this to mean quasi-realistic representation of female slaves (such as nurses), which would hardly be warranted by the texts of the fifth-century tragedians. Aristotle seems to agree with such accusations, which again shows that his idea of acting was that a performer should stay close to the text and avoid excess or imposing his own subtext on the play.

CHAPTER SEVEN

Acting, action and words in New Comedy

Eric Handley

> Only an angel could be a general problem-solver: we mortals have to make fallible guesses from fragmentary information
>
> Steven Pinker, *How the Mind Works* (1997) 30

One must begin somewhere. My own interest in the dramatic qualities of Menander's language began with the first stages of writing notes on the *Dyskolos*, with the need to think about his way of giving actors short choppy sentences, like those spoken by Pan, the prologue speaker, at 17ff.: 'Fighting his partner, not only day by day, but taking in the great part of the night, his life was dreadful; a daughter born; still more so.'[1]

Sentence-connectives like 'and', 'but' and so on are so much a feature of ancient Greek that it is not surprising that their absence rates a technical term, *asyndeton*. When the Cairo codex brought in the modern age of studies in Menander, his early editors were not slow to focus on his fondness for it. Thus Capps, on some words from Daos in the title-scene of *Epitrepontes*, 'Asyndeton is characteristic of Menander's style, especially in narrative passages' (74f./250f.: 'I took the baby up; I went off home with it; I planned to rear it').[2] What makes asyndeton, for our purposes, something more than a feature of style is the recognition, from Aristotle onwards, that it has something to do with drama. We can perhaps make the point best from a passage of the treatise known as Demetrius, *On Style*, in which, as an illustration to his discussion, the author makes a contrast within the field of New Comedy between Menander and Philemon:

(193) The disjointed style is perhaps better for immediacy, and the same style is also called the actor's style [ὑποκριτική] since the asyndeton stimulates dramatic

[1] ταύτῃ ζυγομαχῶν οὐ μόνον τὰς ἡμέρας, / ἐπιλαμβάνων δὲ τὸ πολὺ τῆς νυκτὸς μέρος / ἔζη κακῶς· θυγάτριον αὐτῷ γίνεται· / ἔτι μᾶλλον.

[2] ἀνειλόμην, ἀπῆλθον οἴκαδ' αὔτ' ἔχων, / τρέφειν ἔμελλον: Capps (1910) 54; for more, see the useful survey by Ferrero (1976) to which a little can be added from texts published more recently.

delivery, while the written style is easy to read, and this is the style which is linked closely together and, as it were, safely secured by connectives. This is why Menander, who mostly omits connectives, is acted, while Philemon is read. (194) To show that asyndeton suits an actor's delivery, let this be an example: 'I conceived, I gave birth, I nurse, my dear.'[3] In this disjointed form the words will force anyone to be dramatic, however reluctantly – and the cause is the asyndeton. (Tr. Innes (1995))

The treatise goes on to say that if you put in a connective 'and' between the verbs, the emotional level will be lowered 'and anything unemotional is always undramatic'.

This fragment of information indicates one way in which a dramatic use of language was seen to be different from a non-dramatic use. But in marking out Menander as different from Philemon, it is also a reminder that we are dealing with phenomena that are variable and not constant. If, to the surprise of later critics, contemporary audiences were liable to prefer Philemon to Menander, then it can be asked what other successful methods Philemon had of handling words to telling dramatic effect.

For their first productions in the competitive environment of the Athenian festivals, dramatists relied on their protagonist and the two other actors who were his professional colleagues. One asks how much depended on the actor's art rather than the writer's; and (given long traditions of both writing and acting) how far the two interacted. These were real questions in antiquity, as when we find Aristotle remarking in the *Rhetoric* that 'actors are more important now than poets',[4] or when Terence (*Phormio* 10) puts in the mouth of a prologue speaker the allegation that a rival's play held the boards at its first production thanks to the performance rather than to the writing.

So far our questions relate to the genesis of plays. But New Comedy survived, in one way or another, for something near a millennium. It (by 'it' we mean predominantly Menander) survived very insecurely in the theatre, so far as we know, through the latter part of this long period, but had a life as material for reading and recitation and as a source of improving moral maxims.[5] What, we wonder, were the different contexts for performance (public or private) and for the different kinds of activity that can be covered by the terms 'reading and recitation'? How much of the essence of the plays as originally conceived and performed can be

[3] ἐδεξάμην, ἔτικτον, ἐκτρέφω, φίλε: Men., fr. 685K.-T./456KA, with <ὑπ> εδεξάμην and φιλῶ.

[4] 3.1403b33, tr. Csapo and Slater (1995) 265.

[5] On the survival of Menander, see the recent discussions by Easterling (1995), Blanchard (1997) and Handley (1997b).

held to survive in the Roman theatre and through to the later stages of the Greek tradition?

ACTORS AND DELIVERY

In the background of the passage of Demetrius, *On Style* quoted above is Aristotle, as represented in a passage of the *Rhetoric*.[6] Aristotle distinguishes the style proper to writing (λέξις γραφική), which is supremely precise, from the style of debate (λέξις ἀγωνιστική), which is supremely deliverable (ὑποκριτικωτάτη); the latter may be ethical (ἠθική) or emotional (παθητική): 'this is why actors are always running after plays of this character, and poets after suitable actors'. One can think of poets who are popular as 'reading' poets (like Philemon in Demetrius): the examples given by Aristotle are Chairemon the tragedian and Likymnios the writer of dithyrambs; but in general 'the speeches of writers appear meagre in public debates, while those of the rhetoricians, however well delivered, are amateurish when read'. Asyndeta and repetitions are taken as examples of stylistic features unwelcome in writing that is meant to be read, but exploited by orators in the style of debate, 'for they lend themselves to acting' (ἔστι γὰρ ὑποκριτικά). Examples follow.

The way in which Aristotle's discussion draws at once on forensic oratory and on drama is particularly interesting, and it is worth noting that the rendering of two passages of comedy by an actor called Philemon – not the same man as the comic poet – was sufficiently striking to have been remembered and recalled. In Anaxandrides' *Gerontomania*, he had some special way of speaking the words 'Rhadamanthys and Palamedes' (fr. 10KA) and in the prologue of the *Eusebeis* the word 'I' (fr. 13 KA). There are modern parallels. Edith Evans is well remembered for her role from 1940 onwards as Lady Bracknell in Oscar Wilde's *The Importance of being Earnest*, and in particular for her delivery of the word 'handbag' at a high point in Act I.[7] In ancient as well as in modern times the reputation of great actors could no doubt be built on infinitely many details of sensitive delivery of their words. This is a process in which the writer of the words no longer plays a direct part, even if, to a sensitive interpreter, he is a sleeping partner to be respected. One wonders how far

6 3.1413b2ff., tr. Freese (1926); see also Sifakis, this volume.

7 See Trussler (1994) 292; in advertisements for a recent revival (London, 1999) the handbag has become an icon of the play. There is a similar recollection of Garrick in a note on our passage of Aristotle, *Rhetoric* in Cope (1877) III 149.

ancient dramatists, in their smaller theatrical world, would have shared the feelings expressed by T. S. Eliot (1950, 22):

> ...in the theatre, the problem of communication presents itself immediately. You are deliberately writing verse for other voices, not for your own, and you do not know whose voices they will be. You are aiming to write lines which will have an immediate effect upon an unknown and unprepared audience, to be interpreted to that audience by unknown actors rehearsed by an unknown producer.

In fact, printed copies of modern plays (including T. S. Eliot's) sometimes give directions that relate to the speaking of the words as well as to the actions that are intended to accompany them and to the scenic background at large. From the surviving copies and fragments of Greek plays there is very little of this kind, and a paper by Taplin (1977b) makes it clear that while such instructions may sometimes go back to ancient readings of the text, it is hardly likely that any (or if any, perhaps one or two exceptional instances) can go back to notes for, or deriving from, original productions. One of the very few examples of 'stage directions' in Menander is the marginal note ἡσυχῆ, literally 'quietly' at *Aspis* 93–6, indicating an 'aside'.[8] While in theory such notes could reflect memories of a distinguished actor's performance of the kind we have just been considering, they are much more like observations derived from the text by a commentator or an attentive reader.

The same point arises apropos of a number of notes in the commentary on Terence under the name of Donatus which offer remarks on the delivery of the words, and sometimes on accompanying gestures, or even facial expressions, as on *Phormio* 184, *ERUS ADEST uultu tristi ac superciliis arduis hoc dicendum est*, 'to be said with a bleak expression and a frown'. It has been argued that remarks of this kind spring from a tradition of dramatic performances such as may be reflected in the group of manuscripts with illustrations.[9] Perhaps, as we allowed above, memories of performances sometimes survived. Crucial, it seems, are the references to facial expressions, which cannot derive from a tradition of masked performance as recalled in the miniatures.[10] As is argued in a recent discussion by Jakobi (1996: 7–14), notes of this kind are essentially text-based (to put

[8] Sandbach, in Gomme and Sandbach (1973), aptly compares the fuller form 'he says this aside', ἡσυχῆ δὲ ταῦτα λέγει, as found in the scholia to Aristophanes, *Frogs* 606; there is another ἡσυχῆ at *Aspis* 467.

[9] Jones and Morey (1930–31); *MNC*³ (=Webster (1995)) under 6XP1, with further references; some examples are reproduced in Duckworth (1994) Plates I–VIII.

[10] The old controversy over the history of masked and maskless performances of New Comedy in Latin will not be pursued here, but is usefully outlined by Duckworth (1994) 92–3.

it so, *explications de texte*) and not performance-based. They are relevant to the present discussion in two ways: marginally, in that their composer or composers presumably had comedy somewhere in the background of life, whether as education, scholarly pursuit, entertainment or all three, and the notes are thereby credible witnesses to ways in which the lines were delivered; and more centrally because of a concept of dramatic reading which seems to have played an important part in the survival of Menander and some of his fellow comic poets, and can hardly be left out of consideration when one is concerned with the more directly theatrical side of the story.

PLAYS OUTSIDE THE THEATRE

Aristophanes says that two of the songs of his ageing rival Cratinus were all the rage at symposia (*Knights* 529–30). In *Clouds* (1355–72), Strepsiades complains that his son's party piece was a shocking speech from Euripides' *Aeolus* instead of a lyric by Simonides or a recital from Aeschylus. The often-quoted story of the Athenian captives who gained their release from the quarries in Syracuse by recalling Euripides' plays and being able to sing lyrics from them confirms that plays were thought of as something from which one might well have a stock of favourite passages, whether from schooldays or adulthood, to be called on at will, and hopefully in happier circumstances than those of enduring forced hard labour.[11] This look back to classical Athens shows that the practice of recital (as opposed to theatrical) performances of Menander is one with deep roots.

An interesting sketch of Menander at the symposium, alongside a wide variety of other entertainments, is given by Jones (1991, 192–3). Among the texts referred to is a passage of Plutarch;[12] one might admit objections, says Plutarch, to Old Comedy at a party; but as to New Comedy, 'it has become so completely a part of the symposium that we could chart our course more easily without wine than without Menander'. I am not sure that Jones is on safe ground in arguing from what Plutarch goes on to say about some typical features of the plays and their plots that whole comedies were performed at parties, rather than excerpts or long monologues;[13] but there is plenty of documentation, including passages from Pliny (*Ep.* 3.1.9 et al.), for groups of *comoedi* performing in such

[11] Plutarch, *Life of Nicias* 29.2–3.

[12] *Sympotic Questions* 7. 8 = *Moralia* 712A–B: tr. Minar (1961).

[13] So Fantham (1984) 300.

contexts, or for soloists like the slave-boy in Statius, *Silvae* 2.1.114, who is admired for his beauty as Menander is for his language.[14]

Evidence of several different kinds gives an idea of the nature of these occasions and their role in perpetuating or developing the traditions of spoken dramatic verse. Earlier in the context of Plutarch cited above, a speaker refers to performances of Plato in a way which is of special interest because of the appearance of a scene representing a Platonic dialogue among the Mytilene Menander mosaics to be discussed below: 'You are aware', he says 'that of the dialogues of Plato, some are narrative and others dramatic. Slaves are taught the most lively of these dramatic dialogues, so as to say them by rote. They use a type of presentation appropriate to the personalities of the characters in the text, with modulation of voice and gestures and delivery suited to the meaning.'[15] This is something much more akin to performance than simple reading aloud. It may be set alongside a very similar concept of *hypokrisis* quoted from Longinus, *Ars rhetorica* by Jakobi (1996: 7), in which it is presented as a true representation of an individual's character and emotions, with a deployment of the body and of the voice suitable to the actions involved.[16] It is noteworthy that the discussion goes on to refer both to Demosthenes and to plays in performance. Plainly, the degree of *hypokrisis* present would be likely to vary from occasion to occasion.[17]

In the kind of party depicted by Aulus Gellius (2.23), the friends are represented as taking Caecilius' *Plocium* and comparing it (to Caecilius' disadvantage) with the play by Menander from which *Plocium* derived. A passage of Caecilius was disliked for his introduction of certain mime-like elements: *nescioquae mimica inculcauit* (what precisely is meant by this is a puzzle). This sort of party, if the comparison of plays is to make sense, would need to operate with complete texts (perhaps Gellius and his friends really did). Abridged texts, or texts marked (apparently) for reading, with the different voices indicated by numbers, would be apt for

[14] Green and Handley (2001) 93–4.

[15] 711 B–C, ending with πρόσεστι δ' ὑπόκρισις πρέπουσα τῷ ἤθει τῶν ὑποκειμένων προσώπων καὶ φωνῆς πλάσμα καὶ σχῆμα καὶ διαθέσεις ἑπόμεναι τοῖς λεγομένοις.

[16] ὑπόκρισίς ἐστι μίμησις τῶν κατ' ἀλήθειαν ἑκάστῳ παρισταμένων ἠθῶν καὶ παθῶν καὶ διάθεσις σώματός τε καὶ τόνου φωνῆς πρόσφορος τοῖς ὑποκειμένοις πράγμασι (p. 194 Hammer). The importance of ὑπόκρισις (*actio*, *pronuntiatio*) in the eyes of orators and rhetorical theorists emerges powerfully from the survey of the subject in Katsouris (1981) esp. 12–20.

[17] Demetrius, *On style* 195, distinguishes dramatic reading from full-blown action, in remarking that 'Acting technique offers other aspects to investigate, for example the case of Ion in Euripides, who seizes his bow and threatens the swan which is fouling the sculptures with its droppings. The actor is given wide scope for stage movements by Ion's rush for his bow, by turning his face up to the sky as he speaks to the swan, and by the way in which all the other details are shaped to exploit acting skills. But acting is not our present subject' (tr. Innes (1995)).

less scholarly occasions. An example of an abridgement is a papyrus of the second century AD, *P Oxy.* 409 + 2655, with parts of Menander's *Kolax*, which may have been intended for symposium use, either among the guests or by professional entertainers.[18] The existence of these abridged or part-numbered texts increases our awareness of the possibilities of different kinds of dramatic readings outside the theatre, and hence of the possibilities of interaction between what happened on the stage over the centuries and what happened in the world outside.

An interesting case-study is given by the scenes from Menander found in a house in Chorapha, Mytilene.[19] In recent discussion, it is common ground that the mosaics, a core of them if not all, spring from a long artistic tradition originating in major wall-paintings of the early Hellenistic age (possibly still within Menander's lifetime) which set out to capture key moments of the plays; what is less clear is to what extent and for what reasons they have suffered changes in the course of centuries of transmission, and hence how far they can be trusted as evidence either for original or for contemporary productions.

The continuity of the tradition can be demonstrated acceptably from some leading examples. The Mytilene *Theophoroumene*, with its two young men shown as dancing in honour of Cybele, the Great Mother, has amongst its forebears a very well-known scene from a villa in Pompeii, signed by Dioskourides of Samos; there it was one of a pair bought to ornament a floor-pavement.[20] The other member of the pair also has a relation at Mytilene; it depicts the opening scene of *Synaristosai*, with a party of three women at the end of a meal, and a little servant girl in attendance.[21] There are derivatives of the *Theophoroumene* scene in

[18] See Arnott (1996a) 154–5 with further references. Texts with numbered parts ('algebraic notation'), both of Greek and of Latin New Comedy, are discussed by Jory (1963) and others: an example is *PSI* 1176, of the first century AD (*PCG* VIII.1063), a fragment recently reconsidered in connection with Menander's *Fabula incerta* by Handley (1997a) and Arnott (1998b).

[19] First fully published in Charitonidis et al. (1970); catalogued in *MNC*³ = Webster (1995) under 6DM 2, and assigned there, with caution, to the mid-fourth century AD or later.

[20] Mytilene scene, *MNC*³ 6DM 2.5; Dioskourides scene, *MNC*³ 3DM 2: together in colour in the frontispiece of *IGD* = Trendall and Webster (1971).

[21] Respectively *MNC*³ 3DM 1 and 6DM 2.3; together in colour in Green and Handley (2001) figs. 50–1. Another mosaic, with figures in the order of the Dioskourides scene, but with a second small servant figure in the background at the left, has recently been found in excellent condition at Zeugma in Syria; Sophie Laurent, *Le Monde de la Bible* 132 (jan.–fév. 2001) has a good plate at p. 11, a reference I owe to Alain Blanchard and Colin Austin. The depiction is labelled ΣΥΝΑΡΙΣΤΩΣΑΣ and signed ΖΩΣΙΜΟΣ ΕΠΟΙΕΙ, with the title on the façade of a schematically drawn three-door background and the signature on a dark band which suggests the front of a platform. Otherwise, the figures have moved away from the theatre towards the world of everyday, with plain long dresses and hardly a hint of masks in the presentation of their faces. The scene is still a remarkable witness to the survival of at least some knowledge of the play.

other media, as witness to its survival as a classic – most notably some fine Hellenistic terracotta statuettes from Myrina that represent both the young man with the cymbals and the young man with the tambourine.[22] The theatrical appeal of these representations, and hence their strong theatrical background, seems beyond doubt.[23]

Another side of the story is given in an important recent paper by Csapo (1997). Csapo studies not only the composition of the individual scenes from the house in Mytilene, but that of the whole T-shaped pattern in which those in the dining room floor were set; and he stresses the differences between the Mytilene scenes and their counterparts by Dioskourides. When figures are exchanged (slave in the Mytilene version of *Theophoroumene* instead of girl piper as in Dioskourides), or when left-to-right reversal takes place (old woman on the left in Mytilene *Synaristosai*, perhaps thought of as speaking the first line of the play; speaking on the right in Dioskourides), these variations (it is argued) are not from different productions, or different moments chosen from the same dramatic sequence, but they are modifications by the artist independent of the stage. A comment by me (Handley 1997b: 197) raises the consideration, still to be pursued in detail, that for the designation of acts and for speakers' names (not to mention an exchange like that of *Theophoroumene*) the mosaics still to some extent depend on a text-based tradition. The transposition of characters to left from right may reflect a desire to have the first speaker in the passage concerned on the left hand side, just as in scene-headings, where these occur, the characters regularly read from left to right in order of speaking. Just as, from the theatrical side, in the words of Green (1994a: 164), the mosaics 'are the result of a multiple and recurrent process of up-dating for style of mask, costume and body-language', so other elements from the world outside can be seen or suspected to have intervened: the taste of artist and patron, and the context of symposium reading which (as we have seen) admits Plato in parallel with Menander, and points to the choice of excerpts from both for the purpose.[24]

[22] *MNC*³, under 3DT 16 and 17, with examples illustrated side by side in *IGD* 146.

[23] A similar test case can be found in one of the most widely illustrated scenes from ancient comedy, the relief in Naples (Mus. Naz. 6687) in which an angry old man is restrained by another old man from attacking a revelling youth supported by a slave and accompanied by a girl piper. The play was perhaps Menander's *Methe*; for the relief, see (e.g.) Bieber (1961) fig. 324 and Handley (1997b) fig. 61; it is listed in *MNC*³ under XZ 41, together with its numerous relations, as discussed in some detail by Green (1985).

[24] The scene of *Phaedo* with Socrates, Simmias and Kebes among the representations of Menander at Mytilene may have its textual counterpart in an elegantly written copy from Oxyrhynchus of

Green (1994a: 165) sums up by saying that the Mytilene mosaics and other late derivatives of the tradition 'are not snapshots of the contemporary stage . . . They are the visual equivalent of literary quotations'. If that is the way to look at them, they still show that some of the scenes originally selected to give high points of the plays as theatre were also those that lent themselves to readings. Sometimes, it may be, a significant stage gesture has survived. In the Mytilene scene of *Samia*, Act III, words and picture seem to match very well. The cook, in the background at the left, says (368), 'I'll stand back a little'; then Demeas, centre, 'Don't you hear me? Get out!', with an arm raised in a gesture of dismissal; then Chrysis, right, 'Oh dear, oh dear – wherever to?'[25]

What emerges from this anthology of evidence is a complex – sometimes no doubt mutually supportive – relationship, between speech on stage and speech off stage, whether in a context of oratory, academic study, education or polite entertainment. It may well be that this complex relationship, and not simply the continuing tradition of performance, was cardinal to the long survival of Menander. But action, though it can up to a point be mirrored in dramatic recitation, is a traditional and still powerful element of New Comedy in the theatre, and we must now turn to that.

SCENES OF MOVEMENT AND SPECTACLE

The trend from comedy of action and situation in Aristophanes and his contemporaries to comedy of manners in Menander is one which has been variously delineated.[26] One thing that is clear is that in this genre of comedy, as opposed to Aristophanes in the past, and the writers of New Comedy in Latin in the future, the use of music, and with it the demand for actors to sing, or to sing and dance, is almost at vanishing point. The exceptions are of special interest.

At *Dyskolos* 880, music from the accompanist's pipe is heard.[27] The slave Getas and the cook Sikon are about to carry the misanthrope Knemon out of his house and torment him by dancing up to the door

the proem of Plato's *Phaedrus*, 227a–230e, a very suitable reading on its own, one might think. The handwriting of the Plato is assigned to the third century AD; it is on the back of a register of landowners that was recycled to take it: Turner (1987) no. 84.

25 *MNC*[3] 6DM 2. 2. The scene from *Plokion* (6DM 2. 1) has a very similar composition, and we know that there was a man-and-wife quarrel in the play.

26 There is a sketch by me in the *CHCL* (Handley (1985a)); significant contributions since include the detailed study by Nesselrath (1990) and remarks by Arnott (1996b) in the course of commenting on Alexis; Green (1994a: 70–84) gives a complementary survey of the evidence for changes of emphasis from the archaeological material. Add now Csapo (2000).

27 See Hunter, this volume ch. 8.

and calling in fantastic terms for equipment for the party that is being held in the shrine next door. It is a romp, given additional life and colour by the music. Critics have remarked on the incongruity with the tone of much of the earlier comedy; and part at least of the explanation for that is to be found in a tradition of revelling endings to comic plays, which Menander exploits on this occasion by making his ending a reprise of the borrowing scenes with slave, cook and Knemon earlier in the play (456–521). In this scene, for the only time in surviving Menander, the metre is iambic tetrameter catalectic. The piper is explicitly mentioned in 880; whether that implies that the accompaniment was more prominent than in the scenes in trochaic tetrameters, and whether these in practice were all treated alike, are questions that cannot now be answered. The least we can say is that this is something very different from a play-reading.

Some fragmentary scenes allow us to add a little. *Theophoroumene* was remembered for an occasion when the girl possessed by the goddess sang a song. It was a sequel to the performance by the two young men in the mosaic scene discussed above (p. 171); something of the song (if rightly identified) survives in a papyrus fragment.[28] *Leukadia* was quoted for a song or chant by a temple custodian that seems to come immediately after the opening lines of the play as recovered recently from an Oxyrhynchus papyrus; it helps to set the highly unusual scene on a cliff top.[29] Finally, *Phasma* is quoted for a line in a lyric metre from a context of which we know nothing;[30] a fragment which might be from *Phasma* has a scene in which water for a nuptial bath is brought with due ceremony and accompanied by a singer and a slave to play the pipe, but though there does seem to have been a lyric metre there, its nature is unclear.[31] Notably, in the three cases where we have a context, the music is not part of the stylisation of the scene, as in the ending of *Dyskolos* and in many scenes of Aristophanes and the Latin comic writers in lyrics or tetrameters of different sorts: the songs are such as could occur in a context of the real world, rather like the pipe tune for Pan in *Dyskolos* at 432. These scenes need not have imposed any serious professional demands on the actors; if the Mytilene mosaics of *Theophoroumene* and of *Leukadia* are a token of symposium performance, there seems no reason to suppose that they

[28] Sandbach (1990) 146 ('Fragmentum dubium'), Arnott (1996a), *Theoph.* vv. 31–57; it is in uncomplicated lyric hexameters.

[29] Arnott (1996a) 226ff., anapaestic dimeters; for the Mytilene mosaic scene, hard to interpret, see *MNC*3 under 6DM 2.9.

[30] Fr. 3 K.-T., ithyphallic.

[31] Handley (1992); cf. Arnott (1996a) 84–5, and Perusino and Giacomoni (1999).

would be beyond the range of a normally educated person who took a part. But they are in essence theatre scenes.

The lively stage action in the finale of *Dyskolos* can be compared with a scene on a Paestan red-figure calyx krater signed by Asteas, with two young men named Gymnilos and Kosilos manhandling an old man called Charinos off the top of a chest, with a slave Karion looking on; this is thought to be early work by this painter, and if it was done about 350 BC, it is an apt illustration of the kind of comedy that the *Dyskolos* finale recalls.[32] Another important example is *Samia* Act IV – entirely in swiftly moving trochaic tetrameters, full of conflict and interchanging dialogue, and intercut with sudden exits and entrances. It is on occasions of this kind that the language may take a special colour beyond the range of Menander's regular colloquial style, with alliteration and repetition, with poetic idiom for the sake of elevation rather than satirical allusion or parody, and discourse with abnormal dislocations or patterns. At *Samia* 492, Nikeratos rushes onto the scene from his house with a furious denunciation of Moschion, beginning ὦ κάκιστ' ἀνδρῶν ἁπάντων . . . 'Wickedest of all the wicked . . . ', on which a performer with a strong voice could happily pull out all the stops. 'Nikeratos' language might be thought overdone' says Sandbach; in considering some details of the poetic language used, he warns that 'one cannot say that it was impossible for an Athenian to resort to the language of tragedy if he had strong feelings to express'.[33] Nonetheless, we seem to be dealing with reality enhanced by convention rather than reality itself. There is a similar outburst on another sudden entry at 532 ὦ τάλας ἐγώ, τάλας . . . 'Misery on misery . . . '; the cause of the misery is that Nikeratos found his daughter in the house in the act of suckling. The remark pours out twice with a fascinating variation of pattern, like that of 'O my son Absalom, Absalom my son' or of Polemon's emotional outburst in *Perikeiromene* 'Glykera has left me, she's left me, Glykera . . . '[34] Once again, patterns of this kind may occur in the real world; reality may be enhanced by the dramatist at his choice, and offered as a special gift to the actors who will perform his work.

It is a pity that we have so little direct knowledge of Menander's rivals Philemon and Diphilus. The fragments surviving in Greek, augmented,

32 *IGD* IV, 14.

33 First in a note on 495ff. in Gomme and Sandbach (1973); then on 507.

34 *Samia* 535–6 τὴν θυγατέρ' <ἄρτι> τὴν ἐμὴν τῷ παιδίῳ / τιτθίον διδοῦσαν ἔνδον κατέλαβον; and 540–1 διδοῦσαν τιτθίον τῷ παιδίῳ / ἀρτίως ἔνδον κατέλαβον τὴν ἐμαυτοῦ θυγατέρα; *Perik.* 256f./506f. Γλυκέρα με καταλέλοιπε, καταλέλοιπέ με / Γλυκέρα, Πάταικε: see Feneron (1974) 88 with n. 27.

with inevitable uncertainties, from adaptations such as Plautus' *Casina* and *Rudens* (Diphilus) or *Mercator* and *Mostellaria* (Philemon) suggest that they had ways of exploiting stage spectacle and verbal colour not unlike those exemplified here, in which they inclined more to traditional comedy than Menander regularly does.[35] It is probably no accident that when Plautus has a slave tease his master with the thought that the trickery he has suffered would be an excellent subject for comedy, the two names he chooses to represent that kind of comedy are Diphilus and Philemon; or that Terence, a devoted Menandrean in so many ways, went to Diphilus for the lively scene with the brothel-keeper that he cut in to his adaptation of Menander's *Second Adelphoi*.[36]

An interesting perspective on different styles of comedy in performance, as seen in the Roman theatre of the 160s BC, is given by some words written by Terence for his actor–manager L. Ambivius Turpio to speak as a prologue to the *Heauton Timoroumenos*. For our purposes the essential words come in the appeal for a fair hearing that begins at 35, *adeste aequo animo* . . . 'Allow me to perform in quiet a play that stands still,[37] so that I don't always have to play the Running Slave, the Angry Old Man, the Hungry Parasite and the Shameless Informer, the Grasping Brothel-Keeper, at the top of my voice and with the greatest effort.' A few words later, the speaker engagingly grumbles that the authors of new plays are merciless to an old man like himself: 'if there's one that needs real effort, they run to me; if its a gentle one, off it goes to another company' (43–5).

CONTRASTS IN TONE

An Angry Old Man is what Demeas is in *Samia* at the moment captured by the Mytilene mosaic, when (as we noted, p. 173) he is shown throwing Chrysis out of the house: 'Don't you hear me? Get out!' (369). But what is more interesting here is the battle between anger and self-control that the actor is now asked to portray, as Demeas ascends to this moment of crisis. A key stage in the ascent is the reflective soliloquy which he is given at 324ff., beginning ποῖ σύ, ποῖ, μαστιγία; λάβ' αὐτόν . . . 'Where you going – wants flogging – catch him!' This is said as the slave Parmenon

35 There are brief remarks on this, with some references, in Handley (1985a) at 424.

36 Plaut. *Most.* 1149–51; Ter. *Adel.* 6–11, referring to 155ff.

37 What is given here as 'a play that stands still' is *stataria*, evidently a recognised theatrical term of the time; for more discussion of the passage, see the chapters by Richard Hunter, Peter Brown and Elaine Fantham in this volume.

runs off to escape the threat of a beating for his involvement in the family's misadventures. Demeas' frustration breaks out in a cry of high emotion (a marginal note in the Bodmer copy identifies it as a quotation from Euripides, *Oedipus*): 'O citadel of Kekrops land, O clear air of Heaven . . . ' So far this is comparable with the portrayal of anger we have seen in Act IV of the same play.

Suddenly the mood changes (326). 'O . . . why are you shouting, Demeas? What about, you idiot? Hold on and pull yourself together.' The audience has known of him from the first as a well-to-do man with an adopted son Moschion, whom he has brought up liberally as a single parent; for some time he has had a relationship with the woman from Samos, Chrysis, who gives the play its title, and she is now his established partner. He believes that Moschion has deceived him and had a child by her while he was abroad. He is wrong, and everyone knows he is wrong. But Demeas is not laughably wrong; and the reasoning by which he acquits Moschion of serious passion or malice, and sees him as the young and headstrong victim of seduction by a woman with a sexually experienced past, is a development intended to evoke a measure of sympathy and interest. At the outset of the new chain of thought he turns to the audience as if he were confiding in friends. 'She caught him, perhaps, when he'd drunk too much and was out of control.' The anger transfers to Chrysis: 'The woman's a whore, a damned whore' – and she must go. But that is at a cost: 'Forget about missing her; stop being her lover for good.'[38] The balance of dramatic illusion is delicate; and the range of diction from tragic elevation and periodic flow to gutter language and to staccato sentences gives us some impression of the range and control that the delivery of the speech demands. There is a clear contrast between Demeas here and the more comically and more boisterously treated anger of Nikeratos in Act IV.

Longer-term contrasts of this kind depend for their appreciation on the recovery of long stretches of text, in which the twentieth century has been fortunate. They may be integrated with contrasts of more immediate impact, whether in action or language. This happens very typically with characters of the same type, as with the two old men in the scene from the relief in Naples mentioned above (n. 23). Sandbach makes an attractive case for recognising a contrast at *Samia* 96ff. between the gloomy staccato style with which he credits Nikeratos and

[38] 329, ἄνδρες, vocative, to the audience; 339f., παρέλαβεν αὐτόν που μεθύοντα δηλαδή, οὐκ ὄντ' ἐν αὑτοῦ; 348, χαμαιτύπη δ' ἅνθρωπος, ὄλεθρος; 350, ἐπιλαθοῦ τοῦ πόθου, πέπαυσ' ἐρῶν.

the more relaxed and outward-looking manner of Demeas, his wealthy neighbour.[39] *Dyskolos* offers an example of a four-part contrast, involving the young men Sostratos and Gorgias together with Knemon and Sostratos' father Kallippides from the senior generation. The attitudes and language of the four reflect a complexity of likenesses and differences, not always symmetrical, between youth and age, wealth and poverty, town and country. Costumes and masks offer obvious means of enhancing these features in production, and audiences can be helped to focus on them by references in the text;[40] the contributions of voice and gestures add other dimensions of contrast.[41]

'LIKE IT WAS': SOME FEATURES OF THE NARRATIVE SPEECH

We return to *Samia* to consider Demeas' long speech at the beginning of Act III (206ff., with the loss of a line or so at the beginning). Enough survives of that beginning to show that the speech took off in a high style which matches, and possibly prepares the listener for, its magnitude and importance within the play. In that respect, it is not unlike the long speech in *Sikyonios* (176–271), which sounds its keynote with a reminiscence of its literary forebear in Euripides' *Orestes* (866–956). Here Demeas compares himself to a ship in calm weather struck by a sudden squall.[42] The colourful beginning leads, as in the speech at 324ff. discussed above, to a point at which the audience is involved ('Consider if I'm out of my mind or not', 216); and then, with what is recognisably the beginning of a narrative, the story is told.[43]

Demeas was keen to get everything ready for Moschion's marriage to the girl next door, Nikeratos' daughter. He gave his orders; everything was happening at once; he was trying to help by giving out things from the pantry, and from there he overheard an old woman trying to calm the baby that had been left crying on a couch. 245ff.: 'Oh dear me, it's no time since I was nursing Moschion as a baby like that, and now here he is with a baby of his own...' That, taken with some further

[39] 1970: 121f.; but see Arnott (1998a) 42–3. In the discussion of Sandbach's paper (1970: 137) a parallel is drawn with the contrasting styles of speeches by two young men, Gorgias in *Dyskolos* at 271–87 and Sostratos at 666–90.

[40] See, for example, Handley (1965) on *Dysk.* 257 and 258.

[41] See the chapters by Richard Green and Eric Csapo in this volume.

[42] He may perhaps have drawn on a nautical passage of tragedy, like the narrative in Euripides' *Iphigenia in Tauris* at 1345ff., or the speech which contained Sophocles' two lines about navigation at night (*Achaion syllogos* fr. 143), if indeed they are not themselves part of a simile.

[43] 219, 'The moment I got in there...': see Handley (1965) on *Dysk.* 666–90.

overhearing, taken with a sight of Chrysis comforting the baby at her breast, is the squall that has upset the smooth-sailing ship that he thought he was. 267: 'Recognisably, it's hers: but who on earth the father is – is it mine or . . . I'm not saying, my friends, not even suspecting, just putting to you what I've heard with my own ears, not getting angry yet . . .' He soon will, as we have seen. The low-key narrative of life at home is coloured throughout with the sense of disaster impending, in much the way that Lysias, in 1. 6ff., has his client Euphiletos set the story of his wife's unfaithfulness with Eratosthenes against the domestic background that was the scene of the killing for which he is on trial. The details, in both speeches, are not simply picturesque; the speaker's narration of them is intended to depict his own character at the same time; and the client, or the actor, must handle them plausibly so that they do that.

It is a notable feature of Demeas' narrative that the narrator cuts in direct speech by people other than himself.[44] A speaker who quotes brings a new perspective or a new dimension to what he has to say, and may thereby seem to transport his audience in imagination to another scene. There is a striking example in our earliest extant Greek play, when the messenger who narrates the battle of Salamis in Aeschylus' *Persae* of 472 BC quotes the battle cry that begins 'On, sons of Greece, and set your country free . . .' (402). Whether or not this represents a chant, as Bers (1997: 26) inclines to think, it is (from personal recollection) a moving experience to hear an accomplished Greek actor make the lines stand out of the speech with a resonance akin to the great examples of martial rhetoric that people recall from Nelson, Napoleon, Churchill and others.

At a polar opposite of emotion, but with a similar vivid effect, is Demeas, in the speech we are considering from *Samia*, Act III. In one line (227), he sets the scene in the kitchen from the cries of women preparing the food, as they shout for flour, water, oil and charcoal. Quoted dialogue can be even more interesting from the point of view of performance. It still seems likely, as it did to Osmun (1952: 162–3), that the extensive use of this device is a typically Menandrean development. The dialogue of the old nurse and the servant girl overheard by Demeas later on in the speech is

44 The discussion by Osmun (1952) depends on the texts then available; it seems to have received less notice than it might. Blundell (1980) has good brief observations and more material; there is a new study with useful points by Lamagna (1998); Handley (forthcoming) concentrates on the special case of gappy papyri. Perspective is given to all these studies by Bers (1997), who, for understandable reasons, does little with New Comedy (p. 4; but see p. 118 on passages of *Dyskolos*, and Menander's sparse use of signals like φησί).

a good example, beginning at 252: 'Oh dear, do bath the baby, girls,' says she,[45] 'How can you neglect the little one on his father's wedding day?' Quick as quick 'Oh, you do talk loud,' says the girl, 'Master's in there.' 'No, surely not. Where?' 'In the pantry' – and then she raised her voice a bit 'Mistress wants you, Nurse: off you go, hurry. (He's heard nothing, by great good luck.)' What gives this apparently trivial little exchange its depth is, of course, the context, with the double irony of the unintended (and therefore credible) revelation to Demeas of the baby's parentage and the girl's misplaced confidence that he had heard nothing. It is for the actor to put what spin he can on that; he may have had experience of playing female roles, but here, as earlier, he has to decide what to do as an old man quoting women, and in a situation typical of women's lives, while preserving his own dramatic identity.

A passage of Quintilian, presumably referring to a style of performance of Menander in the later first century AD, suggests that for him at least mimicry could go too far. He is recommending that the orator should distance himself from the more exuberant kind of stage performer: 'For even comic actors seem to me to commit a gross offence against the canons of their art, when, if they have in the course of some narrative to quote either the words of an old man, as, e. g., in the *Hydria* prologue, or of a woman, as in the *Georgos*, they utter them in a tremulous or treble voice, notwithstanding that they are playing the part of a young man.'[46]

The compounding of effects that can be achieved in the acting of quoted dialogue is well illustrated in a long speech in *Misoumenos* Act IV, beginning 'O Lord Zeus, the cruelty of the pair of them, outlandish, inhuman . . .'[47] The slave Getas has been witness to a bitter quarrel between the play's heroine, Krateia, her father, and its hero, the professional soldier Thrasonides, 'The Man She Hated' as the title puts it. The essence of the situation is that Thrasonides has kept Krateia in his house as a war-captive; he loves her, and would like her to live with him as his established partner; but she refuses, and he will not force himself on her. Matters are further complicated when Demeas, the devoted parent, arrives with the object of ransoming his daughter and rescuing her

45 "λούσατ', ὦ τάλαν, τὸ παιδίον" φησίν . . . τάλαν / ὦ τάλαν is an interjection used in comedy only by women, and so characterises the person here quoted: Gomme and Sandbach (1973: 328) on *Epitr.* 258/434. On *Samia* 252ff. and *Mis.*, as quoted below, see also Handley (2001) 25–8.

46 Quintilian *Inst.* 11. 3. 91, tr. Csapo and Slater (1995) 284–5. On this passage see also Csapo, this volume, ch. 5, and Handley (2001) 28f.

47 ὦ Ζεῦ πολυτίμητ' ὠμότητος ἐκτόπου ἀμφοῖν ἀπανθρώπου τε . . . (284ff.; 685ff. Arnott): see Handley (forthcoming) and Lamagna (1998) 292–3; a brief presentation with three other speeches, Handley (1985a) 420–3.

from the situation of being a stateless captive with no proof of identity. The latent reason for the hatred is the deep one that she believes (in fact wrongly) that Thrasonides is responsible for the death of her brother.

Getas is presented as reliving his experience of the quarrel. So introverted is he (we can contrast the extrovert Demeas of *Samia*) that he continues to do this in spite of the presence on stage of Kleinias, who fails to attract his attention, and follows Getas round as he paces up and down with a stream of comments and attempted interruptions, until at last he succeeds in breaking in at 323/724. The comic element in all this offsets the strong emotion of the slave's reflections. It also has the effect, not unfamiliar in comedy, of allowing the presentation to be telescoped.[48] The two actors need to work out the balance of this routine; but an essential function of it is to solve the problems that a direct presentation of the quarrel would have given, both of length and intensity. At the same time it provides the additional dimension of a slave's eye view (one characterised by its strong sense of the values of common humanity), of the strange behaviour of people whose seemingly defensible attitudes have led them into a conflict that looks as if it cannot be resolved.

Damage to the papyrus means that Getas' reflections cannot be followed as fully as we should like throughout. Here the material point is that he mixes narrative and comment with direct quotation, in a manner that an excerpt will perhaps illustrate adequately. We move from hearing of the crux of the argument with Demeas to an account of a passionate appeal to Krateia:

> He went on and on with this one thing, 'She's my daughter: I am here as her father to ask you to release her.' 'And face-to-face, Demeas, I ask you to let me have her as my wife.' (297–9/698–700)

After one of Kleinias' interruptions, Getas goes on:

> Lord help us, he couldn't just be reasonable about it, could he? It was pig versus mule, as they say. But that's not so bad as her – looks away, she does, while he's speaking. 'Oh, Krateia', he says, 'don't leave me, I beg you, don't. You'd never had a man when I took you, and I was your man, the first to love you and cherish you; and I do love you, Krateia, my dearest. What is there about me that pains you? I'll be dead, you'll see, if you leave me.' No answer, none.
> KLEINIAS: What *is* all this?
> GETAS: A barbarian, the woman is, a lioness.

48 A classic, if cruder, example of this technique is Aristophanes' reduction of the prologue speech of Euripides' *Helen* at *Thesmophoriazusae* 855–70.

KLEINIAS: Damn you, you *still* can't see me. How strange.
GETAS: Completely out of his mind. By Apollo here, I'd never have set her free . . .
The Greek way? Happens everywhere, we all know. But pity is right for those who show pity. If you don't show it to me, I've no time or regard for you. You can't? Well, I'm not surprised at all. (302–20/703–21: mostly from Handley (1985a) 423)

The effect of the staccato style of Getas' comments can be given quite well in English. It is, if anything, underscored by the interruptions; and it is in sharp contrast with the high emotional tone of the words he quotes.[49] But there is another effect to notice, when with the words given as 'The Greek way? Happens everywhere, we all know', Getas is not quoting in any natural sense of the term, but putting a point of view as part of an internal debate with himself.[50] This brings us to the consideration that a speaker may not only quote other people (or indeed himself) verbatim, he may present hypothetical utterances of his own or someone else's; or even (as here) a thought or a formulated proposition. There is in this a further challenge to the actor's powers of delivery.

'SPEECH IN SPEECH': SOME FURTHER VARIATIONS

I turn here, under a heading that quotes from the title of Bers (1997),[51] to a passage discussed in Handley (forthcoming), to make the point that the status of apparent quotations is not always obvious; there can be tricky problems for anyone editing a text. At *Dyskolos* 611 ff., Sostratos is trying to persuade Gorgias to join the sacrificial feast: 'I won't take "No" for an answer' he says (οὐκ ἂν ἐπιτρέψαιμί σοι ἄλλως ποῆσαι); then we have πάντ' ἔχομεν, followed by words equivalent to 'For Heaven's sake, who on earth refuses to come to lunch when a friend has made a sacrifice?' (ὦ Ἡράκλεις, / τουτὶ δ' ἀπαρνεῖται τίς ἀνθρώπων ὅλως, / ἐλθεῖν ἐπ' ἄριστον συνήθους τεθυκότος;). πάντ' ἔχομεν, literally, 'We have all (we need)' is known as a form of refusal. The decision is between attributing the words to Gorgias, and leaving them with Sostratos in accordance with the (always fallible) part-marking of the Bodmer papyrus; and if the latter, we have to choose between supposing that Sostratos is quoting

49 It does not greatly matter here that there are different ways of allocating some of the words between speakers.

50 315f./716f., Ἑλληνικόν, καὶ πανταχοῦ γινόμενον ἴσμεν (however punctuated) is an antithetical reaction to οὐκ ἂν ἀπέλυσ(α) 'I'd never have set her free', and it is in turn answered by what follows.

51 Useful background material for this section can be had from Bers' index, s.v. *hypophora*.

a refusal just given off-stage (as in Handley (1965)), and thinking that he is putting what he takes to be Gorgias' thoughts into words: 'No thank you.' If Sostratos is the speaker, the actor needs to show, without a signal like 'you say', that the words are an import into his own discourse and not the same as if he had been refusing something himself. The technique must have been familiar from passages where the verbal echo is immediate and clear. The contrast in tone between the first utterance and the echo can itself be amusing, as when the cook Sikon is confronted by a very angry Knemon at *Dyskolos* 502f. (Σικ.) μηδαμῶς, ἀλλ' ἄφες. (Κν.) ἄφες; 'No way, let me go!' 'Let you *go*?' It is worth noting that echoes of this kind, which are a common feature of rapidly interchanging dialogue in both Greek and Latin New Comedy, may be signalled by the use of forms of indirect speech, particularly in questions: τίνα τρόπον; 'How?', answered by ὅντινα τρόπον; 'How, you ask?', *Dyskolos* 362f.; *quid fecit?* answered by *quid ille fecerit?* Terence, *Adelphoe* 84.

Predictably, the lack of such signals as 'you ask', 'she said', and so on gives special problems when damage to a papyrus copy leaves the sequence of a speech or an argument unclear.[52] As it happens, *Misoumenos* has an extraordinary number of passages in which actors are required, as in the passage discussed above, to reproduce words spoken by other people. Arnott (1996a: 252), in calling attention to this, remarks rightly that the play would have needed capable actors: he lists nine passages from the surviving text, and crowns that with a tenth, a long monologue by Thrasonides, a reflective speech in which he argues with himself somewhat in the way that we have here seen Getas do, but much more elaborately.[53] It is clear from the number of surviving fragments of copies, the record of quotations, and the appearance of a scene from the play among the Mytilene mosaics (*MNC*³ 6DM 2.10) – possibly also on a cake mould from Ostia (ibid., 6FL 1) – that this was one of the really popular plays for a long period of antiquity. One factor in this may have been the appeal of these 'mimetic' speeches for recitations, as well as their effect on the stage.

One reflective speech which has a special interest in regard to acting is the soliloquy of Sostratos at *Dis Exapaton* 18–30 – not least because

[52] Cf. Bers (1997) 118, cited at n. 44 above.

[53] 790–808 Arnott, superseding earlier texts; but still with scope for discussion. In spite of contrary views, I take it that Σιμίχη 'ξελήλυθεν at 790 Arnott is not an indication of the presence of another character, but a hypothetical proposition '*Suppose* Simiche comes out', like πρεσβύτερός τις τῇ θύρᾳ ὑπακήκο(ε) '*Suppose* an old man comes to the door', *Dysk.* 493f. See Balme (2001) 176f.

it is possible to compare and contrast in this regard the version of the speech made by Plautus for *Bacchides* 500–25.[54] The essential point to recall here is that Sostratos is left on stage in the belief that his girl and his best friend are having an affair behind his back. He had hoped to set her up as his mistress with some money diverted from his father; now he has just been asked by the friend's father (who knows nothing of Sostratos' own affair) to intervene and break up a relationship of which he had been given a highly lurid account. In fact the whole situation is false, because there are two girls involved, not one – the *Bacchides* of Plautus' title. Menander has the young man imagine a dialogue between himself and his girl, which can be reconstructed to read something like this (I am taking many details in the reconstruction for granted):

So he's a goner, then; she'll master him in one stroke. Caught Sostratos first, didn't you? She'll deny it of course, that's clear to me – she stops at nothing – and all the gods will come in: 'Hope for no luck if I did' – by Zeus, yes – 'Hope for a bad end if I did.' Back off, Sostratos; perhaps she'll persuade you: 'So you're here as father's little slave-boy, are you?' Yes, for sure – and let her try her persuasion on me when I'm empty handed and penniless. I'll return all the gold to my father, and she'll stop her persuasive pleading as soon as she sees, as the proverb has it, that she's telling a tale to a corpse. But I must go for *him* now. But here – I can see my father coming. (Tr. after Handley (2001) 33)

There is more in this vein at the beginning of the following Act (91–102), when Sostratos and his father part after the gold has been notionally handed over, and the young man anticipates what the girl will now say. The broken style, with rapid changes of reference, and shifts between first, second and third persons, is realistic in the sense that the words can be delivered so as to suggest thoughts pouring into a mind under stress; it also has dramatic movement in showing someone setting those thoughts against each other so as to arrive at a decision. Sostratos does so introspectively. Plautus' young man Mnesilochus, by contrast, is made to carry the situation out to the audience. Plautus gives up the internal dialogue; he makes the situation plainer to the audience – perhaps somewhat laboriously so, but he has reason to do this in that he is about to abridge Menander's version – the style, typically, is marked by more poetic decoration in sound and vocabulary than Menander's; the actor is encouraged to raise laughs from the unexpected twist to the tail of

[54] Cf. Handley (2001); full Greek text in Handley (1997c), with quotations from the Latin and references to the intensive analysis by Zwierlein (1990, 1992).

some of his remarks. A quotation of the first half of the speech may serve to illustrate this:

Whether I'm to think my friend or Bacchis is my worse enemy is quite uncertain. Did she choose him before me? Let her have him, that's fine. There'll be no good come of it – not for me, that is. I hope no divinity does me a favour if I don't, conspicuously in every way – love the girl. I'll make sure she shan't say she's got a man she can mock. I'll go home and – why, I'll grab something from father and give it her. I'll punish her many times over, and bring her to beggary – or rather my father. But am I really sound in mind, telling the tale here and now about what's still to come? (500–10).

Having depicted the young man and his mood in this way, with one eye on the further developments with the gold to come in the later part of the play, Plautus then focuses on preparing for the immediate restoration of the father's fortune which, like Menander, he presents as the next move, including a rendering of the proverb about talking to a corpse (515–19):

She'll never live to mock me. I'm resolved to pay over all the gold to my father. Then she'll try to persuade me when I'm empty-handed and penniless; and then it won't matter to me any more than if she were telling the tale at a tomb to a corpse.

The overall effect still presents a striking contrast with the speech of the young man in Menander.

ROMAN EPILOGUE

To end the story there would be unfair to a histrionic style which seems to have been a special development of Menander's comedy, and which, in different ways, other writers could exploit, not least Terence. Remarkably often, Terence's actors have to quote or echo others' or their own sayings or thoughts, with a range of effects from rapid repartee to the narrative of the highly emotional deathbed speech of Chrysis at *Andria* 284–97, with its dramatic staccato introduction:

Near to death, she sent for me; I came; you all left; we were alone. She began 'Dear Pamphilus, you can see her youth and her beauty; and you know how useless both are to protect her welfare and her virtue . . .'[55]

55 Other examples: *Eunuchus* 234–53 (a slave's lively narrative), ibid. 629–42 (a young man's reflective soliloquy); but see particularly *Andria* 28–171, with comments by Cicero, *De oratore* 2. 326–8, aptly quoted by Shipp (1960) on 117.

One of the most interesting comparisons is the beginning of *Eunuchus*, with its first line, *quid igitur faciam?* (46), taking off from the ἀλλὰ τί ποήσω; which is given from a quotation as the beginning of Menander's play.[56] The broken style is readily recognisable:

quid igitur faciam? non eam ne nunc quidem
quom accersor ultro? an potius ita me comparem
non perpeti meretricum contumelias?
exclusit, reuocat: redeam? non si me obsecret.

What shall I do? Not go to her even now, when she sends for me? Or do I set myself not to put up with insults from call-girls? Shut me out; calls me back: do I go? Not if she begs me.

This was a play-beginning that achieved some fame. Barsby (1999) gives references to quotations of the first line, as above, by Cicero and Quintilian; Horace (*Satires* 2. 3. 259–71) and Persius (5. 161–75) both pick up the motif, reproducing both the young man's indecision and despair and the well-meaning if disillusioned advice that his slave companion offers him. Terence has (64–9):

et quod nunc tute tecum iratus cogitas
'egon illam, quae illum, quae me, quae non . . . ! sine modo,
mori me malim, sentiet qui uir siem',
haec uerba una mehercle falsa lacrimula
quam oculos terendo misere uix ui expresserit,
restinguet.

As to what you're thinking, all angry 'What her? After him? And me? When she didn't? Come on, I'd rather die, and show her what sort of man I am' – these are just words: one tricksy tear she finds it hard to squeeze from her eyes will wipe it all away.

The satirists echo not only the content but the style, no doubt enjoying the technical challenge of converting iambics to dactylic hexameters; and Persius even goes to the length of replacing the names that Terence gave to the characters with those from Menander. If, as we have seen, stage scenes took on a second life in readings at symposia, it is interesting that on this occasion a stage scene could spread its influence in quite another medium, and offer what was perhaps a somewhat different challenge to the reader's voice.

[56] See Barsby (1999) for up-to-date commentary and (pp. 304ff.) the principal remains of the plays on which Terence drew.

POSTSCRIPT

It may seem paradoxical that this intimate style of handling dialogue, and of dialogue within dialogue, should have evolved in the conditions of large open-air theatres, and have been acceptable in them no less than in the closed circle of an after-dinner party among friends. An ancient audience might have been equally surprised at drama on the television screen, with its intimate close-ups, or at large scale in a conventional cinema, at gigantic scale in a drive-in. One accepts the conventions of different media, perhaps unconsciously for most of the time; and yet there is abundant evidence from performers that adaptation to a different medium is not always as easy as it may seem from outside. I quote as an eminent witness Olivier (1982), on stage and film acting:

> They call for the same ingredients but in different proportions. The precise differences may take some years of puzzling work to appreciate; in each case there are many subtle variations according to the character of the actor. It took me many years to learn to film-act; at least ten of these were appallingly rough and ready, from sheer prejudice and ignorance. After that, it was necessary to re-learn how to act on stage, incorporating, though, the truth demanded by cinema and thereby reducing the measure of theatricality.[57]

If this does no more, it at least encourages one to keep open the question of the relationship in antiquity of the media in which the spoken word was deployed and was supreme, whether we think of oratory, drama or the various kinds of literary reading and recitation.

SUGGESTIONS FOR FURTHER READING

The completion of Geoffrey Arnott's Loeb edition of Menander with vol. 3 (2000) greatly facilitates access to the plays and the major fragments. Sandbach (1970) is still a valuable introduction to the dramatic qualities of their language; for detailed interpretation, one relies on commentaries and on many widely scattered discussions, especially in regard to the latest discoveries. On the special device of 'Speech in Speech', as discussed above, the basic survey by Osmun (1952) is updated by Blundell (1980) and Lamagna (1998); but more remains to be said. Visual material relating to New Comedy – that is to say depictions of stage scenes, and representations of actors in costume and of masks – is catalogued by Green and Seeberg in Webster (1995) (=*MNC*[3]); a brief introduction to this material is given by Green and Handley (2001) 71–85, with select

[57] Olivier (1982) 70–1.

bibliography, 122–3; there is a fuller and more broadly based survey in Green (1994a) 105–41; bibliography, 207–26. Many of the texts relevant to the acting and performance of New Comedy are accessible in English in Csapo and Slater (1995) see Part IV, 221–368, with its bibliographical notes, 417–23; one should not neglect recitals and 'after-dinner' performances at symposia, as discussed by Fantham (1984) and Jones (1991). The basic discussion of Roman Comedy by Duckworth (1952) appears in its second edition (1994) with a bibliographical appendix by R. L. Hunter. As with Menander, one depends on individual recent commentaries and discussions for detailed consideration of the acting of the plays; but among recent work, see Moore (1998a) with its extensive bibliography, 31–52.

CHAPTER EIGHT

'Acting down': the ideology of Hellenistic performance

Richard Hunter

CULTURED MOVEMENTS

In Chapter 26 of the *Poetics* Aristotle raises the question of whether epic or tragic mimesis is 'superior' (βελτίων):

> One might pose the question whether epic imitation or tragic is superior. If the less vulgar (ἧττον φορτική) art is superior, and in all cases what is addressed to a superior audience is less vulgar, then it is perfectly clear that the art which imitates indiscriminately is vulgar. Assuming that the audience is incapable of grasping what the performer does not supply in person, they engage in a great deal of movement (as second-rate pipers (οἱ φαῦλοι αὐληταί) spin round if they have to imitate throwing a discus, and drag the chorus-leader about if they have to play the *Scylla*). Tragedy is like that. This is in fact the opinion which older actors held about those who came after them; Mynniskos used to call Kallippides 'monkey' because of his excesses, and Pindaros was viewed in much the same way. The whole art of tragedy stands in the same relation to epic as these do to the others. So it is argued that epic is addressed to decent audiences (θεατὰς ἐπιεικεῖς) who do not need gestures, while tragedy is addressed to second-rate audiences (φαύλους); if, then, tragedy is vulgar, clearly it must be inferior (χείρων).
>
> First of all, this is not a criticism of the art of poetry but of the art of performance. A rhapsode performing epic poetry can make exaggerated use of gestures (like Sosistratos); so can a singer (this is what Mnasitheos of Opus used to do). Next, not all movement is to be disparaged (any more than all dance is), but only that of inferior (φαύλων) persons. This is the objection that used to be made against Kallippides, and is made now against others, on the grounds that the women they imitate are not respectable. Also, tragedy has its effect without movement, just as epic does: its quality is clear from reading. So if tragedy is superior (κρείττων) in other respects, this criticism at any rate does not necessarily apply to it. (*Poetics* 1461b26–1462a14, transl. Heath 1996).

This fascinating text, also discussed by Csapo and Sifakis earlier in this volume, links 'realistic' acting in the form of imitative gestures to the moral qualities of the audience; such exaggerated gestures are the tricks of actors catering to vulgar tastes. So too, Aristotle elsewhere observes that *hypokrisis* ('delivery'), in both drama and oratory, was rightly considered vulgar (φορτικόν), and therefore only the subject of serious study at a comparatively late date (*Rhet.* 3.1403b22–30).[1] For Aristotle, tragic gestures *are* in fact vitally important and, as far as possible, are to be visualised by the poet as he composes (*Poet.* 1455a29–34); they are, however, also to be strictly controlled in the interests of decorum (τὸ πρέπον). When Kallippides played female roles in tragedy, he may have made things too 'realistic'.[2] Plato too had censured excessive 'imitative' effects (cf. *Rep.* 3.396b5–9, 397a3–7), but whereas Plato had been principally concerned with what *mīmēsis* would do to the soul of the imitator, Aristotle's downplaying of the performative element of drama is of a piece with a whole élite attitude to personal bearing and the moral qualities which that bearing reflects.[3] Paul Zanker has expressed it thus:

> In Classical Athens, the appearance and behaviour in public of all citizens was governed by strict rules. These applied to how one should walk, stand, or sit, as well as to proper draping of one's garment, position and movement of arms and head, styles of hair and beard, eye movements, and the volume and modulation of the voice . . . Almost every time reference is made to these rules, they are linked to emphatic moral judgements, whether positive or negative. They are part of a value system that could be defined in terms of such concepts as order, measure, modesty, balance, self-control, circumspection, adherence to regulations, and the like . . . It is no wonder that the individuals depicted on gravestones, at least to the modern viewer, look so stereotyped and monotonous.[4]

With Aristotle's strictures on mimetic performance and the very marginal place he gives to the staging of plays we seem to be watching 'the birth of a new form of élite performance'.[5] After Aristotle, the cultural élite of the later Hellenistic and Roman world would in fact constantly represent themselves as reading or listening to readings of 'the literary classics',

[1] Cf. Wiles (1991) 19–20. For the role of gesture in fourth-century oratory and expressions of similar disapproval cf. Dem. 18.232 (with the note of Wankel (1976)), Hall (1995).

[2] Cf. Janko's note on *Poetics* 1462a10–11 (Janko (1987)).

[3] 'Elites' are, of course, very hard to define and lie, to some extent, in the eye of the beholder, but Aristotle's division of the citizen body (*Politics* 4.1291b17–30) into the *dēmos*, i.e. the 'ordinary people', and the *gnōrimoi*, the 'known'/'notable' ones, who stand out for 'wealth, nobility of birth, *aretē*, education and the like' serves well enough for the (élite) rhetoric (both Greek and Roman) of the whole timespan with which we will be concerned. For some relevant considerations cf. Ober (1989) 11–17.

[4] Zanker (1995) 48–9. Much relevant material is discussed in Bremmer (1991). Plutarch is a central witness for this élite discourse; cf. Hunter (2000).

[5] I owe the phrase to Mary Depew.

including drama,[6] rather than joining public audiences. In this (Platonic) narrative of cultural history, the tyranny of an uneducated audience had destroyed poetry's civilising and educative force; in order to preserve that force, the only proper audience for poetry now was either oneself, or oneself and a few like-minded friends, who would give proper attention to the text, not to a frivolous performance in which it might be clothed. The gradual change from a performative, communal culture to the narrower circulation of 'texts' paradoxically offered a way to preserve, while reshaping to a less universal need, poetry's didactic, communal function.

The subsequent tradition took its cue from Plato and Aristotle and carefully censored excessively 'mimetic' effects. Much of our evidence comes from Roman rhetorical writers who saw that actors had something to teach the aspiring orator but, partly reflecting the contempt for actors which is a standard element of Roman élite discourse,[7] also took pains to warn against excessive mimicry and 'hyper-realism'; the orator was to play the hardest role of all – concealing his theatrical mastery.[8] Of particular importance is the distinction Quintilian draws between the 'movements' of different characters in plays: *in fabulis iuuenum senum militum matronarum grauior ingressus est, serui ancillulae parasiti piscatores citatius mouentur*, 'on the stage, young men, old men, soldiers and matrons move in a stately fashion, whereas slaves, serving-girls, parasites and fishermen move more rapidly' (11.3.112).[9] In part, such prescriptions are to be seen within the long history of élite self-fashioning, characterised by remarkably close attention to 'body language', gait and gesture. Aristotle's μεγαλόψυχος, 'great-souled man', 'walks slowly, has a deep voice and speaks calmly' (*EN* 4.1125a12–14). A character in a play by Alexis comments specifically on the importance of gait:[10]

ἓν γὰρ νομίζω τοῦτο τῶν ἀνελευθέρων
εἶναι, τὸ βαδίζειν ἀρρύθμως ἐν ταῖς ὁδοῖς,
ἐξὸν καλῶς· οὗ μήτε πράττεται τέλος
μηδεὶς γὰρ ἡμᾶς, μήτε τιμὴν δόντα δεῖ

[6] Cf. Dio 18.6–7 on the advantages of having someone read Menander to you.
[7] Cf. Edwards (1993) 98–136.
[8] Cf. Cicero, *De orat.* 2.242, Quintilian 1.111–13, 11.3.91, 181–3 (on the playing of the opening of Terence's *Eunuchus*). On this material cf. Fantham (1982), this volume pp. 370–3. See also Graf (1991) and Connolly (1998).
[9] Cf. 11.3.178 on the differing styles of the comic actors Demetrius and Stratocles. For the Greek background here cf. Wiles (1991) 192–208.
[10] For other relevant passages cf. Arnott (1996b) 741.

ἑτέρῳ λαβεῖν, φέρει δὲ τοῖς μὲν χρωμένοις
δόξης τιν᾽ ὄγκον, τοῖς δ᾽ ὁρῶσιν ἡδονήν,
κόσμον δὲ τῷ βίῳ, τὸ τοιοῦτον γέρας
τίς οὐκ ἂν αὑτῷ κτῷτο φάσκων νοῦν ἔχειν;

(Alexis fr. 265 KA)[11]

For this is one thing which I regard as unbecoming to any gentleman, namely walking gracelessly in the street, when it is possible to do so with beauty. This is something where no one exacts a tax from us, nor must one acquire it by paying a fee to another. Those who do walk with finesse gain an increase in their standing, those who see them are rewarded with pleasure, and *kosmos* is added to life. What man with any pretensions to common sense would not acquire such a prize for himself?

The identity of the speaker is unknown, but the concern with what befits a free man, with *doxa*, 'reputation/standing', which involves the belief that other people look at you in the street, and with 'good order' (*kosmos*) all suggest the values of the élite. As the context is clearly something which has happened or has been narrated in the play, and it is reasonable to suppose that the speaker regards himself as a positive model of how to walk (and perhaps indeed parades around the stage in the approved manner), it is tempting to understand 'the onlookers' here (v. 6) as, in part, a metatheatrical reference to 'the audience'. Be that as it may, in a very similar passage of Plautus[12] a metatheatrical dimension is hard to resist:

liberos homines per urbem modico magis par est gradu
ire, seruile esse duco festinantem currere.

(Plautus, *Poenulus* 522–3)

Free men should proceed through the city at a moderate pace; I regard running and hurrying as what slaves do.

The 'running slave' of Roman Comedy, who enters in haste with an important message,[13] carries a socio-political, as well as a theatrical, resonance. Stage discussion of 'how to walk' can thus shed light on what actors actually did on the stage. Horace expresses his disdain for Plautine farce in comparison with the sophistication and educative value of Greek tragedy (and perhaps also Menander) by representing Plautus as running

[11] For the textual difficulties of vv. 3–5 cf. Arnott (1996b) 741–2.

[12] Arnott (1959) has argued that the Alexis fragment is the original of the Plautine verses which are spoken by the *aduocati*, but the matter seems to me unproven.

[13] For the *seruus currens* as a stock character cf. Ter. *Eun.* 36, *Haut.* 37. I do not mean to imply that there is no Greek background here, cf. Csapo (1993).

in disorderly fashion across the stage, concerned not with art but with getting paid:

> aspice Plautus
> quo pacto partis tutetur amantis ephebi,
> ut patris attenti, lenonis ut insidiosi,
> quantus sit Dossennus edacibus in parasitis,
> quam non astricto percurrat pulpita socco.
> gestit enim nummum in loculos demittere, post hoc
> securus cadat an recto stet fabula talo.
>
> (Horace, *Epist.* 2.1.170–6)[14]

See how Plautus maintains the role of the young man in love, of the careful father, of the pimp who lays traps for you; see what a Dossennus he is among greedy parasites, how he runs across the stage with his shoes loose. He's desperate to pocket the cash and beyond that doesn't care what the play is like.

In view of the persistence of theatrical metaphors for the conduct of ordinary life, it is not surprising that theatrical traditions followed analogous paths to those of the élite's concern with physical and moral deportment. The actor's prologue of Terence's *Heauton Timoroumenos* divides stage roles into two broad types (30–40):

> ne ille pro se dictum existumet
> qui nuper fecit seruo currenti in uia
> decesse populum: quor insano seruiat?
> de illius peccatis plura dicet quom dabit
> alias nouas, nisi finem maledictis facit.
> adeste aequo animo, date potestatem mihi
> statariam agere ut liceat per silentium,
> ne semper seruus currens, iratus senex,
> edax parasitus, sycophanta autem inpudens,
> auarus leno adsidue agendi sunt seni
> clamore summo, cum labore maxumo.

This is not to be regarded as a defence by that man who recently made the people in the street give way to a running slave: why be a slave to a madman? The poet will speak further about that man's errors in the course of future plays, unless he put an end to his slanders. Give this play a fair hearing, and allow me to perform a quiet play in silence, so that I don't always have to act the running slave, the angry old man, the greedy parasite, the shameless trickster, and the rapacious pimp; I'm an old man, and those parts need a lot of shouting and a lot of physical effort.

[14] On this passage cf. Jocelyn (1995).

The point is not just that the actor claims to be too old for 'lively' parts, but that those parts somehow lack dignity; the line from this theatrical concept of a *fabula stataria*, 'a stationary play', one 'lacking violent movement',[15] to the privileged concepts of élite ethics is shown by a passage of Cicero which adapts this language to the practices of oratory:

uolo enim ut in scaena sic etiam in foro non eos modo laudari, qui celeri motu et difficili utantur, sed eos etiam quos statarios appellant, quorum sit illa simplex in agendo ueritas, non molesta. (*Brutus* 116)

As on the stage, so I wish that in the forum also praise should be bestowed not only on those who accomplish rapid and difficult movements, but also on those who are termed 'stationary', in whose acting there is a 'truth' which is straightforward, not irksome.

simplex ueritas indicates a whole 'moral' attitude, not just a style of oratory; so, Aulus Gellius castigates Caecilius for replacing what in Menander is 'taken from the life of men, and is simple and true and gives pleasure' (*de uita hominum media sumptum, simplex et uerum et delectabile*) with buffoonery more suited to mime (*NA* 2.23.12).

It is indeed the plays of Menander, and to some extent New Comedy as a whole, which hold a specially privileged place in this construction of an élite world. No theme is more prominent throughout ancient writing about Menander than his pre-eminence in the reflection of ethical character (τὸ ἠθικόν), and as such he was always likely to appeal to Hellenistic and Roman élites, almost obsessively concerned with how they looked and how they really were inside. For both Greek and Roman élites of the early imperial period, much of the experience of Menander may have come through 'readings' at occasions such as dinner parties, rather than in fully staged theatrical performances.[16] Menander had been fully appropriated into élite *literary* culture; drama has become literature. It is indeed likely enough that readings or performances from drama at dinner parties and other social gatherings avoided excessively imitative effects; such an inference, at least, makes sense of the extreme *mīmēsis* that reigns in Trimalchio's house of horrors in the *Satyrica*.

We must not assume, of course, that reality corresponded closely to the picture painted by a literature concerned to mark out the proper

[15] Cf. further Jocelyn (1995) 243–4.
[16] Cf., e.g., Fantham (1984). For what can be said on the other side cf. Jones (1993) and Green (1994a) 144–71. See also Handley, this volume.

space of the educated. It is certainly possible to identify aesthetic techniques and styles which seem to belong to the 'book culture' of an élite, rather than to a more widespread performance culture,[17] and which were presumably a prime weapon with which the élite marked itself off from the chaos beneath it. Nevertheless, the construction of any *simple* 'élite'–'popular' dichotomy within the rich patterns of Hellenistic performance would simply be untrue to the rich spectrum of 'theatre' which that world offered. Doubtless, some members of the cultured élite stayed away (? ostentatiously) from popular and often vulgar 'mimes',[18] just as they made clear in their writings what kinds of sympotic entertainment they enjoyed, but there is no reason to imagine great gulfs between the classes in what was watched in the theatres: the élite attended and offered enthusiastic patronage for all kinds of theatrical performance. Nevertheless, the ideological picture, the portrait of itself which the élite wished to present, emerges clearly enough. As often, a letter of Pliny, standing in a long tradition of discussion as to what type of entertainment and conversation is proper at gatherings of cultured men (cf. Pl. *Prt.* 347b–348a), suggests the issues with great clarity. With a demonstration of admirable 'philosophical' mildness, Pliny advises a correspondent not to be too angry with the entertainment provided at a dinner party, though he certainly shares his friend's refined taste:[19]

I have received your letter, in which you complain of being highly disgusted lately at a dinner, though exceeding splendid, by a set of buffoons, lewd entertainers and clowns (*scurrae cinaedi moriones*) who were wandering around the tables. But let me advise you to smooth your brow a little. I confess, indeed, I admit nothing of this kind at my own house; however, I bear with it in others. 'And why then' (you will be ready to ask) 'should you not have them yourself?' The truth is, because the soft gestures from a *cinaedus*, the pleasantries from a buffoon, or the idiocies of a clown, give me no entertainment, as they give me no surprise. It is my taste, you see, not my principles, that I plead against them. And indeed, what numbers are there, think you, who find no pleasure in the entertainments with which you and I are most delighted, and consider them either trivial or wearisome! How many are there, who as soon as a reader, a musician, or a comic actor is introduced, either take their leave of the company, or if they continue at the table, show as much dislike to this kind of diversion, as you did at those awfulnesses (*prodigia*), as you call them! Let us bear therefore, my friend, with

[17] Cf. Hunter (1996) 7–13, comparing Theocritus 2 and the *Fragmentum Grenfellianum*.

[18] Cf. below pp. 196–201.

[19] For Pliny's tastes in entertainment cf. also *Ep.* 1.15.2, 3.1.9, 9.36.4. Plutarch speaks elsewhere of entertainment at symposia including 'mime-actors, impersonators (ἠθολόγοι) and performers of Menander' (*Sympotic Questions* 5 proem = *Moralia* 673B); for the subject in general cf. Jones (1991), Davidson (2000).

others in their amusements, that they in return may show indulgence to ours. Farewell. (Pliny, *Ep.* 9.17, transl. Melmoth and Hutchinson (1915), adapted)

MIMING DRAMA

A standard move of the discourse I have been tracing is a contrast between, on the one hand, texts and performance styles which are morally improving and, on the other, the 'debased' traditions of 'mime'. In fact, however, when we move away from élite texts which are concerned to demarcate the boundaries of culture, those boundaries become very hard to find.

'Mime' is a term used by modern scholars to cover a very wide range of ancient performances, from solo singing to 'playlets' performed by a small group of 'actors', almost anything in fact which does not fit the classical categories of tragedy, satyr drama, and comedy. In the present context such looseness is useful, for it is true to the strategy of élite rhetoric.[20] A crucial text here is a tantalisingly brief account, drawing on Hellenistic sources, of types of performance in Athenaeus' *Deipnosophistai* 14.620a–621f (*c.* AD 200). The passage repays detailed consideration.

Athenaeus begins with 'performances' of Homer by the so-called 'Homeristai'.[21] The Hellenistic 'performance' of Homer ranged from private reading and recitation through singing and full-blown acting, and this very spectrum reinforced within élite discourse a distinction between 'serious' study and reading and the theatrical pleasures of the common people. It is telling that Petronius has Trimalchio's 'Homeristai' (*Sat.* 59) engage in violent mimetic action. That such performances are seen as debasements of 'high', educative texts will emerge as a central leitmotif of the mode of self-representation which we are considering. Athenaeus then lists various kinds of solo performer, about most of whom we know very little – *hilarōidoi, simōidoi, magōidoi, lysiōidoi.* It is typical of élite attitudes that Strabo (late first century BC) views the last three of these forms as 'corruptions' of the practices of earlier lyric poets.[22] About the *magōidos* Athenaeus proceeds to report:

The player called a *magōidos* (μαγῳδός) carries tambourines and cymbals, and all his clothes are women's garments. He makes rude gestures (?),[23] and all his actions lack decency (*kosmos*), as he plays the part of adulterous women or bawds

[20] For 'mime' see Reich (1903), Wüst (1932), Cunningham (1971) 3–11, Wiemken (1972), McKeown (1979), Fantham (1989), Csapo and Slater (1995) 369–78, and the essays in Section III of Benz, Stärk and Vogt-Spira (1995) .

[21] Cf. Husson (1993), Nagy (1996) 158–86.

[22] Strabo 14.1.41. The verb Strabo uses is παραφθείρειν.

[23] The exact sense of σχινίζεται is uncertain.

or a man drunk and going on a revel to his mistress. Aristoxenus (fr. 110 Wehrli²) says that *hilarōidia* is serious and derives from tragedy (παρὰ τὴν τραγῳδίαν εἶναι), whereas *magōdia* derives from comedy (παρὰ τὴν κωμῳδίαν). For often *magōidoi* took comic scenarios (ὑποθέσεις) and acted them in their own style and manner.

Such performers scandalise by their absence of decorum and taste, but the hypothesised relation with 'formal drama' sheds important light not only upon mime itself, but also upon élite attitudes to it. Whatever the exact nature of this relationship,[24] such performances are perceived as a 'perversion' of classical drama. With Athenaeus' next category, the *iōnikologoi* and *kinaidologoi*, it is the explicit sexual nature of both verses and performance[25] which élite discourse represents as vulgar, and indeed subversive. It is striking that the most famous such performer, Sotades of Maroneia, was believed to have fallen foul of Ptolemy Philadelphos because he joked about Ptolemy's marriage to his sister Arsinoe (Ath. 14.620f–621a).[26] Just as Sotadean verse (an ionic tetrameter) 'parodies' the repetitive structure and regularity of the hexameter, and the *kinaidos* challenges the assumptions of the male hierarchy by 'performing' as a man who enjoyed the passive role in homosexual intercourse, so Sotades is made to embody a threat to good 'political' discipline. It is of fundamental importance that the discourse of theatrical decorum and *kosmos* is one in which the élite had a real political stake. The excessive theatricality of a Trimalchio threatens to lay bare what is hidden by this veil of ethical values: to turn the 'theatre' of master–slave relations into real theatre, as Trimalchio does, is potentially destabilising in ways which he certainly would never have imagined.

If we turn from what is said in our sources about mimes to the chance survival of papyrus texts, a rather similar picture emerges. The standard collection[27] begins with the so-called *Fragmentum Grenfellianum* (second century BC), a solo song in which a woman (presumably played by a man) adopts the role of *exclusus amator* to complain bitterly that she has been abandoned by her lover.[28] Faint echoes of familiar themes from high poetry, but the substitution of a 'female' voice, mark this text as analogous to, but also pointedly distinct from, the modes of high classical poetry. Two prose texts (2 and 3 Cunningham) of the second or first century BC are 'scripts' for more than one actor, and show themes familiar from

[24] Cf. Hunter (1995) 160–3.
[25] Note Strabo 14.1.41 on the 'mimetic' quality of cinaedic verse.
[26] Cf. Hunter (1996) 78–9. [27] Cunningham (1987) 36–61.
[28] For more detailed discussion cf. Hunter (1996) 7–10. The closest parallel may be the female role in the 'love duet' of Aristophanes' *Ecclesiazusae*, cf. Olson (1988), Parker (1997) 546.

Fig. 30 Three mime actors performing *Mother-in-Law* (Photo: B. Köhlen, M. Gladbach)

New Comedy: hopeless infatuation and a man, the worse for drink, going on a *kōmos* to his beloved. Here we seem to have clear evidence for the close relationship between 'mime' and comedy, which is also asserted by the scholastic tradition and suggested by a terracotta lamp (fig. 30) of the late third century BC showing three performers and inscribed μιμολόγοι, ὑπόθεσις Ἑκυρά, 'mime-speakers, plot, Mother-in-law' (a familiar comic title).[29] So too, the best-known mime-text, the 'Charition mime' (6 Cunningham),[30] restages the escape-plot of Euripides' *Iphigenia in Tauris* on the shores of an outlandishly barbarian India; if the narrative motifs, such as escape by intoxicating the enemy, are familiar enough, the extreme 'vulgarity' of what survives, in which farting plays a major role, seems worlds removed from Euripidean melodrama. This is perhaps less 'parody' than 'para-drama'.

[29] For *hypothesis* as a generic name for a kind of dramatic mime cf. Plut. *Sympotic Questions* 7.8 = *Moralia* 712E. For the lamp cf. Watzinger (1901); Bieber (1920) 176–7.

[30] Cf. Santelia (1991).

A similar picture emerges again from the extant *mimiamboi* of Herodas (first half of the third century BC). These choliambic poems are a curious cross between the traditions of the dramatic mime and the archaic Ionic *iambos* of Hipponax, a cross forged by the literary–historical interests of the sophisticated poets of the high Hellenistic period. Here too, however, the 'high' traditions of epic, forensic oratory (*Mim.* 2),[31] and comedy are replayed at a 'lower' level which casts ambivalent light upon the model texts: thus, for example, the high moral tone of New Comedy is amusingly stained by the common mime-scenario of a mistress who forces her male slaves to satisfy her lust (*Mim.* 5, *Adesp.* 7 Cunningham). The social exchanges of formal drama become revelations of what women 'really' talk about when alone – adultery (*Mim.*1) and masturbation (*Mim.* 6). In feeding off 'high' culture, 'lower' performance traditions, and the literary imitations of them written by Herodas and Theocritus, dramatised the ambivalent status of epic, tragedy and comedy, which – partly because of a deadening fossilisation of roles – could no longer deliver on the grand moral and educational promises which they made and which were made for them. Society had moved on. Elite rhetoric constantly drew attention to the 'lower' traditions of mime in order to advertise what it perceived as its own superiority; mime itself constantly evoked 'higher' traditions, but with a rather more complex agenda.

Of particular interest is a text preserved on a copy probably written in the early first century AD, perhaps not far from its composition date:

π]αιδὸς ἐφύλασσεν ὁ φίλος μου τρυφῶν
τέ]κνον τηρῶν ἐν ταῖς ἀγκάλαις
ἀπορο]ῦμαι ποῦ βαδίσω. ἡ ναῦς μου ἐρράγη.
τὸν κ]αταθύμιον ἀπολέσας ὄρνιθά μου κλαίω
φ]έρε τὸ ἐρνίον τροφὴν αὐτοῦ περιλάβω
τοῦ μαχίμου τοῦ ἐπεράστου τοῦ Ἑλληνικοῦ.
χάριν τούτου ἐκαλούμην μέγας ἐν τῷ βίῳ
καὶ ἐλεγόμην μακάριος, ἄνδρες, ἐν τοῖς φιλοτροφίοις.
ψυχομαχῶ· ὁ γὰρ ἀλέκτωρ ἠστόχηκέ μου
καὶ θακαθαλπάδος ἐρασθεὶς ἐμὲν ἐγκατέλιπε.
ἀλλ' ἐπιθεὶς λίθον ἐμαυτοῦ ἐπὶ τὴν καρδίαν
καθησυχάσομαι. ὑμεῖς δ' ὑγιαίνετε, φίλοι.

(Frag. mim. fr. 4 Cunningham = *GLP* 75 Page)[32]

[31] Cf. Hunter (1995).

[32] Papyrological marks have been kept to a very minimum, and I will not consider here the many problems of the text which do not affect the argument. So too, the old problem of whether or not the text is rhythmical will be left out of account, cf. Cunningham's introductory note.

From its childhood my friend (? Tryphon) guarded it, watching over it like a baby in his arms. I know not whither I may go: my ship is wrecked. I weep for the darling bird that I have lost! Come, let me embrace its chick, this child of the fighter, the beloved, the gallant Greek! For his sake I was accounted a success in life, I was called a happy man, gentlemen, among those who love their pets. I fight for life – my cock has gone astray: he has fallen in love with a sitting hen [or 'with Thakathalpas'], and left me in the lurch. I will set a tombstone above my heart, and be at rest. And you, my friends – goodbye to you! (trans. Page, adapted)

This is a lament for a prize fighting-cock which has apparently not died, but rather fallen in love (with a hen) and fled the coop; the final lines seem to be a resolution to commit suicide. From the earliest days (i.e. the *Iliad*), lamentation was a discourse which gave a special place to the norms and consensual values of society. The importance of the family and respect for parents, as well as the qualities of the deceased, are standard lament themes: the lament is a very public, communal discourse, and this parodic lament obviously gestures towards such traditions. The speaker alludes to his *doxa* – he was 'called fortunate among pet-lovers' – and it is at this moment that we get the address to the audience (ἄνδρες, 'gentlemen'), because reputation and status is precisely a matter of communal consent – this is something which the audience will understand. The speaker is male – it was males who indulged in cock-fighting – but public lamentation was essentially a female discourse, and in the anguish of our speaker we hear distant echoes of the heroines of high literature (cf., e.g., Apollonius, *Arg.* 1.284–91). Here then is a further suggestion that one feature of the mime tradition, certainly not an inevitable or necessary one, was a change of gender voicing by role transference; one aspect of the distinction between 'high' and 'low' performance forms, if the hierarchical terminology is to be retained, lay in the maintenance or subverting of inherited roles and voices. Such transference, as we have seen in the case of *kinaidologia*, makes such traditions (at least potentially) culturally and morally subversive; in the context of the élite rhetoric of *paideia*, such traditions lack *kosmos*, they disturb proper social and moral hierarchies. As Plutarch memorably puts it, 'they throw one's soul into greater confusion than any amount of drink' (*Sympotic Questions* = *Moralia* 712E–F). For a Plutarch, of course, such disturbance is also connected with the frank eroticism of some of these performances. Whereas the sexy Dionysus and Ariadne mime in Xenophon's *Symposium* arouses the diners so much that 'the unmarried swore that they would get married, and the married men mounted their horses and rode off to enjoy their own wives' (*Symp.* 9.7), Plutarch outlaws mimetic *paignia* from the dinner party as staging things which should not even be seen 'by the slaves who fetch our shoes' (*Mor.* 712E–F).

MIMIC ELEMENTS IN NEW COMEDY

New Comedy itself is, of course, a major source for and reflection of élite values, particularly in its focus upon the continuity and stability of the *oikos*, i.e. of the wider family unit and the property which went with it. In the light of the foregoing discussion, it may be worth asking whether our extant New Comedy texts construct a truly homogeneous culture, or whether the plays themselves foreshadow the later developments, and in particular the distinction between 'high' and 'low' performance and acting modes, which we have been tracing.

Of the plays which have survived, it is probably *Dyskolos* which is most obviously concerned with social solidarity and cohesion. What is at issue in *Dyskolos* is socialisation, some kind of normative education, the inculcation of particular social and moral values. Through Knemon, who shuns human society because of his distaste for what he sees as the hypocrisy of human motives (cf. 447–53, 719–20), Menander explores the difference between being μισοπόνηρος 'a hater of wickedness' and being μισάνθρωπος 'a hater of men'; in Knemon the difference may be thought to have collapsed. The result, from one point of view, is a withdrawal which society simply cannot tolerate, because such a withdrawal threatens society itself. At another level, however, the apparently bitter realism of Knemon's *Weltanschauung* is shown to be an inadequate response in the face of communal strategies, such as festive sacrificing, which make up for in positive 'social' results what they may lack in self-analytical frankness. Comedy itself is implicated in this 'noble lie', through the fashioning of a double end to the play around different performance traditions.

At 867–73 the two young men, Gorgias and Sostratos, take their leave of Knemon and of the play, and proceed to join the party inside the cave:

Σω. ἡμεῖς δ' ἴωμεν. Γο. Σώστραθ', ὑπεραισχύνομαι
  γυναιξὶν ἐν ταὐτῷ – Σω. τίς ὁ λῆρος; οὐ πρόει;
  οἰκεῖα ταῦτ' ἤδη νομίζειν πάντα δεῖ. (*Dysk.* 871–3)

SO. Let's go.
GO. Sostratos, I feel very embarrassed – there are women in there . . .
SO. What nonsense! Get a move on. All of this is *oikeion* to you now.

The 'high comedy' thus closes with an expression of properly decent manners and an affirmation that the *oikos* has been preserved and broadened (873, *oikeia*). The closing scene which follows, in which Sikon and Getas tease Knemon mercilessly, functions not merely as a reprise of the earlier door-knocking scenes in which he had abused them, but incorporates into the play a 'low' or farcical reflection of the main action, marked by the use of nearly unparalleled iambic tetrameters to the accompaniment of the *aulos*. The use of music, the extravagant gesture and dancing and the rare, perhaps old-fashioned metre seem something of a throwback to a livelier style of comedy, as though Menander was exploiting his awareness (and that of his audience?) of the general drift of comic history. The values promulgated by the 'high drama' are almost parodied by the self-serving plans of the slave:

θόρυβός ἐστιν ἔνδον,
πίνουσιν· οὐκ αἰσθήσετ' οὐδείς· τὸ δ' ὅλον ἐστὶν ἡμῖν
ἄνθρωπος ἡμερωτέος· κηδεύομεν γὰρ αὐτῷ,
οἰκεῖος ἡμῖν γίνετ'· εἰ δ' ἔσται τοιοῦτος ἀεί,
ἔργον ὑπενεγκεῖν. (*Dysk.* 901–5)

There's a lot of noise; they're drinking – no one will notice. The main thing is that we must make this man tame. We're related to him by marriage, he is a member of the family (*oikeios*). If he's always going to be like this, it won't be easy to put up with.

Oikeios (904) picks up Sostratos' closing words and marks the perverted variation of socialised values which we are about to witness. Knemon must be 'trained' in the ways of the élite symposium: comedy had indeed long used the correct conduct of the symposium as the marker of correct social behaviour (cf. the finale of Ar. *Wasps*). What Getas and Sikon offer in fact is an extraordinary inversion of the *kōmos* in which the *paraklausithyron* (serenade) precedes the drinking; Knemon is forced to witness 'socialised behaviour' turned upside down and made ridiculous, very far from the πότος καλός, 'jolly party' (855–6), which the other characters are now enjoying inside Pan's cave. In what could be taken for an almost paradigmatic confirmation of 'the two cultures' view of the Hellenistic world, the values of comedy are both confirmed and lightly ironised by a scene which derives a quite different kind of humour from an exploitation of the same comic motifs; the smutty, genital jokes of 892 and 895[33] offer a rather low-life perspective upon the formal marriage formula of 842–4:

[33] Just as Sikon takes Getas' question of 891 as the opportunity for a sexual joke on πάσχειν, 'suffer' and 'be penetrated anally', so Getas in 895 puns on Sikon's use of ἀναστῆναι, 'get up' and 'get it up', cf. Hunter (1999) 107, on Theocr. 1.151–2.

ἀλλ᾽ ἐγγυῶ παίδων ἐπ᾽ ἀρότῳ γνησίων
τὴν θυγατέρ᾽ ἤδη μειράκιόν σοι προῖκά τε
δίδωμ᾽ ἐπ᾽ αὐτῇ τρία τάλαντα.

I now betroth my daughter to you, young man, for the begetting [lit. ploughing] of legitimate children, and I bestow a dowry of three talents upon her.

Knemon had wished to remove himself entirely from society; his 'punishment' consists of removal from the realm of 'civilised' comedy into a quite different mode of performance where parodic farce stains the values of the higher mode.

A suggestive parallel for this dramatic technique of doubling and inversion is to be found in Terence's *Adelphoe* ('The Brothers'), which was based on a play of the same title by Menander. Here the abduction of Ctesipho's beloved and the subsequent rough handling of the pimp Sannio, which follows the opening confrontation of the older pair of contrasted brothers, Micio and Demea, and which was, at least in part, added by Terence from the *Synapothnescontes* ('Those who die together') of Diphilus (cf. vv. 6–11), functions as a kind of parodic reprise of the opening debate. Like the fathers, Sannio appeals to notions of *aequum* ('the equitable') and *iniuria* ('wrong'), and like them, the pimp must put up with *iniuria adulescentium* ('the outrages of young men', 207); his threat to exact the full measure of his *ius*, 'legal rights' (163), is a farcical version of the strict legality to which Demea had appealed in his complaints against Aeschinus (84–6) and which Micio had rejected as inappropriate to the business of fatherhood (51–2, 'I do not think it necessary to enforce the full measure of my rights in all things'). When Syrus advises Sannio that it would be to his financial advantage not to insist on the strict letter of his rights, but rather to oblige his clients (*adulescenti esses morigeratus*, 218), we can hardly fail to recall the differences between Micio and Demea which the opening scenes had laid out with such clarity. When Sannio refuses to follow the slave's advice and Syrus observes that Sannio is destined to be a failure as a pimp, *nescis inescare homines* 'you don't know how to entrap men', the language evokes the behaviour of the flatterer and the prostitute to foreshadow what will be an important theme at the close of play. There Demea's assertion that the point of his final charade of generosity was to show Micio that his popularity *non fieri ex uera uita neque adeo ex aequo et bono,|sed ex adsentando indulgendo et largiendo*, 'does not derive from a sincere way of life nor from the pursuit of the equitable and good, but from complaisance, indulgence and extravagant generosity' (987–8) makes the point that not only does Micio's attitude turn others into flatterers (cf. 877–80),[34] but Micio himself is characterised by the hypocrisy and feigned attitudes of the flatterer. In Demea's view, Micio has made the classic mistake of confusing 'friendship' (*philia*) with 'flattery' (*kolakeia* or *areskeia*); his behaviour is that of the Aristotelian *areskos*[35] or the more familiar *kolax*:[36]

> ille suam semper egit uitam in otio, in conuiuiis,
> clemens placidus, nulli laedere os, adridere omnibus.
> (*Ad.* 863–4)

He has passed his entire life in ease and social jollity; always forgiving and calm, never offended anyone, has a smile for everyone . . .

These are the issues which are jokingly previewed in the banter of Syrus and Sannio. So too, Sannio's disingenuous appeal to his own 'free' status (182–3) and Aeschinus' possibly improvised claim that the girl is free-born (193–4) moves to a farcical mode the 'who is free?' theme of the central drama, embodied rather more high-mindedly in Micio's views about the education of *liberi* (57). So too, the debt of reciprocal gratitude which Aeschinus should owe Micio on the basis of the first scene becomes, in the second, a sum of money owed to a greedy pimp. In short, the central themes of the framing play are here replayed in a 'lower', more farcical mode.

From this perspective, Sannio bears an interesting name, which points in two (related) directions. *Sannion* seems to be a word for the penis (cf. Hesychius s.v.), and therefore appropriate to the pimp's trade, but *sannio* appears at Cicero, *De oratore* 2.251 as a word (apparently) for a performer in a clownish and low entertainment; Cicero is discussing appropriate types of humour:

It is also important that not everything which is laughed at is witty. For what could be more to be laughed at than a clown (*sannio*)? But he produces laughter

34 The best commentary on these verses is Arist. *EN* 8.1159a12, 'Because of love of honour most men prefer to be loved rather than to love; that is why most men like flatterers.'

35 Cf. *EN* 4.1126b13–14: 'some men are thought to be obsequious (ἄρεσκοι), viz. those who to give pleasure praise everything and never oppose, but think it their duty to give no pain to the people they meet' (transl. Ross (1915)).

36 Cf. Plut. *How to Tell a Flatterer from a Friend* 2 = *Moralia* 50B: 'Just as false and counterfeit imitations of gold imitate only its brilliancy and lustre, so apparently the flatterer, imitating the pleasant and attractive characteristics of the friend (τοῦ φίλου τὸ ἡδὺ καὶ κεχαρισμένον), always presents himself in a cheerful and blithe mood (ἱλαρὸν καὶ ἀνθηρόν), with never a whit of crossing or opposition.'

with his face, his expression, his voice, his whole body. I could say this is amusing, but in the way a mime-actor is amusing, not as I would wish an orator to be.

What is absurd about this 'buffoon' is precisely that excessive mimicry which we have already seen to distinguish 'serious' from 'clownish' actors and actors from orators. Though Sannion and Sannon are attested historical names, *sannas* is an old word for an idiot,[37] and *sannion* appears with this sense at Arrian, *Epict. diss.* 3.22.83. Among the known bearers of the name is a third-century *kōmōidos* who performed at Delphi (Stephanis no. 2211), and the possibility that such names had 'theatrical currency' in the Greek world, as well as the Roman, is strengthened by the name Sannyrion which Alciphron gives to one of the leaders of the *mimoi* at his farcical 'banquet of the philosophers'.[38] Be that as it may, Novius wrote an Atellan farce called *Sanniones*,[39] and there are thus good reasons to associate the name of Terence's *leno*, as well as the scene in which he appears, with theatrical traditions of a rather 'lower' kind than formal comedy; unsurprisingly, brothel-keepers and slave-traders were familiar characters in the mimic tradition. If this analysis is correct, Terence has pointed to the different levels inscribed in his play by giving his *leno* a name from the traditions of farce and mime. That the themes of the *leno*'s scene replay the themes of the framing drama – a kind of 'play within the play' technique – reminds us of what we have already learned from both Athenaeus and the papyri, namely that 'mimes', both Greek and Roman, often borrowed the plots of 'formal comedy' and performed them in their own style.

Both *Dyskolos* and *Adelphoe* are concerned with 'education' in behavioural and social norms, precisely those themes which later élite moralists saw as most valuable in New Comedy. These plays, moreover, highlight these themes by juxtaposing versions of them as interpreted by different traditions of performance. Such an inclusive practice marks the genuinely theatrical nature of these scripts, a nature which was always

37 Cf. KA on Cratinus fr. 489, Rhinthon fr. 20 KA (where it is tempting to see a 'theatrical' term).

38 Alciphron 3.9.10 Benner and Fobes, cf. Reich (1903) 429–30. 'Sannyrion' is listed among legendary idiots at Aelian, *VH* 13.15. Alciphron's other mime-leader, 'Philistiades', most likely evokes the famous, though very mysterious, mime-poet Philistion (cf. Wüst, *RE* 19.2402–5), and 'Phoibades' the citharode can hardly fail to recall the divine citharode himself, Phoebus Apollo.

39 Cf. Frassinetti (1953) 72; Rawson (1991) 470, discussing Diod. Sic. 37.12 (a *gelōtopoios* called Saunio or Sannio).

likely to be obscured once the texts had moved from the stage to the schoolroom.[40]

SUGGESTIONS FOR FURTHER READING

On the relation between gesture and movement in 'real life' and on the stage see Wiles (1991), the essays in Bremmer and Roodenburg (1991) and Fantham (1982). On Greek and Roman mime see the bibliography listed in n. 20; the standard collection of texts is Cunningham (1987) 36–61. There are helpful editions of Terence's *Adelphoe* by R. Martin (Cambridge 1976) and A. S. Gratwick (1987); modern discussion of the play is most usefully summarised in Goldberg (1986) and Hunter (1985).

[40] I am much indebted to Mary Depew, Pat Easterling, Edith Hall, Susan Lape, David Wray, and many seminar audiences for their helpful criticisms of earlier versions of this chapter.

PART TWO

The professional world

CHAPTER NINE

Nothing to do with the technītai *of Dionysus?*

Jane L. Lightfoot

Until quite recently, few bothered to take the history of Greek theatre beyond the end of the classical period. On the traditional view, drama underwent nothing but decline from the fourth century onwards. The polis had been swallowed up by the Hellenistic kingdoms; drama, especially tragedy, was the self-expression of the polis; therefore . . . and there is hardly any need to complete the syllogism. Yet newer studies emphasise that the transformation of Attic tragedy into an art form of international potency is very far from being a story of decline: drama was one of Athens' most successful long-term exports, and was one of the most important signifiers of Greek culture in the vastly expanded horizons of the Hellenistic world. The main problem in redressing the balance has proved to be the loss of texts themselves, a loss more grievous still for tragedy than for comedy, and one which had been held to speak for itself about the quality of the works involved. But in fact quite a lot of evidence of various sorts does survive for Hellenistic drama, though most of it is not literary. Inscriptions, however, survive in large numbers – civic decrees in honour of esteemed performers; *didaskaliai* and *fasti* and archons' records which list competitors and victors in festivals and the performers who participated in recitals and shows; correspondence between cities about the institution of new festivals or the reorganisation of existing ones; and a large body of evidence relating to the *technītai* or 'Artists' – or better still, 'Artisans' – of Dionysus.

In the *Frogs* (761ff.), Aristophanes had accounted tragedy among the 'great and noble crafts': the *technītai* take their name from the application of *technē* to the performing arts. They are large corporations of musicians, poets and those involved in various ways with dramatic performance, who first appear at the beginning of the third century and are soon spread throughout the Mediterranean – the Greek mainland, Cyprus, Asia Minor, Egypt, eventually South Italy and Sicily, and perhaps Rhodes. They are strange organisations, not quite like anything else even in the Hellenistic period, which saw the formation of leagues and associations and clubs and societies of all kinds, religious and secular, professional and lay. They constituted themselves as cities and appointed officials and issued decrees, while managing to live in the cities where they took up residence as privileged outsiders – in the city but not of it. Like true artists, they had a reputation for awkwardness and unco-operativeness; and also like true artists they had some reputation for riotous behaviour and bohemian living. Above all, they constituted themselves as religious associations and never ceased to refer to and to display acts of piety, especially towards their patron deity Dionysus, the god of Attic drama.

One common account given for the many leagues and societies of the Hellenistic period is that they provided reassuring centres of solidarity for dislocated and rootless populations. But in the case of the *technītai*, the mobility enforced on performers was one of the main reasons for the guilds' existence – along with the natural desire of people with a common interest, a trade, profession or skill, to band together. Performers had to travel. The Hellenistic world saw a proliferation of festivals, the diffusion of drama and festivals of music and athletics as badges of Greek culture throughout the lands conquered and colonised by Alexander and his successors. This also involved a certain confusion of categories. In classical Greece, drama was the domain of the Athenian Dionysia, while music and athletics belonged to the 'sacred games' of the four Panhellenic sites, Olympia, Delphi, Nemea and the Ishthmus; dithyramb was performed at the Dionysia as well as at other festivals. But in the Hellenistic era there was a great expansion of festal complexes containing drama *and* music *and* athletics. Sacred games burgeoned as cities competed for the prestige of hosting a Panhellenic festival, and the distinction between them and the Dionysia was now blurred: a mid-fourth-century epigram speaks of the inclusion of 'sweetly-laughing, grape-crowned comedy' among the sacred games, while Theocritus can refer to the 'sacred games of Dionysus'.[1] One finds a new type of event as well, the *thymelikos agōn*: it was properly a musical competition, yet it seems it could also include drama.[2] Was drama in fact severed from its Dionysian past? It is true that it was no longer confined to festivals of Dionysus. But in some respects the god has extended his domain rather than weakening his hold, for he is regarded as the founder of these

[1] Peek (1955) no. 1495; Theoc. 17.112.

[2] Cf. Lloyd-Jones (1990) 170 with nn. 4–5; *Suppl. Hell.* 705.4, 959.13.

thymelic events too, and when the Athenian guild worshipped him, they did so as Dionysus *Melpomenos*, Dionysus god of song. It is dangerous to deny Dionysus his due, and the Hellenistic Dionysus, rather than slackening his influence, modified it and extended it.

The artists of Dionysus were the professionals who toured this complex circuit under the patronage of a deity whose concern was the whole of theatre and much of music. Since they depended on it for their livelihood, it was logical to band together, because organisations could secure for their members *en bloc* what had previously only been available to privileged individuals, such as grants of immunity from seizure and aggression when travelling abroad (*asylia*), the status of 'sacred' for their persons, or exemption from various taxes and military service. Guild membership could also secure their contracts. Inscriptions show in detail how a city interested in establishing or simply running a festival would send representatives to a guild (or perhaps more than one), courteously reminding them of past goodwill, inviting them to participate, stipulating their requirements, and, most importantly, supplying cash advances; the guild would reply in kind.[3] Penalties were fixed if the guildsmen were to renege on their contracts. It is clear that these procedures were already in place before the formal establishment of the guilds,[4] but now these stand between the city and the individual performers, so squarely that one wonders whether a performer who did not belong to an organisation would have stood much chance of finding work at all. The guilds then seem to have selected the performers from their own membership: they used some sort of procedure designated by the verb *nemein* ('allot'), apparently recalling the classical process of *nemēsis hypokritōn* (the allocation by lot of protagonists to the poets in the City Dionysia), but in fact with only a superficial resemblance to it.[5] For it is not clear that the lot was used by the guilds; nor was it only actors whose parts were assigned in this way; and *nemēsis* is now used of the selection of performers for festivals, not the allocation of pre-selected actors to a creative writer. The terminology, superficially similar, seems in fact to indicate the radical transformation of a classical process. One similarity does, however, remain. While the classical *polis* had seen only to the selection

3 See e.g. the decrees assembled in *DFA* (1988) in the appendix to chapter vii, nos. 3, 4, 11 (= *IK* 28.1 (Iasos) 152).

4 For the organisation of a festival before the inception of the guilds, see the Euboean decree of *c*. 290 BC, *IG* xii/9 207 and p. 176 and *IG* xii, suppl. p. 178 (*DFA* (1988) 306–8 no. 2, Csapo and Slater (1995) 196–200 no. 162). For actors' fines in the fourth century, see Aeschin. *Or.* 2.19.

5 *FD* iii/1 351 l. 35 (228–215 BC); *IG* xii/1 125 =*IGUR* i. 223; *IK* 28.1 (Iasos) 152 ll. 17, 20, 37. Hesych., *Suda*, Photius s.v. νεμήσεις ὑποκριτῶν.

of protagonists, so that selection of the co-performers was up to the leading actors, so too the guild inscriptions speak only of the *nemēsis* of the first actors, who then by some means select their supporting casts, or literally, their crews (*hypēresiai*).[6]

The beneficiaries of this system were singers and instrumentalists, actors and dramatic poets, and those concerned with theatre in other ways, mask-makers and suppliers of costumes. All seem to have been citizens. None is known to have been a woman: actresses seem still to have been unknown, although there is no dearth of women in the musical profession with the highest status of all, that of the citharode.[7] All were performers of relatively high status, for the 'lower-brow' sort of performer – the mimes, conjurers, tight-rope walkers and dancers who were no less part of the festivals, if only on their fringes – are not shown as members of guilds in the Hellenistic period. Their lack of prestige was reflected in their absence from the formal games of the concourse, and some denied that their 'art' was worthy to be called a *technē* at all: Galen and Philodemus seem to want to deny the title *technītai* to trick-artists and conjurers (*thaumatopoioi*), and Philodemus, who has his own axes to grind, would deny it to comic actors too.[8]

The word *technītēs* appears first in the fourth century, before the formation of the guilds, and in one of these passages, Aristotle observes that *technītēs* is the preferred self-designation of those whom others call 'flatterers' or 'fawners' or 'toadies of Dionysus' (*Dionysou kolakes*).[9] One wonders which came first, the insult or the positive phrase, but the former looks to be a depravation of the latter. *Technītai* are endowed with a skill, like artists and sculptors and metalworkers, all of whom can be indicated by the same word, and in a particularly vivid analogy Plutarch indicates how the one sort of craft can be assimilated to the other: actors, he says, are the servants of tragedy, her dressers and litter-bearers, or, better, those who adorn her as if she were an inanimate statue 'as encaustic painters and gilders and dyers'.[10] An epigram from the middle of the fourth century calls a tragic actor a 'horseman of the tragic art'.[11]

6 *IK* 28.1 (Iasos) 152 l. 37.

7 Stephanis (1988) 593–4. On women in guilds generally, see Kloppenborg in Kloppenborg and Wilson (1996) 25.

8 Philodemus *De rhet.* I. p. 59 Sudhaus; Galen *Protr.* 9, I. 20 Kühn; cf. Robert (1938) 106–8.

9 Ar. *Rhet.* 3.1405a23–4; cf. also Chares *apud* Athen. 12.538 f (*FGrH* 125F4) and Theopompus *apud* Athen. 6.254b (*FGrH* 115F281).

10 Plut. *Mor.* 348E.

11 Peek (1955) no. 1698 l. 3, ἡνίοχος τέχνης τραγικῆς.

The actors' specialised skills included not only acting technique itself and voice-production, and perhaps a rhetorical training which could equip the most accomplished performers to be used in embassies,[12] but also expertise with equipment, the boots whose soles rose to ever more alarming heights in the Hellenistic period, and the use of the mask. The expertise required of an actor may explain why dramatic poets are frequently active in public life, whereas actors rarely are: their *technē* required full-time practice. Their expertise may even have led their troupes to confine themselves to the performance of a particular genre, as Oliver Taplin suggests, writing that 'the Artists kept tragedy and comedy separate, performing one or the other'.[13] True, one can point to numerous examples of versatility: we hear of tragic synagonists who are also rhapsodes, and colourful characters such as the champion pugilist who also specialised in muscular roles in tragedy (Heracles, Antaeus, Achilles) and set down no fewer than eighty-eight such victories to his name.[14] Actors often win prizes as heralds at the beginning of contests, but so they should, with their trained delivery and breath control.[15] And there are in fact examples of the crossing of genres, for several are mentioned as actors, lead and supporting, in both comedy and tragedy, one even as a rhapsode as well.[16] But it is hard to know whether these performances in different genres indicate vacillation between the two, or rather if the artist concerned underwent a change of direction at some point in his career.

And no doubt performers were highly remunerated for their specialised craft, though evidence for levels of pay for actors is scant.[17] There is some sensationalist (and sometimes suspicious) anecdote about stars' pay in the fourth century, though their riches are sometimes borne out by more reliable, non-anecdotal forms of evidence: for example, an inscription listing various contributions towards the temple in Delphi records a particularly high one by Theodoros the famous tragedian.[18] Star actors

[12] Cf. the role played by Ktesiphon, Neoptolemos and Aristodemos in the negotiations between Athens and Philip: Dem. *Or.* 5.6, *Or.* 19.12, 18, 94, 315 and hypothesis 2.2; *Or.* 18.21; Aeschin. *Or.* 2.15–17, 19, 52 and hypothesis.

[13] Taplin (1993) 91.

[14] Name unknown, Stephanis (1988) no. 3003 = *IG* v/2 118 = *SIG*[3] 1080.

[15] In [Plut.] *Mor.* 844F, Demosthenes is said to have paid Neoptolemos 10,000 drachmas to train him to deliver 'whole periods' without taking a breath.

[16] E.g. Stephanis (1988) nos. 620; 2137; 822. In the classical period Plato had claimed that rhapsodes and actors could not be the same people (*Rep.* 3.395a).

[17] For prizes in imperial Aphrodisias, see Roueché (1993) nos. 51–3.

[18] *FD* iii/5 3 l. 67. Less credible is Aul. Gell. *NA* 11.9.2, according to whom Aristodemos received a talent for a single performance.

like Neoptolemos might even choose to spend their money on acts of civic euergetism.[19] For ordinary guildsmen in the Hellenistic period evidence is confined to a few inscriptions, one relating to the Sarapieia in Tanagra in about 85 BC, in which sums are mentioned in the form of gold 'crowns' of a certain value for the winner, and cash prizes for the runner-up.[20] It is hard to know whether the figures are representative or not; the sums would be dependent on the endowment and the status of the festival, and the Sarapieia would appear to have been of middling rank. The prizes fall into bands, of which the highest is a crown worth 169 drachmas, won by the aulete, the citharode, the performer of epinician and the actor in old tragedy (for this was one of the many festivals in which revivals of old plays took place beside performances of newly composed ones, and the prize was won by the actors who competed in them). The second highest band was 135 drachmas, for the poets of tragedy and comedy (that is, newly-composed works), the hexameter poet, the citharist, and the actor in the revival of old comedy. The aulode, who presumably accompanied the chorus, got 112.5 drachmas, and the lowest-value first prize was worth 101 drachmas, won by the rhapsode, satyric poet, trumpeter, herald, and the actors in the newly composed tragedy and comedy. There are second prizes in most events, regularly worth 40 and 50 drachmas. Apart from telling us the actual value of the prizes, the inscription is interesting because it gives some indication of the relative statuses of events: old tragedy seems to be perceived to be 'worth' more than new; acting in old tragedy pays better than old comedy, but no distinction is drawn between new tragedy and new comedy.

Another inscription from Euboea, dating from just before the inception of the guilds, contains figures of a rather higher order for the initial hire of the performers, not for the prizes they receive: 600 drachmas of 'Demetrian coinage' for an aulete, 400 for a comic actor and 100 for a tragic actor (but the figure is hard to credit in relation to the others).[21] The same inscription specifies that performers who fail to show up, having entered upon their contract, will forfeit double their hire, a rule which, if applied to a couple of inscriptions showing actors' fines in Epidauros, produces a figure of 200 drachmas for an actor's hire; while in Iasos, the fine was to be 1,000 drachmas for any performer who failed to show: a particularly punitive sum.[22] These performers were clearly well paid.

[19] Dem. *Or.* 18. 114.

[20] *IG* vii/540 = *SEG* 19 (1963), 335, discussed by Calvet and Roesch (1966).

[21] *IG* xii/9 207 ll. 21–2.

[22] Epidauros: *IG* iv/1 (ed. min.) 99, 100; Iasos: *IK* 28.1 152 ll. 19–23.

The figures contrast with what a skilled labourer might earn in a year: 450 drachmas, at one and a half drachmas a day in a working year of 300 days, or 600 drachmas at two drachmas a day if he was very lucky.[23] A musical performer or actor might receive this in a contract for a performance at a single festival – although there is perhaps some ambiguity about whether this sum is to be distributed among the other actors or not. Hellenistic clubs and societies are often associations of the urban poor.[24] Not, so it seems, the *technītai*.

This is not to say that all members of guilds were equally well remunerated, or had equal status. Members of Hellenistic clubs and societies were notionally equal, but in practice statuses within them no doubt tended to fan out. The supporting actors or *synagōnistai* are an interesting case. We saw that in the classical period they were co-opted by the state's chosen protagonist, and that contracts between cities and guilds continue to specify only the required number of leading actors, leaving the selection of the rest of the cast to the will of the guild or the leading actors themselves. The inscriptional marginalisation of the supporting actor is further emphasised by the practice in victor lists and honorific decrees of mentioning only the leading actor by name, even when the rest of the cast were included in his honours.[25] It was not that supporting actors did not have status: they often appear as sacred delegates or *theōroi* from guilds to foreign cities, as at Delphi. But they were not the stars. Whether there was ever tension is hard to say. At Teos the *synagōnistai* actually constituted a separate organisation, but this may have served practical utility, rather than being evidence of a malcontented splinter-group.[26]

Where does this get us? This state of affairs used to be seen as lamentable testimony to the decline in civic spirit at festivals. This lack was, supposedly, intensified by the disappearance of the office of the *chorēgos* and his replacement by a single *agōnothetēs*, who, however civically minded, was nevertheless subsidised with public money and was not in competition with his fellow-citizens in the equipment and training of a choir. But the worst of it was that it was no longer performed by citizen amateurs, but by professional guildsmen with formal contracts. The more notorious incidents in the guilds' histories – the acrimonious rivalry between the guilds based in the Peloponnese and in

23 The figures are taken from Glotz (1926) 359–60.

24 Cf. e.g. Kloppenborg in Kloppenborg and Wilson (1996) 17.

25 An example is *SIG*³ 659 = *FD* iii/1 48: Nikon the τραγῳδός appears alone in the honorific inscription, but is mentioned with his synagonists in the proxeny inscription *SIG*³ 585 nos. 128–30.

26 Michel, *Recueil* 1016 B; *DFA* (1988) 293. They have their own Dionysium and hold common meals.

Athens[27] – were adduced to support the view that theatre had become empty spectacle in the hands of grasping international corporations, its civic and religious elements and the creative excellence of its writers all lost.[28] More recently, however, subtler analyses have been offered. The existence of the guilds themselves proves nothing against the standard of dramatic performance: the principal actors in drama must long have been professionals, and if the same is now true of the members of choruses, this presumably meant that overall standards went up. Contracts between guilds and cities cannot serve as evidence for 'death of the agonistic spirit': cities are no less anxious to secure the best competitors, who in turn are no less anxious to excel; and if more than one guild was present at a festival – which might sometimes have been the case, although whether it was ever general practice is not clear – then inter-guild rivalry could add extra excitement.

Hellenistic theatre used also to be taxed with increasing secularisation, as if the 'taste for spectacle' put at risk the 'sacred character of the theatre', rendering it nothing more than 'a profane diversion'.[29] Yet it is quite clear that the vocabulary of piety and the ritual remain.[30] Many festivals were established following the epiphany of a god: the festival of Artemis Leukophryena in Magnesia on the Maeander is the best-documented example.[31] Festivals are frequently called *thysiai* (literally, 'sacrifices'), and share all the components of their classical predecessors – the *pompē* or procession, the sacrifice at the end, the singing of hymns and the public prayer. The standard terminology is 'hold for the god' or 'hold contests for the god'. The city and its territory would be sacred and inviolable during the festival; its ambassadors had the sacred status of *theōroi*, and in inscriptions piety appears as the most conspicuous virtue of the festival's celebrants and organisers in honorific decrees. It would be unfair and aprioristic to regard this inscriptional language either as mere conventional pietism or as calculated propaganda. Yet it is also too simple to see it as a sincere and true and accurate reflection of people's 'real' feelings. We just do not know how people 'really' felt at sacred games, though it is interesting that even Philodemus – as an Epicurean himself certainly no friend to established religion – asserted that our sense of

[27] *SIG*³ 704–5. [28] See the strictures of Le Guen (1995) 86–7.

[29] Ghiron-Bistagne (1976) 205; *contra*, Le Guen (1995) 87–8.

[30] Dem. *Or.* 21.16 regards all equipment connected with a festival, as well as the persons involved, as sacred for the duration of the festivities.

[31] *IMagn.* 54 is the decree of the *technītai* from Ionia and the Hellespont accepting the invitation to take part.

the divine is particularly keen at festivals.[32] Public decrees, meanwhile, preserve only what their authors wanted to be memorialised about their public conduct. Nevertheless, the data that they furnish is in need of analysis and interpretation.

The prominence of piety, *eusebeia*, in the guilds' self-presentation is especially striking because even skill, the very *technē* of the *technītai*, tends to take second place to it in inscriptions recording their activities and praising their virtues.[33] It is true that, of the other Hellenistic clubs and societies, virtually none is without its religious coloration, because Greek categories of thought did not partition off the sacred as a separate domain. Some societies were heavily involved with cult, others less so; what impresses about the *technītai* is the extent of this involvement for a society which is not expressly a band of worshippers (they never call themselves a *thiasos*, always a *synodos* or a *koinon*[34]). This seems to cohere well with the religious emphasis in festivals. They see themselves and are seen by others as pious organisations because they take part in religious occasions. There is a hard-headed, practical reason: the claim to sacred status is clearly related to the practical need for inviolability for performers travelling across potentially hostile territory. This is already clear in one of the first inscriptions to mention guilds, the Amphictyonic League's recognition of the Athenian *technītai* in 278 BC, which speaks of the 'honours and ceremonies to which the *technītai* are appointed'.[35] The phrase seems to refer to the festivals themselves, and recognition of their part in them leads to a grant of immunity from military service and taxation. The *technītai* might further manifest their piety by staging free performances in honour of the local people and their deity.[36] The most famous occasions on which they did this were the Delphic Pythaides, pilgrimages to Delphi which the Athenian people mounted at sporadic intervals. The Athenian guild took a prominent part on these occasions, and we have several copious decrees praising their piety for staging free performances.[37] They were of course involved in the religious ceremonies, and from the second Pythais we have the two famous poems whose musical notation survives, both of which mention the *technītai* by name – 'Bacchus' great, sacred,

32 Philodemus *De piet.* 27 (765 ff.) and 28 (790 ff.) Obbink.

33 Cf. the praise of the μαγῳδός in the Delphic decree discussed by Robert (1938) 7–11, and his comparisons on 8.

34 But the universal guild in the Roman period was called a ἱερὰ σύνοδος or even a σύνοδος . . . μυστῶν: see *DFA* (1988) 297–8.

35 *SIG*³ 399 ll. 13–14 αἱ τιμαὶ καὶ αἱ θυ[σίαι, ἐ]φ' ἅς εἰσι τεταγμένοι οἱ τεχνῖται.

36 As the Isthmian guild did at the Delphic Soteria: *SIG*³ 489, 690.

37 *SIG*³ 696–9, 711 *L*, 728.

thyrsus-stricken band of *technītai* resident in the Cecropian land', as Limenios, the poet of one of the surviving paeans, somewhat uneconomically puts it.[38]

But piety is a frequent term of commendation for performers who do not figure explicitly as members of guilds (though they may well have belonged to them), performers who give recitals (*epideixeis* or *akroāseis*), not as part of the normal festival events but outside the concourse proper, or in lieu of the festival when it was disrupted by war, or on a wholly separate occasion.[39] Sometimes these recitals were given free of charge, just as the guilds *en masse* might perform free of charge, and this is matter for inscriptional commendation. The greatest bulk of our material of this sort comes from the religious sites of Delphi and Delos and relates to musicians and poets and sometimes lecturers who included historians and *grammatici*, but it appears that there were also wandering dramatists and actors, as when, at the end of the third century, the comic actor Nikophon of Miletus sailed into the harbour in the little town Minoa on Amorgos, dominated by the temples of Dionysus and Pythian Apollo and the theatre on the citadel above, and announced that he and his troupe would perform three plays over the next three days. They did, and Nikophon was honoured for his pains (described as 'performing for the god') with a gold crown of modest proportions.[40] Likewise, the tragedian Dymas of Iasos was honoured by the Samothracians in the first half of the second century BC for his play on the subject of Dardanus, a religious theme which no doubt mentioned Dardanus' brother Iasion and his connection with the mysteries of the local deities the Cabiri.[41] He impressed the Samothracians, whose theatre appears to have been in or beside the sanctuary of the Cabiri.

In all the honorific decrees commemorating such occasions, the piety of the performer is presented as a civic virtue. This seems typical of inscriptional uses of *eusebeia* in the Hellenistic period. It is the standard quality of kings, and Roman emperors inherit the title from them, because they are the ultimate guarantors of civic order and they stand in a special relation to the gods.[42] As well as participants in festivals, the

38 Powell, *Coll. Alex.* pp. 149–59.

39 Some are collected by Guarducci (1929). Note also the Delian archons' records which include lists of all types of performers who render up to the god free ἐπιδείξεις throughout the year, outside the compass of the Apollonia and Dionysia proper (*IG* xi/2 105–34).

40 *IG* xii/7 226; cf. p. 50, and *RE* xv (1932) 1858–9, s.v. Minoa (7).

41 *TrGF* 130 Snell T I–II, with bibliography.

42 Seleucus II: *IK* 24.1 (Smyrna) 573 l. 6; Seleucus I and Antiochus I: Welles (1934) no. 9 l. 10; Antiochus III: Welles no. 44 l. 28; Attalus II (?): Welles no. 62 l. 5; Stratonice: Welles no. 67 l. 2; Philip V: *IK* 21 (Stratonicea) 3 l. 2.

ranks of the pious include priests and priestesses, artisans who work with divine images,[43] and others who participate in cult for the good of the city.[44] Inscriptions tend not to concern private piety until the imperial period (such as in ancestor cult, where *eusebeia* refers to piety towards the blessed dead). Performers, then, are seen to offer a public service, perhaps to be engaged in a collective act of worship. It explains why they are honoured as public benefactors in inscriptions which apply to them the standard euergetic language and confer on them the typical awards for public service: citizenship for Dymas, for the honorands at Delphi in the early first century proxeny, right of prior consultation of the oracle, rights of prior access to lawcourts, *asylia*, tax exemption, the right of sitting in the front seats, 'crowns' of a certain value of gold.[45]

It is important to recognise this for the deliberately constructed ideology that it is: for others they were rabble, and for the fourth-century historian Theopompus they were fit to be mentioned in the same breath as pick-pockets and swindlers and cut-throats.[46] Nevertheless, in the inscriptional record they are the very paragons of piety. Their participation in cult is everywhere apparent. They are often headed by a priest, which is true of many other Hellenistic clubs.[47] They sometimes wore purple: this has been interpreted as the costume of priests of Dionysus – although it is more plausible to see the purple as a generally ostentatious garb (for example, that of kings), though also with likely sacral overtones.[48] And if they wore golden crowns, this will be for victory in sacred games.[49] Religion pervaded their activities. Inscriptions show the guilds in possession of a *temenos* with altar of Dionysus and statues of the god and other benefactors, perhaps flanked by the Bacchic tripods

43 *IG* xi/4 514: an ἀγαλματοποιός in Delos, beginning of the third century BC; *OGIS* 339 l. 47: an official concerned with coinage (which bears a divine image) in Sestos, 133–120 BC.

44 *IG* ii/1 (ed. min.) 649, of a στρατηγός and ἀγωνοθέτης, 294/3 BC; *SEG* 22 (1967), 110 ll. 3–13, of a κοσμητής of ephebes who sacrifices to Athena Polias and the other gods on the day he leaves office, 79/8 BC.

45 100 drachmas for Nikophon (n. 40 above); a donative of 500 drachmas for Polygnota the harpist (*SIG*[3] 738); the figure for Antipater the organist is defaced (*SIG*[3] 737), and for a *choropsaltria* lost (*SIG*[3] 689).

46 [Arist.] *Prob.* 30.10, cf. Aul. Gell. *NA* 20.4; Philostr. *Vit. soph.* 2.16; Theopompus n. 9 above.

47 For exceptions, which include the Athenian guild, see *DFA* (1988) 303. But inscriptions of the Athenian guild do mention a priest of Dionysus (*IG* ii/1 (ed. min.) 1330 ll. 28–33, just before 130 BC). For other clubs, see Wilson in Kloppenborg and Wilson (1996) 7.

48 Csapo and Slater (1995) 240; Sherk (1969) (transl. in 1984: no. 85), with bibliography. For purple as priestly garb, see Athen. 5.211b; according to Athen. 12.534c, it was worn by Alcibiades as χορηγός. Dionysus' dress was typically the saffron κροκωτός; the statue of Dionysus in the πομπή of Philadelphus wore a purple χιτών, κροκωτός, and purple ἱμάτιον (Athen. 5.198c).

49 *SIG*[3] 704 *E* l. 31 and *H* ll. 26–7; cf. *RE*[2] vA (1934) 2491, s.v. τεχνῖται.

which were one of Dionysus' chief emblems.[50] The members might hold common meals, and meet for monthly and annual rites. But these rites did not only involve theatrical and musical deities, Dionysus, the Muses, Pythian Apollo.[51] For the *technītai* seem to have been involved in the more personal, affective cults, as in the case of the guild in Athens who had their own altar in Eleusis to Demeter and Kore, where, on the days of the mysteries, they would sacrifice and pour libations and toast the two goddesses and perform paeans.[52]

What they were most involved in, however, was that notorious new departure in Hellenistic religion, ruler-cult. It is true of many societies that they supported the existing political order, that they were rarely the focus for political discontent.[53] But again, the *technītai* go further than most. This involvement in ruler-cult is signalled in the very title of the artists' guild in Ptolemais-Hermiou, and in Cyprus: 'the *technītai* of Dionysus and the *Theoi Adelphoi*' (referring to the Ptolemy II and his sister and queen, Arsinoe).[54] Theokles, an otherwise unknown poet, seems to refer to an Alexandrian (?) festival called the Soteria at which it was the practice of the *technītai* to sacrifice and to drink the *dikeras* (apparently a two-horned drinking-vessel) in the king's honour.[55] The Athenian and Isthmian–Nemean guilds based on the Greek mainland are not known to have had much involvement in ruler-cult.[56] But the guild of Hellespontine artists based in Teos did, and egregiously so, after uniting with an association of performers for Attalid court entertainments called the 'association of the *technītai* of Dionysus Kathegemon'.[57] Dionysus Kathegemon was the patron deity of the Attalids, but naturally adopted by the associations of Dionysiac *technītai*; indeed, part of the Pergamene theatre was consecrated to the god, part protector of the ruling house, part avatar of drama. The inscriptionally famous Kraton had consecrated a shrine, the Attaleion, beside the Tean theatre, and left it in his will to a priestly

50 Michel, *Recueil* 1011 l. 13 ff., the Isthmian–Nemean guild, 113 BC; Posid. *apud* Athen. 5.212e = F 253 Edelstein–Kidd.

51 Dionysus Melpomenos: Paus. 1.2.5; Dionysus Kadmeios at Thebes: *FD* iii/1 351 l. 22.

52 Michel, *Recueil* 1010 = *IG* ii/1 628 = ii/1 (ed. min.) 1338.

53 S. Walker-Ramisch in Kloppenborg and Wilson (1996) 132–4.

54 *OGIS* 50–1 (Egypt); οἱ περὶ τὸν Διόνυσον καὶ θεοὺς Εὐεργέτας τεχνῖται in *OGIS* 164 l. 5, 166 ll. 4–5 (Cyprus). When the Egyptian guild vote thanks to a benefactor they do it for his εὐσέβεια . . . εἴς τε βασιλέα Πτολεμαῖον καὶ τὸν Διόνυσον καὶ τοὺς ἄλλους θεούς in that order (*OGIS* 51 ll. 19–20).

55 Powell, *Coll. Alex.* p. 173; cf. Fraser (1972) I. 232–3.

56 Though the Athenian guild's honours for Ariarathes verge on the divine (*IG* ii/1 (ed. min.) 1330), and the Isthmian–Nemean guild offers sacrifice for the Romans (*SIG*³ 705 B l. 46, Delphi, 112 BC).

57 τὸ κοινὸν τῶν περὶ τὸν καθηγεμόνα Διόνυσον τεχνιτῶν; cf. Hansen (1971) 460 ff., cf. 452.

institution called the Attalistai whom he himself had founded.[58] As the guild's priest, Kraton offered sacrifices and libations 'to the kings and queens and to the brothers of king Eumenes'. But there was also a separate priest of Eumenes II, whose cult continued under his successor Attalus II, and this priesthood seems to have been institutionally close to the guild. Its holder was also *agōnothetēs*.[59]

The guilds were thus one of many ways in which royal power was presented to its subjects: not only did they undertake royal cult on a large scale (it would not have been imposed on them from above), but they also participated in the festivals and processions which helped to inscribe royal power into the cycle of city life. Their part in processions is to be expected, for the *pompē*, since the classical period, is the occasion for the self-display of the citizenry, and the performers at a festival are a natural addition, even if they come from a foreign community.[60] Thus the *technītai* are one of many elements in the dazzling Dionysiac procession of Ptolemy Philadelphus in Alexandria in the early years of the 270s BC, and they are mentioned, presumably alongside the rest of the citizenry of Teos, in a decree which provides for a new festival called the Antiocheia and Laodiceia, organised in honour of the city's new conqueror at the turn of the third and second centuries BC.[61] Festivals themselves, for which the *technītai* provide the competitors, act as displays of royal power: they do this both nakedly and on a more subtle level, by which the presence of the king is insinuated into the community through the adaptation of a civic calendar and the alteration of the rhythms of a city's life. Many festivals are named after rulers, or the king's name is added to an existing festival, so that a *panēgyris* in honour of an individual is grafted onto a *heortē* in honour of a deity. This happens particularly often with the Dionysia, so that theatrical festivals become bound up with celebrations of royal power;[62] but it can also happen with other deities. In the new city of Alexandria, Ptolemy Philadelphus founded Dionysia in honour of his dynasty's patron god; we do not know the precise events involved, but it seems as likely as not that when Theocritus talks of the sacred contests of Dionysus in which Philadelphus rewarded competitors personally for their *technē*, he is talking about the *technītai*.[63]

58 *DFA* (1988) 292–3; *OGIS* 326.

59 *OGIS* 325, Michel, *Recueil* 1016A ll. 2, 17, 26.

60 See Guettel Cole in Scodel (1993) 28–31.

61 For the τεχνῖται in Philadelphus' πομπή, see Athen. 5.198 b–c; for the Antiocheia and Laodiceia, *SEG* 41 (1991) 1003 II l. 8.

62 On the connection of Dionysia and other festivals with festivals in honour of rulers, see Habicht (1970) 149–50.

63 Theoc. *Id.* 17.112; cf. also Eratosth. *apud* Athen. 7.276b.

This celebration of royal power takes place even in cities which are nominally still 'free' and 'democracies'. Thus in Teos (itself a 'democracy'[64]), protected by a god who patronised both drama and the ruling house, the connection between the guilds and the king was especially close; but Teos was not unique, as we know from the parallel relationship between the Egyptian guild and the Ptolemies. Was the situation reflected in the contents of drama itself? Its loss makes it impossible to say whether any Hellenistic tragedy was as politically engaged as classical had been; whether it dealt with questions of government, of political dialogue, or whether it preferred to use myth for the purpose of aetiology, antiquarian and, as far as possible, depoliticised. But at least it should be recorded that some tragedies seem to have been on historical subjects of the not-too-distant past:[65] Lycophron's *Cassandreis* is often thought to have dramatised the foundation of Cassandreia in 316 BC, and there are other examples of plays which may have offered at least some scope for contemporary political engagement, a relief from the post-Euripidean romantic melodramas which often colour our notions about the nature of much Hellenistic tragedy.

So the view that festivals were no longer lively civic occasions needs correcting: they continued to be occasions for self-display by the community, when its benefactors were rewarded and the city asserted its cohesiveness, its fitness to give and to confer honour.[66] But the communities were changed; and not the least peculiarity of the Hellenistic festival is the fact that its competitors belonged to bodies which characterised themselves as cities – corporations based in cities, as we said before, but distinct and exclusive, cities existing for the sake of citizens with itinerant careers. This is my final point about the *technītai* of Dionysus. Not only do the guilds appoint their own financial, religious, diplomatic, and legislative officials, just like cities.[67] They also issue their own decrees, patterned on the standard civic model. Once more, all these features are shared with other societies, for other clubs and fraternities use civic nomenclature for their officers and issue civic-style decrees. The argument, in the case of other societies, is that they provide fictive polities for those deprived of real political power, the urban poor, in cities which had ceased to have any meaningful political life of their own. But for the *technītai* the guilds were surely more than fantasy poleis for the politically disenfranchised. Their decrees show an astonishing self-assertion for an

64 The βουλή and the δῆμος are mentioned in e.g. *SEG* 41 (1991) 1003 IV l. 3 and 1004 l. 14.

65 Xanthakis-Karamanos (1993) 127.

66 See Guettel Cole in Scodel (1993) 29.

67 For the officials of the various guilds, see *DFA* (1988) 303.

institution whose members, in the classical period, had been itinerant, vulnerable individuals. Whereas actors in the classical period had had to be at the disposal of the city officials, specifically, the archon, performers are now in a position to issue decrees in which they seem to claim equal status, at least in festal matters, with cities themselves. They despatch and receive ambassadors and delegates, *presbeutai* and *theōroi*, and incidentally they seem to be the only institution, apart from the cities themselves, who appoint their own representatives abroad, or *proxenoi*.[68] They use the language of reciprocal honour and the exchange of courtesy, as in one of our earliest documents about the guilds, from the middle of the third century (*SIG*³ 457), where the Isthmian–Nemean guild talk of the courtesies or *philanthrōpa* which they give and receive from the city of Thespiae, presupposing that they are equal partners in the relationship. In Teos, where the two communities were in particular proximity, the city and the *technītai* were linked in the prayers and supplications in the Dionysia, the prytaneum and the assembly. Several documents speak as if a festival is the common property of city and guild.[69] Sometimes there was hostility, when financial interests collided.[70] They might be exempted from the dues and duties to which other communities were bound, especially if they played on their sacred status, although they might also be required to pay a certain annual sum to the community in which they lived.[71]

It is particularly interesting that the guild in the Ptolemais-Hermiou inscription in Upper Egypt refers to itself as a *technīteuma*, a word clearly modelled on *polīteuma*.[72] Just as a *polīteuma* is a self-governing body of citizens, the *technē* has its own political existence, its own rights of self-determination, as a *polis*. But it also recalls the special sense of *polīteuma* to mean an (ethnically) distinctive group, such as Jews or Greeks resident in the Egyptian countryside. The *technītai* are not this; yet they are a distinctive and separate community, and in Ptolemaic Egypt their Greekness, the Greekness of their games and festivals, was a matter for self-advertisement and separation from the indigenous Egyptians. The mobility of the community was another significant point, for mercenaries

[68] *OGIS* 51. ll. 67–72.

[69] *SIG*³ 457 ll. 47–50 οἱ τεχνῖται κοινὸν ὑπολαμβάνοντες εἶναι τὸν ἀγῶνα τῶν Μουσῶν τῇ τε πόλει Θεσπιέων καὶ αὑτοῖς . . .

[70] Welles (1934) no. 53, of the Teans and the guild of artists in Ionia and the Hellespont; Strab. 14.1.29.

[71] See Fraser (1972) vol. II, 870 n. 2 for the freedom of the Egyptian guild from the salt-tax; a piece of land worth 6,000 drachmas was bought by the city of Teos for the Hellespontine guild, to be ἱερὸν and ἀτελὲς ὧν ἡ πόλις ἐπιβάλλει τελῶν (*SEG* 2 (1925) 580 ll. 8–10, cf. Robert 1937: 39–44).

[72] *OGIS* 51 l. 11. On πολιτεύματα, see Ziebarth in *RE* xxi (1952) 1401–2 and references.

also constituted themselves into *polīteumata*, and they, like the *technītai*, were one of the more conspicuous instances of a skilled, mobile work-force in the Hellenistic world.

We have looked at the organisation of festivals and the status of performers in the Hellenistic period, and considered the self-presentation of festivals and guilds, especially with regard to their religious emphases. We have also noted how Hellenistic festivals accommodate the figure of the Hellenistic monarch, and how the guilds are involved in his cult. Inscriptions are extremely informative about the management of festivals and the ideology of their participants, but one of the consequences of the loss of most Hellenistic drama is that we know desperately little about the ways in which religious and political themes were negotiated in this period in the plays themselves. And of course, the loss of the text has also made hopeless any assessment of the bravura displays of their art which were no doubt managed by those skilled technicians, the *technītai*.

SUGESTIONS FOR FURTHER READING

The fullest recent survey of the evidence pertaining to the *technītai* of Dionysus is *DFA* (1988) 279–321, to which add Ghiron-Bistagne (1976) 163–71, 205–6; for sources, see also Csapo and Slater (1995) 239–55, and the prosopography in Stephanis (1988). Still useful are the earlier contributions of Ziebarth (1896) 74–92; *RE*² vA (1934), 2473–558, s.v. Technitai (Poland). On actors' pay, see Ghiron-Bistagne (1976) 179–91. For some recent work on post-classical drama, see Sifakis (1967); Xanthakis-Karamanos (1993); Le Guen (1995); Easterling (1997d) 211–27.

CHAPTER TEN

Actors and actor–managers at Rome in the time of Plautus and Terence

Peter G. McC. Brown

This is a tantalising topic. On the one hand, we have the texts of twenty-six plays by Plautus and Terence (writing *c.* 205–184 and 166–160 BC respectively), the earliest works of Latin literature to have survived, and perhaps the only surviving works of Latin drama that were written for performance on the public stage. On the other hand, they tell us very little about the organisation of the acting profession at the time. There are some references in the plays to the fact that they *are* plays, particularly in the case of Plautus, and it has become fashionable to stress this 'metatheatrical' element in Plautus;[1] but these references give away next to nothing about how things were arranged. Nevertheless, we do have *some* evidence, enough to raise a number of interesting questions – about the status and standing of actors at this time, and also about who took what kinds of financial risk in putting plays on – but not enough to answer them with any certainty. It is also tantalising that, whereas we have a wealth of theatrical terracottas and vases from Southern Italy illustrating Greek drama (of whatever kind), there is no comparable illustrative material for Latin drama.[2]

At a later date, acting was a despised profession at Rome, as it has been in many societies, even though individual actors were sometimes lionised. In particular, there is evidence from later periods that Roman citizens who acted incurred *infamia*, forfeiting many of the privileges of citizenship; and it is likely that *infamia* developed formally out of long-standing informal prejudices.[3] Modern authorities generally agree that most actors at Rome were from the start non-citizens (whether free or slave), but it has been debated whether prejudices against the profession had already taken root by the time of Plautus.

1 E.g. Slater (1985).
2 Taplin (1993) discusses some of the Greek material. The only vase with a non-Greek element is one from the mid-fourth century with the name Santia inscribed in Oscan letters, discussed by Taplin on pp. 40–1.
3 See Levick (1983) 105–10; Edwards (1993) 123–6, (1997).

According to Livy (7.2), officially organised theatrical entertainments (*lūdi scaenici*) were introduced to Rome in 364 BC, with the importation from Etruria of performers (*lūdiones*) who danced to the accompaniment of a reed-pipe; but it was Livius Andronicus (he says) who first composed a play with a plot. It is generally accepted that Livius Andronicus' first production was in 240, and that his innovation (although Livy does not say so) consisted in adapting Greek tragedies and comedies for performance in Latin. Livy's brief account of how the theatre developed at Rome between 364 and 240 is far from clear; but he mentions native performers (*vernāculi artifices*) as being active in this period,[4] and he says they were called *histriones* because *ister* was the Etruscan word for a *lūdio*. He also tells us that Livius Andronicus ('like everyone else at that time') performed his own compositions, but it is not entirely clear that these compositions are the plays with plots.[5] Furthermore, not only is he silent about the Greek models for Livius' plays; he does not record the tradition that Livius was by birth a Greek from Tarentum, nor does he mention the vigorous Greek and Greek-based dramatic traditions of Southern Italy and Sicily of which Romans cannot have been unaware. (There are also strong reasons for believing that drama had developed under Greek influence in Etruria, and that theatrical entertainment there did not consist merely of dancing; and also that key terms of Roman theatrical language came into Latin from Greek via Etruscan – not only *histrio*, which became the standard Latin term for an actor, but *persōna* ('mask', 'character') and *scaena* ('stage').[6] But we have very little to set beside Livy's account.)

One particular piece of evidence about Livius has been taken to strengthen the case for supposing continuity between the Greek and Roman theatrical worlds at the end of the third century, a passage of Festus (333 M):

Thus, when Livius Andronicus in the Second Punic War had written a hymn that was sung by virgins, because the public affairs of the Roman people began to be conducted more successfully, the temple of Minerva on the Aventine

[4] I think it most likely that these were professionals, as accepted by Oakley (1998) 41 (contrast 42 n.1).

[5] Livy 7.2.8. This is the beginning of an anecdote about how Livius introduced the practice of miming the action of accompanied passages while someone else sang the text. But see Oakley (1998) 65–6: we cannot be sure precisely what Livy wrote, or what he meant by it, and in any case 'Most modern scholars have rightly rejected it'; in dramatic works, actors must have been able to sing as well as speak and move. Otherwise Livy says nothing about the involvement of further performers, and possibly *suorum carminum actor* ('performer of his own compositions') refers to solo performances of some kind.

[6] See Oakley (1998) 52.

was officially designated as the place where writers and actors (*histriones*) might assemble and dedicate offerings; this was a tribute to Livius, because he both wrote plays and acted in them.

Although Festus does not use the term, it looks as if there was a guild (*collēgium*) of writers and actors, either already in existence or first established now. Such a guild obviously invites comparison with the Artists of Dionysus (not least in the fact that actors and authors belong to the same guild), and it has indeed been argued that, given Livius' background, 'it is an almost inevitable assumption that the first association of scenic performers in Rome, formed under his guidance, would have been modelled on the contemporary Greek guilds'.[7] Jory also suggests that most Roman actors at this period had probably begun as Artists of Dionysus in Southern Italy, and furthermore that their guild at Rome was under the patronage of Dionysus before it was brought under the wing of Minerva; but there is no positive evidence to support these ideas.[8]

If we accept Festus' way of presenting the matter, official recognition of the guild was an honour; on this basis, it has been taken to indicate that actors at this period enjoyed some respectability, and that it was only later that there came to be prejudices against them.[9] On the other side, it has been argued that the senate's decree was rather an attempt to keep writers and actors in their place, even if it did confer some benefits on them.[10] 'Respectability' is in any case a relative term, and it is unlikely that a Roman citizen ever earned high social standing by performing as an actor.

Livy tells us that one type of performance, the improvised drama known as the *Atellana*, was kept as an amateur preserve by the young men of Rome, who 'did not allow it to be polluted by *histriones*'. Livy adds: 'for that reason it remains established that those who perform in

[7] Jory (1970) 228.

[8] Jory (1970) 225–30, anticipated in some details by Zucchelli (1964) 51–2, and followed by Gruen (1990) 87–8. Festus' wording need not imply that the guild was formed under Livius' guidance, nor (as Jory claims on p. 229) that it consisted largely of foreigners who needed special permission to dedicate offerings to Minerva. What is authorised by the senate is the right to hold regular meetings in a temple, something which required an official decree whatever the status of the guild members (see Waltzing (1895) 81–2); the cases Jory quotes from Livy are quite different, namely cases of foreign states granted permission to dedicate a gold crown on a particular occasion. Leppin (1992) 34–5 remarks on the high proportion of Latin (non-foreign) *cognōmina* among the (small) number of known comic actors from the time of the Roman Republic (a point already noted by Frank (1931) 151), and he offers as an explanation the fact that they were performing works with Latin texts; if this is right, the link with the Artists of Dionysus may not have been as strong as Jory and Gruen suggest. (See also n.12 below.)

[9] So, for instance, Gruen (1990) 89–90, Goldberg (1995) 30–1.

[10] Horsfall (1976) 79–81.

Atellanae are not removed from their tribe and are liable for military service as having no part in the acting profession'.[11] This gives the impression that military service was a privilege from which professional actors were disbarred. Against that, it has been suggested that in origin actors were not so much disbarred as exempted (another similarity with the Artists of Dionysus), because drama had religious connections and it was important to ensure that it could be performed properly – whereas *Atellanae* were not performed at religious festivals at this time.[12] It is hard to progress beyond *a priori* intuitions about this, though we may note the remark elsewhere in Festus (217 M) that actors in the *Atellana*, unlike other actors, were not obliged to remove their masks on the stage; perhaps for actors in other types of drama this was a way of checking (at the end of the performance?) whether they were Roman citizens disgracing themselves by performing on the stage.[13]

At about the time when the temple of Minerva was being assigned for meetings of writers and actors, Plautus started to put on his comedies at Rome. Twenty of his plays survive, together with the six written by Terence in the 160s. Explicit references to actors in these authors come almost entirely in their prologues.[14] The term *histrio* comes in the prologues of three plays by Plautus;[15] *artifex* ('craftsman', 'expert') is found in Plautus at *Poen.* 37 and in Terence (metaphorically, in the body of the play) at *Phorm.* 259.[16] A third noun, *actor*, later used more or less interchangeably with *histrio*, seems at this period to have designated the leading actor in the company: it is found at Plautus, *Bacchides* 213 (metaphorical, but introducing the analogy of Pellio – see below), and twice in the prologue to Terence's *Phormio* (at 33 with reference to his leading actor (whom we know to have been called Lucius Ambivius Turpio), at 10 with reference

[11] Livy 7.2.12: *quod genus ludorum ab Oscis acceptum tenuit iuventus nec ab histrionibus pollui passa est; eo institutum manet, ut actores Atellanarum nec tribu moveantur et stipendia, tamquam expertes artis ludicrae, faciant.* Green (1933) shows against Frank (1931) that *ars ludicra* at the end of Livy's sentence does include acting in general, not just the more trivial forms of entertainment. (For more detail, see Jory (1995) 140–5.)

[12] Frank (1931) 19, Jory (1970) 230–3. Frank suggests that being 'removed from their tribe' was a way of ensuring that citizen actors obtained their exemption. Jory, unlike Frank, believes that most actors at this time were foreigners and therefore not liable to military service; on this view, the granting of exemption was a largely vacuous gesture (cf. n. 8 above).

[13] Cf. Beare (1964) 305, Levick (1983) 107 n. 22. Dumont (1982) suggests that the custom of removing masks at the end of a performance may have been imported from the Greek world of S. Italy.

[14] For a treatment of the terms I discuss, see Knapp (1919), Zucchelli (1964).

[15] *Amph.* 69, 77, 82, 87, 91 (also 90, 152 *facere histrioniam*); *Capt.* 13; *Poen.* 20 (also 4, 44 *histricus*). *Histrio* also comes in the body of the play at *Truc.* 931; it is not found in Terence.

[16] But *Amph.* 69–70 ('the actors or any craftsman') suggests that *artifex* could be a wider-ranging term covering a variety of theatrical trades, and *Poen.* 37 could also be taken in this more general sense.

to an actor (probably the leading actor) in another company).[17] In fact the *actor* was not only the leading actor but the man in charge of the company (for which the word is *grex*, meaning 'flock' or 'herd', but also used more widely of any group of people).[18] We learn most about him from the prologues of Terence, two of which were written to be spoken by Ambivius – as we shall see.

We also hear in two of Plautus' plays of a *chorāgus* who supplied theatrical costumes, and perhaps also props.[19] In his commentary on Terence's *The Eunuch*, line 967, Donatus (writing some 500 years later) suggests that the *chorāgus* was responsible for plotting the movements of the actors; but there is no other evidence for this, and as far as we know there was no 'director' in the modern sense of a separate individual who directs the production.

Etymologically related to *actor* is the verb *agere*, 'to act', nearly always in the sense of performing a play rather than a particular role.[20] Most commonly the subject is the company as a whole (in the first person plural),[21] or the verb is in the passive with the play as its subject;[22] at *Amph.* 88, 94–5 it is the characters Jupiter and Mercury who are said to be performing the play. But Ambivius is the subject in the two prologues of Terence of which he is the speaker (*Haut.* 4–6, 36; *Hec.* 18, 30, 33),[23] and Pellio at Plautus, *Bacch.* 215.[24]

It is above all Terence's prologues that raise questions about the financial relationships between the playwright, the *actor* and the officials responsible for organising the festivals at which the plays were performed. The picture they present takes a lot of background information for granted, and we may well agree with Gruen (1992) 192: 'It is illusory to imagine that we can reconstruct a regular pattern for these transactions – if indeed there was such a thing.' But it is worth setting out the evidence, of which our prize piece is the prologue written in 160 BC to introduce

17 Otherwise *actor* is found in Terence only at *Haut.* 12–13, in the sense of *ōrātor*. It is not found elsewhere in Plautus. *Lūdius*, an alternative for *lūdio*, is found in Plautus at *Curc.* 150 (where *lūdii barbari* appears to mean 'Italian dancers') and *Aul.* 402 (where it is not clear what it means).

18 Plautus, *Asin.* 3; *Cas.* 22; *Pseud.* 1334; Terence, *Haut.* 45; *Pho.* 32.

19 *Persa* 159–60, *Trin.* 858; see Gilula (1996). The word is taken from Doric Greek (with *-a-* as the middle vowel), presumably a sign of the influence of the theatrical world of S. Italy.

20 Of performing a particular role only at Terence, *Phormio* 27 (with the character Phormio, not the actor, as subject!), *Haut.* 37–40, and metaphorically at *Phorm.* 835–6.

21 Plautus, *Capt.* 62, *Mil.* 84; Terence, *Eun.* 19, *Ad.* 3, 12.

22 Plautus, *Capt.* 52, *Cas.* 17, *Men.* 72–3, *Mostell.* 1181, *Poen.* 551, *Pseud.* 720; Terence, *Eun.* 22.

23 See also the *didascaliae* (production notices) to the plays of Terence, preserved in the manuscripts and in Donatus' commentary. These regularly name a further *actor* in addition to Ambivius, probably the *actor* of a later revival, but possibly Ambivius' second-in-command.

24 The verb is intransitive at Plautus, *Poen.* 552, Terence, *Hec.* 44, *Ad.* 24.

the third attempt to perform *Hecyra* (*The Mother-in-Law*), after two previous failures (lines 9–57).[25] Almost certainly, this prologue is the last thing that Terence wrote. He wrote it to be spoken by the *actor*, Ambivius Turpio:

> I am dressed as the prologue-speaker, but I come to you to plead a case. Let my pleading succeed, so that I can enjoy the same rights in my old age as I enjoyed when I was younger . . . Among others, when I first learnt new plays by Caecilius, in some cases I was driven off, in others I had difficulty in holding my ground. Because I knew that success in the theatre was a chancy thing . . . I began to perform the same plays again, so that I could have other, new ones to learn by the same author . . . I made sure they were given a showing; once people had got to know them, they liked them . . . Now, for my sake, hear in all fairness what I want. I am bringing back *The Mother-in-Law* to you. I have never been allowed to perform it in silence . . . When I first began to perform it, there was talk of a boxing match, and there were also hopes of a tight-rope walker, too; slaves were arriving, there was a din, women were shouting – these things made me leave the stage before I'd reached the end. I began to follow my old custom with this new play, and I tried again: I brought it back anew. The first part went down well; but then word got around that a show of gladiators was going to be given: people flocked together, there was an uproar, they were shouting and fighting for a place. While that was going on, it was impossible for me to hold my place.
>
> Now there's no disturbance; all is peace and silence . . . Don't let the art of poetry fall into the hands of a few authors through your doing; let your influence come to the aid and assistance of my influence. If I have never been greedy in setting a price on my skill . . . please grant me this request: do not let his enemies defraud, cheat and laugh at the man who has entrusted his vocation to my safekeeping and himself to your protection. For my sake accept this plea and grant us silence, so that others will want to write, and it will be worth my while in future to learn new plays bought at my price.

Ambivius is made to speak as a man of some authority in the world of the Roman theatre. He boasts of having played a key part in the success of Caecilius, in the generation immediately before Terence's, and towards the end he says of Terence that he 'has entrusted his vocation to my safekeeping' (52–3). Of course this is all done for a purpose, but it must at least have sounded plausible.

Of himself Ambivius says 'I have never been greedy in setting a price on my skill' (49). Naturally there was a financial side to his relations with Terence and the festival organisers (the aediles), but how did it work in

[25] Gruen (1992) 213–18 is over-sceptical in suggesting that this prologue 'did not describe a historical situation at all'; see Parker (1996) 592–601, esp. 600 n. 65.

practice? No doubt he acted as middleman, presenting a budget to the aediles that included a fee for himself and his company as well as the playwright. But what are the implications of the reference at the very end to 'new plays bought at my price' (57)? Did Ambivius pay Terence for it and then sell it on to the aediles (with 'bought at my price' meaning 'bought at my own expense')? Or did his budget include a fee to be paid by the aediles directly to the playwright (the plays being 'bought at a price *suggested by* me')?[26] In either case, who could now be said to own the play? Has it passed out of the hands of the playwright? Does he have any control over its reperformance? Did the plays pass *into* the hands of Ambivius, or of the aediles?[27] And who paid whom to bring a play back for a second (or even a third) attempt after an initial failure? We are not much helped by passages in two earlier prologues; (1) *The Eunuch* 19–21, which says that the aediles had bought the play but not who had sold it to them;[28] (2) the prologue for the second performance of *The Mother-in-Law*, which claims (lines 5–7), 'Now it's absolutely as good as new, and the man who wrote it didn't want to bring it back a second time simply in order to sell it a second time.' This suggests that it is the playwright himself who sells his play, and that he is still in a position to do so even after its first (unsuccessful) performance; but perhaps matters were not so simple.

By contrast with *The Mother-in-Law*, we are told that *The Eunuch* was far and away the most successful play that had ever been put on in Rome up to that time, and that this brought some financial reward. Suetonius, *Life of Terence* 3 says: '*The Eunuch* was acted twice in one day, and it earned a price such as had never been earned before by any comedy of any author, that is to say 8,000 coins.'[29] This was evidently a considerable sum.[30] We do not know who was given the money, nor whether it included the sum originally contracted for. Donatus says it was paid 'to the poet',[31] but he may simply be embroidering Suetonius' account.

26 So Donatus on *Hec.* 57; see Ritschl (1845) 327–8, Brožek (1960) 146–7, Lebek (1996) 33. Suetonius, *Life of Terence* 3 speaks of Terence 'offering' his very first play to the aediles; this could be shorthand for a more complex negotiation, or (if Suetonius' anecdote is to be believed at all) it could reflect the fact that Ambivius had not yet taken Terence under his wing.

27 Gruen (1992) 193 asks, reasonably enough, what interest the aediles themselves would have had in long-term ownership of a dramatic script.

28 Gruen (1992) 192–3 also points out that we do not know how much of the funding for dramatic productions was provided by the state and how much (if anything) by the aediles themselves.

29 Gilula (1989) 75–6 argues that the 'coins' were silver *denarii*.

30 See Gilula (1989), who points out that even if Terence had to share this sum with Ambivius, he made enough out of this and other productions to die quite prosperous two years later (Suetonius, *Life* 6).

31 Don. *Eun. Praef.* 6.

The final passage relevant to these questions comes in Plautus' *Bacchides* ('*The Bacchis Sisters*', written some twenty-five or thirty years earlier), where the slave Chrysalus complains (lines 213–15):

It's not what you say that wounds my heart and annoys me, but the way you say it [lit. 'It's not the subject-matter . . . but the *actor*']. It's the same with *Epidicus*, a play I love as much as myself: there's no play I so hate to see, if Pellio is performing it.[32]

This passage is often quoted as evidence that Plautus and Pellio had fallen out for some reason, but that seems rather literal-minded: for all we know, the joke may even have depended for its effect on the audience's knowledge that Pellio was playing the part of Chrysalus.[33] But it does seem to imply that it was possible for different productions of a play to be put on by different companies. This suggests that the original director did not have control over the reperformance of a play, unless perhaps he decided to sub-contract it. But otherwise we remain very much in the dark about the details of all these arrangements.

Terence used Ambivius' company for all six of his plays. We do not know which character Ambivius himself portrayed in each play, except for *Phormio*, where an anecdote recorded by Donatus (on line 315) confirms what we might have expected, that Ambivius took the title role:

The story is still told about Terence and the drunken Ambivius who, when he was going to perform this play, delivered these lines by Terence yawning, drunk, and scratching at his ear with his little finger; whereupon the author exclaimed that that was how he had thought of the parasite when he wrote it – and he was immediately calmed down, having been angry because he had caught him full of food and drink.

The occasion was probably an early rehearsal of the scene (since Ambivius is said to have been 'about to perform' the play, and Terence has apparently had no previous opportunity to tell him how he envisages the performance of the part). We have no other anecdote of this kind

32 *non res sed actor mihi cor odio sauciat. / etiam Epidicum, quam ego fabulam aeque ac me ipsum amo, / nullam aeque inuitus specto, si agit Pellio.*

33 So Fraenkel (1960) 431. (Frank (1932) 248 had suggested that Pellio was playing Pistoclerus in this scene.) The lines form part of a passage (208–17) deleted by Zwierlein (1992) 199–212 (in the footsteps of Mattingly (1960) 250–2) as being a post-Plautine interpolation composed later in the second century BC. If this is right, the passage is evidence for a period later than Plautus and Terence, though still relatively early. Of Pellio we otherwise know very little. His name is included in the fragmentary production notice for *Stichus*, first performed in 200 BC, where Mattingly and Zwierlein argue that he could be named as the *actor* of a later revival. There is a further possible reference to him at *Men.* 404, but the interpretation is very uncertain.

about Ambivius, and it is interesting that it survived for so long. The story reminds us how much an actor has to add to the words of the text: there is no indication in Terence's text at this point that the actor is to yawn or scratch at his ear; if there are indications in the language that the character is to be portrayed as drunk, they are very slight.[34]

The prologue to *The Self-Tormentor* (163 BC, also by Terence) supports the notion that Ambivius took the title role in *Phormio*, since it includes the following appeal to the audience (lines 35–47):

> Let me be allowed to act a quiet play without interruption, so that I don't always constantly have to play the running slave, the angry old man, the gluttonous parasite, the shameless swindler and the grasping pimp: I'm an old man, and those parts call for a lot of shouting and a great deal of effort... The people who write new plays nowadays show no mercy to an old man: if a play demands effort, it's me they come running to; if it's quiet, they take it to another company. This play contains words, pure and simple: give it a try; see what I'm capable of in both styles.

When Ambivius suggests that it was normally other companies that specialised in quieter sorts of play, he pretends to make it a matter of complaint; but effectively he reminds his audience that *his* is the company that specialises in the plays with the strong comic roles, and that *he* plays the traditional characters they enjoy seeing.

These passages open a window on a world for which we have barely any evidence in the case of Greek drama (though it surely existed there too),[35] a world in which rival companies are in competition with each other for custom; Pellio was the director of one such company in Plautus' lifetime, Ambivius in the time of Terence. We know nothing about their background. Ambivius was presumably not a slave, since he played an independent part of some kind in the negotiations over the productions. But he may have been an ex-slave;[36] however grand he became in his

34 The first reader to have spotted any such indications, as far as I know, is H. D. Jocelyn in a forthcoming paper in *Terenz und die Tradition des Stegreifspiels* in the series ScriptOralia (Tübingen). Ambivius could have conveyed all these gestures while wearing a mask in the actual performance, whether or not he wore one at the rehearsal. I believe that the actors of Plautus and Terence did wear masks, in spite of some ancient evidence to the contrary; see Duckworth (1952) 92–4, Beare (1964) 192–4, 303–9.

35 Demosthenes 19.246–7 probably implies that Theodoros and Aristodemos had different troupes but tells us nothing about the rivalries that doubtless existed between them. One difference between Athens and Rome is that at Athens (at least from a certain date) the actors were assigned to playwrights by the archon (*DFA* (1988) 93–5). In that context, it would have been hard for Ambivius to support Caecilius and Terence in the way Terence's prologues make him claim to have done at Rome.

36 So, for example, Rawson (1985) 112 (repr. 485–6).

own world, we should not imagine him as a member of the best Roman society.

The competitive nature of dramatic production at Rome is complicated by references in the prologues to two of Plautus' plays to a competition between actors:[37] the prize is said to be a palm (a palm-*branch*, presumably), awarded by the aediles, and both passages refer to corrupt lobbying for this prize on behalf of actors. (We have no reason to think that there was a formal competition between *plays* at Rome, as there had been at Athens.) This was perhaps a competition between *companies* of actors, or between the *directors* of the companies, the *actores* themselves (just as at Athens only the protagonists competed for the actors' prizes). We do not know how many different companies there were, nor how many different plays were put on at each festival.[38]

As we have seen, Ambivius liked to take the strong roles himself. It is likely enough that playwrights composed with the talents of their actors in mind, and this may well have been one factor that led Plautus in particular to expand some roles into something far more striking than he would have found in the Greek comedies that he was adapting. So, at any rate, it was suggested by Fraenkel, with particular reference to the part of the scheming slave[39] – but the point could apply just as well (in appropriate cases) to the other roles listed by Ambivius; and we know from Cicero later that in his lifetime Roscius chose to play the part of the pimp Ballio in Plautus' *Pseudolus*, not the part of the slave Pseudolus himself.[40] But Fraenkel perhaps goes too far when he claims that the original Greek plays had been written for a world in which no one member of an association of *technītai* had such power over his colleagues as the *actor* did at Rome. There were star performers in the Greek world as well; dramatists surely took account of their particular talents, and we cannot know that they did not wield great power within their companies.

Evidence for the way in which the Roman *actor* controlled his company is not plentiful, though no doubt Fraenkel was right about it. It has sometimes even been claimed that the other members of the company were typically slaves owned by the *actor*; and a passage at the end of Plautus' *Cistellaria* (*The Casket Comedy*, 782–5) does seem to suggest (if taken seriously) that they were at least firmly under someone's control:

37 *Amphitruo* 64–74, *Poenulus* 36–9; cf. Jory (1988).

38 Taylor (1937) 286 concludes that 'all the regular festivals of the second century provided at least two days in the theatre', with (287) four days at the *Ludi Romani* from 214 onwards. As she notes on p. 301, 'We do not know how many plays were presented in a single day.'

39 Fraenkel (1922) 249–50 = (1960) 240–1.

40 Cic. *Q. Rosc.* 20; cf. Garton (1972) 169–88.

Spectators, you needn't wait for them to come out here to you: no one's going to come out; they'll all finish their business indoors. When that's been done, they'll take off their costumes; after that, anyone who's done wrong will get a beating, anyone who hasn't will get a drink.

Whatever their strict legal status, if they are in danger of corporal punishment from those in charge of them they are not much better off than slaves.[41] But what is the 'wrongdoing' for which punishment is threatened? It seems to be generally assumed that it is bad acting;[42] but perhaps the actors are here (jokingly) threatened with punishment for any misbehaviour committed by the characters they have been playing, even after they have taken their costumes off. In this case (and perhaps in any case) the passage should not be taken seriously as evidence for the realities of life behind the scenes.

Another passage suggests that at least a significant proportion of the actors (perhaps indeed all except the *actor*) were slaves, though not necessarily slaves of the *actor* himself: this is the beginning of the prologue to Plautus' *Asinaria* (*The Comedy of Asses*). The speaker is one of the actors; he addresses the audience and says (lines 2–3): 'May this turn out well for me, for you, and for this company and the masters and those who have hired us' (*gregique huic et dominis atque conductoribus*). The obvious interpretation is that 'the masters' are the owners of those performing in the company, that owners might have slaves trained up to perform in the troupe of an *actor*,[43] and that they have as much interest in the success of the play as the troupe itself and the *conductores* (those who have hired the company, i.e. the aediles).[44] (Some editors have changed the plural

41 This is a further passage deleted by Zwierlein as a post-Plautine interpolation (Zwierlein (1992) 329–31); cf. n. 33. *Asin.* 946 and *Trin.* 990 are sometimes adduced as further evidence that actors were liable to be beaten; but in both cases it is the character in the play who is so liable, not the actor portraying him. At *Amph.* 83–5 there is a clear reference to the beating by officials of any actor 'who has instructed a claque to applaud him, or who has arranged for another actor to be a failure'; but the fact that they were liable to corporal punishment by officials does not show them to have been slaves. At a later date, Roman citizens who acted became *infames*, which rendered them liable to be whipped by magistrates. There is no reason to think that officials would have had any scruples about beating non-slave actors in the time of Plautus.

42 This could be supported by the use of *peccare* in a passage of 'play-acting' at Plautus, *Persa* 624–30, though the verb used in *Cistellaria* is *delinquere*.

43 Cf. Cic. *Q. Rosc.* 27–31 for an example in the first century BC.

44 This passage is ignored by Frank (1931) in his attempt to argue that no slaves acted in the comedies of Plautus and Terence. Jory (1966) prefers to interpret *domini* as 'the masters of those individuals in the company who happened to be slaves', believing that not all members of the company were necessarily slaves. I see some force in the objection of Gruen (1992) 194 that it would be odd to single out the owners of some members of the company in this way if others were not slaves. But we may perhaps take the passage as showing that actors (with the exception of the *actor* himself) were *normally* slaves. (Gruen suggests that the *domini* are 'the stars of the company'; I should be happier with this if it were supported by Plautine usage.)

dominis to the singular *domino* ('the master'), in the belief that the *actor* might be referred to as the *dominus gregis* ('master of the company'); the term is still found regularly in discussions of the Roman theatre, but there is no other evidence for it.)

One man who we know *was* a slave *not* owned by the *actor* was the man who composed the music for Terence's plays, since he is named in the production notices for those plays as 'Flaccus the slave of Claudius'. But we do not know whether he came as part of the package with Ambivius' company or operated entirely separately, nor – sadly – do we have any of his music.

If we accept this one reference in *Asinaria* as establishing a general rule, then it is a provocative idea that in some plays the part of the scheming slave was taken by the one non-slave in the company (the *actor*), while the parts of his master and of other free characters were taken by men who in real life were slaves, perhaps even slaves of the *actor* himself, and certainly under his control as members of the company.[45] But, as we have seen, the *actor* did not always take a slave-role.

This last example shows how slender is the base on which we try to build. The actors of Roman comedy must have been virtuoso performers (with men taking all the women's parts, for instance), and the director of the troupe needed to be a shrewd negotiator and talent-spotter in addition. They must have left their mark on the plays in ways that we can barely begin to guess at. This is true of most drama from most periods, but not all drama teases us with extra-dramatic prologues and epilogues; these may look as if they will satisfy the universal craving to know what an actor's life is really like, but in fact they whet our appetite for more. As other chapters in this volume show, we have evidence from later periods for the organisation, training and techniques of actors in the Roman world; but this is the period from which we have the plays.

SUGGESTIONS FOR FURTHER READING

Gratwick (1982) gives an excellent survey of early Latin drama, including some of the questions discussed in this chapter. The best general introduction in English to Plautus and Terence is Hunter (1985). Duckworth (1952) provides a fuller account, though much of what he

[45] So Dumont (1987) 523; Moore (1998a) 183 claims more generally that 'slave actors played the roles of free men and women, and free actors played slaves' roles'. For a comparable claim made in antiquity about Greek actors (slaves played by leading actor, kings by the least important member of the troupe), see Csapo and Slater (1995) 223, with the warning that 'the cliché may owe more to its attractive paradox than to any normal practice'.

says about Greek New Comedy has been rendered obsolete by the discovery of substantial portions of plays by Menander since 1958. Beare (1964) is still the basic English handbook on the history and staging of Republican Roman drama, though this too is out of date in a number of respects and could do with thorough revision. The actors known by name from this period are listed in Garton (1972) 61. There is some material relevant to this period in Csapo and Slater (1995) chapters IIIC and IVBii.

CHAPTER ELEVEN

*The masks on the propylon of the Sebasteion at Aphrodisias**

John Jory

If a friend invited you to visit a Roman theatre in the imperial period to see a well-known star perform you would have little doubt about the sort of performance you would see. It would not be a comedy or a tragedy but a dance performance and the artist would be a pantomime. These stars attracted huge followings among their supporters and on numerous occasions their rivalry led to violence, so much so that they and their performances were frequently banned. Thanks to their popularity, not only among the people but also with many of the emperors, the bans rarely lasted long.[1] Individual stars mixed with the highest ranks of society and became extremely influential in the imperial household. A few early examples will suffice to outline the picture.

Of the two innovators who gave the pantomime dance its definitive 'Italian' format, Bathyllus, from Alexandria, was a freedman and intimate of Maecenas and Pylades, a Cilician, was on familiar terms with Augustus. Not only was he invited to perform at Augustus' dinner parties but responded to the emperor's questions by quoting Homer or offering dangerous political advice without apparently causing offence. Under Gaius and Claudius, Mnester, a freedman of Tiberius (?), had a charmed if ill-fated life. Showered with kisses in public by his lover Gaius, he also had an affair with Poppaea Sabina, the mother of Nero's Poppaea. Subsequently he was forced by Claudius' wife Messalina to become her bedmate, a liaison for which the emperor eventually put him to death. Paris too experienced the ups and downs of imperial favour. Although a slave, who had purchased his freedom from Nero's aunt Domitia, he was declared freeborn by Nero, and Domitia had to pay back all the money.

* I would like to express my sincere gratitude to Professor R. R. R. Smith for an invitation to visit Aphrodisias, for his hospitality while I was there, and for helpful comments on an early draft of this paper.

[1] Jory (1986b) 59–63.

For a while he and Nero were boon companions until the emperor, who fancied himself as a dancer, had him put to death because, some said, he was a rival.[2]

These dancers were major public figures, and it is interesting to trace their influence on the iconography of the theatre, on the nature of the religious festivals and on society in general. One way of doing this is to investigate the emergence of artistic representations of the pantomime mask, one of the characteristics of the dance performance.

THEATRICAL MASKS AND THE ARTISTIC TRADITION

Representations that reflect theatrical performances are found in Greek art from the sixth century onwards. One of the most common objects represented is the mask, carried by actors before or after a performance, worn on stage or used as decoration.[3] From the Hellenistic period this decorative use of the mask is found in many aspects of Greek art[4] and it has been plausibly argued that it originated with the practice of victorious actors dedicating their masks to Dionysus, after a performance, by suspending them in the god's shrine. On these occasions the mask not only celebrates the role which led to victory but the festivities which come with victory. Over time masks come to be found in all areas of Greek art, both public and private, and the connection with actual performances is often remote, the occurrence of the mask often symbolising little more than a reference to festive occasions, happiness, or just a cultivated and civilised lifestyle. In grave imagery they may symbolise Dionysus, happiness, renewal and a blessed after-life,[5] or they may be apotropaic, since on sarcophagi they frequently occur with the head of a gorgon, a Medusa. They may, however, be purely decorative. In the imperial period masks of tragedy, comedy and satyr-play continue to occur frequently in both Greek and Roman art but, in addition to these masks of the traditional forms of drama, we commonly find the closed-mouth masks of the newly popular pantomime.

[2] Bathyllus, Tac. *Ann.* 1. 54. 3, cf. schol. Pers. 5. 123; Pylades, Macrob. *Sat.* 2. 7. 18–19, Dio 54. 17. 4; Mnester, *CIL* VI 20139, Suet. *Gaius* 55. 2, Tac. *Ann.* 11. 4, Dio 60. 22. 3–4, 60. 28. 3–5, 60. 31. 5; Paris, Tac. *Ann.* 13. 19–22, 13. 27, Ulpian *Dig.* 12. 4. 35, Suet. *Nero* 54. 1.

[3] For an excellent summary of the evidence for Athens in the early period see Green (1991) – for comedy 21ff., tragedy 33ff., and satyr-play 44ff. See also Green (1982) esp. 245–7 and Green and Handley (2001) 75f., 79.

[4] Moretti (1993) 214.

[5] Plut. *Consol. ad Uxor.* 10 = *Mor.* 611 D, Nilsson (1957) 130f.

PANTOMIME

There is now consensus on the broad outlines of the history of Greco-Roman pantomime performances, although some disagreement on the details.[6] Weinreich drew attention to Dioscorides' Alexandrian epigram of the mid-third century BC which recorded Aristagoras dancing the role of a Gallus in some sort of competitive performance, and identified this performance with the type known later in the Roman world as pantomime. He also drew attention to the popularity of the Cybele-Attis myth in pantomime performance throughout the Roman period.[7] Louis Robert discussed an inscription from Priene in the 80s BC which mentions a performer called a *pantomīmos*, and restored the same term on another inscription from Delphi dated 84–60 BC.[8] Thus a form of mimetic dance, the performers of which were occasionally referred to as *pantomimi*, existed in the Greek world from at least the middle of the third century BC. Another term found on an inscription recording a performance in Gortyn in Crete, at the end of the first century BC, by a Roman citizen, Furius Celsus, who was a *mythōn orchēstēs*, a dancer of stories or myths, implies a similar type of dance. It is at about this time that two dancers, Bathyllus and Pylades, from Alexandria and Cilicia respectively, so transformed the dance performance as it was staged in Rome, probably incorporating a number of specifically Italian features from the dancers of the *ludus talarius*,[9] that a contemporary, Aristonikos, referred to it as the 'Italian Dance'.[10] In this fully developed form a solo mute dancer enacted stories that were for the most part taken from the vast repertoire of Greek mythology, although historical dramas also played their part.[11] Unlike the situation in traditional dramatic productions, the

[6] Leppin (1996) 33–40.

[7] Dioscorides *AP* XI 195 in Weinreich (1948) 11 ff., with n.11. (For this role on stage in a mime see Suet. *Aug.* 68, probably in the period 41–39 BC, and possibly the mime *Galli* by Laberius.)

[8] For Priene see Robert (1930) 114–17 (= *OMS* I 662–5) and for Delphi, Robert (1938) 11–13. Apart from these two examples the word *pantomimos* does not occur either on Greek inscriptions or in literary works and Lucian draws attention to the fact that it is a coinage of the *italiotai*, usually identified as the Greek-speaking inhabitants of that land (*Salt.* 67). It is in fact possible that the subjects of both these inscriptions could have been so identified since Robert claims that the Priene inscription has as its subject a *xenos* and that of Delphi a citizen of Dyrrachium. Its first appearance in a Latin transliteration is on an inscription from Naples dated to 2 BC and it is the standard epithet for these performers in Latin epigraphy.

[9] See Jory (1995) 151.

[10] Athenaeus 1. 20 d–e.

[11] Lucian makes a number of general statements about the themes of pantomime, e.g. 'the themes of tragedy and the dance are common to both ...' (*Salt.* 31); 'he [the dancer] will know the more recent happenings that followed the establishment of Macedonian rule, the bold deeds of Antipater as well as those at the court of Seleucus over the affections of Stratonice' (*Salt.* 58); 'beginning with Chaos and the primal origin of the world, he [the dancer] must know everything

solo dancer portrayed each of the characters in the story successively. He was accompanied by a chorus which sang the words of the libretto and an orchestra made up of a variety of musical instruments including auloi, pipes, cymbals, lyres, castanets and even organs. Because the dancer did not speak, the masks he wore differed from the masks of drama in that they had closed mouths. Lucian has this description of the appearance of the dancer: 'It doesn't need me to say that the appearance of the dancer is decorous and becoming, it is obvious to anyone who isn't blind. The mask itself is very beautiful and appropriate to the underlying dramatic theme. Its mouth is not wide open like the others but closed.'[12] It was in this form that pantomime gained its overwhelming popularity in Augustan Rome among all classes of society, not least the members and close associates of the imperial family, a popularity which lasted for half a millennium.[13]

IDENTIFYING PANTOMIME MASKS

By the second century AD pantomime masks can be identified with absolute certainty on a wide range of monuments. Two examples will suffice to illustrate the trend. On a cinerary urn from Rome, dated to the early second century, a dedication to Flavia Sabina is surmounted by three masks. Two have open mouths and represent a tragic young man and a tragic old man. The third mask, with a similar hairstyle and a similar expression to the other two, has a closed mouth and clearly belongs to pantomime (fig. 31).[14] Showing a slight variation on this theme, a fragment of what has been described as the lid of a sarcophagus, also from Rome, dated to the second half of the third century AD with a dedication to Iuste and Iole, has four masks which have been carved under the dedication (fig. 32).[15] On the left are two masks in frontal view, one with an open mouth, one with a closed mouth. The mask on the left, of a young female, may belong to tragedy or comedy; the one to the right of it certainly belongs to the realm of pantomime. Further to the

down to the story of Cleopatra the Egyptian' (*Salt.* 36). The exclusion of events after 30 BC could be interpreted as an indication that stories which featured members of the imperial family were excluded, but panegyrics of the emperor were not unknown (Pliny, *Panegyricus* 64. 1–2).

12 *Salt.* 29. For a preliminary discussion of the masks of pantomime see Jory (1996) 1–27.

13 Zosimus *Historia Nova* VI 1.

14 Now in the Louvre, Paris, inv. no. MA 2148; Sherer (1989) 218 and 221, pl. 104, citing Sinn (1987) 233–4, n. 584, pl. 86b.

15 Now in the Vatican Museum (ex Lateran), inv. no. 31504; Paduano Faedo (1970–71) 448–9, with tav. II 2.

Fig. 31 Two tragic masks and one pantomime mask (Photo: M. and P. Chuzeville)

Fig. 32 Four masks for performances in tragedy, pantomime and comedy (Photo: J. R. Green)

right are two comic masks in profile with characteristically wide open mouths. In these examples the two masks identified as belonging to pantomime each represent well-known types with many parallels existing elsewhere. Where, as here, the context is clearly theatrical, identification of pantomime masks is simple. Where the context is not so clear and we find closed-mouth masks which could be attributed to pantomime together with what are usually identified as 'heads' (which also have closed mouths) it is more difficult to achieve certainty. With this in mind I would like now to look at some friezes from Aphrodisias.

APHRODISIAS AND ROME

Little is known of Aphrodisias before the first century BC, when its people are shown to have been supporters of Rome by a number of inscriptions.[16] They sided with Rome against Mithridates in 88 BC; Sulla dedicated a double-headed axe to her patron goddess Aphrodite,[17] and they took the Julian side in the civil wars of the last half of the century. Julius Caesar dedicated a golden Eros to its Aphrodite, and under Octavian it received a renewed freedom, a number of privileges and direct imperial patronage. The closeness of the relationship is seen in a letter from Octavian to one Stephanos which reads as follows:

> Caesar to Stephanos, greetings. You know how fond I am of my Zoilos. I have freed his native city and recommended it to Antonius. Since Antonius is absent, take care that no burden fall upon them. This one city I have taken for my own out of all Asia. I want them to be protected like my own townspeople. I shall be watching you to see that you carry out my recommendation to the full.[18]

The letter makes it clear that Octavian's affection for Zoilos was a key factor in his decision to grant freedom to Aphrodisias, and that having granted this freedom he was determined that it should continue to have a positive effect on the lives of the inhabitants. The Zoilos of the letter was C. Julius Zoilos, a freedman of Octavian and probably earlier of Caesar. Zoilos himself amassed great wealth and used it to become a very influential citizen of Aphrodisias. He paid for a new and lavish stage building in the theatre and for the first phase of the new marble temple of Aphrodite.[19] Subsequently, despite his freedman status, statues were set up to him by his grateful fellow-citizens, including one in the theatre, and he was made priest of Aphrodite. In addition he held the prestigious honorary post of *stephanēphoros* for ten successive years.[20]

[16] For a full account of Aphrodisias' relations with Rome at this period see Reynolds (1982) 1–106.
[17] Appian *B Civ.* 1. 97. 445. [18] Smith (1993) 11. [19] Smith (1993) 7.
[20] For a full discussion Zoilos' activity and career see Smith (1993) 4–10.

THE SEBASTEION

The connection between Augustus, Zoilos and the theatre is significant in the light of Augustus' own enthusiasm for theatrical shows. Indeed it is quite possible that Augustus' own tastes, representing contemporary performances in Rome, could be reflected in the choice of a number of the theatrical masks found on the friezes which adorned so many of the public buildings in the city. This would be particularly appropriate in the case of the propylon of the Sebasteion. The Sebasteion was a temple complex dedicated to Aphrodite, the *Theoi Sebastoi* (the Julio-Claudian emperors), and the *Dēmos*, with the temple set on a raised platform at the eastern end. Two three-storey porticos with Doric, Ionic and Corinthian ordered columns on the first, second and third storeys, run from West to East. These porticos were decorated on their upper levels by a series of relief panels and statues. The southern portico contained scenes from Greek mythology, including a few with a Roman reference, on the second storey and with Olympian gods, Roman emperors and various allegories on the third. The northern portico had symbolic statues, representing *ethnē* and islands, which had been brought under Rome's control, on the second storey and allegories and probably emperors on the third. At the western end was a two-storey propylon. The whole complex seems to have been designed to link the new cult with the existing patron goddess of the city and the traditional myths which formed the basis of Greek culture.[21] According to R. R. R. Smith, the director of excavations at Aphrodisias, 'The architectural conception of the whole complex is an extraordinary combination of Hellenistic, Roman and original ideas' (fig. 33).[22]

THE PROPYLON FRIEZE

On the first storey of the propylon, facing West and providing the visitor with an imposing first impression of the complex, was a decorative frieze of masks. This frieze survives on twelve fragmentary blocks, eleven of which can be found on public display in the open space in front of the Aphrodisias museum. The remaining block lies at the site of the propylon. These twelve blocks seem to have made up the whole frieze. A total of forty masks are clearly distinguishable and there are signs of the existence of two others, although on one of these damage has destroyed any distinguishing features and the other has disappeared (figs. 34, 35, 36, 37).

[21] Smith (1987) 88–138, and (1990) 89 with (1988) 50–3.

[22] Smith (1988) 51.

Fig. 33 View of Sebasteion at Aphrodisias (Photo: J. Jory)

Fig. 34 Part of Sebasteion frieze (Photo: J. Jory)

Fifteen masks have been designated as tragic, eleven as comic and fourteen as belonging to satyr-play.[23] However, although this classification relates the whole group to the three traditional forms of drama it is not the only classification possible, nor is it necessarily the most

[23] De Chaisemartin (1987) 140.

Fig. 35 Part of Sebasteion frieze (Photo: J. Jory)

Fig. 36 Part of Sebasteion frieze (Photo: J. Jory)

informative, since a number of these masks differ markedly in appearance from the masks of classical drama, the most striking difference being that many have closed or only partially open mouths. It may be useful therefore to explore further what these masks might represent. One possibility, but not the only one as we shall see, is that they, like the ones shown above (figs. 31 and 32), belong to another form of theatre production, the pantomime. This dance form was masked, in this period it included tragic, comic and satyric performances, and it was particularly favoured by Aphrodisias' sponsor, the emperor Augustus.

Fig. 37 Part of Sebasteion frieze (Photo: J. Jory)

THE MASKS ON THE PROPYLON

Nineteen of the surviving masks exhibit the normal wide open mouths of masks of comedy, tragedy and satyr-play, seventeen being comic or tragic and two satyric. These standard masks can be left out of account, although it is worth noting the occasional presence of teeth, an unusual although not unparalleled feature. A mask of an old bearded satyr has five prominent teeth and there are indications of teeth in another, a trumpet mouthed slave, incidentally the only one of the forty surviving masks which is in semi-profile.[24] Of the remaining twenty-one masks, fifteen have closed mouths and six have partly open mouths.

From the depiction of the masks with open mouths it is clear that the sculptor or sculptors were well aware of the typology of the standard masks of tragedy, comedy and satyr-play and that they were capable of reproducing them accurately.[25] Thus if they chose to include in their decorative frieze some masks which were not part of the normal repertoire this was a deliberate choice and did not arise from any ignorance or lack of technique. Why the sculptors of Aphrodisias portrayed some of the masks with closed or partly open mouths may become clearer if we analyse the types of the masks in question.

Among the fifteen masks with closed mouths seven are of satyrs, one of either Dionysus or a maenad, one of a maenad, one of an Attis, one of a Medusa, one of an old bearded male, possibly Hermes, one of Dionysus and two are of Heracles. There is an overwhelming preponderance here of characters belonging to the realm of Dionysus and the Bacchic *thiasos*. Are they then included merely to emphasise the Dionysiac character of the frieze decoration by incorporating members of the *thiasos*? Although this possibility cannot be excluded there are a number of reasons for preferring an alternative explanation. Firstly all the other masks in the series clearly represent characters, like the Pornoboskos, who take part in theatrical performances, and the introduction of masks of members of a Dionysiac *thiasos* seems out of place in that context. Secondly the closed-mouth masks include characters who, although frequently associated with Dionysus, have no direct connection with the *thiasos*. Thirdly there is

[24] For teeth in a similar mask of an old satyr with *korymboi* and wavy beard compare Dwyer (1981) cat. 24. pl. 95, 2; in a mask of a young spiky satyr cat. 23 pl. 95, 1. and of what is probably a maenad see below. For 'a few teeth' on the mask of the 'wolfish old woman' of comedy see *MNC*³ 35. Pollux does not note the teeth in his description of this character, mask number 28, but he does mention the teeth on 'the little old housekeeper', mask 30, 'about two molars in each jaw'. See the discussion in *MNC*³ 38. Teeth seem to have been an 'optional extra' on some masks.

[25] See for example the masks of the Pornoboskos and the comic slave. For illustrations see Green and Handley (2001) figs. 52–5.

sound evidence that Dionysus, Heracles and Attis were popular subjects for contemporary pantomime dances.

While we have no literary evidence for such performances in Aphrodisias at this time we do for Augustan Rome. An epigram in the Planudean Anthology records that the famous Pylades, whom I have mentioned earlier, enthralled Rome when dancing Dionysus, 'When he brought the bacchants from Thebes to the Roman stage Pylades put on the form of the bacchanal god himself, to all mens' delight and terror, for by his dancing he filled the whole city with that deity's intemperate fury.'[26] This 'fury' is a reference to the riots which even in Augustus' time were a regular feature of the pantomime competitions. Bathyllus too was legendary for his light-hearted portrayal of satyrs, evidently a popular topic for the pantomimes of the day.[27] Macrobius relates a story about the same Pylades appearing on stage in the *Hercules Furens*. 'When he appeared in the *Hercules Furens* and seemed to some not to be preserving the movements appropriate to a dancer he took off his mask and chided those who were mocking him: "Fools, I am dancing a madman."'[28] Macrobius goes on to tell another story of Pylades performing the same role at a private banquet *iussu Augusti*, demonstrating again the Emperor's fondness for the dance and the Heracles myth in particular.[29] I have already mentioned Weinreich's demonstration of the popularity of the Attis myth in pantomime in Rome, and his literary references are supported by the introduction of the Attis mask into the typography of the masks found on *oscilla* throughout Rome and Italy.[30] I think then that what we have on the propylon frieze is not a depiction of the members of a *thiasos* but of pantomimic representations of Dionysian and related stories. We know that the Aphrodisians looked to Roman models for a great deal of the carefully thought out sculptural decoration of the North and South porticos of the Sebasteion[31] and it is *a priori* likely that the same thing happened with the selection of masks on the propylon. If this is the case the composition of this frieze was neither haphazardly chosen nor restricted to well-known Hellenistic themes but reflected an attempt to combine the familiar masks of the Greek agonistic festivals with representations of the new Italian dance form which was dominating the Roman stage.

I now come to the six masks not so far discussed. Two, a Papposilenus and a Silenus, have damaged mouths, which could originally have been

[26] *Anth. Plan.* 290 = Antipater of Thessalonica 78 (translation based on Gow–Page), cf. *AP* 9.248 = Boethus 1, see Jory (1996) 9f.

[27] Persius *Sat.* 5.123; Plut. *Mor.* 7.8. 711E–F; Hor. *Epist.* 2.2. 125; *Sat.* 1.5. 63.

[28] *Sat.* 2.7.16–17. [29] *Sat.* 2.7.18.

[30] These *oscilla* are small-scale marble sculptures in relief; Wootton (1999) 314–35.

[31] Smith (1988) 70ff.

Fig. 38 Mask of young female, perhaps a maenad (Photo: J. Jory)

open or shut and which could belong either to satyr-play or pantomime, and four have slightly parted lips. Since these four masks are without the wide open mouths characteristic of traditional drama I am inclined to place them among the closed-mouth category but, because they are a little unusual, we should perhaps look at them in detail.

The first mask with slightly parted lips is that of a young female. (fig. 38). There is some damage to the top of the head and to the nose but the facial features are natural and the expression calm. Two corkscrew curls fall from ear to chin level on either side of the face. A narrow fillet is worn about the forehead and above it there appears to be either a diadem with an ornate centre piece or an arrangement of the hair in an overfold. Inside the mouth there seems to be a full set of upper teeth, very small and very regular. The fillet and the appearance suggest that she is a maenad.

The other three masks in this category are the most difficult to identify since they have no direct parallel in the known types of dramatic or pantomime masks (fig. 39). They occur on a single block. On the left is the mask of a young female with natural features and a smooth face. Her hair is pulled back over the ears. In the middle of the forehead a lock (or brooch?) seems to be looped over the front of the hair above the

Fig. 39 Mask of young female and two young males (Photo: J. Jory)

brow. Although the top of the head is damaged it seems to have been crowned with *korymboi*.[32] The mouth is very slightly open, and chiselling inside the mouth suggests four teeth, although they are not as clearly defined as on other masks. In the centre of the group is a mask of a youthful male with natural features. He is frowning and his mouth is half open. There are no teeth visible. The hair is dressed in thick waves that frame the face to ear level and on his head he may be wearing a type of smooth bonnet. On the right is a mask of a youthful male with natural features. He is frowning and his mouth is half open. There are no teeth visible. The hair is dressed in two layers of thick semi-curls with thinner curls hanging below the ear on either side of the face. In general terms all that can be safely said about these three masks at this stage, as Professor Green has pointed out to me, is that they represent youthful heroes and a heroine. The slightly parted lips suggest by contrast with the wide-open mouths of the comic and tragic masks that these may be heroes of pantomime performances, but so far I have found no parallels for them among known pantomime masks.[33]

32 Clusters of fruit and/or flowers attached or woven into a fillet or wreath.

33 It is possible that the sculptors of Aphrodisias, not yet being as familiar with the masks of pantomime as with those of tragedy and comedy, were influenced by the dramatic models they knew

SUMMARY AND CONCLUSION

I have suggested three possible explanations for the presence of the closed-mouth masks on this frieze alongside the masks of traditional tragedy, comedy and satyr-play. They could be 'generic' representations of theatre masks, they could depict the bacchic *thiasos* and its related stories or they could reflect pantomime performances, prominent among which are those related to the stories of Dionysus. For all the reasons given above, namely (a) the sculptors' expertise in depicting traditional theatre masks, which makes 'generic' masks out of place in the series, (b) the known popularity in contemporary Roman performances of the particular mix of closed-mouth characters chosen, and (c) the deliberate incorporation of elements adapted from Roman models in the decoration of other parts of the Sebasteion, I prefer the third explanation. The closed-mouth masks reflect pantomime performances.

If this is indeed the case and we have pantomime masks depicted on a building of the Julio-Claudian period in Aphrodisias it would be the first example known to me of these masks appearing in Asia Minor.[34] Significantly they form part of the decoration of the Sebasteion, which was no doubt the centre of the imperial cult and the festivals which celebrated it. Pantomime masks are also found in four of the cassettes which decorate the ceiling of the so-called temple tomb in Sidyma, a city which was made a Roman colony under Claudius and which also boasted a Sebasteion.[35] Four more masks appear on the frieze decorating the late first or early second-century South tomb in Cremna in Pisidia, a city which was established as a Roman colony by Augustus.[36] In the same period other masks turn up in Caesarea and Jerash, two of the more romanised cities of the Near East.[37] The fact that these early examples of pantomime masks in the East appear in Roman colonies or highly romanised communities is no accident and reflects the content of festivals celebrating the imperial cult. However, it is not until the latter

in depicting these characters, but this cannot be proved. Large numbers of 'masks/heads' with partially open mouths are found on the North portico of the Agora of Tiberius at Aphrodisias. This is dated to the period AD 14–29.

34 I am leaving aside for the moment the series of ash-chests published by Bianchi and Aravantinos (1991), which they argue had their origins in Asia Minor. Most of those displaying pantomime masks date from the second century AD.

35 Dardaine and Frézouls (1985); Dardaine and Longepierre (1985); Tancke (1989) 126–30, taf. XC, XCI.

36 Mitchell (1995) 53ff., 69–75.

37 A marble pantomime mask, now in the Museo Civico in Milan, is said to have been discovered in Caesarea; see Jory (1996) 13. A number of masks of pantomime are preserved in the Rockefeller Museum in Jerusalem; see Iliffe (1945) 1–26, pls. I–IX, nos. 71, 78–81, pl. V.

half of the second century that these masks become common throughout the Greek East. Undoubtedly this sudden burgeoning of pantomime iconography in the Greek-speaking provinces was influenced by its introduction into the regular Greek agonistic festivals in the early 170s AD.[38] This development is itself a reflection, not only of the popularity of the dance among the Greeks at that time, but also of the enthusiasm for it displayed by the Roman emperors. The sojourn of Lucius Verus in the Eastern provinces and his well-documented passion for the dance and its most accomplished performers may have been the catalyst for the decision to extend the festival programme.[39] It now seems that the general attitude taken by the Greek cities of the East in the late second century towards pantomime performances was anticipated by individual cities where the ties with Rome were strong and the festivals of the imperial cult flourished. The depiction of pantomime masks on the propylon frieze is a manifestation of the wish of the citizens of Aphrodisias to emphasise the very close links between that city and Rome. As with other aspects of the decoration of the Sebasteion they incorporated into a traditional Hellenistic theme Roman references which reflected the personal interests and the cult practices encouraged by their powerful new patrons.

SUGGESTIONS FOR FURTHER READING

For a general account of Aphrodisias and the excavations see Erim (1986). For entertainment in Aphrodisias see Roueché (1993).

For a brief survey of the Roman theatre and its performances see Jory (1986a), and for a fuller account Beacham (1991).

For additional reading on pantomime in Rome see Jory (1981) and (1998).

[38] Slater (1995), Slater (1996a).

[39] *Hist. Aug. Verus* 8: *His accessit, quod, quasi reges aliquos ad triumphum adduceret, sic histriones eduxit e Syria, quorum praecipuus fuit Maximinus, quem Paridis nomine nuncupavit . . . Habuit et Agrippum histrionem, cui cognomentum erat Memfi, quem et ipsum e Syria velut tropaeum Parthicum adduxerat, quem Apolaustum nominavit.* 'In addition he brought pantomimes with him from Syria as if he were bringing kings for his triumph. The most distinguished of these was Maximinus to whom he gave the name Paris . . . He also had with him the pantomime Agrippus, whose cognomen was Memfius. This man too he had brought from Syria like a trophy from the Parthian war. He named him Apolaustus.' Subsequently Paris and Apolaustus were extremely popular in Rome.

CHAPTER TWELVE

Images of performance: new evidence from Ephesus[1]

Charlotte Roueché

Many of the articles in this volume reflect the importance of inscriptions in giving us access to actors in antiquity. Inscriptions give us the names and careers of individual performers, and also record the structure of the festivals in which they appeared; they tend to give information of a kind not available in the literary record, and there is a great deal to be learned from juxtaposing the two categories.

But, while inscribed texts have tended to be considered as 'lower' in the taxonomy of sources than literary texts, they do not represent the 'lowest' form of evidence. The collection and publication of epigraphic material long predated the development of photography; and inscriptions are most cheaply and easily published as texts, with little regard to their physical location. Modern scholarship, with modern resources, is steadily rectifying this situation, and texts are published in the context of their monuments; but the focus is still on texts. While images of performers in an 'artistic' context – in paintings, or in sculpted images – are regularly taken into account, there has been little attempt to look at 'inscribed images' – usually scornfully categorised as graffiti. The normal corpora of inscriptions tend to omit such material unless it is accompanied by words, and it is not considered to be the responsibility of art historians.

[1] I am extremely grateful to the Austrian excavators of Ephesus for their hospitality and unfailing helpfulness to me in the collection of the material presented here, and in particular for providing several of the illustrations; I am particularly grateful to Stefan Karwiese, whose publication of one of the groups of graffiti first alerted me to their importance, and to Dr Ronald Risy, the Photographic Curator of the Austrian Archaeological Institute. I am also very grateful to Glen Bowersock, Denis Feissel, Rebecca Flemming, Hero Granger-Taylor and Ruth Webb for some very constructive comments.

I have used the following abbreviations:

Published inscriptions from Ephesus are referred to as *IEph*: Wankel, Merkelbach et al. (1979–84); the vast majority of the texts can be found on the Packard Humanities Institute CD-ROM no. 7, referred to as PHI.

PLRE refers to Jones, Martindale and Morris (1971–92).

My aim is simply to draw attention to two examples of pictorial graffiti, apparently showing performers, which have been found at Aphrodisias and Ephesus. The images at Aphrodisias were scratched on plaster; those at Ephesus were cut on the stone facing of the *scaenae frons* in the theatre. The graffiti from Aphrodisias have been collected and published; but those at Ephesus, uncovered a century ago, were largely ignored until recently. Some of those with texts accompanying them were eventually published, but the whole dossier has never been assembled and presented in full; so it seems useful to collect and publish them here. The ease with which such material has been overlooked makes it seem highly likely that there is other, similar material waiting to be identified and published at other sites in the Roman empire, which might illuminate the examples presented here.

APHRODISIAS

The material from Aphrodisias depicting performers has already been published, with illustrations.[2] The most important element is a series of drawings on plaster found in rooms in the stage-building of the Odeion/Bouleuterion of the city.[3] These images are fairly varied, but seem mostly to be associated with performance – not least because of several representations of organs.[4] While several of the images are not very specific, there is a group of sketches of three 'kings' – one perhaps standing, the other two enthroned – each of which bears in its left hand a globe surmounted by a cross.[5]

This feature – the orb and cross – suggests a date not earlier than the fifth century AD for these graffiti; a similar date, therefore, to those published below, from Ephesus.[6] There are other similarities between the two groups of graffiti. Above the head of one of the seated 'kings' mentioned above is the name Καρμ̣ι̣λ̣ι̣αινός (11.A.ii), 'Karmiliainos'; above the head of one of the performers presented below, from Ephesus (**7**) is the name Καρμίλις, 'Karmilis', followed by the number Β̄ (two). It is tempting to see this as a reference to a particular mime performer who worked at both Aphrodisias and Ephesus. Also the figure described below as **2**.ii is a forward-facing figure who has two projections – like small

[2] Roueché (1993). [3] Roueché (1993) text 11, with plates iv–vi.

[4] Recognised as such by Moretti (1994) 355 n. 8.

[5] Roueché (1993) text 11.a.ii, and plates iv and v, and, for a detail, figs. 52, 53, 54 below; on these figures see further below.

[6] Alföldi (1935) 117; Arnaud (1984), especially 102–12 for the appearance of the cross on the orb from the reign of Theodosius II.

wings – rising up from his shoulders. This may be the same feature as that found in one of the graffiti at Aphrodisias (II.B.ii, and plate V) where a facing figure seems to have something rising up from each shoulder; but there the feature is much larger, and goes well above his head. The tall figure in a long tunic and stole at Aphrodisias (II.E.i) is paralleled by at least one of the figures at Ephesus (no. **4a** below). The Aphrodisias graffiti include some representations of riders on horseback (II.F) and riders are also found in some of the graffiti at Ephesus; but those are not published here, since they cannot represent anything seen on the stage.

EPHESUS

The Austrian excavations at Ephesus began over a century ago, and the theatre was first excavated in 1898.[7] The excavators at that time made careful records of what they found, including the pictorial graffiti, in the *Skizzenbücher* (notebooks) of the excavation, and took a very large number of squeezes. When the huge task of publishing the *Repertorium* of all Ephesian inscriptions was undertaken, in the 1970s, the editors worked from the *Skizzenbücher*, but had to exercise some selection; they published most of the images which were accompanied by texts, but not all of them, and none of the others.[8]

The inscriptions published here were all found in or near the theatre: nos. **1–4a** are still in situ. The theatre is the subject of a current programme of exploration and study.[9] It seems to have been built in the late second century or first century BC, but it was refurbished several times thereafter. The stage buildings, which still stand to a substantial height, were later remodelled; the façade of the stage building is made up of sculptured panels re-used from an earlier location. It may be that this remodelling should be associated with the repair work done in the theatre by the proconsul Messalinus, according to two epigrams.[10] Messalinus is not known from other sources; but he is honoured in a third inscription at Ephesus, on a base in one of the main streets of the city.[11] That text was cut on a re-used base which had previously recorded honours to Aelius Claudius Dulcitius, proconsul of Asia under Julian (360–3);[12] Messalinus, therefore, was certainly proconsul after that date, probably

7 Heberdey et al. (1912); for the stage-buildings see 53. See also de Bernardi Ferrero (1970) 47 ff.

8 Wankel, Merkelbach et al. (1979–84).

9 For the most recent report see Karwiese (1998), and see Ataç (1999).

10 Published most recently as *IEph* 2043 and 2044.

11 *IEph* 1307.

12 *IEph* 1312; *PLRE* I, Dulcitius 3. Another inscription of Dulcitius, *IEph* 313A, honouring Julian, was re-used in the 'Stadium Road' northwest of the Theatre.

in the late fourth or fifth century. This might suggest that the inscriptions discussed here, which date from after the late-antique re-ordering, are probably late fifth or sixth century; such a date is also suggested by some of the parallels cited below (but see n. 39).

The stage buildings stand to a height of two storeys. The lower storey contains a series of rooms round a corridor; a central door leads out into the area under the stage, and then to the *orchēstra*. The supports of the stage survive, but the stage floor has gone. The second storey formed the back wall of the stage; it was pierced by the normal three principal doors onto the stage. Inscription **1** is cut on the threshold of the central doorway. The stage front was refaced with large blocks concealing decorative moulding, which must originally have served a different function; on these inscriptions **2**–**4a** are cut at a level which will have been directly in front of, or slightly above, performers on the stage. The loss of the stage means that they are now rather difficult to reach, and they have weathered badly over the century since they were uncovered. The wall to the south of the southern door is largely lost. On either side of the central door the wall has two long recessed areas, in which inscriptions **2** and **3** are cut. North of the northern door much of the stage front is lost, but one block remains in situ, with inscription **4a**.

1

The block which forms the architrave of the central doorway from the lower rooms of the stage building into the *orchēstra* also formed the threshold of the doorway above, leading from the upper stage rooms onto the raised stage. On that threshold, a series of drawings have been cut, by someone facing out into the auditorium. These were seen by R. Heberdey, copied by him, *Skizzenbuch* 501, and squeezes taken, but they have never been published.

A long architrave block (H. 0.48, W. 1.94, D. 0.42), inscribed on upper face (letters varying from 0.01 to 0.02). The graffiti are lightly cut with a thin blade, and worn away by use and by exposure. From left:

A group of three figures. There may be lettering above the first two, but the surface is lost; there is certainly writing above the third.

- i One man full face, in short tunic or probably skirt; his arms are foreshortened, perhaps reaching behind his back (0.25). Standing on a square.
- ii To the right, another figure in similar ?skirt, wears tight sleeves with two bands on each; his arms are raised to meet over his head (0.24). He is standing on a square.

Fig. 40 Ephesus, Theatre graffito 1, i–iii (Photo: Charlotte Roueché)

iii To the right, a figure standing on a square is apparently bent over, to his right, to hold a long baton (0.23). Above is a line of very small and worn letters (0.005).

. . .] Τ̣ΟΥ̣Ν *vac.* ΚCΙ *vac.* . . Β̣Λ̣Τ̣- . . CΙΕΛ̣ΥΕ̣. .Ι̣

iv To the right, and at the centre of the stone, a pavilion: columns support a triangular pediment, with a circle at the centre (H. 0.28).
Within, a seated figure seated is raising his right arm. He wears what seems to be a pointed cap.
To the right, letters (0.02):

ΓΕΝΙΑC . Μ̣ . Κ̣Α̣[. . .

Further figures, very unclear.

v To the right, faint images of two figures. One, turned to his left, seems to hold a baton/sword in two hands, pointing out and down. To his left ?a figure facing forward, with ?arms outstretched.
There are traces of lettering above.

Fig. 41 Ephesus, Theatre graffito 1, iv–v (Photo: Charlotte Roueché)

2–4

The following inscriptions were cut on the recessed areas of the façade, and have been numbered from south to north (left to right). The southernmost end of the façade is lost.

2

In the recess south of the central door the facing block is broken; the upper edge and the right hand corner are lost, and the surface of the stone is particularly severely weathered and cracked. There were at least three standing figures, all facing forward; the two complete figures measure 0.67–0.69 in height. Copied by Heberdey, *Skizzenbuch* 500c, and squeezes taken.

i To the left, a standing figure can just be made out; he is bald, with prominent ears. He appears to be wearing a body-suit, covering arms, torso and legs. He may be wearing *bracae*, trousers with feet, as shown, for example, in a tomb-painting at Durostorov;[13] but it seems more likely that this is a full body-suit of the kind worn

[13] Frova (1943) fig. 9.

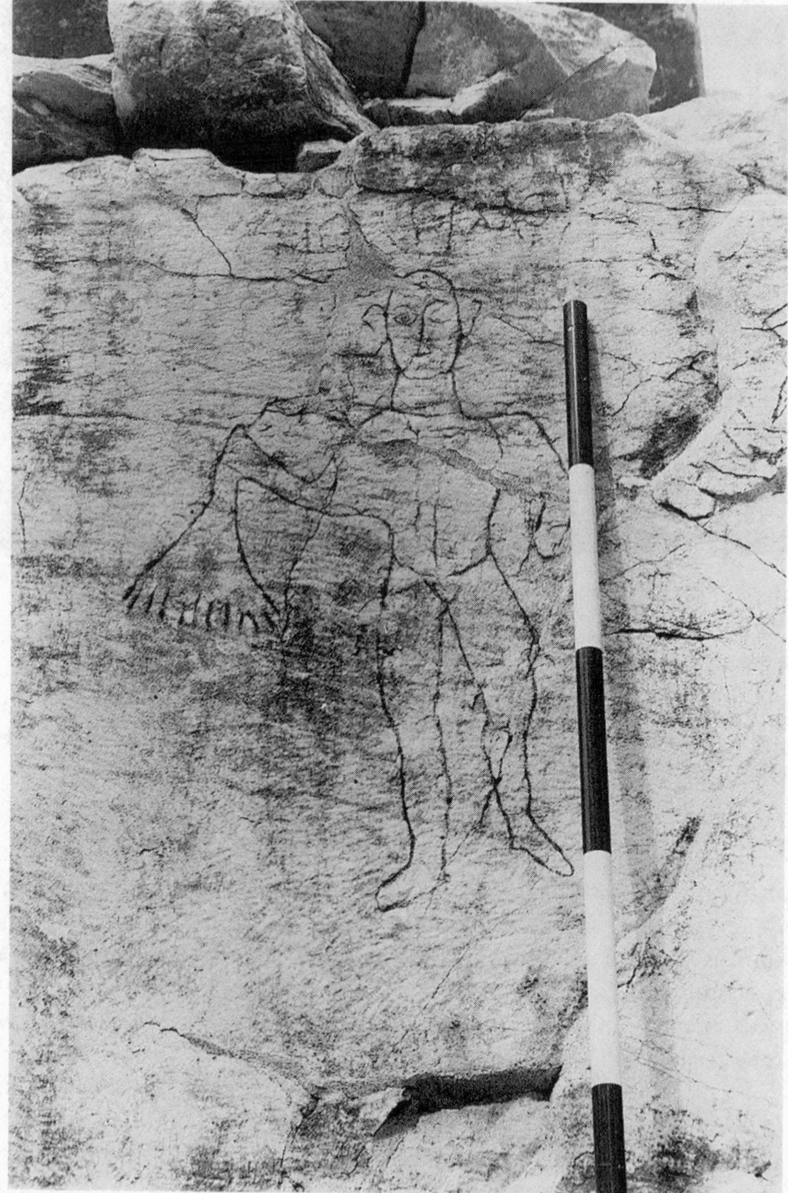

Fig. 42 Ephesus, Theatre graffito 2.i (Photo: Stefan Karwiese)

by actors representing satyrs, as in a mosaic at Antioch.[14] His left arm is bent, and the hand cannot be made out; the right arm is extended, and from the hand hangs what looks like a tasselled shawl.

Above his head, just below the upper moulding, letters (0.04–0.05); the first letter is OY in ligature:

(OY)ṂẸṆEP̣ṂOY *vacat* T [...

ii To the right, another standing figure, also bald and with prominent ears. From each of his shoulders rises a narrow tab – like the end of a ribbon. He wears a tunic with two circles (*orbiculi*) on the skirt; the upper part has a straight neckline, and is crossed by two ?straps which extend to the extreme end of each shoulder. His right arm is held out and up – the hand is lost. His left arm is held out and down, with something long and straight depending from it.

iii To the right the stone is broken away; but down from the break extend the two legs of a third figure, to the same scale.

3

After the central doorway, in the next recess to north, the stone is complete (H.1.28, W. 1.66, D. 0.23). There are no images; some letters (0.02–0.025) are cut at 0.96 above the stylobate; these were also recorded by Heberdey, *Skizzenbuch* 500B, and squeezes taken, but not published. No illustration.

vacat O . ḲIPIṆOC *vacat*

4

In the northernmost recess stands a large block forming the northern end of the facing; it survives to the upper moulding at the upper right corner, but is broken away above and to the left; the back is visible, and shows that the stone originally formed a large entablature, with decorative moulding of the second century BC. The block is now very weathered, and cannot be reached. It is damaged to either side, and most of the upper part is broken away; but it is covered with extensive images. These were recorded by Heberdey, *Skizzenbuch* 500A, photographed at the time of discovery (inv. no. 3.123) and squeezes taken; the main part of the

[14] Levi (1947) 141–8, especially 143, with plate XXVIII; House of Dionysus and Ariadne; I owe this reference to Dr Janet Huskinson.

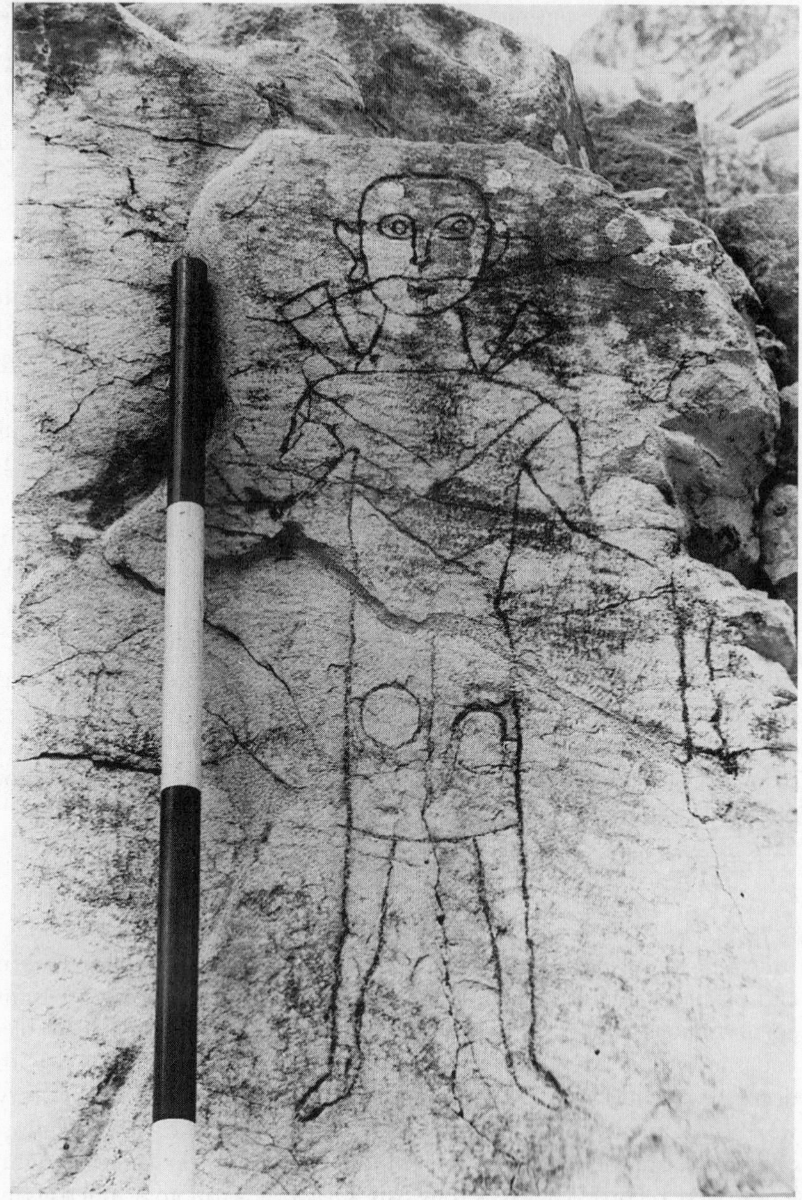

Fig. 43 Ephesus, Theatre graffito 2.ii (Photo: Stefan Karwiese)

Fig. 44 Ephesus: Theatre graffito 2.iii (Photo: Charlotte Roueché)

Fig. 45 Ephesus, Theatre graffito 4a (Photo: Österreichisches Archäologisches Institut)

photograph was published by Stefan Karwiese, Scherrer (2000) 161, abb. 2. A further seven fragments of varying sizes were seen by Heberdey, and squeezes taken. Of these **4b**, a fragment from the upper edge of a block, broken below, definitely joins the upper right corner of **4a** (H. 0.23, W. 0.46, letters 0.025–0.04); it is now in the depot (Domitiansdepot cat. no. 1736), where it was found and photographed by Denis Feissel in 1995. None of the other fragments can be shown definitely to join these pieces, and only two more are substantial enough to be reported here (**4c** and **d**).

4a

Large block, still in situ (H. 1.28, W. 2.34, D. 0.20), broken to left and above.

i At the far left, a figure in a knee-length tunic is broken away above. He is moving to the right, towards the lower part of a standing figure with long robe and stole, almost reaching the hem.

To the right a figure whose head is lost, in a knee-length tunic, with a small ?apron, is facing forwards, but bent to his right. His right arm is extended downwards, perhaps to the head of ?a dog; his left is raised, holding a long bag.

ii To the right, two small figures, of which the upper is largely lost, the lower complete, in knee-length tunics, seem to be moving rapidly to their left, into the frame of an upright rectangle. The lower figure appears to be holding the further of the two uprights. Across this rectangle – to the left of the upper figure, and above the lower one:

λάσανον

Chamber-pot

The stone is broken away above, and there could have been more letters. Immediately to the right stands a four-legged table, with two thin-necked vessels on it. A line reaches from ?the top of the standing rectangle down to the top of the table; the angle suggests that these two figures might be putting up a tent.

iii To the right of this is an ensemble of two seated figures, facing forward, apparently seated on a bench; fragment **4b** apparently formed the upper part.

Fig. 46 Ephesus, Theatre graffito 4b (Photo: Denis Feissel)

4b

The figure to the left is male, with a bald head. He wears a tunic with a scooped neckline (or a necklace?), and a further semi-circle below this, perhaps denoting a large necklace. He has a belt, and his tunic falls to his ankles. His left arm was extended down, but is lost; his right arm is extended down, to the seat on which the second figure sits.

To the left of his head:

. . .]OOΔO

. . .]Χ̣Ι̣C

The figure to the right is apparently female; she is portrayed with curly hair, falling to her shoulders; she wears earrings. Her right arm is extended horizontally to go behind the left shoulder of her companion; her left arm, which is in a tight sleeve with two woven bands, extends down to the bench, where her hand supports her. She has a straight neckline, and *clavi* descend from each shoulder to above her waist, where they end with a circle. She has a waistline, but no belt. Her skirt descends to her ankles; on it are two *orbiculi*.

Above her head:

Cοφρονία[. . .

Sophronia

In front of the knees of the male seated figure two small standing figures are cut, facing forward. They appear to represent decoration on his tunic, and end at the hem. The figure on the left is bald, with his waist demarcated, and probably wearing a simple tunic; his arms are held out and down, and his left arm extends behind the figure to his left. That figure may have a hairline marked. It wears a full-length garment, with long *clavi*. Its right arm is extended to the left shoulder of the figure to its right; the left arm is bent and rests on its hip.

To the right of this ensemble is what appears to be a couch, raised on a support which is cross-hatched.

4c

A large fragment (H. 0.45, W. 0.65), noted by Heberdey in *Skizzenbuch* 500A, and a squeeze taken. Not found again.

Fig. 47 Ephesus, Theatre graffito 4c (Photo: Österreichisches Archäologisches Institut)

To the left, a flying figure, with ?wings or a mantle, bends down to its left, towards a lower figure. This, a ?boy in a short tunic, extends its right arm up towards the first figure, with the left arm extended out behind. Above, traces of letters

. . .]Λ̣ΟΝỊỊ

. . .]IC ΤΙΛΛ

To the right, a second group. A man in a short tunic faces forward. His right arm is bent up to his shoulder, holding a long ?bag. His left arm is extended upwards, to his left, towards a far larger figure, only partially preserved. This figure wears a long robe, to the ankles, with feet showing; on the lower part of the robe are two *orbiculi*. The head is lost, and the left arm: the right arm extends downwads to the head of the first figure.

Above the first figure:

λάϲανον
Chamber-pot

Fig. 48 Ephesus, Theatre graffito 4d (Drawing courtesy of the Österreichisches Archäologisches Institut)

4d

A fragment, broken on all sides, was found in the debris of the north parodos in 1898; it was copied by Benndorf, *Skizzenbuch* 204, in 1898, inventory 204, whence *IEph* 1170 (*PHI* 2874); Domitiansdepot catalogue no. 53. It was found again by Heberdey, and recorded as a fragment of **4**; another squeeze was taken. Not found again (H. 0.19, W. 0.46, D. 0.12).

A figure in a short tunic, facing forwards, with right arm extended and ?carrying something. On the skirt of his tunic are two *orbiculi*. To his right another figure turns away. To the left and below:

Ἀλέκτορ

Alektor

Squeezes survive of four further small fragments, but with no significant traces.

The following are all on loose blocks, not found in context.

5

This was copied by Heberdey, *Skizzenbuch* 397, and squeezes taken, whence published as *IEph* 2091 (whence *PHI* 2892); cited by Csapo

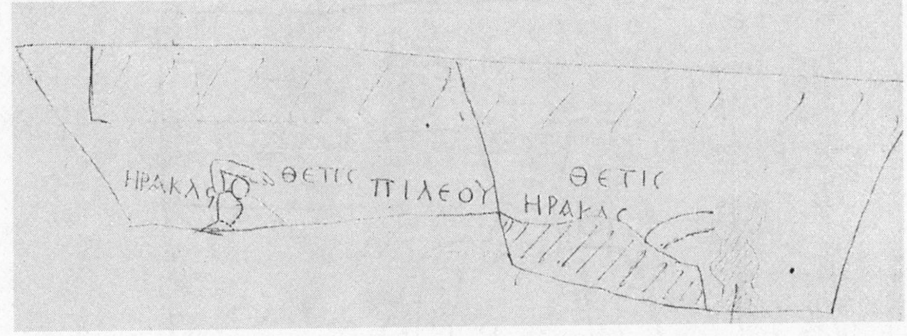

Fig. 49 Ephesus, Theatre graffito 5 (Drawing courtesy of the Österreichisches Archäologisches Institut)

and Slater (1995) 378 no. 21. A fragment was found in the depot by Denis Feissel in 1998 (Domitiansdepot catalogue no. 2208). Despite the description by Heberdey as part of a seat, the drawing resembles the facing of the stage. Dr Feissel has confirmed that the fragment is complete and roughly finished above; it may well have come from the upper edge of one of the facing blocks (H. 0.17, W. 1.20, D. 0.44; letters 0.025). Lunate sigma; scrolls for abbreviation marks.

After the first word there is the upper part of a figure, ?facing downward to his left, with his right arm raised above his head:

Ἡρακλ( ) *figure* Θέτις Θέτις
Πιλέου
Ἡρακλ( )

Herakl(-) Thetis Thetis
(of) Peleos
Herakl(-)

Line 3: Edd. pr. read Ἡφαιστος, which would make good sense, since Hephaistos and Thetis are sometimes shown together, in depictions of the story of the Shield of Achilles. The squeeze is very unclear at this point, but the notebook reading seems to be quite clear.

6

This is another fragment of the facing of the stage, found in fallen debris. It was copied by Heberdey, *Skizzenbuch* 474, and a squeeze taken, and published from his copy as *IEph* 2092.1 (whence *PHI* 2893). It has not been found again.

Fig. 50 Ephesus, Theatre graffito 6 (Drawing courtesy of the Österreichisches Archäologisches Institut)

The fragment is broken away above, but retains the lower moulding (H. 1.20, W. 0.90, D. 0.16); letters (0.045), carefully cut, with triangular trenches and serifs; it is unlike the graffiti of the other texts.

Bust of a man, facing, broken away above. To right of his head:

. . .] OC *vacat*

Below this, according to Heberdey, a line of writing has been erased; this is not apparent on the squeeze

7

A loose block, found in 1898 in the stage buildings, '*Skenegebäude mittelhin*'; now lying in the Theatre-gymnasium depot area. It was drawn by

Heberdey, *Skizzenbuch* 436 (1898), and squeezes taken, whence published as *IEph* 2092.2 (whence *PHI* 2894). Found again in 1994, drawn by H. Cevizoglu, and photographed.

Καρμίλις Β̄.

Karmilis, twice (?) (*or* 'second')

Below, bust of a facing man; he is ?bald, with protruding ears; he is wearing a garment with a straight neck, and *clavi* descending from either shoulder.

Below this

Γω *figure* λλα-

θίο *figure* υ

Of Gollathios

Arranged about the head of a facing man, standing; he is wearing a tunic, with a decoration of circles within a border round the neck and down the front, to the waist, where he wears a belt with a strap hanging down from it; the hem of the tunic has a decoration of triangles. The stone is broken away just below the tunic. He holds a fish in his right hand and ?a knife in his left.

8

A fragment, perhaps a theatre seat (H. 1.20, W. 0.90, D.0.66; letters 0.02–0.03). Found in 1898, and copied by Heberdey, *Skizzenbuch* 506, and squeeze taken; published from this copy *IEph* 2093 (whence *PHI* 2895). Not found again. A figure (*c.* 0.34) facing and turned to his right. He wears a belted tunic with the skirt caught up in folds falling from the belt. His right arm is outstretched, and from it extends a long line – perhaps a rope; his right leg is extended in a stride. His left arm is bent outwards from the elbow, holding ?a spear. There are traces of two ?dogs below, to his left; inscription above his left shoulder, at 0.52 from the right edge. Illustrated at *IEph* 2093.

Πιλεούς.

Peleus

Fig. 51 Ephesus, Theatre graffito 7 (Drawing courtesy of the Österreichisches Archäologisches Institut)

9

A fragment (0.34 × 0.30 × 0.13) found in north parodos. Copied in 1898, *Skizzenbuch* 259 and a squeeze taken, whence *IEph* 2094 (whence *PHI* 2896). Not found again. Letters 0.02. Illustrated at *IEph* 2094.

To the left a structure – something like a cushion on two linear supports. Above and to the right, inscription:

ΠΕΡΛ[...

COMMENTARY

These graffiti clearly offer an important body of evidence for stage performance. There seems no doubt that the graffiti from the theatre at Ephesus all represent performers; some of those in **1** and **2** may be acrobats or dancers, but the majority appear to be actors – presumably mime actors. It is not absolutely certain that all the graffiti on the plaster from the Odeion at Aphrodisias represent stage performers, but it seems likely that most of them do; and, as has been pointed out, there are interesting similarities between the two groups.

What is very unclear is the purpose of these graffiti. The scratched graffiti at Aphrodisias might be seen as outlines of how a scene was supposed to look, which would be a reasonable explanation for graffiti cut behind the scenes with great ease on plaster. But the graffiti at Ephesus are all on stone, and must have been far more demanding to cut; they are large, and were on the façade of the stage buildings. On the other hand, they are cut with a very fine line, and would probably not have been visible from the auditorium, unless the outlined figures were filled out in paint.

Nor is it clear how we should understand the names which accompany the images. Some are clearly description of parts – Herakles, Thetis, Peleus – but others may be the names of individual performers, such as ?Karmilis/Karmilianus, perhaps attested at both Aphrodisias and Ephesus, or Gollathios. Alektor might refer to the minor mythological figure, or be an appropriate stage name for a performer. The representations in **2** appear to present individual performers; those in **4** clearly show scenes from a play. In **1** we seem to see acrobats or dancers, perhaps similar to the group identified as acrobats in a mosaic of the early fourth century at Antioch; the figures there are carrying various pieces of paraphernalia, including a monkey, which may explain why some of the figures in **1** are so hard to determine.[15] In the Ephesus graffito, however, the acrobatic figures are juxtaposed with a central figure seated in a pavilion, who might be a character in a play or a masque. This is a useful reminder that we may be inclined to draw inappropriate distinctions between different kinds of performance; the recent analysis of the use of condemned criminals in staged 'dramas' should be a salutary warning against this.[16] It is worth noting that, in **1**, not only does the seated figure have his feet on a square – which is quite common in depictions of seated dignitaries – but also the 'acrobats' are each shown as standing on a square – perhaps a mark of where they were supposed to stand on stage.

Another noticeable feature in most of these graffiti is the prominent ears of the persons shown. This may perhaps be a convention for showing performers who are not masked, since theatre masks seem to have concealed the ears. The fragments of **4** appear to show several scenes from a play – or more than one play – performed by unmasked actors. Although one name – Sophronia – survives, I have not been able to identify any play with such a character. This must reflect the abundance of mime plays which are lost to us; the closest parallels are provided by the mime papyri edited by Wiemken.[17] The nature of the play must depend on the function of the *lasanon*, carefully labelled in **4a** and **4b**. This term unfortunately has more than one meaning. The plural, *lasana*, is used to describe a trivet or support for a pot. Singular and plural are used to describe a chamber-pot, which could stand on such a support; but the term is also used by in the Hippocratic corpus to describe a pot used to catch the afterbirth when a child is being born.[18] It is not clear, therefore, whether we are dealing with a chamber-pot, deployed for comic effect as in Aristophanes and other comedians, or whether we are seeing the preparations for a birth – which would make good sense of the presence of the empty bed in **4a**. This is an attractive idea; Libanius refers to 'women giving birth' as something which Menander presents.[19] It should be noted, however, that the use of a *lasanon* at childbirth is only recommended in one text, and may therefore not have been widespread. Moreover, the text does not, on either occasion, appear to be closely related to an object. In **4a** it is written across two uprights, which might possibly indicate a door. I would therefore suggest that the

[15] Levi (1947) 273–7 with plate LXIIe; Bath E, Room 3. [16] Coleman (1990).
[17] Wiemken (1972). [18] See Hanson (1994) especially 163–8.
[19] *Or.* 64.73: τὰς παρὰ τῷ Μενάνδρῳ τικτούσας καὶ πολλὰ ἕτερα.

simplest explanation of this term, and its appearance twice, is that it is labelling a location. *Lasana* is used by Theodoret to indicate a public toilet – the place where Arius expired.[20] If the plural can denote a public, multiple toilet, then perhaps the singular can be used to denote a single water-closet, of the kind found fairly extensively in houses of the Roman period.[21] Although this usage is not attested in the singular, it would seem to be the easiest sense to accommodate here; the texts, therefore, may be used to identify either a character, or a part of the setting.

The costumes in **4** suggest that this is a play with a contemporary setting, and Sophronia would seem to be a late antique name; but if the Alektor fragment also belongs here, this may after all be a scene with mythological characters. The figures in **5** are recognisable from mythology, but I have been unable to identify the event which would bring Thetis, Peleus and Heracles on stage together; Peleus reappears in **9**, which is a loose fragment, perhaps from the same scene.

It is clear, however, that most of these depictions represent performers in their costumes; and the costumes suggest a date perhaps in the fifth or sixth centuries AD. Some of the features simply indicate dress found throughout the Roman period – for example the two *clavi*, the vertical stripes, shown on the costume in **7**, are standard, although they are also particularly well attested on the *collobium*, the long-sleeved overtunic of late antiquity.[22] But several features of the costumes are characteristic of late antique dress. The seated figure in **4a**, the standing figures in **2**ii and **4c**, and Alektor in **4d**, all have two circles, *orbiculi*, marked on the skirt of their tunics. This theme appears regularly, for example, on the tunics of figures in the mosaics at Piazza Armerina.[23] The seated woman, Sophronia, in **4**, has typical long sleeves, *strictoria*, ringed with two woven bands, as does the figure in **1**ii. Sophronia also has, woven into her tunic, *clavi* which end above her waist in a circle. A similar decoration appears on two figures in the sixth-century mosaics of the so-called 'Hippolytus Hall' at Madaba; there they are worn by a male figure (Adonis);[24] but a similar adornment appears on a female figure in the Achilles mosaic,

[20] Theodoret, *Haereticarum fabularum compendium*, *PG* 83, 416, l. 23: Εἶτα τῆς γαστρὸς πρὸς ἔκκρισιν ἐπειγούσης εἰς τὰ δημόσια εἰσελήλυθε λάσανα, τὸν ἑπόμενον οἰκέτην ἔξω καταλιπών. The equivalent passage in the Church History uses καθέδρας.

[21] See now the useful study by Neudecker (1994), especially 16–19 for private latrines.

[22] Wild (1994). [23] Carandini et al. (1982) e.g. Room 30, fig. 95.

[24] Piccirillo (1989) 50–60; cf. Buschhausen (1986) and the plates in Piccirillo (1993) 54–5.

of the same period, from another house at Madaba,[25] on a fifth-century ivory of St Menas[26] and embroidered onto a tunic from Panopolis.[27]

Most striking of all the aspects of the costumes are the figures perhaps embroidered on the skirt of the male seated figure in **4a**. Examples of such figurative embroidery on garments are found in Coptic fabrics, for example the shawl of Sabina.[28] The closest parallel to these in art is perhaps provided by the representations of the magi on the gown worn by the Empress Theodora in the mosaics at San Vitale, Ravenna.[29] The images reflect the criticisms made of the rich by Asterius of Amasea for wasting money on embroidered images – of animals, and of hunting, but also of biblical scenes – on their clothes.[30] These figures, therefore, are being presented as typical rich people of the fifth or sixth century. The figures in short tunics may be assumed to be servants. Gollathius, in **7**, is wearing 'oriental' dress – the *skaramangion* – a tunic with decoration at the neck, down the front and at the hem; the sleeve is attached well below the shoulder. There are several parallels, for example, at Palmyra.[31] His belt resembles that worn by Menas in the ivory mentioned above.[32] It may be that he is a performer, who specialised in exotic parts; but he may represent a character, such as the barbarians in the mime-scripts published by Wiemken (1972).

These points suggest that the closest parallels for the Aphrodisias and the Ephesus graffiti are to be found in fifth- or sixth-century mosaics; this agrees with the date of the orbs bearing crosses in the Aphrodisias graffiti. It seems likely, therefore, that these images are offering us a glimpse of stage scenes at this period. They may even tell us more. The parallels cited above are all drawn from mosaics. But some mosaics – for example those at Madaba – resemble the graffiti in more than just details of costume.

For example, the presentation of Aphrodite and Adonis at Madaba described above shows two seated figures (Aphrodite and Adonis), with several other figures in a grouping very like that in number **4a** above; in particular a running figure of Eros to their right closely resembles the

25 Piccirillo (1989) 132–9; (1993) 76–7.
26 Most easily seen in Ousterhout (1990) plate 9s; Menas also has the two *orbiculi* on his skirt.
27 van der Meer and Mohrmann (1958) 341.
28 See Weitzmann (1979) no. 112; cf. for other examples 116, 119, 121, 123, and von Wilckens (1991) chapter 1.
29 Deichmann (1958) plates 360 and, for the decoration, 367.
30 Asterius of Amasea, *Homily* 1, 3–4.
31 For excellent illustrations, see Tanabe (1986) plates 117, 121 (for the sleeve seam), 121, 134, 209–10, 431, 433–5, 437.
32 See note 26.

small running figures at the left side of **4a**. Peleus and Thetis, tantalisingly referred to in **5**, appear in the fifth-century mosaic of the Bath of Achilles found in the Villa of Theseus at Paphos, which has a similar layout, with a series of stylised figures confronting the spectator, rather than interacting with one another.[33]

The mosaics at Madaba include a representation of Hippolytus and Phaedra, which bears a more obvious relationship to theatrical performances.[34] Similar kinds of scene, also from mythology, are found, for example in the House of Dionysos at Paphos; there, it has recently been suggested by Christina Kondoleon that the mythological scenes may represent stage performances.[35] In the case of mosaics, such motifs are often interpreted as reflecting performances which have been sponsored by the patron of the mosaics – and in some cases this may well be the case; but, as Kondoleon points out, they may also illustrate, more fundamentally 'how the people of Rome saw their art'.

It has been easier to see such connections when the scene of a mosaic is entirely narrative. The Adonis and Aphrodite scene at Madaba includes personifications, as do others at this period; but it may be that that too reflects theatrical practice. For example, the closest parallel to the three crowned figures found among the Aphrodisias graffiti is perhaps provided by the three enthroned representations of cities found in the 'Hippolytus Hall' at Madaba;[36] I had previously identified the Aphrodisias graffito figures as 'kings', without being able to find any very helpful parallels. They are all crowned; one is standing, one is seated bearing a cornucopia on its right shoulder, and one, also seated, bears on its right shoulder a ?staff ending in a circular object, decorated, and surrounded by small circles (figs. 52, 53, 54). At Madaba, the three similar figures are labelled as personifications of three cities – Rome, Gregoria and Madaba. They are three seated females, each holding a staff surmounted by a cross in the right hand, and each holding an attribute in her left – a cornucopia, a basket and a container of flowers. Two of the three wear crowns. It may be, therefore, that the Aphrodisias figures also represent personifications, perhaps of cities. If so, since the Aphrodisias

33 Michaelides (1987) no. 50.

34 Piccirillo (1989) 56; (1986) 57. The pair also appear on a late antique mosaic at Sheikh Zouedh, on which see Zayadine (1986) 407–32, especially 423, with other examples from the period.

35 Kondoleon (1994) 300–14; cf. Kondoleon (1991).

36 Piccirillo (1989) 57; (1986) 57. The Madaba mosaics have recently been discussed in a series of lectures by Glen Bowersock, to be published shortly by the Collège de France. I am very grateful to Professor Bowersock for allowing me to see his text, showing that we had separately reached very similar conclusions about the resemblances to the Aphrodisias graffiti.

Fig. 52 Aphrodisias, Odeion graffito (Photo: Mehmet Ali Dögençi, Aphrodisias Excavations, New York University)

graffiti are found in a theatrical context, it seems likely that they – and perhaps both sets of images – should be related to some theatrical presentation – something perhaps more like a masque than a play in the modern sense.

Fig. 53 Aphrodisias, Odeion graffito (Photo: Mehmet Ali Dögençi, Aphrodisias Excavations, New York University)

The similarities between the mosaic scenes and our graffiti seem to confirm the evidence that such mosaics were directly influenced by scenes shown in late antique theatrical shows; mimes as well as pantomimes could be a vehicle for the transfer of 'the tales of the Greeks', for which

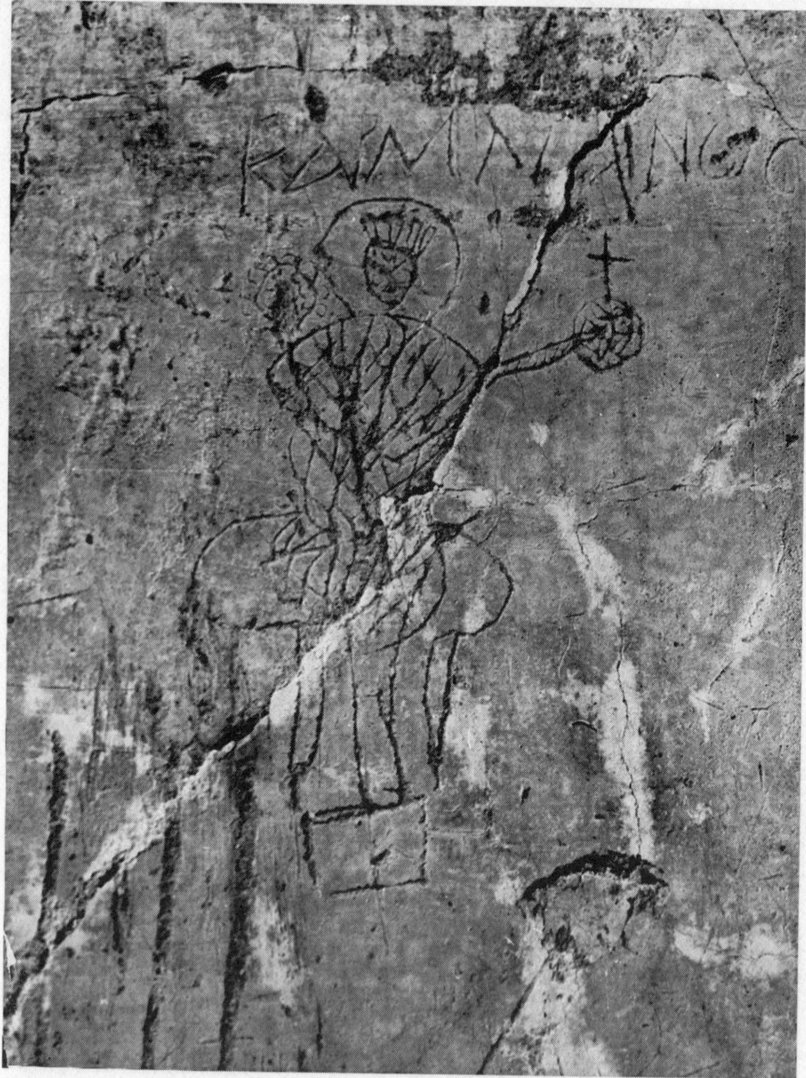

Fig. 54 Aphrodisias, Odeion graffito (Photo: Mehmet Ali Dögençi, Aphrodisias Excavations, New York University)

the festivals were criticised by Joshua the Stylite.[37] If some of the scenes on the late antique mosaics of the eastern Mediterranean were suggested

[37] Josh. Styl. *Chronicle*. ed. W. Wright (Cambridge, 1882) 30, pp. 20–1, 46, p. 35 (late fifth century); cf., for similar criticism in the sixth century, Moss (1935), on Jacob of Serugh.

by theatrical shows, then this would be further evidence of the continuing influence of such shows to add to that which can be extracted from the literary record;[38] it would also show a continuing tradition of theatrical influence on mosaic decoration which had started in the Hellenistic period, but reflecting the style and decor of the contemporary theatre. If this conjecture is correct, then much more information about the late antique theatre may be available to us – lying at our feet – than has previously been realised.[39]

38 See most recently Easterling and Miles (1999).

39 Since writing this, I have had the opportunity for further discussions of the building history of the theatre. It now seems that the remodelling of the *scaenae frons* could have taken place as early as the second century AD, and was probably not part of the late antique work on the theatre. This therefore means that the inscriptions might have been cut at any time from the mid second century until the theatre fell out of use. The other dating criteria, however, remain. I am particularly grateful to Dr Arzu Ozturk and Dr Hilke Thür for their advice on these points.

CHAPTER THIRTEEN

Female entertainers in late antiquity

Ruth Webb

INTRODUCTION

In the cities of the Roman empire women were a common sight in public spectacles as well as private entertainments, performing as musicians, chorus members, mimes, even gladiators. In his commentary on Terence, the fourth-century grammarian Donatus noted that in his day it was possible to see female roles played by women on stage, in contrast to the practice of the author's period.[1] Donatus' remark is a rare piece of evidence for actresses performing in literary comedy, but there is plenty of evidence for their involvement in other types of acting, notably the mime which gained wide popularity throughout the Empire. The best known example, Theodora, the sixth-century performer who dragged herself up from the stage to the palace, comes from the very end of antiquity, but others, both fictional and historical, can be identified from the Hellenistic and Roman periods.

An abundance of evidence from the fourth to the sixth centuries means that women's presence on the stage at this period is particularly well documented. The spread of Christianity into all levels of society provoked an intense re-examination of social practices, including theatrical performances. The sermons of John Chrysostom (late fourth–early fifth century), who saw the lure of the theatre as a major threat to the moral welfare of his flock, are a particularly rich source.[2] We can also trace the increasing attempts to regulate the lives and careers of female entertainers in various pieces of legislation in the Theodosian and Justinianic Codes. The figure of the actress is also used as a negative or positive

[1] Donatus, on Terence, *Andria*, 716, in *Commentum Terenti* ed. P. Wessner I (Leipzig, 1902) 212: *et vide non minimas partes in hac comoedia Mysidi attribui, hoc est personae femineae, sive haec personatis viris agitur, ut apud veteres, sive per mulierem, ut nunc videmus.* See Müller (1909) 40; Leppin (1992) 43. (All dates are AD unless otherwise specified.)

[2] See Theocharidis (1940) and Pasquato (1976).

example in narratives such as Procopius' *Secret History*, the source for the Theodora legend, or the anonymous *Life* of Pelagia, a fifth-century actress who swapped her life on the stage for a life of exemplary asceticism.[3] Theodora's antics are described in lurid detail: she grew up in a theatrical milieu, was a prostitute from an early age, was known for parading through the theatre of Constantinople practically naked and having geese peck seeds from between her thighs. Procopius' scandal-mongering portrait of Theodora has surely made her the best known female performer of the ancient world and does include some incidental details of the world of entertainers and the factions in sixth-century Constantinople. But his blatant bias means that great caution is required from the reader.[4] Moreover, Theodora's notoriety has, if anything, served to draw attention away from the more mundane aspects of performers and their lives. The fictional or fictionalised performers like Theodora and Pelagia certainly have the fullest biographies and by far the best stories, but other female performers are recorded in scattered pieces of evidence. They can provide a balance to a figure like Theodora, and even give cause to question the probability of Procopius' sensational account.

This evidence comes from other literary sources, such as history writing, epigram, prose fiction and rhetorical defences of the stage by two late antique authors: Libanius (fourth century) and Choricius of Gaza (sixth century).[5] Scraps of information in Egyptian papyri of the second and third centuries take us into some of the practicalities of life for performers, while funerary inscriptions bring us face to face with the facts of death. By their very nature, inscriptions and papyri record the women's involvement with others, whether fellow performers or members of the wider communities in which they lived and worked. One example is the epitaph of a female mime, Bassilla, set up by a male colleague at Aquileia in the first half of the third century.[6] The brief but laudatory account of Bassilla's career provides a salutary contrast to the image of the actress conveyed in the stories of Theodora and Pelagia.

The sources used therefore come from a wide range of documents written for a great variety of purposes. They also cover a wide temporal and geographic span. Although the main emphasis is on the second

[3] Procopius, *Secret History* 9; *Life of Pelagia*. [4] See Cameron (1985) 67–83; Fisher (1978).

[5] Libanius, *Reply to Aristides in defence of the dancers* in *Opera*, in vol. IV of R. Foerster's edition (Leipzig, 1908) 420–98, translation in Molloy (1996); Choricius, *Apologia mimorum* in the edition by R. Foerster and E. Richtsteig (Leipzig, 1929) 344–80, also Stephanis (1986).

[6] *CIG* XIV. 2324, now Museo di Aquileia inv. no. 260, see also Kaibel (1878) 609; for an illustration see Scrinari (1973) fig. 344 (= fig. 55 below; see pp. 301–2 for text and translation).

century and later, I will discuss some earlier material. The length of time involved makes it dangerous to suppose that a state of affairs attested for one period can be assumed for others, as social and economic upheavals, as well as the evolution of taste, may well have brought about changes. What is documented for one part of the Empire was not necessarily the case elsewhere, and most importantly, continuity in name may mask differences in practice. Bearing all this in mind, I will first look at the evidence for what women did on stage, then at aspects of their lives off stage. Finally I will discuss the polemics about female performers in Christian authors, particularly Chrysostom, and consider the evidence for the impact of Christianity on their lives. Theodora herself, whose career took place well after Chrysostom's time, shows that the disapproval of the Church was not in itself enough to put an end to the theatre. Nor was such disapproval unique to the Church. In many ways, Christian writers inherited and developed existing prejudices, but there are indications of changes both in perceptions of women on stage at the end of antiquity and in the possibilities actually open to them.

ON STAGE

Terminology

Various terms are used in Greek and Latin sources for female entertainers. Some derive from the arts they practised, as in the case of 'mimes' (Latin *mīma;* Greek *mīmas*) and 'dancers' (Latin *saltātrix*; Greek *orchēstris* or *orchēstria*). Others derive from various words for the stage (Latin *scaenica, thymelica*; Greek *skēnikē, thymelikē* meaning 'woman of the stage') or from the category of performance they specialised in, as is the case with the Latin term *emboliaria* from the Greek *embolimon* or 'entr'acte'. It is not always easy to be sure exactly what is meant by each title, or to gain a clear conception of the categories of performer from the information given by the sources, which encompass many different domains and registers of language. Some of the terms clearly designate broad categories which must have included various types of performer. One example is *scaenica*, a word favoured by the Latin legal vocabulary in use up to the time of Justinian. The definition of *scaena* in legal terms as a place of public performance suggests that in such contexts the label *scaenica* simply identifies the woman as one whose public performances made her subject to *infamia* and classed her among the *probrosae feminae* along with prostitutes, adulteresses, convicted criminals and brothel madames.[7] In such contexts the nature of the performance is of little or no importance. In other contexts, however, *scaena/skēnē* is used in the precise sense of 'stage' as opposed to the *thymele/thymelē* (orchestra).[8] Sometimes *scaenica/skēnikē* may be a precise term for a woman who acted on stage in mime or even comedy, as opposed to the *thymelicae/thymelikai* who could include musicians and chorus members.[9] To add to the complexity, certain terms in use in the everyday language were not acceptable to high-style Greek authors. The lexicographer Phrynichus states sternly that such authors should not use *thymelē* for the place where the chorus and musicians perform but should say *orchēstra* instead.[10] The avoidance of non-classical usages by Atticising authors like Lucian, Libanius, Choricius and Procopius often results in vague circumlocutions or the use of a general (but Attic) term like *orchēsis* ('dance') to designate a variety of arts from dance in general to the very specific (and usually male) art of the pantomime. Other authors have different reasons for using general terms for women of the stage. Chrysostom for example, refers to them all as *pornai* ('harlots'), which tells us a great deal about what he thought of them, but little about precisely what it was they did on the stage that filled him with such horror (and their audiences with such evident delight).

For these reasons it is often difficult to arrive at any neat classification of the types of performance women were involved in, or to be certain how a type of performance mentioned in one kind of source corresponds to others. In general, however, it is clear that women like Bassilla, Theodora and Pelagia acted in the mimes performed in Roman theatres, and sometimes in amphitheatres and hippodromes. Women also appear as singers and dancers, supporting a pantomime, or celebrating a victory in the hippodrome as on the Theodosian obelisk base still standing in Istanbul.[11] Female dancers, like the famous 'Dancing Girls of Cadiz' and the Egyptian 'castanet-dancers', were also hired to perform in more private settings such as banquets or, in Egypt in particular, village festivals.[12]

7 Ulpian cites the definition of the Augustan jurist Labeo in *Digest* 3.2.2.5 according to which a *scaena* was any place, whether permanent or temporary, where people performed in front of the public. See Leppin (1992) 77. On the definition of *probrosae feminae* see Astolfi (1986) 55–6.

8 Vitruvius, *De architectura* 5.7.2. See Frei (1900) 6; Müller (1909) 47.

9 A further complication is that these terms did not necessarily mean the same in Greek and Latin. It is also possible that the range of meaning of an original Greek term changed under influence from Latin usage.

10 Phrynichus, *Ecloga* 135 (142). See also Frei (1900) 6; Leppin (1992) 79–84.

11 Illustrated in Strong (1980) 318 (fig. 254).

12 Fear (1996); Westermann (1924) and Perpillou-Thomas (1993).

Types of performance

Dancers (*orchēstrides, orchēstriai, saltātrices*) are mentioned in inscriptions, in literary epigrams and other types of text, although in law they are not singled out from other types of performers. Some must have been simply dancers like the *orchēstriai* (*P Grenf.* 67) and 'castanet-dancers' *krotalistrides* (*P Oxy.* 475 and *P Cornell* 9) being hired for Egyptian village festivals. The incident recorded in *P Oxy.* 475 (AD 182) shows that they could perform in the open air: a slave boy, Epaphroditos, leaned too far out of a window to watch the *krotalistrides* performing in front of the house and fell to his death. Depictions on Coptic textiles and Egyptian terracotta statuettes give an idea of these dancers' appearance: they are shown holding *krotala* (clappers or 'castanets') and dressed in long tunics which fully cover the body while allowing the movements to show through.[13]

However, the use of the masculine *orchēstēs* ('dancer') by Greek writers to mean specifically pantomime raises the possibility that some women called *orchēstrides* may also have practised this solo mimetic art. At least three of the women called *orchēstrides* in Greek literary sources of the sixth century are described as representing a story silently, through gesture, like the famous male pantomimes discussed by Lucian in *On Dancing*. Aristaenetus' letter to the fictional Panarete (*Epistles* 1.26) refers to the skilful hand movements which she uses to portray different personae. Leontius Scholasticus, also writing in the sixth century, mentions the hand gestures of a certain Rhodocleia (*Anth. Plan.* 283) and speaks of a dancer named Helladia (*Anth. Plan.* 287) who took on the role of Hector. While it was a common, and sometimes controversial, practice for male pantomimes to play female roles, this is an unusual reference to a female performer playing a male role. It is unclear whether these female pantomimes are part of a long but hidden tradition, or a new development of the early Byzantine period.[14] The same ambiguity applies to the Latin *saltātrix* so that, in the absence of further information, it is impossible to be sure whether the women recorded as *saltātrices* were performers of mimetic or non-mimetic dance.[15] In one case the latter does seem a distinct possibility. The 3,000 *saltātrices* who, according to Ammianus Marcellinus (14.6.18), were allowed to remain in Rome

[13] See for example Wessel (1963) fig. 109 and Dunand (1979) plates 46–9; for further discussion of the type of dance performed see Kraemer (1931) and Webb (1997b).

[14] For further discussion see Spruit (1966) 82; Weinreich (1948) 97–105; Theocharidis (1940) 26–7.

[15] For example: Iulia Nemesis in *CIL* VI.10143; Thyas in *CIL* VIII.12925. The feminine *pantomima* is used by Seneca in *Consolatio ad Helviam* 12.6. But it is not clear from the context whether he means the female counterpart of the male pantomimes.

during the famine of 383 were accompanied by choruses and represented subjects from 'the fables of the theatre' (*fābulae theatrales*).[16] These details suggest the pantomime, or something closely resembling it, and therefore seem to confirm that the figures of Helladia and Rhodocleia were not merely figments of the sixth-century literary imagination.

Women certainly played supporting roles in the pantomimes' performances. Libanius mentions women in the pantomimes' chorus (*Reply to Aristides* 87), and the *emboliariae* mentioned in Latin sources provided interval entertainment, though it is not clear of what sort, and could be attached to a particular group or style of pantomimes.[17] Finally, it is clear that there were types of representational performance involving women which did not conform to the generally accepted definition of either mime or pantomime. The dramatic representation of the Judgement of Paris described by Apuleius in *Metamorphoses* 10.29–33 is one example: unlike pantomime, it involved several actors, including women, who are apparently to be thought of as unmasked, but unlike the mime it seems to have been acted out in silence.[18]

Mime

Of all the types of performance involving women we are best informed about the mime, particularly from texts like Choricius' *Apologia*, which defends the mime, from Chrysostom's attacks on the theatre, which often single out aspects of mime, and from papyrus fragments of scripts.[19] Both Bassilla and Pelagia are described as *mīmades*, and *mīmae* are identified in Latin funerary inscriptions and mentioned in the legislation of late antiquity.[20] Theodora is said to have performed on stage with the *mīmoi* and is often referred to in modern sources as a mime, although Procopius himself does not use the term *mīmas* to describe her.[21] His avoidance of this non-classical term may have been due to stylistic preferences, but it conveniently contributes to his depiction of Theodora as a woman with no particular profession or talents.

16 Csapo and Slater (1995) 388–9. See also Puchner, this volume ch. 14.

17 Phoebe (*CIL* VI.10127) and Sophe (*CIL* VI.10128) have both been dated to the first century *AD*. Pliny also mentions *emboliariae* at *HN* 7.158.

18 Similarly, the Dionysus and Ariadne mime described by Xenophon, *Symposium* 9.2–6 does not correspond exactly to either mime or pantomime as we know them from later periods, though in this case the discrepancy can be explained by the early date. See Wiemken (1972) 36, Wüst (1932) 1737 and (1949) 851.

19 See Wiemken (1972), Theocharidis (1940) and Reich (1903).

20 For example *CIL* VI.10111: Luria Privata; *CIL* VI.10112: Thalassia (1st or 2nd century AD).

21 Procopius, *Secret History* 9.13.

Plutarch (*Sympotic Questions* 7.8 = *Mor.* 712 E) distinguishes two main types of mime: the *hypothesis*, involving a lengthy and complex plot; and the *paignion*, a low form of buffoonery (*bōmolochia*) not even fit for slaves.[22] Procopius seems to have had the latter type of performance in mind when he described how Theodora joined in with the buffoonery (*bōmolochiai)* of the mimes and did not mind being boxed around the ears (*Secret History* 9.13–14). But mime performance, particularly the narrative scenarios which Plutarch calls *hypotheseis*, was clearly more demanding than Procopius implies: performers had to be able to speak, sing and convey action through physical gesture.[23] The surviving fragments of mime scripts illustrate the kinds of scene in which female roles figured prominently, one particularly widespread type of plot being the adultery mime.[24] The story of how the emperor Heliogabalus had the sex scenes literally performed in front of him (thereby missing the point of mime as imitation) underlines the erotic potential of these performances, which must have been part of their popularity.[25] Choricius (*Apologia* 33–5), however, shows how such plots could be defended against moral criticism when he claims that the guilty parties are always punished at the end. The fragmentary papyrus, *P Oxy*. 413 (first or second century AD), preserves a partial script for one variation of the theme in which a mistress lusts after a slave and schemes to poison her husband. The same papyrus records a different type of plot, again with a prominent female role: in a story reminiscent of *Iphigenia in Tauris* and the Greek novels, a Greek heroine named Charition finds herself stranded in an exotic location complete with a mixed chorus of nonsense-speaking barbarians.[26]

Papyri also give precious information about the performers and their art. Wiemken suggests that these scripts contain only a general indication of the plot and dialogue, the rest being filled out by the actors (who therefore needed to be able to improvise).[27] Wiemken was also able to reconstruct the troupe for whom *P Oxy*. 413 was written on the basis of the roles. It must have included two women, one leading lady and one

[22] Csapo and Slater (1995) 377.
[23] Reich (1903) 168. Bassilla is portrayed on her stele raising her hand in what is described by Scrinari (1973) 117 as a rhetorical gesture. Chrysostom, *PG* 62. 428, refers to mime plots being conveyed through spectacle and song.
[24] Theocharidis (1940) 83–7; Reynolds (1946).
[25] *Hist. Aug., Heliogab.* 25.4. Reich (1903) 170–1.
[26] On both plots see Wiemken (1972) 48–109 and Winter (1933) 236. Mimes seem also to have performed mythological scenes, see Theocharidis (1940) 87–93. Theodora's act with the goose (p. 283 above) may therefore have been part of a representation of Leda and Zeus.
[27] Wiemken (1972) 153–7.

minor actress (other scripts require only one female part) and four men, with a mixed chorus.[28] The *archimīmae,* like Fabia Arete, who are recorded in Latin inscriptions and the outstanding performers, like Bassilla, must have played lead female roles like that of Charition or the scheming wife.[29] The details of the careers of both Bassilla and Pelagia tell us one further thing about women's roles within the troupes of perfomers: they are both said to have participated in choruses as well as playing as mimes. Pelagia is described as the 'foremost of the female mimes in Antioch and the foremost of the pantomime's chorus girls', while Bassilla is simply said to have won fame for her diverse skills in mimes on the stage (*skēnē*) and in choruses in the orchestra (*thymelē*).[30] The *Life* of Pelagia suggests that these activities may have been concurrent, rather than representing distinct stages in a career, and that a great deal of versatility was demanded of the leading performers.

BEHIND THE SCENES

Procopius' picture of Theodora gives a carefully calculated impression that a career on the stage demanded little more than shamelessness. He does admit that some performers had a modicum of ability, if only to emphasise his point that Theodora had none whatsoever, but the general impression he creates is of a performance so loosely organised that anyone could join in at will. The sources discussed above, however, show that a high degree of skill and training was required from the best performers. They also contain hints of the degree of organisation required to get a group of mimes on the stage, or to get dancers to a village festival. The picture of the unruly lifestyle of performers which recurs in late antique literary sources can be balanced by the occasional glimpses of their organisation contained in papyri and inscriptions.[31] Few refer specifically to female entertainers, but most of the cases discussed below involve women in some capacity. The fact that non-literary sources are so much more informative on the background of performance underlines how little attention the authors of literary and rhetorical texts paid to what went on behind

[28] Ibid., 108 and 173. [29] *CIL* VI.10107. See Leppin (1992) 212; Jory (1996) 44.

[30] For Bassilla (*CIG* XIV 2342.2–4) see Appendix, pp. 301–2; Pelagia is ἡ πρώτη τῶν μιμάδων Ἀντιοχείας· αὕτη δὲ ἦν καὶ ἡ πρώτη τῶν χορευτρίων τοῦ ὀρχηστοῦ. *Life of Pelagia* 78.23–4.

[31] Cassiodorus *Variae* 7.10 refers to the *vita vaga* ('unsettled life') of performers which prompted the creation of the office of the *tribunus voluptatum* to oversee public spectacles and to control the performers. On this office see Lim (1996).

the scenes and helps to put their pronouncements into a wider social context.[32]

The organisation of performers

In the West in particular many performers, both male and female, were slaves either working within a wealthy household or hired out by their owners.[33] Thyas, the *saltātrix* who died in first-century Carthage at the age of fourteen, is said to belong to a woman named Metilia Rufina.[34] The dancers (*orchēstriai*) in *P Grenf.* 67 which a certain Aurelius Theon is contracted to provide for a village festival in third-century Egypt may also have been slaves. Both Licinia Eucharis and the *archimīma* Fabia Arete, recorded in inscriptions from Rome, were freedwomen, and the latter describes herself as *diurna,* probably meaning that she was paid per performance and free to work as a guest artist with various troupes.[35]

Some women appear to have had stable connections with a particular troupe. Sophe is described as *Theorobathylliana*, 'of the group or school of Bathyllus' (the famous pantomime) within which she was in charge of the *emboliariae*.[36] Some *mīmae* also had regular working partners: Bassilla's memorial was put up by the *biologos* (mime) Heraclides, and Ammianus Marcellinus (23.5.3) mentions a married couple of mimes whose performance at Antioch was interrupted by the Persian invasion of the city. The surviving contracts and records from Roman Egypt mention only single male mimes, but they may figure as representatives of a whole group. This would explain the high payment of 496 drachmas made to a *mīmos* in *P Oxy.* 519 (second century) for performing in public games.[37] The same may also apply to the payment made to a pantomime in the same

32 Compare the remarks of Jaffrey (1996) 15–18 on the indifference of the guests at a high-class Delhi wedding to the question of where the uninvited eunuch entertainers came from and how they managed to find out where and when a wedding was being held.

33 See Jones (1991).

34 *CIL* VIII.12925. See Leppin (1992) 306. Nais, who performed the *pyrrhica* (originally an armed dance which became a form of entertainment in the Roman period) was a slave of the imperial household (*CIL* VI.10141) as was Phiale, a *mīma*, recorded in an unpublished inscription mentioned by Leppin (1992) 276.

35 Leppin (1992) 183–4. Seneca *Ep.* 80.7 refers to the acceptance of a daily payment (*diurnum*) as part of the miserable lot of the poor, but free, actor, showing that such payments were not necessarily generous.

36 *CIL* VI.10128 (scratched onto a piece of bone): *Sophe Theorobathylliana arbitrix imboliarum*. The inscription is dated to the Augustan period by Leppin (1992) 297 because of the mention of Bathyllus. See also Weinreich (1948) 48–9.

37 The same suggestion was made by Grassi (1920). If correct, one further conclusion might be that the *mīmoi* who performed in contests from the late second or third century on also took part with their groups, including women. See Robert (1936).

contract.[38] One well-known example of female entertainers' economic and professional independence in Roman Egypt is the early third-century contract (*P Corn.* 9) made between the *krotalistria* Isidora and a woman named Artemisia. Isidora is asked to bring two other dancers with her, suggesting that she acted as a kind of manager or agent for other dancers. The terms are the same as for the dancers supplied by Aurelius Theon (thirty-six drachmas per day plus food) but Isidora and her colleagues were presumably able to keep the totality of the fee for themselves.[39]

Beyond the practical needs for professional organisation, a certain group identity must have existed among performers who were bound together by their work, by the need to travel from city to city in search of employment at festivals and games (as Bassilla did), and who shared the social exclusion of *infamia* in Roman law. It is tempting to read the final message to Bassilla from her fellow actors (*suskēnoi*) at the end of her epitaph in this light. But Procopius' account of Theodora's savage jealousy of her fellow performers, whatever its historical value, provides a corrective to any overly romantic view of stage camaraderie.[40] A more concrete sign of solidarity can however be seen in the tantalising, undated inscription from Rome recording the dimensions of a burial plot belonging to an association of *mīmae*, the *Sociae Mīmae*.[41] Among other things, such associations fulfilled the duty of burial which would normally have been undertaken by the family. It was highly unusual for women to form such a society and the existence of this one underlines both the anomalous social situation of these itinerant professionals and the economic resources available to them.

Training

There is no mention of formal training schools for female artists like those attested for male pantomimes.[42] Aurelius Theon in *P Grenf.* 67

38 *P Flor.* 74 contains a specific request for two pantomimes to perform with their supporting artists (*symphōnia*) but the absence of this stipulation from other contracts does not mean that it was not understood by the parties. It is perhaps significant that when mentioning the high fee of one thousand *denarii* paid to Roscius, Macrobius, *Saturnalia* 3.14.3, states that it was for him alone, not including his troupe (*sine gregalibus*), suggesting that the normal practice was to give an all-inclusive fee to the principal artist who was then responsible for the redistribution.

39 Discussed but with imperfect text in Westermann (1924). The remarks in Webb (1997b) were based on the earlier reading, corrected in Westermann and Kraemer (1926).

40 Procopius, *Secret History* 9.26.

41 *CIL* VI.10109: *Sociarum Mimarum/in FR P XV/in AGR P XII.* See also Leppin (1992) 112; Ausbüttel (1982) 42; Roueché (1993) 126. Charlotte Roueché has suggested to me that the μουσικὸν δάπεδον in which Bassilla was buried may have been a burial ground for actors.

42 Libanius 103–4. Seneca, *Q.Nat.* 7.3.2 mentions the schools of Bathyllus and Pylades.

may have been the trainer of the dancers he managed, and other slaves would have been trained by their owners.[43] The 3,000 dancers mentioned by Ammianus Marcellinus (14.6.18) were accompanied by *magistri*, a term which can mean both trainer and manager. Procopius' account of Theodora's early life shows that one way into the profession was by birth. This was probably the most common way for freeborn women to become performers. The imposition in law of the same restrictions on *scaenicae* and their daughters suggests that the latter were expected to follow in their mothers' footsteps. Theodora's mother, having been widowed and then remarried to the bear-keeper of the Blue faction, is said to have been responsible for putting her daughters on the stage as soon as each came of age (*es hēbēn*). Procopius does not specify the age, but since he states that Theodora became a fully fledged prostitute at about the same time (earlier, he tells us, she had been too young to have intercourse 'like a woman'), he seems to have envisioned this as being around puberty (*Secret History* 8.9). The short life expectancy of the ancient world must have provided an incentive to families or owners to ensure girls started their careers as early as possible, often far earlier than seems to have been Theodora's case. The performers whose ages are recorded died in their teens and early twenties; one *saltātrix*, Julia Nemesis, was only nine when she died.[44] Procopius naturally omits all reference to any formal training Theodora might have had, but other sources insist on the skills of female performers. Bassilla is praised for her excellence (*aretē*) and Latin inscriptions describe female entertainers as 'learned' and 'highly trained', as in the case of Licinia Eucharis who had had an impressive career by the age of fourteen.[45] In the late fourth century, the imposition of a fine of five pounds of gold on any man who took a *thymelica* away from her public duties shows the value placed on these women and suggests that they were not easily replaceable.[46]

[43] The dispute at the origin of Cicero's *Pro Quinto Roscio* arose from an arrangement to train a slave for the stage as a business venture.

[44] *CIL* VI.10143. Eucharis Licinia (*CIL* VI.10096) died at 14 having made her mark in choruses and 'on the Greek stage'; Thyas was also 14 (*CIL* VIII.12925); Phoebe Vocontia *emboliaria* died at 12 (*CIL* VI.10127); Luria Privata, a *mīma*, was 19 (*CIL* VI.10111); Terentia died at 22 (*CIL* VI.10144); Nais (*CIL* VI.10141) and Phiale were 25; see Leppin (1992) 276. No age is given for Bassilla. It is possible that in most cases only women who died while still active were identified as artists and that others who lived on after retirement from the stage, as Theodora did, go unrecorded.

[45] Eucharis Licinia is described twice as *docta et erodita*. The *emboliaria*, Phoebe, is described as *erodita* in *CIL* VI.10127.

[46] *Cod. Theod.* 15.7.5 cf. 15.7.13 which describes a female musician as *erudita*. See Spruit (1966) 201; Blänsdorf (1990) 266.

Social status

However much their art was appreciated by audiences, and recognised as an essential ingredient of public spectacles, the performers themselves suffered from the same stigma of *infamia* as their male counterparts under Roman law, which technically applied throughout the Empire from the edict of Caracalla in 212.[47] Practically, the legal disabilities resulting from *infamia* may not have made a great difference to performers' lives, even where Roman law was applied. But they reflected the *de facto* social exclusion of a group whose members were either born into the profession or were slaves, and whose itinerant life-style marked them off from the communities in which they worked. Roman marriage legislation reveals constant attempts to ensure that people of the stage, like others considered undesirable, remained distinct from the upper echelons of society in particular.

One further consequence of *infamia* was vulnerability to abuse, which was a fact of life for performers in some areas. Cicero's notorious statement in defence of Plancius that the alleged rape of a *mīmula* (note the derogatory diminutive), even if it had taken place, was hardly a crime but recognised as common practice in small towns, is a chilling reminder of the absence of rights for those of low social status.[48] The story of Heliogabalus' insistence on live sex scenes is comparable in its display of the bodies of socially unprotected women with the public acts of bestiality to which low-class female convicts were submitted in the amphitheatres.[49] The frequent association of the theatre with prostitution, as illustrated in the *Secret History*, shows further how visibility and sexual availability were linked in thought as well as in practice. The areas around theatres were known as the haunts of prostitutes and both male and female performers were frequently assumed to be prostitutes themselves.[50] There was, however, a distinction between the category of performer (*scaenica*) and that of prostitute (*meretrix*), even if some women fulfilled both roles.[51]

47 Even after the Edict of Caracalla (also known as the *Constitutio Antoniniana*), local laws and customs continued to be in force, making it difficult to tell what impact, if any, the Roman legislation on actresses may have had in the East. See Evans Grubbs (1995) 41, 97–9.

48 Cicero, *Pro Plancio* 12.30 suggests that Plancius' alleged behaviour towards the *mīmula* was part of the traditional treatment meted out to *scaenici* in general in small towns. The implication is that male actors were also vulnerable to sexual violence.

49 Coleman (1990).

50 Libanius, *Reply to Aristides* 38, refutes Aristides' claim that all dancers (*orchēstai*) were courtesans. The use of the masculine plural may refer to performers in general or just to male pantomimes.

51 See Reich (1903) 171–3; French (1998) 296–7. The intriguing list of names painted on the wall of a third-century house in Dura-Europus contains many women who may have been prostitutes and/or entertainers of some description. See Immerwahr (1944).

Many performers were children of the lower strata of society who remained poor.[52] But in exceptional cases the stage could be a path to wealth. The amounts paid to dancers in the Egyptian contracts compare favourably with the wages of labourers, even if they are hardly lavish.[53] Gifts from wealthy admirers or nobles anxious to display their largesse at public games were a source of extra revenue for male and female performers alike.[54] For women in particular such patronage could take the form of a permanent or semi-permanent liaison with a man of a higher class, Theodora's meteoric rise from the theatre to the palace being the best-known example.[55] Some female mimes in particular seem to have had considerable earning power. The *Sociae Mīmae* in Rome had the resources to create their burial society, while on a more spectacular level, the mime Pelagia is described as dripping with jewels and accompanied by her own slaves as she rides through Antioch.[56] That the wealthy *mīma* was not just a figure of fiction is suggested by the attempt to limit the use of luxurious clothing by *mīmae* in the late fourth century.[57]

The central role of performers in urban life, which brought them possibilities for enrichment and contact with wealthy individuals, combined with their socially marginalised state created tensions which can be traced in marriage legislation.[58] The possibility that female performers might infiltrate the upper orders and that they or their children might divert wealth from legitimate heirs induced a certain amount of anxiety in the authorities at various periods. Roman marriage legislation of the early principate affected male and female performers equally, but later additions were often aimed specifically at female performers and the threat they were seen to pose. From the Augustan period, any marriage between a woman of the stage (along with adulteresses, procuresses and criminals) with an *ingenuus* (free-born man) was not officially recognised and did not provide the parties with the normal advantages of full legal marriage. The same applied to any marriage between a senator or close relation and an actor, actress or child of an actor or actress.[59] The loopholes of this law were progressively tightened, suggesting that such marriages were still taking place, despite the disadvantages. Domitian,

[52] Theocharidis (1940) 111.

[53] For comparisons see Westermann (1924).

[54] Carinus, *Historia Augusta* 20.4 criticises the lavish gifts made by Junius Messalla.

[55] Chrysostom, *PG* 58. 637 mentions an anonymous actress who seduced the brother of an empress, see Theocharidis (1940) 71.

[56] *Life of Pelagia* 78.

[57] *Cod. Theod.* 15.7.11 (393). Csapo and Slater (1995) 329. See Sallmann (1990) 268.

[58] See French (1998).

[59] Lex Iulia et Papia Poppaea of 9 AD. See Astolfi (1986); Spruit (1966) 91–3; Leppin (1992) 75; Treggiari (1991) 61; Daube (1967) 383–4.

according to Suetonius, removed the right of inheritance from *probrosae feminae* like actresses, and Marcus Aurelius declared null all marriages which were not in accordance with the Augustan legislation.[60] In 336 Constantine punished with *infamia* any senator or dignitary (*perfectissimus*) who attempted to pass off a child by an actress or the daughter of an actress as legitimate. In addition any gifts given to the women were to be returned to the legitimate heirs (with the threat of torture for non-compliance).[61] In contrast to the neutral language of the earlier legislation, the rhetorical flourishes typical of the Theodosian Code reveal the fears and prejudices which partly motivated the new law. The hapless aristocrats are described as 'profligates (*perditi*) whose minds are corrupted by the women's poisons'.[62]

The shifting of moral blame for what was, after all, a reciprocal act onto the female performer was not a new tactic but one which became common in Christian polemic, particularly in the writings of Chrysostom, for whom theatre audiences were the passive victims of women of the stage. The extent to which both polemic and legislation come to focus on female performers and their behaviour on and off stage is striking. But it would be inaccurate to qualify the Christian response to female performers as entirely 'anti-feminist'.[63] Both churchmen and legislators of the late fourth and early fifth centuries show an unprecedented concern for the rights of the performer as an individual. This concern, motivated by Christian ideals, exposed the paradoxes inherent in the dependence of members of the highest levels of society on one of the lowest social strata, performers. But the Christianisation of the Empire introduced new paradoxes. Despite the moral disapproval of the stage and the feeling that professions associated with it were unsuitable for Christians, the wording of legislation shows how acutely aware Christian emperors were of the need to provide entertainments for the people.[64] Measures were taken to ensure their provision, and at some point in the fourth century, acting, like other professions and duties, became a hereditary obligation, a measure which formalised the tendency of children to follow their parents onto the stage.[65] The increasingly

[60] Suetonius, *Domitian* 8.3. See Spruit (1966) 100–3; Treggiari (1991) 63.

[61] *Cod. Theod.* 4.6.3; Spruit (1966) 209; Beauchamp (1990) 288–90; Evans Grubbs (1995) 284–300. As Daube (1967) points out, where earlier legislation had imposed the same restrictions on all people of the stage and their children, this law is concerned only with actresses and their daughters.

[62] *Cod. Theod.* 4.6.3: *Ipsas etiam, quarum venenis inficiuntur animi perditorum . . . tormentis (subici) iubemus.* On the language of the Code see Robinson (1997) 38.

[63] The term is from Spruit (1966) 218.

[64] See for example *Cod. Theod.* 15.6.2 (399); Lim (1997).

[65] See Lepelley (1989); Lim (1996).

centralised organisation of spectacles in cities may have facilitated the imposition of such duties.[66]

FEMALE ENTERTAINERS IN CHRISTIAN POLEMIC AND LEGISLATION

Some Christian critics of the theatre, like Tertullian, were most concerned by the pagan, cultic associations of the theatre, and their comments are therefore mostly aimed at the depiction of the pagan gods in the pantomime.[67] The tirades of John Chrysostom have a different emphasis. Again and again he expresses his concern about the danger to the male viewer of the sight of women on stage.[68] Singing and acting out scenes of 'unnatural love' (*atopous erōtas*), these women had a harmful effect on the spectator's imagination.[69] No man was safe from their evil effects; even when he left the theatre the spectator took with him an image of the female performer lodged in his mind. Her invisible presence accompanied him into his own home to threaten his marriage.[70] This striking image plays on the assumed identity between the actress and the role of adulteress she often played. At the same time, it expresses the long-standing idea of the threat posed by the seductive actress to legitimate marriage and society in new terms, as an internalised danger to the individual soul. The same shift from the social to the psychological characterises the Gospel redefinition of adultery as merely looking at a woman with desire (*pros to epithumēsai*) whether consummated or not (Matthew 5.28), a passage to which Chrysostom appeals in his criticism of the theatre. In these terms, merely to look at the spectacles of the theatre was to commit adultery. The presence of women on stage and the popularity of the adultery theme in mime, both aspects of theatrical practice which Chrysostom constantly singles out, contributed to the power of this metaphor of theatre as adultery.

As negative as Chrysostom's comments on female performers were, he also reminded his audience of the basic human dignity of the performer, pointing out the double standards which allowed them to watch a naked woman on stage without compunction simply because she was an actress (the same double standards which had allowed Cicero to claim that the rape of a *mīma* was not a crime at all).[71] His argument that there was

66 Cameron (1976) 218–21.

67 See particularly Tertullian *De spectaculis*; Jürgens (1972); Weismann (1972).

68 See Webb (1997b); Leyerle (1993).

69 Chrysostom, *PG* 62. 428.

70 Chrysostom, *PG* 56. 266–7.

71 Chrysostom, *PG* 57.72; see Brown (1989) 316.

no essential difference in nature (*phusis*) between the actress and the respectable woman was in effect an attempt to reveal and break down the social conventions that had governed the role of theatre in society and to destroy the social fiction of *infamia* that differentiated actors from others. The same message is conveyed in the spectacular conversion stories, of which Pelagia's is one, which illustrated the potential of people of the stage for redemption. Legislation of the late fourth century actually put such ideals into practice by allowing men and women of the stage who underwent genuine conversions to Christianity to leave their profession and by protecting the daughters of *scaenicae* who lived virtuous lives from being forced to follow in their mothers' footsteps.[72]

But the right of the individual to leave the stage had to be balanced against the continuing need for entertainments as part of the fabric of civic life (as illustrated by the chorus line of dancing girls on the Theodosian obelisk base of 390). The tension between Christian ideals and the needs of the state resulted in strict measures being taken to deter false conversions. In a particularly vicious edict of 381, any former actress who failed to lead an exemplary life upon leaving the stage for religious reasons was threatened with being forced back onto the stage with no hope of release until she was a 'ridiculous old woman made ugly by age'.[73] Although the legislation on conversion applied equally to men and to women, it was the female performers who concerned the legislators most, perhaps because they were seen as more morally vulnerable, or dangerous, or perhaps simply because more women were needed for spectacles. Certainly, the availability of skilled performers was a problem in certain places. One threat to the public availability of spectacles was the action of private individuals, as indicated in the fine to be imposed on any man taking a *thymelica* so far away that she could no longer perform her public duties.[74] An edict issued in Carthage in 413 recalled *mīmae* who had formerly been released from their duties, probably after conversion, indicating that these highly skilled performers were in particularly short supply.[75] Such measures suggest that, for whatever reason, the number of women willing to enter a career on the stage was not sufficient to meet the demand. In the mid-fifth century it was felt necessary to protect women, whether slave or free, from being forced onto the stage against their will

72 *Cod. Theod.* 15.7.1 (371); 15.7.2 (371); 15.7.4 (380); Spruit (1966) 198; French (1998) 304–7.

73 *Cod. Theod.* 15.7.8: *retracta in pulpitum sine spe absolutionis ullius ibi eo usque permaneat, donec anus ridicula senectute deformis nec tunc quidem absolutione potiatur*...; Csapo and Slater (1995) 329. See Spruit (1966) 221–2 and Sallmann (1990) 267.

74 *Cod. Theod.* 15.7.5. See p. 292 above.

75 *Cod. Theod.* 15.7.13.

(the repetition of the same prohibition by Justinian in 535 suggests that the original legislation was not effective).[76]

It is not easy to assess the actual impact of legislation on the lives of performers, particularly given the perennial difficulty of enforcing the law in antiquity. One of the few cases in which we can see a result is the Emperor Justin's law of the 520s formally removing the taint of the stage from ex-actresses who mended their ways and thereby allowing his nephew Justinian to marry Theodora.[77] Procopius presents this action as an aberration prompted by Justinian's foolish desire, but in fact the legislation followed the ideology of redemption to its logical conclusion. That it took so long for such a measure to be introduced is a testament to the strength of older social prejudices against actresses which had meant that the taint of the stage, unlike that of slavery, could never be removed however virtuously an ex-actress behaved, an anomaly which is pointed out in the introduction to law. But in other cases, legislation tells us more about the problems than their solutions and points towards the difficulties faced by women who did not have such powerful protectors. How often did the responsible authorities intervene to prevent a woman being forced onto the stage? By what criteria was a woman's behaviour to be judged as 'virtuous'? How many women, one wonders, were able to avail themselves of their right to leave the stage on conversion?[78] The spectacular story of a Pelagia can hardly be taken as representative, and even she is portrayed as needing wealth and unusual determination to be accepted into the church. The shortage of *mīmae* at Carthage suggests that this relatively wealthy group were able to take advantage of the possibilities for social mobility offered by Christianity. But for how many women was abandoning the stage, and their only source of income, an economic possibility?

The rhetoric of the Theodosian Code and of Christian polemic against the stage suggest that the possibilities offered by Christianity were somewhat double-edged. For if sincere converts were given the option to leave their profession and begin afresh, those who stayed in the theatre (as many clearly did) could be assumed to have chosen this life-style of their own free will, whatever their actual social or economic circumstances. The language of Justin's marriage legislation is telling: women are said to choose this life as a result of their innate weakness.[79] Thus while offering,

76 *Cod. Iust.* 1.4.14.1 (457–67). Cf. 5.4.29 and 1.4.33 (535).
77 *Cod. Iust.* 5.4.23; Procopius, *Secret History* 9.51. See Daube (1967).
78 See Lepelley (1989) on a young man's attempts to avoid being forced on to the stage.
79 *Cod. Iust.* 5.4.23 pr.: *indignam honore conversationem imbecillitate sexus elegerint.*

in theory, new possibilities to performers to transform their social status, such legislation, coupled with the attitudes to the stage voiced by polemicists like Chrysostom, threw a new burden of individual moral responsibility onto performers, replacing, or adding to, the old collective social stigma of *infamia*.[80]

CONCLUSION

Procopius' depiction of Theodora's youth in the theatre, with its repeated implications that she chose her career of her own free will, is based on the premiss that a woman's decision to perform in public is a sign of moral turpitude. In the *Secret History*, as elsewhere in the literature of late antiquity, the theatre serves as a metaphor for evil and perversion, and Procopius plays skilfully on the combination of old social prejudices against actresses and the characteristically Christian stress on the moral responsibility of the individual performer.[81] The persistence of a female presence in public performances into the sixth century is however itself an indication that Christian disapproval alone was by no means sufficient to put an end to the various types of spectacle in which women were involved. Although the combination of fourth- and fifth-century polemic and legislation provides a complex picture of élite attitudes and their inherent contradictions, this picture is still partial. The rescripts of the Theodosian Code were specific responses to specific problems which cannot be assumed to have existed throughout the Empire. Outside the major cities, with their tightly controlled bodies of performers, groups of mimes and other performers may well have carried on much as before. Within the cities, certain types of performance may have proved more attractive than others. Even allowing for significant exaggeration, Ammianus Marcellinus' mention of the 3,000 *saltātrices* in Rome in the late fourth century puts the apparent shortage of women available for the public spectacles into context and helps to counter the strong impression given by the legislation that fewer and fewer women were willing to perform.

A final balancing voice is provided by Choricius. The eminently pragmatic arguments which he puts forward in defence of the mime are a welcome contrast to the heated polemic of the Christian extremists and show that it was still possible in sixth-century Gaza to argue on the

80 See Pommeray (1937) 251 on the Christian remodelling of *infamia* to include heretics, i.e. those who choose to reject orthodoxy.

81 See French (1998) 316–17.

basis of public opinion and general practice that such spectacles were a morally harmless (even beneficial) form of entertainment. Choricius has been dismissed as overly rhetorical, and he does state at the outset that he has deliberately chosen a particularly difficult theme in order to display his skills. But contemporary audiences at Constantinople and at Oxyrhynchus, where a group of mimes were billed to perform between races in the hippodrome, confirm that he was not alone.[82] Choricius' appreciation of the mime and his refusal to indulge in moral condemnation of mimes themselves are closer to the matter-of-fact tone of the earlier inscriptions and papyri than to the rhetoric of late-antique lawmakers and churchmen. There is no need to interpret this as a sign of Choricius' paganism; rather his defence of the mime can be seen as an attempt to define a type of performance compatible with Christianity (despite his use of mythological examples within his speech he never tries to defend the enactment of mythological scenes on stage).[83] Justinian, who stipulated that theatrical shows including female performers should be put on by the consuls to mark the beginning of their year of office, would have found it hard not to agree.[84] Ironically, the areas in which women were prominent, non-mimetic dance and mime with its everyday subjects, were less vulnerable to attack on some fronts than was the overtly pagan subject-matter of the pantomime (the Council in Trullo still found it necessary to ban female performers in the late seventh century).[85] The views espoused by Choricius may be anomalous compared to the unanimous rejection of the stage in Christian polemic and legislation, but read against the long history of popular acceptance of such performances they are less surprising.

The intense attention focused on actresses in the late fourth and early fifth centuries highlighted the paradoxes and tensions which had long been inherent in their profession and in their social status. The polemics and legislation which happen to survive are a uniquely valuable window onto élite attitudes to female performers at a time of intense re-examination of social categories and practices. But the sixth-century evidence cited above, together with the apparent references to skilled female pantomimes in the literature of the period, suggest that in the

[82] *P Oxy*. 2707. See Roueché (1993) 58; Cameron (1976) 213 and (on Choricius' rhetorical style) 161, n. 7.

[83] Barnes (1996) argues that Choricius could not, as a Christian, have defended the theatre. I am grateful to Glen Bowersock for allowing me to see the text of an unpublished lecture delivered at the Collège de France in which he argues that the *Apologia* cannot be taken as proof that Choricius was a pagan.

[84] Justinian, *Novellae* 105.

[85] See Walter Puchner's chapter in this volume.

long term, the practical impact of Christianity should perhaps not be overestimated. Procopius may manage to make Theodora into an embodiment of all that certain members of society had always feared that the actress could be, a living example of Chrysostom's seductive and destructive actresses and proof that virtue was incompatible with the stage. But the correspondence tells us far more about Procopius' skill in appealing to long-standing prejudice than about the state of the stage and the lives of performers in his lifetime. While the world in which Bassilla lived, to take one example, was very different from that of Theodora, she is a chance reminder of the anonymous performers who are entirely overshadowed for us, but were still very much part of urban life at the end of antiquity.[86]

APPENDIX: *CIG* XIV 2324: BASSILLA'S STELE FROM AQUILEIA (THIRD CENTURY AD)

τὴν πολλοῖς δήμοισι πάρος, πολλαῖς δὲ πόλεσσι
δόξαν φωνάεσσαν ἐνὶ σκηναῖσι λαβοῦσαν
παντοίης ἀρετῆς ἐν μείμοις, εἶτα χοροῖσι,
πολλάκις ἐν θυμέλαις, ἀλλ' οὐχ οὕτω δὲ θανούσῃ
τῇ δεκάτῃ Μούσῃ τὸ λαλεῖν σοφὸς Ἡρακλείδης
μειμάδι Βασσίλλῃ στήλην θέτο βιολόγος φῶς,
ἣ δὴ καὶ νέκυς οὖσα ἴσην βίου ἔλλαχε τειμήν,
μουσικὸν εἰς δάπεδον σῶμ' ἀναπαυσαμένη
ταῦτα
οἱ σύσκηνοί σου λέγουσιν· εὐψύχει Βάσσιλλα· οὐδεὶς ἀθάνατος

For the woman who formerly gained resounding fame among many peoples and many cities for her varied talents on stage in the mimes, and often in choruses in the orchestra – but this is not how she died – for the mime Bassilla, the tenth Muse, the mime actor Heraclides, skilled in speaking, set up this stele. She has been allotted equal honour in death as in life, resting her body in the ground of the Muses.

[86] This paper has greatly benefited from discussion with Glen Bowersock, Peter Brown, Michael Crawford, Judith Herrin, Richard Lim and Charlotte Roueché and from the comments of the editors and the participants in the Study Day on Group Identities in Late Antiquity held at the Institute of Classical Studies in London, April 1999. It was written with the generous support of a Stanley J. Seeger Preceptorship in Hellenic Studies from Princeton University.

Fig. 55 Memorial stele of the mime actress Bassilla (Reproduced from Scrinari (1973), fig. 344)

That's life!
Your fellow actors say: 'Farewell Bassilla, no one is immortal.'

Note

l.4: ἀλλ' οὐχ οὕτω δὲ θανούσῃ: on the change of case from accusative to dative see Kaibel (1878) 609. This line presents serious difficulties of interpretation. Our translation implies that Bassilla stopped performing before her death but stayed with her former colleagues. For another possible interpretation see Csapo and Slater (1995) 377. The reading of Corbato (1947) is less convincing.

SUGGESTIONS FOR FURTHER READING

Bonaria (1955–56) provides a valuable collection of Greek and Latin sources on all aspects of mime and pantomime, though with no translation or analysis; Csapo and Slater (1995) translate some of the principal sources for this period in their chapters IVBiii on 'Emperors and Theater' and V on 'Mime and Pantomime'; Theocharidis (1940) is a comprehensive and acute study of the evidence for performance in Chrysostom's sermons; Pasquato (1976) is a less rigorous but more easily available study of the same material. Reich (1903) gives a full and judicious survey of the literary evidence for the mime (a projected second volume which would have covered the Byzantine empire was never published). Wiemken (1972) reconstructs mime performances on the basis of the papyrus fragments. Leppin (1992) is a rich study of the historical evidence for performers and their status in the West, including a list of named performers; Spruit (1966) discusses all the legal material pertaining to actors (with a detailed résumé in French). In English, Cameron (1976) explains the background to the organisation of spectacles in late antiquity and early Byzantium, and Roueché (1993) examines the inscriptions from Aphrodisias within a wide-ranging study of the evidence for various types of performance.

CHAPTER FOURTEEN

Acting in the Byzantine theatre: evidence and problems

Walter Puchner

Drama in late antiquity and beyond continues to pose serious obstacles to those wishing to write a single, unified account of its development. The relevant sources remain sparse and do not combine to give a clear picture.[1] Like the history of daily life in general, the history of drama in the Byzantine era can be divided into four major periods. First, there is the early Byzantine era up to the period of Iconoclasm. Various starting-points have been suggested for it, such as the foundation of Byzantium in AD 330, the division of the Roman empire in 395, the date at which Christianity became the official religion, Justinian's accession to power in 527 or the closing of the Athenian Academy in 529. As Vavřínek has pointed out, the period cannot be clearly separated from that of late antiquity which preceded it.[2] This was followed by the period of Iconoclasm, starting as early as the Council in Trullo (691/2) and ending with the Council of Nicaea in 787, the development of John of Damascus' theology of images, and the death of Theophilos in 842. Next came the middle Byzantine era, in the course of which iconographic programmes were consolidated, the liturgy was standardised and the so-called *synaxaria* (Lives of Saints) were re-edited. Finally, there was the period of the Latin empires and the dynasty of the Palaiologoi (1204–1435), which was characterised by growing western influence in both the secular and the religious spheres.

While the early Byzantine period in many ways continued the lifestyle of late antiquity, despite the spread of Christianity and the ban on theatrical performances,[3] decisive changes are likely to have occurred in the relatively 'dark' centuries shortly before and during the period of Iconoclasm.[4] These left the eastern Roman empire radically different from the Hellenistic world. It is crucial to differentiate between the periods, because many of the arguments that are made concerning

[1] Puchner (1981/82), (1984a), (1990). [2] Vavřínek (1985).
[3] Puchner (1997a). [4] Mango (1981).

'Byzantine' theatre in general apply only to early Byzantine times. Furthermore, the participants in this debate come from different disciplines, so that the terms 'drama' and 'theatre' are employed in a variety of ways, from the concrete to the purely metaphorical.[5] The terms *drama* and *theatron* in the Byzantine texts themselves have caused further confusion, since their range of meaning is so broad that it can only be determined in context. Yet another problem is that the debate has been affected by a schematic view of cultural history in general, according to which Byzantium functions as a bridge between antiquity and the Renaissance. Greek nationalism may have played its role in the early phases of the debate about Byzantine 'theatre', especially as the debate took shape in the last decades of the nineteenth century.[6] Since the Second World War Byzantinists have on the whole rather played down, if not ignored, the issue. Such caution has seemed all the more justified in the face of a general lack of evidence from the end of the early Byzantine period onward. The role of drama in Byzantium clearly bears no comparison with the role it plays in antiquity, in the Latin Middle Ages or in the Renaissance.

WAS THERE A 'THEATRE' IN BYZANTIUM? THE HISTORY OF A CONTROVERSY

When Konstantinos Sathas published his voluminous treatise on the music and theatre of Byzantium in 1878, he attempted to link ancient Greek drama with the newly discovered Renaissance theatre of Crete.[7] Sathas based his argument on the character of Byzantium as a bridge between old and new, and on the insight gained in the nineteenth century by the French school of liturgical studies that modern drama had its origins in Christian liturgy.[8] Karl Krumbacher was the first to raise doubts about Sathas' results by pointing out that Byzantine literature did not actually produce any drama.[9] Since then, the disagreement between Sathas and Krumbacher has been rehearsed for over a hundred years, without any fundamentally new data or arguments. Those who play

5 This terminological confusion is apparent in research on the medieval Latin church (Puchner (1991) 12ff.). Some examples: Onasch (1967) and Schulz (1959) 62 speak, in reference to the Byzantine mass, of 'cultic performance' and 'drama'; Wellesz (1947) describes antiphony as 'drama'; Stričević (1967) 120 calls the Ravenna mosaics a 'setting for a liturgical play'; Bréhier (1920) regards the miniatures of the apocryphal Life of Mary by James of Kokkinobaphos as illustrations of liturgical performances; Tinnefeld (1974) deals under the heading 'Mime' with *ioculatores, histriones*, traditional dances and costumes. See Puchner (1981/82) and (1984a).

6 There have also been critics of this trend, for example Mitsakis (1986) 330–53.

7 Sathas (1878). On the Cretan theatre see now Holton (1991).

8 Young (1933). 9 Krumbacher (1897) 644, 647.

down or even refuse to believe in the existence of Byzantine theatre are mostly – though not exclusively – Byzantinists.[10] Among those who have accepted the reality of Byzantine drama the majority have come from a Greek tradition of philologists and cultural historians, but we also find scholars in several other disciplines.[11] Theatre historians were particularly eager to take up the claims made by Vénétia Cottas in her 1931 Paris dissertation on Byzantine theatre.[12] As a consequence, a ghost chapter on the Byzantine church play established itself in the histories of European theatre and survived well into the 1970s.[13]

STAGE TERMINOLOGY AND THE END OF ANCIENT THEATRE

By late Hellenistic times the ways in which tragedy was performed had altered considerably, and much of the evidence survives from contexts other than performances at festivals of Dionysus. At the same time various non-official, more improvisational forms of theatre had sprung up, performed by travelling companies or solo actors. These include mimes, pantomimes, cithara-playing, various forms of singing by *aoidoi* and *tragōidoi*, dancing, and performances by instrumentalists, jugglers and rhetoricians. Stephanis' collection of prosopographical sources for over three thousand 'artists of Dionysus' gives a good picture of these activities.[14] Stephanis' work can also provide a chronological framework for the decline of the performing arts which took place in the course of the early Byzantine era. While in the third century AD our sources still name as many as 200 'artists of Dionysus', this number drops to twenty-three in the fourth to the sixth centuries.[15]

[10] Baud-Bovy (1938), (1975), Marshall and Mavrogordato (1948) 344ff., Dölger (1948) 16ff., Beck (1952) 54 and (1971) 112f., Hunger (1969) 63ff. and (1977–78) 142ff., Mitsakis (1986 [1971]), Tinnefeld (1974), Mango (1981).

[11] 'Greek' tradition: Mistriotis (1894) 697ff., Papamichael (1916), Papadopoulos (1925), Cottas (1931a), (1931b), Koukoules (1955) 110–14, Solomos (1964 [3rd edn 1987]). Philologists and historians: Reich (1903), La Piana (1912), Vogt (1931a, b). Art historians: Bréhier (1913), (1920), and (1950) 411–419, Stričević (1967). Musicologists: Wellesz (1947), Velimirovič (1962).

[12] Cottas (1931a). See Tunison (1907) x, Baty and Chavange (1932) 68ff., D'Amico (1933), Ghilardi (1961) 111ff., Niessen (1949–58) 1240ff., Pernoud (1965) 560 and (1962). These scholars could not test Cottas' results and did not take into account the sharp criticisms of her work published by Kyriakidis (1932) and (1934–37), Maas (1932) and La Piana (1936).

[13] Stadler (1966) 523–8, Berthold (1968) 153–65. There are, however, some theatre historians who have doubted Cottas' results: Laskaris (1938) 32–73, Hunningher (1955) 49, Kindermann (1966) 222–6. See La Piana (1936) 189ff. for bibliography. Other scholars including Erbe (1973), Baldwin (1986), Pontani (1994), as well as some popular accounts (e.g. Nalpantis (1984)), suspend judgement.

[14] Stephanis (1988).

[15] These include male and female dancers in the circus parties or factions in the hippodrome in AD 500, the empress Theodora as mime actress, Memphis the Snub-Nosed (a dancer in Alexandria),

Actors of mimes who become martyrs are attested until the beginning of the fourth century, when Christians ceased to be persecuted: St Ardalion under Maximianus in the East, St Babylas in Cilicia, St Gaianos and St Gelasinos (end of third century) in Heliopolis in Phoenicia, St Pelagia in Antioch, St Porphyrios in Constantinople (362, Stephanis no. 2122), St Porphyrios from Ephesus in Caesarea (*c.* 275), and the aulete Philemon in the Egyptian city of Antinoöpolis under Diocletian.[16] The case of St Gelasinos is characteristic. He was a supporting actor of mimes, who converted to Christianity on the occasion of a parodistic performance of the Christian baptism which was put on in his home town Heliopolis. He was stoned to death by the audience.[17]

Once the classical Greek forms of drama and theatre had largely disappeared, tragedies served above all as canonical texts for school-teaching and for the scholarship that went on in such centres of learning as Alexandria and Constantinople.[18] Tragedy was regarded as part of a cultural heritage in the broadest sense and as such could be alluded to even in the relatively 'low' genre of mime. The extent to which the Greek church fathers were familiar with the texts of tragedy and Old Comedy is astonishing, though of course they reject their content as 'idolatry'.[19] Balsamon, in his commentary on the 62nd canon of the synod in Trullo (691/2), warns against comic and tragic masks as late as the twelfth century.[20] The early church rejects drama and spectacles both because of their part in the allegedly shallow and lascivious entertainment of the time and for deeper theological reasons. The effects of its hostility can be traced in the semantic development of theatrical terminology. The ancient actor, *hypokritēs*, becomes a 'hypocrite' in the modern sense of the word; the verb *hypokrinomai* ('act') now comes to mean 'to pretend' or 'to mislead'; *dramatopoiia* ('dramaturgy') is equivalent to 'intrigue', and *theatrikōs* ('theatrically') means 'in public'. In the face of divine revelation,

a certain Hyperechios (also a dancer), the female dancer Chrysomallo (a favourite of Theodora), as well as an aulete called Aurelios Psenymis, whose name appears on a work contract from the Egyptian city of Hermoupolis in AD 322 (Stephanis nos. 157, 293, 465, 488, 541, 829, 830, 1149, 1156, 1386, 1593, 1639, 2014, 2026, 2122–4, 2194, 2447, 2486, 2630, 2638, 2642).

16 Stephanis nos. 293, 504, 536, 541, 2039, 2122, 2124, 2486. On the dissemination of the legend of Pelagia in the Middle Ages see Usener (1879) and Petitmengin and Cazacu (1981). On the martyrdom of St Porphyrios of Ephesus see van de Vorst (1910): the parody of the baptism ends with a real baptism, followed by miracles and a debate between the holy man and a town councillor.

17 Weismann (1975), Wiemken (1972) 179ff.

18 Müller (1909), Irmscher (1981), (1973).

19 Bibilakis (1996) 147ff., 283ff.; Waszink (1964) 144ff., Easterling and Miles (1999).

20 Rallis and Potlis (1852–56) vol. II, 449–50.

theatre is a lie, and the actor comes to be seen as someone who defiles the idea of man as an image of God.

Theatron generally refers to the hippodrome or any other form of public spectacle and its audience.[21] In the church fathers down to the fifth century, *theatron* refers to a stage building, the amphitheatre, the stadium, the hippodrome, dramatic art or a performance (*poiō theatron* can also mean 'tell a story'); *theatron* can also mean 'public display', 'spectacle', 'audience', 'gathering' (including a church gathering), 'martyrdom' or 'visible world'. Sometimes it has the negative connotations of an abode of demons, the company of the devil, the place of non-transcendental existence, or the opponent of a Christian life. *Theatrizō* can mean 'act in the theatre' or 'display in public', but also takes on the modern meaning of 'mock', 'sneer', 'lie' or 'put up false pretences'.[22] Most notably, in the twelfth century and later, but also in late antiquity, *theatra* are literary and rhetorical events including the reading of homilies, poems and letters, and the performance of panegyric speeches and obituaries under the aegis of the emperor, the patriarch or a high-ranking aristocrat; one could call them the predecessors of the academies of Renaissance Italy.[23] In the *Chronography* of Psellos, the word 'theatre' almost always refers to the hippodrome,[24] but Theodore Metochites (fourteenth century) uses the term in the metaphorical sense of 'world theatre'.[25]

Since there is no dramatic genre in anything like the modern sense of the word, the term 'drama' comes to be used in late Hellenistic and Byzantine romances from Heliodorus, Achilles Tatius and Chariton to Eustathios Makrembolites, who even employs the term in his title.[26] Photius uses the term to refer to the genre of the Hellenistic romance as a whole.[27] Generally speaking, 'drama' refers to an adventurous or tragic life story; the grammarians of the second to the fifth centuries AD

[21] Mango (1981) 342–5. Cf. Hunger (1977–78) 210–11.

[22] Bibilakis (1996) 197ff. and *passim*, with references: the new Christian (negative) connotation can also be detected in other expressions derived from *theatron*, e.g. *theatrizomai* meaning 'make a disgrace of oneself', *theatrikōs* meaning 'superficial' and *theatrismos* meaning 'absurd performance'.

[23] Beaton (1996) 714. Cf. Magdalino (1993) 335–6, Hunger (1991) 131, 236, 255, 318–19 and (1997) 108–9. See also Hunger (1974).

[24] Puchner (1997b) 315ff.

[25] Müller and Kießling (1821) 740, 729, 241, 689, 752, 493, 281, in order of citation. See Beck (1952) 106ff. This metaphorical sense goes back to Epictetus, for whose influence on Christian theology see Kokolakis (1976) 177–85, Hunger (1958) 153ff., Bibilakis (1997) 109–20.

[26] Walden (1894), Yatromanolakis (1990) 725ff. and (1997) 42ff. In his comparison of Heliodorus' *Aithiopika* with Achilles Tatius, Michael Psellos describes the term 'drama' in the novel *Leukippe and Kleitophon* as 'most theatrical' (*theatrikōtatēn*), Dyck (1986) 91–2.

[27] Perry (1974) 74ff., C. W. Müller (1976), Marini (1991).

describe captivating stories about real or fictional events as 'dramatic'.[28] 'Dramatic' elements may therefore be found both in historical writings (Anna Comnena, Psellos, Bryennios) and in works of literary fiction (Makrembolites). From the fifth century onwards the sense of a 'moving event' is predominant, with secondary terms also implying emotional impact (e.g. 'to become a drama' meaning to be unhappy); some derivations also point to a lack of reality (for example, *dramatopoiia* and *dramatourgēma* meaning 'intrigue', and *dramatourgia* as 'mythical story', or 'invention').[29]

A similar development in the meaning of words can also be seen in other terminology concerning the theatre. For example, *skēnē* sometimes means 'outward appearance', 'hypocrisy' or 'heresy' in addition to its more usual meanings. In Psellos it can also mean 'deception', or 'trickery'; Psellos also introduces the word *skēnourgos* in analogy with the term *dramatourgos*, with which it shares the meaning of 'actor' or 'liar'.[30] Only the latter word is known in antiquity. For Psellos, too, *drama* has the meaning of a dramatically acted scene, and the *hypokritēs* has been completely transformed into a court clown. He also employs the generic term 'tragedy' (which the church fathers had still used with a broad spectrum of meanings) in two specific ways: as well as denoting a misfortune or a tragic event, it can also already refer to a song (*tragoudi*) or to sketches and jibes (VI 110, 9–15). The shift whereby 'tragedy' came to mean a 'song' (*tragoudi*) is already complete in the sixth century with Malalas (288. 10), and in ninth-century Arabic translations from the Greek.[31]

28 Nicolai (1867) 82, Hunger (1980) 10, Yatromanolakis (1990) 729ff.

29 Puchner (1997b) 313ff.; Walden (1892), Yatromanolakis (1990) 292, Krumbacher (1900) 485, Bibilakis (1996) 67–77.

30 Bibilakis (1996) 246ff.; Psellos *Chron.* 5. 3. 9–11, 6. 141. 9; Puchner (1997b) 320–1. The mime actor is also described as a 'liar' in the Syrian homily of Jacob of Sarug (1, 25, 100 and *passim*). See Crame (1980), Mass (1935), Frézouls (1959/61).

31 On the term *hypokritēs* see Puchner (1997b) 318–19. In the church fathers *tragōidia* can mean a dramatic work, a theatrical production, a story, the narration of a story, an intrigue, a trick, a plan, an heretical doctrine, torture, misfortune, jest and splendour. *Tragōideō* is used in the sense 'present' something, 'narrate', 'plunge into misfortune', 'describe', 'mock', 'reprimand' and 'prophesy'. *Ektragōideo* means 'present something dramatically', 'narrate in a tragic manner', 'lament with tears', 'sing', 'make something more tragic than it is'; *epitragōideō* means 'describe with exaggeration' *proektragōideō* means 'exaggerate like a tragic actor' (*tragikologia* means 'pathos' or 'bombast'); *tragōdēma* means 'song', 'tragic event' or 'heresy'; *tragōidos* signifies a tragic poet or actor (Bibilakis (1996) 264–300). For 'tragedy' = *tragoudi* see Daiber (1968) 46–7, Schmitt (1970) 197, 202, Niehoff-Panagiotidis (1996) 45ff. *Kōmōidia* and *kōmikos* are also common in the novel (Walden (1894) 41); in patristic texts 'comedy' means the work as well as the production of a comedy, any satire or ridicule, or a joyful event; *kōmōideō* means perform a comedy, have fun, curse, tell lies, reprimand, disapprove, condemn or describe; *kōmikos* can be either the poet or the actor of comedy as well as any ridiculous figure; in Epiphanios *kōmōidopoios* is used in reference to the heretic Manes (Bibilakis (1996) 147–73).

DIALOGUE, DRAMATICITY AND DRAMA

While Byzantine literature does not know any drama in the strict sense, it does display dramatic features across a number of different genres, and it also uses dialogue in the tradition of ancient rhetoric.[32] The *acta* in the hippodrome and at the synods already bore some resemblance to dialogue. These were rhythmic, formulaic, and often chanted, acclamations by the demes and factions, which were often answered in the same style by the heralds of the emperor. In this form, which was in some ways close to literature, one could take political decisions, fight out conflicts or attack individual persons.[33] The relevant material survives in the proceedings of the synods. It is close in character to antiphony and litany and is seen by some scholars as having links with theatre performances.[34] We cannot rule out the possibility that mime actors participated in these public dialogues in the hippodrome. Their role in the hippodrome probably went beyond that of mere entertainers during breaks between the races; in fact, there is one case in which their mini-dialogues can be shown to have had drastic political consequences;[35] after the sixth century, however, both the number of chariot races and the importance of the hippodrome and its factions went into decline.[36]

Elements of dialogue can be found in hymns, homilies and *kontakia* (sermons in verse).[37] Sathas collected the relevant material from the early Byzantine period, but these are not dramas, even though title and prologue sometimes invoke Euripides.[38] Antiphonal elements can be seen most clearly in hymns of Syrian origin, as for example the cycle of hymns on the birth of Christ written by the patriarch Sophronios (634–8), which Egon Wellesz compares with the Italian oratorios of the seventeenth century.[39]

[32] Voss (1970), Hoffmann (1966). On the *Christus patiens* see further below.

[33] E.g. the *Akta dia Kalopodion*, on which see Karlin-Hayter (1973), Irmscher (1970), Baldwin (1981). In general see Tillyard (1912), Maas (1912), Dvornik (1946), Browning (1952), Guilland (1956), Guilland and Paris (1957–70), especially (1968) 24–33, Cameron (1976).

[34] Sathas (1878) 169ff., 289ff., Cottas (1931 a), Solomos (1964) 131–64.

[35] The performance, presented by the emperor Theophilos in the ninth century, portrayed the trick played on a widow by the chamberlain Nikephoros. The chamberlain was immediately punished by being burnt at the stake.

[36] Mango (1981).

[37] For example in the *Praise of the Mother of God* by the patriarch Proclus (434–47, *PG* 65. 736ff.), which furnishes the main piece of evidence for La Piana's theory about dramatic homilies; Kirpičnikov (1892), La Piana (1912).

[38] Sathas (1878) 133ff.; see also Krumbacher (1897) 653. So, for example, in the text *On Free Will* by St Methodios (died 311); see Krumbacher (1897) 654–5.

[39] 'The Syro-Byzantine Nativity cycle was dramatic in the same sense as the Italian oratorio at the beginning of the seventeenth century; it was never intended for representation on the stage . . . It

Hans-Georg Beck has unearthed a delightful little scene in a mediocre Byzantine sermon which goes under the name of John Chrysostom. In this sermon on the Annunciation of Mary, the mother of God finds it hard to believe what the angel tells her about pure conception, while Joseph follows with interest the gradual expansion of his spouse's belly. It is likely that the scene, with its unexpectedly comical elements, harks back to a late Hellenistic mime which had as its theme an adulterous relationship, although whether such fragments of dramatic scenes were in fact read out as dialogue remains doubtful.[40] Remnants of similar scenes from mime are also found in the *Miracles of St Demetrius* and in *Theophanes Continuatus*, but there is no proof for Speck's suggestion that the *Quaestiones physicae* of Theophylact Simocatta and the *Verses on Adam* of Ignatius the Deacon (ninth century, *PG* 117. 1164–74) served as dialogue texts for a school-leaving party.[41] Dialogue and direct speech belong to the rhetorical devices of Byzantine *prosōpopoiia*.[42] The dialogue form survives in the didactic, edifying and panegyric literature of Byzantium down to its latest stages.[43]

Dramatic understanding, and a sensitivity to questions of scene setting, can also be detected in historiographical works, such as the *Alexiad* of Anna Comnena,[44] and especially in the *Chronographia* of Michael Psellos. Here the emperors are sometimes introduced as if they were actors, and

is interesting to note that the first movement towards the development of a mystery play occurs in the Eastern church at such an early date, and yet no attempt was made to develop the semi-dramatic form into an actual liturgy' (Wellesz (1947) 151). See also Baumstark (1923) 101 ff. and Mioni (1937) 27 on the hymns (*kontakia*) of Romanos Melodos. This view has been rejected by Byzantine scholars such as Tomadakis (1965) 126 and Mitsakis (1986), though the poems do of course contain elements of dialogue and dramatic effect.

40 *PG* 60. 756ff., Beck (1978) 113ff. Philologists have frequently underestimated the expressive resources of the solo mime performance, which has led, amongst other things, to the mistaken view that the *Mimiamboi* of Herodas were written for theatrical production; see Puchner (1993c) against Mastromarco (1984). See also Beck (1978) 115.

41 Speck (1996) 36 with references. An analysis of these dialogue texts from the perspective of theatre studies results in no compelling arguments for a theatrical production. For the text of the *Verses on Adam*, with brief notes, see Baldwin (1985) 134–41.

42 Dölger (1948) 14ff. In the *Verses on Adam* it is God, Adam, Eve and the snake who treat of the theme of inherited guilt in 143 lines of dodecasyllabic verse, each speaking three lines in turn. A dialogue of the same kind has Lazarus and the rich man as its theme; Sternbach (1897). In the *Dioptra* of Philip Monotropos there is a debate between body and soul; Beck (1959) 642ff., Hörandner (1964); in the *Dramation* of Michael Haplucheir (twelfth to thirteenth century) a farmer, a scholar, Tyche, the Muses and a chorus discuss the bad social position of the *sophos*; see the edition of Leone (1969) and also Hörandner (1972). The *Cat and Mouse Battle* is conceived as a parody of tragedy (Hunger 1969a), while the *Ethopoiia dramatike* functions as a panegyric on John Kantakouzenos (more examples in Hunger (1977–78) 146ff.).

43 For example, the *Idyll* of Maximus Planudes (Pontani (1973)) or the anonymous dialogue between the shepherds Xenophon and Philemon from the fifteenth century; Sturm (1901).

44 See the remarks of Reinsch (1996) 14.

the author himself participates in the episodes he describes, for example when Michael V is blinded.[45] History is seen as *drama*, as a dramatically presented story, and the historian as the narrator of events is a kind of director who arranges the action on the stage of world theatre in as effective a way as possible.[46] Psellos probably also wrote the short treatise *On Tragedy*, which, together with Tzetzes' *On Tragic Poetry* and *On Hypokrisis*, written by Eustathios, archbishop of Thessalonike, reflects the way in which ancient theatre was seen in the middle and late Byzantine eras.[47]

ACTORS IN EARLY BYZANTINE SPECTACLES

By early Byzantine times the dramatic art of antiquity had been transformed.[48] Comedies had been largely replaced by mimes, while tragedies were the province of the *tragōidos*, who performed excerpts from tragedy wearing a mask and standing on high *kothornoi*. Although he was lavishly dressed and surrounded by silent supporting actors, his art had more to do with vocal and rhetorical display than with theatre.[49] The pantomime required its actor to dance stories taken from tragedy, to the accompaniment of a chorus who sang popular songs. According to Stilpon Kyriakidis, these songs by minor poets represent the beginning of the modern Greek ballad, which is sung in verses of fifteen syllables.[50] The dances themselves were lascivious and erotic in character and emphasised the movement of the hands *(cheirosophistai)*. They were sharply attacked by the church fathers,[51] but defended by some contemporary intellectuals.[52] The genre probably dates back to the principate and perhaps to earlier times; it was common throughout the Greek east (see Jory, this volume, ch. 11).[53] The archbishop Arethas of Caesarea states in the ninth century, in a scholion to Lucian's treatise on dancing, that even in his time a dancer of pantomime was corrupting the young; it remains unclear, however, what exactly is meant here by

45 5. 38ff. See Puchner (1997b), Dyck (1994) 284ff.

46 The idea of history as a 'sequence of episodes on the stage of world theatre' is clearly expressed by Theodore Metochites (see Beck (1952) 96ff., 106–7).

47 Browning (1963), Perusino (1993), Dostálová (1982). The treatise follows Aristotle's *Poetics* closely, but shows an interesting preoccupation with melody, metre and dance ; Puchner (1997b) 297–8. Psellos also wrote a treatise comparing Euripides with George of Pisidia.

48 Müller (1909).

49 Theocharidis (1940) 61. See Hall, this volume, ch. 1.

50 This theory is based above all on two etymologies: the change from *tragōidia* to *tragoudi* and the derivation of *paralogē* ('ballad') from *parakatalogē* ('recitative').

51 For example by Chrysostom *PG* 6. 386. Cf. Kyriakidis (1978) 343, Sathas (1878) 209.

52 For example, in Lucian's treatise *On Dancing*, edited by Kokolakis (1959).

53 Pasquato (1976) 137–65.

'pantomime'.[54] One century earlier we read in the proceedings of the seventh Ecumenical Council that *orchēstika lygismata* were being displayed in the Iconoclast monasteries.[55] Dancing was often linked with heretical liturgies,[56] though the verdicts of the Council in Trullo (691/2), which were being copied as late as the eighteenth century, will have been decisive in banning the pantomime, as they were in many other respects. Lascivious bodily movements, gestures and songs are time and again prohibited, and public dancing and cross-dressing in particular are denounced as pagan customs well into late Byzantine times; sources associated with the church do not differentiate between pantomime, mime, popular forms of fancy dress, dances and songs.[57]

As a result, terms such as *mīmoi, skēnikoi, thymelikoi, mousikoi* and *orchēstai*, although covering a wide spectrum of persons and occupations, in combination seem to refer to an effeminate, unmanly, perverse, obscene and superficial group of people who sing, dance and put on fancy clothes and who imitate others unlike themselves. They indulge their perversion either on the occasion of pagan festivals or in order to earn a living. Because of their corrupt mores they are on a par with whores and pimps. While the early church attacked the pantomime on account of its lasciviousness and the eroticism of its dancing, in the case of the mime it was the primitive obscenity of the drama, with its stereotypical scenes of knockabout and adultery, which caused offence. Female actors stripping on stage, and Christological mimes which parodied the baptism, further contributed to the reputation of a genre of theatre which the church fathers roundly condemned as 'satanic'. Yet preachers had difficulties keeping the eager masses away from this kind of improvised popular theatre, which flourished in the cities (see Webb, this volume, ch. 13).[58]

Nothing has survived of the Byzantine mime, though some papyri found in Oxyrhynchus, and dating back to the first two centuries AD, may give a rough impression of what it could have looked like.[59] The only fragment that survives from the Byzantine period was found in Syria and should be dated to the fifth or sixth century AD.[60] The lack of papyrus finds may be due partly to the hostility of the church, but can also be explained

54 Rabe (1906) 190, Puchner (1983). 55 'Dancers' gyrations': see Kyriakidis (1978) 186.

56 Dölger (1934). 57 Puchner (1987), (1983).

58 Cf. Chrysostom's homily *Pros tous kataleipsantas tēn ekklēsian kai automolēsantas pros hippodromias kai ta theatra*, *PG* 56. 263–70.

59 Wiemken (1972).

60 Link (1904), Vogt (1931b) 623–40. On the existence of mime theatre in sixth-century Syria see also n. 30 above. Archaeological discoveries point in the same direction. See Segal (1985–88), (1987), Kloner (1988), Roueché, this volume, ch. 12.

by the fact that mimes were usually improvised. By contrast with the Roman mime, Greek mimes did not involve clubs, masks and phalloi; the *archimīmus* usually plays the *mōros phalakros* (*stupidus*, 'bald fool'), who is often beaten up by an aggressive character with long hair (see Roueché, this volume).[61] Central motifs of the plot usually include a scene of adultery, a scene where the adulterers are found out, and the verdict of a judge. As we can see from the *Apologia mimorum* of Choricius of Gaza, a fictitious court speech in defence of a 'difficult case', which was written in Palestine under Justinian,[62] the mimes included such characters as medical doctors, rhetors, adulterers, slaves (26), masters, shopkeepers, butchers, cooks, innkeepers, guests, advocates, toddlers, the young lover, the irascible man and the person who tries to appease him (110). The actor has to be a good speaker, for if he repeats himself or hesitates, he is hissed at even more than the rhetors. He must have a good memory and make his entrance onto the stage with confidence. Also important are the movements of the eyes, sweetness of voice and a talent for dancing (124–5). Many sources stress the lascivious dress and trappings of the mime actresses.[63] The Hellenistic theatres were adapted to mime performances by the erection of a wooden stage in the *orchēstra*.[64]

The ivory reliefs of the Consular Diptychs dating to the sixth century do not yield any clear evidence concerning the activity of mime actors.[65] Although they feature such scenes as circus games and performances of mimes and music, the pictures are too stylised to allow for detailed interpretation. Moreover, it is unlikely that the reliefs reproduce the actual celebrations which were held in honour of the new consul, given that diptychs of different date are identical in parts: such pieces were produced in the same style and with the same motifs down to the eleventh and twelfth centuries.[66] We may compare the largely static tradition which

[61] Reich (1903) 616ff., Stephanis (1986) 192–3, *PG* 57. 426 and 59. 28.

[62] Abel (1931), Litsas (1982), Stephanis (1986). Choricius is cited from the edition of Foerster-Richtsteig.

[63] E.g. St Pelagia in *PG* 116. 909B. The *Codex Theodosianus* XV. 7. 11 does not allow actresses to wear precious bracelets and silk dresses embroidered with gold. See Webb, this volume, ch. 13, and Usener (1879) 4, Reich (1903) 102, Traversari (1960), D'Ippolito (1962).

[64] Gregory of Nazianzus already uses the word *skēnē* for a wooden podium (Bibilakis (1996) 252). The same conclusion can be drawn from the *synaxarion* of the holy fool Symeon by Leontios of Neapolis (mid-sixth century Emesa). It reports a miracle in which Symeon wounds a mime by hurling a stone at him, then appears to him in his sleep and tells him that he will be healed as soon as he abjures the stage: text in Rydén (1963) 150.7–19. Cf. Reich (1903), Gelzer (1889), also Rydén (1970).

[65] Delbrueck (1929), Neiiendam (1992) 94–135.

[66] E.g. those held at Constantinople to celebrate the new consuls Anthemios in 515 and Anastasios in 517 (Volbach (1976) 35 no. 16 and 36 no. 20). Neiiendam (1992) 107 infers that the illustrations

Fig. 56 Diptych relief of Anastasios, consul in AD 517, showing scenes with actors (The State Hermitage Museum, St Petersburg)

led Balsamon in the twelfth century to copy the verdicts of the Council in Trullo (691/2). The consuls, who changed annually and whose task it was until AD 541 to regulate public spectacles, commissioned diptychs depicting animal hunts, circus games, mimes, musicians and so on.

The diptych reliefs of Anastasios, consul in 517, feature scenes with actors along with hunts and acrobatic performances.[67] One of the scenes seems to be a parody of the blessing of a child. The child is flanked by two bald mime actors who are tied up and are bitten on the nose by

followed the customary conventions of portrayal of the time, rather than deriving from specific sources (contra Grabar (1968) 245). For the later reliefs see Bank (1977) plates 130, 131, 134, 135; cf. plates 30, 31, 34.

[67] An example of the variety of possible interpretations is the large, masked figure on the lower level of a relief now in St Petersburg (fig. 56), who leans on a small boy and is interpreted by Bieber as the tragic character Teiresias (Bieber (1961) 251), while Green (1985) identifies him as a drunken figure from a comedy.

crabs.[68] We also find a dialogue scene with three actors, which has been interpreted as an episode from tragedy on the basis of such characteristic elements as the *onkos* and the *kothornos*.[69] Next to it we see a parodic healing scene which involves a bald male actor and an actress who provocatively turns to the audience (120–1). The dynamics of bodily movement attest to a primitive realism mixed with crude satire and erotic provocation: the healers pull at one of the blind man's eyelids, while the actress presents herself to the audience with one hand resting on her waist, thus indicating that she is swaying her hips. This may well be the sort of scene evoked by surviving papyrus fragments from Oxyrhynchus. The 'tragic' characters, too, are depicted in realistic ways, each adopting different sitting positions and gesticulating in a manner which allows their bodies to merge in a unified composition.

Performances of mimes were revue-like in character and featured either parodies of daily life (in the so-called 'biological' mime), travesties of myth ('mythological mime') or parodies of the baptism and other Christian rituals ('Christological' mime).[70] When the Christological mime was banned in 546 (*Cod. Just. Nov.* 123, 44), this must have been an important cause for the subsequent decline in dramatic performances. Another factor was Justinian's ban on the public funding of performances during the first years of his reign; in the fifth century we hear of four theatres at Constantinople, but in the sixth century not a single one is mentioned.[71] It is not clear to what extent mime and pantomime were still alive at the time when the 51st and 62nd canons of the Council in Trullo (691/2) enforced the decisive ban, which affected the performances of mime, hunting spectacles, and dancing in the theatre. Despite all restrictions the mime as such had not been illegal until then.[72] After this point it can only be shown to exist in the primitive form of *ioculatores* and *histriones*, who make their appearances in the hippodrome and at the imperial court.

[68] The remains of this relief, which was damaged during the French Revolution, can be reconstructed from a copperplate engraving made in the seventeenth century (Wilthemius (1659)). See Neiiendam plates 40 and 41.

[69] Neiiendam (1992) 119–20.

[70] Reich (1903) 616ff.

[71] Proclus, *Anecdota* 26.8ff. and 59.8ff. ed. Haury; Mango (1981) 341–4, 352.

[72] Rallis and Potlis (1852–56) vol. II, 301–554, Nedungatt and Featherstone (1995) 41–186. On the ban, which concerned shows and costumes, see Tinnefeld (1974), Constantelos (1970), Rochow (1978), esp. 492ff., Magulias (1971), Franceschini (1995), Andrescu (1961) and Mango (1981) 344: 'The mime and the pantomime may have lingered on until the end of the 7th century when they were banned by Canon 51 of the Trullan Council. Does this mean that they were still widespread at the time? The answer is not clear, especially in view of the fact that the same canon also prohibits τὰ τῶν κυνηγίων θεώρια [hunting spectacles] which were, almost certainly, extinct. I know, however, of no clear-cut evidence that would indicate the presence of a theatre in the Byzantine Empire at a later date, apart from the occasional performance given by mummers.'

Texts on ecclesiastical law, such as the synodal commentaries of Zonaras and Balsamon and the edicts of Chomatianos from middle and late Byzantine times, deal with popular masquerades, low-brow farces and pantomimes put on by minor clerics, masked processions of schoolchildren in Constantinople, carnivalesque sketches at the imperial court and a form of carnival celebrated by the church.[73] We should not try to reconstruct a continuous tradition of mime theatre lasting till the fall of Constantinople on the basis of popular masquerades and martial dances such as the 'Gothic Christmas play' (*Gotthikon*, tenth century); nor can the mime be used to explain the origins of the Commedia dell'arte or the Ottoman shadow play.[74] The very repetitiveness of our sources is telling: when Balsamon in the twelfth century talks about comic, tragic and satyric masks and mentions Aristophanes and Euripides, he is displaying his learning rather than referring to any real performances.[75] The language of the synodal verdicts is still alive in the eighteenth century: in 1765, a Greek law-book from Bucharest quotes the 62nd canon of the Council in Trullo in order to stop a public dance by women from taking place as part of the 'paparuda', a ritual processional rain-dance.[76]

CHRIST AND MARY AS STAGE CHARACTERS?

Until very recently the *Christus patiens* was regarded as 'la tragédie chrétienne par excellence'.[77] Although it has usually been attributed to the Greek church father Gregory of Nazianzus the controversy about the authorship and date of this *cento* poem in dialogue form has been exceptionally long and heated.[78] With its 2,531 verses the poem is one of the longest surviving *centos*, borrowing from ancient Greek tragedy (especially Euripides), the Old and New Testaments and the Apocrypha.[79] Its plot centres around a *planctus Mariae* (Lament of the Virgin) in dialogue form,[80] featuring Mary, Christ, John, Mary Magdalene, Nicodemus,

73 Tinnefeld (1974), Puchner (1981/82) 198–205, Kyriakis (1973), Pitsakis (1996), Puchner (1997a) 34, 106–7, Mango (1981) 351.

74 Reich (1903) 616ff., Vogt (1931b), Cottas (1931a) 29–52, Solomos (1964) 15ff., Ljubarskij (1987). On this error in theatre history see Puchner (1997a) 34, 106–7. The thesis that the Byzantine mime lies behind later genres of theatre has been absorbed from Turkish theatre history (And (1951), (1962), criticised by Puchner (1975) 20ff.) as well as from comparative folklore studies (Liungman (1937), Kakouri (1963)).

75 Rallis and Potlis (1852–56) vol. II, 449–50.

76 Zepos (1959), Puchner (1981/82), (1983).

77 Tuilier (1969) 19.

78 Sakkalis (1977), Trisoglio (1996), (1974), Puchner (1993a) 93–4 n. 4.

79 Hunger (1977–78) 102ff., Pollmann (1997).

80 Alexiou (1974) 64–5 and (1975).

Joseph of Arimathea and other speaking characters as well as a chorus which participates in the dialogue and messenger speeches. There are hints of a *teichoskopia* ('viewing from the walls') and additional scenes in which Mary takes centre stage, as well as two scenes featuring the high priest, Pilate and soldiers, which are inserted into a messenger speech and do not involve Mary (2270–94, 2295–377; in these passages the messenger speech changes into staged episodes in direct speech). The *planctus Mariae* of the beginning thus develops into a passion and resurrection play towards the end of the text.[81]

An analysis informed by theatre studies could easily show that the poet is unaware of what it means to stage a play, though he does imitate the dramatic conventions of ancient theatre. He confuses *teichoskopia* and messenger speech, inserts acted scenes into a messenger speech and fails to mark the points in the action at which characters enter and leave the stage. Christ appears several times after his resurrection, acting out the contradictory narratives of all four evangelists. The poet is more concerned with quoting all relevant passages than with producing a unified dramatic plot. Narrated off-stage action often contradicts the on-stage action seen by the audience, particularly after the resurrection. The poem is neither a tragedy meant for production in a theatre nor any other form of drama. Rather, it is a *cento* in dialogue form, which uses quotations from tragedy and imitates some of the dramatic conventions of tragedy without fully understanding their implications. Such a product is more at home in middle Byzantium than in earlier times. Moreover, when Christ is crucified, when his cross is taken by Simon, or when he is lamented, these scenes follow iconographic types which only emerged after the period of Iconoclasm as part of the middle Byzantine iconographical programmes of the passion.[82] The long series of curses which Mary pronounces against Judas points in the same direction. They go better with the more anthropocentric medieval attitudes to Christ and Mary which arose after the era of Iconoclasm than with the high spirituality of the early Christian church. We have thus gained fresh arguments for ascribing to the poem a relatively late date. Since the *cento* quotations presuppose an educated audience, we may think of the schools and scholars of Constantinople in the eleventh or twelfth centuries.[83] The

81 Puchner (1993a) 96ff.

82 Puchner (1993a) 127–34. The *Christus patiens* will hardly have influenced iconography in turn, as is argued by Cottas (1931b): Byzantine sacred painting was too much bound to church doctrine. This also applies to the early Gothic western church (Puchner 1979). See also Puchner (1991).

83 de Aldama (1972), Dostálová (1982), Hörandner (1988).

story of Christ's passion and resurrection as the most sacred 'plot' is dressed up in the language of tragedy as the most beautiful language of the world by the standards of the time. That time did not realise that the result was not a tragedy, despite the reference to Euripides in the prologue and the colophon which assures us that the drama's content is 'true and not invented'.[84]

Another *cento* that stages Mary and Christ is the Cyprus passion cycle. It was composed on Cyprus before 1320, under the rule of the Lusignans, possibly by Konstantinos Euteles Anagnostes.[85] The play is once again of great importance to the debates about Byzantine theatre. It includes a prologue which is addressed to the director of the performance,[86] as well as ten episodes: the awakening of Lazarus, the arrival in Jerusalem, the meal at the house of Peter, the washing of the feet, the treachery, Peter's denial that he is one of the apostles, the humiliation before Herod, the crucifixion, the resurrection, and the touching of the wounds. The episodes generally adhere to the Orthodox Easter cycle from the Saturday before Easter (Lazarus) to the Sunday after (doubting Thomas). They quote the opening words of passages from the Bible and some apocryphal scriptures, and add stage directions in the imperative.

While earlier scholars believed that this scenario is a typical representative of the Byzantine passion play, more recent scholarship stresses that the text stands completely isolated within Byzantine literature; it would seem obvious to assume that we have here a Greek counterpart to the Latin passion play, which came into being under the Lusignans, who adopted western etiquette and maintained close links with France.[87] However, a major difficulty with this theory has been that a western model on this scale is not yet known from the beginning of the fourteenth century; the only possible candidate is the twelfth-century passion play from Monte Cassino, which has a different set of episodes.[88]

Speculation about performances of the Cyprus passion play has centred around the prologue, in which the director is asked to prepare the props, select the actors and ensure that they speak their lines without making mistakes, interrupting each other or provoking laughter. While

84 See further Puchner (1993a) 142–3.

85 Lampros (1916), Vogt (1931b) 37–74; Mahr (1947) restores the *incipit* passages and provides an English translation; author and date are discussed in Baud-Bovy (1938), (1975), Turyn (1964) 117–24, Puchner (1986).

86 Carpenter (1936).

87 See Papadopoulos (1925) 48. On the uniqueness of this work see Baud-Bovy (1938) 322 and Beck (1971) 112.

88 Mahr (1942), (1947) 15ff.; Inguanez (1939), Sticca (1970), Baud-Bovy (1975).

M. Carpenter believes that there was a tradition of mime performances among the crusaders on Cyprus, C. A. Mahr sees the play in the tradition of the Byzantine mime.[89] However, similar prologues are known from the west – for example, the Norman *Jeu d'Adam* (twelfth century) – where the actors involved were clearly non-professionals.[90] A closer analysis of the text from the perspective of theatre studies leads to the conclusion that the text as we have it is unlikely to have served as a script for actual perfomances. First, the play would have involved an enormous cast, including six male and three female protagonists and nine male and two female supporting actors, making forty or fifty actors counting the group of Jews and the children who are present at Christ's arrival in Jerusalem. Moreover, the play involves at least ten different settings, and each episode is made up of two or three parallel actions each requiring a different stage arrangement. More importantly, although the rubrics of the *cento* are phrased in the imperative and addressed to the director, they do not function as stage directions in the usual sense. Rather, they are mere quotations from the Bible transposed into the imperative: although ostensibly there to direct the action on stage, they do not do much to clarify the manifold activities that it involves.[91] Thirdly, the description of stage paintings and props follows the conventions of the iconographic programmes of the *middle* Byzantine period. Mahr adduces in support of his argument the 'Painter's book from the sacred mountain' of Dionysios Phournas,[92] a post-Byzantine compilation which shows traces of western influence. It would be more to the point to study the iconographic programmes of Cypriot churches before 1320.

Thus we are left with a first attempt at writing a passion play suited to an Orthodox context. The experiment was probably inspired by western models. A later attempt in a similar vein is attested on Patmos, where the episode of the washing of the feet, performed on Maundy Thursday,

89 Carpenter (1936) 37ff., Mahr (1947) 15ff. and 82–3: 'Interrupting and cutting-in, no less than improvising, seem to have been habits of the routine actors of mime . . . Apart from the general difficulty in acting out the most sacred events of biblical history before an audience to whom "going to the theatre" was inevitably associated with "laughing," several scenes of the play were potential sources of hilarity in that there existed parallel situations in stock plays of the mime.'

90 Puchner (1984b) 189–90, nn. 136–7.

91 The 'scenic dysfunctionality' and narrativity of the rubrics are not unknown to the medieval western theatre. Compare the *Ludus breviter* or the *Ludus de Passione* from the monastery at Benediktbeuren, which are similar in their thematic structure to the Cypriot passion cycle. In the case of these works contemporary scholarship assumes that the stage directions may have been chanted by an 'Evangelist'. See Noomen (1958), Nagler (1976) 5, Greisenegger (1978) 229ff., Roeder (1974) 24ff.

92 Mahr (1947), Schäfer (1855).

employs a similar compilation of passages from the Bible. It charts the events of the passion up to the moment when Christ is arrested.[93] It is doubtful whether we should link the passion cycle from Cyprus with the long allegorical play (*repraesentatio figurata*) of the presentation of Mary in the temple which Philippe de Mézière put on at Avignon in 1372; Philippe had surely not seen this play during his stay in Cyprus in 1360–68, but composed it himself in order to introduce the Orthodox festival of the presentation of Mary to the west.[94]

'ACTING' IN A CULTURE WITHOUT ORGANISED THEATRE FORMS

It is certainly difficult to imagine that such a long-lived civilisation as that of Byzantium, a civilisation, moreover, which saw itself as the heir of antiquity, could do without any organised form of theatre. This thought becomes even more troublesome when we consider that modern drama started to develop in the Latin west from the ninth and tenth centuries onwards. Christian liturgy provided the starting-point, and it was the western development from the 'liturgical scene' to more complex forms of theatre which time and again led scholars to go in search of a comparable 'church play' in Byzantium.[95] This is why art historians developed theories about the survival of the Roman *scaenae frons* in the Orthodox picture wall (*eikonostasion, templum*), which separates the *naos* (main body of the church) from the sanctuary in the apse.[96] And this is also the reason why scholars have speculated about the influence of the Byzantine church play on book illustrations such as the ones we find in the apocryphal life of Mary by James of Kokkinobaphos.[97] Finally, it has also been argued that church drama influenced Byzantine mosaic frescoes.[98] Liutprand of Cremona is already said in the tenth century to have seen a church play on the apotheosis of Elijah, and later, in the fifteenth century, Bertrandon de la Broquière may have attended a play on the three boys in the furnace; these pieces of information are, however, of doubtful value.[99]

93 Puchner (1977) 319–31 lists the relevant literature and offers a German translation.

94 See Young (1933) vol. II, 244ff., La Piana (1955), Puchner (1993b).

95 On the concepts of 'development' and 'liturgical scene' with reference to the medieval religious theatre see Puchner (1991) 9ff., 12ff.

96 Holl (1906), Schneider (1939) 205ff., Schulz (1959) 62, Kalokyris (1976), (1980) against Felicetti-Liebenfels (1956) 73ff.

97 Bréhier (1913), (1920); contra Lafontaine-Dosogne (1964/65) vol. I, 197–8 and Hutter (1970) 202ff.

98 Stričević (1967), Guldau (1966) 165.

99 Baud-Bovy (1975) 330ff., Puchner (1981/82) 235ff.

Other liturgical scenes such as the awakening of Lazarus from Larnaka or the washing of the feet from Patmos are attested in modern times; but their present 'theatrical' character cannot be traced back to the Byzantine era.[100] The only exception is the rite of *arate pulas, tollite portas*, which enacts the defeat of the gates of hell, very much like the Anastasis icon, the canonical Easter image of the Orthodox church; this rite has been used in the consecration of church buildings from the sixth century onwards.[101] Ritual actions of a symbolic character are also important at other points in the liturgy, such the Descent from the Cross and the Finding of the True Cross on the 14th of September; but only the Descent into Hell at the closed church door, which involves the singing of Psalm 24.7–10 in dialogue, can be regarded as theatre in the wider sense.[102] Here the priest acts the role of Christ for the duration of the psalmodic dialogue, while the deacon plays Satan behind the closed church door. In the meantime, the congregation of believers turns into an audience. From an historical perspective we might call this scene the potential starting-point of a development (which never actually took place) towards the passion play. In the west this development eventually led to the scenes from hell of late medieval times, while in the Byzantine world liturgical 'drama' never lost its character of purely symbolic action.[103]

At this point, the significant question arises of why Byzantium never developed any theatrical forms in the proper sense. It cannot be answered simply with reference to the church fathers' revulsion from the shallow performances of their time or from the pagan origins of the theatre. Rather, the question is in important ways a theological one and as such is closely linked to the phenomenon of Iconoclasm. The ban on pictures which Iconoclasm brought about implied a double ban on theatre. The Third Commandment, proscribing graven images, concerns any form of representation; the medieval religious theatre of the Latin west was in its early stages closely linked with the pictorial language of iconography. When the seventh Ecumenical Council reintroduced the worship of icons, it was subject to a decisive dogmatic restriction, as formulated in the theology of images of St John of Damascus: John closely linked

[100] Puchner (1977) 313–31, (1981/82) 239ff. [101] Puchner (1979), Stiefenhofer (1909) 91.

[102] There is much more extensive bibliography in Puchner (1988) 71–126. This definition of the theatrical situation, which is widely used in theatre scholarship, follows Bentley (1965): a 'communication situation' can be understood as 'theatrical' when person A impersonates person B, while person C watches.

[103] Puchner (1979).

representation to original. The icon was now at the same level as the prototype; it was seen as a sacred object endowed with the power to bestow blessings. As a result, it was radically limited in content and form, a fact which led to the rise of the painters' books.[104] The icon is worshipped – and kissed – as a venerable token of sacred presence. Because it is a mirror image of the transcendental real world, it cannot be produced by human beings for the purpose of educating others in the Christian faith as was done in the Latin church of the west.[105] The deeply symbolic character of the sacred sphere does not allow for the 'materialistic' and 'realistic' tendencies which form the basis of a developed theatre. For human beings to represent the contents of the icon would already mean a desecration of these contents.

In the west, the desire to achieve a more 'vivid' representation of sacred truths provided the basis for the development of religious theatre. This desire was not shared by the eastern church. In fact the outrage which western practices caused among Byzantine observers at the Council of Florence in 1438/9 shows just how divided opinion was. On the occasion of the festival of St John the Baptist, processions took place featuring statues and *tableaux vivants*, which prompted the horrified Byzantine spectators to speak of 'monstrous' miracle plays[106] The same reaction to the obscene and senseless activities of the 'Latins', who allowed human beings to represent holy persons and moments, can be seen in the *Dialogus contra haereses* of Symeon, archbishop of Thessalonike.[107]

No room was left for the development of less restricted forms of representation by the eastern theology of images and the strict harmonisation of all aspects of the Byzantine liturgy.[108] Thus it is misleading to compare the Byzantine liturgy with 'theatre' even in a metaphorical sense. Of course it does contain elements of representation, just as we encounter such elements in courtly etiquette, among jugglers and other performers, or in parodies and fancy dressing on the part of laymen and clerics. But there simply was no organised theatre in the middle Byzantine period. The ban on theatre performances had already preceded the Iconoclasts' ban on images as formulated in the verdicts of the councils. After the times of Iconoclasm, any form of pictorial representation was strictly

[104] Onasch (1967), Ouspensky (1980), Belting (1991) 11 ff.

[105] On the early development of the Latin medieval religious theatre see Drumbl (1981), Schnusenberg (1981).

[106] Pontani (1994) 798ff.

[107] Ch. 23, *PG* 155. 112A–116D (Italian translation in Pontani (1994) 806ff.).

[108] Puchner (1991) 116–17.

controlled by theological doctrine. In the era of the church fathers the 'actor' had already become a sacrilegious 'hypocrite' in the light of the divine truth, someone whose aim it was to defile the 'image of God' which the creator had destined man to be. By the third and fourth centuries AD the ancient art of drama had already become amoral fiction and sacrilege.

PART THREE

The idea of the actor

CHAPTER FIFTEEN

Actor as icon

Pat Easterling

In contemporary English the rather pretentious metaphor 'icon' is steadily taking the place of 'star' (and the older 'idol') as a way of designating performers and others in the public eye – rock musicians, screen actors, footballers, models, princesses – who have an exceptionally magnetic appeal for audiences. What all who achieve iconic status have in common is the extreme seductiveness of their glamour, which depends as much on charisma and physical presence as on particular virtuoso skills. There is no reason, of course, to see this as a purely modern phenomenon: although television and newspaper images can magnify iconic status they hardly create it out of nothing. There may be some value, then, in trying to identify the kinds of charismatic appeal and symbolic function associated with the most popular actors of antiquity, starting from the time – the fourth century BC – when actors became a recognisable category of professionals in the Greek-speaking world.

THE EVIDENCE

There is plenty of evidence from paintings and inscriptions as well as literary texts, though at this distance it is hardly ever easy to identify individuals with certainty or to check the reliability of anecdotes.

Some vase- and wall-paintings, for example, strongly suggest the appeal of famous individual performers, although as a rule we can no longer recover their names. The fact that actors wore masks that completely covered their heads, and more often than not played more than one role in a single performance, certainly cannot have prevented them from being identified: it would be hard, otherwise, to explain why a prize was instituted in 449 BC for the best actor at the Athenian City Dionysia, and why the idea caught on at festivals elsewhere. In any case, there were actors who made their greatest impact through their magnificent voices, like Theodoros, singled out by Aristotle[1] for his extraordinary vocal versatility, and there were others whose physique or special skills made them easily identifiable, like Timotheos of Zakynthos, who was so good at acting the scene of Ajax's suicide that he was given the nickname *Sphageus* ('Slayer').[2]

Three samples from the fourth century BC will illustrate the visual impact of the great performer. One is the famous vase made in Taranto (ancient Taras) in *c.* 340, now in Würzburg,[3] showing an actor holding his mask (fig. 16; this – now anonymous – player has appeared on the front cover of four recent books[4] on Greek drama); another (fig. 57) is the near-contemporary calyx-crater, also from Taranto, now in a private collection in New York, which shows a generic *paidagōgos* figure, one of a series collected and discussed by Richard Green (1996 and 1999),[5] who emphasises the recognisability of the old servant or messenger as the popular intermediary between the world of the heroes and that of the audience. Green also suggests[6] that it was the lead actors who commandeered this sort of part, and we might guess that the picture was specifically recognisable, as representing 'Actor X' in one of his prize-winning roles. In the National Museum at Naples there is a wall-painting from Herculaneum which appears to be a copy of a Greek model dating to *c.* 300 BC.[7] This (fig. 58) shows an actor holding a sceptre, with a purple cloak draped over his knees and a sword resting on it; there are two respectful people at his side, one of them a young woman (or allegorical figure) kneeling and writing an inscription below his tragic

[1] *Rhet.* 3.1404b22; cf. *Rhet.* 3.1403b31 (performers who pay attention to the voice 'nearly always win the prizes in contests'); *Pol.* 7.1336b28: 'Theodoros, the tragic actor, did not allow anyone, not even one of the minor actors, to enter before he did, because the spectators grew attached to the voices they heard first.' (Theodoros = Stephanis (1988) 1157.) Cf. Csapo, this volume, ch. 5, p. 138.

[2] Schol. on Soph. *Aj.* 864: '. . . the impression must be given that he falls on his sword, and the actor must be a strong one (*karteron tina*) so as to compel the spectators to imagine Ajax (doing this). Timotheos of Zakynthos has this reputation, because his acting had a compelling and captivating effect on the spectators, and he was given the name Slayer.' (Stephanis (1988) 2416, where Timotheos is dated fifth–fourth century BC on the ground that the nickname – from the opening line of the suicide speech (*Aj.* 815) – may have been given him in a comedy.)

[3] Martin von Wagner Museum, inv. H 4600.

[4] Csapo and Slater (1995); Easterling (1997a); Pelling (1997a); Albini (1999).

[5] Details in Green (1999) cat. 45.

[6] Green (1996) 29; (1999) 53–4: 'To show a *paidagogos* on his own has its point. He is recognisable. He is a key player.' Green cites two other examples of the figure on his own: one (cat. 44) in the Department of the Classics at Harvard, the other (cat. 36, fig. 2) at Ruvo (Museo Nazionale 1394).

[7] Naples, National Museum no. 9019.

Fig. 57 Actor in the role of *paidagōgos* (Photo courtesy W. Puhze)

mask, which has been set up as a votive offering. The actor himself has been described as 'a matinée idol, handsome, tall and slim with delicate hands and hair elegantly ruffled';[8] evidently the scene represents the prize-winner in costume, dedicating his mask after his victory, and its celebratory function is unmistakable.

Another type of visual record that was particularly popular from the fourth century onwards was the terracotta figurine that could be bought

[8] By John Gould, *CHCL* vol. I, 278.

Fig. 58 Prize-winning actor in tragic costume dedicating his mask (Photo courtesy of the Mansell Collection)

as a souvenir of a dramatic show. Large numbers of these survive, often representing the stock characters in Athenian comedy, and their distribution all over the Greek world shows how much they were in demand.[9] These cheerful little figures are standardised rather than individual, representing the familiar roles in a typical comedy: slaves, nurses, cooks, *hetairai* and so on, but it is at least possible that some of their poses and gestures were originally modelled on those of famous actors,

[9] See Green and Handley (2001) 59–67 for discussion and illustrations; also figs. 24–9 (ch. 4 above). Cf. Garton (1972b) 31, 157.

capturing something that – for a few years at any rate – spectators who had seen a particular great performer might instantly have recognised.

This, of course, can be no more than a guess: the figurines carry no names, and their function is precisely to be generic. Inscriptions, on the other hand, are concerned with the naming of individuals, and they give us victors and dedicators, corroborating evidence from literary sources which suggests that some actors became both extremely famous and extremely rich.[10] Some measure of this distinction can be gauged from such texts as the record of donations for the rebuilding of the Temple of Apollo at Delphi, to which the tragic actor Theodoros of Athens contributed seventy drachmas (*FD* III 5.3.67, 362 BC). As Csapo and Slater point out,[11] this goes way beyond any other private contribution: no one else gave more than fifteen drachmas. Demosthenes (18.114) notes that another famous tragic actor, Neoptolemos, was honoured by the Athenians for his donations when overseer of public works, a service that only a wealthy member of the community could perform.[12]

The combined evidence of inscriptions and literary sources gives the impression that there were several institutional developments crucial to the growth in the prestige and earning power of actors. One of these must have been the opportunity to win cash prizes, and another the development of a competitive market for touring performers. This seems to have entailed deals in which cities intent on hiring particularly sought-after actors provided financial advances to secure them and conversely levied fines if they broke their contract.[13] There is a recurrent anecdote about a conversation between an actor and Demosthenes, in which the orator trumps the actor's boast by saying he was paid more to keep silent than the vast sum – a talent – earned by the actor for appearing in a single competition; the fact that it is variously attributed to Aristodemos, Polos and an unnamed tragic actor on the one hand, and to Demosthenes and Demades on the other[14] does not detract from its usefulness as evidence that the real stars were imagined to earn exceptional fees.

But the stars, though outstanding, were not isolated from networks that enabled them to move effectively round what seems to have rapidly

10 See Mette (1977); Stephanis (1988); Csapo and Slater (1995) especially 221–38; Easterling (1997a) 215–17.

11 Csapo and Slater (1995) 237.

12 Cf. Athenaeus 11.472C, which mentions the dedication by Neoptolemos of gold-plated cups on the Acropolis (Stephanis (1988) 1797).

13 Aeschines 2.19 with schol.; Csapo and Slater (1995) 234–5.

14 Aristodemos/Demosthenes: Aulus Gellius 11.9.2; Polos/Demosthenes [Plut.] *Lives of the Ten Orators* 848B; anon./Demades: Aulus Gellius 11.10.6.

become a circuit.[15] Even in the fifth century, when acting was not yet fully professional, much seems to have depended on the build-up of expertise by theatrical families,[16] and as touring became more and more a feature of the actor's life it became ever more important to have wide-ranging contacts and experience. One of the significant dates in theatre history known from the inscriptional record[17] is 386 BC, when an official contest in revived 'old' tragedies was instituted at the City Dionysia, in acknowledgement, no doubt, of the importance of the actors' troupes, now specifically identified with the protagonists, who took directorial and managerial responsibility for putting on these plays as well as acting in them. It took only a few generations for the more or less informal groupings of theatrical performers to turn themselves into the Artists of Dionysus, with their extraordinary networks of organisation beyond the bounds of any single polis.[18]

The literary sources vary greatly in date and reliability, as one might expect, but they are unanimous in associating leading actors with the patronage of the powerful – Sicilian tyrants as early as Hieron in the fifth century, Macedonian kings, the Ptolemies, Roman generals and (in due course) emperors.[19] Winning the admiration and lavish gifts of monarchs must have been an indicator of success in the sphere of theatrical performance; and with more and more emphasis on the performer as soloist (see Hall, this volume, ch. 1) the range of contexts for performance became wider: reciting, and particularly singing, after dinner in front of the patron's guests was something now for professionals as well as for amateurs.[20] It cannot have been an accident, either, that in the fourth century BC, which saw particularly rapid gains in the fame and influence of the most charismatic actors, the art for which they were most admired, that of speaking compellingly to audiences of all kinds, was equally prized in the sphere of politics and diplomacy.[21] Nor is it surprising that Demosthenes and Aeschines have so much to say about actors[22] or that the anecdotal tradition regularly associates actors with

[15] See most recently Taplin (1999).
[16] For family networks at Athens see Sutton (1987); for later times Chaniotis (1990) 94, with n. 25.
[17] *TrGF* I DID A201–3 (= *IG* II^2 2318). [18] Cf. Lightfoot, this volume, ch. 9.
[19] For sources see e.g. Csapo and Slater (1995) 231–55; Garton (1972b).
[20] Cf. Jones (1991).
[21] Aristodemos and Neoptolemos, for example, evidently acted as spokesmen to the Athenians on Philip's behalf: Aeschines 2.15–19; Demosthenes 19.12, 18, 94, 315. In *On the Peace* Demosthenes criticises the Athenians for taking more notice of Neoptolemos than of himself in a political debate, as if they were watching tragic actors at the Dionysia (5.7).
[22] Cf. Easterling (1999).

famous orators. Thus Andronikos, Neoptolemos and Satyros were all alleged to have been Demosthenes' teachers.[23]

A measure of the prestige of theatrical performers throughout antiquity is the sheer number of stories about them that still survive, in spite of the filtering effect of time and the more or less total loss of a large body of writing on theatre history, by authors like the scholarly king Juba II of Mauretania (late first century BC), Amarantus of Alexandria (first–second centuries AD), Rufus (date uncertain), whose works on dramatic and musical history were excerpted by Sopater (fourth century AD) and summarised in turn by Photius in the ninth century.[24] Photius' account (*Bibl.* 103a) of what Rufus wrote about is telling: 'the different doings and sayings of tragic and comic actors, and the fame of musical composers and performers, both male and female, including an indication of which ones were lovers and friends of kings'. Clearly there was plenty of gossip about the famous in compilations of this sort; as with the life-histories of poets, lawgivers, or philosophers, the anecdotal tradition took on many of the characteristics of fiction, especially the stereotyped story patterns relating to the noteworthy births or deaths of famous people, their memorable sayings, or even sometimes their encounters with helpful animals, a sign of special favour.[25]

SYMBOLIC FUNCTIONS

For our purposes the truth value of ancedotes about actors is not as important as the frequency and durability of these stories. What comes out very clearly is that a few outstanding individuals not only made their mark in their own time but were remembered as paradigmatic figures for centuries afterwards; a couple – Neoptolemos and Polos – even found their way into Stobaeus' *Florilegium*,[26] which guaranteed them canonical status along with many of the most famous people of the Greek world. A handful of others from the fourth century were in nearly the same league: Aristodemos, Athenodoros, Theodoros and Thettalos for tragedy and Kallippides, Nikostratos, Satyros, Philemon and Lykon for comedy.[27]

[23] Andronikos: [Plut.] *Lives of the Ten Orators* 845A–B; Neoptolemos: ibid. 844F.; Satyros: Plut. *Dem.* 27. See Hall, ch. 20 below, with fig. 60.

[24] For Juba and Amarantus see Athenaeus 8.343e–f and 10.414e; for Juba, Rufus and Sopater see Photius, *Bibl.* 103a.

[25] Cf. Fairweather (1974). Cicero *Div.* 1.79 relates a story analogous to that of Pindar and the bees about the infant Roscius' encounter with a snake; cf. Horace *Odes* 3.4.9–20.

[26] 4.34.70, 4.33.28.

[27] For the evidence see the entries in Stephanis (1988).

In later times at Rome Roscius achieved a degree of fame that made him the most celebrated actor of all antiquity,[28] while the pantomime actors Pylades and Bathyllus founded an overwhelmingly influential new genre which was so strongly associated with these two performers that the names Pylades and Bathyllus were adopted by their successors in later generations.[29]

This celebrity must be seen against the background of the growing theatricality of public life, recently documented for the Hellenistic period by Angelos Chaniotis,[30] who points to the development of what he calls a 'culture of onlookers', in which activities in the agora and the gymnasium as well as in the theatre, and events in the assembly and other public contexts, were seen more and more 'as a performance and a spectacle' to be carefully orchestrated by those who wished to exert influence. When political leaders employed professionals to perform roles in public rituals the actors were effectively displacing ordinary citizens, who in the past would have participated directly in festival events. An interesting example of the crossover between theatre and public life is the celebration of a ruler as a New Dionysus, with actors in the costume of his worshippers, attested for Demetrius Poliorcetes, and later for Antony at Ephesus and Alexandria.[31] It is not surprising that the language acquired a great many metaphors from acting and the stage, and the aesthetics of theatrical performance shaped artistic sensibility. All these developments must have had an effect on the way later writers like Plutarch and Diodorus looked at stories of famous actors of the past, but it would be unduly severe not to use them when trying to imagine how these actors were received in their own time.

We can in fact learn something of the impact of the individual performer from stories of public figures more or less consciously using the actor as a model for their own self-presentation (there may be a modern analogy here with politicians' use of television). Plutarch describes how Demetrius Poliorcetes took control of Athens after a siege in 294: the theatre was where he showed himself to the terrified people. He surrounded the stage building and the stage itself with armed men, and then he 'came down as the tragic actors do through (one of) the upper side entrances' (*Life of Demetrius* 34).[32] The solitary figure making

[28] Garton (1972a). [29] Bonaria (1959).
[30] Chaniotis (1997), especially 238–54; the quotations are from p. 252. Cf. Le Guen (1995).
[31] Chaniotis (1997) 241–2. The great procession of Ptolemy II at Alexandria had strong Dionysiac colouring.
[32] Cf. Chaniotis (1997) 238–9.

a dramatic entrance to capture the audience's attention and work on their emotions recalls Diodorus' account of Philip at Aegae: 'At daybreak the procession began. Philip's display was lavish in all its details, including statues of the twelve gods . . . decorated with dazzlingly rich adornment. Along with these a thirteenth statue was paraded, representing Philip himself in a style befitting a god – so the king displayed himself as a throned companion of the twelve gods. When the theatre was full Philip came in wearing a white cloak . . .' (16.92–3). There the theatrical gesture misfired: Philip had told his bodyguard to stand back for his solo entrance, and this gave the assassin his chance. Another passage in Plutarch suggests less studied theatrical effect. This comes in the *Life* of Aratus of Sicyon, the great champion of Greek unity. In 243 he and his men captured Acrocorinth from the Macedonian garrison by a daring night stratagem; when it was over, Aratus came into the theatre before a rapturous crowd, still wearing his breastplate and completely exhausted by the fighting. For a long time he stayed silent, then made a triumphant speech of liberation and gave the citizens the keys of the citadel (*Life of Aratus* 23).[33]

However significant the trend towards the staging (or manipulating) of public feeling on public occasions, it is still important not to underestimate the capacity of the dramatic festivals, the plays – or the recitals – put on at them, and most of all the performers themselves, to exercise a powerful imaginative appeal of their own. Take the famous story about the tragic actor Polos, who used the ashes of his dead son when he played Sophocles' Electra making her great speech over the urn.[34] This can be seen as no more than a typical biographer's anecdote, or at best as evidence for a great professional at work, but Charles Garton put his finger on something more interesting and important when he wrote of the 'magic interlock guaranteed by religion between the stage and life'.[35] For Garton, Polos was responding to the highly charged nature of the theatrical moment when at the same time as throwing himself into the role of Electra he performed in public a ritual of mourning for his

33 Earlier in the same *Life* (18) Plutarch relates how Antigonus Gonatas had himself taken control of Acrocorinth by a different kind of theatrical manoeuvre: he had organised a marriage between his young son Demetrius and the widow of the tyrant of Corinth; the climax of the celebrations was to be a performance in the theatre by Amoibeus (identified by Polyaenus, *Strat.* 4.6.1 as a citharode = Stephanis 159); at the last moment Antigonus slipped away from the theatre and tricked the guards into letting him into the citadel.

34 Aulus Gellius 6.5.

35 Garton (1972b) 33; cf. 37–8. Perhaps there is a similar logic in stories about conversion to Christianity in the theatre: cf. Panayotakis (1997); Puchner (this volume, ch. 14).

son. The more compellingly the actor succeeded in being both Polos and Electra at once, the more he justified his enormous and long-lasting prestige, and the better we can understand why actors at their most inspired, in antiquity as in other periods, could be variously perceived as dangerous, uncanny, or fascinatingly in touch with all that is other and mysterious in human experience. Their capacity to 'play out' the audience's desires, fears or fantasies,[36] and to challenge the stability of identity through cross-dressing and multiple role-playing, must certainly be reckoned with in any discussion of their symbolic function.

A good place to look, if we want to capture something of the distinctiveness of ancient perceptions, is at some accounts of dreams about actors and acting, which will perhaps help to give a sense of the 'collective unconscious' of a society in which theatrical performance was widespread and influential.[37]

Plutarch's description of the death of Demosthenes uses the story of a dream about acting which is rich in relevant detail. How far this goes back is not obvious; Plutarch quotes sources for the main events leading to Demosthenes' death, and there is no reason to doubt the involvement of the actor Archias, but the motif of the dream could have been introduced at any stage in the transmission of the story, or indeed added by Plutarch himself.[38] At all events it has interesting light to throw on Greek notions of the significance of the actor.

The story begins in the *Life of Demosthenes*, ch. 28. This is the final crisis: the Macedonians Antipater and Craterus are reported to be on their way to Athens to establish control after their victory at Crannon; Demosthenes and his associates manage to escape, but the assembly under pro-Macedonian influence condemns them to death. Antipater sends agents to arrest them, under the command of Archias of Thurii,[39] nicknamed '*Phugadotheras*' ('Exile-hunter'). In the narrative as designed by Plutarch the first and presumably most important piece of information about Archias is that he was once a tragic actor and even reputedly trained the great Polos, and the next is that he had himself had training as a rhetor. Given the close links between actors and orators these do not need to be incompatible traditions, but Plutarch's mention of both roles helps to prepare for the close parallelism that will be drawn

36 Cf. Griffith (1999) 58, and Lada-Richards, this volume, ch. 19.

37 Guidorizzi (1988) xxiii–iv: 'i simboli prodotti della imaginazione onirica non sarebbero altro che immagini derivate da un inconscio collettivo'.

38 Cf. Pelling (1997b) 199 on Plutarch's creative use of dreams.

39 For Thurii as a place with theatrical connections see Taplin (1993).

between Archias and Demosthenes.[40] Archias has some of Demosthenes' associates removed from sanctuary at Aegina and sent off to Antipater to be executed; he then goes over to Calauria (Poros), where Demosthenes has taken refuge in the temple of Poseidon, and tries to persuade him to leave voluntarily on the ground that he has nothing to fear from Antipater.

But the previous night, as it happened, Demosthenes had had a strange dream. What he dreamed was that he was taking part in a tragedy and competing with Archias; he did well and won the audience's support, but he was beaten through lack of resources for the production. So when Archias made friendly overtures Demosthenes looked straight at him without getting up [i.e. from where he sat as a suppliant at the altar] and said, 'Archias, you never convinced me in the past with your acting, and you won't convince me now with your promises.' Then Archias got angry and began threatening; 'Now', said Demosthenes, 'you are speaking the words of the Macedonian oracle [i.e. the truth about Antipater's intentions], whereas before you were acting a part. Wait a little while, so that I can send a message to my family.' After saying this he went into the temple and took hold of a papyrus roll as if he were about to write something; then he put his pen to his mouth and bit it, as he often did when he was thinking and writing. He held it to his mouth for a while, then covered his head and bent forward. The guards standing by the door laughed at him for what they took as cowardice and called him soft and unmanly, while Archias came over to him and urged him to get up, repeating the speeches he had made earlier and again promising reconciliation with Antipater. But now Demosthenes realised that the poison was taking effect; he uncovered his head and looked straight at Archias. 'You had better hurry', he said, 'and play the part of Creon: you'll soon have my body to throw out unburied. Dear Poseidon, *I* am leaving your sanctuary while I am still alive, but for Antipater and the Macedonians not even your temple is inviolable.' This was what he said; then he asked someone to help him – he was already shaking and tottering – and as soon as he had stepped forward and passed the altar he fell down, let out a groan, and died. (Plutarch, *Life of Demosthenes* 29)

The dream is thus fulfilled: Demosthenes is indeed a better actor than Archias, but he lacks the material resources to be successful in the 'competition'. The dramatic scene that he enacts, with the aid of speech, action, props and costume, convinces the audience of Thracian guards

40 Earlier in the *Life* Plutarch has emphasised Demosthenes' connections with Satyros : in 7 there is a lively account of Demosthenes learning from the actor how to make a speech come alive. Satyros tells him to recite any speech of Sophocles or Euripides that he knows by heart; he chooses one, and then Satyros demonstrates how an actor would handle it: 'he shaped the same speech in such a way and recited it with such appropriateness of characterisation and delivery that it now seemed like a completely different one to Demosthenes''.

and Archias himself, though they misinterpret his motives. Again, if the contest is to be seen as one of speech between orators, Demosthenes finds the right words to win a moral victory over his deceitful and unworthy opponent: Archias, he says, is fit only to play the unpopular tritagonist's role of Creon in *Antigone*, the role that Demosthenes disparagingly attributed to Aeschines in *On the False Embassy* (247).[41]

There are several different strands of association here. The dream is essentially about a contest between Demosthenes and his opponent, and its use of the theatrical analogy is entirely apt: the most typical contest now (in Demosthenes' time as in Plutarch's) is between individual performers as leaders of troupes, who may also have important solo appearances to make. The dream is also prophetic (just as dreams in drama always were, of course) and is used to give structure and significance to the narrative; it gains extra power from the belief that actors may speak words of ominous significance, giving voice to the 'real' meaning of a situation through the lines of their fictive roles.

It is worth comparing this dream with another theatrical one told by Diodorus (13.97–8) in the context of a critical event in the Peloponnesian War, the battle of Arginusae, before which Thrasybulus (Diodorus should have said Thrasyllus) dreamed that he and six fellow Athenian admirals were playing the roles of the Seven against Thebes in Euripides' *Phoenician Women*, against the Spartan leaders who were taking the parts of the sons of the Seven in the same dramatist's *Suppliants*. The dream was (correctly) interpreted, on the strength of the plots of the plays, as signifying that the Athenians would win, but with significant losses.[42] Here too the dramatic contest functions as an image of conflict, but the emphasis is on the group rather than the individual performer,[43] and the main point is the prophetic nature of the dream. Artemidorus would have had no difficulty with it: 'If anyone dreams that he acts in either a comedy or a tragedy and he remembers his role, the dream will come true in accordance with the plot of the play' (*On the Interpretation of Dreams* 4.37).[44] Compare another

41 Whatever may have been true of the original distribution of parts, it is hard to avoid the conclusion that in the time of Demosthenes and Aeschines the part of Creon was played by the tritagonist. See Demosthenes 18.129 (with Wankel's note) and 19.247; *DFA* (1988) 132–5; Easterling (1999) 157–8, with n. 14; Griffith (1999) 23, n. 73.

42 The seer rightly deduced that it would be a 'Cadmeian victory' for the attacking Spartans; he also predicted the loss of seven Athenian generals, which was (more or less) fulfilled when after the battle the Athenians executed the generals they thought guilty of failing to gather up the dead.

43 If the dream by any chance went back to contemporary traditions it would suit the circumstances of tragic competition in the fifth century quite well; but it looks suspiciously like a later elaboration.

44 Here and elsewhere the translations of Artemidorus are by White (1975).

passage of the same work: 'If the dreamer remembers the words, the dream-fulfilment will correspond to the actual content' (1.56).

This emphasis on the words, or the role, recalls the idea that the actor's words may at any time have an omen-like function: the script and the plot are not of his making, and what he says or sings may work like a *klēdon*, an utterance which turns out to have special significance in a new and seemingly fortuitous context. This could apply even to tunes, as when pipe-players performed 'The Cyclops' shortly before Philip of Macedon suffered the injury that cost him an eye (Didymus on Dem. 12.50–60, quoting Duris).[45] But the most elaborate example comes in Diodorus' narrative of Philip's death in the theatre at Aegae (16.92–3). This includes a detailed account of the entertainment the previous evening, when Philip invites the famous *tragōidos* Neoptolemos to sing something propitious for his planned expedition against Persia. Neoptolemos obliges with a lyric from his repertoire, about death cutting short overweening plans and hopes, but when Philip is assassinated everyone can see that it applies even better to him than to the Persians.[46]

Seeing the actor as a kind of mouthpiece for powers beyond human control was not incompatible, of course, with giving him 'psychagogic' functions. The more compelling the actor, the more effectively he could awaken emotions that lay below the surface and outside the control of the rational consciousness. There is a well-known story about Alexander, tyrant of Pherae in the mid-fourth century BC, who was moved to tears by a tragic performance and walked out, explaining that it was not out of dissatisfaction with the performer, but he was ashamed that he was able to feel pity for the sufferings of actors, and not for his own subjects. Aelian (*Var. hist.* 14.40) names the performer as Theodoros and the part he played as Aerope; in Plutarch's versions (*Fortune of Alexander* 2.1 = *Mor.* 334A; *Life of Pelopidas* 29) the character is the Euripidean Hecuba, and the actor is not named.[47]

The capacity to arouse terror is well documented, too, but not specifically linked in the sources to particular famous actors. It would be interesting, for example, if memories of the acting of the mad Orestes or the mad Pentheus by some famous interpreters lay behind Virgil's evocation of Dido's dreams: 'She would be like Pentheus in his frenzy when

45 Cf. the story of the failed piece of stage business taken as a bad omen by Mithridates, when an image of Victory, with crown in hand, being lowered by machinery broke to pieces before it touched his head (Plutarch, *Life of Sulla* 11).

46 Cf. Easterling (1997d) 218–20 for more details.

47 Cf. Stephanis (1988) on Theodoros (1157) for bibliography.

he was seeing columns of Furies and a double sun and two cities of Thebes; or like Orestes, son of Agamemnon, driven in flight across the stage by his own mother armed with her torches and black snakes, while the avenging Furies sat at the door' (*Aeneid* 4.469–73, trans. West).[48]

None of these associations with the irrational and the supernatural seem, however, to have conflicted with the habit of seeing the actor as the embodiment of fiction and pretence. A couple of passages in Artemidorus make the point succinctly: 'Reciters of mimes and all sorts of jesters [seen in dreams] signify deceits and treachery' (1.76) and 'Actors and players who mount the stage are obviously not to be believed by anyone, since they play parts' (2.69). What is important here is that ancient writers found it possible to use a model which accommodated both truth and falsehood: the paradox that the same person both is and is not Oedipus, for example. Hence, perhaps, the strength, developing from the Hellenistic period onwards, of the 'dramatic simile of life',[49] the perception, given serious elaboration by philosophers, that all the world's a stage. The idea of a drama of life, staged by Tyche or Nature, in which the human being is as much at the mercy of the 'plot' as the actor is controlled by the director, could be used by moralists to promote a proper acceptance of human limitations.[50] But growing recognition that the 'real world' was only 'the greater stage'[51] did nothing to weaken the power of actors: in a culture which is acutely conscious of its own theatricality, it may be the performer who has the best claim to offer images of what reality might be like.

The last word should go to a performer, the tragic actor Neoptolemos, one of the favoured few who on all the evidence seems to have achieved iconic status. His view of the ambivalence of theatre gives a rather different emphasis from that of the moralists. Maximus of Tyre and Marcus Aurelius could suggest, from their different vantage points, that the rationale of dramatic fictions was essentially didactic, either to help you dispel from 'the drama of life' the 'empty' images of Furies and Fates (Maximus),[52] or to help you understand that even the worst things that can happen, such as you see in tragedies, are part of Nature's law: you have to accept your human vulnerability rather than feel threatened by terrors on 'the greater stage' (Marcus Aurelius).[53] Stobaeus[54] records of

[48] Quoted and discussed, along with Lucan's magnificent account of the theatrical dreams of Pompey and of Caesar and his comrades (7.7–28, 760–84), by Pelling (1997b) 204–9.
[49] The title of Kokolakis' study (1960). See also Kokolakis (1976); Chaniotis (1997) 220; 253–4.
[50] Teles, *Peri autarkeias* fr. 2 Hense, p.5; Epictetus, *Enchir.* 17; Marcus Aurelius, *Meditations* 12.36.
[51] See nn. 53 and 54. [52] 13.9. [53] *Meditations* 11.1.6. [54] *Florilegium* 4.34.70.

Neoptolemos that when someone asked him what he was most impressed by in the works of Aeschylus, Sophocles and Euripides he replied, 'Not anything of theirs, but what he himself had witnessed on a greater stage: Philip in procession at the wedding of his daughter Cleopatra and hailed as thirteenth god, and the next day murdered and thrown out.' The point of this story, presumably, is not to belittle the power of the great tragic plots and situations or of those who interpreted them on stage, but to suggest that the dividing line between them and lived experience could never be kept firm. This helps to explain why performers were so much in demand, by the rich and powerful as much as by the ordinary public, and why exceptional performers had so much influence in the shaping of culture.[55]

55 I am indebted to Eric Handley, Janet Huskinson and seminar audiences in Glasgow and at the Center for Hellenic Studies in Washington for helpful discussion and suggestions.

CHAPTER SIXTEEN

Scholars versus actors: text and performance in the Greek tragic scholia

Thomas Falkner

The explanatory material that comes to us in the margins of the manuscripts of fifth-century tragedy has a good deal to say about actors and acting, if not as directly as we should have liked.[1] Although there is general agreement that the tragic scholia are derived primarily from Hellenistic commentaries (albeit with an accretion of Byzantine learning), with much in particular from the great Alexandrian philologists of the early second century BC like Aristophanes and Aristarchus, there is little that is certain about the process by which they came to be excerpted by late antique or early Byzantine copyists.[2] And while it is unlikely that medieval scholars had at their disposal full copies of the Hellenistic sources, it is not clear in what form these materials were available to them: whether the 'mixed' commentaries of late Hellenistic scholars like Didymus;[3] those of anonymous compilers from late antiquity; or perhaps earlier codices already annotated from ancient sources.[4]

Fortunately, the situation is more promising when we relocate these materials in the history of Hellenistic scholarship, where there has been valuable recent work on the artistic principles and intellectual traditions that inform them.[5] Yet it remains true that the tragic scholia are not

[1] Scholia are cited as follows: G. A. Christodoulou (1977) Τὰ Ἀρχαία Σχολιὰ εἰς Αἴαντα τοῦ Σοφοκλέους, Athens; V. De Marco (1952) *Scholia in Sophoclis Oedipum Coloneum*, Rome; W. Dindorf (1852) *Scholia in Sophoclis Tragoedias Septem*, Oxford; P. N. Papageorgius (1888) *Scholia in Sophoclis Tragoedias Vetera*, Leipzig; C. J. Herington (1972) *The Older Scholia on the Prometheus Bound* (*Mnem.* Supp. 19); E. Schwartz (1887), (1891) *Scholia in Euripidem I*; *Scholia in Euripidem II*, Berlin; O. L. Smith (1976) *Scholia Graeca in Aeschylum*, Pars I. Leipzig.

[2] On the transmission generally, see Reynolds and Wilson (1991).

[3] On single-authored and mixed commentaries, see the end of the *Orestes* scholia (παραγέγραπται ἐκ τοῦ Διονυσίου ὑπομνήματος ὁλοσχερῶς καὶ τῶν μικτῶν); cf. Csapo and Slater (1995) 24–5. Only occasionally are the original commentators attributed or even pointed to generally with φασι (sc. οἱ ὑπομνηματισάμενοι); alternate entries are typically introduced with a simple ἄλλως.

[4] See esp. Wilson (1967) and (1982); cf. Barrett (1964) 79: 'it seems hopeless to try to trace the history of the medieval scholia in more than the briefest outline'.

[5] On Alexandrian scholarship, see Pfeiffer (1968) 87–233 and Fraser (1972) vol. I, ch. 8, surveys by Grube (1965) 122–32, Kennedy (1989) 205–10, Reynolds and Wilson (1991) 5–15. On rhetorical

always regarded highly.[6] This is due partly to the tendency to quarry these notes for their content as individual entries. Indeed, it is as repositories of arcane and sundry materials that the scholia are most often employed, shuffled with other curiosities and recycled, too often uncritically, in generations of modern commentaries. This piecemeal approach is in one sense a testimony to the versatility of the Alexandrians, whose range of interests in literary phenomena in many respects matches that of their modern counterparts. But it is also related to the nature of commentary and the process of reducing any text to a series of lemmata, what Glenn Most calls the 'atomization' of the text.[7] Just as commentary levels the text, breaking it down into equal bits and analysing them seriatim, often without consistency of methodological approach or historical context, it offers itself in turn as a series of discrete propositions to be examined in isolation and in reference to a given sub-topic (linguistic, metrical, biographical, historical and so forth), often without due regard for their provenance.

The tendency to regard the scholia as nuggets of erudition is also the result of a model of scholarly production that would recast the scholars at the Library of Alexandria in our image, or rather in the stereotype of closeted academics, living on state support, hermetically sealed from the larger world, engaged in microscopic analysis of obscure subjects of interest only to each other.[8] The image of an Alexandrian Ivory Tower is often assumed to be grounded in the sources.[9] In the first *Iambus* Callimachus, in the voice of Hipponax *redivivus*, admonishes the *philologoi* to cease their disputatious ill-will (*phthonein*) toward each other.[10] So too the famous lines of Timon of Phlius (*c.* 230 BC):

> Many are feeding in populous Egypt, scribblers on papyrus, ceaselessly wrangling in the birdcage of the Muses (*en talarōi/Mouseōn*).[11]

and philosophical influences, see esp. Heath (1987) and Meijering (1987), and now Papadopoulou (1998) and (1999).

6 Cf. Heath (1987) 3. 7 Most (1985) 37.

8 On the founding of Mouseion and Library generally, see Fraser (1972) vol. I, 312–35 and vol. II, 467ff., Pfeiffer (1968) 96–104, Canfora (1989) 3–44, Green (1990) 84–91, and Blum (1991) 95–123.

9 Pollitt (1986) 13f. locates the origins of intellectual exclusiveness in the libraries at Alexandria and elsewhere. Canfora (1987) 43–4 emphasises their isolation and submission to the Ptolemies. Reynolds and Wilson (1991) 6 compare life in an Oxbridge college, while Blum (1991) 97 likens the Mouseion to eighteenth-century royal academies of arts and sciences.

10 Call. *Iamb.* 1 (= fr. 191) *Dieg.* 6.1–6 (the scholars' appetite for polemic is illustrated in *Iamb.* 13).

11 Timon fr. 12 Diels (= Ath. 1.22d), cited in Pfeiffer (1968) 97–8 (his translation). Timon also criticised the excessive zeal of the Homeric editors (Diog. Laert. 9.113).

But in a recent study of Callimachus Alan Cameron challenges the popular understanding of Timon's remark.[12] Although the rivalry of these scholars is explicit (ἀπείριτα δηριόωντες, 'ceaselessly wrangling'), assumptions about their seclusion rest upon a misreading of *talaros*, which means a bird's *nest*: 'There is no suggestion of *caged* birds, of unworldly scholars shut away in a library. The emphasis falls rather on the rivalry and polemic of Alexandrian scholars.' Cameron argues against the over easy dichotomisation of Hellenistic culture (public vs. private, mass vs. learned, oral vs. book),[13] and warns that the tendency to abstract Callimachus from the larger culture has contributed to a view of Alexandrian poetry as sterile, apolitical and frivolous. The argument can be extended to the Mouseion and Library in general, where the tendency to view these poets, scholars and scientists as a cloistered élite can also be misleading. It is helpful to keep in mind the Peripatetic traditions represented in the establishment of the Library, which were hardly isolationist.[14] And to the extent that these institutions were part of a strategy aimed at promoting Hellenisation, it can hardly have been expected for this small army of artists, scholars and scientists to have remained disengaged from the larger culture.[15]

It is here that I would like to locate a discussion of the tragic scholia, where attention to the idea of the actor and its function in the economy of the commentaries can tell us something about the cultural dynamics in which both scholars and actors participated. To be sure, references to 'stage business' in the scholia are far from copious, and their distribution is uneven, even sporadic. Yet the criteria by which these materials were preserved militated against discussion of *scaenica*, and many aspects of dramatic performance must have been better represented in the original commentaries.[16] Both Hellenistic and Byzantine scholars intended their

[12] Cameron (1995) 32, who also argues against the 'monastic associations' given to χαρακῖται for its derivation from χάραξ.

[13] E.g. Gentili (1988) 176: 'The Hellenistic period presents the spectacle of a culture with two totally different aspects, moving along distinct but parallel lines – learned poetry, libraries and erudition on the one hand; and, on the other, festive performances, popular education, and entertainment, which still operate within the oral institutional framework provided by theaters and public competitions.'

[14] E.g. Diog. Laert. 4.1, 5.51, Strabo 13.1.54, Ael. *VH* 3.17, Ath. 1.3a–b, and the 'Letter of Aristeas'. On the role of Neleus, Strato and esp. Demetrius of Phaleron in the creation of the Library, see Pfeiffer (1968) 99–102, Canfora (1989) 16–29, Blum (1991) 99–104 and notes. The Alexandrian achievement in both pure and applied sciences would also have involved extensive contact with the larger culture: see White (1993).

[15] On the true gulf between the Macedonian-Greek and native populations of Ptolemaic Egypt, however, see e.g. Lewis (1986) 4–5.

[16] Cf. Taplin (1977a) 22 n. 1: 'the Alexandrian commentaries . . . may well have given considerable weight to such matters'.

materials as aids for readers and supplements to an understanding of the written text. But Byzantine copyists knew these plays only as texts to be studied by scholars and in schools, and their interest in such matters would be limited largely to what was necessary for the reader to comprehend the written word.[17] As their more bookish concerns narrowed the criteria by which they selected, we must keep in mind the abundant theatricality of the world in which their sources took shape and the 'theatrical mentality' that Pollitt has identified as central to Hellenistic art, architecture and human experience.[18]

This can help account for certain discrepancies. For example, the scholiast observes at *Ajax* 14 (ὦ φθέγμ' 'Αθάνας, 'O voice of Athena'):

This has been very well written. For he [Odysseus] says 'voice' since he does not see her. For it is clear that he does not see her from 'Even if you are unseen, nevertheless . . .', that is, 'invisible'. He only hears her voice, since it is familiar to him. Athena, however, is on stage (ἐπὶ τῆς σκηνῆς). This would certainly be pleasing to the spectator (χαρίζεσθαι . . . τῷ θεατῇ).

The scene resembles the epiphany of Artemis at the end of *Hippolytus*, where the goddess is also unseen by those on stage (Hippolytus recognises her fragrance (1391): ὦ θεῖον ὀσμῆς πνεῦμα), but which passes without comment in the scholia. This may be because in *Ajax* Odysseus actually *describes* the goddess as 'unseen'. The comment is thus anchored in the text, explicating a reference that would otherwise be confusing. In *Hippolytus*, on the other hand, there is nothing in the dialogue that refers directly to Artemis' invisibility, hence no need for the scholiast to turn to ancient sources for clarification.[19]

Similarly, the scholia tell us little about the music of the tragedies, their melodies, dynamics and delivery, a dimension of the text that would have been inaccessible to medieval readers. An exception is at *Orestes* 176,[20] where Electra hushes the entering chorus and prays for the arrival of night (ἐρεβόθεν ἴθι):

[17] Scenes from Greek tragedy remained familiar in the Byzantine visual arts, but these seem to be derived less from performance than from the traditions of fresco, panel painting and illustration in the earliest codices. Weitzmann (1949) relates Byzantine miniatures of Euripidean scenes made during the tenth-century Renaissance to the preservation of classical art objects, including precious manuscripts, in Constantinople. See Puchner, this volume, ch. 14.

[18] Pollitt (1986) 4–7, 230–42; cf. Green (1990) 92–4, 342. On the theatricality of life in antiquity generally, see Easterling (1997a) 218–20 and Chaniotis (1997).

[19] Similarly, although there is a brief mention of Medea on high (ἐπὶ ὕψους) at *Med.* 1317, no attention is paid to the dragon-chariot, which seems to be mentioned on 1320 merely to help the reader understand and why Medea says that Jason will not be able to touch her. The equally spectacular appearance of Apollo *ex machina* at *Or.* 1625 is not discussed.

[20] The scholia from *Orestes* are further discussed below pp. 355–60.

This melody is played on the strings that are called the *nētai* ['lowest' in position, not pitch, of the three strings of the musical scale] and is very high-pitched (ὀξύτατον). And so it is peculiar that Electra makes use of a high-pitched voice (ὀξείᾳ φωνῇ) and also makes these reproaches to the chorus. Rather, she does necessarily make use of the high registers (τῷ ὀξεῖ), for this is appropriate to those singing a dirge, but as lightly (λεπτότατα) as possible.

This valuable information is likewise offered not for its own sake but in reference to the interaction between text and music, seeking to resolve the tension between a song that asks for quiet but is itself acutely tonal, and the textual link explains the note's survival. But the original commentator clearly understood this dimension of the text, was aware of how incongruent the scene might be if badly performed, might perhaps have known of such a performance – in short, had a sensibility that came from a familiarity with these plays not as textbook classics but as living theatre.

Indeed, it is hard to imagine how Alexandrian scholars could not have been influenced by contemporary performance. When Aristophanes of Byzantium praises Menandrian realism[21] this is unlikely to have been the product of reading alone, and his interest in production is reflected in his didascalic hypotheseis, prefaces appended to the texts which include considerable information on both the subject-matter of the plays and the original production, and in the treatise *On Masks* and other philological monographs.[22] Aristarchus would necessarily have addressed questions of performance in the running commentaries he wrote on the tragedies.[23] How much scholars learned from attendance at actual productions we cannot know, but the city surely offered many opportunities to see plays. Alexandria had a history of theatrical and artistic patronage going back to the first Ptolemies (Soter had perhaps tried to lure Menander there, as he had more successfully the poet–scholar Philitas).[24] It boasted a large theatre,[25] and the Ptolemaieia were certainly scenic at least occasionally, with other festivals providing opportunities to book resident companies, travelling troupes, and virtuosi *tragōidoi* and *kōmōidoi* for solo performance. Ptolemy Philadelphus was celebrated for his promotion of Dionysus, theatre and the Artists of

[21] 'O Menander, o life . . .', Syrianus, *Comment. in Hermog.* II.23.6 (= *Men. test.* 32).

[22] On the hypotheseis (conceivably written for each of the 300 tragedies he edited), see Wilamowitz (1909) 143ff., Zuntz (1955) 129–46, Barrett (1964) 47–8, Pfeiffer (1968) 192–6, and Rusten (1982) 357 n. 1. On the Περὶ Προσώπων (*On Masks*) cf. Ath. 14.659a.

[23] Cf. Pfeiffer (1968) 222–4.

[24] Fraser (1972) vol. II, 873 n. 11. On Philitas as 'both poet and critic' (Strabo 14.657), see Pfeiffer (1968) 88ff.

[25] Mentioned in Plut. *Ant.* 69; on its architecture see Bieber (1961) 112 and 291 n. 13.

Dionysus,[26] nowhere more conspicuously than in the Grand Procession in his honour (*c.* 275 BC).[27] This extravaganza, which probably involved theatrical presentations in addition to the procession itself,[28] featured a fifteen-foot statue of Dionysus and tableaux representing scenes from his mythology, preceded by 'the poet Philikos, who was the priest of Dionysus, and all the Guild of the Artists of Dionysus'.[29] Philikos provides an interesting link between performing artists and the poet-scholars of the Library, and as the new creative centre for tragedy Alexandria would have had in residence many poet-scholars writing with an eye to production – the famous Pleiad (of which Philikos may have been a member)[30] included scholars like Lycophron, Philieus and Alexander Aetolus, who was in charge of organising the Library's collection of tragic texts.[31] The prestige of the Artists is further evidenced in two much discussed inscriptions from Ptolemais from the rule of Ptolemy Euergetes (*c.* 240 BC).[32] These suggest the complex internal organisation of the Guild, the careful assigning of duties and responsibilities among them, the range of occupations represented (from performing artists of all kinds to poets, directors and stagehands), and the intimate association the Guild claimed with the royal family, whose cult has been worked into their title: they are 'The Artists of Dionysus and the Brother Gods'.[33] Like the scholars of the Library, the Artists of Dionysus enjoyed the support of the Ptolemies, who had much to gain in turn by associating their rule with popular theatrical culture and the body of Dionysiac myth and ritual.[34]

26 Cf. Theocr. 17.112–16, who also calls him 'loving the Muses', φιλόμουσος at 15.96.

27 On the Grand Procession, described by Kallixeinos in Ath. 5.196a–203b, see esp. Rice (1983); also Green (1990) 159–60, Pollitt (1986) 280–1. The date, only years after the foundation of the Artists of Dionysus in Athens and Isthmia-Nemea in *c.* 279 (cf. *DFA* (1968) 281ff.) suggests the theatrical pre-eminence of Alexandria. Rice (1983) 55 suggests the Alexandrian Guild may in fact represent the first and earliest organisation into Guilds. On the Artists of Dionysus generally, see esp. Stephanis (1988); also Sifakis (1967) 136ff., *DFA* (1968) 279ff., Csapo and Slater (1995) 239–55.

28 Rice (1983) 56–8.

29 πάντες οἱ περὶ τὸν Διόνυσον τεχνῖται Ath. 5.198b–c. Athenaeus' text gives the spelling Philiskos, but see n. 30 below. On the *technītai* see also Lightfoot, this volume, ch. 9.

30 Fraser (1972) vol. II, 859 n. 407 identifies him with Philicus of Corcyra; cf. 608f., 619. He was probably also president of the Alexandrian branch; cf. Rice (1983) 55, *DFA* (1968) 287.

31 Johannes Tzetzes (cited in Csapo and Slater (1995) 22). On the contemporary theatre, of which only fragments survive, see Lesky (1963) 743–50, Sifakis (1967) 1–2, Gentili (1979) 15–32, Fraser (1972) vol. I, 619ff., Xanthakis-Karamanos (1993), Cameron (1995) 47ff.

32 *OGIS* 50, 51; see *DFA* (1968) 287, 310 (trans. Csapo and Slater (1995) 247–9 with bibliography). Rice (1983) 53–4 argues for a date before 243/2, when the cult of Theoi Euergetai was founded.

33 τεχνῖται οἱ περὶ τὸν Διόνυσον καὶ Θεοὺς Ἀδελφούς. There were real financial benefits to be had from royal patronage. Rice (1983) 54–5 notes the substantial privilege of the exemption of the Artists from the salt tax.

34 Ptolemy Euergetes traced his descent from Dionysus (cf. Gow on Theocritus 17.26).

As professional groups working out new forms of community in a cosmopolitan city, the cultures of scholar and actor surely overlapped in significant ways. As custodians of tradition, actor and scholar are advocates for the same client – the one through the intensity and ephemerality of live mass communication, the other more durably to a more restricted and discriminating audience, and these traditions will have been not only complementary but interactive. This is especially the case in regard to the canonisation of the classics, where scholarship sustained a process long since set in motion by actors. Before Aristophanes and Aristarchus set about writing monographs and commentaries on the tragedies, the canon had largely been shaped by traditions of performance. As Easterling has discussed, the single greatest push in the formation of the canon took place in 386 BC, when Athenian revivals of 'old tragedies' were made the responsibility of *tragōidoi* themselves, freeing them from dependence on poets and ultimately from the city, as foreign cities or individuals contracted with actors, and in the arrangements for these performances the tastes of the theatre-going public would find expression.[35] Their role in the process of canonisation was further enhanced by their rising social and political status and professional organisation in the guilds of Artists. Performance and scholarship represent parallel processes by which a selection of plays came to secure their privileged cultural position in everything from festivals to school curricula.

Even through the filter of the scholiasts, the commentaries reveal no bias against performance. Indeed, they speak approvingly of the range of performance related issues – gesture, blocking, delivery, music, costumes, stage machinery. They understand that the language is often only comprehensible in terms of the actor and the physical stage: when Electra says 'and in this way, with unseemly garment . . .' (Soph. *El.* 190–1), the scholiast notes that ὧδε ('in this way') is typical of the way that language excites pity in the audience (*eleeinon*) by pointing to the actors' costume (*to schēma tōn hypokritōn*). Ironically, the scholia are more often adduced in evidence of original conditions of performance, although there is no evidence that the Alexandrians had any special records of fifth-century performances nor any secure sense of performance history. This does not rule out the possibility that some reflect a continuity of practice, and this may encourage us to re-examine our assumptions about fifth-century theatre, but Taplin is right to counsel in this regard that they should be

[35] Easterling (1997a) 212ff. and notes.

used only corroboratively.[36] Consider the many references in them to the use of stage machinery in Aeschylus: the *mēchanē* for the arrival of the chorus at *Prometheus Bound* 128 and 284; or the *ekkuklēma* at *Libation Bearers* 973, as Orestes reveals the bodies of the 'double tyranny'. Then there is the staging of *Eumenides* 64:

> And next there is a display (φαντασία), for the device is turned around (στραφέντα . . . μηχανήματα) to reveal the situation in the shrine. And the spectacle is tragic (ὄψις τραγική): Orestes still holding the bloody sword, and they guarding him in a circle.

It may possibly be the case, as critics have argued in each of these instances, that the practices described in fact date to Aeschylus' theatre. But we can be sure that the commentaries describe the practices of the contemporary stage, reflecting advances in the technical resources and the fondness of Hellenistic audiences for striking display.[37] Equally important are the aesthetics of the commentator, who admires this example of tragic spectacle and appreciates the way in which machinery, props and blocking combine to powerful effect.

Images of the actor and his art are no less revealing, and we may begin with several entries which look beneath the text of a speech to the demands it makes upon the actors. At *Prometheus Bound* 472, the scholiast suggests that the playwright inserted four lines of iambics for the chorus in the middle of Prometheus' exposition of his boons to mankind (436–71, 476–506) 'giving Aeschylus' actor a rest' (διαναπαύουσαι τὸν ὑποκριτὴν Αἰσχύλου). There are many other long speeches in Aeschylus, even in this play, which are not so broken up. But the comment may suggest something of how this rhesis was performed, as a *tour de force* to bring out the virtuosity and physicality of the immobilised protagonist, and the scholar gives the *poet* the credit for having anticipated this and arranged for a breather in mid-speech. Consider also the comment offered at the entrance of the *paidagōgos* at *Phoenissae* 93, who calls down from the *skēnē* roof to Antigone, who is still below. She must remain within until he is sure that she will not be seen 'by one of the citizens on the road':

36 Taplin (1977a) 369: 'It is clear that the scholia and other ancient scholarship often tended to be anachronistic on matters of staging, and simply to describe the way that the scene was or might be played in the later theatre' (see also 407 and 436).

37 Indeed, use of the expression στραφέντα μηχανήματα for the *ekkuklēma* would seem better to describe some later kind of turning or revolving platform. There is probably something like this behind the confused entries on the entrance of Phaedra at *Hippolytus* 171; see Barrett (1964) on 811.

They [the commentators] say that Euripides contrived (μηχανᾶσθαι) this to change the costume of the protagonist (τὸν πρωταγωνιστὴν . . . μετασκευάσῃ) from the character of Jocasta. That is why Antigone does not appear at the same time as him [the *paidagōgos*] but later.

As with the note on 'Aeschylus' actor', a curious bit of stagecraft is explained not by commenting on the 'appropriateness' of the remark or its relation to the dramatic situation but in relation to the realia of performance – the time required by the Jocasta-actor to outfit himself. But why would the Jocasta-actor assume the role of Antigone here, especially since the two will be on stage together later in the play? The comment may allude to the realities of role division by which protagonists, star actors with international reputations, assigned parts to ensure that they might be on-stage as much as possible, showcasing their own versatility (the Antigone-actor gets to sing an aria in this scene) and relegating to the deuteragonist and tritagonist whatever bits were left.[38] The commentator finds nothing objectionable in the doubling up of the roles, which suggests that the practice was standard, and again credits the *poet* for having taken care to allow his actors the time they need.

On a different note are the notorious lines on the entrance of the Phrygian slave at *Orestes* 1366. (The lemma is ἀλλὰ κτυπεῖ, 'but [wait, for] they [the door-bolts] are rattling'):

Someone makes a noise at the doors as he comes out, for this is the practice. But someone might readily agree that these three lines are not from Euripides but rather from the actors, who lest they hurt themselves leaping from the palace roof, open the door a little and then come out wearing the Phrygian's costume and mask. And they added these lines to seem to have reason to come out through the door. But from their own lines they argue against coming out through the doors, for it is clear from the following lines that he has leapt over (ὑπερπεπήδηκεν) [i.e., from the roof of the *skēnē*].

Here it is alleged that contemporary practice has contravened the will of the author, and actors open themselves to criticism on three counts: on the validity of the stage action (they fail to perform the scene as intended); on the integrity of the text (they insert inauthentic material); and on textual comprehension (they fail to recognise the contradiction posed by 1370–2: 'over the cedar beams and Doric triglyphs of the inner chambers'

[38] Already reflected in the fourth century, when 'deuteragonist' and 'tritagonist' acquired derogatory connotations; see Csapo and Slater (1995) 222–3. Sifakis (1995) suggests that already in fifth-century practice the protagonist alone was said to 'act' the play, with roles often so apportioned as to feature his talents.

(κεδρωτὰ πα-/στάδων ὑπὲρ τέραμνα/Δωρικάς τε τριγλύφους). Indeed, in suggesting that the reason is their desire 'not to hurt themselves' (μὴ κακοπαθῶσιν), there is the further implication that they have placed concern for the voices and the bodies that are the instruments of their art (their person is, we remember, sacrosanct and immune) over the express demands of the text.[39]

In fact the lines are plausibly Euripidean and the 'leaping entrance' unlikely, given the height of the *skēnē* and the aria the actor must be prepared to deliver.[40] But the remark takes its place in a larger discourse about the nature of performance which questions the knowledge, judgement and authority by which the actor presumes to represent the playwright. Suspicion and even resentment of the actor are well established in the intellectual traditions, yet given the vigorous approval the scholia give to performance in general, this polemic derives less from Platonic hostility to theatre or Peripatetic preference for the written text than from the kind of complaint Aristotle offers in *Rhetoric* (3.1403b) that 'actors are more important (μεῖζον δύνανται) than poets now in the poetic contests' and from actors' continued ascendancy in the Hellenistic world: their professionalisation, the high pay and other benefits granted them, the royal recognition lavished upon them.[41] Timon's allusion to the rivalry of the scholars and their quarrelsome nature suggests the potential for competition: they may well have been resentful of the patronage, popularity and royal access enjoyed by actors. A second source of tension is related to the kind of authority which the scholarly community claimed on behalf of itself. Hellenistic no less than modern scholars were engaged in not only a search for knowledge but a process of identity formation, by which they defined themselves as a community, valorised their work and promoted their place in society – it was, we recall, Eratosthenes who first appropriated the term *philologos* to describe his scholarly identity.[42] Heinrich von Staden has suggested that we see the ancient commentary as a site of struggle and conflict, of the need to find its unspoken 'plot', its exegetical heroes and villains.[43] One subplot we can try to retrieve is that of the scholar positioning himself in relation to the actor through a

39 The scholars seem to have appreciated the physical vigour required of the actor. Consider their praise for Timotheos of Zakynthos (on *Aj.* 864), whose bravura performance in the suicide of Ajax required him literally to throw himself into his character. On Timotheos, see Lada-Richards, this volume, ch. 19.

40 For brief discussion and bibliography, see Willink's commentary on 1366–8.

41 The ascendancy of the Greek actor is charted in Ghiron-Bistagne (1976) 135–71, Gredley (1984), Slater (1990), Easterling (1997a).

42 Suetonius, *Gram.* 10; see Pfeiffer (1968) 158–9.

43 'Discovery and authority: commentary and the culture of science' (unpublished paper).

rhetorical process of definition and self-definition, marking off tragedy as 'his' territory and defending it from the errors and excesses, real and imagined, of the other.

The commentator's approach is intimated in the illicit (if perhaps anecdotal) circumstances under which Alexandria took possession of these texts, when Ptolemy Euergetes forfeited the deposit of fifteen talents on the archival copies in Athens.[44] On the one hand, the event established the mission of the Library as textual, a continuation of Lycurgus' defence of the text against the alterations of actors and rhapsodes.[45] But the fact that the scholars were not content merely to use or recopy these manuscripts but appropriated them wholesale suggests the kind of authority that possession of these texts seemed to offer. There is in the commentaries a sense of authorial presence whereby the text stands not only as an object of research but as a material link with the poet. And there is a kind of proprietary subtext in the dialectic of scholar and actor: who 'owns' these plays, and in the absence of the poet who best speaks for them?

The difference between actor and scholar is measured by the distance between *script* and *scripture*. For the actor, the text is a malleable object that serves the goals of an evolving art in which no two performances are the same. For the scholar getting the right text and getting the text right are defining issues of methodology and principle, the historic mission of the Library the recovery and elucidation of the *ipsissima verba* of the poet.[46] His commitment to textual integrity and textual fidelity, the *pistis* of the text, signifies his commitment to the poet and his own trustworthiness. The actor becomes the agent of textual infidelity in his willingness to settle for an imperfect text, to change the text, to misattribute lines or introduce inauthentic materials. To be sure, the whole question of 'actors' interpolations' continues to be a matter of serious disagreement: whether their changes are as widespread in our texts as Page and others have claimed,[47] whether the specific passages contested in the scholia had been altered, and whether these scholia report the concerns of second-century BC philologists or later compilers like Didymus and Apollodorus.[48] Yet there is little doubt that actors took liberties with the text, and even where we may dismiss specific charges of interpolations, attention to the larger

44 Galen 17 (I).607; cf. Pfeiffer (1968) 82, 192.

45 Plut. *Vit. Orat.* 841 f.; *DFA* (1968) 100, 155, Pfeiffer (1968) 82.

46 On the Alexandrians' sense of responsibility for the condition of the text, see Reynolds and Wilson (1991) 7–15, Pfeiffer (1968) 105ff., Fraser (1972) vol. I, 320–5, Turner (1968) 100ff.

47 See Page (1934), Reeve (1972/73).

48 For the most recent review, see Hamilton (1974).

rhetoric is a gauge of the scholarly perspective. Actors change the text because they 'misunderstand' (ἀγνοήσαντες *Med.* 85) their own scripts or are ignorant (ἀγνοήσαντες *Med.* 910) of the poet's idiom. They are 'not conversant with the poet's style' (οὐ συμπεριφερόμενοι τῷ τρόπῳ *Med.* 228) or rearrange lines inappropriately or badly (ἀκαίρως *Med.* 356; κακῶς *Med.* 380); they confuse (συγχέειν, συγχέοντας *Med.* 148, 169) the lines of actors and chorus. Where these changes reveal the actor's need for scholarly guidance, more serious are those which (like the interpolation for the Phrygian slave) are done in full knowledge. Actors are suspected of substituting an alternative prologue for *Rhesus* which is pedestrian (πεζός) and unworthy (οὐ πρέπων) of the poet (*Hyp. Rhes.* 11–12). They change the script if they find it difficult to pronounce (τὸ δυσέκφορον *Phoen.* 264) – ease of delivery and projection take precedence over the text. Lines that belong to the chorus are reassigned, with the implication that actors, eager to 'pad' their parts, appropriate such lines to themselves, and the commentators also recognise that this practice has a long history, as at *Medea* 520–1:

> The couplet belongs to the chorus. For already in these times the parts of the chorus were being diminished (τὰ τῶν χορῶν ἠμαύρετο). For the ancient plays were accomplished through the choruses.

This kind of criticism goes beyond specific instances where textual malfeasance is actually charged. To the extent that the actor is understood to be prepared to change the received text, the entire scholarly project is an indictment of his art.

The issue of fidelity is no less central to performance, where again it is the actors' responsibility to deliver to the spectator what the poet 'actually' wrote. The 'boundaries' that governed the performance of the classics was surely not a theoretical question but one that provoked a great deal of controversy, with the eagerness of actors to experiment, the appetite of audiences for something new, and contemporary works that eschewed traditional forms of self-restraint.[49] The persistent focus throughout the scholia on the poet reflects a view of drama as a communication event that involves a particular relationship between the poet and the audience. As Heath observes, the tragic scholia consistently regard drama as a rhetorical medium aimed at producing a certain kind of response: 'The picture is a simple one: the poet tries to secure the

49 See e.g. Wallace (1997) on the relationship between more expressive and sensationalistic drama in the fourth century and charges of decline and 'theatrocracy'. Aristotle recognises that pity and fear can be excited simply through spectacle, this being the sign of the inferior poet (*Poet.* 1453b).

sympathetic attention of his audience, in order to gratify them by the play to which they then attend. . . . this gratification is primarily that which accompanies emotional excitement; indeed, they regard emotion, *pathos*, as the defining quality of the genre.'[50]

The emphasis on emotion is consonant with the poetic and philosophical traditions, from Aristotle's emphasis on 'pity and fear' to more recent echoes of Eratosthenes' arguments for the primacy of 'enchanting' the listener (*psychagōgia*) over Neoptolemus' claim that poetry should offer instruction (*didaskalia*).[51] In the scholia performance is consistently regarded in terms of the experience of the spectator (θεατής), with attention to how the representation of suffering brings pleasure if represented properly and distress if not. As the opening scene of *Ajax* is appreciated for bringing the spectator delight (above, p. 345), the revelation of the hero at 346 evokes 'astonishment' or *ekplēxis*, another key term:[52]

There is an *ekkuklēma* here so that Ajax appears in the midst of the sheep. These things also astonish the spectator (εἰς ἔκπληξιν γὰρ φέρει καὶ ταῦτα τὸν θεατήν), heartrending things in full view (τὰ ἐν τῇ ὄψει περιπαθέστερα). He is shown with his sword, bloody, and sitting amidst the sheep.

Correspondingly, performance should not bring pain or distress. *Hecuba* 484 explains the practice of off-stage murder:

Polyxena has been slain without it being mentioned. It is customary with the tragic poets not to kill in view of the spectators (ἐπ' ὄψει τῶν θεατῶν), for they would have been distressed to see such a sight (ἠνιάθησαν . . . ὁρῶντες τοιαύτην θέαν).

The scholia appreciate both the power of spectacle and the temptation to excess inherent in it, for poet as well as actors. The entry at *Ajax* 815 questions Sophocles' motives in performing rather than reporting Ajax's suicide and entertains a number of explanations:

The scene changes to a deserted place, where Ajax prepares the sword and delivers a speech before his death. For it would be ridiculous for him to enter and fall upon his sword without saying anything. Such scenes are infrequent among the older poets (τοῖς παλαιοῖς), for they are accustomed to report events through messengers. What is the explanation? In *Thracian Women* Aeschylus had

[50] Heath (1987) 10. [51] Cf. Pfeiffer (1968) 166–7.

[52] Aristotle uses ἔκπληξις twice in *Poetics* of tragic plot, not performance, in connection with the 'best kind' of recognitions (1454a4, 1455a17), and singles out *OT* in this regard, which he also commends for its ability to achieve the tragic effects entirely independent of performance. The term has significant Aeschylean associations: cf. *Frogs* 962 (and cf. 144).

already reported the death of Ajax through a messenger. And so perhaps wishing to innovate (καινοτομεῖν) and not to follow in the footsteps of another, or rather wishing to astonish (ἐκπλῆξαι) he placed the deed in full view (ὑπ' ὄψιν). It is irreverent and unfair to randomly criticise one of the older poets (εἰκῇ γὰρ κατηγορεῖν ἀνδρὸς παλαιοῦ οὐχ ὅσιον οὐδὲ δίκαιον).

The commentator is caught between his sense of tragic propriety and his respect for the classics. Sophocles does a better job of arousing emotion without discomforting the audience in his handling of the murder of Clytemnestra (*El.* 1404):

Messengers customarily report the things that have happened inside to those outside. But here, so as not to waste time in the play, he has not written in this way. For it is the suffering of Electra that is being represented. So here the spectator hears her shouting while Clytemnestra is being murdered, and the deed becomes more effective (ἐνεργέστερον) than if it were described through a messenger. The scene is free from vulgar display (τὸ μὲν φορτικὸν τῆς ὄψεως), but it has been made no less vivid (ἐναργές) through her shouting.

The quality of *enargeia*, the ability to make vivid and 'real' through language is crucial in the Greek scholia generally, and is linked in particular to its effectiveness in producing emotions.[53] Sophocles' success in capturing the pathos of Electra and so exciting the emotions of the audience is linked with restraint and the absence of vulgarity.

ORESTES IN ALEXANDRIA

The norms of theatrical propriety are sustained in the criteria by which performance of the classics is evaluated. The actor's responsibility is to be faithful to the author's intentions, and not to exceed these without textual authorisation. The scholia on *Orestes* offer a virtual case-study of the way in which one classic text was performed on the Hellenistic stage and the kinds of strictures these performances drew from contemporary scholars. *Orestes* had provided from its original performance a challenge to actors: according to the scholia, Hegelochos' famous gaffe at 279 'for out of the waves I again see a weasel . . .' provided grist for a generation of comic poets.[54] As the earlier discussion of the entrance of the Phrygian suggests,

[53] Cf. Zanker (1981), Meijering (1987) 21–5, 30–3, 49–52.

[54] Schol. on 279: 'The line is made fun of in comedy because of the actor Hegelochos. Out of breath and unable to observe the elision, he seemed to those listening to say γαλῆν, the animal, not γαληνά, "the calm". And so many of the comic poets ridiculed it, Aristophanes . . . and Strattis in *Anthroporestes*.' Cf. Slater (1990) 391: 'If Aristophanes can have such fun at their expense, actors must now have something of the same public recognition and presence as the other public figures

this is a play that invites an expansive performance, and its use of a range of 'special effects' (culminating in the triple-tiered ending with actors appearing at ground level, on the *theologeion* and the *mēchanē*) would have helped make it a favourite. Its popularity in the fourth century is reflected in the records of performance (*didaskaliai*) that survive from the years 341–339:[55] *Orestes*, with Neoptolemos as protagonist, was performed in 340 as the requisite 'old tragedy', and the criticisms it drew about the same time from Aristotle (*Poet.* 1454a, 1461b) perhaps are further testimony to the frequency of its performance. Aristophanes' hypothesis singles out the play for its popularity on stage (τῶν ἐπὶ σκηνῆς εὐδοκιμοῦντων). The electrifying character of Orestes' on-stage fit of madness is reflected later in references by Virgil (*Agamemnonius scaenis agitatus Orestes*, *Aen.* 4.471) and perhaps also in Ovid (*Orestes / ausus in arcanas poscere tela deas*, *Am.* 1.7.9–10). A wall-painting of the second century AD from a Roman house at Ephesus (fig. 59) portrays lines 233ff., in which Electra cares for her sick brother, and across from it is a scene from Menander's *Sicyonians* which was in turn inspired by that piece of stagecraft.[56]

The visual power of the *mise-en-scène* is further reflected in the care with which it is presented in the Aristophanic hypothesis, where we can see the essential connection the scholar makes between text and performance:

> The arrangement of the drama is as follows. Orestes is situated at the palace of Agamemnon, lying sick from his madness on a little bed, by which Electra sits at his feet. The question arises why she does not sit at his head, for in this way if she were sitting closer to her brother she would seem to be taking better care of him. The poet seems to have arranged things in this way because of the chorus. Orestes, who had fallen asleep only recently and with difficulty, would have awakened if the women of the chorus had taken up their place closer to him. We can assume this from Electra's words 'Quiet, quiet, tread light . . .' And so it is believable that this is the reason for such an arrangement.

It is the poet who has so arranged the opening tableau, and the scholia extrapolate from the text the 'stage directions'[57] by which he has made

he attacks.' That the story is so fully and frequently cited in the scholia may itself suggest a bit of *Schadenfreude*.

55 *IG* II³ 2319–23; see *DFA* (1968) 107–20 and Csapo and Slater (1995) 41–2. For discussion see Easterling (1997a) 214–17.

56 Illustrated in Green and Handley (2001) 97; see also Hall (1997b) 155, who notes the similar juxtaposition of paintings from tragedy and comedy in the so-called 'House of the Comedians' at Delos.

57 The case against actual stage directions (παρεπιγραφαί) in tragedy and satyr play is made in Taplin (1977b).

Fig. 59 Tragic actors in the roles of Orestes and Electra in Euripides' *Orestes* (By permission of the Österreichisches Archäologisches Institut)

this clear: since Electra will later try to keep the chorus from waking up Orestes, she must be located so as best to keep them at a distance. Correspondingly, at the end of the mad scene the text seems to suggest a change in her location, for when she addresses her brother by his 'filthy wretched head of hair' (225) we are told that as she says this 'she sits beside Orestes and draws him to her side'. This, it would appear, is thought to be implicit in the previous couplet, when Orestes asks her for support: 'prop me up, side to side' (ὑπόβαλε πλευροῖς πλευρά).

One can extrapolate to the range of stage business: 'stage-directions' are implicit in the text, and there is no need to go 'beyond' the text to determine them. This recalls the position elaborated by Taplin and others that significant stage action is always implicit in or sanctioned by the text: that a thing done is always a thing said or in some way flagged by the text.[58] Consider the scholium at 168, where Electra first complains that the chorus' howling (θωύξασα) has awakened Orestes:

> Some say that the chorus has made a mournful sound that cannot be written, a shriek or even harsher, the kind of thing which women often do in the utmost misery. For things that cannot be written are revealed by other characters, just as in the comic poet [Aristophanes], when the slave groans, another says: 'Do you hear, how he groans?'

There are serious implications here for the relationship of the scholar and actor: on this assumption, everything the actor needs to know has been indicated by the poet in the text, provided he is knowledgeable and responsible enough to appreciate it. Read in this light, comments throughout the scholia are seen to reflect a consistent approach to stage action. At the opening line of *Ajax* the scholiast notes that the actor playing Odysseus 'should look around in all directions, as though he were afraid that he might be seen', for which there is evidence in his subsequent conversation with Athena. At *Oedipus at Colonus* 1547, as the protagonist makes his final exit into the *skēnē*, we learn that 'the actor does not stumble, but he exits straight as if being led by the god', and Oedipus himsef refers to the guidance of Hermes and Persephone. When at *OT* 1297 Oedipus emerges from the palace and the chorus refers to his suffering as too terrible to behold, we are told that 'perhaps the members of the chorus turn away as they look, unable to behold the suffering'. The principle can be extended to delivery. At *Ajax* 334 we read that Tecmessa's use of *thōussei* to describe Ajax's cry within is emphatic: 'the man playing the part of Ajax should make a very rough sound and howl more like a dog, for that is why the poet said θωύσσει'. The problem, of course, is that even in simple cases what the text 'actually says' is always a matter of interpretation: it is not the mere presence of textual clues that is in question but their identification, selection and relative emphasis. For instance, how do we know when we have a metaphor and when an on-stage action? At *Hippolytus* 215 we are told that the actor playing Phaedra in her longing to join Hippolytus on the hunt 'must arouse himself with both gesture and voice, and with the words "I will go to the woods" jump up as if she were setting out'. Here the move from 'send me to the mountain' to 'I will go to the woods' is said to authorise a

[58] Cf. Taplin (1977a) *passim* and esp. 28–39; '... the significant stage instructions are implicit in the words. The characters of Greek tragedy say what they are doing, or are described as they act; and so the words accompany and clarify the action'.

graphic display of emotion, though there is no certain requirement that these verbs be taken so literally.

In positing a fundamental relationship between language and stage action, commentary takes up the part of the author and his intentions against a performance tradition that has lost its textual moorings. The criticism of certain practices as typical of actors 'nowadays' suggests a degradation in the standards of acting and the tendency to excess: unauthorised display, over-acting and unnecessary padding of the text. So at *Orestes* 57 the scholiast objects to the way that 'some actors today' ignore the author's explicit statement that Helen and the spoils had been sent ahead during the night, and stage her entrance during the day – presumably in an elaborate dumb show before the opening lines are spoken.[59] The principle can be extended to any action that is deemed not to be sanctioned by the text. At *Orestes* 643 the protagonist appeals to Menelaus to give to him nothing of his own possessions but rather the very thing he once received from Agamemnon (which he will identify in the next line as his life, *psychēn emēn*). The scholiast observes that at this point the actors apparently like to gesture as though Menelaus were about to raise an objection, one which has no basis in the text (the lemma is ἃ δ᾽ ἔλαβες):

> When this is said some of the actors raise their hands as though Menelaus were distressed that he is saying that he (Menelaus) had been entrusted with a deposit of money from his father. But for Menelaus to have a suspicion is silly (εὐήθης). For if he did not know the man who was speaking or what he needed, perhaps the thing would be credible. But since he does know, to do this is superfluous and pointless (περιττὸν καὶ ἄπορον).

The error is again linked to an inadequate comprehension of the text and of the character one is playing. In limiting the actor's movements and gestures to what can be anchored in the text, such comments recall Aristotle's objections to the busyness of contemporary actors: 'as though the spectators could not understand if they [actors] did not add something of their own, they stir up all kinds of movement' (*Poet.* 1461 b29–30).

The commentators' rejection of such padding becomes an indictment of routine theatrical elaboration and imagination. Take for instance the oft-cited entry at 268 as Orestes, under attack by Erinyes visible only to him, asks Electra to hand him the weapon which Apollo had given him for just this purpose:

59 Although Willink ad loc. suggests that since such a dumb show might just as well have been allowed as taking place during the night, the practice was more likely to have referred to Helen's regular entrance at 71 with the spoils and via the *parodos* that leads from the harbour, with or without rearranging the discussion at 56–60.

Following Stesichorus, he says that he has taken a bow and arrows from Apollo. And so it is necessary for the actor to take bow and arrows and use them. But the actors who play the hero nowadays ask for the bow and arrows, and not receiving them pretend to use them. But if even a mad man is sane in some respects, we should not be surprised. For the illness takes different forms with those who have it. So too in *Trojan Women*, Cassandra says: 'for just so long will I set aside my ravings'.

The passage can be challenged for the weakness of the argument – what would prevent Orestes from thinking that he had the bow when in fact he didn't? – but it is consistent with the general understanding of stage-action: since there is nothing in the text that refers to his delusion in this respect, we must assume that he does have the bow. The source hunting in Stesichorus' *Oresteia* and the introduction of a parallel situation in *Trojan Women* become supporting arguments which demonstrate the kind of erudition on which the scholar's work is built.

We may conclude by noting the basically realistic and naturalistic set of conventions that are assumed throughout the scholia, especially as these involve physical action on stage: with *Orestes*, as we have seen, Electra must not sing too loud, the chorus must not draw too near, and so forth. The promotion of this aesthetic may be a response to tendencies on the stage that were pushing actors in the direction of over-stylisation and a too much larger-than-life manner of presentation, one also reflected in changes in mask, costume and machinery.[60] This kind of realism apparently extended to matters of casting, as in the note on the suicide of Ajax (*ad* 864) which insists that 'the actor should be stout and strong, to bring the spectators to imagine it is Ajax'.[61] As the scholars would have it, a play that is properly performed invites us to see not the actor but the character. To the extent that the actor embellishes what the poet 'actually says', drawing on his own resources to enhance the text, he rather than the role he plays becomes the object of the audience's attention. Yet the scholarly perspective here would be at odds with the professionalisation of the theatre industry (contracts would often have been arranged to book famous actors in virtuoso roles), the tastes of audiences, which would have been

[60] Cf. Csapo and Slater (1995) 256–8. On realism and the Hellenistic aesthetic, see Pollitt (1986) 141–7, Zanker (1987) *passim*, Green (1990) 92–4.

[61] Cf. Easterling (ch. 15) and Lada-Richards (ch. 19) in this volume. Such physical realism apparently was approved by audiences as well: a third-century BC tragic actor from Tegea (sometimes identified as Apollogenes), who had won many prizes for such heroic roles as Heracles, Achilles and Antaeus, also won a boxing match in Alexandria: here clearly the audience's knowledge that the actor was especially suited to the roles he played enhanced his popularity, if not his performance (*SIG*[3] 1080, trans. in Csapo and Slater (1995) 200).

keenly attentive to just who was behind the tragic masks, and the self-aggrandisement of actors, who would surely tailor their performances to set off their special talents. Just as scholars today might prefer that revivals of Greek tragedy focus more on the play and the performance than on the celebrity of the cast, the production that manages to star Diana Rigg as Medea or Zoe Caldwell as Electra will win its promoters more kudos and a larger box office take. The scholars' argument for a more transparent idea of the actor, like so much of their sustained advocacy of the poet, the text, and the larger performance, will have been largely lost on all but each other in the prevailing theatrical climate.[62]

SUGGESTIONS FOR FURTHER READING

The relevant scholia are collected and discussed in A. Trendelenburg, *Grammaticorum Graecorum de Arte Tragica Iudiciorum Reliquae.* (Bonn 1867), less usefully in K. Weissmann, *Die scenischen Anweisungen in den Scholien zu Aischylos, Sophokles, Euripides und Aristophanes.* (Bamberg 1896); scholia on Euripides in G. Malzan, *De scholiis Euripideis quae ad res scenicas et ad histriones pertinent* (diss. Darmstadt 1908). The definitive history of Hellenistic scholarship remains Pfeiffer (1968). On literary theory in the scholia generally, see Meijering (1987).

[62] I wish to thank the editors for generous assistance and members of the graduate seminar on scholia held at Cambridge University in 1997, where this paper first took shape. It has also benefited from helpful comments by members of the Classical Association of Great Britain and the Classical Association of the Middle West and South, at whose meetings versions of this paper were presented. I am grateful to The College of Wooster for a research leave and other forms of faculty support that made this project possible.

CHAPTER SEVENTEEN

Orator and/et actor

Elaine Fantham

My title is bilingual, because both stage and courtroom professionals were described in classical Latin by the same familiar terms that have survived in English. Although my focus is to be the evidence of Roman writers on rhetoric about actors and acting, it is, I think, important to open with a brief discussion of these key terms. Romans were very conscious of the common element of performance that bound the orator to his theatrical counterpart, but Latin *orator* and *actor*, like their root verbs *orare* and *agere*, were found in the earliest theatrical texts with other senses besides those that survived into the classical period. In the texts of Plautus and Terence both the actor and his director could be said to *agere*: while the Director put on the play *agit* (*fabulam*), the actor played or performed the role *agit* (*partes*). Hence Plautus' jest in *Bacchides*: 'it isn't the action but the performer (*actor*) who strikes my heart with loathing: even the *Epidicus*, a play I love like my own self, I am loath to watch when Pellio is performing (*agit*)'.[1] *Orator*, on the other hand, originally stressed the speaker's role as pleader or intercessor, a sense found in both Plautus and Terence. Both terms converge in a significant passage from the prologue of Terence's *Heauton Timoroumenos*:

> Terence wanted me to be a pleader (*oratorem*) not a prologue speaker. He made the verdict yours, and provided me as advocate (*actorem*), in hope that this advocate can achieve as much by his eloquence as the poet could devise successfully when he wrote the speech that I am about to give.[2]

[1] Plaut. *Bacch.* 213–15 *non res sed actor mihi cor odio sauciat./ etiam Epidicum, quam ego fabulam aeque ac me ipsum amo,/ numquam aeque invitus specto si agit Pellio.* See Brown, in this volume, pp. 228–9 and n. 17. As Brown argues (p. 232), the director Pellio was almost certainly the leading actor, and it is his interpretation as performer which is meant here. See also Brown pp. 228–9 and n. 20 for the use of *actor* for the *dominus gregis* in *Phorm.* 10 and 33, alongside *partes agere* (*Phorm.* 27, 835–6) of playing a part.

[2] *Haut.* 11–15 *Oratorem esse voluit, non prologum;/ vostrum iudicium fecit; me actorem dedit,/ si hic actor tantum poterit a facundia,/ quantum ille potuit cogitare commode,/ qui orationem hanc scripsit quam dicturus sum.* Terence clearly usurps courtroom language to strengthen the advocacy of his prologues.

Beyond the stage, the form of public performance most likely to be required, of Roman public men, was the delivery of a forensic or political speech. In this respect the speaker was an *actor* no less than the stage performer of comedy and tragedy to whom the word was more often applied. Yet it is sometimes difficult to determine which sense of *actor* or *agere* is intended. The orator is an *actor* both because he pleads his case (*causam agit*), and because he enacts the speech he has (normally) himself composed.[3]

Actio, a word not found in early comedy, brings in another complication. The earliest and dominant use of *actio* was as a legal term, to denote the formal and formulaic procedure of the civil courts. In the developed and freer form of public advocacy the speech itself, as a brief or plea, was also called *actio* (like Cicero's *actio prima* against Verres), and so again was its manner of performance. Thus *actio* came to include both visible gesture and oral delivery, *pronuntiatio*. In contrast with the more complex Greek concept *hypokrisis*, this basic noun became the word for acting / performance in courtroom, senate, assembly and theatre.[4]

Our own experience tells us that public speakers often distort the facts. The court defender often has to disguise the truth on behalf of his client, and the politician just as often makes statements he (or she) does not believe to a political gathering. But when the rhetorical theorists who are our main source for Roman methods of acting invoke theatrical practices they are eager to distinguish the reality and veracity of the public speech from the fiction of theatre, and the decorum of the gentleman from the licence of the artist.

For Cicero the stage actor merely imitated reality, whereas the orator engaged with it:[5] the actor was only the performer of a role created by another (the poet) outside himself, but the orator was both originator of his own role and responsible for it.[6] Yet the mature statesman turned repeatedly to the parallel of the actor in the full treatment of *De oratore*, his first great theoretical treatise, using both generic illustrations from the stage and examples of the leading actors of his day to demonstrate

3 Cf. Cic. *De or.* 3.214 *actore mutato . . . quae sic ab illo esse acto constabat oculis, voce, gestu, inimici ut lacrimas tenere non possent.*

4 I am most grateful to the Directors of the *Thesaurus Linguae Latinae* for permission to consult the original Zetteln for both *actio* and *actor.*

5 Typical are *De or.* 2.34 *quis actor imitanda quam orator suscipienda veritate iucundior?*, 2.193 *quid potest esse tam fictum quam versus, quam scaena, quam fabulae?*, 3.214 *oratores qui sunt veritatis ipsius actores reliquerunt, imitatores autem veritatis histriones occupaverunt.*

6 These double aspects of the actor's dependency and speaker's autonomy are reflected in *De or.* 2.194 *neque actor sum alienae personae sed auctor meae.*

the requirements of *actio*, delivery or performance. In his eagerness to press demands on the orator for excellence in performance, Cicero uses examples from the theatre to illustrate the need for natural beauty of voice, body and gesture: he returns to tragedy (rather than comedy) in giving precepts for conveying and arousing emotion, in demonstrating the need for contrast in tone, and above all in the systematic treatment of delivery which ends the treatise.[7]

Cicero's youth, when the writing of Roman drama was already in decline, seems to have been the great period of star actors in both comedy and tragedy. He formed a close friendship with the leading *comoedus*, Q. Roscius Gallus, and knew the slightly younger tragic actor Clodius Aesopus. His intimacy with Roscius is borne out by the speech *Pro Roscio Comoedo*, defending him on a charge of business fraud in 66 BC, by his many allusions to personal conversations with Roscius and his reports of performances by both men. Indeed Macrobius, writing four hundred years later, and probably drawing on lost works of Suetonius, cites Cicero's letters as his source for their friendship.[8] The actor and the orator used to compete by taking an idea or statement and testing whether Roscius could represent it in a greater variety of gesture or Cicero in variety of language. Yet the influence of the two arts was reciprocal, if it is true, as Valerius Maximus claims, that Roscius and Aesopus used to attend court cases in order to adapt forensic gesture for the stage.[9]

These actors were famous in and after their lifetimes, so I include a brief summary of their lives and performances. Although Roscius' name Gallus might suggest he was of freedman origin, his circumstances were too prosperous for him to have been born a slave. He came from the territory of Lanuvium, and circulated the story that as a baby he had

7 See *De or.* 3. 213–27 for the systematic discussion of *actio*. Not *actio*, but *pronuntiatio* is the rubric used by the *Rhetoric for Herennius* for its recommendations on delivery (3.19–27), which deal only briefly with gesture (*corporis motus*, *gestus*). This passage will not be discussed here because like Cicero's *Orator ad M. Brutum* (54–60) it offers no incidental comments on theatrical performance.

8 Macrobius *Sat.* 3.14.10. He or his source seems, however, to have confused Roscius with the tribune Roscius Otho – probably a kinsman – whose theatrical seating law Cicero defended in a consular *contio* of 63 BC.

9 On the contest *utrum ille saepius eandem sententiam variis gestibus efficeret an ipse per eloquentiae copiam sermone diverso pronuntiaret* see Macrobius *Sat.*3.13.12.

On the reverse flow of influence from forensic *actio* to the stage Val. Max. 8.10.2 claims that Hortensius' gesture was so elegant that both Roscius and Aesopus used to attend regularly when he was pleading, in order to transfer to the stage gestures they had found in the judicial forum: *constat Aesopum Rosciumque ludicrae artis peritissimos illo causas agente in corona frequenter adstitisse, ut foro petitos gestus in scaenam referrent.* Since Valerius' other illustrations of the importance of gesture in 8.10 all come from Cicero, this tradition too is probably Ciceronian, but is not found in his extant work.

once been embraced by a snake, but was found by his nurse unharmed – a symbol of future greatness.[10] He must have been born in the 120s BC to be already a star when Lutatius Catulus, the future victor of Vercellae and consul of 102 BC, composed his flattering epigram comparing Roscius to the dawn: *mortalis visus pulchrior esse deo.*[11]

Certainly Cicero, careful to avoid anachronism, makes his former teacher L. Licinius Crassus speak in *De oratore*, set in 91 BC, of seeing Roscius on stage and sharing discussions of his art. Cicero undoubtedly has transferred to his teacher elements of his own experience, but in keeping with the generic tradition of the dialogue, he will also have represented as Roscius' oral teaching maxims like *caput esse artis decere* ('the essence of art is grace'), which could be found in Roscius' treatise comparing oratory and acting, the *librum quo eloquentiam cum histrionia compararet*, cited by Macrobius.[12] But the actor must have begun to perform considerably earlier than the nineties, since Crassus reports the adverse reactions of an older generation (*nostri illi senes*) to Roscius' performance when he wore a mask. This one sentence, *nostri illi senes personatum ne Roscium quidem magnopere laudabant* (*De or.* 3.222), has implications both for the star actor and for the history of the theatre: Cicero acknowledges in *De natura deorum* 1.79 that Roscius had a pronounced squint, but clearly older audiences were used to seeing both Roscius and other performers without masks. While anecdotal versions of theatrical history claim that Roscius introduced the wearing of masks to conceal his squint, a more reliable inference is simply that masks were introduced[13] in the generation before the dramatic date of *De oratore*.

In this period, around 90 BC, Roscius was already taking pupils, so it is not unlikely that some of Cicero's knowledge comes from private study of elocution with him as a boy. We only know that Roscius was usually discontented with his pupils (*De or.* 1.129) but made a success of at least one pupil, Panurgus, whose value he increased 150 fold by his training.[14] Besides his admission to the aristocratic circle of Catulus, Roscius was

[10] Cic. *Div.* 1.79, criticised at 2.66. We might compare Horace's childhood miracle in *Odes* 3.4.17–20, with Fraenkel's note in *Horace* (Oxford (1957) 275), which cites as model the miracle of the infant Iamos described by Pindar *Ol.* 6.45ff.

[11] 'The mortal seemed more handsome than the god', quoted by Cic. *Nat. D.* 1.79. But Cicero adds a revealing comment, discussed below.

[12] *Sat.* 3.14.12. But the book may go unmentioned in Cicero's dialogue because it was not composed until after the dramatic date of 91 BC.

[13] Or re-introduced: I share Brown's belief (p. 233, n. 34) that Plautus' and Terence's comedies were performed in masks, as I have argued in an earlier paper: Fantham (1973).

[14] On Roscius' dispute with his former partner Fannius over the profits from Panurgus, see Lebek (1996) 37.

also an intimate of Sulla,[15] who as Dictator and absolute ruler of Rome gave the actor the gold ring of a Roman *eques* in 81 BC. From this time forward either as a result of his new status or as an affirmation of his own dignity Roscius seems to have performed without accepting a fee.

But what roles did he perform? And what was distinctive about his acting? Roscius would become a byword for artistry in any field,[16] but his own artistry was something perfected by careful rehearsal, for according to Valerius Maximus (8.7.7) he never adopted a gesture on stage that he had not practised at home. He was chiefly known for his *venustas*, which we might translate as 'grace', and this directed him towards comedy rather than tragedy, which made more demands on the actor's voice and less on his action.[17]

Another factor in his preference was that comedy usually exploited nimbler movements, and Quintilian follows his comment on Roscius' preference (11.3.111) for comedy with a list of the comic roles such as slaves, parasites, maidservants and fishermen (!) who move more rapidly than the solid citizens. He does not mention pimps, but Charles Garton has used his vast range of knowledge of Roman theatrical life to create a wonderfully imaginative account of 'How Roscius acted Ballio' largely based on Cicero's statement in his brief for Roscius that this was a favourite role.[18]

If Roscius preferred the role of the pimp in *Pseudolus* to the much longer title role, this may have been for its scope in innuendo[19] as Garton suggests, or perhaps it was a choice of his later years. There are two clues to this in *De oratore*: Roscius is on record as saying that with advancing age he adopted a slower tempo on the accompanying pipe and more leisured singing (1.254), and his mimicry of a tedious old man is cited as famous.[20] And while Pseudolus has an exhausting singing role, the role of Ballio has only the one great *scena ed aria*, a boastful and threatening song with recurring stanzas in many metres (the *canticum* of 133–228).

[15] See Plut. *Sulla* 36, 1–2 (grouping Roscius with the mime Sorex and the Lysiode Metrobios), also Macr. 3.14.13.

[16] Cf. Cic. *De or.* 1.130, 258, Festus 288–9M.

[17] Cf. Cicero's distinction in *De or.* 1.128 *vox tragoedorum, gestus paene summorum actorum est requirendus*, and 1.251 *gestu histrionum . . . tragoedorum voci*.

[18] Garton (1972a) 170–88, starting from Cic. *Q. Rosc.* 20. See also Brown, this volume, p. 234.

[19] In a letter to Paetus (*Fam.* 9.22) Cicero fondly recalls Roscius' intonation on a phrase from an unidentified comedy 'and so she left me – stripped'.

[20] *De or.* 2.242. To judge by the quotation *tibi ego Antipho, has sero, inquit. senium est cum audio*, what was celebrated was the actor's quick change from the young speaker's own voice to his mimicry of the old man. But note below Quintilian's warning to the orator against adopting this theatrical trick.

His part is considerably shorter than that of Pseudolus. But it would be misleading to neglect Roscius as a performer of tragedy; thus to illustrate the art of contrast in oral delivery Cicero comments in *De or.* 3.102 on two passages from tragedy which Roscius regularly performed. First citing from an unknown play, he notes that 'Roscius never acts this verse with that gesture which he is master of,

> The wise man seeks honour, not plunder, as reward of valour,

without immediately dropping his voice, as in the next line,

> But what do I see? A man girt with the sword occupies the sacred place . . .

He cuts himself off, gazes, expresses wonder and amazement.'

Then citing the famous passage from Ennius' *Andromacha* which begins

> What aid am I to seek?'

Cicero comments: 'how mildly, how casually and without gesticulation (*non actuose*) he speaks! For there follows immediately

> O father, O my country, O house of Priam!

where such passionate delivery would be impossible if it had been used up and exhausted by the previous gesture.'

In many ways oratory is closer to tragedy, especially in the pathos of the peroration,[21] and Cicero usually appeals to the art of Clodius Aesopus, whose career began perhaps ten years later than that of Roscius, and ended rather sadly when he disappointed with the huskiness of his voice in his recall to the stage at Pompey's inaugural games of 55 BC. It is probably this episode that has triggered the single reference to Aesopus found in *De oratore*, where Antonius claims that audiences are more critical of actors than orators, hissing Aesopus off the stage *si paulum inrauserit* ('if he grew a little hoarse').[22] Only two years earlier, in 57, Aesopus had moved audiences with his own real tears on Cicero's behalf in his tragic performance in the *Eurysaces* of Accius and subsequently in the praetexta *Brutus*. It is a reflection on the artist's lack of respect for his text that Aesopus not only gave special emphasis to a reference to king Tullius

[21] Often ironically called *tragoediae* e.g. *De or.* 1.219, 228; 2.205, 225. Public oratory often came close to tragedy during the late republic, since it so frequently involved the risk of a noble citizen's *caput* – his life or citizen status – and was played out before a large audience of jurors and onlookers. In this respect the situation of the Roman republic comes closer than the world of the early imperial courts to the courtroom dramas of democratic Athens, as described by Hall (1995), esp. 54ff.

[22] *De or.* 1.259, with which cf. *Fam.* 7.1.2. *is iurare cum coepisset vox eum defecit in illo loco; si sciens fallo.*

that could be applied to Cicero, but inserted into Accius' script lines of his own invention and a whole tragic aria from Ennius' *Andromacha*.[23] He was famed for the passion of his *vultus* and *motus* ('expressions and gestures' *Div.* 1.80),[24] and is said to have been so carried away with violent anger when he was playing the role of Atreus that he killed a slave who ran across the stage (Plut. *Cic.* 5.5).[25] This is a story which Cicero chose to ignore when he was arguing in *Tusculan Disputations* 4.55 that neither the poet nor the actor Aesopus were actually angry when they wrote or performed angry lines such as

> Will no one punish this deed? Bind him, I say!

Drawing the moral that we should play the roles in life best suited to our natures, Cicero praises the judgement of actors who choose to perform not in the best plays, but those which best suit their skills (*sibi accommodatissimas fabulas*, *Off.* 1.114): thus actors who rely on a fine voice choose Accius' *Epigoni* or Pacuvius' *Medus*, whereas experts in gesture play Ennius' *Melanippe* or Accius' *Clytemnestra* – both plays with strong female protagonists: no doubt gesture would dominate in such roles because men could more successfully impersonate women's gait and gesture than their voices. Thus according to Cicero the actor Rupilius (otherwise unknown), constantly revived Pacuvius' highly pathetic *Antiopa*, whereas Aesopus avoided the *Ajax*, perhaps because he was reluctant to spoil his beautiful delivery by playing the madman.[26]

Although Accius, the last great Republican author of tragedies, had died before 80 BC, the revival of old tragedies was still favoured in Cicero's time, and colours his comments on emotion and delivery. At *De or.* 2.193 Antonius notes that he often saw the eyes of the unnamed actor burning through his mask as he spoke these verses from Pacuvius' *Teucer*:

> How did you dare to let him leave your side
> and then come back to Salamis without him?
> Did you not dread to see his father's face?

[23] Cic. *Sest.* 120–3. To fit Cicero's case Aesopus added the phrase *summo ingenio praeditum* (121) and recited the lines quoted above (*O pater, O patria* ... down to *haec omnia vidi inflammari*) with such tears that he even made Cicero's enemies and rivals weep.

[24] This surely implies no use of the mask.

[25] For this excess of subjectivity cf. Lada-Richards, this volume p. 402 and n. 25.

[26] The *Ajax* is probably Ennius' play; we can only assume that the diginified and beautiful speaker Aesopus disliked playing Ajax's mad scenes. On Ajax as typically *attonitus* (frenzied), probably corresponding to his traditional mask, cf. Quint. 11.3.73 cited below. All these plays, revivals in Cicero's time, are now lost. With the exception of the *Antiopa*, praised for its pathos, we do not know why they appealed to the actors.

He adds 'the actor never uttered the word "face" without it seeming to me that Telamon in his anger was maddened with grief; and (in the next few lines) with his voice rising and falling[27] to create a pathetic note . . . he seemed to speak weeping and grieving.'[28]

This stress on the rising and falling pitch of the voice in grief returns in the discussion of *actio* proper at 3.216. Each emotion, Cicero insists, has its own expression, sound and gesture; body, face and voice all sound like the strings of a lyre, as they are struck by the heart's emotion, sharp (rising) or dull (falling) quick, or slow, loud or quiet. Within these categories he lists a greater range of modulations, such as legato, staccato, broken and suspended, or protracted with the pitch rising and falling on each phrase. All these vocal nuances Cicero describes by another synaesthetic comparison as colours in the actor's palette. Thus he associates with anger a sharp excited tone, constantly cutting itself off or broken up, citing Telamon again and the entire role of Atreus. For evoking pity and mourning he suggests the rising and falling full-throated and tearful voice, again with broken effects. Here Medea provides the model:

> where should I turn, what path begin to tread?
> home to my father? or to Pelias' daughters?

Other tragic lines illustrate the humble choking downcast voice of demented Alcmaeon's terror, the strained passionate threatening tone of Atreus' violence, the gay and tender relaxed outpouring of pleasure, and the heavy 'covered over' monotony of bitterness.[29]

On gesture Cicero implicitly defines the actor's practice by his prohibitions; the orator should not represent each phrase but indicate the general theme with restrained gestures of the fingers, extending the arm as if casting a spear, reserving stamping the foot to mark the opening or end of an argument.[30] We will meet the same definition by negatives in Quintilian's discussions.

[27] *inflexa . . . voce.*

[28] It is a topos of rhetorical treatment of the emotions to speak of actors moved to tears. Thus Quintilian discussing pathos in 6.2.35 praises *histriones atque comoedi* for still weeping when they have put aside their masks (or perhaps simply their roles).

[29] It is difficult to render these descriptive terms, only some of which reflect audible effects; if anger is *crebro incidens* (217) but lamentation *interruptum* how do they differ? *demissum* and *abiectum* both convey letting the voice fall in despair, *contentum* urgency, but how to translate the relaxation of *effusum*, or the sense of covering and suppression in *unio pressu ac sono obductum*?

[30] *De or.* 3.220 *manus autem minus arguta, digitis subsequens verba non exprimens. bracchium procerius proiectum . . . supplosio pedis in contentionibus aut incipiendis aut finiendis*. Maier Eichorn (1989) compares *Rhet. Her.* 3.27 *porrectione perceleri bracchi, inambulatione, pedis dexteri rara sub plausione*, and Quint. 11.3.125 below.

Between the time of Cicero and Quintilian comedy and tragedy gave way to mime – first the literary mimes of Laberius, who felt disgraced when Caesar forced him to act in his own play, then the more improvisational and physical comic mime. Tragedy in its turn gave way to the art of the pantomime,[31] and the word *histrio*, formerly used of comic actors, came to denote star dancers such as Pylades and Bathyllus, who relied on gesture without speech. To a great extent the *comoedus* was relegated to become an ornament of élite private life: few were wealthy enough to own a troupe like Ummidia Quadratilla (Pliny *Ep.* 7.24), but many like Pliny himself had a *comoedus* to provide solo dinner entertainment. His *comoedus* Zosimus, according to *Ep.* 5.19, not only performed speeches from comedy but recited prose history and other forms.

The other private function of the *comoedus* was as a teacher of elocution to younger boys. In his chapter on the use of the actor–trainer (1.11) Quintilian starts by rejecting theatrical tricks: he does not want the boy to learn how to speak falsetto like a woman or quaver like an old man, still less to fake drunkenness or the cheeky speech of a slave, or to learn the imitation of lovesickness, greed or fear. All these, like the more extravagant use of voice, arms and pacing around (*vultus*, *manus*, *excursio*) would certainly be standard features in the traditional comedy. Instead Quintilian wants four things from the actor as trainer: he should teach clear pronunciation, correct voice production, synchronisation or at least harmonising of speech and gesture, and the avoidance of mannerisms. The immediate goal of such training is to prepare the boy for appropriate delivery of each part of a speech, and to teach him memorisation and recitation.

But when he comes to discussing delivery as practised by the mature student Quintilian is more informative. The more than thirty pages of his long chapter 11.3 can be divided into prefatory material (1–13), followed by discussion of the voice (14–71), with a transition through comments on facial expression and eyes and neck to the discussion of gesture proper (88–149). Here, the discussion at 125–49 moves from the speaker's use of the feet to consider the varying circumstances of the courtroom, and the control and maintenance of the toga, before leading to a sequential survey of delivery through the phases of a courtroom speech (150–77). Only with the last few sections (178–85) does Quintilian return to wider aspects of delivery associated with the world of the actor.

[31] This is the name of the performer, not the genre.

I shall pass over the positive precepts appropriate to the orator which have been discussed previously both by Fritz Graf and myself.[32] Starting from Cicero's description of gesture as 'body language' or 'bodily eloquence',[33] Quintilian distinguishes between *pronuntiatio* of the voice, which appeals to the ears, and *actio* of face and body, which appeals to the eyes. The stage provides his example of the power of this art, since actors by their interpretive skill and emotional power can both guarantee the survival of plays with inferior texts and overwhelm an audience over pure fiction *rebus quas fictas esse scimus et inanes* ('stories we know to be hollow fiction' 11.3.5). It must have been the case in early imperial Rome as in the modern theatre and opera house, that a 'vehicle', a text or libretto offering a star role or even one exceptionally powerful speech, would be performed beyond its actual literary merit.

Training is all important, but must stop short of anything theatrical: the modern tendency to chant observed in schools and courtroom angers Quintilian because of its resemblance to theatrical intonation 'like the licence of drunks and partygoers' (we are back with his cautions for the younger pupil in 1.11). When the court needs grief and anger, the indignation of the *conquestio* and pity of the *commiseratio*, he sees it as an insult to the dignity of the forum to indulge in the licence of a cabaret (*ludus talarius* 58). But in suggesting that such speakers might as well perform to lyre, pipes and cymbals Quintilian is only echoing Cicero's complaint of a century earlier. It is perhaps easier to understand than to express the rhetorician's distinction between good and bad vocal effects: his indignant repudiation of 'Asiatic' singsong (*cantare* 58, 59) and his admiration for a special tone 'suggesting stage lament, with a dying fall' (*iam cantici quiddam habent sensimque resupina sunt* 11.3.167) in Cicero's famous appeal to the power of poetry at *Pro Archia* 19. In keeping with Quintilian's relish for sheer vocal colour and power are other references such as 11.3.41 *vox . . . toto ut aiunt organo instructa* ('the voice equipped with its full diapason').[34]

The stage naturally provides comparative material for the visual aspects of the orator's delivery. Here Quintilian takes his argument from the art of the pantomime (*saltātio*), which makes itself understood and stirs the emotions without speech (66) showing states of mind (*habitus animorum*)

[32] Cf. Fantham (1982) and Graf (1991). Readers should consult Graf, but in the interests of completeness I will cite some material that overlaps with his comments.

[33] *Quasi sermo corporis* (*De or.* 3.222), *eloquentia quaedam corporis* (*Or.* 59).

[34] Cf. also 167 *pleniore canali* 'with a fuller throttle', 169, *paene extra organum* 'almost beyond its range', and perhaps 50, *apertis, ut aiunt tibiis* 'with the pipes uncovered'.

simply by expression and gait. Of the many kinds of decorum which he goes on to invoke, Quintilian's first requirements are congruence of emotion and tone, and congruence of gesture and gaze. Thus the gaze should always turn towards the direction of the gesture, except when we want to condemn or reject something, so that we seem to turn our face away from the thing we push away with our hands. Later he will describe this gesture, explaining the contradiction; 'to express aversion we thrust our hand / arm out to the left; the left shoulder should be brought forward in unison with the head which will incline to the right' (113). Such gestures of rejection seem very frequent in comedy.[35] Yet in commenting on nodding or shaking the head, Quintilian warns that even stage trainers (*scaenici doctores* 71) think it a fault to gesture only with the head.

We would expect facial expression to be dominant, and Quintilian gives this as the reason why acting coaches (*artifices pronuntiandi* 73) borrow their emotions from the mask associated with each role; thus 'Aerope is sad, Medea savage, Ajax crazed, and Hercules defiant.'[36] In comedy, he notes that this is how the different roles, slaves, pimps, parasites, yokels, soldiers, courtesans, maids, severe and indulgent old men, strict and debauched young men, married women and girls can be told apart at sight. To illustrate the dominance of the mask Quintilian cites the role of the leading father,[37] who ranges between anger and mildness, for whom there is a mask with one eyebrow raised and the other calm; actors, he claims, normally contrive to show the audience whatever side is appropriate to the old man's lines.[38]

In several places Quintilian warns the would-be orator against procedures that are theatrical or appropriate to the pantomime: at 89 he rejects imitation of a doctor taking his patient's pulse or of a lyre player's hands as he plucks the strings: even gesturing to oneself as one speaks about oneself or pointing towards the person referred to are too theatrical.[39]

35 Typically marked by *nolo, aufer, apage, mitte* etc.: cf. Plaut. *Truc.* 358, 751, 861 *non voluptas, aufer nugas, nil ego nunc de istac re ago*, 912 *mitte me, inquam*. Unfortunately it is difficult to match these descriptions with surviving visual representations.

36 Quint. 11.3.73. Cf. Horace *Ars poetica* 125–6 'let Medea be proud and unconquerable, Ino pathetic, Ixion treacherous, Io wandering and Orestes gloomy'.

37 *pater ille, cuius praecipuae partes sunt*; such fathers typically pass from anger with their sons to forgiveness during the play.

38 (11.3.74) *pater ille cuius praecipue partes sunt, quia interim concitatus interim lenis est, altero erecto altero composito est supercilio, atque id ostendere maxime latus actoribus moris est, quod cum iis quas agunt partibus congruat.* The editors remind me that Pollux (4.141) reports a special mask for the minstrel Thamyras who was blinded during the tragedy, with one eye *glaukos* (to represent his blindness) and one black.

39 Compare Suetonius' report (*Nero* 39) of the Atellane actor who mocked Nero by accompanying the text 'farewell father, farewell mother' with gestures of drinking (poison) and swimming, to

It is noteworthy that after repeating the Ciceronian precepts that gesture should echo meaning, not individual words, he claims that this was formerly the practice of more serious actors. But he is essentially conservative: he even criticises *comoedi* who are playing young men but adopt a quavering voice to report an old man's words, as in the prologue to Menander's *Hydria*, or a falsetto for a woman as in the *Georgos*.[40] In contrast with Cicero's praise of this Roscian trick, Quintilian finds such mimicry offensive even in the imitative art of theatre. Later, while reviewing and accepting the more violent gestures of striking the thigh or smiting the brow, Quintilian will claim that it is theatrical to clap the hands or beat the breast (124).[41] Again, raising the hollowed out hand above the shoulder and moving it back and forwards to exhort (103), which he sees as now virtually routine in foreign schools, is seen as wavering and theatrical.[42]

How 'busy' was theatrical gesture? To counter all Quintilian's strictures let us consider some samples from comedy as described by the other actors on stage: Graf has illustrated this from the famous dumb show of deliberation when Palaestrio excogitates his plan in *Miles Gloriosus* (200–10), so I will add a simpler piece of dumb show, when the soldier Stratophanes in *Truculentus* is shut out by the courtesan to whom he has just given extravagant gifts. The rival's cook exultantly describes Stratophanes' look of pain as he seems to eat himself up in envy, his sighs, his gnashing of teeth and slapping of his thigh.[43] This is the gesture which even Quintilian would approve as now accepted (*usitatum*) in the courtroom, fitting the speaker's indignation and effective in rousing

recall how the emperor had disposed of each of his parents: the actor also pointed (*senatum gestu notarat*) to the senators' rows in the theatre as he pronounced the play's envoi (*novissima clausula*) 'Hades is dragging you off by the feet'.

40 11.3.91. On the use of Menander in training orators see 10.2. 69–72 and Fantham (1984).

41 Maier Eichhorn (1989) 133–4 has a valuable note tracing the gesture of distress in striking the thigh back to Homer (*Il.*16.125); she notes that Plut. *Ti.Gracchus* 2.2 attributes it to Tiberius Gracchus (he had Greek teachers and is cited by Cicero for theatrical turns of rhetoric). Quintilian is influenced by the criticism which he quotes from Cicero that Calidius could not have been distressed in his pleading, since he did not express it with these gestures: *non frons percussa, non femur* (*Brut.* 278). Despite her many illustrations of *pectus caedere* Maier Eichhorn does not note that it was not simply a spontaneous gesture, but the ritual gesture of mourning.

42 11.3.103 *est et illa cava et rara et supra umeri altitudinem elata cum quodam motu velut hortatrix manus, a peregrinus scholis tamen prope recepta, tremula, scaenica.* As Maier Eichorn (1989) 96–9 notes, however, editors disagree radically on this. The descriptive phrases seem overcrowded. Should this text be punctuated as two sentences, distinguishing the waving of the hand accepted by foreign schools from a more violent tremulous movement that is theatrical? Or is the text damaged; is *tremula* corrupt, or should it be preceded by a lacuna?

43 *Truc.* 593–4 *sed quisnam illic homost qui ipsus sese comest, tristis, oculis malis?... auscultat observat quam rem agam/... me intuetur gemens/ traxit ex intimo ventre suspiritum/ hoc vide dentibus frendit, icit femur.*

the spectators. But descriptions of gesture are seldom written into the text of comedy and excluded from actual dialogue. Plautus offers description when the audience might otherwise fail to notice e.g. new characters entering and looking stealthily around,[44] or in another passage a piece of dumb show as two young men enter quarrelling.[45] For the most part it was left to the actor to follow his own instinct or more likely a received tradition in choosing his gestures.[46] We can gain some idea of the traditional choreography of gesture from the illustrations that survive in different manuscripts of Terence.[47]

Throughout this chapter Quintilian has chosen his illustrative texts not from comedy and tragedy but from Ciceronian oratory or from the *Aeneid*. He will offer only one demonstration from a stage text (see below), but he does provide some descriptions of individual actors' skills: reversing cause and effect, he adapts Cicero's account of his two great peers: 'the slower the delivery, the greater its emotional power; thus Roscius was rapid and Aesopus weighty in his delivery *because* the former was a comic and the latter a tragic actor'. He allows that within comedy imitation of movement too follows the same dichotomy, as the young men, old men, soldiers and matrons of citizen rank walk more slowly, while slaves and other low characters move more quickly (111–12).[48] Corresponding to these inherited Roman examples, Quintilian turns in his closing section (178–80) to the contemporary Greek *comoedi* Demetrius and Stratocles. We do not know whether these men were known to Quintilian first hand, or another borrowed example, but as comic actors they demonstrate a point: the charm and appeal even of mannerisms (*vitia* 178). Demetrius, who had a sweeter voice, went in for waving his hands and uttering charming cries for the audience and fanning himself with his garment and gesturing with his right side. Stratocles, on the other hand, had a sharper technique and preferred running around and skipping nimbly (is this what is meant by *agilitas*?) and laughing, even when it did not suit his part (180).[49] He was playing to the gallery (*id populo dabat*), even to

44 *Mil.* 990 *viden tu illam oculis venaturam facere atque aucupium auribus.* Cf. *Trin.* 851–2.

45 *Trin.* 622–4 *celeri gradu/ eunt uterque, ille reprehendit hunc priorem pallio,/ haud ineuscheme astiterunt huc aliquantum.*

46 My thinking here is influenced by the long-standing tradition of the D'Oyly Carte Opera company in performing the operettas of Gilbert and Sullivan. Until the expiration of their copyright we could be confident of seeing these operettas with the gestures of the 1870s. More significant examples would be the traditional staging and gestures imposed in the genres of Chinese opera or the Japanese Noh play, but of these I have no experience.

47 For samples of these, see Duckworth (1952) illustrations between 96–7, 240–1, 256–7: for the corpus see Jones and Morey (1930–31).

48 See for similar character implications of fast or uneven gait in Greek drama, Hall (1995) 53.

49 This recalls Petronius' description in *Sat.* 7 (7) of *mimicus risus*. It was obviously a popular feature.

hunching his neck. Stratocles' trademark mannerisms suited him as they would have done no one else, because of his physique and good looks. But if either man had tried on any of the other's tricks it would have been very ugly. The lesson is drawn that we must know ourselves and base our performance not on common rules but on our own nature. In this at least Quintilian is true to Roscius and his maxim *caput esse artis decere* (p. 365 above). But he is not happy to leave his pupils with a dangerous example. So, as a last illustration he notes how an actor will treat the famous opening of Terence's *Eunuchus*, and then rejects the model.

> What am I to do, then? Can't I even go
> now when I'm summoned? or should I steel my self
> not to endure the arrogance of whores?

'The actor will use pauses of hesitation, sliding pitch of voice, a range of hand gestures, and various head movements. But speech has a different flavour, and doesn't want much seasoning: for it depends on enactment, not on pretence (182).'[50]

To judge by Quintilian's incidental comments and his final faint protest, in his time just as poetic diction had become popular in prose oratory, so the delivery of the courtroom was coming closer to that of the stage: *iam recepta est actio paulo agitatior et exigitur – et quibusdam partibus convenit* (184). But the stage itself may have adopted more exaggerated gesture, if we are to go by the claims of Tacitus' modernist orator Aper:

> The crowd of bystanders too ... has grown used to demanding extravagance and beauty of speech, and no more puts up with drab and unkempt old fashioned speech in the courts than it would if a stage player wanted to imitate the gestures of Roscius or Ambivius Turpio.[51]

The stage player in question was probably performing in a salacious mime rather than a decorous comedy, but it is a pity that Quintilian's educational purposes, focused on models of the gentleman's authority, leave in silence the actor's more elegant or provocative gestures. Unfortunately our other informants, the moralising Persius and Juvenal,[52] are more interested in denouncing the sexual responses of the audience, than

50 This passage must surely have been a school exercise, since both Horace (*Sat.* 2.3.258–70) and Persius (*Sat.*5.172–4) cite the same portrayal of amatory indecision.

51 Tacitus *Dialogus de oratoribus* 20.3. We should certainly not assume this represents Tacitus' own preference.

52 Cf. Juvenal 6.61–70 on sexual arousal in response to actors, with Persius 1.80–7 on similar erotic response to oratory.

indicating the actual bumps and grinds of the performers. Coarseness and refinement are after all largely in the eyes of the beholder.

No doubt ancient *actio* also underwent some changes in response to changes in social behaviour: for as fashions in gesture and spoken idiom undergo a gradual transformation in life off-stage, so on-stage too, conventions will gradually be modified to provide a more contemporary style of performance. Even in reconstructing the gestures and techniques of the near-modern stage two generations back we find that still photographs cannot revive the nature of action and achieve the immediacy of the moving camera. So when we attempt to reconstruct the *actio* of the ancient stage by juxtaposing dramatic texts, verbal descriptions and surviving illustrations, we cannot really hope for more than a limited understanding of their living theatre.

SUGGESTIONS FOR FURTHER READING

For the background: Csapo and Slater (1995) esp. 275–85; Fantham (1984). On acting styles: Garton (1972b), esp. 'How Roscius acted Ballio' (pp. 170–88). Other chapters of Garton's book are informative on acting styles, and he provides a list of republican actors in straight theatre and mime. On gestures see in particular Graf (1991). On Quintilian: Fantham (1982); Maier Eichhorn (1989).

CHAPTER EIGHTEEN

Acting and self-actualisation in imperial Rome: some death scenes

Catharine Edwards

Totus mundus agit histrionem[1]

Acting, as a metaphor for human social existence, has a long history. In the fifth century BC, the philosopher Democritus is said to have observed: 'The world is a stage, life is a performance; you come, you see, you go away.'[2] A score of centuries later, Renaissance humanists, familiar with such ancient texts, reworked the trope; a number of Shakespeare's plays return to the idea, *The Merchant of Venice*, *Macbeth*, and *As You Like It*, in which Jacques is famously made to observe: 'All the world's a stage,/ And all the men and women merely players./ They have their exits and their entrances,/ And one man in his time plays many parts' (II.7.139–42). The motto to the original Globe Theatre (quoted above) took this a step further, 'All the world plays the part of the actor.'[3]

Such analogies serve a wide range of functions. They can be read as emphasising a disjunction between the individual and his or her social actions, even perhaps the alienation of the individual from society and its conventions. They may also serve to emphasise the pathos of human life (for all its emotional turmoil, for all its drama, as brief as the duration of a play) or the arbitrariness with which 'parts' are 'assigned' to individuals (the same person plays a king in one play, a knave in another). There is also, perhaps, a suggestion that the outlines of the role are already established, that the individual can exercise only limited control over his or her actions – they follow from the part played.

This chapter will examine some more specifically philosophical uses of theatrical analogies particularly in the context of imperial Rome, though these other associations are significant here, too. While earlier Greek philosophers did make use of theatrical analogies as well as discussing

1 Motto of the original Globe theatre: Chambers (1930) vol. II, 278.

2 Democritus 68 B 115 DK.

3 Kokolakis (1960) 39 sees this as an echo of Petronius *Sat.* 80 via John of Salisbury.

the consequences of acting for human behaviour, such links are much more fully exploited in the Roman world, particularly by those writing in the Stoic tradition. It was in Rome and for a Roman audience that the Stoic Panaetius seems to have developed his 'four *personae*' theory, using the *persona* or mask to denote the different social roles played by one individual. This chapter aims to explore this distinctive development of the Stoic tradition in its Roman context; Seneca, in particular, both in his tragedies and his philosophical writing, exploits theatrical analogies in a number of ways. This new emphasis in Stoicism, I shall suggest, could also be seen as influencing representations (for instance, in Tacitus' historical accounts) of certain aspects of the behaviour of prominent Romans, in particular, how they choose to die. And it is at such moments, I shall argue, that the wider range of associations invoked by theatrical metaphors can come back into play in sometimes disconcerting ways.

PHILOSOPHIES OF ACTING

As the reference to Democritus already suggests, the Stoics were by no means the only philosophers to find acting good to think with. Plato's *Republic* is notoriously concerned at the threat posed by the stage to the well-ordered life of the ideal state. It would be most dangerous, Socrates argues, for one of the Guardians to play a role on stage. 'Do we want our Guardians to be capable of playing parts?', asks Socrates. This is not advisable, they agree, because the same man cannot act many parts as well as he can one (3.394e–395a).

Not only would the Guardians be unable to play more than one part with their customary excellence, but the attempt to represent behaviour which is in any way ignoble might itself corrupt them. They are not to do anything mean or dishonourable; nor should they have experience of representing such behaviour, in case they should become infected with the reality (3.395c5–8). In particular, Guardians are not to play female or servile parts. The only role which could safely be undertaken would be that of a man of noble character acting nobly. Unfortunately, Socrates acknowledges, in the eyes of most people, characters behaving well make poor entertainment. It is safer to ban the theatre altogether from the ideal city. While it is interesting to note in Plato's discussion of acting the suggestion that playing the role of a good man will help make someone good, an idea which clearly foreshadows particularly some of Seneca's comments on acting (discussed below, pp. 381–2), the positive potential of role-playing receives little further attention in Plato's work.

The discussion in Plato's *Republic* is largely concerned with the consequences of acting for human behaviour rather than acting as metaphor. The Cynics, however, seem sometimes to have drawn on the theatre as an analogy. Teles, a Cynic of the third century BC, is said to have compared fortune to a playwright (an idea to be found also in later Stoic writers). To him, too, is attributed the comment that one must know whether one has been given a leading part or not and that there is no point in trying to change the part one has been given.[4] Bion of Borysthenes, it seems, emphasised particularly the different roles or masks assumed by the individual in life. The *prosōpon* or 'mask' doctrine would have been well suited to Bion's own ambiguous career as both Cynic and 'court-philosopher', a combination inevitably involving sophisticated role-playing.[5]

The fragmentary nature of extant Cynic writings makes it hard to judge the extent to which this idea was developed within Cynic philosophy. It was certainly taken up by some Stoics. Ariston of Chios, a follower of Zeno, compares the wise man to a good actor who knows how to play Thersites as well as Agamemnon (*SVF* 1.351). It was in the Roman world, however, that more extended uses of acting as a philosophical metaphor developed. The four *personae* theory attributed to the philosopher Panaetius in the second century BC is set out at some length in Cicero *De officiis* (1.107–21). The first *persona* is universal (the shared rationality of all human beings), the second individual (the physical, mental and temperamental nature of the individual); the third *persona* is what is imposed by chance (wealth, accidents, opportunities), the fourth that which we assume by deliberate choice (for instance one's profession or career).

Cicero explicitly posits the behaviour of actors as a model, in exploring the significance of the second *persona* – the individual's own characteristics:

> Everyone therefore should be familiar with his own natural ability and show himself an acute judge of his own merits and defects; in this respect we should not let actors (*scaenici*) show more good sense (*prudentiae*) than we do. For they choose, not the best plays, but the ones best suited to their own talents. Those who depend primarily on the quality of their voice take the *Epigoni* and the *Medus*; those who rely rather on movement choose the *Melanippa* and the *Clytemnestra*; Rupilius (I remember him) always played in the *Antiope*, Aesopus rarely in the *Ajax*. Shall a player consider this in choosing his role on stage and a wise man

4 *Peri autarkeias* fr. 2 Hense, pp. 5–20.

5 As Moles comments (1985) n. 60.

fail to do so in selecting his part in life?[6] We shall therefore work most effectively in the role to which we are best adapted. (*Off.* 1.114)

Individuals should deploy their knowledge of their own strengths and weaknesses – this second *persona* – the better to equip themselves to live up to the demands imposed by the first *persona* – universal human nature. One should not attempt to assume a role which, however appropriate it might be for someone else, does not fit with one's own personal character. Cicero's choice of illustration to clarify the nature of the second *persona* serves to flesh out the link with the theatre already evoked by the very notion of the *persona* or *prosōpon*. But what exactly is the status of the theatrical analogy here?

POLITICAL THEATRE

Cicero's analogy perhaps suggests a way in which it might make sense to think of the self as something performed. But before exploring the further development of this idea, we might pause to consider its context. The status of theatrical performance in Rome was in many ways problematic. Elaine Fantham, earlier in this volume, discusses the comparisons which were often made between acting and oratory. While orators themselves held oratory to be the higher art, the many points of similarity noted between the two imply that acting itself was accorded considerable value. Yet there are also indications that orators might find the parallels between their own art and that of the theatre profoundly disturbing.[7]

In particular many ancient Roman texts express unease concerning the deception associated with the theatre. The words of an actor were necessarily feigned, archetypally untrustworthy, lacking in *fides* – a particular offence in Rome, where the legal system accorded the spoken word special weight. Actors were subject to a wide range of legal disabilities; they were not permitted to stand for public office, or to serve in the Roman army. Indeed, according to Livy, they were not allowed to vote. Even their bodies were not accorded the degree of protection the law offered those of most other citizens (cf. e.g. Paulus *Sent.* 5.6). All these measures underlined their untrustworthiness – something which also emerges in stories told by many ancient authors.[8]

[6] *Ergo histrio hoc videbit in scena, non videbit sapiens vir in vita? ad quas igitur res aptissimi erimus, in iis potissimum elaborabimus.* The authors of the plays can be identified as follows: *Epigonoi* Accius; *Medus* Pacuvius; *Melanippa* Ennius; *Clytemnestra* Accius; *Antiopa* Pacuvius; *Ajax* probably Ennius.

[7] Cf. Graf (1991); Edwards (1994) 84–5; Gleason (1995) 105–6, 114–16.

[8] Cf. e.g. Livy 24.24.2–3; Tac. *Dial.* 10.5.

It is striking that Romans themselves saw disapproval of actors and the theatre as a particularly Roman characteristic. To quote the preface to Nepos' *Lives*, written in the mid-first century BC:

> Almost everywhere in Greece, it was thought a high honour to be proclaimed victor in Olympia. Even to appear on stage (*in scaenam prodire*) and exhibit oneself to the people was never regarded by those nations as something to be ashamed of. Among us, however, all those acts are regarded as either disgraceful or as base and inconsistent with respectability. (Nepos *pr.* 5)

Cicero and, later, Augustine may also be found contrasting Roman attitudes to the theatre with Greek (Cic. *Rep.* 4.13; Augustine *Civ. Dei* 2.11; 2.13). The theatre was often characterised as an import, alien to true Roman traditions, as well as being associated with false speech and the subversion of gender distinction.

We may wonder, then, how far the 'theatrical' implications of the *persona* theory can be pressed. A few chapters earlier, also on the subject of the 'second *persona*', Cicero, in emphasising the need for consistency throughout one's life, specifically states that this is not to be achieved by *imitating* the nature of others and abandoning that which is one's own (*conservare non possis, si aliorum naturam imitans, omittas tuam*, 1.111). If the essence of acting is imitation (and this is one reason Roman moralists often put forward for abhorring the theatre), then Cicero's theatrical analogy is a distinctly uncomfortable one.

TRUE AND FALSE SELVES?

Sometimes, indeed, acting itself appears to serve as a negative example in Roman moral and philosophical writings. The model of the stage is used to emphasise hypocrisy and deluded self-importance, particularly as associated with public life. The Epicurean Lucretius, for instance, observes in *De rerum natura* that men's true natures emerge only when they are in adversity and 'the mask is torn off' (*eripitur persona*, 3.58).[9]

Seneca, too, can be found using a theatrical analogy to comment on the mismatch between the roles people assume and their true natures:

> I often find this example useful, for I think no other so effectively expresses the drama of human life (*humanae vitae mimus*), in which we are allocated the parts we are to play so badly (*quas male agamus*). There is the man who strides around the stage in padded dress, throws back his head and says: 'I am Lord of the

9 Cf. Petronius *Sat.* 80 (though there are textual problems with the Petronius passage).

Argives ...' And who is this man? He is just a slave; his ration is five measures of grain and five denarii ... the same applies to all those fops whom you see riding in litters above the heads of men and above the crowd; their happiness is merely put on, like an actor's mask (*omnium istorum personata felicitas est*). You would despise them if you unmasked them. (*Ep.* 80.7)

Yet this passage is far from being a condemnation of acting. Rather there are several issues in play – the ease, for instance, with which position can be lost – even the real Lord of the Argives might be reduced to slavery (similar comments are offered in *Ep.* 76.31). This is in line with the Stoic concern that one should prepare oneself mentally against all misfortunes; a distinction is implied between the real self and the social position occupied. The apparent good fortune of some is but an illusion (a matter of 'indifference' in Stoic terms – earlier Seneca comments that 'the merriment of those men called happy is feigned' (*ficta*)). The actor's relation to the drama illuminates the tension in the philosopher's relation to mundane life – like the actor he both is and is not the part he plays.

The importance of constancy of character is something stressed elsewhere by Seneca, again through theatrical imagery:

This is, above all, the sign of a foolish mind: it appears first in one form and then in another, and, which I judge worst of all, it is never like itself. Believe me it is a great thing to play the role of one man. But nobody can act the part of a single person except the wise man: the rest of us slip from one character to another ... We constantly change our mask (*persona*) and put on the very opposite of the one we have discarded. (*Ep.* 120.22)

Seneca suggests we are called upon to play one single role and that we need to play it constantly and well (perhaps a particular challenge for Seneca – that man of many parts). The good actor, who rises to the challenge of providing a good and consistent performance, can be a model for how to live. What is crucial here is the issue of consistency. Like Plato's Socrates in the *Republic*, Seneca seems to disapprove of those who play more than one part. We may perhaps detect some rather problematic slippage here between acting as an analogy and a concern with the effect of acting itself on human behaviour.

THE PHILOSOPHER'S AUDIENCE

A crucial aspect of the acting analogy, particularly as deployed by Seneca, is the role played by the audience. Acting is a success or a failure insofar as it *communicates* the part to those watching. The audience has expectations. The Stoic conception of the self should be seen as, on one level, intrinsically social. Thomas Rosenmeyer comments:

> Stoicism prompts theatrical tropes... The Roman Stoics... focus on playacting in the presence of others... The hero's eagerness to put his suffering or his passions on display matches the Stoic's penchant for exhibitionism and truculence... Stoic heroism is a planned, a highly contrived and intellectualised activity. It achieves its full meaning only if it draws attention to itself as the central spectacle in a crowded arena.[10]

In Stoicism, the actions of an individual acquire meaning insofar as they are witnessed. In Seneca's *Letters*, while the Stoic sage may be imagined as totally self-reliant, humbler mortals may do no more than aspire to this state. For them, the presence of others, so long as these companions are themselves virtuous, serves as a vital stimulus to act virtuously. When such persons are not actually available, Seneca writes, we must try to imagine them present.[11] In *Ep.* 25.5–6, Seneca advises his reader to imagine all his actions are being scrutinised by some great man such as Scipio, or Cato or Laelius. However, this need seems to have its limits. 'When you have made so much progress that you have respect for yourself also, you may send away your tutor,' allows Seneca (cf. *Ep.* 11.8ff.). Is this perhaps the point at which acting ceases to be a relevant analogy?

One might point here to possible parallels with the notion of social role as set out by Erving Goffman in his study of self-presentation in the modern western world. Goffman writes of the self as a 'dramatic effect', rather than a cause of behaviour.[12] The *cause* of behaviour is rather the desire to project a particular kind of self. The stage analogy, here, is then significantly limited. The emphasis of the analogy is on *techniques* of performance. We might want to say, as Goffman does, that ultimately these techniques, though they are important, are incidental. One does need some of the skills possessed by a good actor – but one needs them for a very different purpose from that of stage performance. The objective is rather the communication of a 'character' whose example will influence the behaviour of others.

[10] Rosenmeyer (1989) 47–8. Cf. Boyle (1997) 116. One might note also *De providentia* 2.9, where Seneca envisages the gods as spectators taking pleasure in watching the brave struggle of the virtuous man against misfortune.

[11] For a longer discussion of this particularly in relation to Seneca's advice on how to bear physical pain, see Edwards (1999). Cf. too Rosenmeyer (1989) 52; Boyle (1997) 115–16.

[12] Goffman (1956) 243, 245.

However, we should pause before assuming that the Stoic conception of the self is strictly parallel to the notion of self explored by Goffman, and concluding, therefore, that the theatrical analogy is strictly limited here also. The challenge of conforming oneself to nature demanded, for the serious Stoic, ceaseless self-scrutiny.[13] This might seem far removed from the world of the stage, so focused on external appearances, on persuasive effect. Yet while the advanced Stoic may not require others as an audience, even so an audience is still necessary – even if the Stoic must take on this position for himself. Thus the theatre is internalised – the Stoic must be simultaneously both actor and audience. In another letter on coping with pain, which this time invokes the analogy of the gladiatorial games, Seneca exhorts his reader: 'Be your own spectator; look for your own applause' (78.21). There is a sense, here, in which life can be thought to have meaning only insofar as it is conceived of as spectacle. As Rosenmeyer comments: 'Self-dramatising, seeing oneself as an actor with an audience, entails the admission that life has meaning only as a performance, as an aesthetic experience.'[14] We shall return later to the significance of this for applications of the theatrical analogy to specific historical events.

FATE

Seneca writes of individuals being 'assigned' roles in life. Just as the actor and the audience know in advance what will happen to the Lord of the Argives as the play unfolds – the part is already written – so in real life, for Stoic thinkers, what will befall the individual is already determined by Fate. The good actor accepts the part he has been given and plays it well; similarly the good Stoic will accept willingly whatever Fate has determined for him.

Yet there is also a sense in which it is individuals who are responsible for creating a pattern of expectation both in themselves and in others. They write their own parts. Cicero, in the course of his exposition of Panaetius' theory, discusses the death of Cato. Cato's choice of suicide in preference to Caesar's tyranny was manifestation of his own particular *constantia* and *gravitas* (*Off.* 1.112).[15] His earlier life had served to set up certain expectations about how 'Cato' would behave, setting a trajectory – so

[13] See e.g. Sen. *Ep.* 16.2. [14] Rosenmeyer (1989) 48.

[15] One might compare here Epictetus' comment (1.2.25–9) that, as a philosopher, he would rather die than shave off his beard, though such a sacrifice might seem insignificant to someone else.

that one might see Cato's mode of death as implicit in the earlier course of his own life. Cicero's own *persona* did not, it seems, oblige him (in contrast to Cato) to commit suicide, though Cicero's defensiveness in this respect is interesting (cf. *Ad fam.* 9.18.2; 7.3.4; 4.13.2).[16] As noted earlier, he is at some pains to point out that an action which is appropriate for one person could, because of their different characters, be quite wrong for someone else even under the same circumstances.[17]

We can also see a position similar to that set out by Cicero in Epictetus' use of the notion of the *prosōpon*, 'mask' or 'character'.[18] For Epictetus, living *kata prosōpon* – in accordance with one's character – signifies living up to the role of one who does not 'sell' himself for matters of indifference but pursues only virtue (1.2.7). Such a 'role' is exemplified for Epictetus by figures such as Helvidius Priscus who stand up bravely to political oppression.[19] He recounts a dramatic exchange between Helvidius Priscus and the emperor Vespasian:

> Helvidius Priscus . . . when Vespasian had sent instructions that he should not attend the senate, answered: 'It is in your power not to let me be a senator; but as long as I am one I must attend.' – 'Well then if you do attend, at least be silent.' – 'Do not ask for my opinion and I will be silent.' – 'But I must ask it.' – 'And I must say what seems to me right.' – 'But if you do I will have you killed.' – 'When did I ever tell you I was immortal? You will do your part and I mine: it is yours to kill and mine to die without trembling; yours to banish me, mine to depart without grieving.' (1.2.19–21)

We should note here Helvidius' references to what is expected of one who plays the part of 'senator'. Everyone knows what senators are expected to do in the context of a senatorial meeting. Yet there is also some slippage here. By the end of the conversation, the 'role' is not so much that of the regular senator, respecting the conventions of the *curia*, but rather that of Helvidius the Stoic, who must say what he really thinks, even if it means death. Thus Cicero, Seneca and Epictetus may all be found suggesting that one might envisage one's philosophical project in terms of the consistent performance of a particular role.

[16] Cf. Plutarch *Life of Cato the Younger* 59, 66; *Life of Cicero* 38.1; also Brunt (1975) 15.

[17] Though this should not be thought of as validating the actions of those who, in actualising their own evil characters, go against the requirements of common human rationality (Panaetius' first *persona*). Cf. Gill (1994).

[18] While it has been argued that Epictetus' notion of the *prosōpon* was significantly different from the *persona* of Panaetius, I would follow Brunt in seeing them as largely overlapping. Cf. Brunt (1975) appendix 5.

[19] Gill (1994) 4620.

DRAMA

I have drawn attention to the parallel which might be traced between the pre-set role played by the actor and the Stoic perception of the fatedness of individual lives. Self-consciousness about one's own role is also to be found in plays of the early Empire – written by the same Seneca. A number of characters in discussing their own behaviour repeatedly draw attention to their names. Seneca's Medea wonders if this is this how 'Medea' would behave. 'Medea', says the nurse (171), 'fiam' answers Medea – 'I shall become Medea.' Later – as she lays her plans for killing her children – Medea is made to comment, 'Medea nunc sum' – 'I am now Medea' (910). Discussing the *Thyestes*, another Senecan tragedy, Gordon Braden highlights Atreus' confrontation 'with a self-image to live up to . . . Indeed part of what he sets before himself – like Nero [in *Octavia*] and Medea – is his own name'.[20] Rosenmeyer observes: 'Medea wishes to become Medea, and Hercules Hercules, to conform both to their own expectations and to those of their enemies and friends.' The presence of other persons adds substance to the standing of the individual and is also a kind of existential exercise.[21] Audience and characters always know the end of the story; Senecan drama displays an almost overwhelming sense of historical and literary self-consciousness. As Wilamowitz famously commented, 'this Medea has read Euripides'.[22]

But this particular brand of self-consciousness was not confined to drama. In Roman political life, one could not escape the destiny of one's own name. A particular name might in itself provoke a desire for external fame. What did it mean, for instance, to be called Cato? The moral severity of the Elder Cato was a demanding model to follow. One might read the Younger Cato's choices in life as partially determined by the name he shared with his great-grandfather. The Younger Cato so closely associated himself with the ancient Roman republic that he felt obliged to take his own life when he realised tyranny would prevail. Thus he killed himself, once Caesar's victory in the civil war had become inevitable. Similarly several ancient authors comment on the pressure put on Brutus to take action against Julius Caesar, stemming, in part at least, from the name he bore. According to Plutarch, messages appeared on the base of a statue of L. Brutus, scourge of the Tarquins, 'If only Brutus were alive', and also on the praetor's tribunal in the Forum (when Marcus Brutus occupied that office): 'Brutus, are you sleeping?' and 'You are not really Brutus' (*Life of Brutus* 9.3). His

[20] Braden (1985) 42–6. [21] Rosenmeyer (1989) 52. [22] Wilamowitz (1906) vol. III, 162.

own name obliged Marcus Brutus to follow his famous ancestor and act against tyranny.[23]

Part of Seneca's Letter 120 was quoted above. He continues:

> You should force yourself to play to the very end of life's drama the character which you assumed at the beginning. See to it that men praise you. If not let them at least identify you. (120.22)

The challenge for the would-be Stoic was firstly to establish his own character and then to actualise it, even to the bitter end.

DEATH

Cato affirms his own identity in choosing death at a particular point in history. It may be enlightening to explore the theatrical resonances of a number of descriptions of death, and more specifically suicide, in the context of this Stoic emphasis on the importance of offering a consistent performance of oneself. It was often a commonplace to invoke the parallel with theatre on one's death-bed. This served as a kind of consolation to the dying and those close to them. The emperor Augustus, facing death, is said to have asked his friends: 'whether he had played the comedy of life fitly', *ecquid iis videretur mimum vitae commode transegisse* (Suet. *Aug.* 99.1), before quoting the final lines from a Greek comedy, 'If I have pleased you, kindly signify/Appreciation with a warm goodbye.'[24] The end of life is as inevitable as the end of the play. Whether or not these were Augustus' last words, they were clearly felt by those recounting his end to fit the occasion.

Marcus Aurelius pursues a similar idea, though for a more philosophical purpose, at the close of his *To himself*:

> Why is it hard, then, if you are dismissed from the city not by a tyrant or an unjust judge, but by Nature who brought you in – just as when the master of the show, who has engaged an actor, dismisses him from the stage? 'But I have not spoken my five acts, only three.' 'You are right, but in life three acts are the whole play.' For it is he, who yesterday caused your composition and today your dissolution, who determines when it is complete; you are the cause of neither. Leave the stage, therefore, with good grace, for he, too, who lets you go, is gracious. (12.36)[25]

[23] On the extent to which Brutus may have been motivated by Stoic views, see Griffin (1989) 10–11.

[24] *PCG* VIII.925 (p. 275). I am grateful to Eric Handley for drawing the significance of this to my attention. (Translation Graves (1979).)

[25] Compare the comment made by the character Cato in Cic. *De sen.* that nature, as a careful playwright, will not have neglected provision for the end of the play, *fabula* (2.5).

Paradoxically, the artificial structure of drama is used to make sense of the natural process of life and death.

And Epictetus, also, uses the idea of Fortune as playwright:

Remember that you are an actor in a play, which is as the author wants it to be; short, if he wants it to be short; long if he wants it to be long. If he wants you to act a poor man, a cripple, a public official, or a private person, see that you act it with skill. For it is your job to act well the part that is assigned to you; but to choose it is another's. (*Ench.* 17)

Such comments generate a curious alienation effect, establishing a distance between the subject and the part he or she happens to have played in life. This may be seen as one of many Stoic strategies to reconcile oneself to the prospect of death (or whatever else awaits).

However, a passage from Seneca's *Letters* offers a significantly different perspective while using a similar analogy. This is the emphasis I want to pursue further here. *Ep.* 77 (developing the theatrical metaphor of the previous letter in Seneca's collection, 76.31) concludes as follows:

Quomodo fabula, sic vita non quam diu, sed quam bene acta sit, refert. nihil ad rem pertinet, quo loco desinas. quocumque voles desine; tantum bonam clausulam inpone.

Life is like a play – what matters is not how long the action is drawn out, but how good the acting is. It makes no difference at what point you stop. Stop whenever you choose; but make sure your conclusion's a good one.

The letter has been considering how suicide may sometimes be the appropriate course of action. As we see, it ends presenting life as a play which needs a good *clausula.* Here the Latin *quam bene acta sit* plays both on the sense of 'acting' and also on the sense of 'finishing' – *actum est* (cf. *OLD* 21c). This Stoic is his own playwright. And he takes particular pride in his final lines. Thus might a well-conceived suicide form the equivalent to one of Seneca the playwright's famous concluding *sententiae.* Something memorable, often quoted – witty even.

Yet there seem to be problems with Seneca's theatrical analogies, which are made to fulfil different purposes in different contexts. There is significant slippage between the focus on the multiplicity of roles played by an individual as compared with roles an actor takes on in different plays; self-actualisation as something to be scrutinised (as in Seneca's exhortation – 'Be your own audience!'); the idea of life as fated – we can no more change what will happen than actors can the ending of the play they are performing. This latter notion in particular is effectively deconstructed by Seneca himself. The actor turns playwright and writes his own ending. As often, Seneca pushes metaphors further, to the extent that ultimately he perhaps subverts the Stoic position he elsewhere seems to want to endorse.

DRAMATIC CONCLUSIONS

Here, as often in Latin literature, we are presented with death as moment of truth – 'symbolically . . . the purest moment of life' in the words of Roland Barthes, writing about Tacitus' account of Rome under the Julio-Claudians.[26] Death was a particular preoccupation of the literature of Neronian Rome – besides Seneca's own work we might think particularly of his nephew Lucan's epic or Petronius' *Satyricon*. The high profile of famous deaths in later accounts of the Neronian period is also due in particular to the mass of death literature produced in the years after Domitian – when Tacitus himself was writing, and there seems to have been something of a fashion for death literature, as Connors, Griffin and others have pointed out.[27]

A number of the deaths recounted by Tacitus (and other writers) have striking features in common. This is particularly true of those presented as occurring under the reign of Nero. In many cases Stoic philosophy is at least implicitly presented as informing both the decision to die and also the details of the death. Indeed scholars have sometimes written of a Stoic cult of suicide.[28] This Roman suicide is very much a social act, performed in front of an audience. The suicide acts calmly and deliberately. Pain is borne bravely – the resonant term *constantia* regularly appears. His or her last words play an important part in determining the 'reception' of the death. Griffin comments on 'the theatricality of these scenes', emphasising particularly their length as well as the presence of the audience.[29] Barthes calls Tacitus' treatment of death in the *Annals* 'an obsessional theatre, a scene even more than a lesson'.[30]

The theatrical analogy here, one might argue, serves a wholly different purpose from the theatrical parallels Stoics sometimes use in articulating ideas of the self. Perhaps we should think of two ways of characterising the idea of performance in relation to self-actualisation which are not necessarily linked. But I would like, nevertheless, to explore the possibility that we can make better sense of these theatrical deaths if we look at

[26] Barthes (1982b) 166. [27] Connors (1994); Griffin (1986) 197–8.
[28] Cf. the work of Grisé (1982) and Griffin (1986). [29] Griffin (1986) 65.
[30] Barthes (1982b) 163.

them in the context of Stoic exhortations, in explicitly theatrical terms, to perform one's own personal role well.

The starting point for most discussions of the high profile of suicide under the early principate is the death of the Younger Cato. This death, which could be read as an enactment of the death of *libertas*, becomes a kind of script for subsequent suicides–though, as often in the Roman theatre, some actors showed a considerable talent for improvisation.[31]

Cato himself was drawing on a tradition. He seems to have self-consciously presented his own death as an evocation of that of Socrates (a parallel implied by Cic. *Tusc.* 1.74). Seneca in Letter 24 (also concerned with the subject of suicide in general) rehearses the well-known account of how Cato 'read Plato's book [presumably the *Phaedo*, which gives an account of Socrates' last hours] on that last glorious night with a sword laid at his pillow' (*Ep.* 24.6–8). Plutarch too (possibly using Thrasea's biography of Cato as his source) writes that Cato read Plato's *Phaedo* twice in the hours before he died (Life of the Younger Cato 68)). In Cicero's terms (*Off.* 1.114), Cato had chosen a role particularly suited to his own nature.

The Younger Cato became a Stoic exemplar.[32] His fame did not dim with the passage of time. Cato was turned into a play – or at least Tacitus makes Curiatus Maternus, a character in his *Dialogus*, the author of a tragedy entitled *Cato*. Tacitus has his narrator claim that the enthusiasm with which Maternus had thrown himself into the role of Cato when he gave a recitation of the play (essentially a defence of Cato) caused offence in court circles (2). Indeed many centuries later Cato formed the subject of another politically charged tragedy, this time by Joseph Addison. His *Cato* too (of 1713) seems to have inspired at least one suicide.[33]

Seneca observes, commenting on the gruesome tradition that Cato only succeeded in killing himself at the second attempt by tearing open the wound he had initially inflicted on himself but which had been sewn up by doctors: 'It was not enough for the immortal gods to look upon Cato only once' (*De prov.* 2.12). Many Romans, it seems, aspired to recreate the role of 'Cato' to a degree. Persius, another of Nero's contemporaries,

[31] Connors comments generally on accounts of Roman suicides: 'a text is produced or reenacted in the final moments of life' (1994) 228.

[32] Cf. Griffin (1986). Caesar himself publicised the manner of his death – in the course of his triumph, images were displayed showing the death scenes of leading Republicans. Appian, who relates this (*BC* 2.101), comments that this did not endear Caesar to the crowd.

[33] On Addison's *Cato* see Ayres (1997) 24, 30, 58. When Addison's cousin, Eustace Budgell, committed suicide, he left a note which read 'What Cato did, and Addison approved/Cannot be wrong' (Patrick (1906) 42).

suggests that Roman schoolboys regularly learnt to recite the speech of the dying Cato. He writes of occasions,

> grandia si nollem morituri verba Catonis
> discere non sano multum laudanda magistro.
> (3.45–6)

when I did not want to recite the noble speech of the dying Cato – a speech which would be much praised by my foolish master.[34]

In Roman declamation schools, the 'Death of Cato', we may suppose, was on one level 'performed' regularly. Boyle observes: 'Training in *declamatio*, most especially mastery of the *suasoria*, which required diverse and sustained role-playing, gave to contemporary Romans not only the ability to enter into the psychic structure of another . . . but a substantial range of improvisational skills to create a *persona* at will.'[35] It was all too easy for an educated Roman male to play at being someone else.

Indeed this Cato 'script' seems to have had an influence on the actual death of Seneca himself – as Tacitus describes it, at any rate (*Ann.* 15.60–4). Unlike Cato, Seneca has received an order to commit suicide from the emperor. Like Cato, however, he chooses to spend the hours before his death in philosophical conversation with his friends. He voices criticisms of Nero which, Tacitus writes, were intended for public hearing. One might compare Cato's presentation of his suicide as itself an indictment of Julius Caesar. Seneca's final words are taken down for publication (though suicide is essentially a one-off performance, those who did not catch Seneca's at the time could at least read the script later).

Like Cato, Seneca evokes the death of Socrates, though not through reading the *Phaedo* (or at least that is not mentioned). Rather we are told, when Seneca's attempt to bleed to death (a Roman death, *Romana mors*, as Martial terms it, 1.78) had failed to take effect fast enough, 'Poison, such as was formerly used to execute state criminals at Athens, had long been prepared; and Seneca now entreated his experienced doctor to supply it' (*Ann.* 15.64.3). Seneca next requests that a libation be offered to Jupiter the Liberator (compare Socrates' request that a cock be offered to Asclepius), then expires in a steam bath.[36]

34 On the textual problems associated with these lines, see Tandoi (1965–66).

35 Boyle (1997) 116.

36 One might, as David Levene has commented to me, compare this with the suicide of Otho in Tac. *Hist.* 2.46–50. While the latter is presented as a noble death (in contrast to Otho's otherwise ignoble life) it is not suggested to be philosophically inspired.

Tacitus' *Annals* breaks off in the middle of his account of the death of Thrasea Paetus (Tac. *Ann.* 16.34–5). Thrasea, too, expecting to hear his death sentence, discusses philosophical questions concerning the immortality of the soul with a Cynic philosopher Demetrius. On receiving news of the Senate's decree, Thrasea, like Seneca, slits his veins. He terms the blood which falls on the ground a libation to Jupiter the Liberator – an evocation of the libation requested by Seneca to the same divinity. As Connors comments, he 'seems to construct his last moments as an intertextual re-enactment of Seneca's death scene'.[37] His death can also be read as, specifically, a re-enactment of Cato's re-enactment of Socrates.[38]

To what degree are we justified in treating these deaths as 'performances'? Perhaps my emphasis on scripts, on replays, is straying too far from properly Stoic notions of performing oneself with constancy, even if, or especially if, that means ending one's own life. Nevertheless self-conscious role-playing seems to have a part in all these accounts. We might remember here Epictetus' presentation of Helvidius Priscus, who must say these lines for that is his part. There is also a strong sense that these deaths would lose a crucial part of their meaning if they had no audience. Marcus Aurelius expressed concern at the theatricalisation of suicides. 'How admirable is the soul which is ready and resolved, if it must this moment be released from the body . . . This resolve, too, must arise from a specific decision . . . after reflection and with dignity, and so as to convince others, without histrionic display' (11.3).[39] Yet perhaps his disapproval of the dramatic merely reflects a rather different taste when it comes to the aesthetics of suicide.

From this perspective Seneca has indeed become his own playwright. He has written his own *clausula*. But has he played his part well? Has he been consistent? Could he rather be seen as, in Cicero's terms, imitating someone else's nature and abandoning his own? Can he really become 'Seneca' in playing 'Socrates' or 'Cato'? One might well object that Seneca's death is overwritten. Certainly it seems that Seneca's mode of death did not find universal favour among his contemporaries. It is suggestive to compare here another death, not very Stoic but nevertheless rather histrionic: the death of Petronius, again as recounted by Tacitus (16.18–19). Petronius, arrested by Nero's soldiers and fearing the worst, slits his own wrists – then binds them up again whenever he feels so inclined (in irreverent imitation of Cato?). Waiting to die, he talks with his friends – in the time-honoured way – but Petronius does not discuss

[37] Connors (1994) 228. [38] Geiger (1979) 62–7. [39] Cited by Griffin (1986) 197.

weighty philosophical issues, preferring more trivial topics. He listens to recitations not of discourses on the immortality of the soul but of light lyrics and frivolous poems. His last act is not a sacrifice but the destruction of his own signet ring, after the sealing of a detailed list of Nero's most secret improprieties, to be sent to the emperor. This scene is often read as a parody of a philosophical death. Might this ironic treatment betray Tacitean unease at Stoic death-theatre? One might also conclude that Petronius, just as much as the others, perhaps more so, is dying a death wholly appropriate to his own role as 'Petronius'.

The metaphor of acting encourages the would-be Stoic to think of his or her own behaviour as intrinsically social. It will always have an audience (even if one must sometimes play that part for oneself). The aim is to *project* a good and consistent character. The theatrical metaphor also fits with Stoic fatalism. The play is already written. The individual's only choice is whether to play the part well or badly. The notion of the theatre can also serve to introduce a kind of metatheatrical distancing which itself complements the Stoic preoccupation with self-scrutiny. What does it mean to be 'Medea', to be 'Cato', to be 'Seneca'? Yet the metaphor of acting also allows scope for moves which could be seen as undermining orthodox Stoicism. The fascination of the stage is hard to resist. The most compelling characters are not always the most virtuous. When the Stoic becomes his own playwright, aesthetics may undermine philosophy.

EPILOGUE: FARCE

Theatrical suicides may also have seemed especially appropriate under an actor emperor, though we can never, of course, ascertain how far the theatrical elements characterised the original performances and how far they are the creations of later writers such as Tacitus.[40] The emperor Nero's own death was probably described in the lost latter sections of Tacitus' *Annals*. His end, as presented in Suetonius' account at least (*Nero* 47–9), is highly theatrical. Realising his supporters have finally turned against him, Nero accepts that his position is now impossible and looks to make a traditional Roman exit. He repeatedly pronounces *sententiae* which sound as if they might become famous last words. Yet his apparently final exclamation 'What an artist dies with me!' is succeeded by another; 'My life is scandalous, wretched!', he comments in Latin, then continues in Greek, 'This does not befit Nero, it does not befit him.

[40] On Nero as actor-emperor, see Edwards (1994).

A clear head is what is needed. Come, rouse yourself!' Like the protagonists of Seneca's tragedies, it seems, Nero must live up to his own well-known character. In their turn these words, too, are succeeded by a quotation from the *Iliad*, as horsemen are heard to approach. Even after stabbing himself in the throat, however, Nero is not silent but, in response to a centurion's arrival, croaks out 'Too late' and 'This is fidelity!'[41]

Nero's actions follow a similar pattern. He rushes from place to place and tries out a vast battery of means to kill himself – poison, a gladiator's sword, drowning in the Tiber and finally a dagger. This last in particular could be read as an echo of the death of Seneca, who also had to use a variety of means to squeeze the life from his aged body. In contrast to the calm of Seneca's last hours, the end of Nero's life is frantic. At first he cannot bring himself to plunge the dagger in but begs his companions to help by setting him an example (those of Cato and Seneca, it seems, are not enough). Finally, as his pursuers draw near, he thrusts in the dagger – though even then only with the help of his freedman. Tragedy, then, has descended to farce. In the end, Nero's death – cowardly, inconsistent but above all theatrical – fully lived up to Nero's life. At last he could become Nero.[42]

SUGGESTIONS FOR FURTHER READING

For a helpful and thought-provoking exploration of Roman attitudes to suicide in their historical context, see Griffin (1986). Connors (1994) offers a suggestive discussion of the literary resonance of suicide particularly in Neronian Rome. Rosenmeyer's analysis of the philosophy and rhetoric of Senecan drama (1989) provides some sophisticated insights into the workings of Senecan language.

41 On Nero's last words see Connors (1994) 230.

42 Versions of this chapter have been presented at seminars in Cambridge, Durham, Bristol and Oxford. On all occasions I learned much from the ensuing discussion and am particularly grateful to Pat Easterling, Simon Goldhill, Eric Handley, John Moles, David Levene, Thomas Johansen, Charles Martindale, Miriam Griffin and Matthew Leigh for their thought-provoking comments.

CHAPTER NINETEEN

The subjectivity of Greek performance[1]

Ismene Lada-Richards

Historians of Western theatre from the Renaissance and beyond are fortunate in having a wealth of primary sources offering multiple insights into the stage performer's art. Classicists, on the other hand, have very little by way of primary evidence to match, let us say, Hazlitt's sensitive anatomy of the subjective experience of Kean, an actor whose 'agony and tears, the force of nature overcome by passion . . . beggared description'.[2] Yet, if we were to scrutinise our scraps of evidence, meagre as they are, while consciously looking for the kind of 'subjective' information which abounds in European sources, something of the 'individual', the deeply personal experience of the actor on the ancient Greek stage could perhaps be reconstructed. What did it mean *in practice* for a Greek male citizen to spend his life playing a plurality of persons 'other' than himself and pretending to be involved in incidents which never really happened to him?

My brief attempt to put together a contextualised picture of the Greek stage actor's art will focus on four main areas of his theatrical experience: (a) his preparation for the role and 'secret dialogue' with the 'character' within his part (pp. 395–401); (b) his search for coherence and appropriateness, harmonious correspondence between performing 'self' and impersonated 'character' (pp. 401–7); (c) the opportunities for dazzling displays of histrionic skill offered by the convention of multiple role-playing (pp. 408–12), and (d) his professional aims *vis-à-vis* his audience (pp. 412–15).

'CANCELLING' YOURSELF WITH YOUR PART

An actor in performance is a paradigm of liminality, caught 'in the ironic situation of both being and not-being both himself and the character he

[1] My warmest thanks to the editors for their encouragement and for very many helpful suggestions.

[2] Hazlitt (1930–34) vol. V, 207 (on Edmund Kean's Macbeth).

is playing'.[3] There can hardly be a better illustration of an actor's self-conscious awareness of his own fluctuation between dramatic identity and the reality inherent in his everyday self than Dicaeopolis' declaration in Aristophanes' *Acharnians*:

> δεῖ γάρ με δόξαι πτωχὸν εἶναι τήμερον,
> εἶναι μὲν ὅσπερ εἰμί, φαίνεσθαι δὲ μή.
>
> For I this day must seem to be a beggar,
> Be who I am and yet appear not so.
> (440–1; trans. Sommerstein (1980))

Having gradually acquired the costume and the props of Euripides' tragic character Telephus, Dicaeopolis touches on the very question which lies at the heart of, and effectively determines, a stage performer's attitude towards his role.[4]

If it lies within my power to 'translate' an author's fictions into flesh, clothe them in the reality of a human presence, how do I define *myself* with respect to the manifold new creatures who draw life and breath from my very body on the stage? Do I aim to keep the borders of my own personality intact? Do I choose to simply 'show' to the audience the characters I play, 'describe' and 'demonstrate',[5] but not appropriate or incarnate their feelings and perspective? Or do I aim to 'transform' myself, each time anew, into my characters, to fuse with them so deeply as to ultimately 'become' my part?[6]

Like a seasoned actor, the Aristophanic Dicaeopolis reflects self-consciously upon this twofold way in which the elements of 'actor' and of 'character' can co-exist in a performer's stage presence. An actor may opt to give priority to the dramatic character over his own artistic personality;

3 Sharpe (1959) 30.

4 For the understanding of Dicaeopolis' disguise as artistic, see e.g. Muecke (1982a); Foley (1988); Slater (1993); Lada-Richards (1997).

5 Cf. the Brechtian actor's conception of himself as a showman, a 'demonstrator' of the role, who 'must present the person demonstrated as a stranger' and 'must not go so far as to be wholly transformed into the person demonstrated'; Brecht (1964) 125.

6 The concept of the actor's 'transformation' resulting in his/her ultimate 'identification' with the part was clearly considered in both theory and practice as the highest goal of the actor's art, from the beginning of the seventeenth century through the Romantic exaltation of 'sensibility' and 'sympathetic imagination' and well into the heyday of the Victorian stage. See e.g. Heywood (1612), sig. B4r, G. de Scudéry, *L'Apologie du théâtre* (Paris 1639) 85 (cited in Phillips (1980) 185), Hill (1760) vol. I, 149. From the age of Garrick onwards 'becoming' or 'being' the character seems the most fashionable vocabulary in which to praise theatrical performers. See Hazlitt (1930–34) vol. V, 184, Robson (1846) 34 (on John Kemble), Macready (1875) vol. II, 31 and (1912) vol. I, 282. Finally, 'identification' with the part forms the kernel of Stanislavky's conception of the actor's art: Moore (1966) 76.

he may aspire to become absorbed into the being impersonated, to the point that his own identity leaves off and is virtually invisible (*phainesthai de mē*).[7] However, he may equally well choose to stress the status of the 'who I am' (*hosper eimi*), that is, his own artistic self, over his pretence to be a story-character; in other words, instead of trying to suppress the objective dimension in his acting, he may wish the spectator to be at all times aware that 'what is always present . . . is the presence of the actor on the stage'.[8]

Within the Greek theatrical context, Dicaeopolis' first option represents the aspiration of the actor on the tragic stage: keen to encourage the spectator to surrender, to 'suspend his disbelief' and to lose sight of the very process of artistic transformation, his professional choice is to offer to his audience a unified vision, the image of a thorough merging with his part. Good insights into such an attitude towards the role can be gained through 'self-referential' scenes in tragedy, where the very act of acting draws attention to its own artificiality.

For example, the first episode of Sophocles' *Philoctetes* takes a new turn in line 542 with the entrance of a *nauklēros*, a ship owner, doing trade between Troy and Peparethos. Both the theatre audience as well as Neoptolemus are fully aware that, in reality, the newcomer is only a *False* Merchant, a member of the Argive crew, whom Odysseus, as an 'internalised' stage director,[9] had promised to disguise as a trader (ναυκλήρου τρόποις | μορφὴν δολώσας, 128–9)[10] and unleash into the action, if Neoptolemus were to prove too slow in luring Philoctetes off the island (126–8). But, rather than seeking to 'detach' himself from the role assigned to him within Odysseus' 'play-within-the play' aimed at Philoctetes' deception (54–85), the sailor/actor knows he has to *fuse* with it in one new image, 'I-the character', or 'the condition of I am'.[11] In order to speed up the fulfilment of the Achaean mission on the desert island, he has to trick Philoctetes, the 'intended' audience of his 'performance', into believing that he witnesses a real-life, unrehearsed situation, whereby a *real* Merchant happens to alert Achilles'

7 Cf. the famous Shakespearean actor Richard Burbage's ability to efface himself completely until the play's end: '. . . he never (not so much as in the Tyring-house) assum'd himself again until the Play was done . . .' (extract from *A Short Discourse of the English Stage*, attached to Richard Flecknoe's *Love's Kingdom* (1664), reproduced in Chambers (1923) vol. IV, 370).

8 Wiles (1980) 72.

9 The metatheatrical dimension of Sophocles' *Philoctetes* has been the focus of much recent work; see e.g. Falkner (1998); Lada-Richards (1998); Ringer (1998).

10 Thus drawing attention to the convention of multiple role playing; see Falkner (1998) 35.

11 See Stanislavsky (1961) 174; Magarshack (1961) 75.

son to impending dangers (553–621). In other words, the 'internalised' actor,[12] who lends a body and a voice to the fictitious character created by Odysseus, the 'internalised' playwright, is required to perform his role in such a way as to yield the impression that he does not simply *play at being* a Merchant, that is to say, he does not merely '*act* the character', but, as Hazlitt would put it, he '*is* it, looks it, breathes it'.[13]

It is this same idea of leading the audience to imagine the presence of the character itself[14] that underlies a scholiast's comment on Timotheos of Zakynthos in the role of the Sophoclean Ajax: as he was falling on the sword – with the same skill that prompted Burbage's admirers to believe that 'hee dyed in deed' 'whilst he but seem'd to bleed'?[15] – he offered to his spectators such a 'palpable' reality of body and of flesh that they could bring to mind – 'visualise' (*phantazesthai*) in the language of ancient literary criticism – the *pathos* of the hero himself:

It must be conjectured that he falls on his sword, and the actor must be strongly built so as to bring the audience to the point of visualising Ajax (ὡς ἄξαι τοὺς θεατὰς εἰς τὴν τοῦ Αἴαντος φαντασίαν),[16] as is said of Timotheos of Zakynthos, whose acting carried along and enthralled the spectators (ὅτι ἦγε τοὺς θεατὰς καὶ ἐψυχαγώγει τῇ ὑποκρίσει) [so much] that he acquired the 'tag' Sphageus [The Slayer]. (Schol. Soph. *Aj.* 864)

Nevertheless, if the tragic actor's aspirations are strongly 'Stanislavskian', the Greek comic actor 'never forgets, nor does he allow it to be forgotten, that he is not the subject but the demonstrator'.[17] Greek Old Comedy as a genre is replete with scenes where both character

[12] The False Merchant understands the part assigned to him in theatrical terms, as that of a Messenger, an ἄγγελος (564), while an added layer of 'performative irony' (Ringer (1998) 112–13) arises from the fact that his role is played by the same actor who devised it while impersonating Odysseus in the play's prologue; clear attention to this doubling is drawn by Neoptolemus who asks: How come Odysseus has not sailed out to 'be his own messenger' (αὐτάγγελος)? (568). See further Easterling (1997a) 169–70.

[13] See Hazlitt's (1930–34) vol. XII, 326 admiration of Madame Giuditta Pasta, the famous Italian opera singer, who 'gives herself entirely up to the impression of the part . . . and is transformed into the very being she represents. She does not act the character – she *is* it, looks it, breathes it.'

[14] While being fully aware at the same time that stage characters were professional performers, consciously engaged in the art of imitation and even hoping to win a prize for the best *mīmēsis*. On the audience's 'double' perspective, see Lada-Richards (1997) 66–9 and Easterling's reflections (1997a) 165–7 on the 'collusion' between play and audience.

[15] See the anonymous *Elegy on Burbage*: 'Oft haue I seene him play this part in ieast, / Soe lively, that spectators, and the rest / Of his sad crew, whilst he but seem'd to bleed, / Amazed, thought euen then hee dyed in deed'; extract in Chambers (1923) vol. II, 309.

[16] Cf. Meijering's (1987) 21 translation: 'in order to lead the audience to the illusion of seeing Aias himself'. See also Easterling (1997b) 222.

[17] Brecht (1964) 125.

and actor are simultaneously laid bare to the spectator's view: both the chorus and the actors may intermittently step out of their dramatic roles, and hence expose to the spectator's eyes their real-life selves. For the comedian, then, being an actor means *not* allowing himself 'to become completely transformed on the stage into the character he is portraying'.[18] As Brecht would say, 'He is not Lear, Harpagon, Schweik. He shows them . . . he puts forward their way of behaving to the best of his abilities and knowledge of men; but he never tries to persuade himself (and thereby others) that this amounts to a complete transformation.'[19]

Now, tragedy and comedy may have distinctive modes of acting, yet, whether on the comic or the tragic stage, the first step towards playing a part is to suffer the fictive death of one's former personality: for Agamemnon, son of Atreus, or Creon, son of Menoeceus, to be born, Polos, son of Charicles from Sounion, or Satyros, son of Theogeiton from Marathon (see Lucian, *Necyomantia* 16), must 'die'. One of the best metatheatrical illustrations of the need for the actor's renunciation of his real-life personality can be found in Euripides' *Helen* where, in order to deceive the barbarian Theoclymenus, the captive heroine contrives a fundamentally theatrical escape. In the double role of actor/stage-director, Helen manipulates her appearance[20] and casts her co-player husband into a well-defined part: the role of a performer summoned to play the death of his own, extra-dramatic self.[21] The sailor / 'Menelaus' of Helen's 'internalised' play (1202ff.) can only be 'born' if the real-life king Menelaus is pronounced dead[22] or, as the voice of European anti-theatricalism would put it, if he commits the abominable crime of self-abnegation. Menelaus is no different from Rousseau's stage actor

[18] Brecht (1964) 137. However, generic boundaries should not be conceived as hard and fast with respect to acting modes. On the complexity of the role-play required of tragic messengers, for example, see Lada-Richards (1997) 87–90.

[19] Brecht (1964) 137.

[20] *Helen* 1087–9: she will change her dress and tear at her cheeks. Cf. *Helen* 1186–90.

[21] See *Helen* 1076–8: Menelaus says, 'Yet, whom will you say you heard from about my death?', to which Helen responds, 'You. And *you* make sure you say that, sailing together with Atreus' son, only *you* escaped death and saw him drowning.'

[22] See *Helen* 1050–2: Helen asks, 'Are you willing to be reported dead in word, although you haven't died?', and Menelaus answers, 'I am willing to accept I have died in word, though (in reality) I haven't.' Of course, in a theatre where multiple role-playing is the rule (see below, pp. 408–12) Menelaus' 'internalised' role becomes doubly 'self-reflexive' in performative terms, for it encodes the frequent need for an actor to step onto the stage 'in one guise' after having 'killed himself in another guise'; see Damen (1989) 328–9 and Pavlovskis (1977) 119. More transparently still, in Sophocles' *Electra*, where the same actor is cast into the roles of Orestes and Clytemnestra, the audience is chilled by the off-stage cries of 'Clytemnestra' (1404–15), struck down to her death just before re-emerging on the stage (1424) as the triumphant matricide 'Orestes'.

who, shamefully, 'obliterates himself, so to speak, cancelling himself out with his hero'.[23]

However, the 'death' of the actor's self should not be taken as equivalent with the complete abandonment of himself to delusion and insanity. The Greek actor may be under the aegis of Dionysus (see below), god of ritualised madness, but is also well aware of the necessity never to lose sight of himself on stage, 'let his part "run away" with him', as the famous nineteenth-century French actor Constant Coquelin put it.[24] Thus, even Ion, the rhapsode who feels with the feelings of his characters (see esp. *Ion* 535b–c)[25] in the Platonic dialogue which bears his name, admits that, when reciting, he possesses sufficient self-control to enable him to keep an eye on his spectators, scrupulously observing their reactions:

> For I look down upon them on each occasion from the raised platform and see them weeping and casting fearful looks upon me and sharing in the amazement of my tale. And indeed I have to be exceptionally intent on them, for if I set them crying I will laugh myself because of the money I will get, but if I cause them to laugh, I myself will cry because of the money I will have lost.[26] (Plato, *Ion* 535e)

The clarity of Ion's self-analysis not only parallels Tommaseo Salvini's famous saying that 'an actor lives, cries, and laughs on the stage, but he never stops watching his tears and his laughter';[27] it could also have lent excellent support to nineteenth-century theories on the actor's 'double' or even 'multiple' consciousness, allowing him to *both* feel intensely *and* observe dispassionately, be *both* fully absorbed *and* in perfect possession of his critical faculties.[28] The very construction of stories encoding the danger of overacting,[29] that is, the possibility of the actor's pretended

23 See Rousseau (1948) 108.

24 'Acting and actors' (1887), cited in Cole and Chinoy (1949) 203.

25 Cf. the 'emotionalist' Tommaseo Salvini's saying that when he incarnates a character, he tries to 'think with his brain, to feel with his feelings, to cry with him and to laugh with him, to let my breast be anguished by his emotions, to love with his love and to hate with his hate' (cited in Cole and Chinoy (1949) 409).

26 For a very interesting discussion of Ion's dual role of performer and audience of his own performance, see Dorter (1973) esp. 71–4.

27 Moore (1966) 83; cf. Magarshack (1961) 69.

28 See especially Constant Coquelin's belief in the actor's 'dual personality', Henry Irving's lecture on the actor's 'double consciousness', and William Archer's interviews with famous performers on 'the paradox of dual consciousness'; Cole and Chinoy (1949) 196 (from Coquelin's 'Acting and actors', 1887) and 331 (from Irving's 'The art of acting', 1885); Archer (1888) 150–72.

29 See e.g. Lucian, *On Dancing* 83; on the Roman stage, see Plutarch's story (*Life of Cicero* 5.3) about Aesopus the tragedian 'losing control of himself in the intensity of his passion' and killing a stagehand while playing the role of Atreus.

madness becoming real psychological insanity, indicates that Greek culture is well aware of the borderline between truthful empathy and the clouding of one's sense of separate identity. On a more mundane level, the great actor does not even forfeit his own voice when impersonating his character but, on the contrary, creates *with* it, like the famous Theodoros, whose voice, when contrasted to that of mediocre actors, 'seems to be his own utterance, while theirs seem alien' (Aristotle, *Rhet.* 3.1404b21–4; for another interpretation of this passage see Sifakis, above pp. 153–4).

REMODELLING YOURSELF

In the heyday of nineteenth-century performances of Shakespeare, good acting consisted in perceiving one's role not as a string of verses to be memorised and recited in a dispassionate way,[30] but as a living human being, a fascinating other, whose heart one has to borrow and frame of mind to penetrate.[31] Eliza O'Neill's success, for example, seems to have derived not from 'art or study' but from 'instinctive sympathy . . . a conformity of mind and disposition to the character she was playing, as if she had unconsciously become the very person'.[32]

We may have no equally eloquent insights into the ancient actor's art, but we are privileged to witness a dramatist at work in Aristophanes' *Thesmophoriazusae*, where the tragic poet Agathon explains his art of creating stage characters (146ff.), all the while being a stage character himself in the Aristophanic play. (Meta)theatre lays bare or rather plays upon the truth linguistically encoded in the Platonic and Aristotelian discourse, namely, that the figures of actor and poet merge.[33] In a spirit which anticipates the Romantic doctrine of artistic 'sensibility' or 'sympathetic imagination',[34] Agathon claims that, in order to compose convincingly, a poet must assume the habits (*tropoi*) and mentality

30 Cf. Hazlitt's disapproving remark on one of Mrs Siddons' last appearances as Lady Macbeth: 'in a word, she appeared to act rather from memory than from present impulse'; Hazlitt (1930–34) vol. XVIII, 233.

31 To the eminent performer William Charles Macready, Shakespeare's characters were really 'alive': 'Who is alive if they are not?', he is reported to have said (Pollock (1884) 37).

32 Hazlitt (1930–34) vol. XVIII, 283.

33 This is reflected in the flexibility of the language of *mīmēsis* itself, as *mīmeisthai* can apply both to the poet creating a character (as e.g. in Arist. *Poet.* 1448a1, 1448a26–7; Pl. *Rep.* 3.394d) and to the actor impersonating that character (as e.g. in *Poet.* 1462a10–11; Pl. *Rep.* 3.395cd). See Lucas (1968) on *Poet.* 1448a1. One should also think of the real conditions of early fifth-century theatrical performances, when the poet was acting (initially as the sole actor) in his own dramas; see esp. Arist. *Rhet.* 3.1403b23–4: 'originally the poets themselves acted their own tragedies'; cf. Plut. *Life of Solon* 29.

34 Among a vast literature, see, most importantly, W. J. Bate (1945) and Wasserman (1947).

(*gnōmē*) of his creations.[35] Participating in their mode of existence or, as Keats would say, 'continually . . . filling some other Body',[36] Agathon is, like an actor, skilled in playing parts. If, however, the experience of the actor is embedded in Agathon's poetic composition,[37] the role of the poet is submerged in the artistic task for which Euripides' Kinsman, the Old Man, has volunteered (211–12).[38]

Sent as a woman to infiltrate the Athenian women's gathering at the Demetrian festival of Thesmophoria so that he may have the chance to speak in favour of the persecuted playwright, the Kinsman has been assigned not a role as an artefact, that is to say, an aesthetically designed combination of 'character' (*ēthos*), 'intellect' (*dianoia*) and 'verbal style' (*lexis*), but rather a 'proto-role', a functional position in a loosely worked-out plot (cf. *Thesm.* 184–6). The scenario cannot be carried any further unless he himself devises and constructs *ex nihilo* both the 'words' he will recite[39] and the 'character' within his role. But, just as Agathon feels the need to identify with his prospective characters in order to be able to create them, *mīmēsis* of costume being a preliminary step inducing assimilation of mood, a 'deep' conception of *mīmēsis* is also indispensable for the successful execution of the Kinsman's task: the female character that he conceives of like a poet and imitates like an actor[40] can only be persuasive if it is endowed with the Aristotelian–Stanislavskian quality of speaking 'what is pertinent and appropriate',[41] appropriateness being measured in the Kinsman's case in terms of what could be reasonably expected from the point of view of a female personality.

[35] See especially *Thesm.* 148–52.

[36] See Forman (1935) 228 (letter to R. Woodhouse, Oct. 27. 1918).

[37] For the interpretation of Agathon's work as being partially that of a performer, see Halliwell (1986) 114: 'Agathon is in part being assimilated to the theatrical actor; he is, with a degree of comic exaggeration, doing part of the actor's work in the process of composition.' See also Muecke (1982b) 55.

[38] In some famous eighteenth-century treatises on acting the actor's process of identification with his characters is described in the same terms as the poet's. See Hobson (1982) 206, quoting from Antonio Fabio Sticotti's *Garrick ou les acteurs Anglois* (1769) and Rémond de Ste Albine's *Le Comédien* (1747).

[39] This creative element involved in the execution of the effeminate spy's role is one of the reasons which compelled Euripides to choose Agathon in the first place as his actor: 'only you would be capable of making a speech that would be worthy of me' (187).

[40] The same holds true for Euripides' double role as a poet–actor later on in this same play (871 ff.; 1098ff.): by impersonating his own *dramatis personae* on the stage, Euripides is ultimately required to incarnate through artistic imitation those same characters his poetic *mīmēsis* has created, i.e. to reduplicate through *mīmēsis* the mimetic process which has called forth his own conceptions into dramatic being.

[41] See the Aristotelian definition of *dianoia* as 'the capacity to construct arguments that are pertinent (ἐνόντα) and fitting (ἁρμόττοντα)' (*Poet.* 1450b5).

In other words, in both the perspective of Agathon, the poet–actor, as well as the experience of the Kinsman, the actor–poet, *mīmēsis* cannot leave the imitator's own identity intact. Agathon's theory rests on the very principle that Western anti-thespianism abhors and dreads, that is, 'the belief that "doing" leads to "being"', that 'one may actually become the part one plays',[42] for the part moulds the player to its liking. Euripides' Kinsman, correspondingly, finds out through his own comic suffering the importance of a stage presence 'appropriate to' (*prepousa*) and not discordant with the character impersonated (*tōi hupokeimenōi prosōpōi*).[43]

It is precisely this failed correspondence between the stage actor and his part which paves the way to my further question concerning the Greek performer's preparation for the enactment of his role: would he be content with simply donning a costume and a mask or would he also take care to 'make up and dress his soul', 'tune his inner strings'?[44]

A rehearsal scene[45] performed on the early fourth-century Athenian stage suggests an effort for careful inner preparation and highlights principles which amount to a 'Stanislavskianism' *avant la lettre*. Like an experienced stage director, Praxagora in Aristophanes' *Ecclesiazusae* attempts to train the female members of her cast for the masculine impersonation they are about to perform on the political stage of the city, the Assembly of the Pnyx.

In the first place, what Praxagora is anxious for her actors to accomplish is the right creative state of mind:[46] banishing personal thoughts and feelings and shutting out all conceivable 'interpolations' from their private lives,[47] the women must immerse themselves so thoroughly in their parts as to be able to react in ways that would be most characteristic of their models.[48] Secondly, Praxagora insists that complete and

42 Levine (1994) 20, 21.

43 For such definitions of *hypokrisis* see below n. 61; in Aristotelian terms, the Kinsman's 'female' character is an example of 'inapt and inappropriate character' (*Poet.* 1454a29–30).

44 Magarshack (1961) 68.

45 Signalled explicitly as such: see *Eccles.* 116–17: 'Well, wasn't that exactly why we gathered here, in order to rehearse (ὅπως προμελετήσαιμεν) what we're to say when we go there?' (trans. Sommerstein (1998)); cf. 119. The 'rehearsal' nature of the play's opening scene has been expertly discussed by Slater (1997), who designates it as 'the earliest developed rehearsal scene in comedy' (99).

46 Cf. Magarshack (1961) 69.

47 The women have to cast aside drinking (associated particularly with women by the comic dramatists) (132ff.), carding wool (89ff.), swearing by female deities (155–9; 189–92).

48 See *Eccles.* 248ff., culminating in the injunction to imitate the behaviour (τὸν τρόπον) of country folk (278–9). Cf. Moore (1966) 85: 'An actor should learn to sit, to walk, to dress as an old man, as a fat or a weak one, and so on. At home he should practice his everyday activities as the character, dressing, eating, washing, reading, as the character would.' Cf. Boaden (1825) vol. I, 140–1, 209–10 (on John Kemble).

successful adjustment to the role is a long preliminary process,[49] which cannot be effected *ex abrupto* on the stage: if the actors are accustomed or even prone to certain acts inappropriate to their character, they are bound to reproduce them on the stage, no matter how much care they may take to eliminate incongruities during performance:

> *PRAX.* Swearing by Aphrodite, you fool? A nice thing you'd have done if you'd said that at the Assembly!
> *FIRST WOMAN:* But I wouldn't have said it there.
> *PRAX.* Well, don't get *now* into the *habit* of saying it. (190–2, trans. Sommerstein (1998); cf. 132–5)

Like a Stanislavskian director, then, Praxagora takes her actresses to task for not knowing 'how to carry on playing their parts off stage',[50] and *be in their private lives* what they wish to become on stage.

Equally 'Stanislavskian' is Praxagora's insistence on the need for utmost self-control and absolute self-discipline, so that no jarring elements intrude in the performance (see e.g. 155–9, 165–9) and so that even the 'tiniest . . . fraction' of the part is rendered with absolute precision:[51] '. . . I'm not going to put one foot in front of the other to go to the Assembly, unless these things are got exactly right (εἰ μὴ ταῦτα ἀκριβωθήσεται)', Praxagora declares (*Eccl.* 160–2, trans. Sommerstein (1998)).

But, above everything else, Praxagora understands that her most thorny problem is that of *inner* congruence and adjustment: she has to ensure that her 'feminine-minded company of women' (γυναικῶν θηλύφρων ξυνουσία) is capable of speaking in public (110), a task involving, amongst other things, the adoption of a masculine perspective,[52] since the public sphere is male-dominated. Being well aware that acting which contradicts the 'spirit' of the part or which substitutes the performer's point of view for the frame of mind of the *dramatis persona* incarnated is of no avail, Praxagora is anxious to impress upon her cast that a good impersonation does not merely depend on outer assimilation but is primarily a function of creating one's role in internal and harmonious

49 See Magarshack (1961) 69.

50 Magarshack (1961) 82. Cf. Giatsintova (1955) 125: 'The most remarkable feature of our work is its uninterruptedness. If I am preparing a part, I cannot discard it on my day off; it continues to live within me whatever I may do, whether I am at home, or out skiing, or taking a walk.'

51 Stanislavsky (1961) 157.

52 Cf. Slater's remark (1997) 102 that under Praxagora's guidance the women learn to 'speak not only in a masculine voice but also *from a masculine mental architecture*' (my italics), and Taaffe (1993) 118.

correspondence to the character who lies behind it, in the case of her actresses, 'in a manly way', *andristi*:[53]

Now look, make sure that you speak man's language and speak well . . . (149, trans. Sommerstein (1998))

So Praxagora takes one of her actresses to task because, although playing at being a man, she has sworn by female deities, and this is bound to have a shattering effect, even if in all other respects she has spoken to perfection:

PRAX. By the Two Goddesses, you fool? Where have you put your brain?
FIRST WOMAN: What's wrong? I certainly didn't ask you for a drink!
PRAX. No, but you swore by the Two Goddesses when you were being a *man* – although *otherwise* you spoke very skilfully indeed. (156–9, trans. Sommerstein (1998))

Incongruity then, that is, any kind of disquieting clash between the imitated character and the impersonator's stage presence, could be seen as tantamount to artistic failure, not only in fourth-century Athens but even in so different a context as the pantomime acting of Lucian's day: one of the characters of his dialogue *Nigrinus* expresses his anxiety lest he prove himself similar to those actors who 'many a time, when they have put on the mask of Agamemnon or Creon or even Heracles himself, costumed in a gold-embroidered dress, with terrible eyes and mouths wide agape, project a voice that is small, thin, feminine, and far too humble for Hecuba or Polyxena' (Lucian, *Nigrinus* 11). In fact, it is such a lack of an achieved level of coherence between dramatic character and the actor's own personality which lies behind Dionysus' lamentable performance as an actor set on imitating Heracles in Aristophanes' *Frogs*[54] or Neoptolemus' failure to sustain for long the role of the deserter of the camp, the young man grievously insulted by Odysseus and the Atreids, in Sophocles' *Philoctetes*.

In order to play Heracles successfully Dionysus needs to understand that the mere achievement of a physical resemblance with his prototype

53 I prefer Sommerstein's (1998) ad loc. understanding of *andristi* here as referring to the use of 'appropriately masculine phraseology' to Slater's rejection (1997) 124 n. 14 of the notion of masculine language 'in an anthropological sense' and his preference for vocal timbre, voice quality; see Slater (1997) 101.

54 See especially *Frogs* 109: '. . . I have come in imitation of you (κατὰ σὴν μίμησιν)'. For a full discussion of Dionysus *qua* actor in the *Frogs*, see Lada-Richards (1999) ch. 4.

through the assumption of a lion-skin and club is insufficient.[55] Rather than adjusting the role to himself, he must adjust himself to the role, that is, 'tune' his inner disposition, reflected in the style of his delivery, to the Heraclean appearance (*schēma*) he has donned (*Frogs* 463). However, throughout his performance he only reproduces the image of his own soft and cowardly self,[56] a distinctively Dionysiac *dramatis persona* moulded by a long theatrical tradition of which Cratinus' *Dionysalexandros* is for us the clearest example.

Similarly, Neoptolemus has failed in his role-playing because he never got into the skin of the role Odysseus assigned to him and never 'grasped its rhythm'. It is true that, up to his breaking point at line 895,[57] he succeeded in offering to Philoctetes, his 'internalised' audience, a unified perspective, where artistic self and dramatic pretence were inextricably interwoven.[58] It is also true that he managed to handle the False Merchant's story well in accordance with Odysseus' orders (see especially 130–1), and, in general, that he managed to cling to the Odyssean pre-arranged plot. However, the *dianoia* (intellect) and *ēthos* (character) he constructed for himself within the borders of this plot failed to observe the ancient dramatic and rhetorical standards of propriety (*to prepon*), for, instead of being 'Odyssean', as one would have expected in accordance with the role, both 'intellect' and 'character' were distinctively 'Achillean'. Like one of Lucian's bad actors who, being 'soft' and 'effeminate' himself, plunges into the impersonation of a great hero and, failing to remodel his own nature so as to meet his prototype's standards, is crushed by his own mask,[59] Neoptolemus fails to see the world through the eyes of his character.

Having been asked to play an 'Odyssean' self, placing expediency (*sympheron*) and gain (*kerdos*) above all other considerations, Neoptolemus nevertheless refuses to relinquish his own set of social values.[60] Philoctetes put his finger on Neoptolemus' artistic failure by observing that the youth's

55 Dionysus seems to have taken it for granted that wearing the likeness of Heracles confers upon him an air as fearsome as that of the real hero.

56 See especially *Frogs* 479–502; 579–88.

57 When in full agony he exclaims: 'Alas! what am I to do from now on?'

58 See, e.g., how Neoptolemus introduces himself to Philoctetes: 'I am of Scyros that the sea surrounds [artistic reality]; | I am sailing home [dramatic pretence]. My name is Neoptolemus, Achilles' son [artistic reality]. Now you know everything [dramatic pretence]' (239–41).

59 Luc. *Pisc.* 31.

60 What Odysseus had asked him to do in the play's prologue (54–85) was essentially no different from the demands imposed upon the actor by eighteenth-century theorists of the stage, i.e. to make 'a temporary renunciation of himself and all his connections in common life, and for a few hours . . . forget, if possible, his own identity'; see Wilkes (1759) 92.

ēthos remained distinctively 'Achillean': 'it is not unlike your father, either in word | or in act, to help a good man' (904–5). Unlike the accomplished actor who constructs his *hypokrisis* in such a way as to make it fitting and appropriate to character and situation,[61] Neoptolemus fails to create a stage character 'born of the union of all spiritual and physical elements of the role and the actor'.[62]

Dramatic scenes, then, which (metatheatrically) draw attention to artistic failure, may be taken to highlight the importance of the performative norm. Such a norm, in its turn, could be tentatively reconstructed as the achievement of a much desired amalgam between 'inner' and 'outer' self, with mind and body moving 'in concert',[63] rather than along their own separate paths. That 'singleness' and 'entireness' which Hazlitt so admired on the late eighteenth-century contemporary stage[64] whenever a performer's 'voice answered to her form',[65] could also be conceived as the aspiration of the Greek performer's art: Greek rhetorical handbooks define *hypokrisis* as 'the persuasive disposition of [one's] voice and bearing, appropriate to the underlying character and plot',[66] and some vase-painters depict performers as utterly absorbed in earnest contemplation of their mask,[67] seeking perhaps to co-ordinate their body, voice and entire stage presence with the life and breath of the dramatic figure 'suggested' by that mask.

61 See, e.g. Anon. *Proleg. Rhet.* (in Walz (1832–36), vol. VI, 35, 16–19), where the orator 'in the manner of a first class tragic actor, fine-tunes (καλῶς . . . συσχηματίζεται) to his words both his appearance and expression and voice'; cf. Longinus, *Ars rhetorica* p. 194 Hammer.

62 See Moore (1966) 76.

63 Hazlitt (1930–34) vol. XVIII, 282–3 (on Eliza O'Neill's premature retirement): '. . . her body and mind seemed to be under the guidance of the same impulse, to move in concert . . .'

64 Hazlitt (1930–34) vol. XVIII, 284 (on Eliza O'Neill): 'there was a singleness [i.e. in her general acting style], an entireness, and harmony in it'.

65 See Hazlitt (1930–34) vol. V, 198 (on Mrs Siddons) and Hazlitt (1930–34) vol. XVIII, 408. According to Aristotle, the hearer may be 'deceived' if the orator achieves total correspondence between words (ὀνόματα), voice (φωνή) and countenance (πρόσωπον); *Rhet.* 3.1408b4–10.

66 φωνῆς καὶ σχήματος πιθανὴ διάθεσις, πρέπουσα τῷ ὑποκειμένῳ προσώπῳ καὶ πράγματι (Bekker (1814–21), vol. III, 1165, 744.1). The necessity of the actor's search for 'appropriateness' in his performance is well illustrated in the story Plutarch (*Life of Demosthenes* 7.1–2) relates about the great comic actor Satyros and the young Demosthenes: when the latter recited some tragic monologue rather badly, Satyros, 'taking up the same speech after him, gave it such a form (οὕτω πλάσαι) and recited it with such appropriate sentiment and disposition (καὶ διεξελθεῖν ἐν ἤθει πρέποντι καὶ διαθέσει) that it appeared to Demosthenes to be quite another' (translated by Perrin (1958)).

67 One need only think of the famous Gnathia krater fragment from Tarentum (now in Würzburg; see above, ch. 4 fig. 16 and fig. 54a in *DFA* (1988)), where an actor is engaged in a 'secret' dialogue with the mask he holds in his hand; cf. an Apulian krater of *c.* 400 BC (see fig. 8 in Taplin (1997a)) where an actor (about to play Dionysus?) fixes his eyes on the mask he holds in his hand. On the literary level, cf. Fronto *De eloq.* 2.16.

Yet any discussion of 'coherence' or 'unity of soul and body' in an ancient Greek performance must be appropriately contextualised, for the very obvious reason that our own assumptions of character consistency may be seriously out of tune with the horizon of expectations of ancient viewers, while our own feeling of performative incongruity may not exactly replicate the Greek spectator's understanding of the 'jarring' and the 'out of place'. Bred on the realist dramatic tradition largely revolving round the notions of character wholeness and character development, we find it difficult to get to grips with the idea of *one* actor being called upon to impersonate, become, a series of *different* or even diametrically opposite characters within the action of one single play. In the Greek theatrical tradition, conversely, it is the collocation of several roles in the body of the same actor which constitutes the norm or, better still, one of the most enduring performative conventions. Not only did the Greek theatregoer find nothing incongruous in witnessing the same performer's multiple metamorphoses, either in one single play or in the context of a trilogy; we could even imagine the Greek audience deriving special pleasure precisely from recognising *the same* voice behind a plurality of masks[68] and looking forward to appreciating the subtlety and ingenuity of the performative ironies[69] resulting from the playwright's decision to group his 'characters' in such or such a way before assigning them to the three players the state had given him by lot. Such mental pleasure need not have been either beyond the intellectual capacity of a large and mixed audience or disruptive of the theatrical illusion. The demands placed on classical Greek audiences to appreciate how skilfully an actor had used the 'prima materia' of his voice and body in order to perform his allotted combination of roles were not substantially greater than the demands placed on eighteenth- and nineteenth-century spectators of the English stage, expected to recognise each player's efforts to sustain or invent particular 'points' in the depiction of a character or in the play's action; 'shaken' though they were 'in the very frame and substance' of their hearts, like 'strings . . . perfectly concordant' with the stage performers,[70] they were still sufficiently alert to discern (and to reward with rounds of applause) each actor's individual and distinctive 'points' within a given role.[71]

[68] For the argument that the character of an actor's voice was the primary criterion whereby ancient audiences recognised different performers, see Pavlovskis (1977).

[69] Cf. Jouan (1983) 79; Damen (1989) 321; Johnston (1993) 273; Ringer (1998) *passim*.

[70] John Hill (1755) 10 on the dynamics of contemporary audience response.

[71] See Jackson (1996) 119–21; on the paramount importance of 'the actor's depiction of a specific character at a specific moment' in the eighteenth-century 'connoisseurship of acting', see West (1991) 18ff.

This is obviously no place for scrutinising the so-called 'three actors rule', but no discussion of Greek acting can fail to emphasise that, as Pat Easterling reminds us in her *Cambridge Companion to Greek Tragedy*,[72] the convention of no more than three speaking actors for the cast of an entire play should not be regarded as an artificial state imposition.[73] In a paradoxical way, such a performative requirement can be said to liberate rather than restrict the expression of actors and dramatists alike.[74]

In the first place, the seemingly binding rule celebrated the actor's freedom: as a player of multiple roles, his commitment to his part may not have been so overwhelmingly intense as that of his more modern European counterpart, who constantly strives to 'realize the feelings of his character, and be transported beyond himself',[75] leaving, as it were, the last thought about his own identity back in his dressing room.[76] While professionally engaged in the process of self-transformation, casting requirements never allowed the ancient actor to forget that acting does not entail an irrevocable abdication of the self: there was no other way for 'Agave' to exist as a stage character in Euripides' *Bacchae* than for the actor who played Pentheus to 'return' to 'himself' in order to assume *her* mask and costume, allowing 'her' to display as a prop the sign of his previous *metamorphosis*, the *prosōpon* of the dismembered king of Thebes (*Bacch.* 1200–15, 1277–84; cf. 1139–42). The Greek actor, then, best exemplifies Richard Schechner's perspective on the condition of the stage performer, as a player making 'a journey that ends where it began',[77] that is to say, a player merely 'transported' – as opposed to irreversibly 'transformed' – from one personality to one or more others. Besides, on

[72] (1997a) 153.

[73] For some stimulating discussions of the convention as integral to the Greek theatrical experience and essential to the interpretation of the plays, see primarily Pavlovskis (1977); Jouan (1983); Arnott (1989) ch. 6; Damen (1989); Johnston (1993); Ringer (1998).

[74] From the playwright's point of view the actor's 'shifting' or 'roving' perspective over the action serves as a model for the audience's emotional – and intellectual – response to the entire spectacle: the actor's successive impersonation of contrasting roles becomes one of the dramatist's means of compelling viewers to empathise with a variety of characters and their conflicting arguments, ideas and perspectives.

[75] Garrick (1831–32) vol. I, 359.

[76] See James Boaden on Mrs Siddons: 'When Mrs Siddons quitted the dressing-room, I believe she left there the last thought about herself'; cited in Joseph (1959) 235. Examples of artistic 'over-identification' with the role in British theatres are countless. Johann von Archenholz, a German commentator on the British stage, reports that in 1775, while playing Jocasta in the John Dryden / Nathaniel Lee *Oedipus*, Mrs Bellamy 'was overcome by a sense of tragedy and had to be carried off the stage unconscious. And the audience, too, unable to endure the strain, departed'; Kelly (1936) 54–5. Cf. Downer (1966) 77 on Macready.

[77] Schechner (1977) 125. Schechner had himself directed an important production of Euripides' *Bacchae* in New York in 1968–69. See W. S. Hunter (1991).

a very practical level, it is perfectly conceivable that a Greek protagonist, a candidate for the prestigious acting prize at the City Dionysia (established *c.* 449 BC), would regard the taxing convention of multiple role-playing as rewarding him with ample scope for a full exhibition of histrionic virtuosity:[78] being called upon to incarnate characters of different social status, age, gender, emotional fibre, intellect and set of values, the performer has the chance not only to display the range, depth and cadence of his voice – at best capable of every coloration, timbre or pitch[79] – but also to demonstrate his enormous flexibility[80] and versatility in the projection of widely divergent points of view and the 'realisation' of conflicting moods and passions. For, while we have a tendency to reconstruct a play's action mentally around notions of psychological consistency and unity of character, what holds an ancient Greek play together on the stage is the continuity provided by the actor's own body, that marvellously pliant instrument which lends a presence and a voice to both the matricide son and the murdered mother in Sophocles' *Electra*, or to both the scheming Odysseus and the deified Heracles in the prologue and the closing scene of Sophocles' *Philoctetes*.

Finally, it is the very concept of the actor's 'adjustment' or 'remodelling' of his performing self within the frame of a Greek theatrical production which needs to be explained further at this point.

There are tragedies where the protagonist incarnates only one *dramatis persona* for the entire performance[81] and therefore has the chance to 'get under the skin' of his part, to 'build' his role in a way that would perhaps parallel modern conceptions of wholeness and truthfulness in the presentation of a stage character. However, investing his character

[78] For an appreciation by a later critic of the importance of providing the actor with good opportunities for the display of his acting skills see Demetrius, *On Style* 195, arguing that the shaping of a scene in Euripides' *Ion* had been dictated by the necessity to exploit the actor's talents to the full (πρὸς τὸν ὑποκριτὴν πεποιημένη).

[79] The need for gradation of one's voice and avoidance of monotony in the performer's delivery is stressed just as much in more modern European treatises as in Aristotle, who advises the speaker not to talk flatly and without variation, in the same character and tone (*Rhet.* 3.1413b30–1). Impersonation of different characters would give the actor opportunities for 'perpetually varying his attitudes' (Wilkes (1759) 152; 155).

[80] An actor is by definition 'as the shapeless wax pliable, and in the hand of the artist, ready to be moulded at his pleasure into a Richard or an Horatio, a Castalio or a Zanga'; J. Hill (1755) 59. Epictetus marvelled at the ductility of Polos, who could lend an equally musical and pleasing voice to both Oedipus the King and Oedipus the vagrant beggar of Colonus: ἢ οὐχ ὁρᾷς, ὅτι οὐκ εὐφωνότερον οὐδὲ ἥδιον ὁ Πῶλος τὸν τύραννον Οἰδίποδα ὑπεκρίνετο ἢ τὸν ἐπὶ Κολωνῷ ἀλήτην καὶ πτωχόν; (Epictetus, *Diss.* fr. 11 in Schenkl (1916) 412).

[81] E.g. Medea; Hecuba; Electra in Sophocles' *Electra*; Oedipus in *Oedipus Tyrannus*.

with a 'continuous' emotional life[82] would have seemed a strange ideal to the performer required to shift from the role of the Peasant to that of the Old Man to that of Clytemnestra before exiting as Castor in Euripides' *Electra*; if nothing else, such a player would have no time to perform the mental exercises imposed by Praxagora in order to mould himself into his part, let alone to work himself up for an on-stage display of passion in the same way that the Shakespearean actor William Charles Macready famously did.[83]

Yet such limitations should not be taken to indicate a rigid and inflexible acting style, a cool and detached approach to the role. Even if unable to fashion 'every sentence of the part to his own organs',[84] and even if not possessing the singular skills of the shape-changing Proteus (an enduring metaphor for the actor's pliability of character and 'ductility of mind'[85]), a well-trained actor can be capable of running a full gamut of emotions in quick succession,[86] while abrupt changes of mood and disposition can be encoded even in one and the same stage character,[87] thus imposing extremely high demands on histrionic talent. In performative terms, therefore, the actor's successive impersonation of the *Paidagōgos*, the maiden Chrysothemis and the tyrant Aegisthus in Sophocles' *Electra*[88] is no more difficult than the abrupt transition from the cheerful to the petrified Macbeth of Shakespeare's banquet scene when the Ghost of Banquo enters (Act 3, Scene 4)[89] and no more

82 Cf. Hazlitt (1930–34) vol. V, 190 on Edmund Kean's Iago.

83 According to George Henry Lewes (1875) 38–9, before entering the stage as Shylock, enraged at the flight of his daughter, Macready 'used to spend some minutes behind the scenes, lashing himself into an imaginative rage by cursing sotto voce, and shaking violently a ladder fixed against the wall.' In general, Macready insists on the necessity of the actor's *gradual* identification with his role: Macready (1875) vol. I, 115–16.

84 James Boaden's (1825) 140 assessment of John Kemble's painstaking preparation for his roles.

85 The expression is John Hill's (1755) 61.

86 As Garrick famously did in Paris, when 'in the space of four to five seconds' his expression performed successively a full scale of different emotions; see Diderot (1936) 272; cf. Hedgcock (1911) 38–9. Similarly, Lucian marvels at the pantomime actor's successive impersonation of roles so different in terms of character and mood: Athamas in a frenzy, Ino in terror, Atreus, Thyestes, then Aegisthus or Aerope; 'yet they all are but a single man' (καὶ πάντα ταῦτα εἷς ἄνθρωπός ἐστιν) (*On Dancing* 67).

87 In both ancient and modern drama; in John Hill's famous treatise *The Actor* we read that the 'compleat' player's heart 'should be susceptible of all emotions, and of all equally; he should be able to express all, as well as to feel all in the same force; and to make them succeed to one another ever so quickly; for there are characters which require this'; Hill (1755) 58–9; cf. 68–9.

88 An allocation of roles which had struck Rees (1908) 57 as being 'beyond the power of an ordinary actor' (see *DFA* (1988) 141).

89 Garrick was famous for his expressive change in this scene: 'when the Ghost of Banquo rises, how repeatedly astonishing his transition, from the placidly merry, to the tremendously horrific'

demanding than the artistic 'journey' from Creon, the imperious head of the polis of the beginning of Sophocles' *Antigone*, to Creon, the utterly subdued, mourning father of the tragedy's final scenes. Nor does a tight schedule of entrances and exits within a given play preclude the actor's careful *preliminary* study of his characters, his gradual getting to grips with his allotted set of roles *before* the performance season began.[90]

FILLING YOURSELF WITH PASSION

The previous section argued that metatheatrical insights may point to the conclusion that harmonious correspondence between dramatic character and actor, dramatic mask and acting disposition was a principle firmly embedded in the performative dimension of Greek drama. Taking now this ideal of 'congruity' as a working assumption, I propose to end with an attempt to tackle the most stubborn question of all.

What, if anything, would a Greek performer *feel* when enacting roles full of passion? Was emotion likely 'to have subdued his mind, and moulded his whole form'[91] or would he only feel 'about as much as Punch feels'?[92] To be sure, we will never be enlightened by contemporary surveys or theatre reviews; yet, even so, the subjective dimension of the Greek performative context must not be lamented as entirely lost.

The Platonic construction of Ion, the Homeric rhapsode who, when reciting, slips out of his normal self and feels his soul actually transposed amid the very incidents he is narrating (*Ion* 535b–c) and Aulus Gellius' story about Polos, the tragic actor who created unparalleled verisimilitude by using the urn and ashes of his recently deceased son in order to arouse genuine *pathos* on the stage (*Noctes Atticae* 6.5.7), do more than put into words the eccentricity of individual performers.

(from *The Theatrical Review* (1763) 79; cited in Joseph (1959) 113). In general, all the great actors of the eighteenth- and nineteenth-century stage were admired for the swiftness and expressiveness of their 'transitions' from one mood or emotion to its opposite (see Joseph (1959) s.v. transitions).

90 Actors on the eighteenth-century London stage may have been equally short of time for 'getting into' their character, as they seem to have been expected to play a role at the drop of a hat; see, for example, David Garrick's stiff letter of complaint to an actress who refused to play a character (admittedly belonging to her current repertoire) without a day's notice; Garrick (1963) vol. III, 990–1.

91 Hazlitt (1930–34) vol. XVIII, 233, on John Kemble's acting.

92 Speculation on Garrick's feelings; G. B. Hill (1966 [1897]) vol. II, 248.

Polos' infectious passion and Ion's ability to carry listeners along with him[93] can best be appreciated within the context of a wider admiration for emotionalist, 'involved' acting style,[94] that is to say, for a mode of delivery where the performer hopes to sweep away his spectators with the tide of anguish swelling in his own breast,[95] or, at the very least, to 'transfer' onto them his own vision (*phantasia*) of characters and situation.[96] Ion could have been greatly praised at the height of western empathic acting:

> when I recite something pitiful, my eyes are filled up with tears; when something fearful or terrible, my hair stands on end by fear and my heart pounds. (*Ion* 535c)

Totally submerged in the roles he incarnates, with the ebb and flow of his emotions entirely congruent with the succession of the passions encoded in his text, vibrating with 'that keen sensibility' which 'like electrical fire, shoots through the veins, marrow, bones and all, of every spectator',[97] Ion bears striking resemblance to, let us say, Eliza O'Neill, whose delivery was admired for 'rising and falling with the gusts of passion'.[98] It is not without significance that Plato's picture of a rhapsode sympathetically projected into fictive situations lies behind Diderot's portrayal of the 'involved' performer in his *Paradox on Acting*.[99]

However, irradiating his spectator's body with his own passion would not have been the sole aim of the Greek performer. Styles of acting – as well as the aesthetic appreciation of the actor's art – changed considerably over the centuries, but what seems to have attracted constant praise from Homer to Longinus is the performer's power of 'visualisation', that is to say, his ability to 'see' things with his mind's eyes *so vividly* (*enargōs*) 'as if they were actually present' (Quintilian, *Institutio oratoria*

93 See *Ion* 535e (quoted above, p. 400).

94 Cf. Aristotle's remark that actors seek out those plays whose style (*lexis*) is ὑποκριτικωτάτη, i.e. most appropriate for delivery, giving scope either for the construction of character (ἠθική) or for the expression of emotion (παθητική), and that playwrights in their turn are after actors of such calibre, i.e. capable of conveying both character and passion (*Rhet.* 3.1413b9–12). After all, according to Demetrius (*On Style* 194), 'unemotional' is synonymous with 'unhistrionic': πᾶν δὲ τὸ ἀπαθὲς ἀνυπόκριτον.

95 Hazlitt on Eliza O'Neill: 'it was the tide of anguish swelling in her own breast, that overflowed to the breasts of the audience, and filled their eyes with tears', in Hazlitt (1930–34) vol. XVIII, 282–4.

96 The metaphor is actually an ancient one: see schol. *Odyssey* 4.184, where the 'internalised' audience's compassion is said to be aroused because the 'performer' (Menelaus) 'transferred' (μετήνεγκε) his vision (φαντασίαν) to his listeners (ἐπὶ τοὺς . . . ἀκούοντας); see Meijering (1987) 44. On the emotional response of Greek audiences, see e.g. Pl. *Laws* 7.800d; Isocr. 4.168.

97 Garrick (1831–32) vol. I, 359.

98 Hazlitt (1930–34) vol. V, 199.

99 Diderot (1936) 306.

6.2.29). Here then, once again, the skill of the inspired poet and the good performer merge for, when ignited by 'enthusiasm full of passion', they seem to actually 'see' what they describe and bring their vision to the sight of their audience.[100] Thus, Euripides himself 'saw' the Erinyes and almost compelled his audience to see what he himself had visualised,[101] while according to Aristotle, those orators are most effective in moving their listeners to pity who, 'acting' their part with gestures and cries and displays of feeling, succeed in conjuring up the pitiful circumstances before their very eyes.[102]

It would seem then that the Greek performer's aspiration was to create a channel of communication between stage and auditorium sustained by the transfusion of emotion, the identity of shared feelings. To use Shakespearean language, the Greek actor was fully aware of the necessity to make his audience 'feel for Duncan as brave Malcolm felt'.[103] Orchestrating the passions of their spectators and leading them skilfully to tears was the performative ideal of Kallippides and Theodoros,[104] excellent examples of actors playing 'to the audience's hearts'.[105] In any case, it would be reasonable to assume that, if Greek audiences were 'following sympathetically' at the sight of people 'singing and beating their breasts' (Plato, *Rep.* 10.605d), their response could only have been aroused by performers visibly involved in their roles.[106] It was Theodoros enacting the role of Aerope 'with excessive passion' (*sphodra empathōs*) who moved the tyrant Alexander of Pherae to tears (Aelian, *Varia*

[100] See 'Longinus'' definition of *phantasia* as the process whereby 'inspired by strong emotion, you seem to see what you describe and bring it vividly before the eyes of your audience' (ἃ λέγεις ὑπ' ἐνθουσιασμοῦ καὶ πάθους βλέπειν δοκῇς καὶ ὑπ' ὄψιν τιθῇς τοῖς ἀκούουσιν) (*On Sublimity* 15.1). Similarly, criticism of Shakespearean players is full of praise for the performer's skill in conceiving a strong idea or passion and transmitting it to the audience, compelling it to 'see' or otherwise 'feel'. See Gentleman (1770) vol. 1, 108 on Garrick as Macbeth visualising the fictitious dagger and Knowles (cited in Bartholomeusz (1969) 121) on Mrs Siddons in the sleepwalking scene.

[101] 'Long.' *On Sublimity* 15.2. [102] *Rhet.* 2.1386a32–4. See Sifakis this volume, pp. 155–8.

[103] From manager Elliston's prologue (spoken by himself) to a 1809 performance of *Macbeth* at the Royal Circus; text in J. Bate (1996) 105.

[104] Kallippides was said to be exceedingly proud of his ability 'to fill the seats with weeping audiences' (Xen. *Symp.* 3.11), while in Theodoros' perspective the wonder of his art resided in his skill to make spectators 'tearful and wailing' (Plut. *Mor.* 545F)

[105] The attitude denounced by Brecht (1964) 15.

[106] Cf. the French actor Talma's saying that 'It is only by an excess of sensibility that he [i.e. the actor] can succeed in producing deep impressions, and move even the coldest souls. The power that raises must be greater than the power raised'; Talma (1883) 14. A similar causal relationship between speaker/orator and listener pervades rhetorical treatments of *enargeia* and *phantasia*. See Webb (1997a) esp. 117–21 (with ancient references) and, in a more general perspective, cf. Arist. *Rhet.* 3.1408a23–4.

historia 14.40);[107] it was the passion animating Phaedrus' recital which brought Socrates to a state of stunned bewilderment (*ekplēxis, Phaedrus* 234d); and it was clearly the vibrant ardour of two actors/lovers which aroused a pantomime audience in Xenophon's *Symposium* (9.3–7).

Western anti-theatricalists may have accused the stage actor of mummery and feigned feelings, but even the patchy picture of the Greek performative context that can be pieced together from our scanty evidence yields an altogether different impression: from Demosthenes' demand for 'pain' (*algos*), which comes directly from the soul instead of tears flickering on the voice,[108] to Aristotle's observation that it is genuine emotional involvement that leads to the effect of the 'most persuasive' (*to pithanōtaton*),[109] the performer is never allowed to be cool, mechanical and calculating, driven by the head or brain rather than the heart – to borrow from the language of the famous eighteenth-century controversy between the 'emotionalists' and 'anti-emotionalists' in the art of acting. Lack of first-hand accounts makes judgements hazardous, but it would seem that the Roman orators' widely publicised conviction that it is only genuine feeling which can arouse the listener's emotions[110] found its first 'realisation' in the performative ideals of the Greek stage actors. To put it in another way, I would like to believe that a player with 'a heart / which could not feel emotions, nor impart',[111] a player who performs without weeping in the agony of grief, blushing with shame, glowing with love, trembling with terror,[112] would have been aesthetically intolerable within the Greek theatrical context.[113]

107 In another version of the same story (Plut. *Life of Pelopidas* 29.5), where the actor performs in Euripides' *Trojan Women*, Alexander leaves the theatre embarrassed by his own sensibility: '. . . he was ashamed to have the citizens see him, who had never taken pity on any man that he had murdered, weeping over the sorrows of Hecuba and Andromache'; on the tyrant's response, see further Lada-Richards (1996) 96–7, and Hall, this volume, ch. 20.

108 See Dem. 18.287 μηδὲ τῇ φωνῇ δακρύειν . . . ἀλλὰ καὶ τῇ ψυχῇ συναλγεῖν.

109 *Poet.* 1455a30–1: 'For given the same natural talent, the most convincing (πιθανώτατοι) are those [i.e. poets] who are themselves in the grip of passion (οἱ ἐν τοῖς πάθεσίν εἰσιν).'

110 See, e.g. Cic. *De or.* 2.189–90; Quint. *Inst.* 6.2.26–8; 11.3.2, etc. Most importantly, in order to enhance their argument, both Cicero and Quintilian resort to the theatrical realm and draw a comparison with the intense emotional link uniting the actor with his part; see, e.g. Quint. *Inst.* 6.2.35: 'I have often seen actors, both in tragedy and comedy, leave the theatre still drowned in tears after concluding the performance of some moving role'; Cic. *De or.* 2.193–4.

111 Churchill (1763) 16.

112 See Salvini, cited in Archer (1888) 51 and also quoted with approbation by George Bernard Shaw (1889) 14.

113 However, one has to acknowledge at this point the existence of the Stoic view on the orator/actor as totally unmoved by the passions he displays, merely pretending to be under their sway; see, e.g. Sen. *De ira* 2.17.1 ('for the actors too move their audience with their declamations not when they are angry but when they skilfully imitate an angry man'); Cic. *Tusc.* 4.25.55.

CONCLUSION: THE PARADOX OF ACTING

A famous passage in Plato's *Republic* highlights the paradoxical position of the 'imitative' poet, a creature who inspires amazement and awe (*hieron kai thaumaston*) through his wisdom and unequalled mimetic power,[114] but who must, all the same, be expelled as a danger and a threat to the polis' masculine integrity (3.398a–b). Constantly fluctuating between deviations from the 'normal' male self, the Greek performer too is a supreme crosser of boundaries, a man who, by profession and through his skills in imitation, participates in a multiple reality and, in so doing, challenges and puts at risk the dividing lines of the rigidly structured community to which he belongs. The paradox attached to the mimetic poet becomes applicable *par excellence* to him who earns his living through performative *mīmēsis*.

If successful, the ancient actor is admired and lavishly rewarded for his exceptional artistic skills: not only special histrionic prizes but also public honours and, as the fourth century progresses, even political power are increasingly within his grasp. Yet this same individual pays, as it were, the price for his extraordinary resemblance to the figure of the public speaker, the demagogue/orator. As Demosthenes puts it with respect to Aeschines (an actor on both the theatrical and the political stages of Athens): treating his court cases as stage dramas, he becomes through his acting experience 'all-dreadful', 'terrible': *pandeinos* (Dem. 19.20).[115] The actor's exceptional voice,[116] coupled with his expert training in the gestures and the tropes of delivery (the common ground between acting and declaiming), turns him into a dangerous wizard (*goēs*), a sophist (*sophistēs*) and a rogue (*phenax*),[117] who captivates and enchants his audience and, in so doing, may lead them astray. A late rhetorical handbook captures very strikingly the dangerous psychagogical effect of expert delivery:

> histrionic power . . . knows how to guide the spectator seizing him with plots and enchantments, with seductions and deceptions. For, although argument and logical proof can persuade [the listener] perforce, histrionic delivery entices

[114] *Rep.* 3.398a: 'clever enough to assume all shapes and imitate (μιμεῖσθαι) everything'.

[115] Demosthenes is, of course, hardly an unbiased voice on the matter.

[116] For which 'a memorable image' (most famously applied to Aeschines) can be 'the music of the Sirens . . . and its associations – glamour, power, danger – '; Easterling (1999) 154; just as the Sirens enchant their listeners and lead them to their destruction, so the vocal performance of the trained orator acts to the detriment of its hearers (Aesch. 3.228).

[117] On the interconnection of these terms in the context of misleading oratory see Lada-Richards (1993) 128 n. 41.

the mind of the judge through illusion (*apatē*) and drags it towards that which the speaker believes to be true.[118]

What professional qualities would turn distrust into admiration, what artistic gifts would tip the balance in the actor's favour and earn him general acclaim and fame? By what means could he hope to command respect and to become successful?

I have suggested in this chapter that, beyond the ability to project himself imaginatively into the position of another character – the *dramatis persona* created by the author – the actor is expected to adjust himself to that character, that is to say, to find the right 'key' and 'tune' on which the character can be evoked, 'constructed' and presented on the theatre's *skēnē*. Moreover, not only does the actor have to 'feel himself into' his part, sharing somebody else's frame of mind and being infected by a string of 'alien' passions, but, equally importantly, he has to draw upon his powers of visualisation (*phantasia*), so that his own bodily performance can direct the mind of the spectator to the play's characters and events. It would not be an exaggeration to claim that the tragic actor in particular can be seen as the successor of the Muse-inspired bard: both *aoidos* and tragic stage performer 'make present' for the sake of their audience heroes belonging to a legendary past and both share the unique ability to 'cast a spell', to bewitch, captivate and enthral.[119]

Finally, no discussion of the nature of ancient acting can afford to neglect the vital link between the stage performer/dancer and Dionysus. For, in sharp contrast to the frustratingly elusive 'frame of mind' of the Greek performer, iconography, archaeology, epigraphy and literature across periods and genres converge on a picture of the ancient actor as living and breathing under the aegis of the patron god of theatre himself. Like the Dionysiac devotee worshipping the god either in the private ambience of an organised *thiasos* or in the public openness of wild mountain glens, the actor relinquishes temporarily the safe boundaries of individuality and personal identity. Without becoming actually 'possessed' to the extent of losing control over himself and his performance (see above, pp. 412–14), he plunges into characters and situations which are alien to himself and his everyday experience. To put it differently, in the Dionysiac theatre's perspective, the 'subjectivity' of

118 Longinus (*Ars rhetorica* p. 195 Hammer, 1–5).

119 In this respect, one might even argue that, as an 'inspired' τεχνίτης, the ancient actor 'deconstructs' the polarisation of *physis* and *technē* so important to ancient poetics and literary criticism from Pindar onwards.

the performer is ultimately of a Dionysiac nature, for both the actor's 'stepping out' of himself and the spectator's sympathetic fusion with the acting stage figure become possible through the Dionysiac experience of *ekstasis*.

SUGGESTIONS FOR FURTHER READING

For aspects of ancient Greek acting, see Ghiron-Bistagne (1976), Walcot (1976), *DFA* (1988), Arnott (1989), N.W. Slater (1990), Green (1994a), Csapo and Slater (1995), Lada-Richards (1997). On multiple role-playing in the Greek theatre, see Pavlovskis (1997), Jouan (1983), Damen (1989), Ringer (1998). On metatheatre and acting matters, see Taaffe (1993), Slater (1993) and (1997), Ringer (1998), Lada-Richards (1997), (1998), and (1999) ch. 4. On Brecht and 'epic' acting, see Brecht (1964), Willett (1977); on Stanislavsky and 'Method' acting, see Stanislavsky (1961), Moore (1966). For useful miscellanies of actors' views on acting, see Archer (1888), Cole and Chinoy (1949). For actors in Shakespeare's own time, see Chambers (1923), Bentley (1984), Gurr (1992). For Garrick see Garrick (1963), Joseph (1959), West (1991); for a collection of mezzotints illustrating Garrick's performances see Lennox-Boyd et al. (1994); for Macready, see especially Downer (1966). Very informative on acting and the history of the English stage are Hazlitt (1930–34), Bartholomeusz (1969), Donohue (1970).

CHAPTER TWENTY

The ancient actor's presence since the Renaissance

Edith Hall

There was a player once upon a stage,
Who striving to present a dreery passion,
Brought out the urne of his late buried sonne,
It might the more affect him, and draw teares.

These lines are spoken by the hero of an early seventeenth-century revenge tragedy, *Orestes* (Act III scene 5), written by Thomas Goffe for performance at Christ Church, Oxford. Orestes is comparing his own 'real' grief at the death of his father with that displayed by a (here unnamed) 'player'. The ancient actor once aroused his own emotions by handling his dead son's ashes while performing. Goffe's Orestes is referring, of course, to one of the most famous of all ancient anecdotes about actors (and one which several chapters in this volume have discussed), the story Aulus Gellius relates concerning the way Polos, in the fourth century BC, had played Sophocles' *Electra* (*Noctes Atticae* 6.5.7). The comparison Goffe's Orestes makes is particularly appropriate because his own play is itself modelled, at least in part, on that ancient tragedy.[1]

Earlier in the present volume Pat Easterling's study of the iconic status of star actors argued that the ancient anecdotal tradition which attached to famous performers like Polos is important less for its truth value than for the frequency with which the anecdotes were recounted in Greek and Latin authors, and for their durability across the many centuries of 'antiquity'. This chapter is intended to serve as a sort of conclusion by using a few examples to suggest that the charisma of the ancient actor, especially the famous star performer, the ancient professional whose art, social status and image have formed the subject of the essays in this volume, has actually had a durability which has allowed him to survive far beyond antiquity to haunt the imagination of the Renaissance and the modern world.

[1] Goffe (1633); see Hall (1999b) 262–4. The Polos anecdote, as Holford-Strevens (1999) 238 n. 58 points out, has been important to theorists of acting as late as the twentieth century.

The 'metatheatrical' trope inspired by Polos in Goffe's Jacobean revenge tragedy provides but one example amongst many of the popularity and familiarity from the Renaissance onwards of ancient narratives concerning actors. It was, of course, a dominant trend in Renaissance and Jacobean tragedy that it consistently and self-consciously referred to its own status as theatre, and, inspired by a tradition which owes more to ancient philosophy than drama (see Edwards, this volume), to its characters as 'actors' within the fictive world of the stage. Ancient Greek tragedy, at any rate, had scrupulously avoided such generic self-referentiality, probably because its authors were attempting to reconstruct an 'authentic' Homeric world when theatre had not yet been invented.[2] But to dramatists like Shakespeare and Goffe, who enjoyed reminding their audience that they were watching 'players', the figure of the ancient actor, especially the famous star individual, was extremely attractive.

The extent of Shakespeare's access to ancient playscripts, Greek or Roman, is of course famously controversial, although scholars are increasingly happy to accept that he knew far more Greek tragedy, via Latin translations, than they used to believe possible.[3] Yet it is indisputable that his tragedies are rich in self-reflexive and self-conscious theatricality,[4] and this dimension is enhanced by his knowledge of accounts he found in ancient authors of actors in Greece and Rome. His plays set in the Greek and Roman worlds show an awareness that antiquity enjoyed a rich theatrical life. A fine example is the moment towards the end of *Antony and Cleopatra* when the Queen of Egypt fears that she and Antony will become the subjects of ribald, cross-dressed comedy at Rome (5.2.216):

> The quick comedians
> extemporally will stage us and present
> our Alexandrian revels. Antony
> shall be brought drunken forth, and I shall see
> some squeaking Cleopatra boy my greatness
> I' th' posture of a whore.

But it is not just general accounts of ancient actors' performances that feature in tragedy of this era. Roscius' name, in particular, was familiar not only to playwrights but also to their audiences, and is invoked with some frequency. Henry the Sixth, for example, asks the Duke of Gloucester, who is about to stab him, 'What scene of death has Roscius now to act?' (*Henry VI Part III*, V.vi.10).

[2] Easterling (1985) 6. [3] Schleiner (1990); Kerrigan (1996) 173. [4] See e.g. Grene (1988).

The post-Renaissance afterlife of the ancient star actor has attracted little scholarly attention, with the exception of Charles Garton's idiosyncratic but stimulating monograph, *Personal Aspects of the Roman Theatre.* The final chapter traces the 'Rosciad idea' in English literature until the nineteenth century. Roscius' name continued to be used to denominate brilliant actors, such as David Garrick, or the early nineteenth-century child prodigy William Betty, advertised to his public as 'The Young Roscius'; Roscius also lent his name to numerous treatises and polemics on acting, which in the eighteenth century were often given the title *Rosciad.*[5]

Roscius, preserved for posterity largely through the works of the orator Cicero, enjoyed just as vigorous an afterlife in the science of rhetoric. Treatises on rhetorical delivery for consultation by the public speaker, from the Renaissance through to the nineteenth century, drew, as their predecessors had, on Cicero and Quintilian. The authors of such treatises found in these Roman writers many references to the parallel art of acting, some of which have been discussed by Fantham in this volume. Some even went back beyond Cicero to Demosthenes, for example John Bulwer's *Chironomia* of 1644. Bulwer's frontispiece (fig. 60) dynamically illustrates his view of the debt owed to the stage by orators such as Cleon and Hortensius, whose vigorous gestures are portrayed on the upper level. The main picture depicts on the left Andronikos (Stephanis no. 179), the Greek tragic actor reported in the seventh of the *Lives of the Ten Orators* attributed to Plutarch to have taught Demosthenes the importance of delivery (*hypokrisis*, *Mor.* 845A–B; cf. Handley, this volume p. 170). Andronikos holds his right hand in a dramatic gesture above his famous pupil's head. Demosthenes practises his delivery in a mirror inscribed with the precept he learned by studying with the actor, that delivery was the first, second and third most important thing in oratory: 'actio, actio, actio'. The Greek actor and orator are balanced by portraits of the Romans Roscius and Cicero on the right.[6]

But Roscius has been far from the only ancient actor to figure in later works, whether rhetorical or theatrical literature. The hero of *Hamlet*

[5] Garton (1972b) 203–29.

[6] Perhaps the most influential of such treatises, however, was Michel Le Faucheur's *Traitté de l'action de l'orateur ou de la Prononciation et du geste* (Paris 1657), the standard work in the eighteenth century, translated into English, German, Spanish and Latin, and the inspiration behind many imitations. See e.g. the headmaster Gilbert Austin's *Chironomia; or a Treatise on Rhetorical Delivery: Comprehending many Precepts, both Ancient and Modern, for the Proper Regulation of the Voice, the Countenance, and Gesture* (London 1806). On all these matters see Barnett (1987).

Fig. 60 Acting and rhetoric: Andronikos and Demosthenes balanced by Roscius and Cicero (By permission of the British Library)

prefaces the famous 'play-within-a-play' scene in the second scene of the second act with a light-hearted reference to Roscius (397), but also seems aware of an 'actor' anecdote preserved in Plutarch. Hamlet, struck by the remarkable manner in which one of the leading players has impersonated Hecuba's grief, soliloquises (558–67):

> Is it not monstrous, that this player here,
> But in a fiction, in a dream of passion,
> Could force his soul so to his whole conceit,
> That, from her working, all his visage wann'd;
> Tears in his eyes, distraction in 's aspect,
> A broken voice, and his whole function suiting
> With forms to his conceit? And all for nothing?
> For Hecuba!
> What's Hecuba to him, or he to Hecuba,
> That he should weep for her?

Hamlet goes on to ask what this actor would do if he had the same cause for passion as Hamlet – amongst other things he would 'drown the stage with tears' and 'make mad the guilty'. It is difficult to believe that Hamlet is not here inspired by Sir Thomas North's English translation of Plutarch's *Lives*, first published in 1579, in particular by the story preserved in the *Life of Pelopidas* about the tyrant Alexander of Pherae in the fourth century BC (29.4–6). In North's version Alexander, who suffered from a 'gilty conscience', watched an outstanding tragic actor (named in another version of the same story preserved by Aelian (*VH* 14.40) as none other than Theodoros: see Lada-Richards, this volume, pp. 414–15) in a performance of Euripides' *Trojan Women*. The 'cruel and heathen tyran' was forced to leave the theatre abruptly (like Hamlet's uncle Claudius) because 'he was ashamed his people shoude see him weepe, to see the miseries of Hecuba and Andromacha played'.[7] The availability of Erasmus' version of Euripides' *Hecuba* may be one inspiration behind this famous passage,[8] but Plutarch's anecdote seems to fit Hamlet's sentiments more precisely.[9]

7 North in Wyndham (1895) 323. See also Lucas (1928) 52–3.

8 See Purkiss (2000) 46.

9 One of the focuses of this volume has been the development of different acting styles, and the individual actors associated with them (Csapo, Sifakis, Handley, Hunter); it is, therefore, fascinating that the use of the ancient actor in the famous 'player' scene in *Hamlet* is probably implicated in a commentary on contemporary acting. Some scholars believe that the performances in the scene are inspired by the different acting styles associated respectively with Shakespeare's company of actors, the Chamberlain's Men, who favoured increasingly naturalistic delivery and gestures, and their rivals the Admiral's Men. See Gurr (1963) and (1980) 99–101, 111–12.

Indeed, Plutarch's 'actor' anecdotes were particularly popular. John Milton reminds his reader of Plutarch's account of the Phocian who performed tragic lyrics from the parodos of Euripides' *Electra*, which would have entailed singing lines designed both for the actor playing Electra and for the chorus. The venue was a banquet at the end of the Peloponnesian War, and the performance so moved the allied generals who were considering razing Athens to the ground that they decided against this policy (*Vit. Lys.* 15.2–3). Milton saw parallels between the Peloponnesian War and the English Civil War. Pondering in 1642 the possibility that the King's army might take London, his eighth *Sonnet* remembers that 'the repeated air/Of sad *Electra's* Poet had the power/To save the *Athenian* walls from ruin bare' (lines 12–14).

The ideological context of the battle between King and Puritan had already provided a stimulus to the revivification in English prose of the ancient actor. Puritan opponents of the theatre consistently reprocessed the more vitriolic attacks on actors they found in church fathers such as Tertullian, while its apologists demonstrated the antiquity and dignity of the acting profession by describing ancient examples such as Aesopus and Roscius. The main lines of the debate can already be traced in the actor–dramatist Thomas Heywood's *Apology for Actors* of 1612 and the anonymous 1615 response to it, *A Refutation of the Apology for Actors*. The debate, as Jonas Barish demonstrates in his brilliant study of antitheatricalism from Plato onwards, culminated in the 'megalomaniac' William Prynne's *Histriomastix* ('Scourge of Players') of 1633, just under a decade before the theatres were actually closed in 1642.[10] Prynne's lengthy title includes his claim to have drawn on no fewer than seventy-one '*Fathers and Christian Writers*' in order to prove that stage-plays are pernicious corruptions, and that the professions of both dramatist and player are '*unlawfull, infamous and misbeseeming Christians*'.

One of the most important defences of the acting profession against such charges was, however, made in a play set in imperial Rome. Philip Massinger's *The Roman Actor* featured as its hero an attested ancient pantomime dancer, the Egyptian-born Paris, during the reign of the emperor Domitian. Massinger, however, transformed Paris into a tragic actor of spoken drama. This was almost certainly because Massinger was using Philemon Holland's 1606 English translation of Suetonius' life of Domitian. Holland had misunderstood the Latin term *pantomīmus* which Suetonius used in one reference to Paris (12.10), translating it as 'player

[10] Barish (1981) 80–8.

and counterfeit',[11] and Massinger, apparently in ignorance, reproduces the error.

The Roman Actor was first performed at Blackfriars, London, in 1626 by the King's Men. It used the figure of Paris to mount a stirring defence of the stage and the acting profession against the increasingly vehement denunciations which they were facing at the time. James I had already been forced into forbidding bear-baiting and stage-playing on the Sabbath, and the closure of the theatres had become a real threat. Massinger's response was to create an appealing hero out of ancient writers' references to Paris, the empress' love for him, and his murder on the orders of the emperor. Paris is a brave, attractive professional, with whom, as a fellow-actor, Massinger seems strongly to have identified.[12]

The choice of an ancient actor as hero gave Massinger the opportunity to display the power and versatility of contemporary acting skills in 'plays within the play' based on stories in Horace and Ovid. More importantly, it allows the opportunity for a passionate speech in defence of the stage, with powerful relevance to Massinger's audience, when Paris addresses the Senate on behalf of his profession after becoming the spokesman of the actors in ancient Rome. Paris' speech (Act I.iii) advances arguments which were becoming traditional amongst apologists for the theatre, the most important of which was the view that drama helps its audience to attain virtue by offering, in emotionally persuasive form, the positive moral examples of noble heroes. Philosophers, says Paris, can deliver moral precepts, which are seldom read.

> But does that fire
> The blood, or swell the veins with emulation
> To be both good and great, equal to that
> Which is presented in our theatres?
> (I.iii.80–3)

He argues that if 'a good actor, in a lofty scene' impersonates Hercules, Camillus or Scipio, 'All that have any spark of Roman in them . . . contend to be/like those they see presented'. There is more in a similar vein, and it proved popular. The tragedy was revived in 1690–92 and several times in the eighteenth century. But it was Paris' speech, excerpted and

[11] See Holland in Whibley (1899) 238 and 245.

[12] Sandidge (1929) 21–3. Besides Suetonius, Massinger's sources included Dio Cassius, Martial's epitaph for Paris (xi.13), Juvenal (6.87, 7.87) and Eutropius' *Epitome de Caesaribus* (xi.11).

performed, which kept the reputation of this Jacobean tragedy alive even into the nineteenth century.[13]

By the nineteenth century, however, the intuitive British identification with Rome had been replaced in the theatre by interest in the Greeks, foreshadowing the new philhellenism of the last quarter of the century. This is reflected in the type of ancient actor found revivified on the contemporary stage. The first work on which W. S. Gilbert and Arthur Sullivan collaborated, for example, staged an invented sequence from the life of Thespis, traditionally the first known actor. *Thespis*, which opened at the Gaiety Theatre on Boxing Day 1871, dramatised the take-over of Olympus by the 'original' actor–manager Thespis and his troupe of actors. Although almost all the music and some of the dialogue has been lost, it is clear that *Thespis* was one of the last in a tradition of popular burlesques of classical themes culled from Greek tragedy, Greek and Roman epic, and above all Ovid's *Metamorphoses*. These classical burlesques, a staple of the Victorian theatre since the 1830s, entailed rhyming couplets, contemporary jokes, endless punning and alliteration, transvestite actors, virtuoso dancing, songs set to popular tunes, extravagant spectacle, and a nearly continuous self-conscious commentary on the classical tradition of literature, myth and theatre.[14] Frank Talfourd's *Electra in a New Electric Light*, for example, performed at the Haymarket Theatre in 1859, is a burlesque recasting of Sophocles' famous tragedy, performed with classical dress and scenery.[15] In the fifth act, the audience was treated to the highly self-referential spectacle of an 'internal', on-stage audience '*witnessing the performance of a Strolling Company of* ACTORS *on a Thespian cart*'.[16] This was probably inspired by Horace's picture in the *Ars Poetica* of Thespis as the inventor of the tragic Muse, whose company of itinerant players sang and acted his poems from a wagon (275–7). The display helped Talfourd's audience reflect upon the history of the Greek theatre which the current entertainment was so satisfyingly debunking.

It is against this tradition of classical burlesque that *Thespis* needs to be understood. The cast consisted of several Olympians (Jupiter, Apollo, Mars, Diana, Venus and Mercury), grown old and so bored that they make an agreement to change places with Thespis and his troupe of players, who have comically 'Hellenised' punning names such as Timidon, Tipseion, Preposteros and Stupidas.[17] Although the gods take back their power at the end of the play, much fun is had in the interim (see fig. 61). The part of Mercury was created for Nelly Farren,

[13] Sandidge (1929) 4–5. [14] Hall (1999c) 355–6. [15] Hall (1999b) 285–7.
[16] Talfourd (1859) 23–4. [17] Rees (1964) 102.

Fig. 61 First performance of *Thespis* (Drawing courtesy of the Archive of Performances of Greek and Roman Drama, University of Oxford)

incomparable in the tights of travesty roles (one reviewer said that the actresses in *Thespis* were dressed in a manner 'more than ordinarily indecent'),[18] while Thespis was played by J. L. Toole, one of the most distinguished comic actors of his day.[19] Although the show was unsuccessful, the name of Thespis continued to be familiar, and informed at least light-hearted works for the stage in the twentieth century. Stephen Sondheim's 1962 musical *A Funny Thing Happened on the Way to the Forum*, for example, is still in the popular repertoire today. Its prologue, usually delivered by the slave Pseudolus (a direct descendant of the leading character in Plautus' *Pseudolus*, a play in antiquity particularly associated with Roscius (see Brown, this volume)), opens by invoking the aid of the first known actor: 'O Thespis, we place ourselves in your hands.'[20]

At least one ancient female theatrical performer, the remarkable mime dancer and Byzantine empress Theodora, has had a significant afterlife, explored in the Epilogue to Robert Browning's fascinating book *Justinian and Theodora* (1971). She inspired an important play by Victorien Sardou, *Théodora*, and the title role was appropriately played in the Paris premiere of 1884 by the great diva of the late nineteenth-century stage, Sarah Bernhardt. Theodora has also featured in novels, including Robert Graves' much admired *The Count Belisarius* (1938), and at least one motion picture.

More recently, an ancient actor has been the subject of an entire movie. Giorgos Stampoulopoulos' 1991 film *Two Suns in the Sky* (*Duo Ēlioi ston Ourano*) is a study of a travelling actor and his colleagues, dedicated to Dionysus, in the late fourth century AD. A Greek–French collaborative enterprise, *Two Suns in the Sky* is the biography of the fictional Timotheos of Antioch, 'the greatest *tragōidos* of his era', whose speciality was performing in Euripides' *Bacchae*. The film, which dramatises the controversial role of theatre and the status of actors during the confrontation of Christianity and paganism in late antiquity, discussed by Webb, Roueché and Puchner in this volume, contains several plausible and exciting reconstructions of the way in which tragedy was being performed by this era.[21]

It is not only rhetorical, theatrical and cinematic media which have consistently engaged with the figure of the ancient actor. Actors have also made important appearances in prose fiction since antiquity. They feature in both extant Latin novels, performing at Trimalchio's feast in Petronius' *Satyrica* and in entertainments described in Apuleius' *Golden*

[18] *The Examiner*, quoted in Rees (1964) 78. [19] Ayre (1972) 406.
[20] Shevelove, Gelbart and Sondheim (1963) 5.
[21] I am extremely grateful to Pantelis Michelakis for help on this.

Ass; in Achilles Tatius' Greek novel *Leucippe and Cleitophon*, written in the second century AD but set several centuries earlier, there is an exciting episode featuring a professional actor (3.20, see Hall, this volume, ch. 1). Achilles Tatius' travelling player provides a prototype for all the ancient actors who have appeared in modern fiction since it began to find inspiring settings in the Greek and Roman worlds. An important example is Henryk Sienkiewicz's influential Polish novel *Quo Vadis*, first published in 1896 but subsequently translated into no fewer than thirty-five languages. It features a set-piece banquet attended by Lucan, Petronius and other famous contemporaries, in which Nero performs as a citharode. But the climax is inspired by ancient pantomime (on which see Jory, this volume), when the dancer Paris spectacularly performs the various adventures of Io, daughter of Inachus,[22] a myth which Sienkiewicz probably knew is attested as the subject of an ancient pantomime (Lucian, *On Dancing* 43). The entertainments at the banquet scene of *Quo Vadis* have been recreated in the several cinematic versions of this famous novel made from 1912 onwards, notably the 1951 MGM classic, directed by Mervyn LeRoy. The composer of the musical score, Miklós Rózsa, was an historian of music interested in recreating the authentic melodies of antiquity. He persuaded Peter Ustinov (Nero) to give a citharodic performance of *Song of Seikilos*, a dirge which was inscribed, with musical notation, on a first-century stele in Caria.[23]

The ancient actor has remained a recurrent feature of historical novels written much more recently than *Quo Vadis*, which have been inspired by actors of Old Comedy, of tragedy and of mime in Cicero's Rome.[24] By far the most important 'ancient actor' novel, however, is Mary Renault's bestseller *The Mask of Apollo* (1966), which recreates the increasingly international world of the fourth-century Greek theatre in loving detail, seen through the eyes of Nikeratos, a gifted Athenian tragic actor. Renault invented Nikeratos, but her choice of name was probably inspired by the Athenian with a penchant for tragic diction called Nikeratos in Menander's *Samia* (on whom see Handley, this volume). Moreover, the 'real' figures of the famous stars Theodoros and Thettalos loom large

22 Sienkiewicz (1941) 53–4. 23 See Palmer (1975) 38–40.

24 The narrator and hero of Tom Holt's *The Walled Orchard* is Eupolis, one of the rivals of Aristophanes, who relates an engaging story of the day when his leading actor gets too drunk to perform (Holt (1997) 564–73). Joanne Daly's *An Actor in Rome* (1971) is a fictionalised biography of Roscius, also featuring Aesopus and Eucharis, a mime actress, whose gifts and very early death are commemorated by a stele at Rome (*CIL* VI 10096, see Garton (1972b) 251, and Webb, this volume). John Arden's *Silence among the Weapons* (1982) tells the story, set in the same period, of an Ephesian comic actor turned actors' agent. Davies (1995) involves a travelling troupe of actors in Syria during Roman imperial times. Thanks to Nan Dunbar and Peter Brown for help on this.

in her narrative. Renault was a lifelong lover of the theatre, numbering actors amongst her friends, but the important influence behind her novel was certainly the great Euripidean scholar Gilbert Murray, whose lectures Renault had attended while reading for her English degree at Oxford in the late 1920s. For *The Mask of Apollo* Renault plundered the works of Margarete Bieber, T. B. L. Webster and A. W. Pickard-Cambridge, producing a narrative distinguished by its historical accuracy. It also offers imaginative reconstructions of the physical reality of the ancient theatre, especially at the point when a rival actor tries to kill Nikeratos by tampering with the theatrical machine.[25]

One of the arguments developed in this book is that the techniques and talents of the ancient actor exerted a profound impact on the form taken by both theatrical literature and other, related genres. He has also played an important role in the emergence of new genres since the Renaissance, and in theoretical debates about them. The founding fathers of modern ballet in the eighteenth century, for example, including Jean-Georges Noverre, adopted ancient pantomime artists as their generic ancestors. They pointed out that distinguished dancers such as Pylades and Bathyllos had performed serious, extended versions of myth in an art-form distinct from tragic theatre, but enjoying equivalent status to it.[26]

Discussions of the practices of the ancient actor had also been fundamentally involved in the controversies surrounding the invention of opera, for the Italian humanists tended to believe that ancient actors performed all their lines as song and recitative.[27] One of the earliest members of the Florentine Camerata was Vincenzo Galilei (father of the astronomer), whose polemical *Dialogo della musica antica e della moderna* (Venice 1581) examined a wide range of ancient sources on music, pointed to Plato and Aristotle's views on the ethical and emotional force of music, argued that polyphonic modern music was incapable of expressing words with sufficient passion, and became the foundation text for early experiments in solo recitative.[28] Consequently, when Ottavio Rinuccini and Jacopo Peri collaborated at Florence as librettist and composer on what is now regarded as the earliest opera, *Dafne* (1598), they sincerely believed that they were recreating the forgotten art of the ancient *tragōidos*. Rinuccini wrote of *Dafne* in 1600:

[25] Sweetman (1993) 35–6, 240–4.
[26] See Goodden (1986) 112.
[27] See Donington (1981) 81, 99.
[28] See Donington (1981) 82–3.

It has been the opinion of many . . . that the ancient Greeks and Romans sang entire tragedies on the stage; but such a noble manner of reciting has not only not been renewed, but, so far as I know, not even attempted until now by anybody, and this I thought a defect of modern music, very far inferior to the ancient.[29]

A year later Peri explained his musical method, which entailed what would now be known as 'recitative', as an attempt to recreate the 'harmoniousness' of the way in which speech was imitated by music in the Greek and Roman theatres. He reasoned that this must have gone beyond ordinary speech but have fallen short of the 'melodiousness' of full-blown song.[30] Subsequent discussions of the role of song in serious theatre continued to use the ancient actors' manner of performance to justify their arguments.[31]

Theoretical treatises on acting also often illustrated their arguments from what was known of the practices of ancient Greek and Roman players. William Cooke appends to his *The Elements of Dramatic Criticism* (London 1775), *A Sketch of the Education of the Greek and Roman Actors; Concluding with Some General Instructions for Succeeding in the Art of Acting.* Diderot, as Lada-Richards has shown, used the discussion of the nature of rhapsodic performance in Plato's *Ion* in his *Paradox on Acting* (1773, although not published until 1830), and Diderot's treatise concludes with references to ancient anecdotes about the emotional involvement of Polos (see above) and Aesopus in their roles.[32] When the critic William Archer published *Masks and Faces*, his important response to Diderot, in 1888, this ancient evidence was once again recycled.[33] The prejudices of ancient writers on the theatre offered plentiful material to their nineteenth-century counterparts with axes to grind. William Donne, Examiner of stage plays in the Lord Chamberlain's Office, inveighing in literary magazines against vulgar entertainments, pointed to the way the ancient drama of Roscius and Aesopus had 'degenerated' into the pantomime of Bathyllus and Pylades; Percy Fitzgerald, disparaging the vulgarity of mid-Victorian popular entertainers while pleading for the resurrection of more serious, intellectual drama, drew numerous disapproving parallels between the practices of contemporary artistes in the music hall and the ancient *scurra*.[34]

29 This translation of part of Rinuccini's dedication to his next libretto, *L'Euridice*, is taken from Donington (1981) 104–5.

30 Peri, dedication to his score of *L'Euridice*, translated in Donington (1981) 105.

31 See e.g. Ralph (1731) 10–11.

32 Diderot in Diderot and Archer (1957) 70–1.

33 Archer in Diderot and Archer (1957) 106, 196.

34 Donne (1863) 79, 233 (articles reproduced from *Fraser's Magazine* and the *Westminster Review* respectively); Fitzgerald (1870) 251.

Yet to other nineteenth-century critics the ancient theatre was a useful site for defining their own ideals of acting by way of contrast and comparison. The Victorians attached great importance to emotional and psychological realism, portrayed by minute alterations in the facial expression; George Henry Lewes is not untypical when he writes:

> The immensity of the [Greek] theatre absolutely interdicted all individualizing; spectators were content with masks and attitudes where in the modern drama we demand the fluctuating physiognomy of passion, and the minute individualities of character.[35]

The difference between the masked performance of the ancient actor and the 'fluctuating physiognomy of passion' required of Victorian performers is discussed by Lewes' close contemporary Robert Browning in the opening narrative of *Balaustion's Adventure* (1871). This discussion leads directly into Browning's programmatic defence of the legitimacy of transforming ancient playscripts into dramatic monologues such as Balaustion's own solo 'performance' of Euripides' *Alcestis*. The dramatic monologue – a new, Victorian form for the content of poetry once performed by masked actors – is defended on the ground that poetry can do alone the work of words, of visual art and of music (308–35). Browning thus found ancient actors helpful when meditating on his own experiments in form. At the climax of *Aristophanes' Apology* (1875), Browning appropriates Plutarch's anecdote (previously used by Milton, see above) about the Phocian who saved Athens by performing lyrics from Euripides' *Electra*. The Phocian *tragōidos* is revealed in this Browning version to be none other than Euthukles, a figure symbolising the redemptive power of poetry who, as the husband of Balaustion/Elizabeth Barrett Browning, is to be closely associated with Browning himself.

The ancient actor and his art have also exerted a profound influence in the arena where their presence is most appropriate, the modern theatre. By the late nineteenth century there occurred the first of many serious attempts to reconstruct certain distinctive aspects of the experience undergone by the ancient actor and his audience, especially in connection with music, movement, costume and equipment, discussed earlier in this volume by Wilson, Valakas and Green. In 1886, for example, the actors in a performance of Aeschylus' *Agamemnon* at the Paris Opéra used stately movements and wore elaborate masks carefully modelled on a variety of the tragic masks described in Pollux's *Onomasticon*.[36] The identification

[35] Lewes (1875) 150.

[36] Girard (1894–5) part 2, 117 and n. 3. In England some learned gentlemen, for example Thomas Francklin, a former professor of Greek at Cambridge who translated plays for the London

with the ancient actor became even more acute when the dramatic setting changed from the proscenium arch to open air (and often reconstructed ancient) theatres, heralding the emergence of a style of acting inspired by ancient art and archaeology (see Valakas, this volume). Jean Mounet-Sully, who famously took the part of Oedipus in the late nineteenth and early twentieth centuries, played in (amongst other places) the Roman theatre at Orange (Arausio). Mounet-Sully visited museums and pored over books to achieve the appropriate 'geste'. He was also a noted sculptor and drew inspiration for his own (maskless) performance from a mask that he had cast in his own studio.[37] But attempts at the authentic recreation of ancient acting styles in performances of ancient plays is probably of less significance than the more subterranean influence exerted by the practices of the ancient theatre on important theatrical movements, developments in dramatic aesthetics, and the works of modern playwrights. The Symbolists, the director Gordon Craig, and the dramatic authors W. B. Yeats, Eugene O'Neill, T. S. Eliot and Samuel Beckett, for example, all significantly learned from and in turn contributed to the twentieth-century revival of interest in the techniques used by actors in the theatres of the ancient Greeks.[38]

Falkner's chapter in this volume showed how in Hellenistic times the art of the ancient tragic actor formed a bridge between the world of the scholar and the world of popular entertainment. The ancient plays by the Greek and Roman tragedians have always occupied a privileged place in subsequent western culture, enjoying lives both within the academy and far beyond it in the world of public performance. Translated, adapted, and enacted, ancient drama has rarely, since the Renaissance, been long absent from the public stage. This chapter has sketched an argument that the concept and figure of the ancient actor has enjoyed a parallel but often separate revival in the Renaissance and modern worlds. It has touched on a striking number of the top 'star' names that have already been encountered in this volume – Polos, Andronikos, Theodoros, Thettalos, Roscius, Aesopus, Paris, Pylades and Bathyllus.

The brilliant essayist and theatre critic William Hazlitt opened his second essay on the acting profession with the familiar lament that it is 'the misfortune of actors for the stage, that they leave no record behind

stage, were advocating a return to masked acting as early as the eighteenth century (see Pye (1792) 533).

37 See 'Vernay' (1888) 139. For a photograph of Mounet-Sully performing Creon in Sophocles' *Antigone*, see fig. 12.

38 See Dorn (1984) 63–83, Walton (1999), Macintosh (1994), Macintosh (1997), and her chapter on Symbolism in Hall and Macintosh (2004). The present chapter could not have been written without her generous help and advice.

them except that of vague rumour, and that the genius of a great actor perishes with him, "leaving the world no copy"'.[39] Yet the traces left by the greatest actors of antiquity far exceed 'vague rumour'. Actors from the sixth century BC to the Christian era, and exponents of tragedy, comedy, mime and pantomime, have all left sufficient records of their 'genius' to inspire not only scholars but also creative writers. It is impossible to foretell what metamorphoses will be undergone by these ancient players in the course of the twenty-first century, but even this brief survey of their presence from the Renaissance onwards suggests that the survival of interest in them beyond the 'Classics' academy looks no less likely than that of the famous plays which they performed.[40]

SUGGESTIONS FOR FURTHER READING

Besides the study of Roscius' *Nachleben* in Garton (1972b), the presence of the ancient actor during and subsequent to the Renaissance has received little systematic attention. Barish (1981) shows how ancient prejudices against the acting profession have been recycled by more recent antitheatricalists, especially Protestants; Barnett (1987) makes some interesting points about eighteenth-century connections between oratory and acting; Macintosh (1997) outlines the story of the discovery in the nineteenth and twentieth centuries that ancient tragedies could still work in performance.

39 Hazlitt (1917) 76. 'On Actors and Acting II', was first published as Essay 39 of *The Round Table* in 1817.

40 I would like to express my gratitude to the Arts and Humanities Research Board, whose funding of the research project 'History of Performances of Greek and Roman Drama' at the University of Oxford greatly enhanced this chapter.

Glossary

GREEK WORDS

agōn	contest
agōnothetēs	director of contests
akroāsis, pl. akroāseis	recital
amoibaion	lyric exchange
aoidos	bard
asylia	immunity as traveller
aulētēs, pl. aulētai	male piper
aulētris, pl. aulētrides	female piper
aulōidia	solo singing, to piped accompaniment
aulos, pl. auloi	pipe, usually in pairs
biologos	mime actor in parody of everyday life
bōmolochia	buffoonery
cheirosophistēs	skilled gesticulator
chitōn	tunic
chitoniskos	short tunic
chlamys	short cloak
choraulēs	piper
chorēgia	office of *chorēgos*
chorēgos, pl. chorēgoi	sponsor of choruses
choreia	dance by chorus
choropsaltria	female harpist
choros	group in performance, chorus
chous	pitcher
dēmos	sovereign people
dianoia	thought, meaning
didaskalia, pl. didaskaliai	record of dramatic productions
didaskalos	poet–trainer
ekkuklēma	trolley/platform wheeled out to reveal a scene from inside the stage building
ekstasis	mental distraction
embolimon	*entr'acte*
endosimon	'keynote'

epideixis, *pl. epideixeis*	recital, display
epinīkion	victory ode
epiparodos	re-entry of chorus
ethnos, *pl. ethnē*	nation, class, tribe
ēthos	character, disposition
eusebeia	piety
exodos	closing scene of a tragedy
exōmis	slave's garment
gelōtopoios	mime performer: 'laughter-maker'
harmonia, *pl. harmoniai*	musical 'mode': melodic type
heōrtē	festival in honour of a deity
hilarōidia	type of song
hilarōidos	type of singer
hīmation	outer garment
hypēresia, *pl. hypēresiai*	crew, supporting cast
hypokrisis	delivery
hypokritēs	actor
hypokritikē	the art of delivery, the art of acting
hypothesis	scholar's introductory preface to a play, mime with complex plot, scenario
ionikologos	type of mime actor
kinaidologos	type of mime actor
kithara	cithara
kitharisma	piece of music played on the cithara
kitharistēs	player on the cithara
kitharistria	female player on the cithara
kitharōidos	musician who plays and sings to the cithara
klismos	chair
koinon	public authority
kommos	sung dialogue between actor and chorus
kōmoidos	singer in comic chorus, comic actor
kōmōidoumenos	object of ridicule in comedy
korymboi	clusters of fruit and/or flowers attached to a wreath
koryphaios	chorus leader
kothornos	high boot worn by tragic actors
krokōtos	saffron-coloured female dress
krotala	clappers used by dancers
krotalistris, *pl. krotalistrides*	castanet dancer
kroumata	melodies
kroupeza	rattle, clapper
lexis	diction, style
lyrikos	lyre-player
lysiōidos	female impersonator
magōidia	type of mime performance

magōidos	magode, type of mime performer
melopoiia	songwriting
melos, pl. melē	song
metastasis	exit (of chorus)
mīmas, pl. mīmades	female performer of mime
mīmēsis	imitation
mīmos, pl. mīmoi	male performer of mime
mousikē	poetry/music/dance
mousikos	person skilled in *mousikē*
mousikos agōn	contest in *mousikē*
mythos	plot, myth
mythōn orchēstēs	'dancer of stories/myths'
nemēsis hypokritōn	allocation of protagonists to playwrights
nomos, pl. nomoi	nome, musical composition
nosos	sickness
ōidē	song, ode
onkos	artificial crown of hair above the forehead, worn by tragic actors from the Hellenistic period onwards
opsis	spectacle
orchēsis	dance
orchēstēs	male dancer
orchēstra, pl. orchēstrai	orchestra (in architectural sense): place where chorus and musicians perform
orchēstria/orchēstris	female dancer
paidagōgos	tutor, slave who accompanied schoolboys
paideia	education, culture
paignion	slapstick mime
panēgyris	festival in honour of an individual
pantomīmos, pl. pantomīmoi	pantomime (performer)
paraklausithyron	doorstep serenade
parodos	entrance song/side-entrance to stage
phantasia	representation of images, imagination
phorbeia	leather straps worn around cheeks and over head by piper
pīlos	traveller's hat
pinax	dedicatory tablet
poikilia	elaboration
polis, pl. poleis	city-state
politeuma	self-governing body of citizens
pompē	procession
pornoboskos	pimp
presbeutēs, pl. presbeutai	ambassador
prosodion	processional ode
prosōpopoiia	dramatisation, creation of characters

prosōpon	face, mask, character
prōtagōnistēs	leading actor
protomai	foreparts of an animal in visual art
proxenos	representative of a *polis* abroad
pseudokorē	pretend maiden
rhapsōidia	recitation of epic poetry
schēmata	gestures
sikinnis	type of dance performed by satyr-chorus
skēnē	stage-building, stage
skēnikē	female stage performer
skēnikos	theatrical
skēnographia	scene-painting
skeuē	costume(s), properties
skiagraphia	'shadow painting', scene painting
stephanēphoros	crown-wearing (of certain magistrates)
symphōnia	supporting artists
symposion	drinking party
synagōnistēs, *pl.* *synagōnistai*	supporting actor
synodos	meeting, company, guild
technē	art, skill
technītēs, *pl.* *technītai*	performing artist
technīteuma	theatrical profession
temenos	sacred precinct
thaumatopoios, *pl.* *thaumatopoioi*	trick-artist, conjurer
theātai	audience
theologeion	platform for gods' appearances in the theatre
theōros, *pl.* *theōroi*	sacred delegate at festival
thiasos	band of worshippers
thymelē	orchestra (in architectural sense), stage (in general sense)
thymelikē	female performer
thymelikos agōn	competition in musical and/or dramatic performance
thysia, *pl.* *thysiai*	sacrifice, festival
tragōidia	tragedy
tragōidos, *pl.* *tragōidoi*	tragic actor, tragic singer
xenos	foreigner visiting or living in an adopted city

LATIN WORDS (many of these are loanwords from Greek)

acta	acclamations
actio	legal procedure, speech in court, performance
actor	(leading) actor in charge of company, performer
ago	stage (a play), act (a part)
archimīma, pl. archmīmae	leading lady in mime
archimīmus	male lead in mine
artifex	craftsman, performer
artifex pronuntiandi	acting coach
canticum, pl. cantica	song
chorāgus	supplier of equipment to dramatic company
choraules	piper
citharoedia	performance on the cithara
citharoedus	performer on the cithara
cognōmen, pl. cognōmina	surname of family or individual
collēgium	guild
comoedus	comic actor
conductor	hirer of company
corporis mōtus	deportment
curia	court, meeting place of the senate
didascalia	production notice
diurnum	daily payment
diverbium	speech, spoken dialogue
emboliaria	female performer in entr'acte
fābula	play
fābula saltātōria	danced performance
fasti	festival calendar
gestus	gesture
grammaticus, pl. grammatici	scholar, grammarian
gregāles	members of a troupe
grex	company
histrio, pl. histriones	performer
hypocrita	actor
infamia	offical disgrace involving loss of certain rights
ioculātor	jester
krotalistria	castanet dancer
lēno	pimp
lūdi scaenici	theatrical entertainments
lūdio, pl. lūdiones	performer
lūdius, pl. lūdii	performer
lūdus tālārius	cabaret

magister	trainer, manager
meretrix	prostitute
mīma, dim. mīmula	female performer of mime
mīmus	male performer of mime
orātor	public speaker
oscillum, pl. oscilla	small mask hung from trees to promote fertility
partes	parts in a play
pantomīma	female pantomime performer
persōna	mask, character
probrosae feminae	disreputable women
pronuntiatio	delivery
pyrrhica	type of dance, originally performed in armour
saltātio	dance, pantomime
saltātor	male dancer
saltātrix	female dancer
satura	variety performance, satire
scaena	stage/place of public performance
scaenica/scaenicus	actress/actor
scaenicus doctor, pl. scaenici doctores	stage trainer
scurra	buffoon
servus currens	running slave
spectātōres	audience
symphoniaci	musicians performing in a band
thymelica	female performer
tibia	pipe
tibicen	piper
tragicus cantor	tragic singer
tragoedia cantata	performance by *tragoedus*
tragoedia saltata	pantomime
tragoedus	tragic singer, tragic actor
tribunus voluptatum	overseer of public spectacles

Works cited

Abel, F. M. (1931) 'Gaza au VIe siècle d' après le rhéteur Choricios', *Rbi* 40: 5–31

Albini, U. (1999) *Nel nome di Dioniso. Vita teatrale nell' Atene classica*. Milan (1st edn Milan 1991)

Aldama, J. A. de (1972) 'La tragedia *Christus Patiens* y la doctrina mariana en la Capadocia del siglo IV', in J. Fontaine and C. Kannengiesser, *Epektasis. Mélanges patristiques offerts au Cardinal Jean Daniélou*, 417–32. Paris

Alexiou, M. (1974) *The Ritual Lament in Greek Tradition*. Cambridge

(1975) 'The lament of the Virgin in Byzantine literature and modern Greek folk song', *Byzantine and Modern Greek Studies* 1: 111–46

Alföldi, R. (1935) 'Insignien und Tracht der Römischen Kaiser', *MDAI(R)* 50: 1–171

Allen, W. (1972) 'Ovid's *Cantare* and Cicero's *Cantores Euphorionis*', *TAPhA* 103: 1–14

And, M. (1951) 'Byzantine theatre', in P. Hartnoll, ed., *Oxford Companion to the Theatre*, 143–4. Oxford (4th edn with corrections Oxford 1985)

(1962) *Bizans Tiyatrosu*. Ankara

Andrescu, C. (1961) 'Kritik am Tanz – ein Ausschnitt aus dem Kampf der griechischen Kirche gegen heidnische Sitte', *ZKG* 72: 216–62

Anon. (1615) *A Refutation of the Apology for Actors*. London

Archer, W. (1888) *Masks or Faces? A Study in the Psychology of Acting*. London

Arden, J. (1982) *Silence among the Weapons: Some Events at the Time of the Failure of a Republic*. London

Arias, P. E., M. Hirmer and B. B. Shefton (1962) *A History of Greek Vase Painting*. London

Arnaud, P. (1984) 'L'image du globe dans le monde romain', *MEFRA* 96: 53–116

Arnott, G. (1959) 'The author of the Greek original of the *Poenulus*', *RhM* 102: 252–62

Arnott, P. D. (1962) *Greek Scenic Conventions in the Fifth Century BC*. Oxford

(1989) *Public and Performance in the Greek Theatre*. London and New York

Arnott, W. G. (1995) 'Menander's manipulation of language for the individualisation of character', in de Martino and Sommerstein, 147–64

(1996a) *Menander*, II. Cambridge, MA and London

(1996b) *Alexis: The Fragments. A Commentary*. Cambridge

(1998a) 'First notes on Menander's *Samia*', *ZPE* 123: 35–44

(1998b) 'Menander's Fabula Incerta', *ZPE* 123: 49–58

Artaud, A. (1958) *The Theater and Its Double*, transl. M. C. Richards, New York (French original 1938)

Astolfi, R. (1986) La *Lex Iulia et Papia*. Padua

Ataç, I. (1999) 'Neue Beobachtungen am Theater von Ephesos', in P. Scherrer, H. Taeuber and H. Thür, eds., *Steine und Wege: Festschrift für Dieter Knibbe zum 65. Geburtstag*, 1–6. Vienna

Ausbüttel, F. M. (1982) *Untersuchungen zu den Vereinen im Westen des römisches Reiches*. Kallmünz

Austin, G. (1806) *Chironomia or a Treatise on Rhetorical Delivery: Comprehending Many Precepts, both Ancient and Modern, for the Proper Regulation of the Voice, the Countenance and Gesture*. London

Ayre, L. (1972) *The Gilbert and Sullivan Companion*. London and New York

Ayres, P. (1997) *Classical Culture and the Idea of Rome in Eighteenth-Century England*. Cambridge

Bacon, H. H. (1961) *Barbarians in Greek Tragedy*. New Haven and Connecticut

Bain, D. (1984) 'Female speech in Menander', *Antichthon* 18: 24–42

Bakhtin, M. M. (1981) *The Dialogic Imagination: Four Essays*, ed. M. Holquist. Austin, Texas (Russian original 1975)

Baldwin, B. (1981) 'The date of a Circus dialogue', *REByz* 39: 301–6

(1985) *An Anthology of Byzantine Poetry*. Amsterdam

(1986) 'Byzantine drama: was there any?', *17th International Byzantinological Congress. Abstracts of Short Papers*, 20–1. Washington, DC

Balme, Maurice (2001) *Menander. The Plays and Fragments, Translated with Explanatory Notes*. Oxford

Bank, A. V. (1977) *Byzantine Art in the Collections of Soviet Museums*. New York and Leningrad (3rd edn enlarged Leningrad 1985)

Barba, E., and N. Savarese (1991) *A Dictionary of Theatre Anthropology. The Secret Art of the Performer*, transl. R. Fowler. London and New York

Barish, J. (1981) *The Antitheatrical Prejudice*. Berkeley, Los Angeles and London

Barker, A., ed. (1984/89) *Greek Musical Writings*. Vol. I: *The Musician and His Art* / Vol. II: *Harmonic and Acoustic Theory*. Cambridge

Barlow, S. A. (1986a) *Euripides. Trojan Women*. Warminster

(1986b) 'The language of Euripides' monodies', in J. H. Betts, J. T. Hooker and J. R. Green, eds., *Studies in Honour of T. B. L. Webster*, vol. I, 10–22. Bristol

Barner, W. (1971) 'Die Monodie', in W. Jens, ed., *Die Bauformen der griechischen Tragödie*, 221–75. Munich

Barnes, T. D. (1996) 'Christians and the theater', in Slater (1996b) 161–80

Barnett, D. (1987) *The Art of Gesture: the Practices and Principles of 18th Century Acting*. Heidelberg

Barrett, W. S. (1964) *Euripides. Hippolytos*. Oxford

Barsby, J. (1999) *Terence. Eunuchus*. Cambridge

Barthes, R. (1982a) *L'obvie et l'obtus. Essais critiques III*. Paris

(1982b) 'Tacitus and the funerary baroque', in S. Sontag, ed., *Barthes: Selected Writings*, 162–6. London

Bartholomeusz, D. (1969) *Macbeth and the Players*. Cambridge
Bartsch, S. (1994) *Actors in the Audience*. Cambridge, MA and London
Bate, J. (1996) 'The Romantic stage', in Bate and Jackson, 92–111
Bate, J., and R. Jackson, eds. (1996) *Shakespeare: An Illustrated Stage History*. Oxford
Bate, W. J. (1945) 'The sympathetic imagination in eighteenth-century English criticism', *ELH* 12: 144–64
Baty, G., and R. Chavange (1932) *Vie de l' art théatral: des origines à nos jours*. Paris
Baud-Bovy, S. (1938) 'Sur un *Sacrifice d'Abraham* de Romanos et sur l'existence d'un théâtre religieux à Byzance', *Byzantion* 12: 321–34
(1975) 'Le théâtre religieux, Byzance et l' Occident', *Hellenica* 28: 328–49
Baumstark, A. (1923) *Vom geschichtlichen Werden der Liturgie*. Freiburg
Beacham, R. C. (1991) *The Roman Theatre and its Audience*. London
Beare, W. (1950) *The Roman Stage: A Short History of Latin Drama in the Time of the Republic*. London (2nd edn London 1955; 3rd edn London 1964)
Beaton, R. (1996) 'The Byzantine revival of the ancient novel', in G. Schmeling, ed., *The Novel in the Ancient World*, 713–33. Leiden, New York and Cologne
Beauchamp, J. (1990) *Le statut de la femme à Byzance 4e–7e siècles*. Paris
Beazley, J. (1955) 'Hydria-fragments in Corinth', *Hesperia* 24: 305–19
Beck, H.-G. (1952) *Theodoros Metochites. Die Krise des byzantinischen Weltbildes im 14. Jahrhundert*. Munich
(1959) *Kirche und theologische Literatur im byzantinischen Reich*. Munich
(1971) *Geschichte der byzantinischen Volksliteratur*. Munich
(1978) *Das byzantinische Jahrtausend*. Munich
Bekker, I., ed. (1814–21) *Anecdota graeca*. Berlin
Bélis, A. (1986) 'La Phorbéia', *BCH* 110: 205–18
(1988) 'Κρούπεζαι', *scabellum*', *BCH* 112: 323–39
Belting, H. (1991) *Bild und Kult. Eine Geschichte des Bildes vor dem Zeitalter der Kunst*. 2nd edn. Munich
Bentley, G. E. (1984) *The Profession of Player in Shakespeare's Time, 1590–1642*. Princeton, NJ
Bentley, R. (1965) *The Life of Drama*. London
Benz, L., E. Stärk and G. Vogt-Spira, eds. (1995) *Plautus und die Tradition des Stegreifspiels. Festgabe für Eckard Lefèvre zum 60. Geburtstag*. Tübingen
Bergemann, J. (1994) 'Die bürgerliche Identität der Athener im Spiegel der attischen Grabreliefs', in E. Pöhlmann and W. Gauer, eds., *Griechische Klassik. Vorträge bei der interdisziplinären Tagung des Deutschen Archäologenverbandes und der Mommsengesellschaft vom 24.–27.10.1991 in Blaubeuren*, 283–94. Nuremberg
(1997) *Demos und Thanatos. Untersuchungen zum Wertsystem der Polis im Spiegel der attischen Grabreliefs des 4. Jhs. v. Chr. und zur Funktion der gleichzeitigen Grabbauten*. Munich
Bernarbò Brea, L. (1981) *Menandro e il teatro greco nelle terracotte liparesi*. Genoa
Bernarbò Brea, L., and M. Lavalier (1991) *Meligunis Lipara V: Scavi nella necropoli greca di Lipari*. Rome
Bernardi Ferrero, D. de (1970) *Teatri classici in Asia Minore* 3. Rome

Bers, V. (1985) 'Dicastic *thorubos*', in P. Cartledge and D. Harvey, eds., *Crux: Essays in Greek History Presented to G. E. M. de Ste. Croix*, 1–15. London
(1997) *Speech in Speech. Studies in Incorporated Oratio Recta in Attic Drama and Oratory*. Lanham, Maryland and London
Berthold, M. (1968) *Weltgeschichte des Theaters*. Stuttgart
Berti, F., and C. Gasparri, eds. (1989) *Dionysos. Mito e Mistero*. Bologna
Beschi, L. (1967–68) 'Il monumento di Telemachos, fondatore dell' Asklepieion ateniese', *ASAA* 29–30: 381–436
Bianchi, L., and M. Bonnano Aravantinos (1991) 'Una tradizione di scultura funeraria microasiatica a Ostia', *BArch* 8: 1–32
Bibilakis, J. (1996) '῾Η θεατρικὴ ὁρολογία στοὺς Πατέρες τῆς ᾿Εκκλησίας. Συμβολὴ στὴ μελέτη τῆς σχέσεως ᾿Εκκλησίας καὶ Θεάτρου'. Dissertation. Athens
(1997) '῾Η σκηνὴ τοῦ βίου: Ἡ παραβοὴ τοῦ κοσμοθεάτρου στοὺς ἐκκλησιαστικοὺς Πατέρες', Σύναξη 62: 109–20
Bieber, M. (1920) *Die Denkmäler zum Theaterwesen im Altertum*. Berlin and Leipzig
(1961) *The History of the Greek and Roman Theater*. 2nd edn Princeton
Blänsdorf, J. (1990) 'Der spätantike Staat und die Schauspiele im Codex Theodosianus', in J. Blänsdorf, ed., *Theater und Gesellschaft im Imperium Romanum*. Tübingen
Blanchard, A. (1997) 'Destins de Ménandre', *Ktèma* 22: 213–25
Blázquez, J. M. (1975) *Castulo* I. Madrid
Blum, R. (1991) *Kallimachos. The Alexandrian Library and the Origins of Bibliography*, trans. H. Wellisch. Madison (German original 1977)
Blundell, J. (1980) *Menander and the Monologue*. Göttingen
Boaden, J. (1825) *Memoirs of the Life of John Philip Kemble, Including a History of the Stage, from the Time of Garrick to the Present Period*. London
Bonaria, M., ed. (1955–56) *Mimorum Romanorum fragmenta*, 2 vols in one. Genoa
(1959) 'Dinastie di pantomimi latini', *Maia* 11: 224–42
ed. (1965) *Romani Mimi*. Rome
Bond, G. (1963) *Euripides. Hypsipyle*. Oxford
Bowra, M. (1958) 'A love-duet', *AJPh* 79: 376–91
Boyle, A. J. (1987) *Seneca. Phaedra*. Liverpool
(1997) *Tragic Seneca: An Essay in the Theatrical Tradition*. London and New York
Braden, G. (1985) *Anger's Privilege: Renaissance Tragedy and the Senecan Tradition*. Yale
Braemme, F. (1976) *Katalog over teatervidenskabelige kilder i Nationalmuseets Antiksamm-ling*. Copenhagen.
Braun, E. (1982) *The Director and the Stage. From Naturalism to Grotowski*. London
ed. and trans. (1991) *Meyerhold on Theatre*. Rev. edn London (1st edn London 1969)
Brecht, B. (1964) *Brecht on Theatre: The Development of an Aesthetic*, ed. and trans. J. Willett. London
Bréhier, L. (1913) 'Le théâtre à Byzance', *Journal des Savants* 1913: 357–61, 395–404
(1920) 'Les miniatures des *Homélies* du moine Jacque et le théâtre religieux à Byzance', *MMAI* 24: 101–8

(1950) *La civilisation byzantine*. Paris
Bremer, J. M. (1976) 'Aristotle, *Poetics*, 1449b27–28', in J. M. Bremer, S. L. Radt and C. J. Ruijgh, eds., *Miscellanea tragica in honorem J. C. Kamerbeek*, 29–48. Amsterdam
Bremmer, J. (1991) 'Walking, standing, and sitting in Ancient Greek culture', in Bremmer and Roodenburg, 15–35
Bremmer, J., and H. Roodenburg, eds. (1991) *A Cultural History of Gesture from Antiquity to the Present Day*. Oxford
(1997) *A Cultural History of Humour from Antiquity to the Present Day*. Cambridge
Breuer, C. (1994) *Reliefs und Epigramme griechischer Privatgrabmäler vom vierten bis zweiten Jahrhundert als Zeugnisse bürgerlichen Selbstverständnisses*. Cologne
Brommer, F. (1959) *Satyrspiele. Bilder griechischer Vasen*. 2nd edn Berlin
Broneer, O. (1953) 'Isthmia excavations, 1952', *Hesperia* 22: 182–95
Brooks, R. A. (1981) *Ennius and Roman Tragedy*. New York
Brown, P. (1989) *The Body and Society: Men, Women and Sexual Renunciation in Early Christianity*. London
Browning, R. (1952) 'The riot of AD. 387 in Antioch: the role of the theatrical claques in the later Roman empire', *JRS* 17: 13–20
(1963) 'A Byzantine treatise on tragedy', in L. Varcl and R. F. Willetts, eds., Γέρας. *Studies Presented to George Thomson on the Occasion of his 60th Birthday*, 67–81. Prague
(1971) *Justinian and Theodora*. London
Brožek, M. (1960) 'Einiges über die Schauspieldirektoren und die Komödiendichter im alten Rom', *StudClas* 2: 145–50
Brunt, P. A. (1975) 'Stoicism and the principate', *PBSR* 43: 7–35
Bulle, H. (1930) 'Von griechischen Schauspielern und Vasenmalern', in *Festschrift für James Loeb zum sechzigsten Geburtstag*, 5–37. Munich
Burian, P. (1997) 'Myth into *muthos*: the shaping of tragic plot', in Easterling (1997a), 178–208
Burkert, W. (1994) 'Orpheus, Dionysos und die Euneiden in Athen: Das Zeugnis von Euripides' *Hypsipyle*', in A. Bierl and P. von Möllendorff, eds., *Orchestra: Drama, Mythos, Bühne*, 44–9. Stuttgart and Leipzig
Buschhausen, H. (1986) 'La sala dell'Ippolito', in Piccirillo, 117–27
Butcher, S. H. (1929) *The Poetics of Aristotle*. 4th edn London
Bywater, I. (1909) *Aristotle. On the Art of Poetry*. Oxford
Calvet, M., and P. Roesch (1966) 'Les Sarapieia de Tanagra', *RA* 1: 297–332
Cameron, Alan (1976) *Circus Factions: Blues and Greens at Rome and Byzantium*. Oxford
(1995) *Callimachus and his Critics*. Princeton
Cameron, Averil (1985) *Procopius and the Sixth Century*. London
Canfora, L. (1989) *The Vanished Library*, trans. M. Ryle. Berkeley (Italian original 1987)
Capps, E. (1910) *Four Plays of Menander*. Boston and London
Carandini, A., A. Ricci and M. de Vos (1982) *Filosofiana, the Villa of Piazza Armerina*. Palermo

Carpenter, M. (1936) 'Romanos and the Mystery Play of the East', *University of Missouri Studies* 9: 21–51

Chaisemartin, N. de (1987) 'Recherches sur la frise de l'Agora de Tibère', in J. de la Genière and K. Erim, eds., *Aphrodisias de Carie. Colloque du centre de recherches archéologiques de l' Université de Lille III* (13 November 1985), 135–54. Paris

Chambers, E. K. (1923) *The Elizabethan Stage*, 4 vols. Oxford

(1930) *William Shakespeare. A Study of Facts and Problems*. Oxford

(1935) *Shakespeare*. London

Chaniotis, A. (1990) 'Zur Frage der Spezialisierung im griechischen Theater des Hellenismus und der Kaiserzeit auf der Grundlage der neuen Prosopographie der dionysischen Techniten', *Ktèma* 15: 89–108

(1997) 'Theatricality beyond the theater. Staging public life in the Hellenistic world', *Pallas* 47: 219–59

Charitonidis, S., L. Kahil and R. Ginouvès (1970) *Les mosaïques de la maison du Ménandre à Mytilène*. Bern

Churchill, C. (1763) *The Rosciad*. 8th edn London

Cockle, W. H. (1975) 'The odes of Epagathus the choral flautist: some documentary evidence for dramatic representation in Roman Egypt', in *Proceedings of the XIVth International Congress of Papyrologists* (Oxford 24–31 July 1974), 59–65. London

Cole, T., ed. (1955) *Acting: A Handbook of the Stanislavski Method*. Rev. edn. New York

Cole, T., and H. K. Chinoy (1949) *Actors on Acting*. New York

Coleman, K. M. (1990) 'Fatal charades: Roman executions staged as mythological enactments', *JRS* 80: 44–73

Coles, R. A. (1968) 'A new fragment of post-classical tragedy from Oxyrhynchus', *BICS* 15: 110–18

Collard, C. (1975) *Euripides. Supplices*. Groningen

Collard, C., M. J. Cropp and K. H. Lee (1995) *Euripides. Selected Fragmentary Plays*. Vol. 1. Warminster

Colvin, S. (1999) *Dialect in Aristophanes and the Politics of Language in Ancient Greek Literature*. Oxford

Comotti, G. (1989a) 'La musica nella tragedia greca', in De Finis, 43–61

(1989b) *Music in Greek and Roman Culture*, trans. R. V. Munson. Baltimore and London (Italian original 1979)

Connolly, A. (1998) 'Was Sophocles heroised as Dexion?', *JHS* 118: 1–21

Connolly, J. (1998) 'Mastering corruption. Constructions of identity in Roman oratory', in S. R. Joshel and S. Murnaghan, eds., *Women and Slaves in Greco-Roman Culture*, 130–51. London

Connors, C. (1994) 'Famous last words', in J. Elsner and J. Masters, eds., *Reflections of Nero: Culture, History, and Representation*, 225–35. London

Constantelos, P. (1970) 'Canon 62 of the Synod in Trullo and the Slavic problem', Βυζαντινά 2: 23–35

Cooke, William (1775) *The Elements of Dramatic Criticism*. London

Cope, E. M. (1877) *The Rhetoric of Aristotle*, rev. and ed. J. H. Sandys. Cambridge (original London 1867)

Corbato, C. (1947) 'L'iscrizione sepolcrale di una mima ad Aquileia romana', *Dioniso* 10: 188–203

Cottas, V. (1931 a) *Le théâtre à Byzance*. Paris.

(1931 b) *L' influence du drame Christos Paschon sur l' art chrétien à Orient*. Paris

Courtney, E. (1980) *A Commentary on the Satires of Juvenal*. London

Craik, E. M. (1990a) 'The staging of Sophokles' *Philoktetes* and Aristophanes' *Birds*', in Craik (1990b), 81–4

ed. (1990b) *'Owls to Athens': Essays on Classical Subjects Presented to Sir Kenneth Dover*. Oxford

Crame, W. (1980) 'Irrtum und Lüge. Zum Urteil des Jacob von Sarug über Reste paganer Religion und Kultur', *JbAC* 23: 96–107

Cropp, M., and G. Fick (1985) *Resolutions and Chronology in Euripides: The Fragmentary Tragedies* (*BICS* Suppl. 43). London

Csapo, E. (1993) 'A case study in the use of theatre iconography as evidence for ancient acting', *AK* 36: 41–58

(1997) 'Mise en scène théâtrale, scéne de théâtre artisanale: Les mosaïques de Ménandre à Mytilène, leur contexte sociale et leur tradition iconographique', in Le Guen, 165–82

(2000) 'From Aristophanes to Menander? Genre transformation in Greek comedy', in Depew and Obbink, 115–33

(forthcoming a) 'The production and performance of Greek comedy in antiquity', in G. Dobrov, ed. (forthcoming) *A Companion to the Study of Greek Comedy*. Leiden

(forthcoming b) 'The politics of the New Music', in Murray and Wilson (forthcoming)

Csapo, E., and W. J. Slater (1995) *The Context of Ancient Drama*. Ann Arbor

Cunningham, I. C. (1971) *Herodas' Mimiamboi*. Oxford

(1987) *Herodae Mimiambi cum appendice fragmentorum mimorum papyraceorum*. Leipzig

Dacier, A. (1692) *La Poétique d'Aristote*. Paris (repr. Hildesheim 1976)

Daiber, H. (1968) 'Die Arabische Übersetzung der Placita Philosophorum'. Dissertation. Saarbrücken

Dale, A. M. (1954) *Euripides. Alcestis*. Oxford

(1969) '*Ethos* and *dianoia*: "character" and "thought" in Aristotle's *Poetics*', in T. B. L. Webster and E. G. Turner, eds., *Collected Papers of A. M. Dale*, 139–55. Cambridge

Daly, J. (1971) *An Actor in Rome*. London

Damen, M. (1989) 'Actor and character in Greek tragedy', *Theatre Journal* 41: 316–40

(1990) 'Electra's monody and the role of the chorus in Euripides' *Orestes* 960–1012', *TAPhA* 120: 133–45

D'Amico, S. (1933) 'La "querela" fra Chiesa e teatro', *Nuova Antologia* 370, no. 1480: 217–32

Dardaine, S., and E. Frézouls (1985) 'Essai de typologie des monuments funéraires de Sidyma', *Ktèma* 10: 211–17

Dardaine, S., and D. Longepierre (1985) 'Essai de typologie des monuments funeraires de Sidyma', *Ktèma* 10: 219–32
Daube, D. (1967) 'The marriage of Justinian and Theodora: legal and theological reflections', *Catholic University of America Law Review* 16: 380–99
Davidson, J. (1986) 'The circle and the tragic chorus', *G&R* 33: 38–46
(2000) '*Gnesippus' paigniagraphos*: the comic poets and the erotic mime', in D. Harvey and J. Wilkins, eds., *The Rivals of Aristophanes*, 41–64. London
Davies, L. (1995) *Last Act in Palmyra*. London
Dearden, C. W. (1976) *The Stage of Aristophanes*. London
Decleva Caizzi, F. (1993) 'The porch and the garden: early Hellenistic images of the philosophical life', in A. Bulloch et al., eds., *Images and Ideologies. Self-definition in the Hellenistic World*, 303–29. Berkeley
De Finis, L., ed. (1989) *Scena e spettacolo nell'antichità. Atti del convegno internazionale di studio* (Trento 28–30 March 1988). Florence
Deichmann, F. W. (1958) *Frühchristliche Bauten und Mosaiken von Ravenna*. Baden
Delbrueck, R. (1929) *Die Konsulardiptychen und verwandte Denkmäler*. Berlin
Del Corno, D. (1975) 'Alcuni aspetti del linguaggio di Menandro', *SCO* 24: 13–48
(1979) 'Vita cittadina e commedia borghese', in A. Barigazzi et al., eds., *La crisi della polis*, 265–98 (Storia e civiltà dei Greci, 5). Milan
(1997) 'La caratterizzazione dei personaggi di Aristofane attraverso i fatti di lingua e di stile', in Thiercy and Menu, 243–52
Depew, M., and D. Obbink, eds. (2000) *Matrices of Genre. Authors, Canons and Society*. Cambridge, MA and London
De Sainte Albine, R. (1747) *Le Comédien*. Paris
Devine, A. M., and L. D. Stephens (1981) 'A new aspect of the evolution of the trimeter in Euripides', *TAPhA* 111: 43–64
(1983) 'Semantics, syntax, and phonological organization in Greek: aspects of the theory of metrical bridges', *CPh* 78: 1–25
Dicken, M. (1999) 'The distribution of messenger roles in fifth-century Greek tragedy'. MA thesis, McMaster
Dickie, M. (1993) 'Palaistrites/palaestrita: callisthenics in the Greek and Roman gymnasium', *Nikephoros* 6: 105–51
Diderot, D. (1936) 'Paradoxe sur le comédien', in F. C. Green, ed., *Diderot's Writings on the Theatre*. Cambridge (1st edn Paris 1773)
Diderot, D., and W. Archer (1957) *The Paradox of Acting* and *Masks or Faces*. New York
Dihle, A. (1981) *Der Prolog der Bacchen und die antike Überlieferungsphase des Euripides-textes*. Heidelberg
Diller, H. (1979) 'Sophokles: Die Tragödien', in G. A. Seeck, ed., *Das griechische Drama*, 51–104. Darmstadt
Dindorf, L., ed. (1870) *Historici Graeci Minores*, vol. 1. Leipzig
D' Ippolito, G. (1962) 'Draconzio, Nonno e gli "Idromimi"', *A&R* 7: 1–14
Dodds, E. R. (1960) *Euripides' Bacchae*. 2nd edn. Oxford
Dölger, F. J. (1934) 'Klingeln, Tanz und Händeklatschen im Gottesdienst der christlichen Melitianer in Ägypten', *Antike und Christentum* 4: 245–65
(1948) *Die byzantinische Dichtung in der Reinsprache*. Berlin

Donington, R. (1981) *The Rise of Opera*. London and Boston
Donne, W. B. (1863) *Essays on the Drama and on Popular Amusements*. 2nd edn. London
Donohue, J. (1970) *Dramatic Character in the English Romantic Age*. Princeton
Dorn, K. (1984) *Players and Painted Stage: The Theatre of W. B. Yeats*. Brighton
Dorter, K. (1973) 'The *Ion*: Plato's characterization of art', *Journal of Aesthetics and Art Criticism* 32: 65–78
Dostálová, R. (1982) 'Die byzantinische Theorie des Dramas und die Tragödie *Christos Paschon*', in *XVI. Internationaler Byzantinistenkongress, Akten II* (Vienna 4–9 October 1981), 73–82. Vienna
Dover, K. J. (1987) *Greek and the Greeks: Collected Papers* I. Oxford
(1993) *Aristophanes. Frogs*. Oxford
Downer, A. S. (1966) *The Eminent Tragedian: William Charles Macready*. Cambridge, MA and London
Drumbl, J. (1981) *Quem quaeritis. Teatro sacro dell' alto medioevo*. Rome
Duckworth, G. E. (1952) *The Nature of Roman Comedy*. Princeton (repr. Bristol 1994)
Dumont, J. C. (1982) '*Cogi in scaena ponere personam*', *REL* 60: 123–7
(1987) *Servus: Rome et l'esclavage sous la république*. Rome
(1997) '*Cantica* et espace de représentation dans le théâtre latin', in Le Guen, 41–50
Dunand, F. (1979) *Religion populaire en Egypte romaine: les terres cuites isiaques du Musée du Caire*. Leiden
Dunbar, N. (1995) *Aristophanes. Birds*. Oxford
Dvornik, F. (1946) 'The circus parties in Byzantium: the evolution and suppression', Βυζαντινά-μεταβυζαντινά 1: 119–33
Dwyer, E. J. (1981) 'Pompeian oscilla collections', *MDAI(R)* 88: 247–306
Dyck, A., ed. (1986) *Michael Psellus. The Essays on Euripides and George of Pisidia and on Heliodorus and Achilles Tatius*. Vienna
(1994) '*Psellus tragicus*: observations on *Chronographia* 5.26ff.', *ByzF* 20: 269–90
Easterling, P. E. (1985), 'Anachronism in Greek tragedy', *JHS* 105: 1–10
(1990) 'Constructing character in Greek tragedy', in Pelling (1997a), 83–99
(1993a) 'The end of an era? Tragedy in the early fourth century', in Sommerstein, Halliwell, Henderson and Zimmermann, 559–69
(1993b) 'Gods on stage in Greek tragedy', in J. Dalfen et al., eds., *Religio Graeco-Romana, Festschrift für Walter Pötscher, Grazer Beiträge* Suppl. 5, 77–86. Graz
(1995) 'Menander: loss and survival', in Griffiths, 153–60
(1997a) *The Cambridge Companion to Greek Tragedy*. Cambridge
(1997b) 'Form and performance', in Easterling (1997a), 151–77
(1997c) 'A show for Dionysus', in Easterling (1997a), 36–53
(1997d) 'From repertoire to canon', in Easterling (1997a), 211–27
(1999) 'Actors and voices: reading between the lines in Aeschines and Demosthenes', in Goldhill and Osborne, 154–66
Easterling, P. E., and R. Miles (1999) 'Dramatic identities: tragedy in late antiquity', in R. Miles ed., *Constructing Identities in Late Antiquity*, 95–111. London and New York

Edmunds, L., and R. W. Wallace, eds. (1997) *Poet, Public and Performance in Ancient Greece*. Baltimore and London

Edwards, C. (1993) *The Politics of Immorality in Ancient Rome*. Cambridge

(1994) 'Beware of imitations', in J. Elsner and J. Masters, eds., *Reflections of Nero: Culture, History, and Representation*, 83–97. London

(1997) 'Unspeakable professions: public performance and prostitution in ancient Rome', in J. P. Hallett and M. B. Skinner, eds., *Roman Sexualities*, 66–95. Princeton

(1999) 'The suffering body: philosophy and pain in Seneca's letters', in J. I. Porter, ed., *Constructing the Body in Classical Antiquity*, 252–68. Ann Arbor

Eire, A. L. (1997) 'A propos de l'attique familier de la comédie aristophanienne', in Thiercy and Menu, 189–212

Eitrem, S., L. Amundsen and R. P. Winnington-Ingram (1955) 'Fragments of unknown Greek tragic texts with musical notation (*P Oslo* inv. no. 1413)', *SO* 31: 1–87

Elam, K. (1980) *The Semiotics of Theatre and Drama*. London and New York

Eliot, T. S. (1950) *Poetry and Drama*. (The Theodore Spencer Memorial Lecture, Harvard University, 21 November 1950) London

Else, G. F. (1967) *Aristotle's* Poetics*: The Argument*. Cambridge, MA

England, E. B. (1891) *The Iphigeneia at Aulis of Euripides*. London and New York

Erbe, B. (1973) 'En undersøgelske af byzantinsk teater' *Acta Universitatis Bergensis, Series humanarum Litterarum* 1972.2. Bergen

Erim, K. T. (1986) *Aphrodisias, City of Venus Aphrodite*. London

Evans, E. C. (1969) *Physiognomics in the Ancient World*. Philadelphia

Evans Grubbs, J. (1995) *Law and Family in Late Antiquity*. Oxford

Fairweather, J. A. (1974) 'Fiction in the biographies of ancient writers', *AncSoc* 5: 231–75

Falkner, T. M. (1998) 'Containing tragedy: rhetoric and self-representation in Sophocles' *Philoctetes*', *ClAnt* 17: 25–58

Fantham, E. (1973) 'Towards a dramatic reconstruction of the fourth Act of Plautus' *Amphitruo*', *Philologus* 117: 197–214

(1982) 'Quintilian on performance: traditional and personal elements in *Institutio* 11.3', *Phoenix* 36: 243–71

(1984) 'Roman experience of Menander in the late republic and early empire', *TAPhA* 114: 299–310

(1989) 'Mime: the missing link in Roman literary history', *CW* 82: 153–63

Fantuzzi, M. (1990) 'Sulla scenografia dell' ora (e del luogo) nella tragedia greca', *MD* 24: 9–30

Fear, A. T. (1996) 'The Dancing Girls of Cadiz' in I. McAuslan and P. Walcot, eds., *Women in Antiquity*, 177–81. Oxford (repr. from *G&R* 1991)

Felicetti-Liebenfels, W. (1956) *Geschichte der byzantinischen Ikonenmalerei*. Olten and Lausanne

Feneron, J. S. (1974) 'Some elements of Menander's style', *BICS* 21: 81–95

Ferrero, M. G. (1976) 'L'asindeto in Menandro', *Dioniso* 47: 82–106

Fisher, E. A. (1978) 'Theodora and Antonina in the *Historia Arcana*: history and/or fiction', *Arethusa* 11: 253–79
Fitzgerald, P. (1870) *Principles of Comedy and Dramatic Effect*. London
Flashar, H. (1991) *Inszenierung der Antike: Das griechische Drama auf der Bühne der Neuzeit 1585–1990*. Munich
Foley, H. P. (1988) 'Tragedy and politics in Aristophanes' *Acharnians*', *JHS* 108: 33–47
Follmann, A.-B. (1968) *Der Panmaler*. Bonn
Forman, M. B. (1935) *The Letters of John Keats*. Oxford
Fortenbaugh, W. W. (1985) 'Theophrastus on delivery', *Rutgers University Studies* 2: 269–88
Fraenkel, E. (1922) *Plautinisches in Plautus* (*Philologische Untersuchungen*, 28). Berlin
(1950) *Aeschylus. Agamemnon*. 3 vols. Oxford
(1960) *Elementi Plautini in Plauto*. Florence
(1977) *Due Seminari Romani di Eduard Fraenkel*. Rome
Franceschini, E. B. (1995) 'Winter in the great palace: the persistence of pagan festivals in Christian Byzantium', *ByzF* 21: 117–34
Frank, T. (1931) 'The status of actors at Rome', *CPh* 26: 11–20
(1932) 'Two notes on Plautus', *AJPh* 53: 243–51
Fraser, P. M. (1972) *Ptolemaic Alexandria*. 2 vols. Oxford
Frassinetti, P. (1953) *Fabula Atellana. Saggio sul teatro popolare latino*. Genoa
Freese, J. H. (1926) *Aristotle. The Art of Rhetoric, Aristotle XXII*. Cambridge, MA and London
Frei, J. (1900) *De Certaminibus Thymelicis*. Basle
French, D. (1998) 'Maintaining boundaries: the status of actresses in early Christian society', *VChr* 52: 293–318
Frézouls, E. (1959/61) 'Recherches sur les théâtres de l' Orient syrien', *Syria* 36: 202–27 / 38: 54–86
Froning, H. (1971) *Dithyrambos und Vasenmalerei*. Würzburg
Frost, K. B. (1988) *Exits and Entrances in Menander*. Oxford
Frova, A. (1943) *Pittura Romana in Bulgaria*. Rome
Fuchs, G. (1904–05) *Die Schaubühne der Zukunft*. Berlin
Gaca, K. (1999) 'The sexual and social dangers of *Pornai* in the Septuagint Greek stratum of Patristic Christian Greek thought', in L. James, ed., *Desire and Denial in Byzantium*, 35–40. Aldershot
Galilei, Vincenzo (1581) *Dialogo della musica antica e della moderna*. Venice
Gardiner, C. P. (1987) *The Sophoclean Chorus. A Study of Character and Function*. Iowa City
Garrick, D. (1831–32) *The Private Correspondence of David Garrick with the Most Celebrated Persons of his Time*. 2 vols. London
(1963) *The Letters of David Garrick*, eds. D. M. Little and G. M. Kahrl. 3 vols. London
Garton, C. (1972a) 'How Roscius acted Ballio', in Garton (1972b), 170–88
(1972b) *Personal Aspects of the Roman Theatre*. Toronto
Geddes, A. G. (1987) 'Rags and riches: the costume of Athenian men in the fifth century', *CQ* 37: 307–31

Geiger, J. (1979) 'Munatius Rufus and Thrasea Paetus on Cato the Younger', *Athenaeum* 57: 48–72
Gelzer, H. (1889) 'Ein griechischer Volksschriftsteller des 7. Jahrhunderts', *HZ* 61: 1–38
Gentili, B. (1960) 'Paracataloghè', in *Enciclopedio dello Spettacolo,* vol. VII, 1599–1601. Rome
(1979) *Theatrical Performances in the Ancient World: Hellenistic and Early Roman Theatre*. Amsterdam
(1988) *Poetry and Its Public in Ancient Greece*, trans. A. T. Cole. Baltimore (Italian original 1985)
Gentleman, F. (1770) *The Dramatic Censor or Critical Companion*. 2 vols. London
George E. (1994) *The Nature of Roman Comedy: A Study in Popular Entertainment*. 2nd edn. Norman, Oklahoma (1st edn Princeton 1952)
Ghilardi, G. (1961) *Storia di Teatro,* I. Milan
Ghiron-Bistagne, P. (1974a) 'Die Krise des Theaters in der griechischen Welt im 4. Jh. v.u.Z', in Welskopf, vol. I, 335–56
(1974b) 'Images du théâtre grec', *REG* 87: 361–8
(1976) *Recherches sur les acteurs dans la Grèce antique*. Paris
Giatsintova, A. S. (1955) 'Case history of a role', in Cole, 125–9
Gill, C. (1986) 'The question of character and personality in Greek tragedy', *Poetics Today* 7: 251–73
(1988) 'Personhood and personality: the four-*personae theory in Cicero De officiis* I', *OSAPh* 6: 169–99
(1994) 'Peace of mind and being yourself: Panaetius to Plutarch', *ANRW* 2.36.7: 4599–640
Gilula, D. (1985–88) 'How rich was Terence?', *SCI* 8–9: 74–8
(1996) 'Choragium and choragos', *Athenaeum* 84: 479–92
Girard, P. (1894/5) 'De l'expression des masques dans les drames d'Eschyle', *REG* 7: 1–36/8: 88–131
Gleason, M. (1995) *Making Men: Sophists and Self-presentation in Ancient Rome*. Princeton
Glotz, G. (1926) *Ancient Greece at Work: An Economic History of Greece*. New York
Goffe, T. (1633) *The Tragedy of Orestes*. London
Goffman, E. (1956) *The Presentation of Self in Everyday Life*. London
Goldberg, S. M. (1986) *Understanding Terence*. Princeton
(1995) *Epic in Republican Rome*. Oxford
Goldhill, S. (1990) 'Character and action, representation and reading: Greek tragedy and its critics', in Pelling, 100–27
(1994) 'Representing democracy: women at the Great Dionysia', in R. Osborne and S. Hornblower, eds., *Ritual, Finance, Politics: Athenian Democratic Accounts Presented to David Lewis*, 347–69. Oxford
(1999) 'Programme notes', in Goldhill and Osborne, 1–29
Goldhill, S. and R. Osborne, eds. (1999) *Performance Culture and Athenian Democracy*. Cambridge
Gomme, A. W., and F. W. Sandbach (1973) *Menander: A Commentary*. Oxford

Goodden, A. (1986) *Actio and Persuasion: Dramatic Performances in Eighteenth-Century France*. Oxford
Gould, J. (1978) 'Dramatic character and "human intelligibility" in Greek tragedy', *PCPhS* 24: 43–67
Gow, A. S. F. ed. (1965) *Theocritus*. Cambridge
Grabar, A. (1968) *L'art de la fin de l'antiquité et du moyen âge*. Paris
Graf, F. (1991) 'Gestures and conventions: the gestures of Roman actors and orators', in Bremmer and Roodenburg, 36–58
Grassi, T. (1920) 'Musica, mimica e danza secondo i documenti papiracei greco-egizi', *Studi della scuola papirologica* 3: 117–35
Gratwick, A. S. (1982) 'Drama', in *CHCL*, vol. II, 77–137. Cambridge
(1987) *Terence. The Brothers*. Warminster
Graves, R. (1938) *The Count Belisarius*. London
trans. (1979) *Suetonius: The Twelve Caesars* (Harmondsworth 1957), rev. M. Grant. Harmondsworth
Gredley, B. (1984) 'The discovery of the second actor', *Themes in Drama* 6: 1–14
Green, J. R. (1982) 'Dedications of masks', *RA* 2: 237–48
(1985) 'Drunk again. A study in the iconography of the comic theatre', *AJA* 89: 465–72
(1989) 'Greek theatre production 1971–86', *Lustrum* 31: 7–95
(1991) 'On seeing and depicting the theatre in classical Athens', *GRBS* 32: 15–50
(1994a) *Theatre in Ancient Greek Society*. London and New York
(1994b) 'The theatre', in J. Boardman, ed., *The Cambridge Ancient History. Plates to Volumes V and VI. The Fifth and Fourth Centuries B.C.*, 150–66. Cambridge
(1995a) 'Theatrical motifs in non-theatrical contexts on vases of the later fifth and fourth centuries', in Griffiths, 93–121
(1995b) 'Theatre production: 1987–1995', *Lustrum* 37: 7–202, 309–19
(1995c) 'Oral tragedies? A question from St Petersburg', *QUCC* 51: 77–86
(1996) 'Messengers from the tragic stage' (the A. D. Trendall Memorial Lecture), *BICS* 41: 17–30
(1997) 'Deportment, costume, and naturalism in comedy', in Le Guen, 131–43
(1999) 'Tragedy and the spectacle of the mind: messenger speeches, actors, narrative, and audience imagination in fourth-century BCE vase-painting', in B. Bergmann and C. Kondoleon, eds., *The Art of Ancient Spectacle*, 37–63. New Haven and London (Studies in the History of Art, 56)
Green, J. R., and E. W. Handley (2001) *Images of the Greek Theatre*. London 1995. Reprinted
Green, P. (1990) *Alexander to Actium*. Berkeley
Green, W. M. (1933) 'The status of actors at Rome', *CPh* 28: 301–4
Greisenegger, W. (1978) *Die Realität im religiösen Theater des Mittelalters. Ein Beitrag zu Rezeptionforschung*. Vienna
Grene, D. (1988) *The Actor in History: A Study of Shakespearean Stage Poetry*. Philadelphia and London

Grenfell, B. P., and A. S. Hunt, (1903) 'Farce and mime', *The Oxyrhynchus Papyri* 3: 41–57
eds. (1906) *The Hibeh Papyri*. London
Griffin, M. (1976) *Seneca: A Philosopher in Politics*. Oxford
(1986) 'Philosophy, Cato and Roman suicide', *G&R* 33: 64–77 and 192–202
(1989) 'Philosophy, politics and politicians at Rome', in J. Barnes and M. Griffin, eds., *Philosophia Togata*, 1–37. Oxford
Griffith, M. (1983) *Aeschylus. Prometheus Bound*. Cambridge
(1999) *Sophocles. Antigone*. Cambridge
Griffiths, A., ed. (1995) *Stage Directions: Essays in Ancient Drama in Honour of E. W. Handley* (*BICS* Suppl. 66). London
Grisé, Y. (1982) *Le suicide dans la Rome antique*. Montreal
Grube, G. M. A. (1965) *The Greek and Roman Critics*. Toronto
Gruen, E. S. (1990) *Studies in Greek Culture and Roman Policy*. Leiden
(1992) *Culture and National Identity in Republican Rome*. London
Guarducci, M. (1929) 'Poeti vaganti dell'età ellenistica: Ricerche di epigrafica greca nel campo della letteratura e del costume', in *Memorie della R. Academia Nazionale dei Lincei. Classe di scienze morali, etc.* ser. VI vol. II, 627–65. Rome
Guidorizzi, G. ed. (1988) *Il sogno in Grecia*. Rome and Bari
Guilland, R. (1956) 'La disparition des Courses', in *Mélanges offerts à Octave et Melpo Merlier* I, 31–47
Guilland, R., and E. Paris (1965/66/68/70) 'Etudes sur l'hippodrome de Byzance', *Byzantinoslavica* 26: 1–39 / 27: 26–40 / 29: 24–33 / 31: 1–11
Guldau, E. (1966) *Eva und Maria. Eine Antithese als Bildmotiv*. Graz and Cologne
Gurr, A. (1963) 'Who strutted and bellowed?', *Shakespeare Survey* 16: 95–102
(1980) *The Shakespearean Stage. 1574–1642*. 2nd edn. Cambridge (3rd edn Cambridge 1992)
Habicht, C. (1970) *Gottmenschentum und griechische Städte*. Munich
Haigh, A. E. (1907) *The Attic Theatre*. 3rd edn. Oxford
Hall, E. (1989) *Inventing the Barbarian: Greek Self-Definition through Tragedy*. Oxford
(1995) 'Lawcourt dramas: the power of performance in Greek forensic oratory', *BICS* 40: 39–58
(1996a) *Aeschylus. Persians*. Warminster
(1996b) 'Is there a *polis* in Aristotle's *Poetics*?', in M. S. Silk, ed., *Tragedy and the Tragic. Greek Theatre and Beyond*, 295–309. Oxford
(1997a) 'The sociology of Athenian tragedy', in Easterling (1997a) 93–126
(1997b) 'Theatrical archaeology', *AJA* 101: 154–8
(1999a) 'Actor's song in tragedy', in Goldhill and Osborne, 96–122
(1999b) 'Sophocles' *Electra* in Britain', in J. Griffin, ed., *Sophocles Revisited: Essays Presented to Sir Hugh Lloyd-Jones*, 261–306. Oxford
(1999c) 'Classical mythology in the Victorian popular theatre', *International Journal of the Classical Tradition* 5: 336–66
(2000) 'Female figures and metapoetry in Old Comedy', in D. Harvey and J. Wilkins, eds., *The Rivals of Aristophanes: Studies in Athenian Old Comedy*, 407–18. Swansea

Hall, E., and F. Macintosh (2004) *Greek Tragedy and the British Stage 1660–1914*. Oxford

Hall, E., F. Macintosh and O. Taplin, eds. (2000) *Medea in Performance 1500–2000*. Oxford

Halleran, R. (1985) *Stagecraft in Euripides*. London

Halliwell, S. (1986) *Aristotle's* Poetics. Chapel Hill and London

(1990) 'The sounds of the voice in Old Comedy', in Craik (1990b), 69–79

(1993) 'The function and aesthetics of the Greek tragic mask', in N. W. Slater and B. Zimmermann, eds., *Intertextualität in der griechisch-römischen Komödie*, 195–211. Stuttgart

Hamilton, R. (1974) 'Objective evidence for actors' interpolations in Greek tragedy', *GRBS* 15: 387–402

(1978) 'A new interpretation of the Anavysos chous', *AJA* 82: 385–7

Handley, E. W. (1965) *The Dyskolos of Menander*. London and Cambridge, MA

(1985a) 'Comedy', in *CHCL*, vol. I, 355–425. Cambridge

(1985b) 'Comedy. From Aristophanes to Menander', in *CHCL*, vol. I, 398–414. Cambridge

(1985c) 'Menander and the New Comedy', in *CHCL*, vol. I, 414–25. Cambridge

(1992) *The Oxyrhynchus Papyri* LIX, no. 3966. London

(1997a) *The Oxyrhynchus Papyri* LXIV, no. 4409. London

(1997b) *The Oxyrhynchus Papyri* LXIV, no. 4407. London

(1997c) 'Some thoughts on New Comedy and its public', in Le Guen, 185–200

(2001) '*Actoris opera*: words, action and acting in *Dis Exapaton* and *Bacchides*', in Renato Raffaeli and Alba Tontini, eds., *Lecturae Plautinae Sarsinates IV: Bacchides*, 13–36. Urbino

(forthcoming) '*POxy*. 4407: Menander, *Dis Exapaton* 18–30', in J. A. López Férez, ed., *Estudios actuales sobre textos griegos (La comedia)*. (Madrid, 22–5 October 1997) Madrid

Hansen, E. V. (1971) *The Attalids of Pergamum*. Ithaca and London

Hanson, A. E. (1994) 'A division of labor', *Thamyris* I: 157–202

Harmon, A. M. (1936) *Lucian, with an English Translation*, vol. III. Cambridge, MA and London

Hartigan, K. V. (1995) *Greek Tragedy on the American Stage: Ancient Drama in the Commercial Theatre, 1882–1994*. Westport CT and London

Hausrath, A., and H. Hunger, eds. (1970) *Corpus Fabularum Aesopicarum*, vol. I. 2nd edn. Leipzig

Hawthorn, R. Y. (1967) *The Handbook of Classical Drama*. London

Hazlitt, W. (1917) 'On actors and acting II', in G. Sampson, ed., *Hazlitt: Selected Essays*, 76–80. Cambridge

(1930–34) *The Complete Works*, ed. P. P. Howe, 21 vols. London

Heath, M. (1987) *The Poetics of Greek Tragedy*. Stanford

trans. (1996) *Aristotle. Poetics*. London

Heberdey, R. et al., eds. (1912) *Das Theater in Ephesos* (Forschungen in Ephesos, II). Vienna

Hedgcock, F. A. (1911) *A Cosmopolitan Actor: David Garrick and his French Friends.* London
Held, G. F. (1985) 'The meaning of ἦθος in the *Poetics*', *Hermes* 113: 280–93
Henderson, I. (1957) 'Ancient Greek music', in E. Wellesz, ed., *The New Oxford History of Music,* vol. 1, 336–403. London
Hense, O. (1909) *Teletis Reliquiae.* 2nd edn. Tübingen
Herington, J. (1985) *Poetry into Drama: Early Tragedy and the Greek Poetic Tradition.* Berkeley
Herrmann, A. (1994) 'Statuette of a standing Greek comic actor', in *Passion for Antiquities,* 218–19. Malibu
Heynen, C., and R. Krumeich (1999) '10 Sophokles: Unsicheres', in Krumeich, Pechstein and Seidensticker, 1–40
Heywood, T. (1612) *An Apology for Actors,* London, ed. A. Freeman. New York and London 1973
Higgins, R. A. (1954) *Catalogue of the Terracottas in the Department of Greek and Roman Antiquities, British Museum,* vol. 1. London
Hill, A. (1760) *The Dramatic Works of Aaron Hill,* 2 vols. London
Hill, G. B., ed. (1966) *Johnsonian Miscellanies,* 2 vols. London (1st edn Oxford 1897)
Hill, J. (1755) *The Actor or A Treatise on the Art of Playing.* London (reissued New York 1972)
Himmelmann, N. (1994) *Realistische Themen in der griechischen Kunst der klassischen und archaischen Zeit.* Berlin
Hobson, M. (1982) *The Object of Art: The Theory of Illusion in Eighteenth-century France.* Cambridge
Hörandner, W. (1964) 'Die Wiener Handschriften des Philippos Monotropos', Ἀκροθίνια: 23–40
(1972) 'Prodromos-Reminiszenzen bei Dichtern der nikäischen Zeit', *ByzF* 4: 88–104
(1988) 'Lexikalische Beobachtungen zum *Christos Paschon*', in E. Trapp et al., *Studien zur byzantinischen Lexikographie,* 183–202. Vienna
Hoffmann (1966) *Der Dialog bei den christlichen Schriftstellern der ersten vier Jahrhunderte.* (Texte und Untersuchungen, 96) Berlin
Holford-Strevens, L. (1999) 'Sophocles at Rome', in J. Griffin, ed., *Sophocles Revisited: Essays Presented to Sir Hugh Lloyd-Jones,* 219–59. Oxford
Holl, K. (1906) 'Die Entstehung der Bilderwand in der griechischen Kirche', *ARW* 9: 365–84
Holt, T. (1997) *The Walled Orchard.* London
Holton, D., ed. (1991) *Literature and Society in Renaissance Crete.* Cambridge
Honzl, J. (1976) 'The hierarchy of dramatic devices', in L. Matejka and I. R. Titunik, eds., *Semiotics of Art. Prague School Contributions,* trans. S. Larson, 118–27. Cambridge, MA (Czech original 1943)
Horsfall, N. M. (1976) 'The Collegium Poetarum', *BICS* 23: 79–95
Hourmouziades, N. C. (1984) Ὅροι καὶ Μετασχηματισμοὶ στὴν ἀρχαία ἑλληνικὴ Τραγωδία. Athens
Howard, A. (1893) 'The αὐλός or tibia', *HSPh* 4: 1–60

Hughes, A. (1991) 'Acting style in the ancient world', *Theatre Notebook* 45: 2–16
Hunger, H. (1958) 'Der Ἠθικός des Theodoros Metochites', in Πεπραγμένα του Θ΄ Διεθνοῦς Βυζαντινολογικοῦ Συνεδρίου, vol. III, 153 ff. Athens
(1969a) *Der byzantinische Katz-Mäuse-Krieg.* Vienna
(1969b) *Die byzantinische Literatur der Komnenenzeit.* Graz, Vienna and Cologne
(1974) 'Klassizistische Tendenzen in der byzantinischen Literatur des 14. Jahrhunderts', in *Actes de XIVe Congrès Intern. des Etudes Byzantines,* vol. I, 134–51. Bucharest
(1978) *Die hochsprachige profane Literatur der Byzantiner,* 2 vols. Vienna
(1980) *Antiker und byzantinischer Roman.* Heidelberg
(1991) Βυζαντινὴ Λογοτεχνία. Ἡ Λόγια κοσμικὴ γραμματεία τῶν Βυζαντινῶν, vol. I. 2nd edn. Athens
(1997) Βυζαντινὴ Λογοτεχνία. Ἡ Λόγια κοσμικὴ γραμματεία τῶν Βυζαντινῶν, vol. II. 2nd edn. Athens
Hunningher, B. (1955) *The Origin of Theatre: An Essay.* Amsterdam
(1956) *Acoustics and Acting in the Theater of Dionysus Eleuthereus.* Amsterdam
Hunter, R. L. (1985) *The New Comedy of Greece and Rome.* Cambridge
(1995) 'Plautus and Herodas', in Benz, Stärk and Vogt-Spira, 155–69
(1996) *Theocritus and the Archaeology of Greek Poetry.* Cambridge
(1999) *Theocritus. A Selection.* Cambridge
(2000) 'The politics of Plutarch's comparison of Aristophanes and Menander', in S. Gödde and T. Heinze, eds., *Skenika. Beiträge zum antiken Theater und seiner Rezeption,* 267–76. Darmstadt
Hunter, W. S. (1991) *The Dionysus Group.* New York
Husson, G. (1993) 'Les homéristes', *JJP* 23: 93–9
Hutter, I. (1970) 'Die Homilien des Mönches Jakobos und ihre Illustrationen. Vat.gr.1162–Par.gr.1208'. Dissertation. Vienna
Hutton, J. (1982) *Aristotle's Poetics.* New York
Huys, M. (1993) '*P. Oxy.* LIII 3705: a line from Menander's *Periceiromene* with musical notation', *ZPE* 99: 30–2
Ieranò, G. (1997) *Il Ditirambo di Dioniso.* Pisa and Rome
Iliffe, J. H. (1945) 'Imperial art in Trans-Jordan. Figurines and lamps from a potter's store at Jerash', *Quarterly of the Department of Antiquities in Palestine* 3: 1–26
Immerwahr, H. R. (1944) 'Appendix II: Dipinti from G5, C2' in M. I. Rostovtzeff et al., eds., *The Excavations at Dura-Europos: Preliminary Report of the Ninth Season of Work 1935–1936,* 203–65
Inguanez, D. M. (1939) 'Un dramma della Passione del secolo XII', *Miscellanea Cassinese* 17: 7–55
Innes, D. C. (1995) *Demetrius. On Style.* Cambridge, MA and London
Irmscher, J. (1970) 'Ἄκτα διὰ Καλοπόδιον', in *Orbis Mediaevalis, Festgabe für A. Blaschke,* 78–88. Weimar
(1973) 'Antikes Drama in Byzanz', in D. Hofmann et al., eds., *Die gesellschaftliche Bedeutung des antiken Dramas*', 227–38. Berlin
(1981) 'Warum die Byzantiner altgriechische Dramatiker lesen', *Philologus* 125: 236–9

Jackson, R. (1996) 'Actor-managers and the spectacular', in J. Bate and R. Jackson, 112–27
Jaffrey, Z. (1996) *The Invisibles: A Tale of the Eunuchs of India*. New York
Jakobi, R. (1996) *Die Kunst der Exegese im Terenzkommentar des Donat*. Berlin and New York
Janko, R. (1987) *Aristotle. Poetics I with the Tractatus Coislinianus*. Indianapolis
Jocelyn, H. D. (1967) *The Tragedies of Ennius*. Cambridge
(1995) 'Horace and the reputation of Plautus in the late first century BC', in S. J. Harrison, ed., *Homage to Horace*, 228–47. Oxford
Johnson, W. A. (2000) 'Musical evenings in the early empire', *JHS* 120: 57–85
Johnston, B. (1993) 'The metamorphoses of Theseus in *Oedipus at Colonus*', *Comparative Drama* 27: 271–85
Jones, A. H. M., J. R. Martindale and J. Morris (1971–92) *Prosopography of the Later Roman Empire*, 3 vols. Cambridge
Jones, C. P. (1991) 'Dinner theater', in W. J. Slater, ed., *Dining in a Classical Context*, 185–98. Ann Arbor
(1993) 'Greek drama in the Roman empire', in Scodel, 39–52
Jones, J. (1962) *On Aristotle and Greek Tragedy* (reissued Stanford 1980)
Jones, L. W., and C. R. Morey (1930–31) *The Miniatures of the Manuscripts of Terence prior to the Thirteenth Century*. 2 vols. Princeton
Jory, E. J. (1963) '"Algebraic" notation in dramatic texts', *BICS* 10: 65–78
(1966) 'Dominus Gregis?', *CPh* 61: 102–4
(1970) 'Associations of actors at Rome', *Hermes* 98: 224–53
(1981) 'The literary evidence for the beginnings of imperial pantomime', *BICS* 28: 147–61
(1986a) 'Continuity and change in the Roman theatre', in J. H. Betts, J. T. Hooker and J. R. Green, eds., *Studies in Honour of T. B. L. Webster*, vol. I, 143–52. Bristol
(1986b) 'The early pantomime riots', in A. Moffatt, ed., *Maistor, Classical, Byzantine and Renaissance Studies for Robert Browning*, 59–63. Canberra
(1988) 'Publilius Syrus and the element of competition in the theatre of the Republic', in N. Horsfall, ed., *Vir Bonus Discendi Peritus. Studies in celebration of Otto Skutsch's Eightieth Birthday* (*BICS* Suppl. 51), 73–81. London
(1995) 'Ars Ludicra and the Ludus Talarius', in Griffiths, 139–52
(1996) 'The drama of the dance: prolegomena to an iconography of Imperial pantomime', in Slater (1996a), 1–27
(1998) 'The pantomime assistants', in T. W. Hillard, R. A. Kearsley, C. E. V. Nixon and A. M. Nobbs, eds., *Ancient History in a Modern University*, vol. I, 217–21. Michigan and Cambridge
Joseph, B. (1959) *The Tragic Actor*. London
Jouan, F. (1983) 'Réflexions sur le rôle du protagoniste tragique', in *Théâtre et spectacles dans l'antiquité: Actes du Colloque de Strasbourg* (5–7 November 1981) (Travaux du Centre de recherche sur le Proche-Orient et la Grèce antiques, 7), 63–80. Leiden
Jürgens, H. (1972) *Pompa Diaboli: die lateinischen Kirchenväter und das antike Theater*. Stuttgart

Kaibel, G., ed. (1878) *Epigrammata Graeca ex lapidibus conlecta*. Berlin

Kaimio, M. (1988) *Physical Contact in Greek Tragedy. A Study of Stage Conventions*. Helsinki

(1993) 'The protagonist in Greek tragedy', *Arctos* 27: 19–33

Kalokyris, K. I. (1976) *The Ancient Theatre and its Influence on Greek Orthodox Tradition*. Athens

(1980) Μελετήματα χριστιανικῆς ὀρθόδοξης ἀρχαιολογίας καὶ τέχνης. Thessaloniki

Kakouri, K. (1963) Διονυσιακά. Athens

Kambitsis, J. (1972) *L'Antiope d'Euripide*. Athens

Kamerbeek, J. C. (1963) *The Plays of Sophocles. Commentaries*, 1, *The Ajax*. 2nd edn. Leiden

Karlin-Hayter, P. (1973) 'Les ἄκτα διὰ Καλοπόδιον', *Byzantion* 43: 84–107

Karwiese, S. (1998) 'Ephesos 4: Theater', *ÖJh* 67, Beiblatt: *Grabungen* 1997: 24–9

Katsouris, A. G. (1981) Ρητορικὴ Ὑπόκριση. Ioannina (3rd edn Ioannina 1989)

Kay, N. M. (1985) *Martial Book XI: A Commentary*. London

Kelly, H. A. (1979) 'Tragedy and the performance of tragedy in late Roman antiquity', *Traditio* 35: 21–44

Kelly, J. A. (1936) *German Visitors to English Theaters in the Eighteenth Century*. Princeton

Kennedy, G. A., ed. (1989) *The Cambridge History of Literary Criticism*. Vol. 1: Classical criticism. Cambridge

Kerrigan, J. (1996) *Revenge Tragedy: Aeschylus to Armageddon*. Oxford

Kiilerich, B. (1988) 'Physiognomics and the iconography of Alexander the Great', *SO* 63: 51–66

Kindermann, H. (1966) *Theatergeschichte Europas*, vol. 1. 2nd edn. Salzburg

King, H. (1998) *Hippocrates' Woman*. London and New York

Kirpičnikov, A. (1892) 'Reimprosa im 5ten Jahrhundert', *ByzZ* 1: 527–30

Kloner, A. (1988) 'The Roman amphitheatre at Beth Guvrin. Preliminary report', *IEJ* 38: 15–24

Kloppenborg, J. S., and S. G. Wilson (1996) *Voluntary Associations in the Greco–Roman World*. London and New York

Knapp, C. (1919) 'References in Plautus and Terence to plays, players, and playwrights', *CPh* 14: 35–55

Knauer, E. R. (1985) 'Ex oriente vestimenta. Trachtgeschichtliche Beobachtungen zu Ärmelmantel und Ärmeljacke', *ANRW* II.12, 3: 578–741

Knoepfler, D. (1993) *Les imagiers de l' Orestie: Mille ans d' art antique autour d' un mythe grec*. Zurich

Koerte, A. (1959) *Menandri quae supersunt*. Leipzig

Kokolakis, M. (1959) 'Pantomimus and the treatise Περὶ ὀρχήσεως', *Platon* 11: 1–56.

(1960) *The Dramatic Simile of Life*. Athens

(1976) Τὸ δρᾶμα τοῦ βίου εἰς τὸν Ἐπίκτητον. Φιλολογικὰ Μελετήματα εἰς τὴν Ἀρχαίαν Ἑλληνικὴν Γραμματείαν. Athens

Kondoleon, C. (1991) 'Signs of privilege and pleasure: Roman domestic mosaics', in E. Gazda, ed., *Roman Art in the Private Sphere*, 105–15. Ann Arbor

(1994) *Domestic and Divine: Roman Mosaics in the House of Dionysos*. Ithaca
Koster, W. (1975) *Scholia in Aristophanem*. I A: *Prolegomena de comoedia*. Groningen
Kott, J. (1974) *The Eating of the Gods. An Interpretation of Greek Tragedy*, trans. B. Taborski and E. J. Czerwinski. London (Polish original 1971)
Koukoules, Ph. (1955) Βυζαντινῶν βίος καὶ πολιτισμός, vol. VI. Athens
Kraemer, C. J. (1931) 'A Greek element in Egyptian dancing', *AJA* 35: 125–38
Krien, G. (1955) 'Der Ausdruck der antiken Theatermasken nach angaben im Polluxkatalog und in der pseudoaristotelischen "Physiognomik"', *JhOAI* 42: 84–117
Krierer, K. R. (1988) 'Mimik als Stigmatisierungsfaktor in Darstellungen sozialer Randgruppen in der antiken Kunst', in I. Weiler and H. Graßl, eds., *Soziale Randgruppen und Außenseiter im Altertum* (Graz 21–3 September 1987), 339–48. Graz
Krumbacher, K. (1897) *Geschichte der byzantinischen Literatur*. 2nd edn. Munich
(1900) Ἱστορία τῆς Βυζαντηνῆς [*sic*] Λογοτεχνίας, trans. G. Sotiriadis, vol. II. Athens
Krumeich, R., N. Pechstein and B. Seidensticker, eds. (1999) *Das griechische Satyrspiel*. Darmstadt
Kyriakidis, S. (1932) Review of Cottas (1931 a), Ἐπετηρὶς Ἑταιρείας Βυζαντινῶν Σπουδῶν 9: 446–51
(1934–37) Review of Cottas (1931 a) *Laog*. 11: 281–4
(1978) Τὸ δημοτικὸ τραγούδι. Συναγωγὴ μελετῶν, ed. A. Kyriakidou-Nestoros. Athens
Kyriakis, M. J. (1973) 'Satire and slapstick in seventh and twelfth century Byzantium', Βυζαντινά 5: 289–306
Lada-Richards, I. (1993) 'Empathic understanding: emotion and cognition in classical dramatic audience response', *PCPhS* 39: 94–140
(1996) '"Weeping for Hecuba": is it a "Brechtian" act?', *Arethusa* 29: 87–124
(1997) '"Estrangement" or "reincarnation"? performers and performance on the classical Athenian stage', *Arion* 5: 66–107
(1998) 'Staging the *ephebeia*: theatrical role-playing and ritual transition in Sophocles' *Philoctetes*', *Ramus* 27: 1–26
(1999) *Initiating Dionysus: Ritual and Theatre in Aristophanes' Frogs*. Oxford
Laflotte, D. B. (1899) 'Théâtre antique, gestes modernes', *Le Théâtre* (cited from Barba and Savarese (1991), 166)
Lafontaine-Dosogne, J. (1964/65) *Iconographie de l' enfance de la Vierge dans l' empire byzantin et en Occident*, 2 vols. Brussels
Lamagna, M. (1998) 'Dialogo riportato in Menandro', in E. García Novo and I. Rodríguez Altageme, eds., *Dramaturgia y puesta en escena en el teatro griego*, 289–302. Madrid
Lampros, S. (1916) 'Βυζαντιακὴ σκηνοθετικὴ διάταξις τῶν παθῶν τοῦ Χριστοῦ', Νέος Ἑλληνομνήμων 12: 381–407
Landels, J. (1999) *Music in Ancient Greece and Rome*. London

La Piana, G. (1912) *Le Rappresentazioni Sacre nella Letteratura Bizantina dell' Origini al Secolo IX con Rapporti al Teatro Sacro d' Occidente*. Grottaferrata

(1936) 'The Byzantine theatre', *Speculum* 11: 171–211

(1955) 'The Byzantine iconography of the presentation of the Virgin Mary to the Temple and a Latin religious pageant', in K. Weitzmann, ed., *Late Classical and Medieval Studies in Honor of Albert Mathias Friend, Jr.*, 261–71. Princeton

Laskaris, N. (1938) Ἱστορία τοῦ Νεοελληνικοῦ θεάτρου, vol. 1. Athens

Latte, K. (1954) 'Zur Geschichte der griechischen Tragödie in der Kaiserzeit', *Eranos* 52: 125–7

Lavagne, H. et al. (1989) 'Le goût du théâtre dans l'art funéraire: notices 93 à 108', in C. Landes, ed., *Le Goût du théâtre à Rome et en Gaule romaine*, 207–25. Lattes

Lebek, W. D. (1996) 'Moneymaking on the Roman stage', in Slater, 29–48

Le Faucheur, M. (1657) *Traitté de l'action de l'orateur ou de la Prononciation et du geste*. Paris

Le Guen, B. (1995) 'Théatre et cités à l'époque hellénistique: "Mort de la cité" – "Mort du théâtre"?', *REG* 108: 59–90

ed. (1997) *De la scène aux gradins: théâtre et représentations dramatiques après Alexandre le grand* (*Pallas*, 47). Toulouse

(2001) *Les associations de technites dionysiaques à l'époque hellénistique*, deux tomes; *Etudes d' Archéologie Classique* XI, A. D. R. A. Nancy

Lennox-Boyd, C. et al., eds. (1994) *Theatre: The Age of Garrick*. London

Leone, P. (1969) 'Michael Haplucheir, dramation', *Byzantion* 39: 251–83

Lepelley, C. (1989) 'Trois documents méconnus sur l'histoire sociale et religieuse de l'Afrique romaine tardive, retrouvés parmi les spuria de Sulpice Sévère', *AntAfr* 25: 235–62

Leppin, H. (1992) *Histrionen: Untersuchungen zur sozialen Stellung von Bühnenkünstlern im Westen des Römischen Reiches zur Zeit der Republik und des Principats*. Bonn

(1996) 'Tacitus und die Anfänge des Kaiserzeitlichen Pantomimus', *RhM* 139: 33–40

Lesky, A. (1963) *A History of Greek Literature*, trans. J. Willis and C. de Heer. 2nd edn. New York

(1966) 'Neroniana', in W. Kraus, ed., *Gesammelte Schriften*, 335–51. Bern

(1983) *Greek Tragic Poetry*, trans. M. Dillon. New Haven and London (trans. of *Die tragische Dichtung der Hellenen*. 3rd edn 1972)

Levi, D. (1947) *Antioch Mosaic Pavements*. Princeton

Levick, B. (1983) 'The *Senatus Consultum* from Larinum', *JRS* 73: 97–115

Levine, L. (1994) *Men in Women's Clothing: Anti-theatricality and Effeminization 1579–1642*. Cambridge

Lewes, G. H. (1875) *On Actors and the Art of Acting*. London (repr. New York 1957)

Lewis, N. (1986) *Greeks in Ptolemaic Egypt*. Oxford

Leyerle, B. (1993) 'John Chrysostom on the gaze', *Journal of Early Christian Studies* 1: 159–74

Lim, R. (1996) 'The *Tribunus Voluptatum* in the later Roman empire', *Memoirs of the American Academy in Rome* 41: 163–73

(1997) 'Consensus and dissensus on public spectacles in early Byzantium', *ByzF* 24: 159–79

Link, J. (1904) *Die Geschichte der Schauspieler nach einem syrischen Manuscript der Königlichen Bibliothek*. Berlin

Litsas, F. K. (1980) *Choricius of Gaza. An Approach to his Work*. Chicago

(1982) 'Choricius of Gaza and his descriptions of festivals at Gaza', *JÖByz* 32: 427–36

Liungman, W. (1937) *Traditionswanderungen Euphrat-Rhein*. Helsinki

Ljubarskij, J. N. (1987) 'Der Kaiser als Mime. Zum Problem der Gestalt des byzantinischen Kaisers Michael III', *JÖByz* 37: 39–50

Lloyd, G. E. R. (1979) *Magic, Reason and Experience: Studies in the Origin and Development of Greek Science*. Cambridge

Lloyd-Jones, H. (1990) *Greek Comedy, Hellenistic Literature, Greek Religion and Miscellanea: The Academic Papers of Sir Hugh Lloyd-Jones*. Oxford

Loraux, N. (1981) 'Le lit, la guerre', *L' Homme* 21: 37–67

(1985) *Façons tragiques de tuer une femme*. Paris

Lucas, D. W. (1968) *Aristotle. Poetics*. Oxford

Lucas, F. L. (1928) *Euripides and his Influence*. New York

Luppe, W. (1973) 'Textkritische Bemerkungen zu Plutarchs Vergleich von Aristophanes und Menander', *Philologus* 117: 127–30

Maas, P. (1912) 'Metrische Akklamationen der Byzantiner', *ByzZ* 21: 28–51

(1927) 'Σιμωιδοί', *RE* III.A1: 159–60

(1932) Review of Cottas (1931a), *ByzZ* 32: 396–7

MacDowell, D. M. (1988) 'Clowning and slapstick in Aristophanes', in J. Redmond, ed., *Themes in Drama, 10: Farce*, 1–13. Cambridge

Macintosh, F. (1994) *Dying Acts: Death in Ancient Greek and Modern Irish Tragic Drama*. Cork

(1997) 'Tragedy in performance: Nineteenth and twentieth century productions', in Easterling (1997a), 284–323

MacMullen, R. (1984) *Christianizing the Roman Empire*. New York and London

Macready, W. C. (1875) *Macready's Reminiscences and Selections from his Diaries and Letters*, ed. Sir F. Pollock. 2 vols. London

(1912) *The Diaries of William Charles Macready 1833–1851*, London, ed. W. Toynbee. 2 vols. London

Magarshack, D. (1961) 'Introduction', in Stanislavsky, 11–87

Magdalino, P. (1993) *The Empire of Manuel A. Komnenos 1143–1180*. Cambridge

Magulias, H. J. (1971) 'Bathhouse, inn, tavern, prostitution and the stage as seen in the lives of the saints of the sixth and seventh centuries', Ἐπετηρὶς Ἑταιρίας Βυζαντινῶν Σπουδῶν 38: 233–52

Mahr, C. A. (1942) *Relations of Passion Plays to St Ephrem the Syrian*. Columbus

(1947) *The Cyprus Passion Cycle*. Notre Dame and Indiana

Maier Eichhorn, U. (1989) *Die Gestikulation in Quintilians Rhetorik*. Frankfurt and New York

Manakidou, E. P. (1997) ‘Ἱστορημένα ὑφάσματα: μία κατηγορία μικρογραφικῶν παραστάσεων πάνω σὲ ἀττικά ἀγγεῖα’, in J. H. Oakley, W. D. E. Coulson and O. Palagia, eds., *Athenian Potters and Painters: The Conference Proceedings*, 297–308. Oxford
Mango, C. (1981) ‘Daily life in Byzantium’, *JÖByz 31*: 337–54
Marini, N. (1991) ‘Δρᾶμα: possibile denominazione per il romanzo greco d’ amore’, *SIFC* 84: 232–43
Marshall, C. W. (1997) ‘Comic technique and the fourth actor’, *CQ* 47: 77–84
Marshall, F. H., and J. Mavrogordato (1948) ‘Byzantine philology’, in N. Baynes and H. S. B. Moss, eds., *Byzantium: An Introduction to East Roman Civilisation*, 221–51. Oxford
Martin, R. (1976) *Terence. Adelphoe*. Cambridge
Martino, F. de and A. H. Sommerstein, eds. (1995) *Lo Spettacolo della voci*. Bari
Mass, C. (1935) ‘Jacob of Serugh’s homilies on the spectacles of the theatre’, *Muséon* 48: 87–112
Massinger, P. (1629) *The Roman Actor*. London
Mastromarco, G. (1984) *The Public of Herondas*. Amsterdam
Mastronarde, D. (1994) *Euripides. Phoenissae*. Cambridge
Mattingly, H. B. (1960) ‘The first period of Plautine revival’, *Latomus* 19: 230–52
McClure, L. K. (1995) ‘Female speech and characterization in Euripides’, in de Martino and Sommerstein Part 2, 35–60
(1999) *Spoken Like a Woman: Speech and Gender in Athenian Drama*. Princeton
McKeown, J. C. (1979) ‘Augustan elegy and mime’, *PCPhS* 25: 71–84
Meijering, R. (1987) *Literary and Rhetorical Theories in Greek Scholia*. Groningen
Melmoth, W. (1915) *Pliny: Letters, with an English translation* (London 1747), rev. W. M. L. Hutchinson. London and Cambridge, MA
Mette, H. J. (1977) *Urkunden dramatischer Aufführungen in Griechenland*. Berlin and New York
Michaelides, D. (1987) *Cypriot Mosaics*. Nicosia
Minar, E. L. (1961) *Plutarch. Quaestiones Convivales* (*Plutarch. Moralia* IX). London and Cambridge, MA
Mioni, E. (1937) *Romano il Melodo*. Padua
Mistriotis, G. (1894) Ἑλληνικὴ Γραμματολογία, I. Athens
Mitchell, S. (1995) *Cremna in Pisidia*. London
Mitsakis, K. (1986) ‘Κοντάκιο καὶ θρησκευτικὸ θέατρο’, in K. Mitsakis, Βυζαντινὴ Ὑμνογραφία, 330–53. Athens (1st edn Athens 1971)
Moles, J. (1985) ‘Cynicism in Horace Epistles 1’ in F. Cairns, ed., *Papers of the Liverpool Latin Seminar*, vol. V, 33–60
Molloy, M. E. (1996) *Libanius and the Dancers*. Hildesheim
Moore, M. B. (1997) *Attic Red-Figured and White-Ground Pottery. The Athenian Agora*, XXX. Princeton
Moore, S. (1966) *The Stanislavski System: The Professional Training of an Actor. Digested from the Teachings of K. S. Stanislavski*. London

Moore, T. J. (1998a) *The Theater of Plautus: Playing to the Audience*. Austin, Texas
(1998b) 'Music and structure in Roman Comedy', *AJPh* 119: 243–75
Morenilla-Talens, C. (1989) 'Die Charakterisierung der Ausländer durch lautliche Ausdrucks-mittel in den *Persern* des Aischylos sowie den *Acharnen* und *Vögeln* des Aristophanes', *IF* 94: 158–76
Moretti, J. C. (1993) 'Des masques et des théâtres en Grèce et en Asie Mineure', *REA* 95: 207–23
(1994) 'Showbiz à Aphrodisias', review of Roueché (1993), *Topoi* 4: 351–61
Moss, C. A. (1935) 'Jacob of Serugh's Homilies on the spectacles of the theatre', *Le Muséon* 48: 87–112
Most, G. (1985) *The Measures of Praise*. Göttingen
Muecke, F. (1982a) '"I know you – by your rags": costume and disguise in fifth-century drama', *Antichthon* 16: 17–34
(1982b) 'A portrait of the artist as a young woman', *CQ* 32: 41–55
Müller, A. (1909) 'Das Bühnenwesen in der Zeit von Constantin d. Gr. bis Justinian', *Neue Jahrbücher für das klassische Altertum, Geschichte und deutsche Literatur* 23: 36–55
Müller, C. G., and T. Kießling, eds. (1821) *Theodori Metochitae Miscellanea*. Leipzig
Müller, C. W. (1976) 'Chariton von Aphrodisias und die Theorie des Romans in der Antike', *A&A* 22: 115–36
Murnaghan, S. (1987/88) 'Body and voice in Greek tragedy', *YJC* 1: 23–43
Murray, P., and P. Wilson, eds. (forthcoming), *Mousikē: Music and Culture in Ancient Greece*. Oxford
Nachtergael, G. (1977) *Les Galates en Grèce et les Sōtéria de Delphes*. Brussels
Nagler, A. M. (1976) *The Medieval Religious Stage. Shapes and Phantoms*. New Haven and London
Nagy, G. (1996) *Poetry as Performance*. Cambridge
Nalpantis, D. (1984) 'Τὸ βυζαντινὸ θέατρο', 'Αρχαιολογία 12: 44–52
Nedugant, G., and M. Featherstone, eds. (1995) *The Council of Trullo Revisited*. Rome
Neighbarger, R. L. (1992) *An Outward Show: Music for Shakespeare on the London Stage 1660–1830*. Westport, Connecticut and London
Neiiendam, K. (1992) *The Art of Acting in Antiquity. Iconographical Studies in Classical, Hellenistic and Byzantine Theatre*. Copenhagen
Nesselrath, H. G. (1990) *Die attische Mittelere Komödie*. Berlin
Neudecker, R. (1994) *Die Pracht der Latrine*. Munich
Nicolai, A. (1867) *Über Entstehung und Wesen des griechischen Romans*. Berlin
Nicolaou, I. (1989) 'Acteurs et grotesques de Chypre', in R. Etienne, M.-T. Le Dinahet and M. Yon, eds., *Architecture et poésie dans le monde grec. Hommage à Georges Roux*, 270–84. Paris
Niehoff-Panagiotidis, J. (1996) 'Graeco-Arabica 2: Ein griechischer Vulgarismus in arabischer Übersetzung', *WO* 27: 45–50
Niessen, C. (1949–58) *Handbuch der Theater-Wissenschaft*. Emsdetten

Nilsson, M. P. (1957) *The Dionysiac Mysteries of the Hellenistic and Roman Age*. Lund
Noomen, N. (1958) 'Passages narratifs dans les drames médiévaux français. Essai d' interprétation', *RBPh* 31: 761–85
Nordquist, G. (1992) 'Instrumental music in representations of Greek cult,' in R. Hägg, ed., *Ancient Greek Cult Practice from the Epigraphical Evidence (Proceedings of the First International Seminar on Ancient Greek Cult, organized by the Swedish Institute at Athens)*, 143–68. Stockholm
(1994) 'Some notes on musicians in Greek cult,' in R. Hägg, ed., *Ancient Greek Cult Practice from the Epigraphical Evidence (Proceedings of the Second International Seminar on Ancient Greek Cult, organized by the Swedish Institute at Athens)*, 81–93. Stockholm
Oakley, J. H. (1990) *The Phiale Painter*. Mainz
(1991) '"The death of Hippolytus" in South Italian vase-painting', *NAC* 20: 63–83
Oakley, S. P. (1998) *A Commentary on Livy Books VI–X*, vol. II (Books VII and VIII). Oxford
Ober, J. (1989) *Mass and Elite in Democratic Athens*. Princeton
Ober, J., and C. Hedrick, eds. (1996) *Demokratia: A Conversation on Democracies, Ancient and Modern*. Princeton
Olivier, L. (1982) *Confessions of an Actor*. London
Olson, S. D. (1988) 'The "love duet" in Aristophanes' *Ecclesiazusae*', *CQ* 38: 328–30
(1998) *Aristophanes. Peace*. Oxford
Onasch, K. (1967) *Die Ikonenmalerei. Grundzüge einer systematischen Darstellung*. Leipzig
Osmun, G. F. (1952) 'Dialogue in the Menandrean monologue', *TAPhA* 83: 156–63
Ouspensky, L. (1980) *Théologie de l' icône dans l' église orthodoxe*. Paris
Ousterhout, R. (1990) *The Blessings of Pilgrimage*. Urbana
Owen, A. S. (1936) 'The date of Sophocles' *Electra*', in *Greek Poetry and Life: Essays Presented to Gilbert Murray on his Seventieth Birthday*, 145–57. Oxford.
Padel, R. (1990) 'Making space speak', in Winkler and Zeitlin, 336–65
Paduano Faedo, L. (1970/71) 'Contributo allo studio dei sarcofagi con Muse', *SCO* 19/20: 442–9
Page, D. (1934) *Actors' Interpolations in Greek Tragedy*. Oxford
Palmer, C. (1975) *Miklós Rózsa: A Sketch of his Life and Work*. London and Wiesbaden
Panayotakis, C. (1997) 'Baptism and crucifixion on the mimic stage', *Mnemosyne* 50: 302–19
Papadopoulos, A. A. (1925) Τὸ θρησκευτικὸν θέατρον τῶν Βυζαντινῶν. Athens
Papadopoulou, Th. (1998) 'Tradition and invention in the Greek tragic scholia: some examples of terminology', *SIFC* 16, 3rd ser.: 202–32
(1999) 'Literary theory and terminology in the Greek tragic scholia: the case of *plasma*', *BICS* 43: 203–10
Papamichael, G. (1916) Ἐκκλησία καὶ Θέατρον. Alexandria

Parker, H. N. (1996) 'Plautus vs. Terence: audience and popularity re-examined', *AJPh* 117: 585–617
Parker, L. P. E. (1997) *The Songs of Aristophanes*. Oxford
Pasquato, O. (1976) *Gli spettacoli in S. Giovanni Crisostomo: Paganesimo e Cristianesimo ad Antiochia e Constantinopoli nel IV secolo* (Orientalia Analecta, 20). Rome
Patrick, D., ed. (1906) *Chamber's Cyclopaedia of English Literature* (London 1857–58). Rev. edn. London and Edinburgh
Paulsen, T. (1992) *Inszenierung des Schicksals: Tragödie und Komödie im Roman des Heliodor*. Trier
Pavis, P. (1996) *L' analyse des spectacles: théâtre, mime, danse, danse-théâtre, cinéma*. Paris
Pavlovskis, Z. (1977) 'The voice of the actor in Greek tragedy', *CW* 71: 113–23
Peek, W., ed. (1955) *Griechische Versinschriften*, i: *Grab-Epigramme*. Berlin
Pelling, C., ed. (1990) *Characterization and Individuality in Greek Literature*. Oxford
ed. (1997a) *Greek Tragedy and the Historian*. Oxford
(1997b) 'Tragical dreamer: some dreams in the Roman historians', *G&R* 44: 197–213
Peredolskaya, A. (1964) *Attische Tonfiguren aus einem südrussischen Grab*. Bern
Pernoud, R. (1965) 'Le théâtre au moyen-âge', in E. Dumur, ed., *Histoire des Spectacles*, 553–78. Paris
Perpillou-Thomas, F. (1993) *Fêtes d'Egypte Ptolémaïque et romaine d'après la documentation papyrologique grecque*. Louvain
Perrin, B. (1958) *Plutarch's Lives with an English Translation*, vol. VII. Cambridge, MA and London
Perry, B. E. (1967) *The Ancient Romances. A Literary-Historical Account of their Origins*. Berkeley and Los Angeles
Perusino, F., ed. (1993) *Anonimo (Michelle Psello?). La tragedia greca*. Urbino
Perusino, F., and A. Giacomoni (1999) 'Un canto di risveglio nella commedia nuova', in B. Gentili et al., eds., *Per Carlo Corbato. Scritti di filologia greca e latina offerti da amici e allievi*, 101–7. Pisa
Petitmengin, P., and M. Cazacu (1981) *Pelagie la Pénitente. Metamorphoses d'une légende*. Paris
Pfeiffer, R. (1968) *A History of Classical Scholarship from the Beginnings to the End of the Hellenistic Age*. Oxford
Pfister, M. (1988) *The Theory and Analysis of Drama*, trans. J. Halliday. Cambridge (German original 1977)
Pfuhl, E. (1927) *Die Anfänge der griechischen Bildniskunst. Ein Beitrag zur Entwicklung der Individualität*. Munich (repr. in K. Fittschen, ed. (1988) *Griechische Porträts*, 224–52. Darmstadt)
Phillips, H. (1980) *The Theatre and Its Critics in Seventeenth-Century France*. Oxford
Piccirillo, M., ed. (1986) *I Mosaici di Giordana*. Rome
(1989) *Chiese e mosaici di Madaba*. Rome
(1993) *The Mosaics of Jordan*. Amman
Pingiatoglou, S. (1992) 'Eine Komödiendarstellung auf einer Choenkanne des Benaki-Museums', in H. Froning, T. Hölscher and H. Mielsch, eds., *Kotinos: Festschrift für Erika Simon*, 292–300. Mainz
Pinker, S. (1997) *How the Mind Works*. London

Pintacuda, M. (1978) *La musica nella tragedia Greca*. Cefalù

Pitsakis, K. (1996) 'Μορφὲς "δρωμένων" σὲ βυζαντινὲς νομικὲς πηγὲς', in Λαϊκὰ δρώμενα. Παλιὲς μορφὲς καὶ σύγχρονες ἐκφράσεις (Komotini, 25–7 November 1994), 153–71. Athens

Pöhlmann, E. (1960) *Griechische Musikfragmente: Ein Weg zur altgriechische Musik* (Erlanger Beiträge, 8). Nuremberg

(1970) *Denkmäler altgriechischer Musik*. Nuremberg

(1997) 'La scène ambulante des Technites', in Le Guen, 3–12

Pöhlmann, E. and M. L. West (2001) *Documents of Ancient Greek Music: the Extant Melodies and Fragments*. Oxford

Pollitt, J. J. (1972) *Art and Experience in Classical Greece*. Cambridge

(1986) *Art in the Hellenistic Age*. Cambridge

Pollmann, K. (1997) 'Jesus Christus und Dionysos. Überlegungen zu dem Euripides-Cento *Christus Patiens*', *JÖByz* 47: 87–106

Pollock, L. J. (1884) *Macready as I Knew Him*. London

Pommeray, L. (1937) *Etudes sur l'infamie en droit romain*. Paris

Pontani, A. (1994) 'Firenze nelle fonti greche del Concilio', in P. Vitti, ed., *Firenze e il Concilio del 1439* (Florence 29 Nov.–2 Dec. 1989), 753–812. Florence

Pontani, Ph. M. (1973) *Maximi Planudis Idyllium* (Istituto di Studi bizantini e neogreci, 7). Padua

Potts, L. J. (1962) *Aristotle on the Art of Fiction*. Cambridge

Prag, A. J. N. W. (1986) *The Oresteia: Iconographic and Narrative Tradition*. Warminster

Prynne, William (1633) *Histriomastix*. London

Puchner, W. (1975) *Das neugriechische Schattentheater Karagiozis* (Miscellanea Byzantina Monacensia, 21). Munich

(1977) *Brauchtumserscheinungen im griechischen Jahreslauf und ihre Beziehungen zum Volkstheater* (Veröffentlichungen des Österr. Museums für Volkskunde, 18). Vienna

(1979) 'Zur liturgischen Frühstufe der Höllenfahrtsszene Christi. Byzantinische Katabasis-Ikonographie und rezenter Osterbrauch', *Zeitschrift für Balkanologie* 15: 98–133

(1981/82) 'Τὸ Βυζαντινὸ Θέατρο. Θεατρολογικὲς παρατηρήσεις στὸν ἐρευνητικὸ προβληματισμὸ τῆς ὕπαρξης Θεάτρου στὸ Βυζάντιο', Ἐπετηρὶς τοῦ Κέντρου Ἐπιστημονικῶν Ἐρευνῶν 11: 169–274. Nicosia

(1983) 'Byzantinischer Mimos, Pantomimos und Mummenschanz im Spiegel griechischer Patristik und ekklesiastischer Synodalverordnungen. Quellenkritische Anmerkungen aus theaterwissenschaftlicher Sicht', *Maske und Kothurn* 29: 311–17

(1984a) 'Τὸ Βυζαντινὸ Θέατρο. Θεατρολογικὲς παρατηρήσεις στὸν ἐρευνητικὸ προβληματισμὸ τῆς ὕπαρξης Θεάτρου στὸ Βυζάντιο', in W. Puchner, Εὐρωπαϊκὴ Θεατρολογία. Ἕνδεκα μελετήματα, 13–92, 397–416, 477–94. Athens

(1984b) Ἱστορικὰ Νεοελληνικοῦ Θεάτρου. Athens

(1986) 'Θεατρολογικὲς παρατηρήσεις γιὰ τὸν "Κύκλο τῶν Παθῶν" τῆς Κύπου', Πρακτικὰ Β΄ Διεθνοῦς Κυπριολογικοῦ Συνεδρίου, vol. II, 447–66. Nicosia

(1987) 'Zum Nachleben des Rosalienfestes auf der Balkanhalbinsel', *Südost-Forschungen* 46: 197–278
(1988) Ἑλληνικὴ Θεατρολογία. Δώδεκα μελετήματα. Athens
(1990) 'Zum "Theater" in Byzanz. Eine Zwischenbilanz', in G. Prinzing and D. Simon, eds., *Fest und Alltag in Byzanz*, 11–16, 169–79. Munich
(1991) *Studien zum Kulturkontext der liturgischen Szene. Lazarus und Judas als religiöse Volksfiguren in Bild und Brauch, Lied und Legende Südosteuropas*, 2 vols. (Österreichische Akademie der Wissenschaften, philosophisch-historische Klasse, Denkschriften, 216). Vienna
(1993a) 'Theaterwissenschaftliche und andere Anmerkungen zum "Christus Patiens"', *AAWW* 129: 93–143
(1993b) 'Die "Repraesentatio figurata" der Präsentation der Jungfrau Maria im Tempel von Philippe de Mézières (Avignon 1372) und ihre zypriotische Herkunft', Θησαυρίσματα 23: 91–129
(1993c) 'Zur Raumkonzeption der Mimiamben des Herodas', *WS* 106: 9–34
(1997a) *Akkommodationsfragen. Einzelbeispiele zum paganen Hintergrund von Elementen der frühkirchlichen und mittelalterlichen Sakraltradition und Volksfrömmigkeit* (Kulturgeschichtliche Forschungen, 23). Munich
(1997b) 'Θεατρολογικὲς παρατηρήσεις σὲ βυζαντινοὺς ἱστοριογράφους. Ἡ περίπτωση τοῦ Μιχαὴλ Ψελλοῦ', *EEAth* 31: 283–329
Pugliese Carratelli, G. (1990) *Magna Grecia*, vol. IV: *Arte e artigianato*. Milan
Purkiss, D. (2000) 'Medea in the English Renaissance', in Hall, Macintosh and Taplin, 32–48
Pye, H. J. (1792) *A Commentary Illustrating the Poetic of Aristotle by Examples taken chiefly from the Modern Poets*. London
Quadlbauer, F. (1960) 'Die Dichter der griechischen Komödie in literarischen Urteil der Antike', *WS* 73: 40–82
Questa, C. (1984) *Numeri Innumeri: Ricerche sui cantica e la tradizione manoscritta di Plauto*. Rome
Raaflaub, K. (1983) 'Democracy, oligarchy, and the concept of the "Free Citizen" in late fifth-century Athens', *Political Theory* 11: 517–44
(1984) 'Zur Freiheitsbegriff der Griechen', in C. E. Welskopf, ed., *Soziale Typenbegriffe im alten Griechenland und ihr Fortleben in den Sprachen der Welt*, vol. IV, 180–405. Berlin
Rabe, H. (1906) *Scholia in Lucianum*. Leipzig
Rallis, G., and M. Potlis (1852–56) Σύνταγμα τῶν Θείων καὶ Ἱερῶν Κανόνων τῆς Ὀρθοδόξου Ἀνατολικῆς Ἐκκλησίας, 6 vols. Athens
Ralph, J. (1731) *The Taste of the Town or A Guide to All Publick Diversions*. London.
Rasmussen, T., and N. Spivey, eds. (1991) *Looking at Greek Vases*. Cambridge
Rau, P. (1967) *Paratragōdia: Untersuchungen einer komischen Form des Aristophanes* (Zetemata, 45). Munich
Rawson, E. (1985) 'Theatrical life in Republican Rome and Italy', *PBSR* 53: 97–113 (repr. in Rawson (1991) 468–87)
(1991) *Roman Culture and Society. Collected Papers*. Oxford

Rees, K. (1908) *The So-called Rule of Three Actors in the Classical Greek Drama*. Chicago
Rees, T. (1964) *Thespis: A Gilbert and Sullivan Enigma*. London
Reeve, M. (1972/73) 'Interpolation in Greek tragedy', *GRBS* 13: 247–65, 451–74 / 14: 145–71
Rehm, R. (1992) *Greek Tragic Theatre*. London
Reich, H. (1903) *Der Mimus: ein Litterar-Entwicklungsgeschichtlicher Versuch*. Berlin
Reinhardt, K. (1949) *Aischylos als Regisseur und Theologe*. Bern
Reinsch, D. R. (1996) *Alexias Anna Komnene*. Cologne
Renault, M. (1966) *The Mask of Apollo*. London.
Revermann, M. (1997) 'Comic business'. Dissertation Oxford
Reynolds, J. (1982) *Aphrodisias and Rome* (*JRS* Monographs, 1). London
Reynolds, L. D., and N. G. Wilson (1991) *Scribes and Scholars*. 3rd edn. Oxford
Reynolds, R. W. (1946) 'The Adultery Mime', *CQ* 40: 77–84
Rice, E. E. (1983) *The Grand Procession of Ptolemy Philadelphus*. Oxford
Ringer, M. (1998) *Electra and the Empty Urn: Metatheater and Role Playing in Sophocles*. Chapel Hill and London
Rispoli, G. M. (1996) 'La voce dell'attore nel mondo antico: Teorie e techniche', *Acme* 49: 3–28
Ritschl, F. (1845) *Parerga zu Plautus und Terenz*. Berlin
Robert, L. (1930) 'Pantomimer in griechischen Orient', *Hermes* 65:106–22
(1936) ''Αρχαιολόγος', *REG* 49: 235–54
(1937) *Etudes Anatoliennes: Recherches sur les inscriptions grecques de l'Asie Mineure*. Paris
(1938) *Etudes épigraphiques et philologiques*. Paris
(1984) 'Discours d'ouverture', in Πρακτικὰ τοῦ Η' διεθνοῦς συνεδρίου ἑλληνικῆς καὶ λατικῆς ἐπιγραφικῆς (Athens 3–9 October 1982), 35–45. Athens
Roberts, W. R., and I. Bywater (1954) *The Rhetoric and the Poetics of Aristotle*, trans. W. R. Roberts (*Rhetoric*) and I. Bywater (*Poetics*). New York (repr. New York 1984, with an introduction by E. P. J. Corbett)
Robinson, O. F. (1997) *The Sources of Roman Law: Problems and Methods for Ancient Historians*. London
Robson, W. (1969) *The Old Play-goer*. Ed. R. Gittins. London (1st edn 1846)
Rochow, I. (1978) 'Zu "heidnischen" Bräuchen bei der Bevölkerung des byzantinischen Reiches im 7. Jahrhundert', *Klio* 60: 483–97
Roeder, A. (1974) *Die Gebärde im Drama des Mittelalters*. Munich
Roesch, P. (1982) *Etudes béotiennes*. Paris
(1989) 'L'aulos et les aulètes en Béotie', in H. Beister, J. Buckler and S. Lauffer, eds., *Boiotika: Vorträge vom 5. Internationalen Böotien-Kolloquium zu Ehren von Prof. Dr. S. Lauffer*, 203–14. Munich
Rosenmeyer, T. G. (1989) *Senecan Drama and Stoic Cosmology*. Berkeley
Ross, W. D. trans. (1915) *The Works of Aristotle*, vol. IX. Oxford
Rossi, L. E. (1989) 'Livelli di lingua, gestualità, rapporti di spazio e situazione drammatica sulla scena attica', in De Finis, 63–78
Rostagni, A. (1956) *Scritti minori*. Turin

Rothwell, K. (1992) 'The continuity of the chorus in fourth-century Attic comedy', *GRBS* 33: 209–25.
Rotolo, V. (1957) *Il pantomimo. Studi e testi.* Palermo
Roueché, C. (1993) *Performers and Partisans at Aphrodisias in the Roman and Late Roman Periods. A Study based on Inscriptions from the Current Excavations at Aphrodisias in Caria.* London
Rousseau, J.-J. (1948) *Lettre à Mr. D'Alembert sur les Spectacles.* Ed. M. Fuchs. Lille and Geneva (1st edn 1758)
Russell, D. A. (1990) '*Ēthos* in oratory and rhetoric', in Pelling, 197–212
Russo, C. F. (1994) *Aristophanes: An Author for the Stage.* London and New York.
Rusten, J. (1982) 'Dicaearchus and the *Tales from Euripides*', *GRBS* 23: 537–67
Rydén, L. (1963) *Das Leben des heiligen Narren Symeon von Leontios von Neapolis* (Studia Graeca Upsalensia, 4). Uppsala
(1970) *Bemerkungen zum Leben des heiligen Narren Symeon von Leontios von Neapolis* (Studia Graeca Upsalensia, 6). Upssala
Sakkalis, I. (1977) Γρηγορίου Θεολόγου, Ἅπαντα τὰ Ἔργα. Vol. VIII. 1. Ὁ Χριστὸς Πάσχων, 2. Ἔπη Δογματικά (Ἕλληνες Πατέρες τῆς Ἐκκλησίας, 24). Athens
Sallmann, K. (1990) 'Christen vor dem Theater', in J. Blänsdorf, ed., *Theater und Gesellschaft im Imperium Romanum*, 243–59. Tübingen
Sandbach, F. H. (1970) 'Menander's manipulation of language for dramatic purposes', in Turner, 113–43
(1990) *Menandri reliquiae selectae.* Rev. 2nd edn. Oxford (1st edn Oxford 1972)
Sandidge, W. L. (1929) *A Critical Edition of Massinger's The Roman Actor.* Princeton
Santelia, S. (1991) *Charition Liberata (P.Oxy. 413).* Bari
Sathas, K. (1878) Ἱστορικὸν δοκίμιον περὶ τοῦ θεάτρου καὶ τῆς μουσικῆς τῶν Βυζαντινῶν ἤτοι εἰσαγωγὴ εἰς τὸ Κρητικὸν θέατρον. Venice (repr. Athens 1979)
Schäfer, G. (1855) Ἑρμηνεία τῆς Ζωγραφικῆς. *Das Handbuch der Malerei vom Berge Athos.* Trier
Schechner, R. (1977) 'Towards a Poetics of Performance', in R. Schechner, *Essays on Performance Theory 1970–1976*, 108–39. New York
Scheithauer, A. (1997) 'Les aulètes dans le théâtre grec à l'époque hellénistique,' *Pallas* 47: 107–27
Schenkl, H (1916) *Epicteti Dissertationes ab Arriano Digestae.* Leipzig
Scherrer, P., ed. (2000) *Ephesus. The New Guide.* Selcuk and Vienna
Schleiner, L. (1990) 'Latinized Greek drama in Shakespeare's writing of *Hamlet*', *Shakespeare Quarterly* 41: 29–48
Schmidt, M. (1993) 'Tracce del teatro comico attico nella Magna Grecia', in *Vitae Mimus. Forme e funzioni del teatro comico greco e latino* (Pavia 18 March 1993), 27–41. Pavia
(1995) 'Τῆς γῆς οὐχ ἁπτόμενος. Nochmals zur Choenkanne Vlastos aus Anavyssos', *MH* 52: 65–70

Schmitt, E. (1970) *Lexikalische Untersuchungen zur arabischen Übersetzung von Artemidors Traumbuch*. Wiesbaden

Schneider, C. (1939) 'Das Fortleben der Gesamtantike in den griechischen Liturgien', *Kyrios* 4: 185–221

Schnusenberg, C. (1981) *Das Verhältnis von Kirche und Theater. Dargestellt an ausgewählten Schriften der Kirchenväter und liturgischen Texten bis auf Amalarius von Metz (A.D. 775–852)*. Bern

Schulz, H.-J. (1959) 'Die "Höllenfahrt" als "Anastasis". Eine Untersuchung über Eigenart und dogmengeschichtliche Voraussetzung byzantinischer Osterfrömmigkeit', *Zeitschrift für katholische Theologie* 81: 1–66

Schütrumpf, E. (1970) *Die Bedeutung des Wortes ēthos in der Poetik des Aristoteles* (Zetemata, 49). Munich

(1987) 'The meaning of ἦθος in the *Poetics* – a reply', *Hermes* 115: 175–81

Scodel, R., ed. (1993) *Theater and Society in the Classical World*. Ann Arbor

Scrinari, V. S. M. (1973) *Catalogo delle sculture romane del Museo di Aquileia*. Rome

Scudéry, G. de (1639) *L'Apologie du Théâtre*. Paris

Seaford, R. (1984) *Euripides. Cyclops*. Oxford

Seale, D. (1982) *Vision and Stagecraft in Sophocles*. Chicago

Segal, A. (1985–88) 'Theatres in ancient Palestine during the Roman-Byzantine period', *SCI* 8–9: 145–65

(1987) 'Theatres in Eretz – Israel in the Roman–Byzantine period', *Eretz – Israel* 19: 106–24

Segal, C. P. (1986) *Interpreting Greek Tragedy. Myth, Poetry, Text*. Ithaca and London

(1995) 'The female voice and its contradictions: from Homer to tragedy', in J. Dalfen, G. Petersmann and F. F. Schwarz, eds., *Religio Graeco-Romana: Festschrift für Walter Pötscher*, *Grazer Beiträge* Suppl. 5, 57–75. Graz

Seidensticker, B. (1999) 'Philologisch-literarische Einleitung', in Krumeich, Pechstein and Seidensticker, 1–40

Shapiro, A. (1987) 'Kalos-Inscriptions with Patronymic', *ZPE* 68: 107–18

Sharpe, R. B. (1959) *Irony in the Drama: An Essay on Impersonation, Shock, and Catharsis*. Chapel Hill

Shaw, B. (1889) 'Acting, by one who does not believe in it', repr. in D. H. Lawrence, ed., (1961) *Platform and Pulpit*, 12–23. New York

Sherer, A. (1989) 'Le goût du théâtre dans l'art funéraire', in C. Landes, ed., *Le goût du théâtre à Rome et en Gaule romaine*. Lattes

Sherk, R. K. (1969) *Roman Documents from the Greek East: Senatus Consulta and Epistulae to the Age of Augustus*. Baltimore

(1984) *Translated Documents of Greece and Rome*, vol. IV: *Rome and the Greek East to the Death of Augustus*. Cambridge

Shevelove, B., B. Gelbart and S. Sondheim (1963) *A Funny Thing Happened on the Way to the Forum*. London

Shipp, G. P. (1960) *Terence. Andria*. 2nd edn. Oxford

Sienkiewicz, H. (1941) *Quo Vadis*, trans. M. Gardner. London and New York

Sifakis, G. M. (1967) *Studies in the History of Hellenistic Drama*. London, Toronto and New York

(1979) 'Boy actors in New Comedy', in G. W. Bowersock, W. Burkert and M. C. J. Putnam, eds., *Arktouros: Hellenic Studies presented to B.M.W. Knox*, 199–208. Berlin and New York

(1995) 'The one-actor rule in Greek tragedy', in Griffiths, 13–24

(1997) '*Agōnismata* in Thucydides and Aristotle', *BICS* 42: 21–7

Simon, E. (1968) '*Tereus*. Zur Deutung der Würzburger Schauspiele-Scherbe', *Festschrift des Kronberg-Gymnasiums, Aschaffenburg*, 155–67. Aschaffenburg

(1982) *The Ancient Theatre*, trans. C. E. Vafopoulou-Richardson. London (German original 1972)

Sinn, F. (1987) *Stadtrömische Marmorurnen*. Mayence

Slater, N. W. (1985) *Plautus in Performance*. Princeton

(1987) 'Transformations of space in New Comedy', in J. Redmond, ed., *Themes in Drama* vol. IX, *The Theatrical Space*, 1–10. Cambridge

(1990) 'The idea of the actor', in Winkler and Zeitlin, 385–95

(1993) 'Space, character, and ἀπάτη: transformation and transvaluation in the *Acharnians*', in Sommerstein, Halliwell, Henderson and Zimmermann, 397–415

(1997) 'Waiting in the wings: Aristophanes' *Ecclesiazusae*', *Arion* 5: 97–129

Slater, W. J. (1995) 'The pantomime Tiberius Julius Apolaustus', *GRBS* 36: 263–92

(1996a) 'Inschriften von Magnesia revisited', *GRBS* 37: 195–204

ed. (1996b) *Roman Theater and Society*. Ann Arbor

(1997) 'L'*hegemon* dans les fêtes hellénistiques', in Le Guen, 97–106

Smith, R. R. R. (1987) 'The imperial reliefs from the Sebasteion at Aphrodisias', *JRS* 77: 88–138

(1988) '*Simulacra gentium*: The *Ethne* from the Sebasteion at Aphrodisias', *JRS* 78: 50–77

(1990) 'Myth and allegory in the Sebasteion', in C. Roueché and K. T. Erim, eds., *Aphrodisias Papers: Recent Work on Architecture and Sculpture*, 89–100. Ann Arbor

(1993) *The Monument of C. Julius Zoilos*. Mainz

Snyder, J. (1979) '*Aulos* and *kithara* on the Greek stage', in T. Gregory and A. Podlecki, eds., *Panathenaia: Studies in Athenian Life and Thought in the Classical Age*, 75–95. Kansas

Solomos, A. (1964) Ὁ ἅγιος Βάκχος ἤ ἄγνωστα χρόνια τοῦ ἑλληνικοῦ θεάτρου 300 π.Χ.-1600 μ.Χ. Athens (3rd edn, Athens 1987)

Sommerstein, A. H. (1980) *Aristophanes. Acharnians*. Warminster

(1987) *Aristophanes. Birds*. Warminster

(1995) 'The language of Athenian women', in de Martino and Sommerstein, 61–85

(1998) *Aristophanes. Ecclesiazusae*. Warminster

Sommerstein, A. H., S. Halliwell, J. Henderson and B. Zimmermann, eds. (1993) *Tragedy, Comedy and the Polis. Papers from the Greek Drama Conference* (Nottingham 18–20 July 1990). Bari

Speck, P. (1996) 'Ideologische Ansprüche – historische Realität. Zum Problem des Selbstverständnisses der Byzantiner', in A. Hohlweg, ed., *Byzanz und seine Nachbarn*, 19–45. Munich

Spengel, L., and C. Hammer, eds. (1894) *Rhetores Graeci*. Leipzig

Spigo, U. (1992) 'Esemplari di ceramica a figure rosse a decorazione sovradipinta siceliota ed italiota al Museo Regionale di Messina', *Ricerche di Archeologia. Industria poligrafica della Sicilia* (*Quaderni dell'attività didattica del Museo Regionale di Messina*, 2). 9–27

Sprague, R. K. (1972) *The Older Sophists. A Complete Translation*. South Carolina

Spruit, J. E. (1966) *De juridisch en sociale positie van de romeinse acteurs*. Assen

Stadler, E. (1966) 'Das Theater der Antike und des Mittelalters', in M. Hürlimann, ed., *Atlantisbuch des Theaters*, 459–550. Zurich

Stanislavsky, K. S. (1961) *Stanislavsky on The Art of the Stage*, trans. D. Magarshack. 2nd edn. London

Stephanis, I. E. (1986) Χορικίου Σοφιστοῦ Γάζης Συνηγορία Μίμων. Thessaloniki

(1988) Διονυσιακοὶ Τεχνῖται. Συμβολὲς στὴν Προσωπογραφία τοῦ Θεάτρου καὶ τῆς Μουσικῆς τῶν Ἀρχαίων Ἑλλήνων. Heraklion

Sternbach, L. (1897) 'Στίχοι Ἰγνατίου εἰς τόν Λάζαρον καὶ εἰς τὸν πλούσιον', *Eos* 4: 151–4

Stevens, P. T. (1937) 'Colloquial expressions in Euripides', *CQ* 31: 182–91

(1945) 'Colloquial expressions in Aeschylus and Sophocles', *CQ* 39: 95–105

(1976) *Colloquial Expressions in Euripides*. Wiesbaden

Sticca, S. (1970) *The Latin Passion Play: Its Origins and Development*. Albany

Sticotti, A. F. (1771) *Garrick ou les acteurs Anglois: ouvrage contenant des observations sur l'art dramatique, sur l'art de la représentation et le jeu des acteurs*. Paris

Stiefenhofer, D. (1909) *Die Geschichte der Kirchweiche vom 1.–7. Jahrhundert*. Munich

Strauss Clay. J. (1992) 'Pindar's twelfth Pythian: reed and bronze', *AJPh* 113: 519–25

Stričević, G. (1967) 'Drama as an intermediary between Scripture and Byzantine painting', in H. von Einem, ed., *Stil und Überlieferung in der Kunst des Abendlandes* (21st International Congress for the History of Art), vol. I, 106–27. Berlin

Strocka, V. M. (1977) *Die Wandmalerei der Hanghäuser in Ephesos* (*Forschungen in Ephesos* VII. 1). Vienna

(1988) 'L' arte ad Atene durante la guerra di Peloponneso', in E. La Rocca, ed., *L' esperimento della perfezione. Arte e società nell' Atene di Pericle*, 147–79, Italian translation by G. Bejor. Milan (German original 1975)

Strong, D. (1980) *Roman Art*. Harmondsworth

Sturm, J. (1901) 'Ein unbekanntes griechisches Idyll aus der Mitte des 15. Jahrhunderts', *ByzZ* 10: 433–52

Sutton, D. F. (1971) 'The relation between tragedies and fourth place plays in three instances', *Arethusa* 4: 55–72

(1980) *The Greek Satyr-play* (*Beiträge zur klassischen Philologie*, 90). Meisenheim am Glan

(1987) 'The theatrical families of Athens', *AJPh* 108: 9–26

Sweetman, D. (1993) *Mary Renault. A Biography*. London
Taaffe, L. K. (1993) *Aristophanes and Women*. London and New York
Taillardat, J. (1962) *Les Images d'Aristophane*. Paris
Talfourd, F. (1859) *Electra in a New Electric Light: An Entirely New and Original Extravaganza in One Act*. London
Talma, F. J. (1883) *Talma on the Actor's Art*. London
Tanabe, K. (1986) *Sculptures of Palmyra* I (Memoirs of the Ancient Orient Museum, Tokyo, I). Tokyo
Tandoi, V. (1965–66) '*Morituri verba Catonis*', *Maia* 17 : 315–39 and 18: 20–41
Tancke, K. (1989) *Figuralkassetten griechischer und roemischer Steindecken*. Frankfurt am Main
Taplin, O. (1977a) *The Stagecraft of Aeschylus. The Dramatic Use of Exits and Entrances in Greek Tragedy*. Oxford
(1977b) 'Did Greek dramatists write stage instructions?', *PCPhS* 203: 121–31
(1978) *Greek Tragedy in Action*. London, Berkeley and Los Angeles
(1993) *Comic Angels and other Approaches to Greek Drama through Vase-Paintings*. Oxford
(1995) 'Opening performance: closing texts?', *Essays in Criticism* 45: 102–5
(1997) 'The pictorial record', in Easterling (1997a), 69–92
(1998) 'Narrative variation in vase-painting and tragedy', *AK* 41: 33–9
(1999) 'Spreading the word through performance', in Goldhill and Osborne, 33–57
Taylor, L. R. (1937) 'The opportunities for dramatic poerformances in the time of Plautus and Terence', *TAPhA* 68: 284–304
Theocharidis, G. C. (1940) *Beiträge zur Geschichte des byzantinischen Profantheaters im IV. und V. Jahrhundert, hauptsächlich auf Grund der Predigten des Johannes Chrysostomos, Patriarchen von Konstantinopel*. Thessaloniki (Diss. Munich 1937)
Thesleff, H., ed. (1961) *The Pythagorean Texts of the Hellenistic Period*. Åbo
Thiercy, P., and M. Menu, eds. (1997) *Aristophane: La langue, la scène, la cité*. Bari
Tillyard, H. J. W. (1912), 'The acclamations of emperors in Byzantine ritual', *ABSA* 18: 239–60
Tinnefeld, F. (1974) 'Zum profanen Mimos in Byzanz nach dem Verdikt des Trullanums (691)', Βυζαντινὰ 6: 321–43
Tomadakis, N. B. (1965) Εἰσαγωγὴ εἰς τὴν βυζαντινὴν φιλολογίαν. 2nd vol.: Ἡ βυζαντινὴ ὑμνογραφίακαὶ ποίησις. Athens
Townsend, R. F. (1986) 'The fourth-century skene of the Theater of Dionysos at Athens', *Hesperia* 55: 421–38
Traversari, G. (1960) *Gli Spettacoli in acqua nel teatro tardo-antico*. Rome
Treggiari, S. (1991) *Roman Marriage: Iusti Coniuges from the Time of Cicero to the Time of Ulpian*. Oxford
Trendall, A. D. (1995) 'A phlyax bell-krater by the Lecce painter', in A. Cambitoglou and E. G. D. Robinson, eds., *Classical Art in the Nicholson Museum*, 125–131. Mainz
Trisoglio, F. (1974) 'Il *Christus Patiens*: rassegna delle attribuzioni', *Rivista di Studi Classici* 27: 351–423

(1996) *San Gregorio di Nazianzo e il Christus Patiens. Il problema dell' autenticità gregoriana del dramma.* Turin

Trussler, S. (1994) *The Cambridge Illustrated History of British Theatre.* Cambridge

Tuilier, A. (1969) *La Passion du Christ. Tragédie.* Paris

Tunison, J. S. (1907) *Dramatic Traditions of the Dark Ages.* Chicago and London

Turner, E. G. (1968) *Greek Papyri: An Introduction.* Oxford

ed. (1970) *Ménandre.* Geneva = *Entretiens sur l' antiquité classique* 16

(1987) *Greek Manuscripts of the Ancient World.* 2nd edn, revised and enlarged by P. J. Parsons (*BICS* Suppl. 46). London

Turyn, A. (1964), *Codices Graeci Vaticani saeculis XIII et XIV scripti annorumque notis instructi*, vol. I. Vatican

Usener, H., ed. (1879) *Legenden der Hl. Pelagia.* Bonn

Van de Vorst, C. (1910) 'Une passion inédite de S. Porphyre le mime', *AB* 29: 258–75

Van der Meer, F., and C. Mohrmann (1958) *Atlas of the Early Christian World.* London

Van Hoorn, G. (1951) *Choes and Anthesteria.* Leiden

Vavřívnek, V. (1985) 'The eastern Roman empire or early Byzantium? A society in transition', in V. Vavřívnek, ed., *From Late Antiquity to Early Byzantium* (16th International *Eirene* Conference), 9–20. Prague

Velimirovič, M. (1962) 'Liturgical drama in Byzantium and Russia', *Dumbarton Oaks Papers* 16: 349–85

Vernant, J.-P., and P. Vidal-Naquet, eds. (1986) *Mythe et tragédie en Grèce ancienne.* Paris

'Vernay', L. (1888) 'Chez Mounet-Sully: A propos d'Oedipe Roi', *Revue d'Art Dramatique* 11: 136–40

Vetta, M. (1993) 'La voce degli attori nel teatro attico', in R. Prestagostini, ed., *Tradizione e Innovazione nella Cultura Greca da Omero all'età ellenistica: Scritti in onore di Bruno Gentili*, vol. II, 703–18. Rome

(1995) 'La voce degli attori nel teatro attico', in de Martino and Sommerstein, 61–78

Vogt, A. (1931 a) 'Le théâtre à Byzance et dans l' empire du IVe aux XIIIe siècle. I. Le théâtre profan', *Revue des questions historiques* 59: 257–96

(1931 b) 'Etudes sur le théâtre byzantin', *Byzantion* 6: 37–74, 623–40

Volbach, W. F. (1976) *Elfenbeinarbeiten der Spätantike und des frühen Mittelalters.* Mainz

Voss, B. R. (1970) *Der Dialog in der frühchristlichen Literatur* (Studia et Testimonia Antiqua, 9). Munich

Walcot, P. (1976) *Greek Drama in its Theatrical and Social Context.* Cardiff

Walden, J. W. H. (1894) 'Stage-terms in Heliodorus's *Aethiopica*', *HSPh* 5: 1–43

Wallace, R. W. (1995) 'Speech, song and text, public and private. Evolutions in communications media and fora in fourth century Athens', in W. Eder, ed., *Die athenische Demokratie im 4. Jahrhundert v. Chr.*, 199–224. Stuttgart

(1997) 'Poet, public, and "theatrocracy": audience performance in classical Athens', in Edmunds and Wallace, 97–111

Walton, M. (1999) *Gordon Craig*. Revised edn. London
Waltzing, J.-P. (1895) *Etude historique sur les corporations professionelles chez les Romains*, vol. I. Louvain
Walz, C., ed. (1832–36), *Rhetores Graeci*, 9 vols. Stuttgart and London
Wankel, H. (1976) *Demosthenes. Rede für Ktesiphon über den Kranz*. Heidelberg
Wankel, H., R. Merkelbach et al. (1979–84) *Die Inschriften von Ephesos* (Inschriften griechische Städte aus Kleinasien, 11–17). Bonn
Warmington, E. H. (1936) *Remains of Old Latin*. London and Cambridge, MA
Wasserman, E. R. (1947) 'The sympathetic imagination in eighteenth-century theories of acting', *Journal of English and Germanic Philology* 46: 264–72
Waszink, J. H. (1964) 'Die griechische Tragödie im Urteil der Römer und des Christentums', *JbAC* 7: 139–48
Watzinger, C. (1901) 'Mimologen', *MDAI* 26: 1–9
Webb, R. (1997a) 'Imagination and the arousal of the emotions in Greco-Roman rhetoric', in S. M. Braund and C. Gill, eds., *The Passions in Roman Thought and Literature*, 112–27. Cambridge
(1997b) 'Salome's sisters: the rhetoric and realities of dance in late antiquity and Byzantium', in L. James, ed., *Women, Men and Eunuchs: Gender in Byzantium*, 119–48. London
Webster, T. B. L (1939) *Greek Art and Literature, 530–400 B.C.* Oxford
(1963) 'Alexandrian epigrams and the theatre', in *Miscellanea di Studi Alessandrini in Memoria di Augusto Rostagni*, 531–43. Turin
(1967) *The Tragedies of Euripides*. London
(1970) *Sophocles. Philoctetes*. Cambridge
Wehrli, F. (1967) *Die Schule des Aristoteles*. II: Aristoxenos. 2nd edn. Basle and Stuttgart
Weinreich, O. (1948) *Epigrammstudien* I: *Epigramm und Pantomimus*. Heidelberg
Weismann, W. (1972) *Kirche und Schauspiele: die Schauspiele im Urteil der lateinischen Kirchenväter unter besonderer Berücksichtigung von Augustin*. Würzburg
(1975) 'Gelasinos von Heliopolis, ein Schauspieler-Märtyrer', *AB* 93: 39–66
Weitzmann, K. (1949) 'Euripides scenes in Byzantine art', *Hesperia* 18: 159–222
(1979) *The Age of Spirituality*. New York
Welles, C. B. (1934) *Royal Correspondence in the Hellenistic Period: A Study in Greek Epigraphy*. New Haven
Wellesz, E. (1947) 'The Nativity drama of the Byzantine church', *JRS* 37: 145–51
Welskopf, E. C., ed. (1974) *Hellenische Poleis, Krise, Wandlung, Wirkung*, vol. III. Berlin
Wessel, K. (1963) *Koptische Kunst: die Spätantike in Ägypten*. Recklinghausen
West, M. L. (1990a) *Studies in Aeschylus* (=*Beiträge zur Altertumskunde*, 1). Stuttgart
(1990b) 'Colloquialism and naive style in Aeschylus', in Craik (1990b), 3–12
(1992a) *Ancient Greek Music*. Oxford
(1992b) 'Analecta musica', *ZPE* 92: 1–54
(1999) 'Sophocles with music? Ptolemaic music fragments and remains of Sophocles (Junior?), *Achilleus*', *ZPE* 126: 53–65

West, S. (1991) *The Image of the Actor: Verbal and Visual Representation in the Age of Garrick and Kemble*. London

Westermann, W. L. (1924) 'The Castanet Dancers of Arsinoe', *JEA* 10: 134–44

Westermann, W. L., and C. J. Kraemer (1926) *Greek Papyri in the Library of Cornell University*. New York

Whibley, C. (1899) *Suetonius. History of the Twelve Caesars, translated into English by Philemon Holland anno 1606*, vol. II. London

White, K. D. (1993) '"The base mechanic arts"? Some thoughts on the contribution of science (pure and applied) to the culture of the Hellenistic age', in P. Green, ed., *Hellenistic History and Culture*, 211–20. Berkeley

White, R. J. (1975) *The Interpretation of Dreams: Oneirocritica by Artemidorus* (translation and commentary). Park Ridge, NJ

Whitmarsh, T. (1998) 'Reading power in Roman Greece: the *paideia* of Dio Chrysostom', in Y. L. Too and N. Livingstone, eds., *Pedagogy and Power*, 192–213. Cambridge

Wiemken, H. (1972) *Der griechische Mimus: Dokumente zur Geschichte des antiken Volkstheaters*. Bremen

Wilamowitz-Moellendorff, U. von (1959) *Einleitung in die griechische Tragödie*. Darmstadt (repr. from 3rd edn 1895; 4th repr. 1909)

Wilckens, L., von (1991) *Die textile Künste: von der Spätantike bis um 1500*. Munich

Wild, J. P. (1994) 'Tunic no. 4219', *Riggisberger Bericht* 2: 9–36

Wiles, D. (1991) *The Masks of Menander*. Cambridge

Wiles, J. T. (1980) *The Theater Event: Modern Theories of Performance*. Chicago and London

Wilkes, T. (1759) *A General View of the Stage*. London

Wille, G. (1967) *Musica Romana: die Bedeutung der Musik im Leben der Römer*. Amsterdam

Willett, J. (1977) *The Theatre of Bertolt Brecht: A Study from Eight Aspects*. Rev. edn. London

Willink, C. W. (1986) *Euripides. Orestes*. Oxford

Wilson, N. G. (1967) 'A chapter in the history of scholia', *CQ* 17: 244–56

(1982) 'The relation of text and commentary in Greek books', in C. Questa and R. Raffaelli, eds., *Atti del convegno internazionale Il Libro e Il Testo*, 105–10. Urbino

Wilson, P. (1999) 'The *aulos* in Athens', in Goldhill and Osborne, 58–95

(2000) *The Athenian Institution of the Khoregia: The Chorus, the City and the Stage*. Cambridge

Wilthemius, A. (1659) *Diptychon Leodiense ex consulari factum episcopale et in illud commentarius*. Liège

Winkler, J. J., and F. I. Zeitlin, eds. (1990) *Nothing to Do with Dionysos? Athenian Drama in Its Social Context*. Princeton

Winter, F. (1903) *Die Typen der figürlichen Terrakotten*. Berlin and Stuttgart

Winter, J. G. (1933) *Life and Letters in the Papyri*. Ann Arbor

Wood, E. M. (1996) 'Demos versus "we the people": freedom and democracy, ancient and modern', in Ober and Hedrick, 121–37

Wootton, G. E. (1999) 'A mask of Attis. Oscilla as evidence for a theme of pantomime', *Latomus* 58: 314–35

Wüst, E. (1932) 'Mimus', *RE* 15: 1727–64

(1949) 'Pantomimus', *RE* 18: 833–69.

Wylie, L. (1997) *Beaux Gestes. A Guide to French Body Talk.* Cambridge, MA

Wyndham, G., ed. (1895) *Plutarch's Lives of the Noble Grecians and Romans Englished by Sir Thomas North anno 1579*, vol. II. London

Xanthakis-Karamanos, G. (1980) *Studies in Fourth Century Tragedy.* Athens

(1993) 'Hellenistic drama: developments in form and performance', *Platon* 45: 117–33

Yalouris, N. (1986) 'Die Anfänge der griechischen Porträtkunst und der Physiognomon Zopyros', *AK* 29: 5–7

(1992) 'Mosaiken eines spätrömishcen Gebäudes in Elis', in H. Froning, T. Hölscher and H. Mielsch, eds., *Kotinos: Festschrift für Erika Simon*, 426–8. Mainz

Yatromanolakis, G. (1990) 'Τὸ Ἀρχαῖο Ἑλληνικὸ Μυθιστόρημα καὶ ἡ ὁρολογία του', in Yatromanolakis, Ἀχιλλέως Ἀλεξανδρέως Τατίου, Λευκίππη καὶ Κλειτόφων, 719–34. Athens

(1997) 'Εἰσαγωγή', in A. Sideris, Ἡλιόδωρος, Αἰθιοπικὰ ἢ Τὰ Περὶ Θεαγένην καὶ Χαρίκλειαν, 15–88. Athens

Young, K. (1933) *The Drama of the Medieval Church*, 2 vols. Oxford

Zanker, G. (1981) '*Enargeia* in the ancient criticism of poetry', *RhM* 124: 297–311

(1987) *Realism in Alexandrian Poetry: A Literature and its Audience.* London

Zanker, P. (1995) *The Mask of Socrates. The Image of the Intellectual in Antiquity*, trans. A. Shapiro. Berkeley

Zayadine, F. (1986) 'Peintures murales et mosaïques à sujets mythologiques en Jordanie', in L. Kahil et al., eds., *Iconographie classique et identités régionales*, 407–32 (*BCH* Suppl. 14). Athens

Zeitlin, F. I. (1990) 'Playing the other: theatre, theatricality and the feminine in Greek drama', in Winkler and Zeitlin, 63–96

Zepos, P. I., ed. (1959) Μιχαὴλ Φωτεινοπούλου Νομικὸν Πρόχειρον (Βουκουρέστιον 1765). Athens

Ziebarth, E. (1896) *Das Griechische Vereinswesen.* Leipzig

Zimmermann, B. (1991) *Greek Tragedy. An Introduction*, trans. T. Marier. Baltimore and London (German original 1986)

Zucchelli, B. (1964) *Le denominazioni latini dell'attore.* Brescia

Zuntz, G. (1955) *The Political Plays of Euripides.* Manchester

Zwierlein, O. (1990/92) *Zur Kritik und Exegese des Plautus*, vol. I / vol. IV. Stuttgart

Index of major ancient passages cited

General index

NOTE: references in italics denote illustrations